Amazing 3-D Games
Adventure Set

Welcome to the world of *ACK-3D*! This color gallery shows many of the features provided with the *ACK-3D* engine and the tools you can use to easily create your own amazing 3-D games.

Using *ACK-3D* and the power of WinG, you can develop games like the Windows version of *Station Escape*. This game is included on the companion CD-ROM with complete source code. You can use the game as a model to build your own 3-D creations.

The engine provides everything you need to create both DOS and Windows games. This game shows the kind of fast animated objects you can put in your games. As you move around the objects, you'll experience them in 3-D.

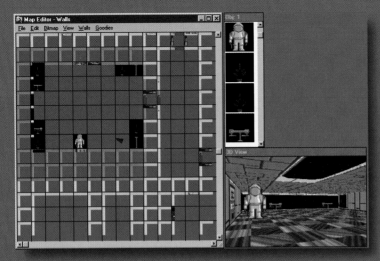

Use the provided visual map editor to create your games interactively. As you design the maps for your game, you can explore them in 3-D by viewing them in the powerful 3D View window. This editor greatly automates the process of building games.

The map editor also lets you place stationary and movable objects in your 3-D worlds. A custom dialog box is provided so that you can easily animate your objects.

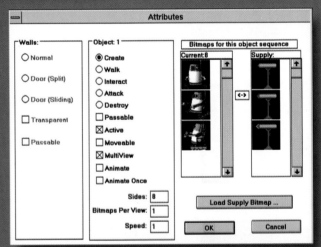

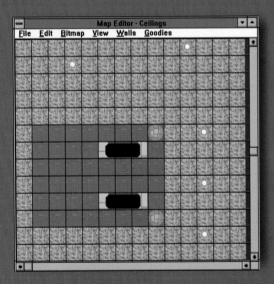

It's also easy to add fully-textured floors and ceilings using the visual map editor.

You can use the DOS-version of the map editor also to view and change your game maps.

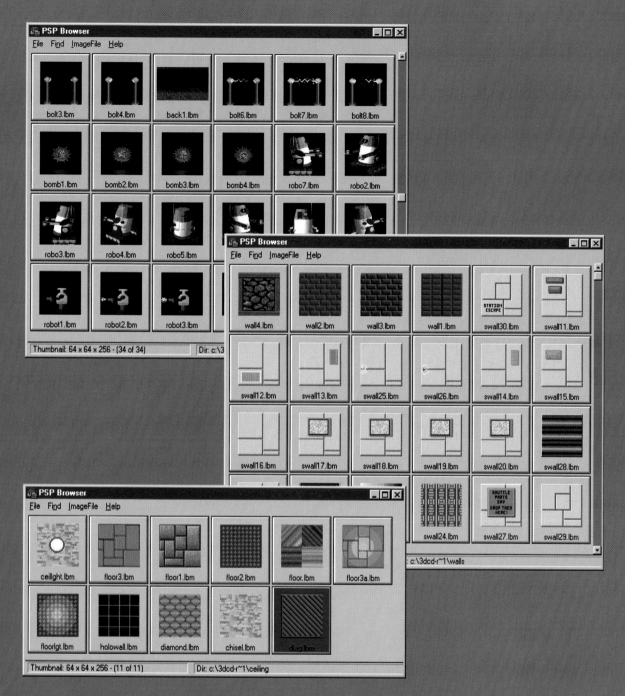

To create the art for your game, use a bitmap painting program and create all of the wall, object, and floor bitmap components as 64×64 pixel building blocks. These windows show some of the bitmaps used to create the Windows version of the *Station Escape* game provided on the companion CD-ROM.

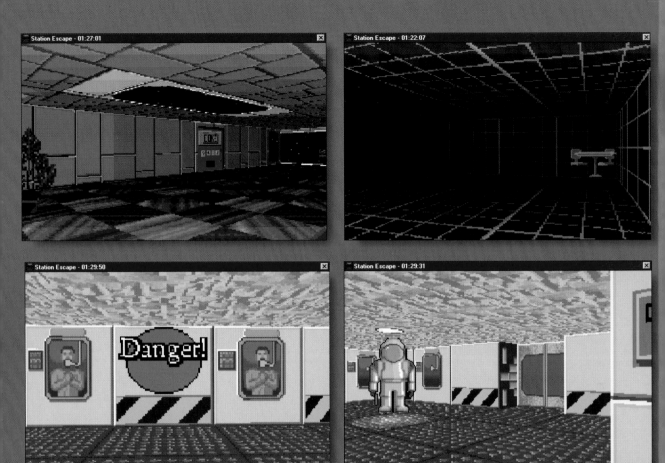

Here are more scenes from the Windows version of the *Station Escape* game. You can use creative light shading effects to change the mood in your games and give your player a real sense of adventure.

The companion CD-ROM provides a playable version of the popular 3-D *Slob Zone* game, which was developed with the *ACK-3D* engine. Try your luck at this fast-action game, where the goal is to gather all the trash you can and fight off enemies using weapons like water balloons, soap, and deodorant. Check out the incredible artwork.

Amazing 3-D Games
Adventure Set

Lary Myers

Edited by Keith Weiskamp

 CORIOLIS GROUP BOOKS

Publisher	*Keith Weiskamp*
Copy Editor	*Diane Green Cook*
Proofreader	*Jenni Aloi*
Interior Design	*Bradley Grannis*
Layout Production	*Bradley Grannis and Michelle Stroup*
Publicist	*Shannon Bounds*
Indexer	*Stephen Bach*
CD-ROM Engineer	*Anthony Potts*

Trademarks: All brand names and product names included in this book are trademarks, registered trademarks, or trade names of their respective holders.

Distributed to the book trade by IDG Books Worldwide, Inc.

Library of Congress Cataloging-in-Publication Data

Myers, Lary
    Amazing 3-D Games adventure set / Lary Myers : edited by Keith Weiskamp
        p. cm.
    Includes Index
    ISBN 1-883577-15-2 : $39.99

Printed in the United States of America

10 9 8 7 6 5 4 3 2 1

Acknowledgments

A book is a container, a receptacle of the thoughts, ideas, and experiences of the people involved in its making. It is also a conduit, tranferring those attributes onto you, the reader. Without writers, editors, and publishers, there would be no books for you to read; without readers, there would be no need for books. Together we make it possible for the distribution and advancement of knowledge from generation to generation.

And so it is a great pleasure that I have been given the opportunity to share the culmination of several years of research and coding. For, like you, I am an avid reader and enjoy seeing the fruits of such labors laid out in black and white. Yet this achievement is but one step along the way to even more exciting things in the future as technology advances and we approach the end of a millennia.

I did not walk these steps alone. There were, and still are, a great many people who traveled along with me. To all of you, I extend my sincerest thanks and best wishes on the electronic infoways that lay in waiting before you. To Mark Betz, who as a former System Operator of the Gamers forum on CompuServe, allowed me to upload a program simply called XTEST, which began the entire development process for *ACK-3D*. Jaimi McEntire, who took the primitive engine under his experienced wing, and began a correspondence and friendship that has grown over the years. With the help of Andrew Welch, Frank Sachse, Ron Sachse, Bart Stewart, Steven Salter, and especially Kenneth Lemeiux, I was able to mold the 3-D engine into a playable demo called *Station Escape*, that was well received in the aforementioned Gamers forum. Bob Provencher, who then as the Sysop of Gamers, allowed me to join in on some wonderful online conferences with others in the gaming community and further expand my pathways into the exciting world of 3-D games. Diana Gruber, who could always make me laugh and lifted my spirits when the waters became cloudy. She is, by far, the most dynamic lady in the gaming world. James R. Shiflett, who believed in me and produced the first commercial *ACK-3D* application as a screen saver. Closer to home, I wish to thank Denise Sicluna for her careful reading of some of my chicken scratches, sometimes referred to as writing.

Without question, Keith Weiskamp has been the sole person who kept me on track during the writing of this book and the further development of the software explained within. To Keith and everyone at the Coriolis Group who took part in this project, and to everyone out there in gameland, I extend my heartfelt appreciation and best wishes to each and every one of you! Lastly I want to mention my two children Elizabeth and Lee, who I hope have a chance to understand the meaning of life and the myriad paths that always present themselves.

About the Author

Lary L. Myers is a key software developer and game designer. His high-performance 3-D game engine and tools have been used by many leading game companies to create their commercial games. He is the former system operator of the popular Gamers forum on CompuServe.

This book is dedicated to my mother, whose endless desire to write and immutable spirit instilled within me the desire to always reach for the stars.

Contents

Chapter 12   Working with Bitmaps   381

Chapter 13   The WinG Connection   417

Chapter 14　Creating a Windows App with ACK-3D　445

Introduction

A few years ago, id Software, a pioneering game development company based in Texas, created a game named *Wolfenstein 3-D* that created quite a stir in the PC gaming industry. In early 1994, id released its blockbuster game, *DOOM,* which sent a tidal wave throughout the gaming industry. Never before had a company put together such exciting 3-D-like games for the PC market. The rapid success of both *Wolfenstein 3-D* and *DOOM* was quite an event—even *USA Today* and NPR radio picked up on the story and praised id for its innovative technology and marketing approach.

These games unleashed a hot graphics technology for PCs that was previously only found on machines with high-end graphics capabilities. Now you can learn how to use some of this exciting 3-D-like technology to create your own applications from games to screen savers to multimedia projects for your PC.

id and other leading game-development companies have mastered the art of creating games with rendered 3-D-like worlds—worlds where you can quickly explore 3-D objects and fight off menacing enemies. This technology was perfected by developing powerful 3-D game engines that provided most of the components needed to assemble a game or other type of 3-D adventure. With the right 3-D engine, such as the one I'll present in this book, you can create the types of games and products you've just dreamed about.

Who Needs This Book

Do you want to learn what goes on behind the scenes of a 3-D action game like *Wolfenstein 3-D* or *Terminator Rampage*? Do you want to know how to build an exciting 3-D game using a powerful prebuilt 3-D engine? Do you want to know how to create your own flexible 3-D engine? Well, you've come to the right place. This book takes you step by step through the basics needed to understand and create your own 3-D action or adventure game. Using your imagination along with the software provided, you can build a game of your own design, populate it with objects that are stationary or moving, and create a 3-D universe like you've never seen before.

The best part is that you don't need to be a game-programming expert to follow along and create your own 3-D-like worlds. After you get a few key background concepts under your belt, such as ray casting and 3-D rendering, you'll be amazed at what you can create using the 3-D game engine provided. All of the code I'll present was developed with Borland C++ 4.0, 4.5, and TASM, although I used straight C to make it easy to follow.

What You Get

This book is like no other book on graphics or PC programming. You won't just be writing a set of simple routines to draw graphics or perform sprite animation. Nope. I'll go all the way and show you how to create a professional-quality 3-D engine that you can use for all types of exciting applications. The core of the engine you'll get has been tested and used by commercial software companies to write professional games including the sample *Slob Zone* game provided on the companion CD-ROM.

I wrote the 3-D game engine and support utilities with the help of other game developers over a three year period, although I've been working with this technology and fine-tuning my ideas for over a decade. Here's what you get:

- A full-featured 3-D game-development engine called *ACK-3D* with complete source code and documentation. The engine is designed to work with a 32-bit flat model so that you can unleash the real power of your PC using full 32-bit address space. No longer are you limited to just 640 K of memory! The engine is especially designed to work with both DOS and Windows. (More on this in a moment.)

- A visual map editor provided to help you interactively create layouts (floors, walls, and ceilings) for your 3-D worlds and then populate your worlds with objects.

- A library of support routines to help you write fast-action games and other products that require the use of the keyboard, mouse, and graphical interfaces.

- A resource compiler to help you combine the different files needed to construct a 3-D world, including bitmap images, objects, and level maps.

- Fun and easy-to-use demonstration programs that show you how to use the *ACK-3D* engine.

- A complete 3-D action game with full source code that you can play for hours of enjoyment.

- Sample games that were written by commercial companies using the *ACK-3D* engine.

An Amazing Engine

If you have followed the gaming world while you hang around on the Internet or on online services like CompuServe, you've probably seen gamers use the term *engine* a time or two. (In fact, if you've played *DOOM*, you might have already encountered the engine that Id has made available for customizing *DOOM*.) The engine I'll present is an actual 3-D programmer's tool. It uses powerful ray-casting technology and provides all of the essentials that you need to easily build 3-D-like worlds.

But the engine is much more than just a library of functions. Its unique and flexible architecture makes it ideal for creating many types of animated 3-D worlds. The engine renders scenes in real-time using a hand-optimized ray-casting technique to give you very fast and smooth animation. You can easily build walls and t.avel through first person, three-dimensional scenes in no time at all. But you don't have to stop with just simple walls because the *ACK-3D* engine allows you to turn walls into doors. You can also create more depth and realism to your 3-D worlds by adding ceilings and floors.

A Special Note about Platforms

When I first started developing the *ACK-3D* engine, I worked mainly with DOS. (Back then, Windows wasn't considered a viable platform for games or 3-D animation!) As I've continued to develop the engine, the market for Windows games and multimedia products has exploded. But the big problem with Windows is that it adds more overhead than DOS for programming fast-action graphics. Fortunately, Microsoft has recently released a special API (DLL) called *WinG*. With this API, you can create special types of bitmaps, access them directly, and blast them on the screen to create faster and smoother animation than possible using the standard graphics functions provided with Windows.

As my engine evolved, I took special care to implement the low-level screen routines in separate modules so that the core of the engine would be easy to port to different platforms. In fact, a few months after uploading an early version of the engine to the popular Gamers forum on CompuServe, I noticed that a number of developers were actively porting the engine to different platforms, including UNIX. This actually gave me the inspiration to figure out the WinG API and develop a version of *ACK-3D* that could run under Windows. My initial goal was to make it run as fast as the DOS version. After porting it, I was surprised at how close I got. So, in this book, I'll present both a DOS and Windows version of the *ACK-3D* engine. As you explore the code, you'll probably be amazed at how much of the same code is shared between the two versions.

The main benefit of this approach is that you'll see firsthand what is involved in writing an engine and creating a game that can work on multiple platforms. Most of the source code discussions focus on the general aspects of the code and 3-D graphics techniques. Along the way, you'll learn a bit about DOS Mode X, WinG, and the art of performing fast animation under DOS and Windows.

How to Use This Book

I wrote this book for C and C++ programmers who want to learn about the art of creating animated 3-D worlds. All of the tricky 3-D concepts originally are presented at a very conceptual level to help you grasp the concepts. Let's face it, 3-D programming is tricky, and you'll need all the help you can get to create 3-D programs. The best part of the book's organization is that you can learn the difficult concepts while you use the *ACK-3D* engine to create your own worlds.

In Part 1, you'll start your 3-D adventure by learning all about the techniques of 3-D animation and gaming. You'll see how concepts like *ray casting, point of view,* and *rendering walls, ceilings, and floors,* come into play.

But you don't have to wait too long to start your 3-D adventure. In Part 2, I'll quickly get you on the road to creating and dissecting the *ACK-3D* engine. We'll start by creating all of the data structures we need to implement the engine. Then, we'll work our way into the code and explore how the ray-casting engine is designed and coded. Along the way, you'll learn how to use powerful optimization techniques and programming tricks, such as table look-ups and fixed-point math, to get the engine running as fast as possible. We'll also take a close look at what is involved in supporting both DOS and Windows. One chapter is devoted to DOS and Mode X graphics, and another chapter takes you inside WinG and fast Windows bitmap animation.

In Part 3, we'll put the engine to work by designing and developing 3-D games. You'll learn how to use the powerful visual map editor to create the components—walls, doors, ceilings, floors, objects—of your 3-D worlds. Then, we'll finish by creating a fun-to-play 3-D game using all of the tools we've developed.

What You'll Need

To create your own 3-D games, you'll need the Borland C++ 4.0 or 4.5 compiler, a 386 or later PC with a VGA display, and the software tools provided on the companion CD-ROM from this adventure set. As I've said, the code was created with Borland C++ 4.0 and also tested with 4.5, but it can be ported to other compilers with minimal effort. Some of the source supplied on the accompanying CD-ROM was written in assembler using Borland's TASM assembler. Assembly code was used for optimization of the critical routines.

If you plan to get even more serious about 3-D game development, or you want to see just how fast some of the 3-D games provided on the companion CD-ROM can run, you'll need a complete multimedia-like gaming system that includes the following hardware and software:

- A 386DX/33 or better processor (486DX/33 or faster is highly recommended)
- At least 2 MB of memory (4MB is recommended)
- Microsoft, Novell, or IBM DOS
- A VGA system or better
- Microsoft-compatible mouse
- A standard sound board (optional)
- A CD-ROM drive

Last but not least, you'll want to have the following on hand as you read this book and develop your games:

- Graph paper and pencil
- A ruler or other straight-edge
- A calculator

Contacting Me

When I'm not snowed under, trying to add more extensions to the *ACK-3D* construction kit, I like to hang out on some of the online services like CompuServe. (In fact I used to be the System Operator of the popular Gamers forum on CompuServe until I got talked into writing this book.) You can send E-mail to me as CIS 72355,655. You can also reach me via snail mail (postal service) by contacting The Coriolis Group at 7339 E. Acoma Drive, Suite 7, Scottsdale, AZ, 85260. If you have a FAX to send, use (602) 483-0193. You can also send Internet E-mail to the Coriolis Group at orders@coriolis.com. If you have a web browser, point your browser to http://www.coriolis.com/coriolis.

Of course, being a busy programmer, I can't answer every letter or question but I'll do my best to respond. I'm always interested in hearing about projects that are developed with the *ACK-3D* kit, so, if you're doing something interesting, please let me know. I hope you enjoy using *ACK-3D* as much as I enjoyed developing it for you.

Lary Myers
March 1995

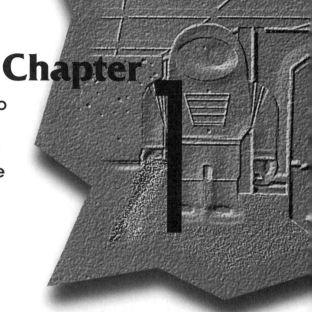

Here's your chance to step into the world of 3-D games and find out how this technology is changing the landscape of the PC game industry.

Entering the World of 3-D Games

You've probably waited a long time to get your hands on some real code and tools so that you can create your own 3-D-like games and interactive adventures—worlds where you travel through mazes and buildings that are inhabited by animated 3-D objects.

In this chapter, I'll take you on a quick tour through the evolution of 3-D games on the PC. Then, we'll explore the key features used to create 3-D games; these features are based on the powerful graphics programming technique called *ray casting*. In some ways, you'll be surprised at the simplicity of these 3-D games, and in other ways, you'll be surprised by the creativity and clever tricks that developers use to create them. Having the "historical perspective" will help you understand where the technology has come from and where it is going.

Before we complete the chapter, we'll explore the different components that go into a 3-D game or interactive world. We'll also discuss the steps that developers use to create hot 3-D games.

An Evolutionary Matter

If you've played computer games for any time at all, you've probably noticed that 3-D games have grown more sophisticated. And lately, the 3-D technology used in PC-based games has really come of age. In the early days of PC games, a game named *Wizardry* was released (you might not remember this one because it was developed for the Apple platform). *Wizardry* placed you in a first person-like environment where you could view the world around you as if you were standing directly in front of your screen looking in, as shown in Figure 1.1. This game was a fantastic way to represent many kinds of adventures, from a trek through a dark dungeon to a frantic race against time trying to escape from a building of horrors. The goal of a game like this is to give you the illusion that you could walk into the game and interact with the world inside. This was quite a departure from the technique used in popular side scrolling games like *Commander Keen*, as shown in Figure 1.2. In a "side scroller" game like this, you view the screen as a flat panel having an animated scene that can move only from side to side. (Side scrollers are great games to play because they usually give you many levels of adventures to encounter.)

The 3-D-like approach used in *Wizardry* imposed a few serious limitations. As you moved forward, you would take a giant step into the next block of a maze. As you turned, you would whip around 90 degrees to face to the left or right, coming full circle in just four turns. This was not exactly the way you or I would move around in real life, at least under normal conditions. The limit-

Figure 1.1   Playing a 3-D game where you can "walk inside."

Figure 1.2   *A sample side scroller game named* Commander Keen.

ing factor in a game like this was that the walls, which gave the player the 3-D perspective, were created out of simple polygons. The awkward navigation of a game like *Wizardry* kept the player from really experiencing the true potential of 3-D as we know it in the real world. Yet, many hundreds of games exist today that use this same approach to put you in a wide variety of settings. I created several games using the polygon type of walls, my favorite being *The Dungeons of Ashka*, which I first created on the now almost extinct TRS-80 computer. (Don't tell me you still have one of these machines in your closet like I do!)

Fortunately, computers (at least most of them) got better and *much* faster over time. Once the PC AT came along, a whole new world of gaming possibilities opened up, and 3-D adventures began to take on a more realistic overtone. For example, *The Bard's Tale* by Chris Crawford put you above ground in a town where the walls seemed to flow past as you moved forward (see Figure 1.3). Although you could turn only in 90-degree units, the game felt surrealistic as the walls moved smoothly past while you walked down a street. This was also true of the underground sewers and dungeons that you encountered in the game as you pursued your quest. This approach was truly a delight to gamers and another milestone in the evolutionary process of 3-D games.

Also during this time, 3-D-like flight simulator games began to run much more smoothly. Figure 1.4 shows a typical flight simulator using simple 3-D graphics. These games were quite different from other 3-D-like games because they accurately simulated the flight characteristics of popular aircraft.

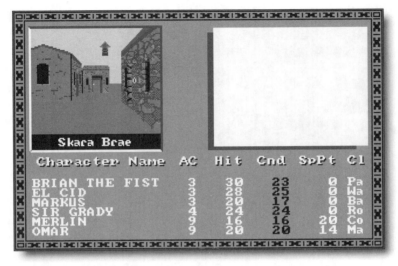

Figure 1.3　*A sample scene from* The Bard's Tale *game.*

Figure 1.4　*Simulating flight with a 3-D-like flight simulator.*

The approach behind these games was to create mathematical models to simulate the motion of flight in three dimensions. In this respect, games like these were considered "true 3-D." Unfortunately, their landscapes were not exactly state-of-the-art: Mountains and buildings were often represented by filled-in polygons, which gave the appearance of a world where things were devoid of detail compared to the real world. But, they were 3-D-like and you could spin around, tilt up and down, and fly over and under objects to your heart's content.

Since their introduction to the PC market years ago, 3-D flight simulators have come a long way; much farther, in fact, than I would have guessed. Even on a moderately fast PC you can zoom across the sky in an F-16 and shoot up enemy aircraft, all with complete freedom of movement. Many of the advancements in today's popular virtual reality field actually are based on the pioneering work of 3-D flight simulator technology. If you are ever in Las Vegas, you owe it to yourself to go to the Luxor and take their mini full-motion simulator game out for a test flight. This simulator, created by Sega, combines graphics with a motion device to give you the sense of real flight. What's amazing is that the graphics look exactly the same as you see on your PC screen; however, the motion aspect tricks your body into thinking that you really are immersed in a 3-D environment.

3-D Comes of Age (Well, Sort Of)

The real potential of 3-D graphics for PC games emerged when *Wolfenstein 3-D* was released. This highly popular action game, created by id Software and published by Apogee, took the gaming world by storm from the moment it was available on bulletin boards around the country. John Carmack, developer of the game, placed you in a free moving world where you could turn at any angle and walk forward and back in a fluid motion of unbelievable speed (see Figure 1.5). The walls of this environment were beautifully texture mapped with graphics that caused many "ooh's" and "aah's" from both the player and those who happened to be looking over the player's shoulder, which was

Figure 1.5 Wolfenstein 3-D *in action.*

often a large crowd. Here was a game that simulated a fast-moving 3-D environment, perfect for adventuring below the surface in a mystical dungeon, or within the confines of a building.

Keep in mind that *Wolfenstein 3-D* was another evolutionary step in 3-D gaming, although it presented its own restrictions on the way the player interacted with the environment. After the initial excitement of the game wears off (or I should say, if the excitement wears off), you begin to notice some of the limitations. The first, and most debated one, was the fact that the environment was not true 3-D because you couldn't walk under an object and you couldn't look up at the ceiling overhead or down at your feet. The second limitation was very noticeable soon after you began playing: The walls were constructed of blocks at 90 degree angles as shown in Figure 1.6. There were no diagonal walls, or even different height walls in this game. These limitations caused many gamers and reviewers to use the term *2-D and a half* to describe the graphics of *Wolfenstein 3-D*. (It's tough when you are the first to develop new technology—you tend to get a lot of arrows in your back.)

Debating whether this technology is "true 3-D" is a big waste of time in my opinion. What's important is how fun and engaging games like *Wolfenstein 3-D* are for the player. Once this technology was released, many other games appeared on the scene, each having its own unique way of displaying a free-moving first person perspective in a maze-type setting. Let's look at some of the more popular games that used this 3-D approach:

Figure 1.6 *How the walls are represented in* Wolfenstein 3-D.

- *Ken's Labyrinth*

  This was the first game to come out after *Wolfenstein 3-D* was released. Ken basically had the same dream as I did—to create an environment using the extremely popular *Wolfenstein 3-D* look and feel.

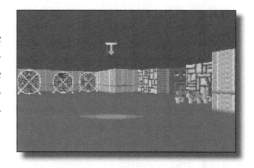

- *Blake Stone*

  This game was a very popular Apogee release that was similar to *Wolfenstein 3-D* except that the action takes place in a science fiction environment. The most noticeable feature added to this game was that the floors and ceilings were texture mapped. (Until this point, only

  walls had been texture mapped in 3-D-like games.) The texture-mapped ceilings and floors gave the game a much more realistic setting. *Blake Stone* also provided unique transparent walls, which added a new dimension to PC 3-D games. With transparent walls, you could see through a section of a maze into another area and create items such as doorways that led into other rooms.

- *Shadow Caster*

  This was a fantasy game, produced by three cooperating companies, which first demonstrated a variety of new features, including a scrolling background, characters swimming in water, and multi-height walls. I especially liked the multi-height walls idea introduced in this

  game because they allowed you to walk through scenes that seemed much more three-dimensional.

- *Terminator Rampage*

  This game was a spinoff of
  Wolfenstein 3-D. The graphics techniques and 3-D technology behind
  the game were not very different
  from *Wolfenstein,* but the approach
  of designing a 3-D game around a
  popular movie plot was a novel
  idea and probably helped the
  game's sales. As far as I know, this
  was one of the first games based
  on a movie plot. Today, big-screen
  producers from Hollywood and
  game developers from as far away
  as Holland are getting together left
  and right to create the last word in
  electronic entertainment.

- *Isle of the Dead*

  This was a really gruesome game that used some old techniques in new
  ways. For example, when you first start the game, you see a shoreline. But
  the shoreline wasn't created using any new sophisticated 3-D programming
  and animation techniques. Believe it or not, the ocean waves that appear in
  the shoreline were simulated using walls and floor textures like those found
  in other maze-style games. This game really opened my eyes to the creativity that was possible by using just the *Wolfenstein*-style engine.

- *Legends of Valour*

  This was a good game with exte-
  rior and interior views that depict
  a small town with multi-height
  walls. This is another ray casting
  style of game, very well done.

- *Depth Dwellers*

  This shareware game used high walls and a unique method of showing doors opening. Its smooth animation and wide variety of weapons made this game fun to play.

- *Arena*

  This game provided a huge environment that incorporated many of the features used in the other games we've explored. The game provides both above and below ground level 3-D scenes to give the player the illusion that he or she can travel around in a very large world.

When we build our 3-D engine, we'll be using many of the graphics techniques found in games like *Wolfenstein 3-D*, as well as some new features seen in later generation games like *DOOM* and the ones we've just explored. The essential goal is to use the free-moving, first-person navigation that first made *Wolfenstein 3-D* so popular. Once you understand how to create and use this type of technology, you can modify and adapt it to many types of settings. The beauty of having a well-designed engine is that you can realistically modify it when new technology comes your way. As I present the *ACK-3D* engine, I'll try to point out techniques, such as *BSP trees*, and parts of the source code that could be extended to add powerful new features.

Enter the World of DOOM

We can't leave the subject of 3-D action games without exploring the game hit of the 90s—*DOOM*. In this game, you suddenly are thrust into a fantastic world of diagonal walls, steps that can be walked up and down, elevators and wide doors that give you the sensation that you are moving around in a world of tremendous chunks of metal, inside and outside views, alcoves, and much more, as shown in Figure 1.7.

Figure 1.7　*DOOM—the game that really turns heads.*

DOOM is very appealing to both game players and developers because of its tremendous leap in 3-D-like technology, and besides it's really fun to play! John Carmack, *DOOM's* creator, used a new philosophy to create the surreal world of *DOOM.* Of course, the entire mechanics of how *DOOM* is written is beyond the scope of this book, but you might want to know some of the key development issues that go on behind the scenes. As we develop our engine throughout this book, I'll point out some of the approaches that our engine uses to create scenes as compared to the methods that *DOOM* employs. But before we move on and explore the elements that go into the design and creation of a 3-D game, let's look at a few of the concepts behind *DOOM.*

In the traditional *Wolfenstein 3-D* approach to rendering scenes, walls are represented as individual bitmap images, as shown in Figure 1.8. The walls must be placed at grid points in a 2-D map. This type of representation works well for creating scenes that are based on geometric shapes.

DOOM, on the other hand, treats walls as line segments with endpoints that are no longer restricted to grid points on a 2-D map. Rays are still cast out from a player, except line intersections are now used to determine the bitmap to display. Rooms are defined in *sectors* to speed up the rendering process, with each sector capable of having its own set of attributes to define attributes, such as height, floor and ceiling bitmaps, lighting, and so on. But is this true 3-D? Well, no, but it's still an amazing achievement to the player, the one who is most important to a successful game. When the players sit down to spend an evening battling evil forces, do they really care if method A or B was used, or do they

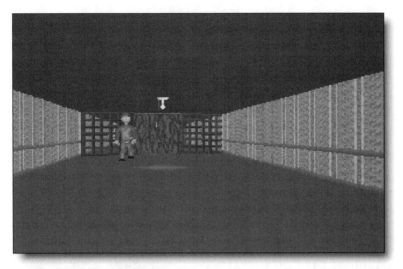

Figure 1.8 *Representing walls as bitmaps.*

only care just how much fun the darn game is? I believe the latter, and that's why I'm presenting the *ACK-3D* engine to you, complete and ready to roll so that you can start creating your own fun and exciting adventures!

The Features of a Ray-Casted, 3-D Game

You've probably played some (or maybe all) of the games we've been exploring, but you probably haven't thought much about what makes these types of games tick. (Unless, of course, you've tried to write one before.) Although the 3-D scenes presented in these different games may vary widely, the basic techniques of both playing and designing the games are similar. The more obvious components, such as rendered walls, floors, ceilings, movable objects, and stationary objects are labeled in Figure 1.9. Of course, there are other features such as story levels, story lines, 3-D animation, secret doors, and so on that are difficult to show in a stationary picture, so we'll need to take a closer look.

DESIGN TIP

Playing the Slob Zone Game

Before you spend too much time just reading about ray-casted, 3-D games, you should try out the game *Slob Zone* provided on the companion CD-ROM. This is a complete ray-casted, 3-D game created with the *ACK-3D* engine that features rendered walls, ceilings, and floors, moving doors, sound and music, animated and stationary objects, and a detailed maze through which you can travel.

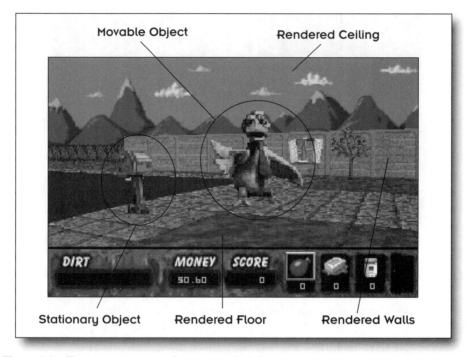

Movable Object   Rendered Ceiling

Stationary Object   Rendered Floor   Rendered Walls

Figure 1.9   *The key components of a ray-casted, 3-D game.*

The game is easy to play. You can use the arrow keys or the mouse to move around in 3-D space.

First, What Is Ray Casting?

I've used the term ray casting a few times already in this book, but I haven't actually explained what it is. Although we'll be exploring the process of ray casting in detail in the next chapter, let's explore this concept now so that you can have a better understanding of what's needed to create the types of games we are discussing.

Ray casting is simply a technique of determining where objects are placed in a scene as a person moves around. As an example, Figure 1.10 shows a simple scene that contains a few walls. If you were to walk into that scene and move forward, you'd want to know where the walls are placed so that you wouldn't run into them. Of course, you can see them with your eyes, but a computer program cannot. But what a program can do is cast out rays to see what's in view. Usually, these rays are cast in an arc so that the walls and other objects that are directly in front of a player as well as those off to the side can be found.

Mysterious Mazes

Many game developers like to refer to ray-casted, 3-D games as maze games, since they actually take place in a maze-like environment. For example, when you move around in the *Station Escape* game, you are moving around in the maze shown in Figure 1.11. Here we are also showing what one section of the maze looks like as it's rendered on the screen. If you move forward and run into a wall, you have to go backwards and find a different way around the wall.

In this respect, creating a 3-D game like *Station Escape* involves building a maze and then deciding where you want to put different objects into the maze. But don't let this seemingly rigid maze structure limit your thinking of what can be created. You can represent most settings in the real world as a maze—your house, office, downtown Manhattan, even an amusement park. All you need to do is apply some creativity to the way you design your walls, floors, and ceilings.

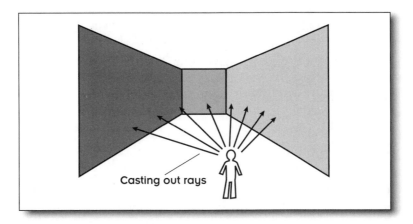

Casting out rays

Figure 1.10 *Using ray-casting techniques to find objects in our view.*

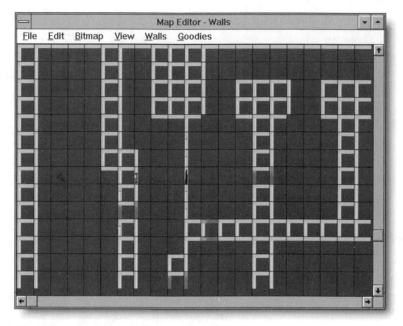

Figure 1.11   *The maze used in the* Station Escape *game.*

Rooms, Walls, Floors, and Ceilings

The components that give shape to a maze in a 3-D world are rooms, walls, floors, and ceilings. Rooms are constructed simply by placing walls in the maze. The walls themselves are created out of bitmaps. But a wall doesn't have to just look like those cheap partitions you find in a used office furniture store. A wall can be the side of a mountain, a wave at the shoreline, a doorway into a store, a dense row of trees at the edge of a forest, or even the side of a school bus. Essentially, a wall is a stationary object that can only be placed at a boundary point in a maze grid.

When you create your games, you have complete control over what your walls look like and where they are placed. Once you design a layout for your maze, you can create different types of walls (using a painting program) and then place the walls into your maze. Figure 1.12 shows samples of bitmap wall textures that have been created for different games. The more life-like you create your walls and the more textures you use, the better your 3-D world will look.

On the companion CD-ROM, you'll find a set of bitmap files that contain images for creating your own walls and objects. These bitmap files are provided in both .PCX and .BBM format. Each bitmap file contains a 64×64 pixel wall or object bitmap.

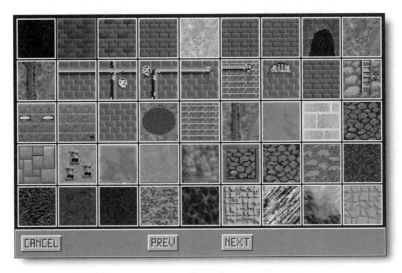

Figure 1.12   *Creating walls using bitmap textures.*

Oops, Don't Forget the Story

If you've taken a few minutes to play the *Station Escape* game, you've probably noticed that the game takes place in a space station. The game is actually designed around an intriguing science fiction story I created. I won't present the whole story now because I want to save it for later when we actually create the entire game, but it starts like this:

> *Slowly, ever so slowly, your eyes begin to focus as you awaken from the cold sleep of cryogenic freeze. Every muscle in your body is screaming at you to stay right where you are, but you know you need to move around to get the circulation started. You shiver as your body temperature rises above freezing back into the normal range for the living. Your head still hasn't cleared but it seems that something is amiss. Nobody is here, at least in the field of vision you care to try to see. Rubbing your neck, you begin looking around the cryogenic lab. Nothing, nobody, nowhere. Odd, the entire thawing process must have been done by the central computer, but why? And then you hear it. The station's alarm klaxon sounding the evacuation tone. Still groggy, you remember the briefing before you went into freeze, "Should the station require evacuation, the computer will automatically bring everyone out of frozen sleep."*

Figure 1.13   *The start-up screen for Station Escape.*

The story is further enhanced by the start-up screen that appears when you start the game, as shown in Figure 1.13. As you might guess, the space station needs some serious repair and it's your job to quickly fix it.

So why go into all of this story detail? The story is what keeps the game together. It makes the game seem larger than life and enhances the setting of the game. After all, traveling around in a maze for no reason can get really boring after a few minutes. When you set out to design your own games, take the time to come up with a good story and then build the graphical world (maze, walls, ceilings, floors, and objects) to pull the player into the story. You should think of the story as your foundation. The better you make it, the better your chances are of having a great game.

Levels of 3-D Worlds

Most 3-D games provide multiple levels of adventure to keep players hooked for hours and maybe even days. Each level of your game can easily be constructed from a maze map. You can also introduce different objects in different levels. The levels also give you a chance to change your scenery and keep your game from getting too boring. As an example, Figure 1.14 shows different scenes from the game *Slob Zone*. This game was also written with the *ACK-3D* engine, and a special version of it is included on the companion CD-ROM so that you can see the types of games that can be created with the engine.

In this respect, many 3-D games are not all that different from arcade-style side scrollers where the main goal is to navigate your way through a level

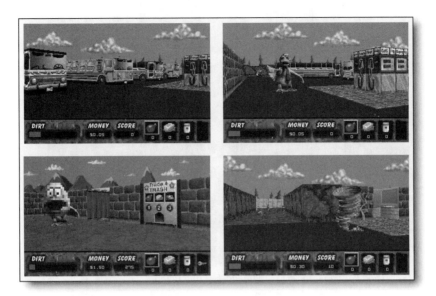

Figure 1.14   *Different views available in the* Slob Zone *game.*

until you collect enough points to move up to another level. You can use all of the standard tricks, such as having your player locate and pass through a secret door to move to another level or rescue a captured crystal. And if you're really into violence, you can set up your games so that the player has to wipe out all of the aggressive villains in order to move up to a new level.

A Little Lighting, Please

You've seen that 3-D scenes are constructed from walls that you can navigate around, but these walls would not look very realistic if they could not be displayed in different ways as a player moves around. Many 3-D games, such as *Wolfenstein 3-D* and *DOOM*, use special lighting and shading techniques to give players the sensation that they are moving about in a real 3-D world. As an example, Figure 1.15 shows how objects will change color (darken) as a player moves farther away from them.

There are many types of lighting and shading techniques that can be used in a 3-D game. Most of them involve changing colors in the color palette used to display walls as a player moves. We'll look at different types of lighting and shading techniques that can be performed when we create the *ACK-3D* engine.

Stationary and Animated Objects

The features that really give a 3-D game its unique personality are the stationary and animated objects that are used. As players work through a maze

Figure 1.15　*Using lighting effects to create life-like animation.*

scene, they can encounter all kinds of stationary objects—desks, chairs, coke machines—and animated objects—monsters, fire balls, and whatever else your imagination can conjure.

After I completed the first version of the *ACK-3D* engine over a year ago, I put together a few sample game demos to test some of the engine's features. I'm not an artist by trade so most of the objects I put into my 3-D creations were very simple. I sent the demos around to other developers and what surprised me the most were the animation changes they made and the types of objects they incorporated into their versions. My all-time favorite was the wild duck that throws eggs (see Figure 1.16) created by Andrew Hunter for the *Slob Zone* game. This was a real stroke of genius; it further opened my eyes to the endless possibilities you can create with animated objects.

All Those Secret Touches

The final touches that go into a 3-D game are all the secret tricks that make players stand up and take notice. These are usually the ideas that come to you in the middle of the night or when you are daydreaming. I like to keep a notebook close at hand and jot down my ideas, even if they seem crazy at the time.

How *ACK-3D* Came to Be

After traversing the hallways of *Wolfenstein 3-D* (and later *DOOM*) and blasting the enemies (these games were shoot-em-ups in gamers' terms), I wanted

Figure 1.16 *The famous wild duck created by Andrew Hunter for the* Slob Zone *game.*

to create an engine that would allow me to expand upon the environments presented. My starting point was to model the 3-D-like techniques presented in *Wolfenstein 3-D* and then add features such as multi-height walls, fully textured floors and ceilings, highly animated 3-D objects with multiple views, and so on. I wanted to be able to take the player into fantasy dungeons, museums, pyramids, or a basic workplace using the free moving 3-D-like environment. The first question that popped into my head was, how'd they do it? I started experimenting with the technology, and after a number of months of trial and error, I was building 3-D worlds.

Unfortunately, when I started, there were no books available on actual game programming, let alone 3-D game programming. (Although, since that time a few books have emerged that claim to tell you all about the secrets of writing games like *DOOM*, they end up really selling you short!) I was working in the dark to figure out what works and what doesn't. (You should have seen some of my first attempts!)

Being a "tool-oriented" developer, I wanted to go one more step and create a tool so that gamers who didn't know, or want to know, how to program, could still create a variety of playable 3-D scenarios using their own imagination. That's how the *Animation Construction Kit*, or *ACK-3D*, came into being (heck, my initial filename for the engine was called XTEST; I had to come up with a better name than that!). With a kit, based upon a library that allows programmers to interface into their own games, the untapped potential of the 3-D environment could become a reality.

Along the way, I also wanted to add enhancements to the original design of the *Wolfenstein* engine, as a sort of evolutionary process that would make it much more appealing to game designers. This was my goal, and after much head scratching and a lot of help from other game designers, *ACK-3D* in its initial library version became a reality. This book describes the internal workings of the engine to satisfy another of my goals, the release of the methods used to create the 3-D environment to the general public. With the discussion and software provided here, not to mention your imagination, my hope is that we will see the biggest, meanest, most enjoyable games ever introduced into the gaming community. If I help to play a part in that process, my goal has been met, and I can sit back and say "I actually helped here." Let's get moving in that direction, shall we, and let the fun begin!

A Truly General Construction Kit

Our emphasis so far has been on just ray-casted, 3-D games, but keep in mind that you can use the *ACK-3D* engine to create all kinds of applications that could benefit from interactive 3-D "walk-through" type graphics. Here are some examples of applications that could be created:

- Screen savers
- Educational programs
- Walk-through demos
- 3-D multimedia
- Navigational mapping programs

Where to Start?

After reading this chapter, you might be feeling a little overwhelmed by all of the components that go into a 3-D interactive world. To put everything in perspective, here's a step-by-step checklist to help you understand the process involved in creating a 3-D game.

Step 1: Create a story or theme for your 3-D game. Try to develop your story as much as possible before you begin to create the components of the game (for example, walls, objects, ceilings, floors, and so on).

Step 2: Create the concepts for the initial levels of your game.

Step 3: Create bitmap images for the components of the game—walls, doors, ceilings, floors, stationary objects, movable objects. The techniques for doing this are explained in Chapter 12.

Step 4: Use the *ACK-3D* visual map editor to design a maze and put in all of the game components. The editor will automatically create the data structures and resource files needed to use the *ACK-3D* functions.

Step 5: Write your game code using the *ACK-3D* engine functions. Your program must control all of the logic for your game, as well as make calls to the key *ACK-3D* functions to initialize the engine and generate 3-D scenes. You'll learn all about how to build games with the *ACK-3D* functions in Part 3 of this book.

Step 6: Try out your game and keep fine-tuning it until you think you're finished. Then, spend a little more time testing it and smoothing out the rough spots.

Step 7: Enlist the help of everyone you know to beta-test your game. Try to find people who are really picky and aren't afraid to give you their two cents' worth.

Step 8: Fix every problem you can and get your game out to market!

In the next chapter, we'll get our feet wet as we start to unravel the technology behind ray-casting engines.

2

What really goes on behind the scenes of a 3-D maze game? Read this chapter and you'll be well on your way to fast ray casting in 3-D.

Exploring the Techniques of Casting 3-D Worlds

B efore we jump in and start to code our *ACK-3D* engine, let's take some time to discuss the technology behind 3-D ray casting and animation. I want to make sure you are "up to speed" on what goes on under the hood, before throwing a bunch of code listings your way and saying, "Now see, this is how it's done." By the time you finish this chapter, you'll have a solid conceptual understanding of what ray casting is and how you can use this technique to display walls and 3-D-like objects in perspective. This was one of the biggest hurdles I had to get over in creating the *ACK-3D* engine. I spent many long hours trying to figure out the best methods for creating graphics that would be fast enough to display texture-mapped walls in real time. The real challenge isn't just knowing the basics of how walls and objects are created in a 3-D, maze-type game, but knowing how to create 3-D-like worlds where your players can move around at the speed of light.

We'll start our 3-D technology tour by exploring the basics of both ray tracing and ray casting. Then, we'll explore the key techniques and concepts required to set up a maze-type, 3-D game, including walls, point of view, field of view, calculating wall heights, and much more. In the second part of the chapter, I'll show you some of the actual optimization tricks that the *ACK-3D* engine uses to generate fast 3-D-like animation. I'll need to introduce some calculations, so get out your trig and geometry books from high school and hang on.

Soon you'll be casting rays and letting your imagination whisk you away toward your own 3-D adventure.

To Ray Cast a World

Buzzwords are everywhere. The one associated with the technology we'll be using in this book to create our 3-D worlds is called *ray casting*. Ray casting is actually a spinoff of a technique you may be familiar with called *ray tracing*. Ray tracing has been around since the 1960s, and it is used to create very accurate-looking pictures of real life with detailed lighting effects, mirroring, and texture. Most of the 3-D graphics images you see in traditional books on computer graphics are created using ray-tracing techniques. For example, Figure 2.1 shows an interesting 3-D-like image that was created using a high-end, ray-tracing program. But back in the 1960s and 1970s when this technique was in wide use by large organizations, such as NASA and Evans and Sutherland, it took quite a powerful computer to handle all of the graphics processing required. As PCs have become much faster, ray-tracing software, such as *POV-RAY* and

Figure 2.1　*An image created using ray tracing techniques.*

SIMPLRAY, has migrated to the desktop. (See the reference section in the back of this book for a list of books and software that feature ray-tracing techniques.)

If you haven't experimented with ray tracing software on your PC, I suggest you do so. With many of the programs that are available, you can specify parameters, such as light sources, shading, texture, perspective, and so on. Then, the program builds a 3-D scene for you, right before your eyes. This is a good and fun way to learn about the concepts involved in 3-D computer graphics, such as perspective, shading, scaling, and texture mapping. Of course, you won't be able to walk around your 3-D creations like you can in an interactive 3-D game.

So how does ray tracing work? In a nutshell, ray tracing involves modeling real-world objects by simulating the light rays that reflect off the objects. This might sound complicated, but it's actually quite simple conceptually. Let's say you are in a room looking at a glass of beer. (Now stand back a few feet; otherwise you might be tempted to pick it up and drink it!) As Figure 2.2 shows, you are the *viewer*, the glass of beer is the *object*, and the window in your room is the *light source*. Light comes from the light source, bounces off the glass of beer, and comes to you. The light coming from the window to the

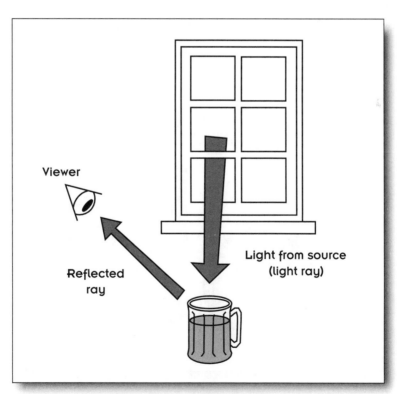

Figure 2.2   *How ray tracing works (conceptually).*

beer glass is called the *light ray* and the light from the glass to you is called the *reflected ray*. This reflected light brings you the colors of the glass so that you can see it. Okay, we're done. Go pick up that glass of beer and have at it.

Of course, keep in mind that our example has been simplified a bit in terms of how light rays actually travel. In reality, many of the light rays that originate from a light source, collide with objects and bounce off in many different directions (like kids in a playground). Some of the rays get absorbed and some of them continue on and bounce off other objects, never reaching the viewer's eye. This dynamic ballet of light rays is responsible for creating the types of images that we see in the world.

To program ray-tracing techniques with a computer, you need to sort of simulate the way light travels in the real-world. Actually, because light rays bounce around all over the place and many of them don't actually come to the viewer, ray tracing in a computer is usually performed by starting with the viewer and projecting rays backwards toward an object. By taking this "back-wards" approach, as shown in Figure 2.3, we won't miss too many of the important reflected light rays needed to make an image appear.

What's the best way to simulate light rays? Over the years, programmers have evolved a technique of using what is called a *camera* or *pin-hole model.*

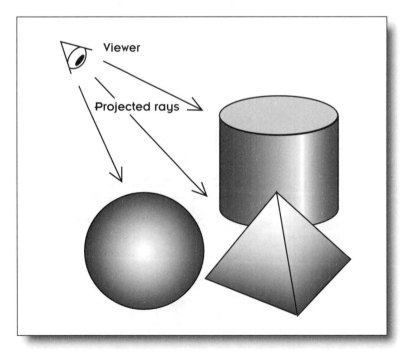

Figure 2.3   *How the computer models light rays when ray tracing.*

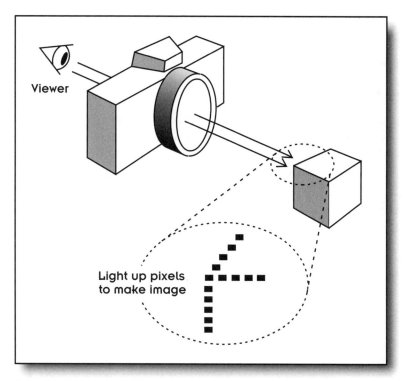

Figure 2.4 *Computer ray tracing using the camera model.*

As Figure 2.4 shows, the camera serves as the viewer. It takes a "picture" of an imaginary object illuminated by imaginary light sources. When a "picture is taken," rays are projected backward toward an object. The object is represented in the computer as a collection of pixels or points. When a ray hits a particular location of the object, the ray tracer sets the appropriate pixels to make that part of the object light up. As you might guess, you can create all kinds of interesting and realistic imaging effects, such as shadows, reflections, and highlights, by experimenting with your light source. In the world of computerized ray tracing, the data and calculations that support these imaging effects are called the *lighting model.*

The Real Drawback Is Speed

The biggest drawback to the ray-tracing approach we've been exploring is speed (or I should say, lack of speed!). In fact, ray tracing is so slow that it is pretty much impossible to create a dynamic, real-time environment on anything short of the fastest super computers, and then at a cost of thousands of man-hours worth of effort. Not exactly the kind of process suitable to the gaming or entertainment industry. Imagine how impatient you or your kids would get if they had to wait an hour for an image to be updated as they moved around in their Super Nintendo 3-D game. No way!

A Better Way of Modeling

But there is a solution. Game programmers are a clever bunch, and they are always finding unique ways to speed up how things are done. In this case, by trimming down the ray-tracing process, and imposing some limitations on the model used to create an environment, a quicker method of simulating objects with light rays is possible. And that's where ray *casting* comes in. Recall that ray tracing took a beam of light and traced its path from a light source to an object, maybe to yet another object, and then to the eye of the viewer. As shown in Figure 2.5, ray casting strips this process down into a path from the eye of the viewer to the first obstacle it encounters.

Here's another way to look at how this ray-casting process works. Imagine yourself sitting on the floor in an empty room (with no glass of beer available). As shown in Figure 2.6, lines start out from a single point in front of you and fan out until they hit the bottom of the walls of the room. When one of

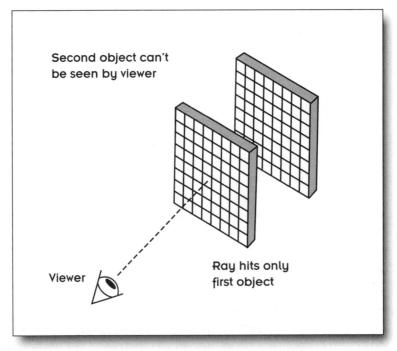

Figure 2.5   *Simplifying the process of viewing objects with ray casting.*

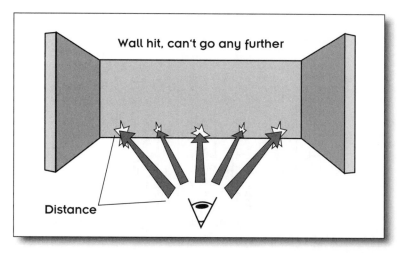

Figure 2.6   *Modeling a room with ray casting techniques.*

those lines hits the wall, it stops and the information about that line—such as its distance from you and where it came into contact on the wall—gives you all that is needed to display that wall on the computer screen. In this respect, ray casting allows us to easily model a world that is constantly in motion. As you move, the computer can easily calculate where objects—like walls, ceilings, and even monsters—should be placed. That, in a nutshell, is the underlying concept of a ray-casting engine. Ah, but we're not done yet!

We can also redefine the number of rays that are cast by only casting a ray for each column of the video screen (in our case, 320) as shown in Figure 2.7. This significantly reduces the time required to create a scene. Because we don't really need to look at every pixel of the screen, we only have to cast rays from the player out across a flat two-dimensional map.

Lost in a Maze

By now you're probably thinking, "Wow, I can just cast this ray out and find any old wall, no matter where it's located, then display the bitmap for that wall and, and, ..." Well, not yet; we need to discuss a little more about some of the things that restrict the way we display our 3-D worlds. Let's take our adventure a little deeper and wander into a maze (literally) of the actual technology behind the ACK-3D game engine and games like *Wolfenstein 3-D.* There are many hidden rooms to discover in our maze, so let's get going.

As we uncover the engine, keep in mind that our goal is to render a 3-D, maze-type world with walls, ceilings, floors, and so on from a 2-D represen-

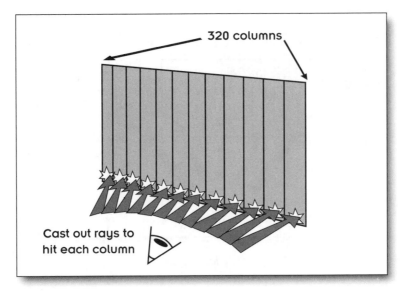

Figure 2.7　*Casting out 320 rays to cover the computer screen.*

tation. To get there, we'll need to use some math tricks. But don't panic yet because the math isn't as scary as you might first think. To help you out, I've tried to keep the math discussions as conceptual as possible, and I've grouped them into this section of the book so that you can refer back to them if needed, without seeing complicated math equations spread all over the place.

A Wall Is a Wall Is a Wall

The main component we'll be displaying in our 3-D environment is a wall— a flat, ordinary, everyday wall. But this wall could have dusty stones of an ancient dungeon, pictures of all the presidents, art from the impressionistic period, or even samples of wallpaper for prospective customers. All we need to worry about now is how to get our wall displayed on the screen. The first step in doing that is knowing how to determine just what walls we are looking at as we move around.

It All Depends on Your Point of View

Before we get any further, we need to discuss the term *Point of View*, or *POV* for short. The POV represents both the person sitting in front of the computer in the real-world and some of the attributes as far as the 3-D engine is concerned. When we begin our process of casting out rays to find what's out there, we need to start at a single point—just as we did when we had you sitting on the floor of an empty room and we drew lines from your position to the walls of the room. (Of course, don't try this at home—your spouse and kids or your parents may object to you moving all the furniture out and marking up the floor with a bunch of chalk lines!) As Figure 2.8 indicates, this single point is called the *Point of View* and is represented by the following three attributes:

- X coordinate
- Y coordinate
- Angle we are currently facing

(There are several more attributes we can attach to the Point of View, such as the height off the floor, but for now, we'll only use these three attributes, since they form the basis for our engine.) With this information, we know just where to start casting rays and in what direction they will go. We don't need to be concerned with any walls behind us or even off to the left or right of us, because these walls will not be displayed on the computer screen.

Another term we will encounter is the *Field of View*, or *FOV*. This term tells us how much of the world we see at any particular moment. The *ACK-3D* engine uses a 64 degree Field of View to ray cast scenes. The larger the FOV, the more area you will see at any one time, and the smaller the FOV gets, the less you will see, akin to tunnel vision.

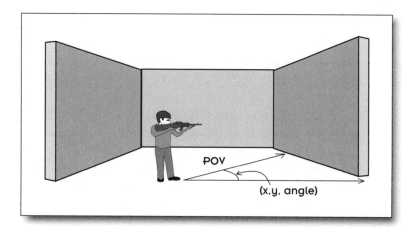

Figure 2.8 *Starting with a Point of View (POV).*

DESIGN TIP

I chose an FOV of 64 degrees for *ACK-3D* simply by trial and error. After trying different settings for the FOV, 64 degrees turned out to produce the best looking scenes on the screen. If you do some experimentation, you'll find that the wider you make the FOV, the more stretched out the walls appear, while a narrower FOV creates a claustrophobic-looking scene with scrunched walls. An FOV of 64 degrees is both pleasant to the eye and a bit easier to work with in terms of the math that is required, as we'll see later on.

How High Is a Wall?

Okay, we're sitting in our room and we've cast out rays and discovered that there is a wall in front of us that our ray has hit. So now what? How do we take the distance to that wall and turn it into something we can use? Since the apparent size of a wall changes with different distances, we can build a relationship of distance to height. We want the height of the wall to be smaller the farther the wall is from our POV, as it would be in the real world. This method allows us to scale our wall dynamically as we move around in our 3-D environment. The actual height used to draw walls in 3-D, ray-casted environments is based on individual preference, but for the purposes of this book, and some special optimization reasons, I've chosen to use this formula to relate height to distance:

Height = (64 * 256) / distance

The value 64 also happens to be the size of the bitmaps we'll be using with our engine. Each wall is constructed by using sections of 64×64 bitmaps, as shown in Figure 2.9. You'll learn how to create these bitmaps and build maze environments using the visual map editor later in this book. The value 256 will become apparent when we look at the optimization techniques used to perform our ray casting.

But don't trust my calculations. Let's run some tests on this relationship to make sure it does what we want. Get out some graph paper that has wide spaces between the grid lines. (You don't need to have a lot of grid lines, so the more space between them the better.) If you don't have graph paper, use a napkin—a lot of great things have been invented using napkins. Now draw a box that is two squares by two squares and put a point in the cross hairs in the center. That's you, the POV, standing in the center of a room made up of four squares (see Figure 2.10). Because we are using bitmaps that are 64 pixels wide and 64 pixels tall, we can safely say that each square of our room is 64 by 64 in size. This becomes very important as we calculate our distances.

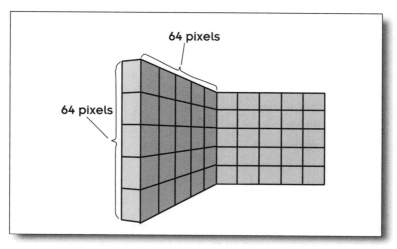

Figure 2.9 *Constructing walls using 64x64 bitmap sections.*

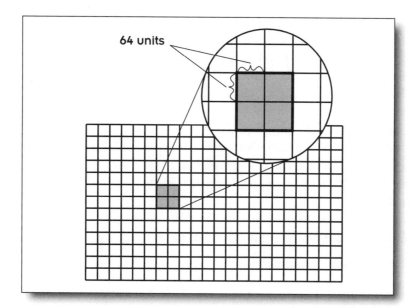

Figure 2.10 *Creating a room made up of 64x64 units.*

DESIGN TIP

Take note of the grid configuration shown in Figure 2.10. I'm frequently asked why each grid of the map is 64x64. The reason is that the width of the bitmaps we use for the walls is 64 pixels, as shown in Figure 2.11. If we wanted to use a different grid size, such as 128, we would have more grid space than pixels of the bitmap. (Ah, but we could double each column of the wall and make it fill the entire grid,

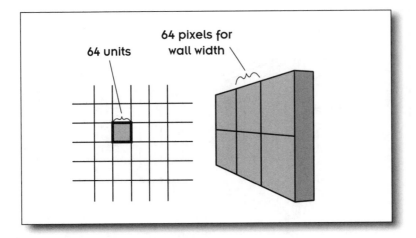

Figure 2.11 *Using walls with a width of 64 pixels.*

but that's another story.) For now, let's make the size of each grid square equal to the width of the bitmaps we will be using. Note that the height of a wall doesn't enter into this discussion. Because we are standing up the walls on their edge, we really don't care how high the bitmap is, at least in relation to the size of the grid square.

For our example, let's say that the POV is facing to the right for now, although it could be any angle. Draw a line from the POV out to the right until it touches the wall on the right (see Figure 2.12). This is our single ray of the wall slice directly in front of us. How far is the wall? Since the ray only traveled the distance of one grid square from the POV to the wall, the distance we have is exactly the same as the size of the grid square, or 64. This distance can then be plugged into our equation:

Height = (64 * 256) / 64

It works so far! The 64 on the top and bottom factor out and we are left with:

Height = 256

This gives us the number of rows on the screen we need to draw for this single section of the wall.

Now here comes the real test: Move the POV dot from the center of the room to the right by one half of a grid square. You should still be on the same line to the wall that you just drew. Here, the distance to the wall is 32, one half of what it was before, so:

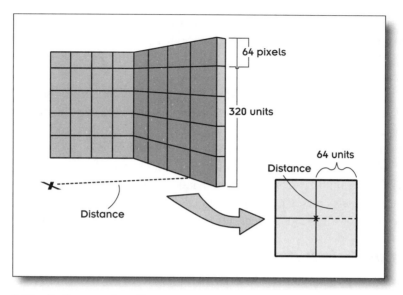

Figure 2.12   *Casting a ray from the room.*

Height = (64 * 256) / 32 which says....
Height = 2 * 256 = 512

So now our wall is twice the height it was before (which incidentally is higher than the computer screen in the 320 columns by 200 rows display mode we are using, which allows us to only see a portion of the wall).

Now we know that we can use this relationship for determining how high the wall needs to be at any given distance.

A Distant Problem—The Fisheye Effect

It was bound to happen; things were just going too smoothly until now. As our world begins to take shape, we find an interesting anomaly presented to us. Looking at our display of walls, we see that the wall directly in front of us is much higher than the walls on either side of the screen, even when we are facing a wall head on. This happens because the straight line distance from the POV to the walls at the side is greater than the distance from the POV to the walls directly in front. This result doesn't look good; it almost makes you think that the screen has turned into one of those fun house mirrors at an amusement park. The effect even has a name—the *fisheye effect* (do fish really see like this?). Interesting enough, the very process we just went through is what causes the fisheye effect to occur.

Put your POV dot in the center of the room again and this time draw a diagonal line from the POV up to the upper-right corner of the room (see Figure 2.13). Notice something? Yep, the line from the POV to the corner is longer than the line from the POV out to the right, which would be directly in front of you if you were facing toward the right. And since we just created a handy-dandy equation that tells us the height decreases as the distance increases, we find that walls will appear smaller off to the left and right of the POV for any particular Field of View. What happened here is that we based our distance calculations on circular trigonometric functions on top of a rectangular map. While the math is correct, the deviation from a polar to a rectangular coordinate system causes our "fisheye" problem. Let's take a closer look at what's going on behind the math and then we'll find a way to solve our problem.

Solving the Fisheye Problem

If you were creating a game called *The Nightmare in Funhouse City* or something like that, you'd be all set. You could use the simple height equation to calculate the distance to all of your walls. But to create a general-purpose engine that models real-world scenes, we'll need to fine-tune our approach.

We need to compensate for the polar to rectangular mapping. What we need is a little trigonometry. When we calculated the height of a wall using our first equation, we were working with Cartesian coordinates. If you remember from high school, a fellow named Pythegoras came up with a very clever way of determining the hypotenuse of a right triangle, as shown in Figure 2.14. (Remember the Pythagorean theorem?) Here the longest side of the triangle or hypotenuse is calculated by using the formula:

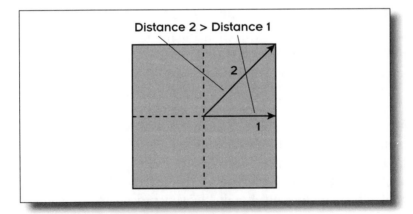

Figure 2.13　*Detecting the fisheye effect.*

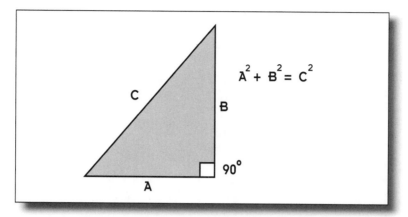

Figure 2.14 *Using the Pythagorean theorem to calculate the hypotenuse of a right triangle.*

$A^2 + B^2 = C^2$

If you stood this triangle up, you could say that its height B (or the height of a wall) is equal to:

$B^2 = C^2 / A^2$

or

$B = \sqrt{C^2 / A^2}$

where A represents the distance. Now doesn't this equation look very similar to the one we used to calculate the height of a wall from a given point? It is similar; however, in our other equation, we used a few tricks, which we'll explain later, so that the equation can be calculated faster by the computer. (We don't want to waste our time performing square roots if we don't need to.)

But the fisheye problem is the one we are most interested in solving. To solve it, we need to explore polar coordinates. In the Cartesian system, all points and relationships are expressed using x and y coordinates. In the polar system, on the other hand, all points are located using a distance and a direction. The distance component can be specified using any type of units—feet, inches, or pixels; the direction component can be specified using units such as north, south, left, right, or degrees (angles). Figure 2.15 shows one of the more common units used to navigate in a polar coordinate system. Here, we have a circle based on a 360-degree measurement system. For each position we move to in this region, we can record it by using a distance and an angle. If you recall, this is the type of system we've been using to describe our POV.

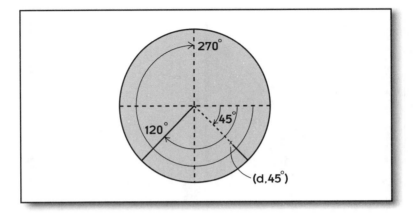

Figure 2.15 *Working with a polar coordinate system.*

To see how this all comes together, let's try our triangle shown in Figure 2.14 by combining a polar coordinate system with a Cartesian one. The result is shown in Figure 2.16. Looking at the triangle again, we can see that by using the cosine of the viewing angle against the distance, we convert back into rectangular coordinates. Unfortunately, this is yet another calculation in a time critical part of our code, but the result is well worth the added effort.

DESIGN TIP

Although we are using a bit of math to calculate coordinate positions and trig functions, you'll find that we won't actually include many of these equations in our code. We'll use pre-generated lookup tables to get as much raw speed as possible. The art of creating really fast 3-D games is a balancing act. You want your 3-D animations to look as realistic as possible, yet at the same time your games must be fast! To accomplish both goals, you'll want to find ways to off load as much time intensive processing as possible, and this typically involves using lookup tables.

From 2-D to 3-D

We've been discussing ray casting so far as if everything we're doing is in a 3-D world. But our computer model actually works in two dimensions to *simulate* a 3-D world. To understand the concepts we're about to explore, you might want to get out some more graph paper and keep your geometry books open because we're still not finished with the math stuff. Don't worry if you have a little trouble visualizing how 2-D worlds are represented in three

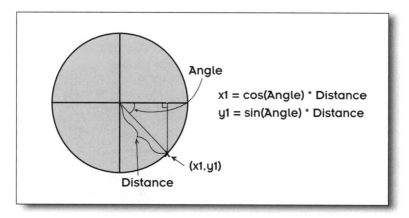

Figure 2.16 *Combining a polar coordinate system with a Cartesian one.*

dimensions. This is one of the hardest conceptual parts of creating 3-D animation, and it takes some getting used to before you can easily move from two to three dimensions.

Our first step is to use a two-dimensional map to create a maze. As Figure 2.17 shows, our maze has borders (walls) in both the x and y planes. Notice how the walls describe the physical boundaries of the map.

If you look closely, you'll see that the map is made up of cubes, each having a fixed size. For our purposes we'll use 64×64 units for each square. This allows an object (or player) to move 64 units in either the x or y direction before moving into another square. The total map is made up of a number of squares to form rows and a number of rows to form a two-dimensional structure.

You're now probably wondering how you can move about in such a maze. It's actually quite easy. In fact, this is where the POV concept introduced earlier comes in. We'll define a player as a location on the map having the three key properties: x coordinate, y coordinate, and the angle that the player is currently facing. You can see how this relationship is set up in Figure 2.18.

What Can We See?

Once we know where the player is and the current angle the player is facing, we can begin to determine what the player can see at a given moment in time. But before anything can be displayed, we need to decide on the FOV that will be used. Recall that *ACK-3D* uses a 64 degree FOV to show the walls in a realistic setting. This means that the player will see all walls and items from 32 degrees to the left of the current viewing angle up to 32 degrees to the right of the current angle. Figure 2.19 illustrates this 64 degree FOV.

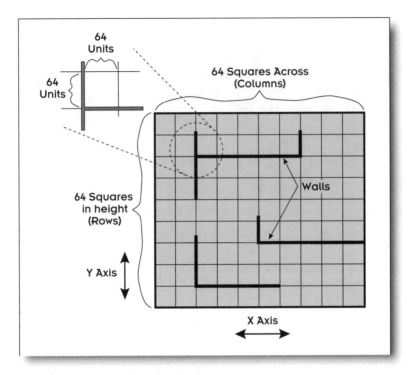

Figure 2.17   *Creating a two-dimensional maze.*

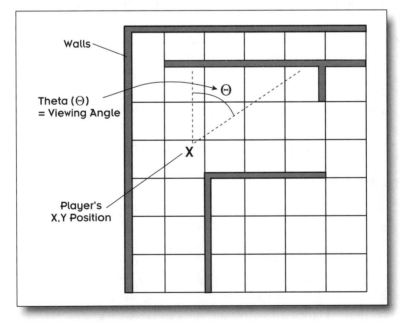

Figure 2.18   *Representing a player in the maze.*

Now here's where things get a little interesting (you might even need your 3-D glasses to follow along—maybe there's a copy in the back of this book). If we superimpose Figure 2.19 with Figure 2.18, guess what we get. An FOV that encompasses the walls in front of the player at the current viewing angle. Figure 2.20 shows what this looks like.

What the user (player) should see at this point is shown in Figure 2.21. Here the double border represents the screen with the walls displayed inside.

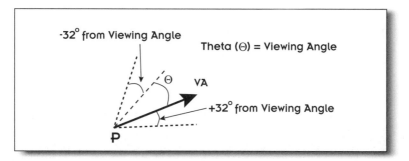

Figure 2.19 *The 64 degree FOV used with ACK-3D.*

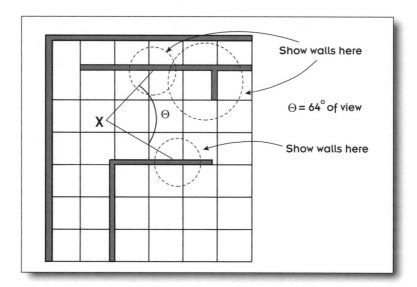

Figure 2.20 *Putting the POV in a maze.*

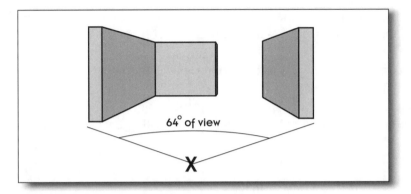

Figure 2.21   *The view the user sees while moving in the maze.*

Getting Back to 3-D

So, how do we get from a flat two-dimensional map to the appearance of 3-D walls? Recall that the trick is to calculate the height of the walls as a function of distance. Given the current x, y coordinates of the player and the x, y coordinates of the wall, we can use trigonometry to figure out the distance between the player and the wall. The tough part is to perform these calculations with the speed necessary to show realistic movement in our 3-D environment. Some books and articles explain the concepts behind the calculations, but then they give examples and programs that don't provide the right kinds of optimizations to make the 3-D animation fast enough. Not here; we're planning to go all the way.

But before we get to the optimizations, let's look at the brute force method of determining how far the walls are. The first thing to remember is that we will be casting a ray for each column of the screen. Using VGA mode 13h, this gives us 320 columns by 200 rows. So, 320 rays, one for each screen column, will be cast out to fill the screen with our field of view.

Let's begin by setting some initial values for the player. Earlier I said that each square was 64×64 units in size. Looking back at Figure 2.16, we see that the player is in square 1,1, about 3/4 the way down from the top of the square and about 1/4 the way over from the right side of the square. This puts our player at roughly location 80,112. (The current viewing angle will be 0 for this part of the discussion.)

Since we are going to use the trig functions provided in the standard C libraries, we can draw a polar coordinate system where the angle increases in a clockwise direction, giving us Figure 2.22.

Okay, get ready—here comes the math stuff for the ray-casting process!

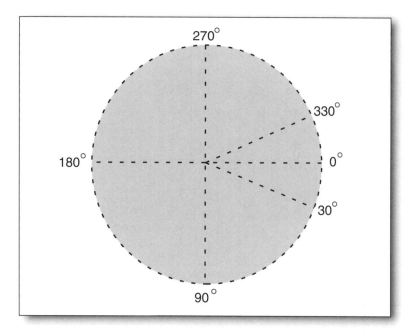

Figure 2.22 *Using a polar coordinate system where angles increase in a clockwise direction.*

For our example, we'll begin our ray casting 32 degrees to the left of the current view angle, or at 328 degrees, and continue until we are 32 degrees to the right of the viewing angle, which will be at +32 degrees. This gives us a total sweep of 64 degrees as shown in Figure 2.23 As you can see from looking at this figure, we can form a right triangle from the player position to the starting point at angle 328 (-32), which we'll call angle *a*. Using this right triangle, there are some important trigonometric relationships that come into play:

Tan a = Opp/Adj
Cos a = Adj/Hyp
Sin a = Opp/Hyp

What we've done here is draw an imaginary line from the player out to some point at angle 328 (-32). But how far do we draw the line? As far as needed to encounter a wall or until we leave the outside boundaries of the map. For this example, let's assume our map is 10 squares across by 8 rows down, as shown in Figure 2.24. (*ACK-3D* uses a 64×64 map size but that is more than we need for our discussion at this point, so let's keep things small.) That gives us a total of 80 squares. The maximum width of our map is there-

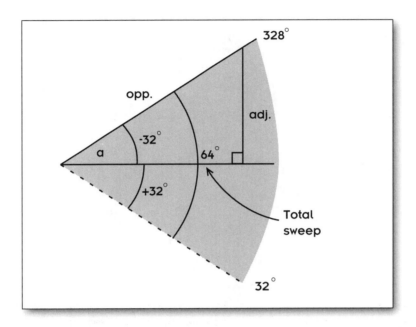

Figure 2.23   *The total sweep for ray casting.*

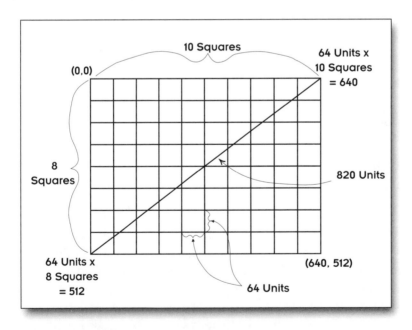

Figure 2.24   *The smaller map used for the ray tracing example.*

fore 64 units multiplied by 10 columns (640 units). The maximum height is 64 units multiplied by 8 rows (512 units). The maximum distance we ever have to look is given by our faithful Pythagorean theorem, which we introduced earlier:

$$C^2 = A^2 + B^2$$

or

$$C^2 = 640^2 + 512^2$$

which gives us 819.5999 or 820 units.

So, 820 units is the total distance we'll cast each ray. But as we cast each ray, we'll check along the way for a wall or a boundary condition. We can use the well established *Bresenham's line-drawing algorithm* to plot each point along the line to see what it strikes. (The sidebar, *Bresenham's Line-Drawing Algorithm Upclose* explains the basics of this technique.)

Bresenham's Line-Drawing Algorithm Upclose

Bresenham's line-drawing algorithm has been used for years by graphics programmers to generate fast lines on a computer display. Many books have covered this popular technique, and in fact Michael Abrash's bible on graphics programming for the PC, *Zen of Graphics Programming*, devotes over two chapters of discussion just to this algorithm. So why does this algorithm get so much attention? It's fast as lightning.

The next question you probably have is how does it work? To understand it, you need to know a little bit about how pixels are displayed on the screen to create the appearance of a line. The limited resolution of our screens makes it difficult to drawing nice looking lines without having a lot of "jagged" patterns. If you draw a line from one coordinate position to another, say 10,10 to 120, 30, you must approximate a straight line by selecting different pixels. Unfortunately, some of the pixels won't exactly be in the "true" path of the line and that's what causes the jaggies. (The only exception to this is lines drawn at a horizontal, vertical, or 45 degree diagonal.)

Bresenham's algorithm gives us a method to quickly approximate a line from one coordinate to another. It is fast because it does not use floating-point operations, such as division or multiplication. Usually, graphics programmers implement this algorithm in assembly to make it as fast as possible. After all, the basic line-drawing routine serves as the foundation of any graphics library, and if there was ever a place for highly optimized code, this is it.

Figure 2.25 shows the basic idea behind the algorithm. Here each pixel displayed to create the line will fall exactly on the true line or will be on one side or the other of the line. The less deviation we have between the pixels that fall on the true line and those that fall to the sides, the better the line will look. In the case of our example line, the line moves farther in the x direction than it does in the y direction (110 units as compared to 20 units). The x dimension of the line is considered to be the *major dimension* and the y dimension is the *minor dimension.* The algorithm draws the line by incrementing each coordinate position by a unit of one pixel in the major dimension (x), and then it determines which y coordinate goes with the x coordinate to plot the point at the right location. As you might guess, the line can be drawn using a single tight loop.

The secret to the algorithm is found in the way that it calculates the minor coordinate positions that go with the major coordinate positions. Because most minor positions that are selected won't be truly on the line, the best we can do is select the ones that result in the least amount of errors as the line continues. The algorithm does this by adapting this technique:

1. Every time a new minor coordinate is selected to pair with a major coordinate, the algorithm keeps track of the running error between the minor coordinate selected and the actual coordinate of the true line.
2. If the running error (distance) is greater than the distance between the minor coordinate of the true line and the next minor coordinate position, the algorithm uses the new minor coordinate position instead of the previous one.

Although this algorithm might sound a little complex, it's actually quite straightforward. And if you trace through the example line shown in Figure 2.25, it will start to make sense.

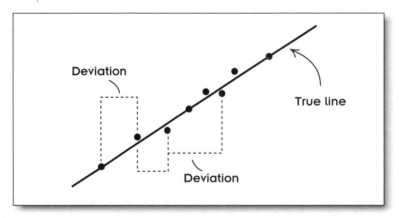

Figure 2.25　*Drawing a line using Bresenham's line drawing algorithm.*

Sweeping Rays

As you may have already surmised, we don't need to advance our ray casting sweep by whole degree increments. Instead, we move in 64/320 degrees or 0.2 increments to give us a 64 degree Field of View in 320 columns of the video screen.

When each ray is casted, we need to determine the actual endpoints of the ray. Fortunately, if we return to our techniques of using a polar coordinate system, we can use the following equations to determine the x and y coordinates of a point on a circle:

X1 = X + (cos(angle) * distance)

*Y1 = Y + (sin(angle) * distance)*

Where does the circle come from? It is the arc that we've casted moving from 328 degrees to 32 degrees, as shown back in Figure 2.23. Using the numbers we presented earlier for the position of our player (80,112) and the maximum distance to a wall, here's how we determine our new coordinates:

X1 = 80 + (cos(328) * 820)

*Y1 = 112 + (sin(328) * 820)*

which gives us:

X1 = 775

Y1 = -332

Of course, these new coordinates take us to a position that is well off the map, as shown in Figure 2.26. Passing the coordinates 80,112,775,-332 into a line-checking routine, we begin to see if any walls intercept the line. The technique is to check every point in the line segment (as shown in Figure 2.26) to find the possible intersection points. Notice that these intersection points are where the line crosses a grid boundary. At each point along the line, we calculate a special map position, which we use as an index to look into a map array. This array keeps track of which grid boundaries have walls. When we build our data structures for the *ACK-3D* engine in Chapter 4, we'll discuss how this wall-checking system works in much more detail. For our example here, let's use the following equation to calculate a map position into the wall array:

```
Map Position = ( Y / 64 ) * 10 + ( X / 64 )
```

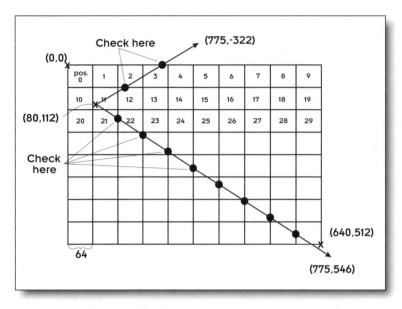

Figure 2.26　*Checking a line segment to determine if it intersects any walls.*

Recall that our sample map was 10 squares across and each square was 64 by 64 units in dimension. What this equation does is force any x, y coordinate into a boundary position that is represented by our map array. For example, if we plugged in the coordinates for the starting point of the line (80, 112), the equation would calculate the wall map position for the wall that turns out to be position 11:

```
Map Position = (112 / 64) * 10 + (80 / 64)
             = (1 * 10 + 1) = 11
```

Looking back at Figure 2.26, we see that our first intercept when checking the ray that is cast at 32 degrees will come when the line passes into the square at location 2,0 in the map. Notice that the x, y coordinates at this point are approximately 128,148. So the first thing we do is use these coordinates with the equation that calculates the wall map position:

```
Map Position = (128 / 64) * 10 + (148 / 64)
             = (2 * 10 + 2) = 22
```

If we looked up position 22 in the map array, we'd find out that a wall had been struck. Next, we need to determine the distance to that wall. We'll call the intersection point *Wx* and *Wy* to distinguish it from our actual line endpoints; in this case, (775, 546). Using the Pythagorean theorem again, we can determine the distance to the wall:

$$C^2 = A^2 + B^2$$
$$C^2 = (Wx - x)^2 + (Wy - y)^2$$

Let's plug in the actual coordinate values into our equation:

$$C^2 = (128 - 80)^2 + (148 - 112)^2$$

which gives us:

Distance = 60 units

Using this distance, we can look up the height from a precalculated table to see how high the wall should appear on the screen. (This may seem like a magic number but recall that we base the height of the wall on the distance to that wall and then apply a constant value that we have determined looks good on the screen.)

We continue this process for each column of the screen until we have displayed 320 columns of graphic walls, each column showing the walls at a certain height, which gives the illusion of distance.

A Quick Summary of the Basic Ray-Casting Process

I used the ray-casting process we just explored in the first version of the ACK-3D engine that I created. The technique works; however, there are some tricks we can use to optimize it. But before we jump in to fine-tune it, let's review the actual steps that are involved.

1. Take the current viewing angle of the player and subtract 32 from it to get the starting ray-casting angle. This will allow us to produce a sweep of 64 degrees (32 degrees on each side of the viewing angle).

2. Calculate an x and y endpoint using the player's current x, y coordinates, the cast angle, and a maximum distance to cast the ray.

3. Using Bresenham's line-drawing algorithm, plot each point along the line and look for an intercept with a wall or the point where the line goes outside the map boundaries.

4. Use the possible intersection point coordinates to calculate an index into a map array to see if a wall is present at this location. If a wall is found, return the Wx and Wy point of the wall intercept.

5. Using the player's x, y coordinates and the wall Wx, Wy coordinates, calculate the distance to the wall using the Pythagorean theorem.

6. Use the distance calculated as a table lookup value to get the height of the wall to display.

7. Add 0.2 to the cast angle and go back to step 2 until 320 rays have been cast. (The 0.2 value is the angle increment used to cover 64 degrees of our sweep using 320 rays.)

Believe it or not, that's all there is to it. But we can do better. We can make our ray-casting process more efficient. To keep things simple, we could stop here and implement this algorithm. After all, this is only a book and most books usually don't go all the way and show you the most optimized techniques for generating graphics. The problem is that when we start to optimize algorithms, we get more into black art programming techniques and these techniques are often tricky to explain.

Since we're concerned about the art of creating ray-casting code that is as fast as possible, let's go the extra mile and put in the optimizations. After you see how fast the code is, you'll definitely agree that it's worth the effort.

To start, let's look at a few of the bottlenecks in our current ray casting algorithm:

Speed Casting a line and checking every point in the line for walls is slow. Especially because we need to do this for 320 rays! If you had a slow computer, you could even see the screen being updated as the rays were cast from left to right. We're actually wasting processing time here because it is not necessary to check every point on a line for a potential wall intersection. Obviously, this is the first place that we're going to look for optimizations.

Accuracy We used floating-point math to calculate the needed increments in angles and distance for the ray-casting process. (Recall that we were sweeping in .02 degree increments.) But if we wrote our code using this approach, we'd have a big problem with rounding errors. (Originally, I did write my code this way, and many friends and professional game developers who looked at the code pointed out this problem to me.)

Intercepts We didn't have an easy way to determine if we had hit a wall on the x or y borders of a grid square. One method that could have been used was to determine if the Wx and Wy points fell on an even 64 boundary, but this was never tried. Once we found the correct intercept, we still had the problem of determining which column of the wall should be drawn. (Recently, some game developers have been discussing the merits of casting both x and y rays at the same time instead of casting each ray separately as we've been doing. But I've found that this approach doesn't really speed up the ray casting process. More on this later.)

Our First Steps into a 3-D World

By this point, we are now able to freely maneuver around in our little room and can even approach the doorway we've designed, although it won't open just yet—hey, it's locked for now! What we need is more rooms, maybe some hallways connecting them, and a look at how we can speed things up a little (okay—a lot). Read on! We need to go back and re-examine our ray-casting algorithm. Right out of the gate there is one major optimization that we can do that will really speed things up. Unfortunately, it will introduce one of the major limitations of this type of engine—90 degree walls that are eight feet thick.

Recall that our ray-casting approach used the Bresenham algorithm for plotting lines, to cast out from our POV and determine if a wall was hit. This approach will reliably tell us if a wall is present at a given location and give us the distance to that wall. It does this by looking at each point along the line to see if it was on one of the wall boundaries we had drawn on our map. While this method works, it is terribly inefficient since we don't need to look at all those points in between the POV and the wall, as shown in Figure 2.27.

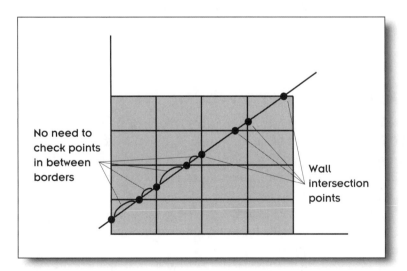

Figure 2.27 *The big time waster—looking at each point for a wall intersection.*

Optimized Ray Casting—The Real *ACK-3D*

For our optimized ray-casting system, we'll still build our map (floor plan) with 64×64 squares. We'll also be using the player's key properties: the x, y coordinate pair and the current angle that the player is facing. The total viewing angle will also remain at 64 degrees with a sweep from -32 degrees to the left to +32 degrees to the right of the current player angle.

In optimizing our system, our first order of business is to get rid of floating-point calculations. By using fixed-point numbers, we can greatly speed up the overall process. I won't get into all of the details of how fixed-point numbers work right now (we'll explore this topic in Chapter 5). Essentially the technique of using fixed-point numbers instead of floating-point numbers involves shifting the bits of a given number to the left to retain the fractional part of the number. This new value is then used in a calculation and the result is shifted back to the right to remove the fractional part. *ACK-3D* uses two fixed-point ranges to perform its calculations, the first being a 16-bit shift and the second being a 20-bit shift (which we'll get into later).

Our second optimization involves using tables for most of the housekeeping calculations. Because we knew that our viewing angles are in 0.2 degree increments, we can precalculate sine and cosine tables (as well as tangent tables) ahead of time. Our full circle can therefore become 360 / 0.2 or 1,800 entries in the tables. Every angle from 0 to 360 will be calculated, multiplied by 65,536 (our 16-bit shift for fixed point), and written out to a file. Then, if we need to find the cosine of 330 degrees, we can use the value 1,650 (330/0.2) to look up the cosine table and get the value 56,759 (after rounding). The same holds true for sine and tangent tables (and some others) as well.

Much Faster Drawing for Ray Casting

Now, we need to figure out how we can speed up drawing an imaginary line from the player to a point off in the distance. If you look closely at one of the maps presented earlier, you'll notice that each square is a fixed distance from each other. We can use this information to speed up our casting process. Let's break the process down further in that we only want to look for walls that fall on the x side and then walls that fall on the y side of the square. This means that we have to cast two rays for every angle, but it also means we know in advance which intercepts will occur.

Figure 2.28 shows our section of the map with only the x walls marked; the y walls (which we'll ignore for now) all fall on the single lines. (X walls are walls that a player will encounter as the player moves in an x direction—right or left—and y walls are the walls encountered as the player moves up or

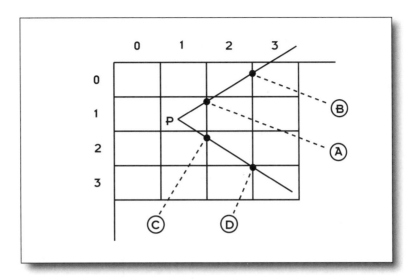

Figure 2.28 *Using a ray to detect only x walls.*

down.) From this, we can see that a ray, looking only for x walls, will intercept at points A and B at angle 328. We also see that points C and D will be
struck at our rightmost angle of 32 degrees. This gives us a method to optimize the ray-casting algorithm using the following steps:

1. Again, we'll cast using a range of 64 degrees; to do this we subtract 32
    degrees from the current player angle to get the starting angle for casting.
2. Determine the y intercept of the current square based on the angle and the
    x coordinate. (Note that the x coordinate will be the right side of the current
    square if our viewing angle falls between 270 degrees and 90 degrees and
    it will be the left side of the current square if our viewing angle falls be-
    tween 90 degrees and 270 degrees.) This x, y intercept of the current square
    will be the first point we check for a wall, as shown in Figure 2.29.

By using the tangent or inverse tangent of the viewing angle, we can calculate the y or x offset, depending on which ray we are casting. This gives us a
starting point in the current square to begin looking for walls.

We know that the width of each square is 64, so we can easily determine
the next y coordinate that our ray will fall on if we increase (or decrease) the
x intercept by 64. This can be precalculated and placed in a table. We continue stepping through both the x and y coordinates using simple addition
until a wall is hit or we pass the boundaries of the map. By using the
Pythagorean theorem again (hey, this guy is really popular in this book), we
see that we only need to traverse a maximum of 13 (rounded) points along

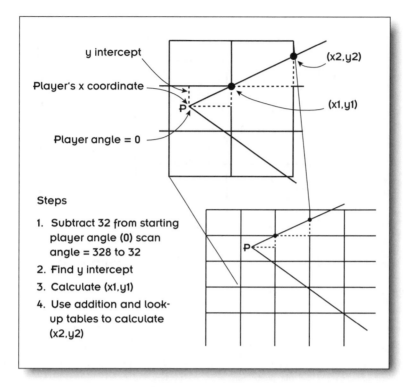

Figure 2.29 *The process of optimizing the ray-casting technique.*

any given line (820/64). (Recall that our first method required 820 points; this is a great savings!)

3. Once a wall is struck, use the y coordinate to determine what column of the wall to display (y AND 63) and the x coordinate to determine the distance.

4. Next, we flip the process around and perform a ray cast for walls that fall along the y side of the square, using the x coordinate to determine the column of the wall and the y coordinate to determine the distance.

5. Comparing the distance from the x ray and the distance from the y ray to see which one is closer, we get the actual wall and wall column to display.

6. Finally, we advance our view angle by one unit in our 1,800 entry circle and loop back to step 2 until 320 ray pairs have been cast.

Now you have it; all of our secrets have been revealed—well, most of them.

Determining the Height of a Bitmap

Once we know the distance to a wall, we need to look up the display height of the bitmap from our table. This table is precalculated and is based on dividing the distance into an experimentally derived number (that means I tried a variety of values until I found one that looked the best!). For *ACK-3D,* this turned out to be 18,000. (Note: This number is always changing as I've been fine tuning the engine, but overall a number around 18,000 is a good place to start.) All distances from 1 to our maximum distance (which turns out to be 2,048 units) are divided into this number to get a height value to draw the bitmap. Heights that are too big or too small are set to the maximum or minimum values, respectively. The minimum height for a wall will be 8 units, and the maximum height will be 960 units.

As shown in Figure 2.30, the height values are stored in a lookup table. The index into the table is the distance to the wall (0 to 2047), and the height can range from 8 to 960. In the *ACK 3-D* engine, this table is represented as a single-dimensioned array.

A Pixel Here, a Pixel There

We now have the techniques to create an engine that displays walls at various heights depending on how far the wall is away from us. So far we've been using lines of different colors to represent our walls. Nice, but far from the realistic designs we want to display. Now we need to come up with a means to display our actual bitmap data on the screen. This is called *texture mapping,* a process that uses the individual pixels of the bitmap for each corresponding position on the screen. Once we know the height of the wall, we can scale the corresponding texture bitmap to fit within that height. Scaling is

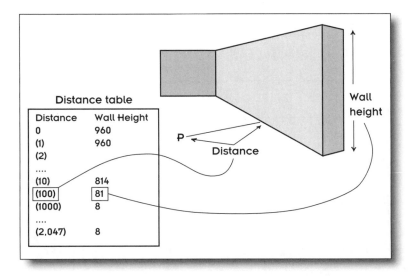

Figure 2.30 *Using a distance/height table to determine the height of a wall.*

a very straightforward process of multiplying the original height of the bitmap by the scale factor to which you wish to scale:

```
New Size = Original Size * Scale Factor;
```

For example, say we want to make our bitmap twice the size of the original. We would use a scale factor of 2 and plug it into the above equation. A scale factor less than 1 would cause our bitmap to shrink in size. The trick with scaling isn't the math involved but finding a way to do it so that it's fast enough for 3-D animation. When we explore bitmaps later in this book, we'll take apart the code and unravel the fast techniques used to scale and display our bitmaps.

I Want Outta Here—Give Me a Door!

Whoops! We've constructed a room that has us standing inside and looking at the walls in front of us, but how do we get out of this room and really start exploring? What we need here is a good old-fashioned door, preferably one that we can open and close on demand. It turns out that doors are essentially walls with a twist. To represent doors in the *Wolfenstein 3-D* style, we nudge the distance to them so they appear a little further away than a wall, as shown in Figure 2.31 because the distance is a little greater, the height is a little smaller, giving the door the appearance of being inset into the surrounding walls. We can build this support right into the ray-casting routines themselves so the actual display process doesn't even know it's displaying a door, it just thinks it has another slice of wall that is a little further away than the other slices around it.

There is a small caveat to this door trick that you will probably notice later when you look at the code for casting rays. Since we have embedded the

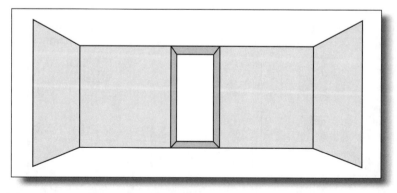

Figure 2.31   *The tricks used for displaying a door.*

walls by adjusting the distance, we need to take into account the part of the side wall that may be visible when you look at the door from an angle other than straight on. The calculation buried in the ray-casting routines compensates for this effect and correctly determines the bitmap column of the side wall that should be displayed.

Ungluing Your Feet

Swell, we have walls, we even have a door beckoning to us to walk through, but we're stuck in one place, glued to the floor. How do we move our POV around this place? The first thing we need to know is how fast we want to move. This is important since we could move so slowly that it would impede game play, or so fast that things would jump around so much we could become dizzy. (Some people have reportedly become nauseous while playing *Wolfenstein 3-D* or *DOOM*, which was almost unheard of in any games before the release of these games.)

The distance we want to move can be determined in a variety of ways depending on what input device is used, such as the keyboard or mouse, and what is currently happening in our 3-D world. Right now, all we need to know is that the value is greater than 1 and less than some huge value that would cause us to jump right through the walls from one square into another. Let's use 6 just for our examples. That gives us a good value where it will take a few steps to traverse our 64×64 grid squares.

Two calculations tell us where we'll end up after we move. They are given next. (Hopefully, you're still hanging in there with all of this math stuff).

Suppose we have the variables **xPlayer** and **yPlayer** to represent where we are at a given point in time, and **PlayerAngle** to represent what direction we are facing. We can use a little trig to move our POV:

```
Distance = 6
xPlayer = xPlayer + (cos(PlayerAngle) * Distance)
yPlayer = yPlayer + (sin(PlayerAngle) * Distance)
```

Voilà! We now have new x and y coordinates to represent the location of the POV. Notice that we didn't change the angle we are currently facing, just the location. (Let's hope that door is directly in front of us!)

By using the two equations above, we now have a means of moving the player, or POV, around in our 3-D world. All we need to do now is hook in these calculations to the particular input device we wish to use. By creating a function that uses the current POV location and angle and a distance, we can keep the movement algorithm separate from the main application using our 3-D library.

To turn around in our world, we merely change the angle we are facing, taking into account that if we turn from 359 degrees to 360 we are really facing angle zero, and if we turn to the left from angle zero to less than zero, we are really facing angle 359. The engine itself doesn't have a turn function; the application using the engine determines how the POV will turn.

DESIGN TIP

This doesn't mean you can't add a turn function to the engine itself. For example, you could add a routine that takes a positive or negative value for a change in the angle and then adds it to the current Player Angle. Of course, you'll need to perform the checks I just introduced to see if the angle has gone below zero or above 359 degrees. This is one of those reader exercises, isn't it?

Objects within Our World

Dealing with objects turns out to be a completely different problem from processing walls, one that wasn't apparent from the effort put into the wall algorithm. The goal was to present an object to the user that did not show the same effects with angles as the walls; in other words, I didn't want objects to have corners when looking at them diagonally. This meant the distance to the object should not be dependent on either the x or the y ray but should be based on a line of sight ray cast from the player's current position.

After much experimenting and head scratching, I decided to support objects by using more traditional 3-D methods. The challenge with this approach is to keep the code optimized enough to get the processing speed we need. (As you've probably discovered, traditional 3-D animation is slow on PCs. The brute force method would involve putting all of the objects' x and y coordinates in a lookup table. Each object could then be translated to base 0,0 from the player and rotated into the field of vision. If the final x, y location of the object fell within the 64 degree field of vision, the object would be visible and handled by the drawing routines. But what if there were many objects in this table? The time expended to check each object would become a function of the number of objects that exist. No, we'll need a more efficient way to handle our objects.

The solution is to combine the ray casting with the object lookup process I just described. Using this approach, we could eliminate all objects not within the current field of vision and thereby reduce the amount of calculations needed. Here's a summary of how this process works:

1. During the ray-casting process, we look in the object map to see if an object exists. If so, the object is added to a list, and a flag is set to indicate that the object has been seen. This flag prevents other near-angle rays from adding the same object to the list. After all, only one entry is needed.

2. Sort the objects in the list by moving closer objects toward the end of the list and farther objects toward the top of the list. This way when the objects are later drawn, the closer ones will hide objects that may be farther away and at the same angle.

3. Continue the ray-casting process past the object just found. This allows us to find additional objects and finally any walls that may be in the line of sight. What gets returned to the caller of the ray-casting routine is always the wall information, never any objects (since objects are stored in a global list).

4. Once all the rays for the entire screen are cast, we draw the walls into the off-screen video buffer. Now its time to check for the objects.

5. Using the object list built during ray casting, we perform the laborious task of translating and rotating the objects' coordinates relative to the player's position and angle. This gives us final coordinates that we can use to determine where to place the object on the screen and in what column to begin drawing the object. As we begin drawing, the distance to the object is checked against the distance to the corresponding wall. If the wall is closer, the object is not drawn in that column. We don't need to check the current object against all the other objects because they were sorted by distance when found; they'll cover up objects farther away by default.

6. This process continues until all of the objects have been displayed in the list. Each time the routine is called to draw the screen, we clear out the object seen flags and set the object count back to zero. This allows us to start fresh when finding any objects in our Field of View.

More Object Considerations

The other consideration we need to take into account to support objects in our 3-D world is that more than one object could occupy the same grid square at the same time. We either have to restrict this from happening (not what I wanted to do) or define two different types of objects, one being movable and one being fixed. We'll take the latter approach because it's more interesting and challenging. Actually, all we need to do is assign a "moveable" attribute to an object to indicate that it should be automatically placed in the list of objects that is checked each time a screen is rendered. These objects are not stored in the object map as fixed objects are, so they must be checked using the process we just discussed in the previous section. But keep in mind that the more moveable objects there are, the more brute force checks that must be made. If you have too many objects, speed could become an issue. With all of this in mind, here is the revised list of steps required to support our objects:

1. Begin the rendering process.
2. Copy all moveable objects to the object list that will be checked after all the rays are cast.
3. Begin casting rays and check for any fixed objects. If found, add the fixed objects to the object list.
4. Once the rays are cast, check to see if any objects are in the object list. (There will always be moveable objects in this list.)
5. Begin the calculations using the x and y coordinates of the objects to determine where they fall in the current Field of View. (Note that the moveable objects may or may not be visible in the FOV.)
6. Add the objects to the slices that will be displayed when the walls themselves are shown.
7. Display the wall or object slices into the off-screen buffer and return to the application.

What's Next?

Okay, now we've seen the techniques involved in displaying both walls and transparent objects into our off-screen buffer, ready for the application to display whenever it chooses. The *ACK-3D* engine provides a ready made routine to blit the buffer onto a 320x200 screen, but the application is free to display it itself, if desired. In fact, the Windows version of the *ACK-3D* engine does just that; it renders the view using the ray casting engine, then uses the new WinG library to display the view into a Windows window. How's that for portability?

It's now time for us to move on and start creating the code to implement the powerful ray casting techniques. In the next chapter, I'll show you which source and header files we'll be creating. In Chapter 4, we'll take a close look at the underlying data structures needed to create the general-purpose, ray-casting engine. As you begin to work with the code, you might want to refer back to this chapter to review the foundation concepts and algorithms that make the ray-casting engine work. Of course, as you were reading this chapter, the question "How do we implement this technique?" probably came up a time or two. Well, hold on—you're about to find out!

Chapter 3

What does it take to support a 3-D engine? Here's your chance to learn how an engine is arranged and how its different components communicate with your application.

Working toward a 3-D Game Engine

The most challenging part of writing 3-D games and other types of interactive 3-D applications is making sure that you have the right tools available. 3-D programming techniques have been floating around for years, but much of this technology hasn't been picked up by PC programmers because it would have been too slow to use in the past. Now that PCs are so much faster, more memory is available, C and C++ compilers can crank out 32-bit code, and platforms like Windows can support faster bitmap graphics with the aid of DLLs like WinG, the flood gates are opening.

Almost weekly some PC programmer uploads a new 3-D-like engine on a bulletin board or network such as the Internet or CompuServe. The goal of these engines is to provide the basic framework or tools to create 3-D rendered scenes. You can learn a lot by playing with these engines and exploring the types of 3-D views that can be built. To create your own 3-D worlds, you'll need to know how a real engine works and how the different components of the engine communicate with each other and your applications.

In this chapter, we'll explore the main components of an engine, in particular the *ACK-3D* engine. You'll see that code for an engine can be written to be used with both DOS and Windows platforms (or other platforms if you are interested in porting it). I'll also show you which source files are needed to implement the engine, and which parts of the engine are coded in C and which parts are coded in assembly to get the performance we need.

Why Create an Engine?

When I first started working with the 3-D ray-casting concepts presented in the previous chapter, I put all of my code into a few big source files. What a mistake that was! This technique kept me from achieving my goal of creating general-purpose 3-D code that could be used for a variety of applications, such as adventure games, screen savers, 3-D walk-through demos, and other projects that I might dream up when I was feeling creative. The better approach (which I soon adopted) was to separate the code that performed the 3-D rendering from the rest of the application that I was building. The actual code for processing keyboard and mouse input, memory management, creating and moving objects, and so on, could easily be placed in the application that would build upon the underlying base of the 3-D rendering functions. What I was left with was a powerful 3-D engine that could be easily ported to other platforms, such as Windows or UNIX, because the engine itself was essentially a mathematical or structural model and did not require too much specific platform code.

As Figure 3.1 shows, the engine and the application code I'll present in this book includes two distinct components—the 3-D library, which we'll refer to as the *ACK-3D* engine, and the application code for a particular project. The engine contains all of the code for constructing or rendering the elements for 3-D scenes—floors, ceilings, walls, and controlling the POV. The application code is responsible for handling the main interface with the player and contains the routines that are specific to the particular project being written. In Part 2 of this book, we'll focus on the engine. Then, in Part 3, we'll show you how to create interactive 3-D games using the engine.

Putting It All in Perspective

If you are still having a little trouble conceptualizing what the *ACK-3D* engine actually does and how it relates to the applications you can build, take a look at Figure 3.2. You can think of the engine as the process between your application's logic and the video screen. Within the engine are a variety of functions to

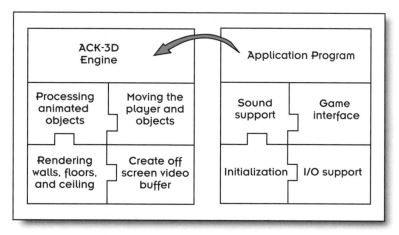

Figure 3.1   *The two distinct areas of the* ACK-3D *system.*

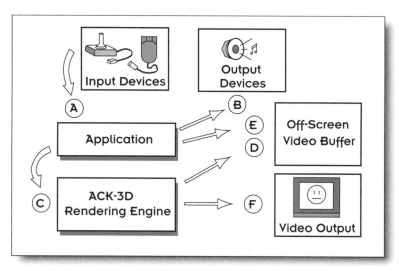

Figure 3.2   *How the processes in a 3-D application created with* ACK-3D *communicate with each other.*

handle the actual building of 3-D scenes based on the parameters supplied by your application. Some of these parameters include the current x, y position of the POV, the angle the POV is facing, and so on. Your application makes a function call to the engine to render the current scene into an off-screen buffer that can then be processed by your application if needed. This approach makes it easy for you to use the engine to generate a basic scene and then overlay graphics on top of the scene before the scene is displayed.

To take all of this one step further, let's see how the various processes shown in Figure 3.2 communicate with each other. Notice that input devices, such as the keyboard, mouse, or joystick, send information to the application to change parameters, such as the current x, y position of the player. The application also handles output devices, such as a Sound Blaster card or PC speaker, on its own by sending the appropriate data to the output device. After an application receives new parameters from input devices, it makes function calls to the *ACK-3D* engine to render a new scene. Then, *ACK-3D* generates the current scene into an off-screen buffer and then returns to the application. At this point, the application can overlay its own custom graphics onto the off-screen buffer. Finally, the application calls an *ACK-3D* function to display the current scene onto the actual video screen. But this last step can also be accomplished by the application.

The best part about working with a custom engine like *ACK-3D* is that your application can even perform its own display, leaving the path open for using the engine in other graphic environments like Windows (as you'll see next). Other utility functions are also provided with *ACK-3D* so that you can move the POV, check for wall and object collisions, load in graphic bitmaps, and so on. This approach gives your application code the power and flexibility to perform all kinds of tasks on its own, yet the engine provides all of the essential 3-D processing functions so that you can still do a lot without writing thousands of lines of code.

Wow! ACK-3D Does Windows

The first version of *ACK-3D* was written using Borland C++ 3.0. After Watcom released its 32-bit protected mode compiler, I created a 32-bit version of the engine, which as you might guess, really speeds up the 3-D processing. Then, I moved the engine over to Borland C++ 4.0 and also tested it with Borland C++ 4.5. After finishing a few technical coding details on the engine for DOS 32-bit protected mode, Microsoft released a special DLL for Windows called WinG. WinG has only been available for a short time, but its release has really stirred up a lot of activity among PC game developers. With WinG, you can perform bitmap graphics much faster under Windows than you could in the past. (We'll cover some of the important areas of WinG programming in Chapter 13.)

As a test to see how portable the *ACK-3D* engine really was, I decided to port *ACK-3D* to Windows and make use of WinG. In this book, I'll provide you with both the Windows and DOS versions of the engine. In some respects the Windows version is simpler than the DOS version because it does not require all of the low-level screen support, or the interface support (mouse and keyboard) functions.

Components of the *ACK-3D* Engine

Let's now look at the various components of the *ACK-3D* engine itself. These components are used in both the DOS and Windows versions. The six main parts of the engine include:

- Initialization and Setup
- Data and Graphic File Loading
- Rendering or Building the View
- POV Movement and Collision Detection
- Object Movement and Collision Detection
- Displaying the View Buffer to the Screen

For the most part, this is the order that an application would make use of the engine. By separating these sections, the application designers are free to make their own choices about which functions to use and which ones to do themselves, with the exception of a few mandatory routines. Let's discuss them one by one to see how the various files and functions are used. Later in this chapter I'll present the files and functions used as support utilities, Windows support, and the Map Editor support.

ACK-3D Files

All of the files that make up the DOS and Windows version of the core *ACK-3D* library are included on the disk that accompanies this book, and begin with the three letter prefix of Ack. As Table 3.1 shows, the names of the files closely parallel the different sections of the engine. Notice that the files are grouped by category and that both .C and .ASM source files are listed. Table 3.2 lists the .H header files needed to compile the .C source files.

Communicating with the Engine

You're now probably thinking, "This 3-D engine approach sounds great, but how do I get my applications to use the engine and communicate with it?" To simplify the connection, *ACK-3D* provides a special structure named **ACKENG** for building a complete POV. This structure, which we'll explore in detail in Chapter 4, can be placed in the data segment of your program or it can be dynamically allocated in memory. When you write an application, you must correctly create and set up this structure before using the engine. If you don't set it up properly, watch out! Your 3-D world won't materialize.

Table 3.1 *Source Files Used to Implement the Core ACK-3D Engine*

File	Description
Data and initialization routines:	
ACKDATA.C	Defines the global data variables required for the engine.
ACKINIT.C	Initialization routines for the engine. Includes functions for loading trig tables, opening and closing resource files, allocating memory, and reading and processing map files.
Main 3-D ray-casting routines:	
ACKBKGD.C	Defines the key function for generating a solid floor and ceiling.
ACKDOOR.C	Provides all of the door-processing routines for checking the current status of doors, locating empty door slots, and so on.
ACKFLOOR.C	Routines for drawing floors and ceilings for a scene.
ACKOVER.C	Routines for processing screen-size images into a compiled form that can be later superimposed on top of the rendered image buffer.
ACKOBJ.C	Routines for processing the objects displayed in a scene.
ACKPOV.C	Support routines for moving the Point of View (POV) and objects, and for performing collision detection.
ACKVIEW.C	The main functions for the ray-casting engine. Provides the interface routines for rendering the view, floors, and ceilings. Also provides the main function for checking for the presence of objects.
ACKWRAP.C	Special wrap-up routine that must be called before exiting in Borland C++ if the keyboard and timer vectors were plugged.
ACKRTN.INC	Include file used by the assembly modules. This file defines the macros and equates used by the internal assembly routines.
ACKRTN.ASM	The first part contains the low-level code used to set up interrupt vectors, control the keyboard, and display bitmaps and text on the screen. The routines in this file are primarily used with the DOS version. The second part provides the main functions for casting rays in the x and y planes.
ACKRTN1.ASM	Code for drawing single slices of walls.
ACKRTN3.ASM	Ray casting routines for creating multi-height walls as well as low-resolution wall slice drawing.
ACKRTN4.ASM	Routines to draw non-shaded wall slices as well as the background images for mountains and such. Also provides some support routines for speeding up the system timer.

Table 3.1 *Source Files Used to Implement the Core ACK-3D Engine (Continued)*

ACKRTN5.ASM	Routines for drawing floors and ceilings. Routines with the letters "NS" at the end of the routine name indicate that the routine does not perform light shading (NS = No Shading).

Bitmap processing routines:

ACKGIF.C	Routines to read in .GIF images. (This code is stubbed out for now.)
ACKIFF.C	Routines to read in Deluxe Paint .BBM and .LBM images.
ACKLDBMP.C	Interface routines for loading bitmaps (walls or objects). This file also contains the key functions for creating and setting up objects.
ACKPCX.C	Routine to read in .PCX images.

Utilities:

ACKUTIL.C	Miscellaneous support routines, including memory tracking, setting up the keyboard and timer vectors in Borland C++, and palette support functions.

Table 3.2 *Header Files Used to Implement the Core ACK-3D Engine*

File	Description
ACK3D.H	Defines the main data structures for creating objects, doors, and communicating with the *ACK-3D* engine. Also includes the function prototypes for the main *ACK-3D* functions.
ACKENG.H	Defines all of the constants and data structures needed to build walls with *ACK-3D*.
ACKEXT.H	Defines all of the external variables used by the engine.
IFF.H	Defines the data structures and constants needed for processing bitmap images. (This file is included by the ACKIFF.C module.)

The **ACKENG** structure is defined in the header file ACK3D.H. As Figure 3.3 shows, this structure takes care of all of the essentials required to build a 3-D world. Notice that there are variables for storing the current location and angle of the player, the actual map arrays for the walls and objects, pointers to the screen buffer, overlay buffer, and background buffer, as well as dimensions of the viewport for building your walls.

When you write programs to use the engine, you simply allocate storage for this structure and then initialize it by assigning values to some of its members. Then, when one of the *ACK-3D* functions is called, the function uses the data stored in the structure to determine how to perform an operation, such as rendering a scene.

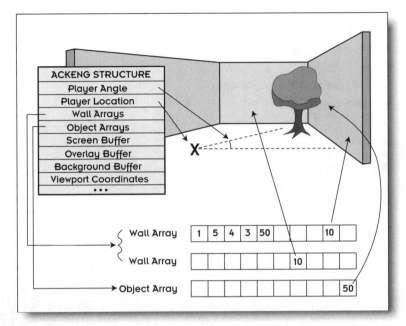

Figure 3.3 *The features of the ACKENG structure.*

DESIGN TIP

To use *ACK-3D*, you only need to be concerned with the overall library itself and the key data structures like **ACKENG**. The library file ACK3D.LIB is included on the CD-ROM already built, so you can quickly begin using it in the examples that are presented in this book.

A Closer Look at the *ACK-3D* Engine Functions

Now that you know which files are used to implement the *ACK-3D* engine, you're probably wondering about the functions that are provided in each of the .C files. Each file contains a set of user-callable routines and internal routines that are used by the engine to create and process 3-D scenes. Most of the functions that start with the three letter prefix Ack are set up to be user-callable routines. Tables 3.3 through 3.13 list all of the functions found in the .C source files. Each table represents one or more of the .C source files presented in Table 3.1. The only file that's not presented is ACKDATA.C because this source file does not define any functions. After these functions are presented, I'll discuss the assembly code for the engine.

Table 3.3 *Functions Defined in ACKINT.C*

Function	Description
AckSetupWindow()	Initializes variables for accessing the viewport window where a view will be displayed.
AckInitialize()	Initializes the *ACK-3D* interface structure and reads in the trig tables from either the standalone TRIG.DAT file or from a resource file that was opened before this call. This function *must* be called before calling AckBuildView() and AckDisplayScreen(). The AckInitialize() function must always be called to initialize the engine before any of the other engine functions are used.
AckOpenResource()	Opens a resource file for use by any *ACK-3D* routine that requires a filename. Only one resource file can be opened at a time. A resource file can be used to combine different data files that the *ACK-3D* engine needs, such as TRIG.DAT and map files created by the Map Editor.
AckCloseResource()	Closes a resource file if one is opened.
BuildWallDstTables()	Internal function used to pre-define height tables for the wall drawing code.
AckBuildTables()	Internal function called from AckInitialize() to read in the trig tables and allocate memory for the various buffers.
AckReadMapFile()	Reads a map file and processes any multi-height walls.
AckBuildHeightTables()	Internal function used to create height and distance tables for objects.
AckBuildGrid()	Internal function called by AckReadMapFile() to process the objects in a map. Both moveable and stationary objects are processed with this function.

Table 3.4 *Functions Defined in ACKBKGD.C and ACKOVER.C*

Function	Description
AckBuildBackground()	Generates a solid floor and ceiling. This function is used only if floors and ceilings are not active.
AckCreateOverlay()	Creates an overlay buffer that contains non-transparent information for an image. The position and length of the non-transparent areas are stored for later processing after the drawing phase. Theoretically, the amount of information stored in the overlay buffer could exceed the actual size of the image.

Table 3.5　*Functions Defined in ACKDOOR.C*

Function	Description
CheckDoors()	Internal function that checks all the active doors to see their current state. If a door's column offset is non-zero, it is either opening or closing, so the speed of the door is added in and then the door is checked to see if it is fully opened or fully closed.
FindDoor()	Internal routine used to locate a door from its map coordinate and return its index position.
FindDoorSlot()	Internal routine used to find an empty slot for a door. If the door already occupies a slot and it is in a non-closed state, this function returns an error.
AckCheckDoorOpen()	Checks directly in front of the POV to see if a door is there. If so, and the door is not locked, this function sets it to begin opening.

Table 3.6　*Functions Defined in ACKFLOOR.C*

Function	Description
SetupFloors()	Internal function called during the initialize process to set up the floor and light shading arrays.
AckDrawFloorHz()	Draws the floor and ceiling horizontally.
AckDrawOneFloor()	Draws a floor that contains only one type of bitmap. This is a much faster process and may be useful in some applications.

Table 3.7　*Functions Defined in ACKOBJ.C*

Function	Description
AckGetObjectAngle()	Internal function called by FindObject(). The application may also use this function if it needs to find the angle between two points. DX and DY are the deltas between the two points (that is, DX = X1 - X and DY = Y1 - Y).
long_sqrt()	Internal function that returns the square root of a long value.
FindObject()	Internal function called by AckBuildView() that checks the list of objects found during the ray cast and places the object slices into the wall slices.

Table 3.8　*Functions Defined in ACKPOV.C*

Function	Description
AckCheckObjPosn()	Internal function called by AckMovePOV() and AckMoveObjectPOV(). Checks the passed x and y coordinates against the actual object coordinates.

Table 3.8 *Functions Defined in ACKPOV.C (Continued)*

Function	Description
AckMovePOV()	Moves the POV based on a specified angle. After moving, but prior to returning, the position of the POV is checked for collisions.
AckMoveObjectPOV()	Moves an object using a specified angle and distance. After moving, this function checks for collision with other objects and the POV.
AckCheckObjectMovement()	Runs the list of objects and checks for any animation that should occur for that object.
GetWallX()	Internal function that checks to see if a wall is present along an x coordinate boundary.
GetWallY()	Internal function that checks to see if a wall is present along a y coordinate boundary.

Table 3.9 *Functions Defined in ACKVIEW.C*

Function	Description
AckRegisterStructure()	Transfers certain variables from the interface structure to global variables so that they can be accessed faster by the drawing functions. The interface structure is kept by the application, and there can be more than one of them for different views. Each time a new view needs to be processed, this function *must* be called before calling the drawing routines.
AckBuildView()	Renders the current scene into the off-screen buffer based on the POV coordinates and angle. This function does not display the scene once it is rendered; thus, the application can overlay graphics into the buffer before it is actually displayed.
ShowNone()	Stub function for slices that do not contain walls.
BuildSlice()	Internal function to cast the x and y rays and build a slice structure for each column of the viewing window.
BuildSliceMulti()	Creates the ray cast for multi-height walls so that any wall that is taller than the walls in front of it will be displayed.
AckCheckHit()	Internal function called by AckCheckDoorOpen() to check for a collision with a wall within a certain distance.

Table 3.10 *Function Defined in ACKWRAP.C*

Function	Description
AckWrapUp()	Frees up buffers and closes any resource file that may be open. After calling this function, do not call AckBuildView() or AckDisplayScreen().

Table 3.11 *Functions Defined in ACKIFF.C, ACKGIF.C, and ACKPCX.C*

Function	Description
CloseFile()	Utility function provided for closing a specified bitmap file.
iffswab()	Internal function used by AckReadiff() to swap bytes.
ByteFlipLong()	Internal function used by AckReadiff() to flip bytes in a long word.
AckReadiff()	Reads and processes a Deluxe Paint .BBM or .LBM format file and returns the resulting buffer to the caller.
get_next_code()	Returns the next unencoded byte while reading
AckReadgif()	Reads and processes a .GIF format image and returns the resulting buffer to the caller. (This function is only a stub for now.)
AckReadPCX()	Reads and processes a 256 color .PCX file and returns the resulting buffer to the caller.

Table 3.12 *Functions Defined in ACKLDBMP.C*

Function	Description
BlankSlice()	Internal function used to determine if the column of a bitmap contains only transparent colors; if so, the column is marked to be skipped during the draw phase.
AckLoadBitmap()	Loads a bitmap of different formats based on the setting of bmLoadType in the ACKENG interface structure. The loaded bitmap is placed into either the wall bitmap array or the object array based on the value of BitmapType passed to this function.
GetExtent()	Internal function that returns a pointer to the file extent.
AckLoadWall()	Calls AckLoadBitmap() with the TYPE_WALL flag set so the bitmap is placed in the wall array.
AckLoadObject()	Calls AckLoadBitmap() with the TYPE_OBJECT flag set so the bitmap is placed in the object array.
AckCreateObject()	Creates an object structure. This function *must* be called before the object data can be initialized in the NEWOBJECT structure.
AckSetObjectType()	Sets up an object into one of the pre-defined sequences (CREATE, DE-STROY, and so on). Movable objects are placed into a special list that is used later in the drawing phase.
AckSetupObject()	Fills in an object structure with a communication structure passed by the application. This allows the application to set up the key fields, such as the number of sides the object has, the number of bitmaps displayed for each side, and so on.

Table 3.13   *Functions Defined in ACKUTIL.C*

Function	Description
AckSetupKeyboard()	Establishes a hook into interrupt 9 for keyboard handling. The application can access which key is pressed by looking at the AckKeys[ ] global array. (DOS version only)
AckSetupTimer()	Establishes a hook into the user timer interrupt. The application can access a counter by looking at the AckTimerCounter global variable. (DOS version only)
AckMalloc()	Utility routine used to track memory usage by the *ACK-3D* engine and applications.
AckFree()	Matching routine for AckMalloc(). This routine must be used to free memory if AckMalloc() is used to allocate memory.
AckLoadAndSetPalette()	Reads a palette from a file and immediately sets it into the VGA registers. (DOS version only)
AckSetupPalRanges()	Sets up the palette range for light shading. The incoming ranges are in a 16x256 array where there are 16 different distance levels, each having a full-color translation table for light shading.
AckGetObjectHit()	Returns the index of the last object hit by the POV.
AckGetWallHit()	Returns the map location of the last wall hit.
AckDeleteObject()	Sets an object to inactive. The memory used by the object is not freed by this routine.
AckSetNewBitmap()	Sets a new wall or object index into the map array specified.
AckFreeBitmap()	Obsolete routine for real mode. Flat model memory can be freed by the application. Real mode requires XMS memory to be handled. This routine is maintained for backward compatibility with the older versions.

Moving into Assembly

You've now seen all of the C source functions required to implement the *ACK-3D* engine. Hopefully, you're not too overwhelmed! Many of the functions presented perform the background work of calculating intersections and distances to walls, loading bitmaps, and so on. The actual number of functions you need to know about to make calls to the *ACK-3D* engine from your application program is relatively few.

The complete engine could be written using just C code. In fact, my original version was developed with just C. As I began to fine tune the engine, I converted some of the time-critical code to assembly. When you use the engine and see for yourself how fast it is, I'm sure you'll agree with me that using the assembly code is worth the effort. Tables 3.14 through 3.18 list all of the assembly routines that are used. As you are looking them over, keep in mind that all are called internally by the *ACK-3D* C functions. You don't have to call any of these routines from your application programs. Most of the routines listed in Table 3.14 are provided for DOS support only. For example,

---

Table 3.14 *Functions Defined in ACKRTN.ASM*

Function	Description
AckInkey	Checks for a keystroke and returns 0 if a keystroke is not found. If a key is found, the routine returns the scan code/character pair in AX. This routine should *not* be used if the keyboard vector has been changed by calling the AckKbdInt routine described next.
AckKbdInt	Sets up an interrupt 9 (Int 9) keyboard handler. It places keys into a keyboard array so they can be checked by an application.
AckDisplayScreen	Used in the DOS version to call the assembly language routine. This provides one level of an API that keeps the application from requiring modification if you change the way the screen is displayed. This would be a good place to hook in displays to other videos without having to change your application code.
AckPutVideo	Puts a single byte into video memory.
AckGetVideo	Retrieves a single byte from the video memory.
AckCopyToVideo	Copies a block from the data segment buffer to the video screen.
AckInitVideoSelector	Retrieves a selector to video memory and stores it in the VidSeg global.
AckGetIntVector	Retrieves a protected mode interrupt vector.
AckSetIntVector	Sets a protected mode interrupt handler.
AckSetPalette	Sets the 256 palette registers from a buffer of RGB values provided.
AckSetVGAmode	Switches to 320x200 256 color mode 13h. This routine should be called before using any of the VGA display routines to write to the screen.
AckSetTextmode	Switches to 80x25 16 color mode 13h.
AckDrawPage	Actual routine that displays a buffer onto the video screen. Called by AckDisplayScreen to provide a common interface with the application.
xRaySetup	Prepares various global variables for use by the xRayCast routine.
xRayCast	Performs the actual ray cast by looking for intersections with walls and objects in the x plane.
yRaySetup	Prepares various global variables for use by the yRayCast routine.
yRayCast	Performs the actual ray cast by looking for intersections with walls and objects in the y plane.

routines like **AckSetVGAmode**, **AckSetTextmode**, **AckPutVideo**, and **AckDisplayScreen** perform low-level DOS screen access and can't be used in a Windows application.

Table 3.15 *Functions Defined in ACKRTN1.ASM*

Function	Description
ShowCol	Draws a single wall or object slice into the off-screen buffer. This routine draws solid walls that have no transparent colors.
ShowColMask	Draws wall or object slices that contain transparent colors. This is a slower routine than ShowCol since every pixel must be checked for transparency.
DrawSolidCeiling	Fills the off-screen buffer with the solid ceiling color. This routine is called before any walls are drawn.
DrawSolidFloor	Fills the off-screen buffer with the solid floor color. This routine is called before any walls are drawn.
DrawWalls	The main routine for drawing all the wall and object slices. This routine loops through the SLICE structures for the number of columns in the actual display window.

Table 3.16 *Functions Defined in ACKRTN3.ASM*

Function	Description
ShowColLow	Draws a single slice of a wall or object in low-resolution mode, which doubles every column for speed.
ShowColMaskLow	Draws a single slice with transparency in low-resolution mode, which doubles every column for speed.
xRayCastMulti	Performs the same task as xRayCast except it only checks for multi-height walls. This allows taller walls to be seen behind normal height walls.
yRayCastMulti	Performs the same task as yRayCast except it only checks for taller walls that may be behind normal height walls.
CheckHitMap	Routine called by BuildUpView to check to see if a movable object is in view in the map while building a scene.
BuildUpView	Main routine that cast rays and builds up the slices for walls and objects.

Table 3.17 *Functions Defined in ACKRTN4.ASM*

Function	Description
AckTimerHandler	Handles the system timer interrupt when the clock is running faster. This routine will call the real timer interrupt at the appropriate intervals to keep the system clock updated properly.

(continued)

Table 3.17　*Functions Defined in ACKRTN4.ASM (continued)*

Mymemset	Support routine to replace memset(). Some compilers do quite a bit of overhead checking before actually copying bytes, so I've provided this routine to replace the standard library routine.
AckSpeedUp	Speeds up the internal system clock by a specified factor. Useful for performance timings and generating sound on the PC speaker (which is not used by *ACK-3D*).
AckSlowDown	Returns the system clock to normal speed.
DrawBackDrop	Draws the appropriate part of the background bitmap into the off-screen buffer. Use this routine if you don't want to combine the operation with the ceiling draw functions.
ShowColNS	Displays a wall or object slice without light shading.
ShowColMaskNS	Displays a transparent wall or object slice without light shading.

Table 3.18　*Functions Defined in ACKRTN5.ASM*

Function	Description
AckDrawFloorNS	Draws a textured floor and ceiling that does not have light shading.
AckDrawFloorOnlyNS	Draws only a textured floor (assumes solid ceiling) without light shading.
AckDrawCeilingOnlyNS	Draws only a textured ceiling (assumes solid floor) without light shading.
DrawSolidCeilAndFloorNS	Draws a solid ceiling and textured floor without light shading.
DrawSolidCeilAndFloor	Draws a solid ceiling and textured floor with light shading.
DrawSolidFloorAndCeilNS	Draws a solid floor and textured ceiling without light shading.
DrawSolidFloorAndCeil	Draws solid floor and textured ceiling with light shading.
DrawSolidCeilSolidFloor	Draws a solid ceiling and solid floor with light shading.

Supporting the DOS and Windows Interface

So far we've concentrated on the main C and assembly files that are used to support the core *ACK-3D* engine. If you compile and link all of these files, you'll end up with the engine library (ACK.LIB) that you can use to create either DOS or Windows applications. What's missing from this library is the DOS code for additional features such as sound, mouse, and higher-level keyboard support. In addition, the core engine source files provide no direct Windows support. So how can we create real 3-D applications with the engine library?

Essentially, I included a number of other source files that provide all of the basic support you'll need to create games and other 3-D applications. These files are grouped into the four categories shown in Figure 3.4.

To write DOS applications, you'll need support for the mouse, keyboard, and sound. (The screen interface support is wired into the engine code already.) Table 3.19 shows you the DOS support files that are available. Of course, as you start to develop your own games, you'll come up with your own unique needs.

Thanks to WinG, providing Windows support is not as hard as you might think. I came up with some useful high-level C++ classes to encapsulate the key *ACK-3D* functions and data structures. Table 3.20 lists the actual files used to interface with the WinG API. Again, I provided a useful C++ class to make it easier for you to access the WinG functions. I'll explain how all of this

Table 3.19 *DOS Application Support Files*

File	Description
MOUSE.C	Provides low-level support of the mouse functions, such as reading the mouse position and button status.
KIT.H	Header file that must be included by DOS applications that use the *ACK-3D* library.
MOUSE.H	Header file used for MOUSE.C.

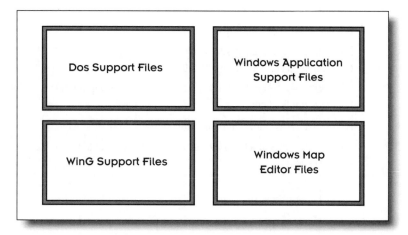

Figure 3.4 *Types of support files available for creating 3-D applications with* ACK-3D.

works in Chapters 13 and 14. Table 3.21 lists the support files that are provided to help you build your own Windows applications. These files are also used with the Windows-based map editor. ACKINFO and ACKSUP.CPP define a set of useful functions for reading in data files for Windows applications. ACKWIN.CPP defines six functions that can greatly help you streamline the work of building a Windows application that uses the *ACK-3D* engine. Some of the functions included in these files, such as **InitACKEngine()** are designed to be generic so that you can add in your own code.

Our last stop is the files used for the map editor (see Table 3.22). These files are used to create the standalone Windows editor, as shown in Figure 3.5. We'll be using this editor to put our 3-D scenes together. As you create your 3-D worlds, you'll find this application to be a very valuable resource.

Table 3.20 *WinG Support Files*

File	Description
WING.H	Microsoft's standard header file for WinG support. This file defines the structures and function headers for the WinG functions.
WINGDLL.H	Defines a high-level interface class for WinG named WinGdll.
WINGDLL.CPP	C++ source code to support the high-level WinG interface class.
WINPALL.CPP	C++ source code to support Windows indentity palettes.

Table 3.21 *Windows Support Files*

File	Description
DOS-KEYB.H	Defines scan codes for keyboard input.
ACKINFO.CPP	Provides support functions for loading and processing resource files. (This file can also be used with DOS applications.)
ACKSUP.CPP	Windows C++ support functions for the map editor and for creating other Windows applications.
ACKWIN.H	Header file for Windows implementation of the *ACK-3D* engine.
ACKWIN.CPP	Generic Windows functions for use by any Windows application that uses the *ACK-3D* engine.

Table 3.22 *Map Editor Source and Header Files*

File	Description
ACKEDIT.H	Main header file for the Windows 3-D visual map editor.
ACKRES.H	Header file that contains the resource definitions used by the map editor.
ACKEDIT.RC	Windows resource file for the map editor.
ACKEDIT.CPP	Windows C++ functions for the map editor.
ACKDLG.CPP	Windows C++ functions for creating dialog boxes and controls.

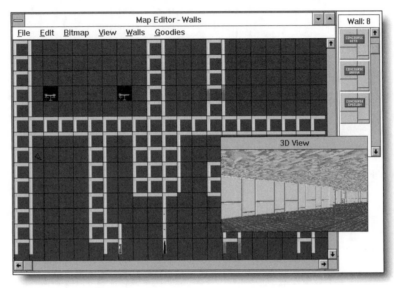

Figure 3.5 *The Windows-based map editor.*

Chapter 4

To support the *ACK-3D* engine, we'll need special data structures to communicate between the 3-D library routines and an application. We'll also need structures to support the important ray-casting techniques.

Putting the Data Structures Together

f you're like me, you've probably written many programs only to discover that the data structures you designed for them end up limiting how your program can grow. In the early design phases of thinking over the kinds of functions needed in a program and mapping out the data structures, it's hard to anticipate everything needed—especially if you are creating a program as complex as a 3-D engine. The best you can do is design your data structures so that they are as flexible as possible to withstand the major coding changes that occur over time.

The development of the *ACK-3D* engine was certainly a lesson in planning for me. As the system has evolved and I've discovered faster and better ray-casting techniques, I've had to change many lines of code (more than I'd like to remember) and extend many of the initial data structures. Every time I added a new feature, such as an object that can have multiple views as you walk around it, the first place I needed to turn to was the internal data structures. By now, they've been so fine-tuned that you'll find internal support for most of the features you'll want to add into your 3-D worlds, from secret doors to transparent walls to awesome 3-D-like animated objects.

Now that we have the basic 3-D ray-casting theory under our belt, and we've explored the basic concepts of the game engine, it's time to dig in and start building our 3-D adventure kit. Our first stop along the way will be the data structures used to implement the *ACK-3D* engine. We'll pick up from where we left off in Chapter 3 and discuss the main data structure—**ACKENG**. Then, I'll describe the other important data structures needed to implement the *ACK-3D* engine. Along the way, you'll learn the basics of using some of the structures—that is, which fields you should and should not set. As we explore the internal data structures, you'll gain a much better understanding of how the important ray-casting techniques are implemented. Later, in Chapter 11, when we explore techniques for initializing the *ACK-3D* engine, I'll reintroduce the main structure **ACKENG** so that you can see how it should be created by your applications, initialized, and passed to *ACK-3D* functions.

The Underlying Data Structures

To build a 3-D engine with the power and flexibility of *ACK-3D*, we'll need an ample supply of data structures for representing 3-D worlds. For example, we'll need a way to store bitmaps for walls, doors, ceilings, and floors. We'll also need a way to store information about wall height and information about objects so that they can be animated as the POV changes in a scene. And most important of all, we'll need a way to pass data back and forth from an application to the core 3-D functions in the engine so that we can make sure our scenes get updated as a player moves around in a 3-D world.

It may seem that we'll need many types of data structures to support something as complex as 3-D scenes that are constantly changing. When you actually see the data structures that are required, you'll be surprised at how few of them are used and how straightforward they are.

We'll focus our code explorations on two different header files, ACK3D.H and ACKENG.H, with a slight diversion into one of the source files, ACKDATA.C. Once you have a good understanding of how these files are organized and how the data structures are designed and coded, you'll be in a much better position to understand how the engine works, use the callable *ACK-3D* functions, and make changes to the engine. (You might even feel bold enough to make a few changes to the data structures to add some new features!)

The data structures we'll examine include:

- **ACKENG**   This structure is defined in ACK3D.H to serve as the main interface structure.
- **OBJSEQ** and **NEWOBJECT**   These structures are defined in ACK3D.H to support animated objects.

- **DOORS**   This structure is defined in ACK3D.H to support doors.
- **SLICE**   This structure is defined in ACKENG.H to support ray casting.
- **Slice[ ]**   This array is defined in ACKDATA.C to support ray casting.
- **DistanceTable[ ]**   This array is defined in ACKDATA.C to keep track of wall-height data.

The first four structures listed here are defined in ACK3D.H. We'll refer to them as *communication* or *interface structures* because they are used directly by the *ACK-3D* functions that you call from your applications. As the term "interface structure" indicates, these structures are used to communicate information to your applications so that you can easily generate 3-D scenes. For example, the **NEWOBJECT** structure stores information about a stationary or movable object, such as a monster or a table, that you could put into a 3-D scene. Within your application, it's your job to make sure that this structure gets initialized properly. Then, when certain *ACK-3D* functions are called and the structure is passed, it's their job to make sure that important information is updated in the structure when certain events occur, such as the object being moved in a scene. In this respect, *ACK-3D* uses structures like these to communicate with your applications.

We'll also be looking at some of the internal array structures, such as **xGrid[ ]** and **yGrid[ ]** that are included in the main interface structure **ACKENG**.

DESIGN TIP

The **ACKENG** structure is by no means complete; in fact, every time I go back and look at it, I see where I could have changed things to further separate the engine side from the calling application side. The old woe of programming, "A program is never finished" definitely applies in this case. Don't hesitate to jump in and change things; that's what this book is all about. Together we are going to build a 3-D environment that can be used in a variety of ways.

Creating the ACKENG Structure

In Chapter 3 we discussed the basics of how applications communicate with *ACK-3D* by using the **ACKENG** structure. Here's the complete code for this structure defined in ACK3D.H:

```
// Main interface structure used between the application and the ACK engine.
// This structure MUST be allocated or defined before any ACK calls are made.
typedef struct {

    UINT       xGrid[GRID_ARRAY];      // Map for x walls
    UINT       yGrid[GRID_ARRAY];      // Map for y walls
```

```
UCHAR      *mxGrid[GRID_ARRAY];    // Wall data for multi-height x walls
UCHAR      *myGrid[GRID_ARRAY];    // Wall data for multi-height y walls

UCHAR      *bMaps[MAX_WALLBMPS];   // Pointers to wall bitmaps
UCHAR      *oMaps[MAX_OBJBMPS];    // Pointers to object bitmaps

UCHAR      *ScreenBuffer;  // 64k buffer for screen
UCHAR      *OverlayBuffer; // Buffer for compiled overlay
UCHAR      *BkgdBuffer;    // Buffer for ceiling and floor

short      xPlayer;        // Player's current x position (from 0 to 4095)
short      yPlayer;        // Player's current y position (from 0 to 4095)
short      PlayerAngle;    // Player's current angle (from 0 to 1919)

short      DoorSpeed;      // Door open/close speed
short      NonSecretCode;  // Wall code for secret door

UCHAR      TopColor;       // Base color of ceiling
UCHAR      BottomColor;    // Base color of floor
UCHAR      FloorBitmap;    // Bitmap number for single floor
UCHAR      CeilBitmap;     // Bitmap number for single ceiling
UCHAR      LightFlag;      // Light shading flag (0 = light shading off,
                           //   1 = light shading on)
UCHAR      PalTable[PAL_SIZE];    // Stores data for lighting and shading
                                  // 16 solid colors, 32 zones

short      WinStartX;             // Value of left side of viewport
short      WinStartY;             // Value of top side of viewport
short      WinEndX;               // Value of right side
short      WinEndY;               // Value of bottom side
short      CenterRow;             // Value of (WinEndY-WinStartY)/2
short      CenterOffset;          // Center row times bytes per row
short      WinWidth;              // Value of WinEndX - WinStartX
short      WinHeight;             // Value of WinEndY - WinStartY
UINT       WinLength;             // Number of dwords in window
UINT       WinStartOffset;        // Value of WinStartY * 320

UINT       SysFlags;       // General system flags for display attributes
UCHAR      bmLoadType;     // Bitmap load flags (BBM, GIF, PCX, etc.)

short      MaxObjects;                    // Total objects in map
NEWOBJECT  *ObjList[MAX_OBJECTS+1];       // Current objects in map
DOORS      Door[MAX_DOORS];               // Doors moving at one time
} ACKENG;
```

Make sure you read the two comment lines—especially the second one. In Chapter 11, I'll show you exactly how to allocate and initialize an **ACKENG** structure before using any of the engine functions. For now, let's concentrate on the individual fields of this structure.

This structure looks a little complex at first, but don't worry, because it's actually easy to follow. The first two array fields, **xGrid[ ]** and **yGrid[ ]**, are used to store map data for building 3-D scenes. The constant used to declare the arrays, **GRID_ARRAY**, is defined in ACK3D.H as:

```
#define GRID_ARRAY  (GRID_WIDTH+2) * (GRID_HEIGHT+2)
```

where **GRID_WIDTH** and **GRID_HEIGHT** are set to the value 64. This is the full size of the grid map used to determine what the POV sees at any given time. (Hang in there if this all seems like a mystery to you because we'll unravel it a little later in this chapter when we explore how the arrays are used to build 3-D scenes.)

The next set of fields in **ACKENG** include ***mxGrid[ ]** and ***myGrid[ ]**. These are arrays of pointers that contain wall data for multi-height walls. (The reasoning behind using pointer arrays was that multi-height walls would be the exception rather than the rule so why take up more memory with pre-allocated arrays?) The actual bitmap graphic images for walls and objects in our 3-D worlds are referenced using the arrays of pointers ***bMaps[ ]** (bitmaps) and ***oMaps[ ]** (object bitmaps), respectively.

In earlier chapters, we mentioned that *ACK-3D* creates scenes by placing data in an off-screen buffer and sending the buffer data to the screen later. This scene data is referenced by the pointer ***ScreenBuffer**. The overlay data that your application can add is accessed by using ***OverlayBuffer**. Finally, the data for the floors and ceilings in your scene is accessed using ***BkgdBuffer**. Normally, an application won't need to access the **OverlayBuffer** and the **BkgdBuffer**, because these get combined into the **ScreenBuffer** as a full scene when the rendering is completed. The application can then manipulate the contents of the **ScreenBuffer** before it is actually copied to the video screen. You'll learn more about how DOS screens are supported in Chapter 7 and how Windows screens are supported in Chapters 13 and 14.

The next section contains the three important fields—**xPlayer**, **yPlayer**, and **PlayerAngle**—that your application must set before calling any of the *ACK-3D* functions to build a scene. These three fields determine the actual location of the player in the map and what direction the player is currently facing. The fields, **DoorSpeed** and **NonSecretCode**, are used as door attributes within your 3-D worlds.

Another important set of fields in the interface structure, **TopColor**, **BottomColor**, **LightFlag**, and **PalTable[ ]**, is used to set colors and light shading for 3-D scenes. We'll look at how the first three of these fields should be set in the next section. The palette array, called **PalTable[ ]**, controls how the *ACK-3D* engine performs light shading. The array contains 16 ranges of 256 colors, each of which is used to substitute for the actual colors of the bitmap based on the distance the player is from a wall or object. The other two fields in this group, **FloorBitmap** and **CeilBitmap**, are used to specify the bitmap numbers for floors and ceilings, respectively. These fields only come into play if you decide you want to use a single bitmap for the floor and ceiling; otherwise, the global **FloorMap[ ]** and **CeilMap[ ]** arrays in ACKDATA.C are used.

The next group of fields, starting with **WinStartX** and ending with **WinStartOffset**, specifies the size and coordinates of the display region used to render scenes on your screen. *ACK-3D* supports display regions up to 320 pixels wide and 200 pixels high, which consist of the entire video screen in the normal VGA 256 color mode (mode 13h).

The last group of fields includes **SysFlags**, **bmLoadType**, **MaxObjects**, ***ObjList**, and the array **Door[ ]**. The flag field, **SysFlags**, is used to keep track of the display attributes that the engine uses to generate a scene. In ACK3D.H, you'll find a set of flags that are available for setting this field, as shown here:

```
// These defines are used for the SysFlags field in the ACKENG structure.
#define SYS_SOLID_BACK    0x8000     // On if solid color bkgd vs picture
#define SYS_SOLID_FLOOR   0x4000     // On if solid vs texture floor
#define SYS_SOLID_CEIL    0x2000     // On if solid vs texture ceiling
#define SYS_NO_WALLS      0x1000     // On if walls are NOT to display
#define SYS_SINGLE_BMP    0x0800     // On if 1 bitmap for floor & ceiling
```

As you can see, a variety of display options are available, such as displaying a scene without walls or displaying a floor as a solid instead of as a texture. These flags are actually used internally by some of the *ACK-3D* functions for setting the **SysFlags** field.

The **bmLoadType** field keeps track of the type of bitmap files that *ACK-3D* can load. The three settings for this field include **BMLOAD_BBM**, **BMLOAD_GIF**, and **BMLOAD_PCX**. The **MaxObjects** field stores the total number of objects used in a scene, and the ***ObjList[ ]** array stores pointers to each of the objects used. This array is used internally so that *ACK-3D* functions can easily process objects as you move around in a scene. Finally, the field **Door[ ]** is an array that references the moving doors used in a scene. We'll be looking at the **DOORS** structure a little later in this chapter.

Fields You Must Set in ACKENG

Before calling the *ACK-3D* engine to initialize it, you must assign values to some of the fields in **ACKENG**. The other fields will automatically be set and updated by *ACK-3D* functions. Let's look at the fields you must set. First, the following four fields, which contain window coordinate data, must be initialized so that the engine can calculate values for the other key window sizing variables:

WinStartX   The leftmost pixel coordinate of the viewport

WinEndX   The rightmost pixel coordinate of the viewport

WinStartY   The upper pixel coordinate of the viewport

WinEndY   The lower pixel coordinate of the viewport

As Figure 4.1 shows, the viewport is the region where scenes are displayed on your screen. With this data in hand, *ACK-3D* can calculate values for the other six positioning fields defined in **ACKENG, CenterRow, CenterOffset, WinWidth, WinHeight, WinLength,** and **WinStartOffset** on its own.

Before calling the *ACK-3D* function to construct the background for a scene, these fields must be filled in:

TopColor   Color value of the ceiling

BottomColor   Color value of the floor

LightFlag   Turn light shading on or off

Notice that the first two fields control the way floors and ceilings are drawn. Floors and ceilings are considered background items because they are drawn independently of the walls and objects that are actually moved as a player's POV changes. The settings for the top and bottom colors only apply if a solid ceiling and floor is used.

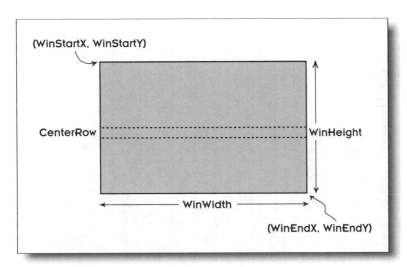

Figure 4.1   *Using a viewport to create scenes.*

Finally, before calling the **ACKBuildView()** function to actually build the POV, these fields must be assigned values:

xPlayer   X coordinate for the POV

yPlayer   Y coordinate for the POV

PlayerAngle POV angle in *ACK-3D* units

By now you should be familiar with these settings. The *ACK-3D* engine relies on the POV fields above to build the current scene. But what you might not realize is that by changing these values, you can easily build a variety of scenes one after the other. For example, Figure 4.2 shows a scene that was created by setting the **PlayerAngle** field to 0 before building the view. If you change **PlayerAngle** to 180 degrees and then build the view, you'll see the scene shown in Figure 4.3. Notice how the POV has changed. This feature of changing coordinates and angles and then building views gives you a lot of flexibility when designing 3-D games.

Representing 3-D Worlds with Map Arrays

As I've mentioned, several arrays are used to build 3-D POV scenes. These arrays are referred to as *map* or *grid arrays* because they "map out" the positions of the walls used to create a maze. But before we get too far into the details of how the arrays are constructed and used, let's stand back for a moment and explore once again how we move around in a 3-D world.

Figure 4.2   *Building a view by setting PlayerAngle to 0.*

Figure 4.3 *Building a view by setting PlayerAngle to 180.*

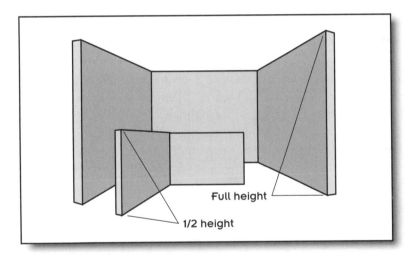

Figure 4.4 *A scene created with different walls.*

Imagine that you have a scene set up like the one shown in Figure 4.4. As you look into the scene, you should see a wall along the back and walls half-way around the sides. You should also see walls directly in front of you and also to your right and left. In this scene, the walls directly in front of you were made half-size so that you could see over them to notice the walls in back.

This is the type of map (or maze) that we need to represent as a data structure. The structure is needed so that we can easily determine where the walls are located. For any given position in the map, we need to know if there is a wall in front, behind, to the left, or to the right of us.

Your first attempt might be to set up this structure as a two-dimensional array. Let's try this approach. Figure 4.5 shows one possible way to represent the map shown in Figure 4.4 using a two-dimensional array. Here, each array location corresponds to an (x,y) coordinate position in the map. As the player moves around in the map, we would need to look up the array location that corresponds to the new position to see if there are any walls. But here's the problem, what do we store in each array location so that we have the wall data that we need? Remember that we must know where the walls are at all four sides of a given position. Of course, we could set up the array to be an array of structures and each structure could contain left, right, front, and back wall data. But this could get too complex and add too much overhead. After all, we want to be able to move around in our 3-D world as fast as possible. Fortunately, there is a simpler and more efficient way to create our map data structures.

Going for the Edges—Mapping a Maze with Two Arrays

If we think of the map or maze as a grid system laid out in squares like graph paper, a new solution presents itself. Instead of representing actual map coordinate positions, that is the location in a grid square within four walls, let's represent the edges. As shown in Figure 4.6, each location in the map is really a square that has two x (right and left) and two y (top and bottom) components or wall positions. For example, the map position (0, 0) has *xa* and *xb* as left and right walls and *ya* and *yb* as top and bottom (or front and back) walls. Position (0, 0) has the pairs (*xa*, *xb*) and (*ya*, *yb*), position (1, 0) has the pairs (*xb*, *xc*) and (*yc*, *yd*), and so on.

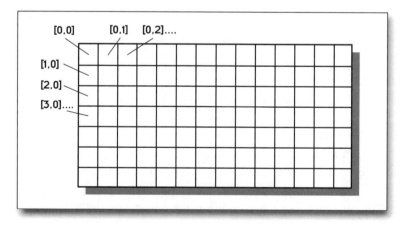

Figure 4.5　*Representing the map using a two-dimensional array.*

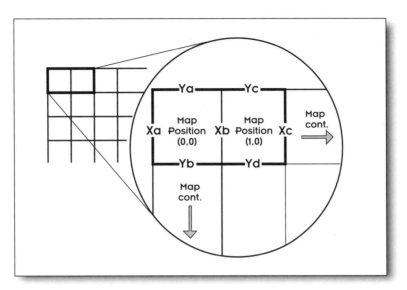

Figure 4.6   *Representing the edges of a map.*

What we really need is a way to store data for walls displayed in the x-plane and walls displayed in the y-plane. In *ACK-3D*, walls are simply displayed and referenced as bitmap images. Thus, we only need to store a bitmap ID code for each wall position. We can actually store the wall ID codes by using two single-dimensioned arrays. It turns out that these are the arrays **xGrid[ ]** and **yGrid[ ]** defined in the **ACKENG** structure. The **xGrid[ ]** array stores the bitmap IDs for the walls that appear in the x plane and **yGrid[ ]** stores bitmap IDs for the walls that appear in the y plane. Let's look at the actual code used to set up the map and the two grid arrays. Then, you'll see how the grid arrays are accessed to determine where walls are placed in the map.

Setting Up the Map and Grid Arrays

All of the definitions needed to set up the map and grid arrays can be found together in ACK3D.H, as shown here:

```
#define GRID_MASK 0xFFC0     // Use FF80 for 128 and FFC0 for 64
#define GRID_SIZE 64         // The size of an individual grid unit
#define GRID_WIDTH  64
#define GRID_HEIGHT 64
#define GRID_MAX  GRID_WIDTH * GRID_HEIGHT
#define GRID_XMAX BITMAP_WIDTH * GRID_WIDTH
#define GRID_YMAX BITMAP_WIDTH * GRID_HEIGHT
#define GRID_XMAXLONG (GRID_XMAX * FP_MULT)
#define GRID_YMAXLONG (GRID_YMAX * FP_MULT)
```

```
// The main grid array used with the ACKENG structure
#define GRID_ARRAY  (GRID_WIDTH+2) * (GRID_HEIGHT+2)
```

As shown in Figure 4.7, the map for representing 3-D scenes is constructed of individual grid squares where each grid square is 64×64 units. *ACK-3D* uses a total map configuration of 64×64 grid squares to determine what the POV sees at any given time. This configuration makes the total width and height of the map:

height = 64 grid squares × 64 units per grid square = 4,096
width = 64 grid squares × 64 units per grid square = 4,096

In Chapter 2 we used a grid map of 10×10 to keep the grid small for a conceptual presentation. But all of the concepts introduced apply here, even though the actual map is a little bigger. As an example, recall that the player can move a total of 64 units left or right or up or down before traveling from one grid square (or map position) in the maze to another. As it turns out, the size of each wall bitmap is also 64×64. (That's why each grid square is 64 units in width and height.)

The **xGrid[ ]** and **yGrid[ ]** arrays are designed to represent each map position. Here are the definitions as found in the **ACKENG** structure:

```
UINT    xGrid[GRID_ARRAY];  // Map for x walls
UINT    yGrid[GRID_ARRAY];  // Map for y walls
```

As we've mentioned, one array represents the walls along the x axis and the other represents the walls along the y axis. As a player moves around in 3-D

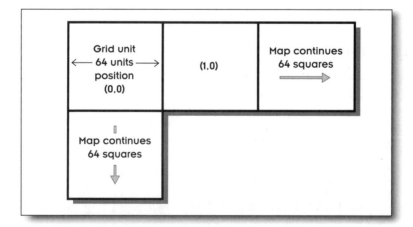

Figure 4.7   *The actual map used by* ACK-3D.

space, we can keep track of where walls are actually located by examining the x and y map arrays.

The map editor included with *ACK-3D* is used to create the data for these arrays, which is then saved to a file and later read into memory by calling the **AckReadMapFile()** function. This approach helps you automate the process of creating and changing your walls. The two arrays are used during the rendering process to facilitate finding the line of sight intersections between the player's position and the surrounding walls.

Let's take a closer look at how these arrays are constructed. This discussion will give you insight into the inner workings of the *ACK-3D* engine. You first might be wondering why the map array has a size of 64×64 units. This size was chosen to facilitate the calculations required to determine the relationship between a player's position (as he or she moves around in a 3-D space) and the corresponding location in the map array. As Figure 4.8 shows, each entry in the map array stores a value.

In this array, a value of 0 represents a blank square (no wall) and a non-zero value represents a wall bitmap value. (Walls can have bitmap values that range from 1 to 255.)

But recall that the *ACK-3D* engine uses two arrays (**xGrid[ ]** and **yGrid[ ]**) so that wall information can be broken into walls that fall on x-planes and walls that fall on y-planes. To support this type of representation, Figure 4.9 shows how the x and y map arrays reference actual wall locations in the map.

These two arrays are basically what becomes of the original map shown in Figure 4.7 for the engine to see walls in either the x or y planes. So how do we determine which map location corresponds with the current (x, y) position in a 3-D scene? Here are the calculations:

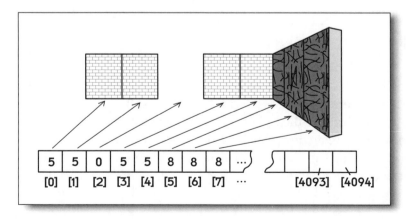

Figure 4.8 *Using a map array to represent walls in a scene.*

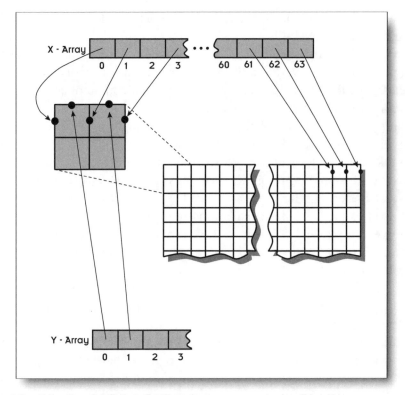

Figure 4.9 *Using the xGrid[] and yGrid[] arrays to access actual wall locations.*

```
int MapPosn;        // Location to look at in map

MapPosn = (y & 0xFFFC) + (x>>6);  // Calc (y/64 * 64)+(x/64)
xGrid[MapPosn];                   // This would be the left x wall
xGrid[MapPosn + 1];               // This would be the right x wall

yGrid[MapPosn];                   // This would be the top y wall
yGrid[MapPosn + GRID_WIDTH];      // This would be the bottom y wall
```

In English, this code translates to this: As a player is positioned at a location (x,y) in a 3-D scene, check the **xGrid[ ]** array for walls in the x direction to see if there are any walls to the right or left of the player. Then, check the **yGrid[ ]** array to see if there are any walls in front of the player. (The coordinate scale for x and y that are used in these calculations are based on the actual height and width of the grid where both x and y can range from 0 to 4,095.) A value of 0 stored in all four of these locations indicates that there is nothing at this square in the map.

Let's step through an example to see how the calculations work. Assume that you are at the location y=96 and x=200 in the map, as shown in Figure 4.10. The actual calculation for the map position would be 67 as shown here:

```
(96/64 * 64) + (200/64)
(1 * 64) + 3
67
```

As Figure 4.10 indicates, location y=96, x=200 corresponds to position row = 1 and column = 3 in the map. To see what walls are to the left and right of you at this map position, these two **xGrid[ ]** array locations are checked:

```
xGrid[67]
xGrid[68]
```

To see what walls are in front, these positions in **yGrid[ ]** are checked:

```
yGrid[67]
yGrid[131]  // calculation is position + grid width
```

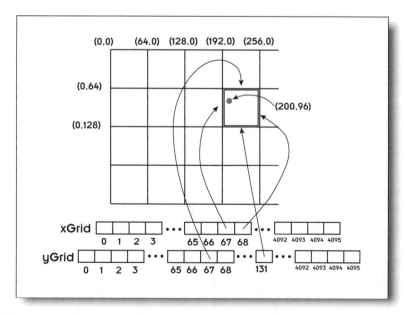

Figure 4.10 *Calculating array positions using a given map position.*

Essentially, we are checking the same position as in the **xGrid[ ]**, except that for the bottom wall, we need to check the array position that corresponds with the wall that is all the way at the bottom of the map.

DESIGN TIP

One unique feature of the *ACK-3D* engine is that a grid location (map square) can be assigned from one to four walls, making it possible for walls to be paper thin instead of an entire cube. Some neat effects can be achieved, such as alcoves and entryways with signs over them, by using a single wall that is both transparent and passable. Another feature is that different bitmaps can be used for each of the four sides of a map square, which further enhances the visual effects of a 3-D environment.

Representing Walls and Objects as Bitmaps

Recall that the **ACKENG** structure contained two bitmap arrays for storing actual wall and object data:

```
UCHAR   *bMaps[MAX_WALLBMPS]; // Pointers to wall bitmaps
UCHAR   *oMaps[MAX_OBJBMPS];  // Pointers to object bitmaps
```

Actually, they are just simple arrays of pointers that reference the wall and object bitmaps, respectively. The two constants are defined as:

```
#define MAX_WALLBMPS  256    // Total wall bitmaps allowed
#define MAX_OBJBMPS   256    // Total object bitmaps allowed
```

Each bitmap stored is 64×64 pixels, as shown in Figure 4.11. Each byte represents one pixel and may have a color value from 0 to 255. As shown, it takes 4,096 bytes of memory for the 64×64 size bitmap. If all 256 wall bitmaps are used in an application, the total memory required for storage is about 1 MB. Another 1 MB is needed if you use the maximum number of objects (256) in an application. As you can see, bitmaps can eat up a lot of memory. But if you plan ahead, you can create basic bitmap textures that can be used to build a variety of walls and objects.

All of the walls and objects that are used in a 3-D world are built from basic 64×64 bitmap building blocks. As an example, Figure 4.12 shows some of the actual bitmaps that are used to create walls in the *Station Escape* game provided on the companion CD-ROM. The 64×64 bitmap building blocks can be

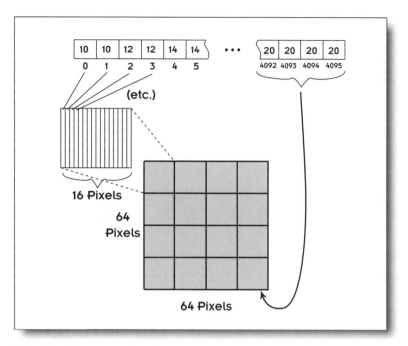

Figure 4.11   *How bitmaps are stored.*

created by any painting program that stores images in one of these formats: Deluxe Paint II (.BBM) by Electronic Arts, Graphics Interchange Format (.GIF) designed by and used on CompuServe, or .PCX by ZSoft Corporation. The *ACK-3D* engine itself requires that bitmaps be in a raw image format as shown in Figure 4.11; however, a special function named **AckLoadBitmap()** is provided to read in .BBM, .GIF, or .PCX files. (Actually, the function to read in .GIF files is not included with the *ACK-3D* engine at this time because of pending legal issues. See Chapter 12 for more information.)

Walls are actually constructed using the *ACK-3D* map editor by piecing the 64×64 bitmap building blocks together. We'll explore techniques for building walls out of bitmaps in Chapter 12.

An important point to keep in mind when using *ACK-3D* functions to create views is that *ACK-3D* reads bitmaps in normal row order, where there is a row of color bytes one after the other, like this:

```
1,2,3,...    An arbitrary bitmap of 64x64
1,1,1,...
4,2,4,...
....
```

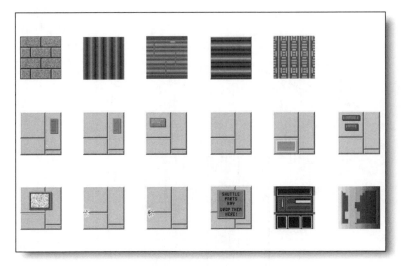

Figure 4.12   *Some of the bitmap images used to build walls in* Station Escape.

The bitmap is then "rotated" 90 degrees so that it is in column order, which makes it easier to use when drawing the bitmaps in vertical slices. After this rotation, here's what the bitmap data looks like:

```
1,1,4,....    Bitmap rotated 90 degrees
2,1,2,....
3,1,4,....
```

Supporting Multi-Height Walls

We've examined the structures that are used for storing standard wall data, but what about multi-height walls? For this feature, you'll find these two arrays included in **ACKENG**:

```
UCHAR   *mxGrid[GRID_ARRAY]; // Wall data for multi-height walls
UCHAR   *myGrid[GRID_ARRAY]; // Wall data for multi-height walls
```

This time around, we need to store pointers to actual multi-height wall data. This allows us to create scenes with different size walls, as shown in Figure 4.13.

Earlier I mentioned the ***mxGrid[ ]** and ***myGrid[ ]** arrays in the **ACKENG** structure. These two arrays are specifically designed to support multi-height walls with the *ACK-3D* engine. A multi-height wall is two or more wall blocks stacked on top of each other. I use pointer arrays here instead of pre-allocated arrays because I think multi-height walls are typically treated as an exception rather than a standard. Because the data required to store the wall information for multi-height walls can be variable in length, it seems logical to use point-

Figure 4.13 *Using multi-height walls in a 3-D scene.*

ers instead of assuming the maximum length of data and allocating an entire array when most of it would be empty. Thus, ***mxGrid[ ]*** and ***myGrid[ ]*** are NULL filled except where a multi-height wall appears (which may be none, or more). A flag is set in the standard wall arrays, **xGrid[ ]** and **yGrid[ ]**, to indicate that a particular wall is indeed multi-height to further speed the checking needed during the display phase of the rendering process.

Multi-height walls can be used to add some neat effects, like billboards and skyscrapers or even an entire room that is taller than the surrounding rooms. There is one caveat with the current engine however; floors and ceilings are created using preset numbers for the height of the viewer so they tend to "float" when used in conjunction with multi-height walls. I might change this in future versions of the engine (or you might want to do it yourself as a fun weekend project) but for now, multi-height walls should be limited to outside scenes.

Supporting Doors

If you thought your 3-D worlds were limited to just walls and objects that can move around within the walls, you're in for a pleasant surprise. The *ACK-3D* engine allows you to create doors, such as the ones shown in Figure 4.14, that can be opened and closed as a player moves around in a scene. If you look closely at the **ACKENG** structure, you'll see the following field declaration that paves the way for adding doors:

```
DOORS   Door[MAX_DOORS];   // Doors moving at one time
```

Here, **Door[ ]** is defined as an array of structures of type **DOORS**. The constant **MAX_DOORS** is set to the value of 10 in ACK3D.H. (This value allows you to have up to ten moving doors in an application at one time, which has been more than sufficient in everything I've seen so far. The actual number of doors allowed in the entire maze is limited only by the practicality of not having a door in every wall!) The **Door[ ]** array is used to keep track of the status of doors that are currently in motion. (opening or closing). Although doors are actually similar to walls when it comes to performing ray casting to build a scene, we'll need a special structure to store the coordinates and moving components of a door. The structure used is **DOORS,** which is also defined in ACK3D.H:

```
typedef struct {
        short     mPos;          // Stores position info for a door
        short     mPos1;
        short     mCode;         // Bitmap ID of the door
        short     mCode1;
        UCHAR     ColOffset;     // Column offset for the door
        char      Speed;         // Speed setting for opening and closing the door
        char      Type;          // Code for the door type
        UCHAR     Flags;         // Door attribute settings
} DOORS;
```

A set of flags is also defined to set attributes for doors:

```
// These defines are used to set the Flags field in the DOORS structure.
#define DOOR_OPENING  0x80     // Set if door is currently opening
#define DOOR_CLOSING  0x40     // Set if door is currently closing
// Other attributes that can be assigned to the Flags field.
```

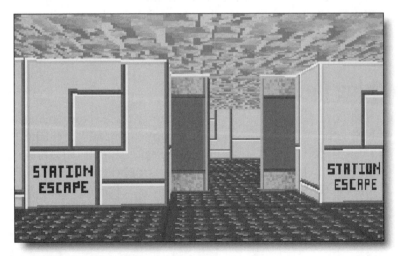

Figure 4.14 *Using movable doors in a 3-D scene.*

```
#define DOOR_TYPE_SECRET   0x8000
#define DOOR_LOCKED        0x4000
#define DOOR_TYPE_SLIDE    0x2000
#define DOOR_TYPE_SPLIT    0x1000
```

Your application can easily check the status of a door by looking at the **Flags** field in the **DOOR** structure for either a **DOOR_OPENING** or **DOOR_CLOSING** setting. You can keep a door open permanently by changing the **Speed** field to zero once the door is fully open. (The **Flags** field changes from **DOOR_OPENING** to **DOOR_CLOSING**.) You can also keep a door open by setting the **ColOffset** field to a value greater than 64 for as long as your application wishes to keep the door open. The drawback to this method is that your application must continually update the field after calling the main scene building function, **AckBuildView()**. The best time to check the status of your doors is after you call **AckBuildView()** because each time this function is called, it causes the doors to be updated in the structure (whether the door is currently visible or not).

DESIGN TIP

Because of the way doors are represented, you can incorporate neat sound effects as doors open and close. By checking the status of a door, an application can "whoosh" the door shut even if the player is not currently looking at the door. A quick calculation of the distance of the door from the player could also be used to control the volume of the sound, making an even more realistic effect of a door closing in the distance!

Let's move on and discuss each of the fields in the **DOORS** structure so that you can better see how doors are represented:

mPos	Map position for one side of a grid square
mPos1	Map position for the other side of a grid square
mCode	Bitmap code that represents the door
mCode1	Bitmap code for the door on the other side
ColOffset	Current column offset of the door
Speed	The speed setting for opening and closing the door
Type	Type of door
Flags	Current door action (**DOOR_OPENING** or **DOOR_CLOSING**)

Figure 4.15 shows how the position-related fields, such as **mPos** and **mPos1**, are used to represent a door. Notice that everything is included to determine where the door is located in a grid square.

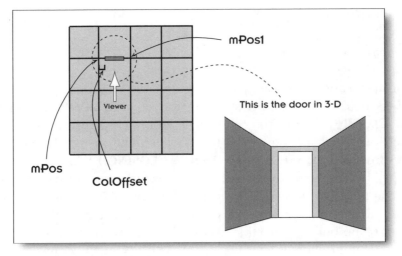

Figure 4.15   *The components of a door.*

ACK-3D allows you to turn any wall into a door. You can also assign your doors different attributes so that they will operate in different ways. Here are the four attributes that are supported:

DOOR_TYPE_SLIDE   Door slides from left to right the full width of the panel

DOOR_TYPE_SPLIT   Door opens from the center out

DOOR_TYPE_SECRET   Door is a secret panel that moves away from the player until the door block strikes another wall

DOOR_LOCKED   Indicates door cannot be opened until this flag is cleared

You can set the **Flag** field to one of these settings when a door is opening so that your application can determine the current state of the door.

One important difference to keep in mind between secret doors and normal doors is that secret doors remain flush with the surrounding walls, while normal (sliding or split) doors are recessed into the walls by one-half the width of a wall block. Secret doors also recess into the surrounding walls, while normal doors simply open sideways and then close again.

Doors can be opened at various speeds by setting the **Speed** field of the door structure to values greater than 1. (The maximum speed setting is 255.) Normally, you'll want to set the speed value to 16 or less so that the player can see the door open or close smoothly. (Of course, if you want to see a door slam, try a higher setting!)

Representing Objects

Okay, now let's look at how objects are represented with *ACK-3D*. Objects can be either stationary or movable. For example, if you want to create a 3-D world that looks like a shopping mall, you could create counter tops with cash registers as stationary objects and "shoppers from hell" who move around at a furious pace as movable objects. Fortunately, both types of objects can be handled exactly the same—the stationary objects just never change their position. The objects you create can also share bitmaps and can be composed of more than one bitmap. This technique allows you to create a variety of object types. If an object uses different bitmaps, it can remain in one place or its bitmaps can be displayed in sequence to create animation effects. We'll refer to these as *object sequences* in this book. You can also use multiple bitmaps to show different views of an object as the POV moves around in your 3-D world.

So, how can we represent these flexible features in the form of a data structure? Actually, we'll need to use two structures, **NEWOBJECT** and **OBJSEQ**. If you look closely at the **ACKENG** interface structure, you'll find two field declarations that will give you your first clue of how objects are set up:

```
short    MaxObjects;              // Total objects in map
NEWOBJECT *ObjList[MAX_OBJECTS+1]; // Current objects in map
```

The first field, **MaxObjects**, stores the number of objects (254) that can be used in an application. The second field, ***ObjList[ ]**, consists of an array of pointers to structures of type **NEWOBJECT**. (This means we're just about ready to sneak in another data structure.) Again, this is an array stored within the interface structure and accessible to your application as well as the *ACK-3D* engine. Each object is represented by an entry in this array. The **AckInitialize()** function automatically fills in the initial x and y coordinates of an object when it finds one in the map file. The rest of the object data must be filled in by your application before the object can be used. Let's take a closer look at the **NEWOBJECT** structure and see how objects are represented.

Inside the NEWOBJECT Structure

The **NEWOBJECT** structure is designed to hold all of the key attributes needed to set up and move an object around. Some of these attributes include coordinate positions, object ID, speed and direction for animation, views, bitmaps, and so on. Special fields are also provided so that you can create an object with multiple object sequences for extended animation. This code shows the actual definition of **NEWOBJECT** found in ACK3D.H:

```
typedef struct {
  char    Active;           // Determines object status: 0=Inactive, 1=Active
  UCHAR   Flags;            // Misc flags for this object
  char    Speed;            // Speed of obj (used by application)
  short   Dir;              // Direction of obj (used by application)
  short   x;                // Current x,y location in grid
  short   y;
  short   mPos;             // Current map location in grid
  UCHAR   id;               // Object id
  short   CurrentType;      // Create, Destroy, etc. is current
  UCHAR   *CurrentBitmaps;  // Current bitmap list
  short   Sides;            // Number of views
  short   aFactor;          // Angle factor
  short   BitmapsPerView;   // Number of bitmaps in each view
  UCHAR   CurrentBm;        // Current bitmap number
  UCHAR   Maxbm;            // Max bitmap number for this view
  OBJSEQ  Create;           // Stores structures for the 5 object sequences
  OBJSEQ  Destroy;
  OBJSEQ  Walk;
  OBJSEQ  Attack;
  OBJSEQ  Interact;
  } NEWOBJECT;
```

The best way to see how this structure works is to discuss each of the main fields. Let's start at the top and work our way down. The first two fields, **Active** and **Flags**, are used to determine how an object should be set up and displayed:

Active   Indicates if an object should be displayed or not (0 or 1 setting)

Flags   Determines how objects are animated and controlled

For setting the **Active** field, two defines are provided with ACK3D.H:

```
#define OBJECT_ACTIVE 1 // Active and may be movable
#define OBJECT_INACTIVE 0 // Won't be displayed
```

The **Flags** field, on the other hand, can be set using any of these flags, which are also defined in ACK3D.H:

OF_PASSABLE   Object can be walked through

OF_ANIMATE   Object bitmaps are animated

OF_MOVEABLE   Object can be moved

OF_MULTIVIEW   Object has multiple sides

OF_ANIMONCE   Animate once then stop

OF_ANIMDONE   One shot animation is completed

These settings provide you with quite a bit of flexibility for animating your objects. Because they serve as flags, you can combine some of them to create various animation effects. For example, if you set the **Flags** field using the following assignment statement:

```
NEWOBJECT Obj1;
Obj1.Flags = OF_MOVEABLE & OF_MULTIVIEW;
```

you could create a movable object that has multiple sides. Keep in mind that you need to set other fields before actually using this object.

The next group of fields in **NEWOBJECT** includes the following:

Speed   Speed of object for use by the application

Dir   Direction of object for use by the application

x   Current x location of object in grid

y   Current y location of object in grid

mPos   Current actual map location in grid

id   Object id for use by the application

Most of these fields, such as **x**, **y**, **mPos**, and **id** are first set by *ACK-3D* when you initialize the engine by calling **AckInitialize()**. In addition, position information is updated and stored in the related fields as an object is moved around by calling one of the *ACK-3D* object processing functions, such as **AckMoveObjectPOV()**. The **Speed** field is one you'll want to set in your application before creating the object. It tells the **AckMoveObjectPOV()** function just how fast you want the object to move. A setting of 0 allows no movement of the object.

We also need a field to keep track of the type of object sequence that will be used for a given object' that's where the **CurrentType** field comes in. This field can be assigned to one of the following values:

NO_CREATE   Initial creation of the object; normally has the **OF_ANIMONCE** flag set so it doesn't repeat

NO_DESTROY   Opposite of create; normally done once at the end of the object's life cycle

NO_WALK   Normally used for continuous animation, such as walking

NO_ATTACK   Another one shot animation sequence for attacking

NO_INTERACT   Can be used for interaction with the player or other one shot animation sequences

To support the bitmaps and views needed for an object, we'll be using these fields:

CurrentBitmaps   Current bitmap list for this object
Sides   Number of views (sides) for this object
aFactor   Angle factor (used by the *ACK-3D* library)
BitmapsPerView   Number of bitmaps in each view
CurrentBm   Current bitmap number being displayed
Maxbm   Maximum bitmap number for this view

Last, but not least, we need fields to store special structures for the five types of object sequences that are supported in *ACK-3D*:

Create   Stores the data to describe how an object appears when it is activated
Destroy   Stores the data to describe how an object appears when it is deactivated
Walk   Stores the data to describe how an object walks
Attack   Stores the data to describe the action when the object and player are in combat with each other
Interact   Stores the data to describe when the player and object are interacting with each other

All of these fields are defined as type **OBJSEQ**. Essentially, they store the data structure needed to represent an object as it sequences through different stages of its "existence": creation, destruction, walking, attacking, and interacting with the player. The names for these sequences were chosen arbitrarily and were meant to be a generic means of grouping the various phases of an object. You can use these sequences for whatever you need; for example, the attack sequence could easily be used for animation showing a monkey eating a banana. (Must be time for lunch, I'm thinking of food already!)

Supporting Object Sequences

It's now time to take a quick peek at what is actually stored in an object sequence structure. Recall that object sequences are used to define the various phases of an object. These phases can be defined and used by your application at any point. Here's the definition for **OBJSEQ** found in ACK3D.H:

```
typedef struct {
  UCHAR flags;                    // Flags for this sequence
  UCHAR bitmaps[MAX_OBJ_BITMAPS]; // Bitmap numbers in this sequence
```

```
    short bmSides;              // Number of views in sequence
    short bmBitmapsPerView;     // Number of bitmaps in each view
    short AngleFactor;          // Used internally to support
                                // the object sequence
    UCHAR MaxBitmaps;           // Maximum bitmaps in this sequence
    } OBJSEQ;
```

The **Flags** field is used to store the animation attributes for this object sequence. This field can be assigned the same flag settings used to set the **Flags** field in the **NEWOBJECT** structure (**OF_PASSABLE**, **OF_ANIMATE**, and so on). The second field, **bitmaps[ ]**, is an array that stores the bitmap number for each bitmap being used by this object sequence. In this way, each sequence can have its own list of bitmaps to display, based on the state of the object. The *ACK-3D* engine will use this bitmap number to index into the **oMaps[ ]** array when it actually needs to display the objects bitmap.

Next, we have **bmSides**. This field specifies the number of different sides or views that are used for an object. For example, if the object were a table, it would have four views: front, back, and two sides. In this case **bmSides** would be set to 4.

The other view related field is **bmBitmapsPerView**. This field indicates the number of bitmaps used to make up each view of the object. In our table example, we would set this field to 1 since there is no animation taking place. This setting tells the *ACK-3D* engine that we only want to see one bitmap for each of the four sides of the table as the player walks around it.

Using Multiple Views

The technique of creating objects that can have multiple bitmaps for each view is a clever way of animating objects, one that goes way back to the early sprite animation days on those dusty old computers. As an example, suppose you wanted to display a table with a flickering candle on top of the table in your 3-D world. For each of the four views of the table as shown in Figure 4.16, you could create bitmaps to make the candle look like it is flickering. (That is, draw the candle flame in different positions.) Let's assume that three are needed for each view. You would also want to be able to walk around the table and see the candle flickering from each of the four sides. Thus, the field **bmBitmapsPerView** would be set to 3 to indicate that each side or view has three bitmaps and **bmSides** would be set to 4 to indicate that the object will have four sides. By judicious use of these two fields, you can create some amazing sequences of animation and 3-D effects; use your imagination and let the sky be your limit.

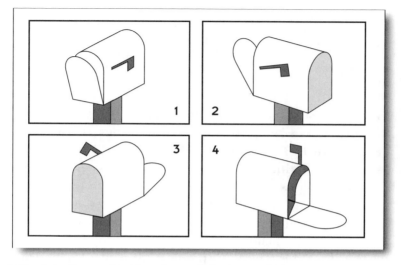

Figure 4.16 *Animating an object by using multiple views and bitmaps.*

Structures for Ray Casting

Now that we're finished looking at the main data structures used to support the *ACK-3D* engine, it's time to start slicing up walls. That is, we'll explore the internal data structures needed to implement our ray-casting routines.

The structures we're about to look at now aren't actually used directly by the application programmer when calling any of the main *ACK-3D* functions for building scenes. They're tucked away in the two files ACKDATA.C and ACKENG.H. But nevertheless, it's important for you to know how these structures are used so that you can better understand how ray casting is performed in *ACK-3D*.

If you recall from Chapter 2, the ray-casting process involves casting out rays from a given position to see if there are any objects that need to be displayed. In our case, we need to construct walls or 3-D objects, such as monsters, giant chickens that can fly, or desks—you get the idea. So how do we support this process? As Figure 4.17 shows, we divide the screen into 320 columns to display our scenes. Wherever you put yourself within this region, you'll have 320 columns of viewing. As you scan from left to right, a part of a wall or object could intersect any of these columns. We then need to determine which objects in the grid arrays are in our view, and we need another basic array to store information about which walls or objects to put on the screen in a particular screen column location.

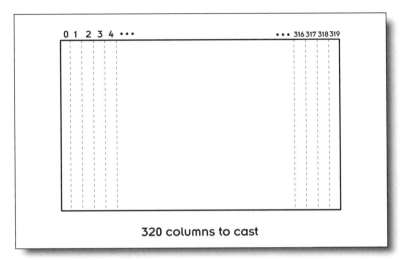

Figure 4.17 *Setting up the screen for ray-casting scenes.*

The next question is, what do we store in each array location? To build a scene, we need specific information, such as the bitmap image (of a wall or object) displayed at a particular column location, the distance between the current POV and the wall or object, the column location of the wall or object, and so on. The array used to build a scene is defined in the source file ACKDATA.C. Here is its definition:

```
SLICE Slice[VIEW_WIDTH];
```

In this case, **VIEW_WIDTH** is defined as the value 320. As shown, the array holds structures called **SLICE**s. We use the term *slice* because the data that is stored represents a "slice" or section of a wall. The actual **SLICE** structure is defined in ACKENG.H as:

```
// Holds info for the current wall section found during the ray casting
// process. During this process, ACK-3D casts out rays, looks for
// a wall at a given screen column position, and if a wall (slice) is
// found, information about the slice is stored in this structure.
typedef struct _slicer {
    UCHAR   **bMap;  // Pointer to wall or object bitmap found while ray casting
    UCHAR   *mPtr;        // Grid pointer to reference multi-height wall data
    short   bNumber;             // Bitmap number of the wall or object found
    unsigned short  bColumn;     // Screen column location of the found slice
    short   Distance;            // Distance from the POV to the slice
    short   mPos;                // Position of the slice in the associated map
    unsigned char      Type;     // Indicates if the slice is a wall or object
    void (*Fnc)(void);           // Pointer to a function to draw wall or object
```

```
    unsigned char Active;           // Indicates if a wall or object is displayable
                                    // or not
                                    // The next two pointers are used if the current
                                    // slice is part of a transparent wall
    struct _slicer *Prev;           // References the wall slice in front of the
                                    // current slice
    struct _slicer *Next;           // References the wall slice behind the
                                    // current slice
    } SLICE;
```

To understand how this **SLICE** structure is used, you'll need to recall the ray-casting technique we explored in Chapter 2. First, the *ACK-3D* engine takes the player's POV and examines the grid arrays to see if a wall is around. Figure 4.18 shows how the **SLICE** data structure is built. If there is a wall, the slice that corresponds to the appropriate screen column position is constructed. The pointer ****bMap** stores a reference to the wall bitmap that will be displayed. (Note the "pointer to pointer" reference, since we're actually storing a pointer into our bitmap array that contains pointers.) If the wall is a multi-height wall, ***mPtr** is used to reference the wall. The **SLICE** structure also holds the bitmap number for the wall (**bNumber**) and the screen column location (**bColumn**) where the wall will be displayed.

At this stage, you're probably wondering how the engine can determine where the wall bitmap should be displayed on the screen. We know the screen column position, but how is the row position determined? That's where

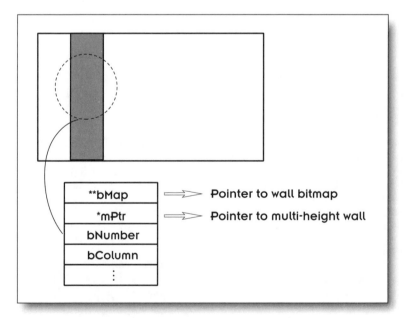

Figure 4.18 *Using slices to build up a scene.*

the **Distance** field comes in. This field stores the actual distance from the player to the slice. With this information, the engine can easily calculate the true position of the slice on the screen. Notice also that the **SLICE** structure stores the position of the grid arrays where the slice data is stored.

So far, I've been associating the term slice with a section of a wall. Now brace yourself for a little curve:

A slice can actually be a section of a wall or a section of an object.

But don't feel tricked—I just wanted to introduce one concept at a time to keep things simple. The field **Type** keeps track of the kind of slice that is being stored and displayed. The field is always assigned one of these two values:

```
#define TYPE_WALL 0
#define TYPE_OBJECT 1
```

Because a slice can be either a wall or object, we need some way to determine the function to call when the bitmap is rendered into the off-screen buffer. That's where **(*Fnc)(void)** comes in. In English, this indicates a pointer to a function that has no arguments. When the actual slice is determined, a pointer to the function that will actually draw the slice is plugged into this field. That way, when it comes time to actually draw, expensive testing of the type of slice is not needed. The draw manager just makes a call to the proper routine stored in this field. Here is a quick example to show how this works:

```
void ExampleRoutine(void)
{
SLICE sa;
if (Wall is intercepted)
  sa.Fnc = WallDrawRoutine();
if (Object is intercepted)
  sa.Fnc = ObjectDrawRoutine();
}
```

This example is by no means real or even useful, but it does illustrate what the **Fnc** field is used for. The actual **WallDrawRoutine()** and **ObjectDrawRoutine()** functions would then be called in the slice drawing function as follows:

```
void DrawSlices(void)
{
SLICE *sa;
sa = Slice;
while (sa->Next != NULL)
  sa->Fnc();
}
```

As you can see, the routine above doesn't know or care what actual function is being called; it just blissfully calls the pointer contained in the **Fnc** field of the slice structure. That is why at the very top of the **BuildSlice()** function you will see this field being set to a do nothing routine, just in case (heaven forbid) that no wall slice is found and no objects appear within this slice.

The last field is the **Active** variable, which is used to determine if a wall or object is actually going to be displayed or not. This field gives the application an easy way of "turning off" an object without actually having to delete it from the object list.

The Magic of Transparent Walls

One of the more interesting features of the *ACK-3D* engine is that it supports transparent walls. This feature enables you to build scenes containing walls that you can "see through" to view walls or objects that are behind them. A transparent wall can be used to create door ways, alcoves, partial walls, walls with windows, and just about anything else you can dream up. The basic idea behind transparency is that a wall object is rendered in such a way that the walls or objects behind it are also displayed. This technique gives the player the illusion that they can see through an object or wall. Figure 4.19 shows a scene from *Slob Zone* that uses a transparent wall. Notice that one of the walls has a doorway you can see through to view the walls behind it. The more you experiment with the concept of transparency, the more you'll discover how powerful it is. Keep in mind that the price you pay for this power is less

Figure 4.19 *Creating a scene with transparent walls.*

speed. A different routine must be called for transparent walls, which needs to check every pixel of the bitmap to see if it is transparent or not, causing a slowdown in the display.

So how can we implement transparent walls? Do we need another data structure? Actually, we can use the **SLICE** structure. Look closely at the definition of **SLICE** and you'll see these two fields hiding at the bottom:

```
struct _slicer *Prev;
struct _slicer *Next;
```

To see how these fields are used, let's build a wall that has an opening in the middle so that it looks like a doorway. We'll put another wall behind the first wall that contains a see-through window. Finally, we'll put a tree behind the window. If you were looking into this scene, as shown in Figure 4.20, you could see through the doorway and the window, and locate the tree. As this scene is being constructed for the screen, one **SLICE** structure would contain the data for the doorway slice. Its *****Next** field would reference a second **SLICE** structure that stored the data for the wall slice that contained the window. The *****Prev** field for this window slice would point to the first **SLICE** and its *****Next** field would reference a third slice—the tree object. Because we can also store an object as a slice, we'd treat the tree as if it were a wall. In the tree slice, *****Prev** would point to the window slice and *****Next** would be set to **NULL** to indicate that we've reached the end of the line. So what we have here is a simple doubly-linked list that can be traversed to locate walls or objects behind walls.

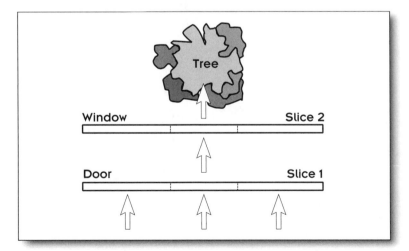

Figure 4.20 *Using a linked list to reference transparent walls.*

Once we have a data structure like this, rendering a scene with transparent objects is actually quite straightforward. As shown in Figure 4.21, the process involves casting a ray to locate the first intersection, in this case, the wall with the doorway. But since this wall is transparent, the ray caster continues casting the line to find the next intersection in the path. This process continues until the last wall or object is found. To keep things as fast as possible, the linked list is set up during the initialization process and is kept around until the application exits. This method eliminates the need for expensive memory allocation each time the scene is rendered.

When a scene is actually drawn on the screen, the engine traverses the linked list of slices using the ***Next** pointers to locate the one that is the furthest behind the others. Then, the list is traversed in reverse order. Each time a new slice is found, it is created. This gives the player a feeling of true depth. Another possible approach is to just build the list of slices and then perform a sort on the entire list afterwards, but I'll leave that experiment up to you.

How High Is a Wall

If you recall from Chapter 2, we spent a bit of time discussing the relationship between the players' position and the height of a wall that they see as they move away from the wall or toward the wall. What we discovered is that we need to keep track of the height of a wall bitmap for different distances from

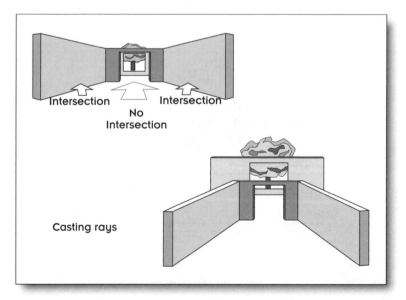

Figure 4.21   *Casting rays to pass through transparent walls.*

the POV. The array designed for this job is called **DistanceTable[ ]**, and it is defined in ACKDATA.C as:

```
short DistanceTable[MAX_DISTANCE + 1];
```

Here, **MAX_DISTANCE** is defined as the value 2048. This value is the maximum distance in units that a player can be from a wall and still see the wall. Each location of the array stores a height value for displaying a bitmap. These values can range from 8 units (minimum height of a bitmap) to 960 units (maximum height of a bitmap). When we explore the **AckBuildHeightTables()** function later in this book, I'll show you how the height calculations are made. The **DistanceTable[ ]** array is initialized when the *ACK-3D* setup routines are first called. It is designed to be a global array so that the key rendering functions can use it whenever scenes need to be updated.

Introducing ACKENG.H and ACK3D.H

I've been showing you pieces of the two key header files for setting up the *ACK-3D* structures, but now it's time to show the complete files. At this stage, you might want to look over these files and review the data structures that we've explored in this chapter. Now that you have a good road map, you should be able to follow along without too much head scratching. As you look at these header files, keep in mind that they both work with the DOS and Windows version of the *ACK-3D* engine. If you ever want to experiment with the engine and add new features, these are the files you should work with first.

```
// ACKENG.H header file for supporting ray casting routines.
// This file contains the main data structure named SLICE and definitions
// required to support the ray casting routines. The data structures defined
// in this file are not to be used directly by the programmer who is using
// the functions in the ACK-3D library. To locate data structures for the
// ACK-3D interface, see the file ACK3D.H. Copyright 1995 by Lary Myers.
#define TRANS_WALLS     0
#define FLOOR_ACTIVE    1
#define USE_XMS         0          // Set to 0 if XMS not desired
#define MAX_RBA         500        // Number of RBAs in resource header
// Fixed point constants used to perform fixed point calculations.
#define FP_SHIFT        16         // Number of shifts used to represent
                                   // fixed-point numbers

#define FP_MULT         65536
#define FP_HALF         32768
#define VIEW_WIDTH      320        // The number of columns in a view (screen)
#define MAX_DISTANCE    2048       // The max distance from the POV to a wall slice
#define TYPE_WALL       0          // Bitmap type codes
```

```
#define TYPE_OBJECT      1
#define TYPE_PALETTE     2
#define MAX_HEIGHT       960    // Maximum height of a wall
#define MIN_HEIGHT       8      // Minimum height of a wall
#define MAX_UPDOWN       30     // Maximum up or down spots for each level
#define MAP_STARTCODE    0xFC   // Force player to this square
#define MAP_UPCODE       0xFD   // Go up to previous level
#define MAP_DOWNCODE     0xFE   // Go down to next level
#define MAP_GOALCODE     0xFF   // Finish line!
#define ST_WALL          1      // Flag to indicate if a bitmap item is
                                // a wall or object
#define ST_OBJECT        2
#define COLS_PER_BYTE    1      // Use 1 for normal mode 13h, 4 for modeX
#define BYTES_PER_ROW    320    // Use 320 for normal mode 13h, 80 for modeX
#define DWORDS_PER_ROW   (BYTES_PER_ROW / 4)    // Number of double words to
                                                // represent a screen row
#define SCREEN_SIZE      64000
// Holds information for the current wall section found during the ray-casting
// process.
// During the ray-casting process, ACK-3D casts out rays, looks for a wall at a
// given screen column position, and if a wall (slice) is found, information
// about the slice is stored in this structure.
typedef struct _slicer {
  UCHAR    **bMap;        // Pointer to wall bitmap found while ray casting
  UCHAR    *mPtr;         // Grid pointer to reference multi-height wall data
  short    bNumber;       // Bitmap number of the wall found
  USHORT   bColumn;       // Screen column location of the found slice
  short    Distance;      // Distance from the POV to the slice
  short    mPos;          // Position of the slice in the associated map
  UCHAR    Type;          // Indicates if the slice is a wall or object
  void     (*Fnc)(void);  // Pointer to a function to draw wall or object
  UCHAR    Active;        // Indicates if a wall or object is displayable or not
  // The next two pointers are used if the current slice
  // is part of a transparent wall
  struct _slicer *Prev;  // References the wall slice in front of the
                         // current slice
  struct _slicer *Next;  // References the wall slice behind the current slice
  } SLICE;


// ACK-3D.H header file for the engine interface.
// This file contains the main data structures and definitions
// required to support the ACK-3D engine. The data structures defined are the
// ones you use to set up the communication links between your application and
// the ACK-3D library. The four main data structures set up in this header file
// include: ACKENG, DOORS, NEWOBJECT, and OBJSEQ.

// USED TO RID OURSELVES OF THE MANY CASTING PROBLEMS
#define CAST(t,f) (t)(f)
// Internal definitions used to simplify field declarations.
typedef unsigned long   ULONG;
typedef unsigned short  USHORT;
typedef unsigned char   UCHAR;
```

```
// Error codes returned from ACK-3D functions. You can use these error codes
// in your applications to debug the function calls.
#define ERR_BADFILE         100    // File not found, usually bad filename
#define ERR_BADCOMMAND      101    // Bad command found in the .INF file
#define ERR_BADOBJNUMBER    102    // Object number out of range
#define ERR_BADSYNTAX       103    // Invalid syntax in the .INF file
#define ERR_LOADINGBITMAP   104    // Error while reading a Bitmap file
#define ERR_BADDIRECTION    105    // Error in direction field of objects
#define ERR_BADSTARTX       106    // Error in initial x position of player
#define ERR_BADSTARTY       107    // Error in initial y position of player
#define ERR_BADANGLE        108    // Error in initial player angle
#define ERR_BADMAPFILE      109    // Error in map file header
#define ERR_READINGMAP      110    // Error during read of map file
#define ERR_BADPICNAME      111    // Error in bitmap filename
#define ERR_INVALIDFORM     112    // Error in .BBM or .LBM format
#define ERR_NOPBM           113    // Error in .BBM format
#define ERR_BADPICFILE      114    // Error reading a bitmap file
#define ERR_NOMEMORY        115    // Out of memory error
#define ERR_BADPALFILE      116    // Error reading raw palette file
#define ERR_BADWINDOWSIZE   117    // Invalid window size for engine
#define ERR_TOMANYVIEWS     118    // Out of range object views
#define ERR_BADOBJECTNUM    119    // Invalid object index
#define ERR_BADOBJTYPE      120    // Invalid object type


// Defines for angle sizes used with the ACK-3D engine.
// These values are used as table look up indexes. The range is from 0 to 1800
// where each value represents an angle increment of 0.5 degrees;
// 0 = 0 degrees and 1800 = 360 degrees.
#define INT_ANGLE_1     5
#define INT_ANGLE_2     10
#define INT_ANGLE_4     20
#define INT_ANGLE_6     30
#define INT_ANGLE_32    160
#define INT_ANGLE_45    225
#define INT_ANGLE_90    450
#define INT_ANGLE_135   675
#define INT_ANGLE_180   900
#define INT_ANGLE_225   1125
#define INT_ANGLE_270   1350
#define INT_ANGLE_315   1575
#define INT_ANGLE_360   1800


// These values are returned by the AckMovePOV() and AckMoveObjectPOV() functions.
#define POV_NOTHING 0    // Nothing was hit
#define POV_XWALL   1    // An x wall was hit
#define POV_YWALL   2    // A y wall was hit
#define POV_OBJECT  3    // An object was hit
#define POV_PLAYER  4    // The player was hit by object
#define POV_SLIDEX  5    // Sliding along an x wall
#define POV_SLIDEY  6    // Sliding along a y wall
#define POV_NODOOR  0    // No door was opened
#define POV_XDOOR   1    // An x door was opened
```

```
#define POV_YDOOR       2      // A y door was opened
#define POV_XSECRETDOOR 3      // An x secret door was opened
#define POV_YSECRETDOOR 4      // A y secret door was opened
#define POV_DOORLOCKED  0x80   // Bit is on if door is locked


// Defines required to support bitmaps.
// Each bitmap used in ACK-3D is 64x64 pixels in size.
#define BITMAP_WIDTH    64
#define BITMAP_HEIGHT   64
#define BITMAP_SHIFT    6      // Bits to shift for bitmap width
#define BITMAP_SIZE (BITMAP_WIDTH * BITMAP_HEIGHT)

// Defines used to set up map grid. The grid is used with the ACKENG structure.
// Each grid component is 64x64 units in size.
#define GRID_MASK       0xFFC0 // Use FF80 for 128 and FFC0 for 64
#define GRID_SIZE       64         // The size of an individual grid unit
#define GRID_WIDTH      64
#define GRID_HEIGHT     64
#define GRID_MAX        GRID_WIDTH * GRID_HEIGHT
#define GRID_XMAX       BITMAP_WIDTH * GRID_WIDTH
#define GRID_YMAX       BITMAP_WIDTH * GRID_HEIGHT
#define GRID_XMAXLONG (GRID_XMAX * FP_MULT)
#define GRID_YMAXLONG (GRID_YMAX * FP_MULT)

// The main grid array used with the ACKENG structure
#define GRID_ARRAY  (GRID_WIDTH+2) * (GRID_HEIGHT+2)

// Defines to specify maximum sizes for the various components used with
// ACK-3D, including wall bitmaps, light zones, shading palette, views, multi
// height walls, doors, object bitmaps, and objects.
#define MAX_WALLBMPS    256      // Total wall bitmaps allowed
#define MAX_ZONES       8        // Number of light zones
#define PAL_SIZE        4096     // Shading palette ranges
#define MAX_VIEWS       47       // Total sides to an object
#define MAX_MULTI       3        // Max height for multi-height walls
#define MAX_DOORS       10       // Max number of doors that can be opened or
                                 // closed at one time
#define MAX_OBJBMPS     256      // Total object bitmaps allowed
#define MAX_OBJECTS     254      // Total objects allowed in map
// Defines to set up different wall types.
#define WALL_TYPE_TRANS 0x0800   // Transparent wall
#define WALL_TYPE_MULTI 0x0400   // Wall is 1.5 times high
#define WALL_TYPE_UPPER 0x0200   // Wall is above floor level
#define WALL_TYPE_PASS  0x0100   // Wall can be walked through
#define TYPE_WALL       0
#define TYPE_OBJECT     1
#define RES_LOW         1        // Resolution is low for walls, floor, and ceiling
#define RES_MEDIUM      2        // Resolution is low only for floor and ceiling


//*****************************************************************
// Definitions and data structures used to represent and process objects.
// These defines specify the two settings for the Active field in the
// NEWOBJECT structure.
```

```
#define OBJECT_ACTIVE   1      // Active and may be moveable
#define OBJECT_INACTIVE 0      // Won't be considered moveable

// These defines specify values for the Flags field in the NEWOBJECT structure.
// They are used to indicate the type of animation available for an object.
#define OF_PASSABLE     0x80   // Object can be walked through
#define OF_ANIMATE      0x40   // Object bitmaps are animated
#define OF_MOVEABLE     0x20   // Object will move x,y
#define OF_MULTIVIEW    0x10   // Object has multiple sides
#define OF_ANIMONCE     0x08   // Animate once then stop
#define OF_ANIMDONE     0x04   // One shot animation is completed

// These defines specify values for the CurrentType field in the NEWOBJECT
// structure. They are used to indicate the current status of the object.
// The names given are arbitrary and can be used for a variety of purposes.
#define NO_CREATE    1
#define NO_DESTROY   2
#define NO_WALK      3
#define NO_ATTACK    4
#define NO_INTERACT  5

// The Object Sequence structure. This structure is used by the NEWOBJECT structure.
#define MAX_OBJ_BITMAPS 32        // Max bitmaps per sequence type
typedef struct {
  UCHAR flags;                         // Flags for this sequence
  UCHAR bitmaps[MAX_OBJ_BITMAPS]; // Bitmap numbers in this sequence
  short bmSides;                       // Number of views in sequence
  short bmBitmapsPerView;              // Number of bitmaps in each view
  short AngleFactor;    // Used internally to support the object sequence
  UCHAR MaxBitmaps;     // Max bitmaps in this sequence
  } OBJSEQ;

// The definition of the main object structure—NEWOBJECT.
typedef struct {
  char    Active;          // Determines object status: 0=Inactive, 1=Active
  UCHAR   Flags;           // Misc flags for this object
  char    Speed;           // Speed of obj (used by application)
  short   Dir;             // Direction of obj (used by application)
  short   x;               // Current x,y location in grid
  short   y;
  short   mPos;            // Current map location in grid
  UCHAR   id;              // Object id
  short   CurrentType;     // Create, Destroy, etc. is current
  UCHAR   *CurrentBitmaps; // Current bitmap list
  short   Sides;           // Number of views
  short   aFactor;         // Angle factor
  short   BitmapsPerView;  // Number of bitmaps in each view
  UCHAR   CurrentBm;       // Current bitmap number
  UCHAR   Maxbm;           // Max bitmap number for this view
  OBJSEQ  Create;          // Stores structures for the 5 object sequences
  OBJSEQ  Destroy;
  OBJSEQ  Walk;
  OBJSEQ  Attack;
  OBJSEQ  Interact;
  } NEWOBJECT;
```

```
//****************************************************************************
// The definitions and data structure that are used to represent doors.
// The default value for the Speed field in the DOORS structure.
#define DEFAULT_DOOR_SPEED  2
// These defines are used to set the Type field.
#define DOOR_XCODE       60            // Map codes for the various doors
#define DOOR_SIDECODE    61
#define DOOR_YCODE       62
// These two defines are used to set the Flags field in the DOORS structure.
#define DOOR_OPENING     0x80          // Set if door is currently opening
#define DOOR_CLOSING     0x40          // Set if door is currently closing
// Other attributes that can be assigned to the Flags field.
#define DOOR_TYPE_SECRET 0x8000        // Secret door
#define DOOR_LOCKED      0x4000        // Locked door
#define DOOR_TYPE_SLIDE  0x2000        // Sliding door
#define DOOR_TYPE_SPLIT  0x1000        // Split door
// The main DOORS structure
typedef struct {
  short mPos;          // Stores position info for a door
  short mPos1;
  short mCode;         // Bitmap ID of the door
  short mCode1;
  UCHAR ColOffset;     // Column offset for the door
  char  Speed;         // Speed setting for opening and closing the door
  char  Type;          // Code for the door type
  UCHAR Flags;         // Door attribute settings
} DOORS;


//****************************************************************************
// The defines and data structure for the main interface structure—ACKENG.
// These defines are used for the LightFlag field in the ACKENG structure.
#define SHADING_ON    1  // Set if distance shading is on
#define SHADING_OFF   0
// These defines are used for the SysFlags field in the ACKENG structure.
#define SYS_SOLID_BACK   0x8000      // On if solid color bkgd vs picture
#define SYS_SOLID_FLOOR  0x4000      // On if solid vs texture floor
#define SYS_SOLID_CEIL   0x2000      // On if solid vs textured ceiling
#define SYS_NO_WALLS     0x1000      // On if walls are NOT to display
#define SYS_SINGLE_BMP   0x0800      // On if 1 bitmap for floor & ceiling
// These defines indicate how bitmaps will be loaded. They are used with the
// bmLoadType field.
#define BMLOAD_BBM    0  // Bitmaps will be loaded using BBM format
#define BMLOAD_GIF    1  // Bitmaps will be loaded using GIF format
#define BMLOAD_PCX    2  // Bitmaps will be loaded using PCX format

// The main interface structure used between the application and the ACK-3D engine.
// This structure MUST be allocated or defined before any ACK-3D calls are made.
typedef struct {
  USHORT   xGrid[GRID_ARRAY];      // Map for x walls
  USHORT   yGrid[GRID_ARRAY];      // Map for y walls
  UCHAR    *mxGrid[GRID_ARRAY];    // Wall data for multi-height
                                   // x walls
  UCHAR    *myGrid[GRID_ARRAY];    // Wall data for multi-height
                                   // y walls
```

```
    UCHAR    *bMaps[MAX_WALLBMPS];  // Pointers to wall bitmaps
    UCHAR    *oMaps[MAX_OBJBMPS];   // Pointers to object bitmaps
    UCHAR    *ScreenBuffer;         // 64k buffer for screen
    UCHAR    *OverlayBuffer;        // Buffer for compiled overlay
    UCHAR    *BkgdBuffer;           // Buffer for ceiling, floor
    short    xPlayer;               // X value from 0 to 4095—stores current
                                    // position
    short    yPlayer;               // Y value from 0 to 4095—stores current
                                    // position
    short    PlayerAngle;           // Angle value from 0 to 1799
    short    DoorSpeed;             // Door open/close speed
    short    NonSecretCode;         //  Wall code for secret door
    UCHAR    TopColor;              // Base color of ceiling
    UCHAR    BottomColor;           // Base color of floor
    UCHAR    FloorBitmap;           // Bitmap number for single floor
    UCHAR    CeilBitmap;            // Bitmap number for single ceiling
    UCHAR    LightFlag;             // 0 = no light shading, 1 = ON
    UCHAR    PalTable[PAL_SIZE];    // 16 zones of 256 colors each
    short    WinStartX;             // Value of left side of viewport
    short    WinStartY;             // Value of top side of viewport
    short    WinEndX;               // Value of right side
    short    WinEndY;               // Value of bottom side
    short    CenterRow;             // Value of (WinEndY-WinStartY)/2
    short    CenterOffset;          // Center row times bytes per row
    short    WinWidth;              // Value of WinEndX - WinStartX
    short    WinHeight;             // Value of WinEndY - WinStartY
    USHORT   WinLength;             // Number of dwords in window
    USHORT   WinStartOffset;        // Value of WinStartY * 320
    USHORT   SysFlags;     // General system flags—determines display attributes
    UCHAR    bmLoadType;  // Bitmap load flags (BBM, GIF, PCX, etc.)
    short    MaxObjects;  // Total number of objects in map
    NEWOBJECT *ObjList[MAX_OBJECTS+1];
                                    // Current objects in map
    DOORS    Door[MAX_DOORS];  // Doors moving at one time
} ACKENG;

// Structure used to build the palette ranges for light shading
// There are 16 color ranges (or zones) each containing 256 colors.
typedef struct {
  unsigned char start;    // Starting color for this range
  unsigned char length;   // Length of range
} ColorRange;

//********************************************************************
// Function prototypes for the user callable ACK-3D functions.
//********************************************************************
// The user callable functions defined in ACKINIT.C.
//********************************************************************
// Reads trig files, builds wall and object maps, and performs the general
// initialization tasks. This function also sets up the distance table used
// by ACK-3D.
short AckInitialize(ACKENG *ae);
// Opens a resource file and prepares for reading.
short AckOpenResource(char *ResFileName);
```

```
// Closes the currently open resource file.
void AckCloseResource(void);
// Reads the map file and sets up the map grids.
short AckReadMapFile(ACKENG *ae,char *MapFileName);


//***********************************************************************
// The user callable functions defined in ACKLDBMP.C.
//***********************************************************************
// Loads a bitmap and places it in either a wall bitmap array or an object
// bitmap array.
short AckLoadBitmap(ACKENG *ae,short BitmapNumber,short BitmapType,char *bmFileName);
// Loads a wall bitmap and places it into the wall array.
short AckLoadWall(ACKENG *ae,short WallNumber,char *bmFileName);
// Loads an object bitmap and places it into the object array.
short AckLoadObject(ACKENG *ae,short BmpNumber,char *bmFileName);
// Fills in an ObjList structure with the information passed in.
short AckCreateObject(ACKENG *ae,short ObjNumber);
// Sets up an object into one of the pre-defined sequences (CREATE, DESTROY,
// and so on).
short AckSetObjectType(ACKENG *ae,short oNum,short oType);
// Fills in an object structure with a communication structure passed by
// the application.
short AckSetupObject(ACKENG *ae,short oNum,short oType,OBJSEQ *os);


//***********************************************************************
// The user callable functions defined in ACKIFF.C, ACKGIF.C, and ACKPCX.C
//***********************************************************************
// Reads in a .LBM or .BBM file and returns a buffer.
UCHAR *AckReadiff(char *FileName);
// Reads a 256 color .GIF file and returns a buffer.
UCHAR *AckReadgif(char *FileName);
// Reads in a 256 color .PCX file and returns a buffer.
UCHAR *AckReadPCX(char *filename);


//***********************************************************************
// The user callable functions defined in ACKVIEW.C.
//***********************************************************************
// Assigns the current engine structure to various global variables.
// This function MUST be called before AckBuildView() is called.
void AckRegisterStructure(ACKENG *ae);
// Draws the current view into ScreenBuffer.
void AckBuildView(void);
// Returns the angle (0-1800) between two objects.
short AckGetObjectAngle(long DeltaX,long DeltaY);
// Checks if a collision occurs. Used by AckCheckDoorOpen() routine.
short AckCheckHit(short xPlayer,short yPlayer,short ViewAngle);


//***********************************************************************
// The user callable functions defined in ACKPOV.C.
//***********************************************************************
// Used by AckMovePOV() and AckMoveObjectPOV() to check collision with objects.
short AckCheckObjPosn(short xPlayer,short yPlayer,short oIndex);
```

```
// Runs the list of objects to check movement.
void AckCheckObjectMovement(void);
// Moves the POV by the specified amount at the specified angle.
short AckMovePOV(short Angle,short Amount);
// Moves the object POV by the specified amount at the specified angle.
short AckMoveObjectPOV(short ObjIndex,short Angle,short Amount);


//***********************************************************************
// The user callable function defined in ACKOVER.C.
//***********************************************************************
// Reads overlay file and compiles it into the OverlayBuffer.
short AckCreateOverlay(ACKENG *ae, UCHAR *OverlayScreen);


//***********************************************************************
// The user callable function defined in ACKBKGD.C.
//***********************************************************************
// Builds background buffer from TopColor, BottomColor, and LightFlag.
short AckBuildBackground(ACKENG *ae);


//***********************************************************************
// The user callable function defined in ACKDOOR.C.
//***********************************************************************
// Check if a door in front to open
short AckCheckDoorOpen(short xPlayer,short yPlayer,short PlayerAngle);


//***********************************************************************
// The user callable function defined in ACKWRAP.C.
//***********************************************************************
// Frees memory buffers.
short AckWrapUp(ACKENG *ae);


//***********************************************************************
// The user callable functions defined in ACKUTIL.C.
//***********************************************************************
// Internal memory allocation for development purposes
void *AckMalloc(size_t mSize);
// All memory allocated with AckMalloc() must use AckFree() to free memory.
void AckFree(void *m);
// Reads in a palette file and sets the screen palette.
short AckLoadAndSetPalette(char *FileName);
// Fills in the shading palette table.
void AckSetupPalRanges(ACKENG *ae,ColorRange *ranges);
// Returns the object index number of the last object hit.
short AckGetObjectHit(void);
// Returns the map location of the last wall hit.
short AckGetWallHit(void);
// Removes the specified object from the map.
short AckDeleteObject(ACKENG *ae,short ObjectIndex);
// Sets a new bitmap or changes image in the bitmap array.
short AckSetNewBitmapPtr(short BitmapNumber,UCHAR **Maps,UCHAR *NewBitmap);
// Frees up the memory used by the bitmap.
short AckFreeBitmap(UCHAR *bmType);
```

```
//*************************************************************************
// The user callable functions defined in ACKRTN.ASM.
//*************************************************************************
// Sets a previously loaded palette.
void AckSetPalette(UCHAR *PalBuffer);
// Places video in standard 320x200 mode 13h.
void AckSetVGAmode(void);
// Places video in 80x25 color text mode 3.
void AckSetTextmode(void);
// Displays the contents of ScreenBuffer and OverlayBuffer if desired. short
AckDisplayScreen(void);
```

Time to Code

In this chapter we covered most of the major data structures that you'll need to create ray-casted 3-D scenes. We learned how to interface with the *ACK-3D* engine and how to represent a maze-type world with objects by using simple one-dimensional grid arrays. We also learned how doors, stationary objects, and movable objects are represented. Then, we worked our way down a level and explored the flexible slice structure that is used during the ray-casting process to build scenes. We even took a peek at how transparent walls are represented and constructed in a scene. Our final destination was to create the two key header files, ACK3D.H and ACKENG.H, which contain all of the code for the main data structures used by the engine.

As you read through this book and start to explore the ray-casting and game code in later chapters, you'll want to refer back to this chapter to review the main data structures. The more you know about how they are designed and used, the easier it will be for you to follow the code and make changes to it. There are a lot of neat tricks that can be performed using these structures and many more enhancements that can be made to ease the use of the engine. I wanted to give you a nice place to start and the flexibility to make whatever changes you like, without having to redesign things from the ground up.

In the next chapter we'll start to create the actual code for the ray-casting engine. We have a lot of code to write, so let's get started.

Chapter

To understand how a 3-D engine is designed and coded you must know how to navigate in a 2-D world and then be able to project your motion in 3-D.

Working Your Way through a Map

We're about to embark on a two part adventure. In this chapter, you'll learn how to write code to help you work your way through a map. Then, in Chapter 6 you'll learn how to build 3-D scenes as you travel in a 2-D map representation. Along the way, you'll learn about some useful techniques for representing floating-point numbers as fixed-point numbers. All of our key map navigation routines will be placed in the source file ACKPOV.C. This is the first C source file that we'll investigate. There's a lot of territory to cover, so let's get started.

Introducing ACKPOV.C

If you recall from Chapter 3, ACKPOV.C is the *ACK-3D* file that provides the main functions for controlling how a player and objects move around in a map. Some of the functions in this module are internal routines—that is, your application program does not call them directly. The three functions in ACKPOV.C that can be called by your games or other 3-D programs include:

- **AckMovePOV()** This moves the player's POV using a specified angle and distance.
- **AckMoveObjectPOV()** This moves a specified object using an angle and distance.
- **AckCheckObjectMovement()** This checks all active objects used in a map to determine if they need to have their bitmaps changed to animate them.

Since our goal in this chapter is to create the code for these functions, we'll also need to take a close look at the code in the internal routines, such as **GetWallX()**, that are required to bring the main functions to life. To help you work your way through the functions defined in ACKPOV.C, Figure 5.1 shows the calling hierarchy of the three main functions. But before we jump in and start writing code, we need to take a closer look at how we can navigate and control motion in a map or maze.

Moving Around—From 2-D to 3-D to 2-D

When you move around in a 3-D maze-type game, you're not really moving around in three dimensions. Of course, it's our job as programmers to try to trick the player as much as possible into thinking that he or she is traveling in three dimensions. The world that we model in a game is really constructed from a two-dimensional map as we saw in Chapter 3. Any location in the map can be represented with an x and y coordinate point, as shown in Figure 5.2. This representation is the way you might view the world you live in if you were looking at your handy AAA travel map while you planned a trip down the coast from San Francisco to Los Angeles. In such a case, you're free to take any route you want, but you can only move north, south, east, or west.

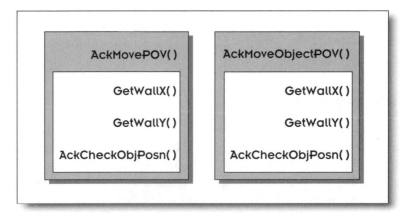

Figure 5.1 *Calling hierarchy for the main functions defined in ACKPOV.C.*

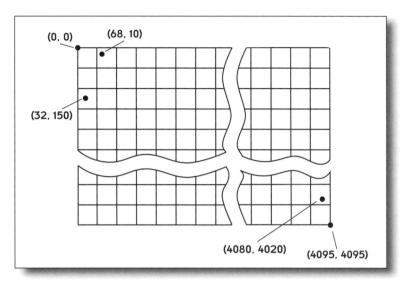

Figure 5.2 *Moving around in a two-dimensional map.*

If you get in your car and start driving to Los Angeles, the world won't look like a two-dimensional map any more. You'll see trees, road signs, other cars, lots of cows, but hopefully not too many highway patrol cars. Everything you see is in three dimensions. To simulate this with computer graphics, we need a different type of coordinate system, as shown in Figure 5.3. Here, I've introduced a third axis called the *z-axis*. The z-axis is hard to visualize on a flat piece of paper, but just imagine that it appears as a straight line that comes right out of this page into your face. By adding this third axis, we can now model the real world—every location in our day to day 3-D world can be represented with three coordinates (x, y, z).

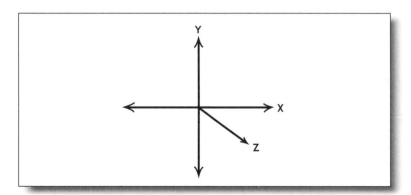

Figure 5.3 *The basic 3-D coordinate system.*

Now here comes the big problem, a computer screen operates in a two-dimensional world. You can't climb inside your computer and move forward. You can only move up, down, left, or right. So what we need is a way to travel around in a 2-D map, model a 3-D image for a given location in the map, and then project or render that 3-D model on a 2-D plane (the computer screen). (And we have to do this as fast as lightning to keep our player from getting bored.)

Movement in a 2-D Map—Introducing AckMovePOV()

Our starting point is to come up with a way of moving around in our 2-D map. The 2-D map contains all of the components that are needed to implement a game, such as walls, doors, and static and dynamic objects. In designing a game in this manner, you get to pretend you are an architect and create a floor plan to your liking. But creating a 3-D maze game is even more challenging than just designing a floor plan because you need a way to support real-time motion.

As a player moves around, we'll need to keep track of where the player is and what the player encounters as he or she moves. If the player runs into a wall, you must stop the player in his or her tracks. If the player encounters a menacing enemy who is firing a ray gun, you must allow the player to quickly move around and get out of the line of fire. Shortly, I'll show you how to create the code for game navigation, but first we need to come up with an easy (and fast) way of representing motion.

Angles and Distance

In using the classic (x, y) Cartesian coordinate system, we're taught that we can move from one point to another by specifying an x and y (horizontal and vertical) distance. (You weren't completely asleep during high school geometry, I hope.) For example, if you are at position x = 10, y = 20 and you want to go to position x = 30, y = 42, you can get there by moving 20 units in the x direction and 22 units in the y direction, as shown in Figure 5.4.

But when we move around in a 2-D map that we need to represent as a 3-D scene, it is much easier for us to think in terms of angles and distances. Thus, if we are at a given location and we want to move to a new position, we can get there by moving at a specified angle and distance as shown in Figure 5.5.

This approach involves using a polar coordinate system like the one introduced in Chapter 2. Using such a system, we can easily calculate a new coordinate position by using these two formulas

```
x1 = xp + cos(a) * d
y1 = yp + sin(a) * d
```

where the starting position is (xp, yp), the angle is *a*, and the distance is *d*.

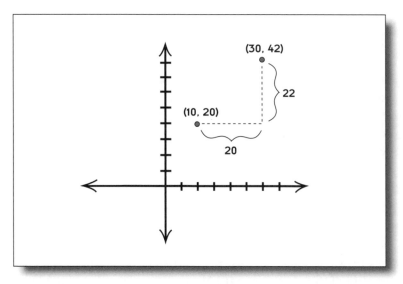

Figure 5.4 *Moving in two dimensions by calculating horizontal and vertical distances.*

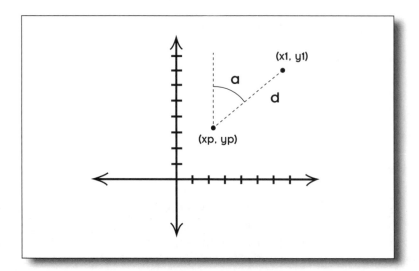

Figure 5.5 *Using an angle and distance to specify movement.*

To see how these equations work, let's use some real numbers. Let's say we are at position (10,10) and want to move 50 units at an angle of 30 degrees. The calculations would be:

```
x1 = xp + cos(30) * 50
x1 = 10 + 43.3
x1 = 53.3
```

```
y1 = yp + sin(30) * 50
y1 = 10 + 25
y1 = 25
```

That's all there is to it. But when we need to perform calculations like these in our code, we can use a few of the optimization tricks that we introduced in Chapter 2. Recall that we've done away with floating-point math and substituted fixed-point math and lookup tables for cosines and sines. Therefore, the actual x, y coordinate calculations for a new position look like this:

```
// Calculate the x,y distance of movement using an angle and distance
x1 = xp + (long)((CosTable[Angle] * Amount) >> FP_SHIFT);
y1 = yp + (long)((SinTable[Angle] * Amount) >> FP_SHIFT);
```

Here we simply look up the cosine and sine values for the angle, multiply these values by the distance (**Amount**), and shift the result to the right by 16 places to get rid of the fractional part. Now you have a sneak preview of how the **AckMovePOV()** function calculates a new coordinate position.

Working with Fixed-Point Math

Before we go any further into the mysteries of moving around in a 3-D world, let's take a little time to explore what's involved in using fixed-point math. Fixed-point math is one of those programming topics you hear a lot of people talking about but you seldom see it explained very well. For now, I'll cover some of the general techniques behind fixed-point math and then I'll show you exactly how fixed-point math is implemented with *ACK-3D*. Before we get underway, however, I'd like to thank 3-D programming wizard Brian Hook, who contributed some of the text and examples for this discussion.

Floating-point math has traditionally been painfully slow with PCs. After all, the hardware required for fast floating-point math was not part of the main CPU until the 80486DX came on the scene. In the past, developers who wanted to use floating-point calculations in their applications had to emulate these calculations in software or write code that could only run on the latest machines. Either approach is suicide if you are trying to develop products for the game or entertainment markets.

The better approach is to skip floating-point math altogether and switch over to fixed-point math. In theory, this means representing real numbers, such as 12.4567, using only integers. The problem is that when we get rid of the decimal point, so to speak, we have less range and precision to work with. But the gain in speed is well worth it.

Shifting Those Decimal Points

So how can we represent real numbers as integers? One way would be to use scaled integers. For example, you could take a real number like 3.333 and multiply it by a *fixed constant* or *scale value*, such as 1,000, to represent the number as an integer in the computer. In this case, you'd end up with the number 3,333, which is called the *fixed-point representation* of 3.333. You could then perform calculations with this number and when you finish calculating, you could divide the number by the scale value to bring it back to the world of floating-point numbers.

The value in question should always be scaled by a fixed amount. Therefore, the point at which the integer is divided into a whole and fractional part (*radix point*) is fixed in its position—which also means that the precision and range of the value are fixed. In representing the number 3.333, using our example, the radix point is fixed at the thousandths position.

There is a slight problem with using this method to represent floating-point numbers: speed of converting numbers. Each time a number is converted from a floating-point value to an integer, a multiplication must be performed. When you go the other way—integer to floating point—a division is required. A better method is to scale numbers by a power of two instead of a power of ten. This allows us to use fast bit shift operations for our conversions.

The biggest drawback with using the "power of two" method to represent floating-point numbers is that the range of numbers we can represent will be limited. For example, if fixed-point numbers are stored in long integers (32 bits), you only have 32 slots to represent a number. This might sound like a lot, but it really isn't because you need space to store both parts of a number: its integer part and its fractional part. The challenge is deciding which bits to use for the actual number being represented (the number's *range*) and which bits to use for the scale factor (the number's *precision*). For example, Figure 5.6 shows an example where 20 bits are used for a number's range and the remaining 12 bits are used for the precision. In this case, the largest number

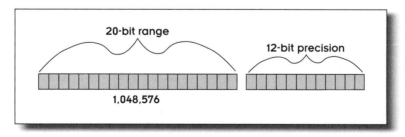

Figure 5.6   *Representing a number with 20 bits of range and 12 bits of precision.*

that can be represented is 2 (20) or 1,048,576. Where to make this split is highly application dependent, so before you choose a range and precision, put some careful thought and planning into your needs. You also have to be careful that the amount you shift the fractional part doesn't push the integer part of the number off the right side of the bits! If you are writing a true 3-D application, such as a flight simulator, you might need to go for precision and accuracy. If you are writing a *DOOM*-style game, read on.

Taking the Middle Ground

If you've looked at any of the code in the *ACK-3D* files, you probably have a good idea of the scaling approach taken. In fact, the ACKENG.H file presented in the previous chapter contains these three defines that should clue you in:

```
#define FP_SHIFT16
#define FP_MULT 65536
#define FP_HALF 32768
```

Essentially, I've taken the middle ground. All fixed-point numbers are stored as 32-bit long integers—this is the default register size of the 80386 CPU. The range is set at 16 bits, which leaves 16 bits for precision. The even split gives us both a reasonable amount of range (0 to 65,536) and precision or accuracy.

To support this system, routines must be written to perform basic mathematical operations between fixed-point values. First, we need a way to convert both integers and floating-point numbers to fixed point and back again. Integers are easy to convert. This just involves performing a 16-bit left shift, as shown here:

```
result = int_val << 16
```

If we were actually converting a true floating-point number, we'd need to first multiply the number by 65,536.0 and typecast the result to a long integer. This step would effectively convert both the "integer" part of the number and the fractional part. To retrieve the floating-point equivalent from the fixed-point number, we simply do the reverse (divide the long integer by 65,536 and store it). If you wanted to get fancy, you could define a set of simple macros to do the conversion dirty work for you, as shown here:

```
typedef long FIXEDPOINT;

#define FLOATTOFIX(a) ( (FIXEDPOINT) ( (a) * 65536.0 ) )
#define INTTOFIX(a) ( (FIXEDPOINT) (a) << 16 )

#define FIXTOINT(a) ( (int) ( ( ( (a) + 0x8000 ) ) >> 16 ) )
#define FIXTOFLOAT(a) ( ( (a) + 0x8000 ) / 65536.0 )
```

Performing Operations with Fixed-Point Numbers

For the most part, the *ACK-3D* engine will only be performing simple calculations on the floating-point numbers that are represented as fixed-point numbers. The most common of these operations is looking up a floating-point value (such as an angle or result of a trig function) that is stored in a table as a fixed-point value and then converting it for a coordinate calculation. Of course, you can do much more with fixed-point numbers: addition, subtraction, multiplication, and division.

Addition and subtraction are quite straightforward. In fact, fixed-point addition and subtraction are the same as long integer addition and subtraction, and thus no special routines are required. Multiplication and division are a bit trickier, however, so let's take a closer look.

The problem with multiplication is that when two fixed-point values are multiplied, the scale values are multiplied also, giving a fixed-point result that is scaled too far. In our case, the bits needed to store the precision (fractional) part of the number alone would be 32 leaving no room for the other part of the number. This is what you'd call a serious overflow problem!

This dilemma could be solved by scaling the initial values so that the final result will be scaled correctly after the multiplication. Here's an example:

```
long FixMulFix( long a, long b))
{
   return ( (a >> 8) * (b >>8) );
}
```

In this case, each number (*a* and *b*) is shifted to the right by eight bits before the multiplication. But we are we trading one problem for another. In this case, resolution is lost because of the scaling. If you performed calculations like this over and over in a program like a 3-D game or flight simulator, you'd really notice the compounding calculation errors. (You'd probably end up in a place in your maze that you couldn't get out of or you'd land your plane in a ditch—ouch!)

The real solution to a problem like this is found in assembly language. When a multiplication operation is performed on a 80386 processor, the result is actually a 64-bit value store in two 32-bit registers—edx contains the high double word (dword) and eax contains the low dword. Here's how such an operation could be performed by using inline assembly code with a C function:

```
long MulFix(long a, long b)
{
   long result;
```

```
asm move   ax, [a]
asm move   bx, [b]
asm imul   ebx1            // Multiply eax by ebx
asm shrd   eax, edx, 16    // Shift result back 16 bits
asm mov    [result], eax   // Return the correct result
return     result;
}
```

The first number is placed in the eax register and the second number is placed in ebx. The multiplication is performed by the **imul** instruction. The key here is the **shrd** instruction, which is executed on the result of the **imul** instruction. This tells the processor to shift eax to the right 16 bits, but instead of placing zeros in eax's high word, the CPU replaces eax's high word with edx's low word. edx itself is left unmodified. Thus, if the registers were set to these values before the **shrd** instruction

```
edx = 0123456h
eax = 89abcdefh
```

the result of the operation **shrd eax, edx, 16** would be:

```
edx = 0123456h
eax = 89abcdefh
```

No overflow, no loss of precision! Isn't assembly language handy at times like this? Efficient C or C++ compilers that allow 32 bit code will also perform the above C calculations in much the same way, but be wary! Sometimes the actual code produced is not what you'd expect.

Now, what about division? As you might have guessed, we can't use the "pre-scaling" approach because we'll lose too much precision. Once more the 386's 32-bit registers and instructions come to the rescue and provide us with the solution. This time the **idiv** instruction can be used. This instruction takes as its divisor a 32-bit number but it produces a dividend weighing in at 64 bits. Let's look at the code required and then we'll discuss how it works:

```
long DivFix(long a, long b)
{
  long result;

  asm move   ax, [a]
  asm cdq                    // Extend eax into edx:eax
  asm shld   edx, eax, 16    // Shift edx:eax left by 16
  asm sal    eax, 16
  asm move   bx, [b]         // Get the divisor
  asm idiv   ebx             // Perform the division
```

```
asm mov    [result], eax   // Return the correct result
  return     result;
}
```

The division solution isn't as straightforward as the multiplication code. The trick is to first load eax with the dividend, then convert it into a quadword stored in the edx:eax register pair. We then shift the high word of eax into the low word of edx and shift eax left by 16 bits. Are you still with me? This effectively shifts the 64-bit value (edx:eax) left by 16, making it a 16:32 fixed-point value. edx is then loaded with the divisor, the **idiv** instruction is executed, and the result stored in eax comes out just the way we want it—a 32 bit value with 16 bits of precision (fractional part).

If this floating-point math stuff really interests you, take a look at the routines and examples provided on the companion CD-ROM. These examples, created by Brian Hook, include source code for performing many types of fixed-point calculations including matrix multiplication. You might find this code very useful for your own special game development work.

Getting Back to AckMovePOV()— What's Out There Anyway?

Okay, enough with the math stuff. Let's get back to our 3-D world and see what really happens as we move around in our map.

As you try to move in a two-dimensional map using a specified angle and distance, one of six conditions can occur, as shown in Figure 5.7:

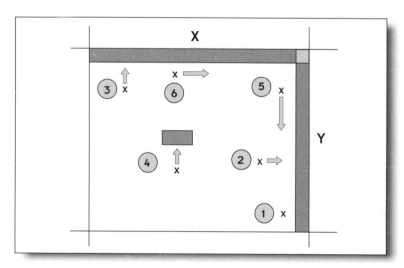

Figure 5.7 *Events that occur as you move in a map.*

1. You might already be up against a wall or object and nothing will happen.
2. You can run into a wall along the y direction.
3. You can run into a wall along the x direction.
4. You can run into a stationary or movable object.
5. You can move (slide) along a wall in the y direction.
6. You can move (slide) along a wall in the x direction.

These are the actual events that we'll need to support when we write the **AckMovePOV()** function to help us navigate in a map. We'll check the player's previous coordinate position with the new location to determine the outcome. Then, we'll need to update the player's current location and return a status flag to the application that calls **AckMovePOV()**.

The **AckMovePOV()** function is defined in the source file ACKPOV.C. As you might guess, it only requires two parameters: **Angle** and **Amount**. Let's look at the code for the entire function and then we'll step through it so that you can see how it checks for the different cases we just described. As you examine the code, keep in mind that the **if** conditions that check for walls are also checking to see if an object is encountered. Here is the complete **AckMovePOV()**:

```
short AckMovePOV(short Angle,short Amount)
{
   short x1,y1,HitResult;                // New coordinate position
   short xp,yp;                          // Starting player coordinates
   short xLeft,xRight,yTop,yBottom;      // Coordinates for grid square
   short mPos;                           // Map position for xGrid[], yGrid[]
   USHORT mCodeX,mCodeY;                 // Return codes for x,y wall arrays

HitResult = POV_NOTHING;                 // We haven't hit anything yet
xp = aeGlobal->xPlayer;                  // Get the current x,y player coordinates
yp = aeGlobal->yPlayer;

xLeft = xp & 0xFFC0;                     // Determine coordinates of the boundaries
yTop = yp & 0xFFC0;                      // of the grid square we're in
xRight = xLeft + GRID_SIZE;
yBottom = yTop + GRID_SIZE;

// Calculate the x,y distance of movement using the angle and distance
// x1,y1 = the new coordinate position of the player
x1 = xp + (long)((CosTable[Angle] * Amount) >> FP_SHIFT);
y1 = yp + (long)((SinTable[Angle] * Amount) >> FP_SHIFT);

// Calculate current map position for the xGrid[] and yGrid[] arrays
mPos = yTop + (xp >> 6);                 // Current Map Posn
```

```
// It's time to see what happens when we move
if (x1 < xp)                    // Are we moving left?
  {
  if (GetWallX(mPos))           // Wall found in current square (left edge)
    {                           // We crossed the wall or we're too close
    if (x1 < xLeft || abs(x1-xLeft) < 28)
      {
      x1 = xp;                  // Use the previous x position
      HitResult = POV_SLIDEX;   // We're possibly sliding along the left x wall
      }
    }
  }

if (x1 > xp)                    // Are we moving right?
  {
  if (GetWallX(mPos+1))         // Wall found in current square (right edge)
    {                           // We crossed the wall or we're too close
    if (x1 > xRight || abs(xRight-x1) < 28)
      {
      x1 = xp;                  // Use the previous x position
      HitResult = POV_SLIDEX;   // We're possibly sliding along
                                // the right x wall
      }
    }
  }

if (y1 < yp)                    // Are we moving up?
  {
  if (GetWallY(mPos))           // Wall found in current square (top edge)
    {                           // We crossed the wall or we're too close
    if (y1 < yTop || abs(y1-yTop) < 28)
      {
      y1 = yp;                  // Use the previous y position
      HitResult = POV_SLIDEY;   // We're possibly sliding along
                                // the top wall
      }
    }
  }

if (y1 > yp)                    // Are we moving down?
  {                             // Wall found in current square (bottom  edge)
  if (GetWallY(mPos+GRID_WIDTH))
    {                           // We crossed the wall or we're too close
    if (y1 > yBottom || abs(yBottom-y1) < 28)
      {
      y1 = yp;                  // Use the previous y position
      HitResult = POV_SLIDEY;   // We're sliding along the bot
                                // tom wall
      }
    }
  }
```

```
// A wall or object hasn't been hit yet—we must look further
// The current grid sqaure will be divided into four regions:
//   A = top left; B = top right; C = bottom left; D = bottom right
// Each of these regions will be checked to see if the player's new position (x1,y1)
// is close to a wall or object that borders one of these regions.
// Each grid square is 64x64 units, so each region to check is 32x32 units.
if (!HitResult)
  {                                          // Check region A—top left area of grid
  if (y1 < (yTop+32))                        // New y position falls in top half
    {
    if (x1 < (xLeft+32))                     // New x position falls in left half
      {
      mCodeX = GetWallX(mPos-GRID_WIDTH); // Check adjacent x wall (to left)
      mCodeY = GetWallY(mPos-1);          // Check adjacent y wall (above)

      if (mCodeX && y1 < (yTop+28))          // Adjacent x wall found and new y coord
        {                                    // is within 28 units
        if (x1 < (xLeft+28))        // New x coord is within 28 units of edge
          {
          if (xp > (xLeft+27))      // Previous x position was outside range
            {
            x1 = xp;                // Use previous x position
            HitResult = POV_SLIDEX;
            }
          else
            {
            y1 = yp;                // Use previous y position
            HitResult = POV_SLIDEY;
            }
          }
        }

      if (mCodeY && x1 < (xLeft+28))  // Adjacent y wall found and new x coord.
        {                             // is within 28 units
        if (y1 < (yTop+28))           // New y coord. is within 28 units of edge
          {
          if (yp > (yTop+27))         // Previous y position was outside range
            {
            y1 = yp;                  // Use previous y position
            HitResult = POV_SLIDEY;
            }
          else
            {
            x1 = xp;                  // Use previous x position
            HitResult = POV_SLIDEX;
            }
          }
        }
      }
    // Check region B—top right area
    if (x1 > (xRight-32) && !HitResult)        // New x is at top right
      {
      mCodeX = GetWallX(mPos+1-GRID_WIDTH); // Check adjacent x wall (to right)
      mCodeY = GetWallY(mPos+1);            // Check adjacent y wall (above)
```

```
        if (mCodeX && y1 < (yTop+28))          // Adjacent x wall found
          {
          if (x1 > (xRight-28))
            {
            if (xp < (xRight-27))
              {
              x1 = xp;                          // Use previous x position
              HitResult = POV_SLIDEX;
              }
            else
              {
              y1 = yp;                          // Use previous y position
              HitResult = POV_SLIDEY;
              }
            }
          }

        if (mCodeY && x1 > (xRight-28))         // Adjacent y wall found
          {
          if (y1 < (yTop+28))
            {
            if (yp > (yTop+27))
              {
              y1 = yp;                          // Use previous y position
              HitResult = POV_SLIDEY;
              }
            else
              {
              x1 = xp;                          // Use previous x position
              HitResult = POV_SLIDEX;
              }
            }
          }
        }
      }
// Check region C-bottom left area
if (y1 > (yTop+32) && !HitResult)               // We are below upper half of square
  {
  if (x1 < (xLeft+32))                          // and on the left half of square
    {
    mCodeX = GetWallX(mPos+GRID_WIDTH);         // Check adjacent x wall (to left)
    mCodeY = GetWallY(mPos-1+GRID_WIDTH);       // Check adjacent y wall (below)

    if (mCodeX && y1 > (yBottom-28))            // Adjacent x wall found
      {
      if (x1 < (xLeft+28))
        {
        if (xp > (xLeft+27))
          {
          x1 = xp;                              // Use previous x position
          HitResult = POV_SLIDEX;
          }
        else
```

```
          {
          y1 = yp;                   // Use previous y position
          HitResult = POV_SLIDEY;
          }
        }
      }

  if (mCodeY && x1 < (xLeft+28))    // Adjacent y wall found
    {
      if (y1 > (yBottom-28))
        {
        if (yp < (yBottom-27))
          {
          y1 = yp;                   // Use previous y position
          HitResult = POV_SLIDEY;
          }
        else
          {
          x1 = xp;                   // Use previous x position
          HitResult = POV_SLIDEX;
          }
        }
      }
}
// Check region D—bottom right area
if (x1 > (xRight-32) && !HitResult)      // Check right side of square
  {
  mCodeX = GetWallX(mPos+1+GRID_WIDTH); // Check adjacent x wall (to right)
  mCodeY = GetWallY(mPos+1+GRID_WIDTH); // Check adjacent y wall (below)

  if (mCodeX && y1 > (yBottom-28))      // Adjacent x wall found
    {
    if (x1 > (xRight-28))
      {
      if (xp < (xRight-27))
        {
        x1 = xp;                   // Use previous x position
        HitResult = POV_SLIDEX;
        }
      else
        {
        y1 = yp;                   // Use previous y position
        HitResult = POV_SLIDEY;
        }
      }
    }

  if (mCodeY && x1 > (xRight-28))      // Adjacent y wall found
    {
    if (y1 > (yBottom-28))
      {
      if (yp < (yBottom-27))
        {
```

```
        y1 = yp;                      // Use previous y position
        HitResult = POV_SLIDEY;
        }
      else
        {
        x1 = xp;                      // Use previous x position
        HitResult = POV_SLIDEX;
        }
      }
    }
   }
  }

if (AckCheckObjPosn(x1,y1,0))        // We've hit an object—not a wall
  return(POV_OBJECT);

// We've hit an x wall and we're not sliding
if (HitResult == POV_SLIDEX && y1 == yp)
  HitResult = POV_XWALL;

// We've hit a y wall and we're not sliding
if (HitResult == POV_SLIDEY && x1 == xp)
  HitResult = POV_YWALL;

aeGlobal->xPlayer = x1;              // Update player's new x,y position
aeGlobal->yPlayer = y1;
return(HitResult);
}
```

Although this looks like a lot of code, **AckMovePOV()** performs two simple operations. First, it calculates a new coordinate position (**x1, y1**) when a player moves from his or her current position to a new one specified by an angle and distance. Then, it returns a status condition for the new position in the maze; that is, we need to know if the player *will* run into something like a wall or other object if he or she moves to the new position. In a sense, this will actually tell us *how* the player should be moved. The status code returned can be one of the following:

POV_OBJECT   Indicates the player has come upon an object

POV_XWALL   Indicates the player has run into an x wall

POV_YWALL   Indicates the player has run into a y wall

POV_SLIDEX   Indicates a player has run into a y wall and is moving in the x direction (sliding along the wall)

POV_SLIDEY   Indicates a player has run into an x wall and is moving in the y direction (sliding along the wall)

These status codes are defined in ACK3D.H.

Calculating Coordinates

AckMovePOV() first calculates the position of the player, which is easy to do because this information is stored in a global structure of type **ACKENG**. This code reveals the name of the global structure:

```
xp = aeGlobal->xPlayer;
yp = aeGlobal->yPlayer;
```

The structure **aeGlobal** is actually defined in the header file ACKEXT.H as:

```
extern ACKENG *aeGlobal;
```

You'll see this global variable hanging around a lot whenever we explore the *ACK-3D* engine source files. It was set up within the **AckRegisterStructure()** function so it doesn't have to be passed as a parameter to many of the support functions, thus cutting down on the overhead when a function is called from the application. You'll need to call **AckRegisterStructure()** from your application program when it initializes the engine. We'll explore it in more detail when we look at how views are created in Chapters 6 and 7.

Once we determine the player's current coordinates, we need to know the actual coordinates of the grid square in which the player is located. (Recall from the previous chapter that a game map is laid out as a 2-D structure having 64x64 individual grid squares. Each grid square itself is 64x64 pixels in size.) To determine the coordinates (left, top, right, and bottom) of the actual grid square, we use this code:

```
xLeft = xp & 0xFFC0;        // Determine the coordinates of the boundaries
yTop = yp & 0xFFC0;         // of the grid square we're in
xRight = xLeft + GRID_SIZE;
yBottom = yTop + GRID_SIZE;
```

To see how this works, assume that a player is at position 100, 200. The first two lines of code would produce the values:

```
xLeft = 100 & 0xFFC0;       // calculates (xp/64) * 64
yTop = 200 & 0xFFC0;        // calculates (yp/64) * 64
```

or

```
xLeft = 64
yTop = 192
```

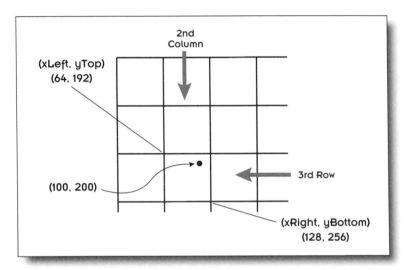

Figure 5.8   *Determining the coordinates for a grid square by using the player's current x, y position.*

As shown in Figure 5.8, this calculation gives us the actual coordinate of the upper corner of the grid square that the player is in when the player is at location 100, 200. Notice here that we've also filled in the values for **xRight** and **yBottom** (128 and 256). (If you recall from Chapter 4, **GRID_SIZE** is set to 64.) Figure 5.8 also indicates that this is the grid square that is positioned in the map as second from the right and third from the top. (We'll come back to this in a minute when we calculate the actual map position.)

Next, **AckMovePOV()** goes about its work by determining the new (x, y) coordinate position for the player. We've already explored how this is done using simple polar coordinate equations. But what you might not realize is that we're not actually using a real angle specified in degrees to calculate a cosine or sine value. Recall from Chapter 2 that our engine can cast arrays from 0 to 360 degrees in 0.2 degree increments. That means that we can have 1,800 different angles to work with (360 degrees / 0.2 degree increment). Instead of working with actual degrees, our code uses integer indexes from 0 to 1,799, where these indexes correspond with angles (see Table 5.1 for some examples of this relationship). Now, if you look at one of the equations that calculates a new coordinate position, it should make much more sense to you:

```
x1 = xp + (long)((CosTable[Angle] * Amount) >> FP_SHIFT);
```

Here, we look up a cosine value in the array **CosTable[ ]** by using an index value from 0 to 1,799. The **CosTable[ ]** array is initialized by reading cosine data from a file when the *ACK-3D* engine is initialized. Since we don't want to deal with floating-point math, this array stores cosine values that have been shifted to the right by 16 bits; that is, each cosine value is multiplied by 65,536 (see Table 5.1).

Again, let's plug in some real numbers. Assume that **AckMovePOV()** has been called with the values **Amount = 100** and **Angle = 150**. This means that we are requesting the player to move 100 units at 30 degrees (30/0.2 = 150). Using the new coordinate calculation for the x position, we get:

```
x1 = 100 + (long)((56755 * 100) >> FP_SHIFT)
x1 = 100 + 86
x1 = 186
```

The value 56,755 is the cosine of 30 degrees shifted 16 bits to the left for fixed-point representation. Here's what we have for the new y coordinate position:

```
y1 = yp + (long)((sinTable[Angle] * Amount) >> FP_SHIFT)
y1 = 200 + (long)((32768 * 100) >> FP_SHIFT)
y1 = 200 + 50
y1 = 250
```

Figure 5.9 verifies that these calculations make sense. Notice that this movement involves taking the player from one grid square into another. The question you might be asking now is, what will the player encounter as he or she moves in this path?

Locating a Wall or Object

Most of the remaining code in **AckMovePOV()** is dedicated to checking for the conditions outlined earlier: Will the player hit a wall and try to go forward?, will the player try to slide along a wall?, will the player encounter an object?, and so on.

The work of finding out what's in the player's path starts with this code:

```
mPos = yTop + (xp >> 6);
```

Table 5.1   *Relationship between Some Integer Indexes and Degrees*

Index	Degree	Cosine	Value Stored
1	0.2	.999993	65,535
2	0.4	.999975	65,534
5	1.0	.999847	65,526
100	20	.939692	61,584
900	180	-1	0
1,799	360	1	65,536

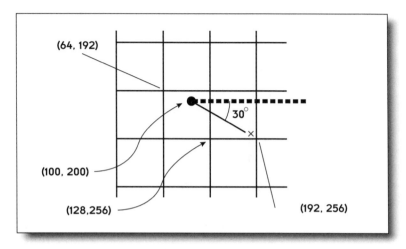

Figure 5.9 *Moving the player from position (100,200) to (186,250).*

Here we calculate an array index, **mPos**, that is used to later access the **xGrid[ ]** and **yGrid[ ]** arrays. If we used our numbers from Figure 5.9, this index would be:

```
mPos = 192 + (100 >> 6);
mPos = 193
```

This is essentially the index into the array location that represents the third row, second column of the 2-D map or maze, which in turn represents our 3-D world. (If you don't recall exactly how this indexing system works, you might want to go back and review Chapter 4.) Now we have everything we need to determine what's out there in the map.

I won't take you through every line of code in **AckMovePOV()**. Essentially, this code is organized into two parts. The first part checks the map for the various conditions: player moving left, right, up, or down. If the player en-counters a wall (or object) as the player moves in one of these directions, the **HitResult** flag is set and the second part of the conditional code is skipped. (I'll show you an example of how this logic works shortly.) The last set of instructions actually determines which status code is returned.

The second set of conditional statements gets a little trickier. If this code is reached, we know that the player has not encountered a wall at any of the four grid squares' borders (left, right, top, or bottom). When this happens, we need to find out what is outside the immediate grid. For example, there could be a wall that runs adjacent to one of the grid borders, as shown in Figure 5.10, which could affect the player's movement if the player gets too close. I'll later explain in detail how this situation is handled but for now the basic

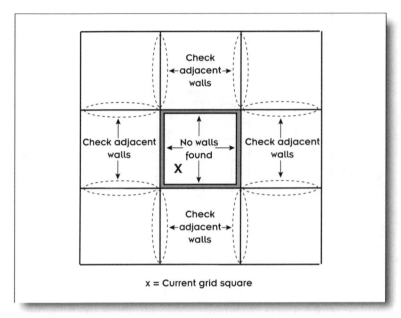

Check
←adjacent→
walls

Check adjacent
walls

No walls
←found→
X

Check adjacent
walls

Check
←adjacent→
walls

x = Current grid square

Figure 5.10   *Checking outside the immediate grid for adjacent walls or objects*

approach involves dividing the player's current grid square into four regions: upper-left, upper-right, lower-left, and lower-right. Each 32x32 region is then checked with the player's movement to see if the player is approaching any adjacent walls or objects.

Moving Left, Right, Up, or Down

Once you know how the basic testing algorithm works in the first section of conditional code, you'll be able to follow all of the conditions that are tested. Let's look at one of them to get you started. The following code checks to see if the player is moving to the right, which is exactly what is happening in our previous example as the player moved from (100,200) to (186,250):

```
if (x1 > xp)                    // Are we moving right?
  {
  if (GetWallX(mPos+1))         // Wall found in current square (right edge)
    {                           // We crossed the wall or we're too close
    if (x1 > xRight || abs(xRight-x1) < 28)
      {
      x1 = xp;                  // Use the previous x position
      HitResult = POV_SLIDEX;   // We're possibly sliding along the right x wall
      }
    }
  }
```

Let's step through this code using our sample numbers. The new x position (**x1**) is greater than the previous x position (**xp**). (Recall **xp** is 100 and **x1** is 186.) This indicates that the player is moving to the right. (The player is also moving down but we can only check one condition at a time!) Next, the function **GetWallX()** is called to see if a wall (or other object) is located at the grid square's right border. Notice that we are checking the location **mPos+1**; the location **mPos** would be to the left of the player. **GetWallX()** is really simple and requires only a few lines of code:

```
// Checks the XGridGlobal[] array to see if a wall is present at
// a given map location
UINT GetWallX(short mPos)
{
  UINT  mCode;

mCode = xGridGlobal[mPos];
if (mCode & WALL_TYPE_PASS)
  mCode = 0;

return(mCode);
}
```

The array that is being checked is actually named **xGridGlobal[ ]** instead of **xGrid[ ]**, but they are the same; **xGridGlobal[ ]** is simply a global variable that the engine code sets up in the **AckRegisterStructure()** function and uses to access the array without indirect addressing into the **ACKENG** structure. **GetWallX()** returns a wall code for the array position that is being checked. These codes are defined in ACK3D.H, and they are loaded into the array when the *ACK-3D* engine is initialized. Note that if a wall is found and it possesses a **WALL_TYPE_PASS** attribute, **GetWallX()** will return a value to indicate that no wall is present. This allows the player to move through some walls that were set up to be passable by the game designer (you!). You can create some nice effects with the passable flag, such as cave entrances, one-way mirrors, and so forth.

Keep in mind that **GetWallX()** has a cousin named **GetWallY()**. This second function checks the **yGridGlobal[ ]** array (**yGrid[ ]**), which stores the wall information for the y walls.

DESIGN TIP

If a wall or object is found, a non-zero value is returned. **AckMovePOV()** then checks to see if the player will run into the wall or is trying to cross over it. In our case, **x1** is greater than **xRight,** which means that the player is trying to cross. The code then saves the previous x position and sets a flag (**HitResult**) to indicate that a wall will be hit. (The previous x coordinate is saved because the player has hit a wall and therefore cannot move in the x direction.) In this early stage, the flag value saved is **POV_SLIDEX** to indicate that the player could be trying to slide along an x wall in the y direction or the player has gotten too close to the wall. At the tail end of **AckMovePOV()**, this status will be updated after other conditions are checked.

If you continue to walk through **AckMovePOV()** using our example, you'll see that the next step checks to see if the player is moving up and then down. If the player does not encounter a wall while moving left, right, up, or down, **HitResult** won't be set and a new set of conditions must be checked.

Checking Adjacent Walls

As I mentioned before, if the player does not encounter a wall at one of the grid square's borders while moving, additional testing is required. The best way to understand what happens next is to study Figure 5.11. Notice that the grid square has been divided into four regions: A, B, C, and D. The code that does the processing for each of these regions is referenced in the listing using

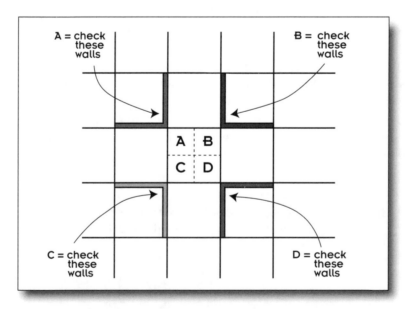

Figure 5.11 *Checking for adjacent walls outside the grid square.*

these region names so that you can easily follow along. In addition, Figure 5.11 shows the possible locations for adjacent walls. These walls must be checked for in each region. Basically, we need to determine which region of the grid square the player is moving in and then check for proximity to possible walls directly outside the grid square.

Here is the beginning of the code that performs this second level testing:

```
if (!HitResult)
  {                            // Check region A—top left area of grid
  if (y1 < (yTop+32))          // New y position falls in top half
    {
    if (x1 < (xLeft+32))  // New x position falls in left half
      {                        // Check adjacent x wall (to the left)
      mCodeX = GetWallX(mPos-GRID_WIDTH);
      mCodeY = GetWallY(mPos-1);       // Check adjacent y wall (above)
      if (mCodeX && y1 < (yTop+28))    // Adjacent x wall found and new y coord
        {                              // is within 28 units
        if (x1 < (xLeft+28))          // New x coord is within 28 units of edge
          {
          if (xp > (xLeft+27))        // Previous x position was outside range
            {
            x1 = xp;                   // Use previous x position
            HitResult = POV_SLIDEX;
            }
          else
            {
            y1 = yp;                   // Use previous y position
            HitResult = POV_SLIDEY;
            }
          }
        }
      }
```

First, notice that the **HitResult** flag has not been set to indicate that the player has encountered a wall or object yet. The next two **if** statements check to see if the player is in region A—the top-left corner of the grid square. Then, the x and y grid arrays are checked by calling the **GetWallX()** and **GetWallY()** functions. The remaining code shown performs the work of testing the player's location in relation to the x wall that is adjacent to the grid square. If the player's new x position is within 28 units of the left border, one of two conditions will be triggered:

- The player is trying to move in the x direction (left) from a position outside of the upper-left region and therefore, the player can't be allowed to move left (in the x direction) because the player is getting too close to the edge of the adjacent wall. (Movement will be restricted to up and down along the adjacent wall.)

- The player is trying to move in the y direction (up) from outside the region and movement will be restricted to the x direction.

These two conditions are illustrated in Figure 5.12. Notice how the picture really helps remove the complexity from the code. (All of the **if** statements and coordinate checking can make your head spin a little. The main thing to get out of this discussion is that we are attempting to keep the player from passing through, or even becoming partially embedded within a wall or object no matter what angle we use to approach it. That requirement is why all of the different checks need to be performed. If you are a *Wolfenstein* fan, you'll notice the similarities here with the movement characteristics of this popular game.)

Essentially, the code that tests for the other regions is the same. The only difference is that other map positions must be checked and compared with the player's starting and ending points. After all of this checking is completed, we get to the end of the function and encounter this conditional statement:

```
if (AckCheckObjPosn(x1,y1,Angle,0))    // We've hit an object-not a wall
   return(POV_OBJECT);
```

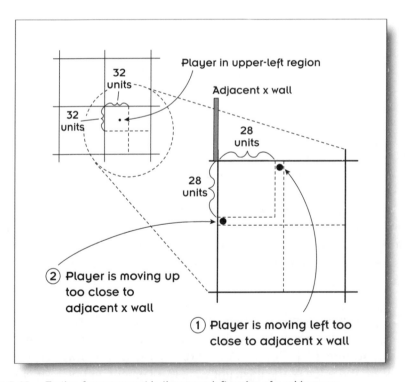

Figure 5.12   *Testing for movement in the upper-left region of a grid square.*

Guess what? Now it's time to see if the thing in front of the player is actually a wall or an object.

Is There an Object in View?

The **AckCheckObjPosn()** function requires three parameters: the player's ending (x,y) position, the angle the player is moving, and an index value that is used to indicate that a specified object should not be tested. (If this parameter is set to 0, all the objects used in a game will be checked to see if the player will encounter one.) Once called, this function determines what grid square the player is in after moving to **x1, y1**. A variable named **MapPosn** is assigned an index value that corresponds to the map position. This index value is used to test the object list array, **ObjList[ ]**, where the information about objects is stored:

```
result = POV_NOTHING;              // Initialize to nothing found
MapPosn = (yPlayer & 0xFFC0) + (xPlayer >> 6);  // Calculate grid square the
                                   //   player will be in
maxObj = aeGlobal->MaxObjects;   // Total number of objects used
oList = &aeGlobal->ObjList[0];   // Reference the list of objects
```

The processing work involves spinning through a loop to check each object in the **ObjList[ ]** array. Each object is tested to see if it is active and passable:

```
for (i = 0; i < maxObj; i++)     // Loop and check each object in the list
  {
  oPtr = oList[i];               // Point to current object
  if (oPtr == NULL)              // No object here; skip to next object in list
    continue;

  if (!oPtr->Active || oPtr->Flags & OF_PASSABLE) // Object is not active
                                   //   or is passable
    continue;
```

This code takes advantage of the fact that all of the objects used in an application are stored in an array of structures that can easily be accessed using a pointer. This array is set up when the main *ACK-3D* engine initialization routines are called. If you remember from the previous chapter, the object structure contains a lot of useful information to keep track of and process objects, such as the object's speed, current grid location, x and y, location in a grid, object iD, and so on. The component we are concerned with now is **mPos**—the object's current grid location in the map. To see if an object is in the player's square, this simple condition statement is used in **AckCheckObjPosn()**:

```
if (MapPosn == oPtr->mPos && i != oIndex) // We've found an object
  {
  LastObjectHit = i;                       // Store the object's index
  return(POV_OBJECT);
  }
```

Here, the player's grid position is compared to an object's position. If they match, guess what? A flag is returned (**POV_OBJECT**) to indicate that an object has been found. Notice also that the number of the object in the list is saved in the variable **LastObjectHit**. This **if** block is contained inside a **for** loop that continues to increment until each object in the list has been tested or a match has been found. If **AckCheckObjPosn()** comes up empty handed, **POV_NOTHING** is returned.

Moving Objects with AckMoveObjectPOV()

So far we've been treating our code development work from the standpoint that only a player can move around. If you wrote a game like this, it would get quite boring. To spice things up (and add that great element of surprise), you can also move objects around in your map. The function for moving objects is **AckMoveObjectPOV()**, and as you might have guessed, its code is very similar to the code found in **AckMovePOV()**.

AckMoveObjectPOV() is called with three parameters:

ObjIndex	The index number of the object to be moved. This index is a reference into the object array
Angle	The angle to move the object
Amount	The distance to move the object

The first lines of code in **AckMoveObjectPOV()** set up a reference to the actual object being moved:

```
oList = &aeGlobal->ObjList[0];  // Reference the start of the object list
oPtr = oList[ObjIndex];         // Set a pointer to the object being moved
if (oPtr == NULL)               // No object is available to move
  return(0);
```

Next, the actual coordinates of the object are obtained (**xp**, **yp**) and the new position of the object is calculated (**x1**, **y1**) as well as the coordinates of the grid square in which the object is found. We've already discussed how these calculations work when we explored **AckMovePOV()**. Once we have all of the coordinates and index values we need, the first thing we need to know is if the object that we are moving will encounter another object in its grid square. Here's the call that does this work:

```
oNum = AckCheckObjPosn(x1,y1,Angle,ObjIndex);
if (oNum > 0)
  return(POV_OBJECT);
```

Does this look familiar to you? This time around **AckCheckObjPosn()** is called with a value set for **ObjIndex** so that this object (the object we are moving) won't be tested to see if it runs into itself!

If the object checking routine fails, the **HitResult** flag is set to **POV_NOTHING** and away we go. Essentially, all of the conditions tested in **AckMovePOV()** must be checked here: To see which direction the object is moving. (If you already forgot how this logic works, you might want to go back and review the description of **AckMovePOV()**.)

Once all of the tests have been made, the object's coordinates are updated:

```
oPtr->x = x1;        // Update the new x,y coordinates for the object
oPtr->y = y1;
oPtr->mPos = MapPosn; // Update the grid map position for the object
```

A Little Bit of Object Animation

As we've seen, **AckMoveObjectPOV()** takes care of the work of moving an object around in a map and checking to see if the object encounters another object or wall in its path. To actually animate the objects used in an application, we need a function to check the status of the objects used so we can determine which ones need to be animated and updated. This task can be easily accomplished with the function named **AckCheckObjectMovement()**. This function, defined in ACKPOV.C, is designed to be called from your application after you've moved objects around in your map.

What does this function actually do? It runs through the list of objects used in a program and it updates each object that can be animated. This "animation update" is achieved by assigning each object a different bitmap to display. But before we get into the details of how **AckCheckObjectMovement()** operates, let's stand back a moment and discuss how objects are animated.

Each object used in a game is assigned a series of bitmaps. As an example, Figure 5.13 shows some bitmaps used to create an enemy spaceman. To give this object an animated life, we simply display the different bitmaps in their assigned sequence. At any given time, we can determine the state of the animation sequence by checking to see which bitmap is currently displayed for the object.

The object structure we introduced in the previous chapter (**NEWOBJECT**) provides a field (**CurrentBm**) to keep track of which bitmap should be displayed for an object at any given time. A number of other fields are provided, such as **Flags**, **Active**, **Dir**, and **Speed**, so that we can easily keep track of the current state of an object. By checking these fields, we can tell if an object is movable, in which direction it is going, how fast it should be moved, whether it can be animated only once or multiple times, and so on.

Now that you're a little more familiar with the techniques behind object animation, let's return to **AckCheckObjectMovement()**. The first two tasks that this function performs determine the number of objects used in an application and set up a pointer to the list of objects:

```
maxObj = aeGlobal->MaxObjects;   // Get the number of objects used
oList = &aeGlobal->ObjList[0];   // Reference the list of objects
```

Next, a **for** loop is used to step through the list of objects and determine which bitmap references need to be updated:

```
for (i = 1; i < maxObj; i++)     // Loop to check each object in the list
  {
  oPtr = oList[i];               // Access current object in list
  if (oPtr == NULL)              // No object here; skip
    continue;

  if (!oPtr->Active)             // Object is not active; skip
    continue;
```

Figure 5.13 *Animating an object using a sequence of bitmaps.*

```
  if (!oPtr->Speed)       // Object has no speed setting; skip
    continue;

  if (!(oPtr->Flags & OF_ANIMATE))  // Object is not set up for animation
    continue;
```

Notice that in each iteration, four conditions are tested. If all of these conditions fail, we know that the object is active, has a **Speed** setting, and that it is set up to be animated. The actual animation process consists of bumping the bitmap sequence by one so that the next bitmap in the list will be used to animate the object. Here's the code that performs this task:

```
  dx = oPtr->CurrentBm + 1;      // Use the next bitmap
  if (dx >= oPtr->Maxbm)         // We're at the end of the list of bitmaps
    {
    if (oPtr->Flags & OF_ANIMONCE)// Object should only be animated once
      {
      oPtr->Flags &= ~OF_ANIMATE; // Reset flags to indicate that we're done
      oPtr->Flags |= OF_ANIMDONE; // animating the object
      dx = oPtr->CurrentBm;       // Keep current bitmap number
      }
    else
      dx = 0;                     // Start at the beginning of the set of bitmaps
    }
  oPtr->CurrentBm = dx;           // Store the next bitmap as the current one
```

The field **CurrentBm** stores the sequence number of the bitmap that is currently displayed for the object. By increasing this value by one, we can move to the next bitmap in the sequence. But before increasing this number, we need to check to make sure that the object can still be animated and that we haven't reached the end of the bitmap sequence. If we get to the end, we start over at the top (bitmap 0).

The Complete ACKPOV.C

```
// This file defines the functions for player and object movement in the
// the game map.
// (c) 1995 ACK Software (Lary Myers)
#include <windows.h>
#include <stdlib.h>
#include <stdio.h>
#include <dos.h>
#include <mem.h>
#include <io.h>
#include <fcntl.h>
#include <time.h>
#include <string.h>
#include <sys\stat.h>
#include "ack3d.h"
```

```
#include "ackeng.h"
#include "ackext.h"
//**************************************************************************
// Internal function called by AckMovePOV(). Checks the passed x and y
// coordinates of the player against the object coordinates to see if the
// player will encouner an object.
//**************************************************************************
short AckCheckObjPosn(short xPlayer,short yPlayer, short oIndex)
{
  short     i,result,maxObj;
  short     MapPosn;
  NEWOBJECT **oList;
  NEWOBJECT *oPtr;
result = POV_NOTHING;                        // Initialize to nothing found
MapPosn = (yPlayer & 0xFFC0) + (xPlayer >> 6); // Calculate grid square the
player is in maxObj = aeGlobal->MaxObjects;   // Total number of objects used
oList = &aeGlobal->ObjList[0];                      // Reference the list of objects
for (i = 0; i < maxObj; i++)       // Loop and check each object in the list
  {
  oPtr = oList[i];                   // Point to current object
  if (oPtr == NULL)                  // No object here; skip to next object in list
    continue;
  // Object is not active or is passable
  if (!oPtr->Active || oPtr->Flags & OF_PASSABLE)
    continue;                            // Skip to next object in list
  // Object is found in the player's grid position
  if (MapPosn == oPtr->mPos && i != oIndex)
    {
    LastObjectHit = i;        // Store the number of the object found
    return(POV_OBJECT);       // Return flag to indicate an object is found
    }
  }
return(result);
}
//**************************************************************************
// Internal function called by AckMovePOV() to see if a wall or object is
// located in the player's current grid square. This function checks for walls
// or objects in the x-plane using the xGrid array. The bitmap code for the wall
// or object is returned. A value returned of 0 indicates that no wall or object
// is present or that the wall is passable.
//**************************************************************************
USHORT GetWallX(short mPos)
{
  USHORT  mCode;
mCode = xGridGlobal[mPos]; // Get bitmap code at specified map position
if (mCode & WALL_TYPE_PASS) // Passable walls can be walked through
  mCode = 0;
return(mCode);
}
// ************************************************************************
// Internal function called by AckMovePOV() to see if a wall or object is
// located in the player's current grid square. This function checks for walls
// or objects in the y-plane using the yGrid array. The bitmap code for the wall
// or object is returned. A value returned of 0 indicates that no wall or object
```

```
// is present or that the wall is passable.
//****************************************************************************
USHORT GetWallY(short mPos)
{
  USHORT  mCode;

mCode = yGridGlobal[mPos];  // Get bitmap code at specified map position
if (mCode & WALL_TYPE_PASS) // Passable walls can be walked through
  mCode = 0;
return(mCode);
}


//****************************************************************************
// Moves the POV based on Angle for Amount. After moving but prior to
// returning, the position of the POV is checked for collisions.
//****************************************************************************
short AckMovePOV(short Angle,short Amount)
{
  short x1,y1,HitResult;        // New coordinate position
  short xp,yp;                  // Starting player coordinates
  short xLeft,xRight,yTop,yBottom;// Coordinates for grid square
  short mPos;                   // Map position for xGrid[], yGrid[]
USHORTmCodeX,mCodeY;            // Return codes for x,y wall arrays

HitResult = POV_NOTHING;        // We haven't hit anything yet
xp = aeGlobal->xPlayer;   // Get the current x,y player coordinates
yp = aeGlobal->yPlayer;
xLeft = xp & 0xFFC0;      // Determine coordinates of the boundaries
yTop = yp & 0xFFC0;       // of the grid square we're in.
xRight = xLeft + GRID_SIZE;
yBottom = yTop + GRID_SIZE;
// Calculate the x,y distance of movement using the angle and distance
// x1,y1 = the new coordinate position of the player.
x1 = xp + (long)((CosTable[Angle] * Amount) >> FP_SHIFT);
y1 = yp + (long)((SinTable[Angle] * Amount) >> FP_SHIFT);
// Calculate current map position for the xGrid[] and yGrid[] arrays
mPos = yTop + (xp >> 6); // Current Map Posn
// It's time to see what happens when we move
if (x1 < xp)              // Are we moving left?
  {
  if (GetWallX(mPos))      // Wall found in current square (left edge)
    {
    if (x1 < xLeft || abs(x1-xLeft) < 28)   // We crossed the wall or we're too close
      {
      x1 = xp;                 // Use the previous x position
      HitResult = POV_SLIDEX; // We're possibly sliding along the left x wall
      }
    }
  }
if (x1 > xp)                // Are we moving right?
  {
  if (GetWallX(mPos+1))       // Wall found in current square (right edge)
    { // We crossed the wall or we're too close
    if (x1 > xRight || abs(xRight-x1) < 28)
```

```
        {
        x1 = xp;                    // Use the previous x position
        HitResult = POV_SLIDEX; // We're possibly sliding along the right x wall
        }
      }
    }
if (y1 < yp)                        // Are we moving up?
  {
    if (GetWallY(mPos))             // Wall found in current square (top edge)
      {
      if (y1 < yTop || abs(y1-yTop) < 28)// We crossed the wall or we're too close
        {
        y1 = yp;                    // Use the previous y position
        HitResult = POV_SLIDEY; // We're possibly sliding along the top wall
        }
      }
  }
if (y1 > yp)                        // Are we moving down?
  {
    if (GetWallY(mPos+GRID_WIDTH))// Wall found in current square (bottom edge)
    { // We crossed the wall or we're too close
    if (y1 > yBottom || abs(yBottom-y1) < 28)
      {
      y1 = yp;                      // Use the previous y position
      HitResult = POV_SLIDEY; // We're sliding along the bottom wall }
      }
  }
// A wall or object hasn't been hit yet—we must look further.
// The current grid sqaure will be divided into four regions:
//  A = top left; B = top right; C = bottom left; D = bottom right
// Each of these regions will be checked to see if the player's new position
// (x1,y1) // is close to a wall or object that borders one of these regions.
// Each grid square is 64x64 units, so each region to check is 32x32 units.
if (!HitResult)
  {                                 // Check region A—top left area of grid
  if (y1 < (yTop+32))       // New y position falls in top half
    {
    if (x1 < (xLeft+32))  // New x position falls in left half
      {
      mCodeX = GetWallX(mPos-GRID_WIDTH);    // Check adjacent x wall (to left)
      mCodeY = GetWallY(mPos-1);             // Check adjacent y wall (above)
      if (mCodeX && y1 < (yTop+28)) // Adjacent x wall found and new y coord
        {                                // is within 28 units
        if (x1 < (xLeft+28))           // New x coord is within 28 units of edge
          {
          if (xp > (xLeft+27))         // Previous x position was outside range
            {
            x1 = xp;                   // Use previous x position
            HitResult = POV_SLIDEX;
            }
          else
            {
            y1 = yp;  // Use previous y position
            HitResult = POV_SLIDEY;
```

```
        }
      }
    }
  if (mCodeY && x1 < (xLeft+28))    // Adjacent y wall found and new x coord
    {                               // is within 28 units
    if (y1 < (yTop+28))             // New y coord is within 28 units of edge
      {
      if (yp > (yTop+27))           // Previous y position was outside range
        {
        y1 = yp;                    // Use previous y position
        HitResult = POV_SLIDEY;
        }
      else
        {
        x1 = xp;                    // Use previous x position
        HitResult = POV_SLIDEX;
        }
      }
    }
  }
// Check region B—top right area
if (x1 > (xRight-32) && !HitResult)    // New x is at top right
  {
  mCodeX = GetWallX(mPos+1-GRID_WIDTH); // Check adjacent x wall (to right)
  mCodeY = GetWallY(mPos+1);            // Check adjacent y wall (above)
  if (mCodeX && y1 < (yTop+28))         // Adjacent x wall found
    {
    if (x1 > (xRight-28))
      {
      if (xp < (xRight-27))
        {
        x1 = xp;                    // Use previous x position
        HitResult = POV_SLIDEX;
        }
      else
        {
        y1 = yp;                    // Use previous y position
        HitResult = POV_SLIDEY;
        }
      }
    }
  if (mCodeY && x1 > (xRight-28))    // Adjacent y wall found
    {
    if (y1 < (yTop+28))
      {
      if (yp > (yTop+27))
        {
        y1 = yp;                    // Use previous y position
        HitResult = POV_SLIDEY;
        }
      else
        {
        x1 = xp;                    // Use previous x position
        HitResult = POV_SLIDEX;
```

```
              }
            }
          }
        }
      }
// Check region C—bottom left area
if (y1 > (yTop+32) && !HitResult)     // We are below upper half of square
  {
  if (x1 < (xLeft+32))                 // and on the left half of square
    {
    mCodeX = GetWallX(mPos+GRID_WIDTH);   // Check adjacent x wall (to left)
    mCodeY = GetWallY(mPos-1+GRID_WIDTH); // Check adjacent y wall (below)
    if (mCodeX && y1 > (yBottom-28))       // Adjacent x wall found
      {
      if (x1 < (xLeft+28))
        {
        if (xp > (xLeft+27))
          {
          x1 = xp;                        // Use previous x position
          HitResult = POV_SLIDEX;
          }
        else
          {
          y1 = yp;                        // Use previous y position
          HitResult = POV_SLIDEY;
          }
        }
      }
    if (mCodeY && x1 < (xLeft+28))         // Adjacent y wall found
      {
      if (y1 > (yBottom-28))
        {
        if (yp < (yBottom-27))
          {
          y1 = yp;                        // Use previous y position
          HitResult = POV_SLIDEY;
          }
        else
          {
          x1 = xp;                        // Use previous x position
          HitResult = POV_SLIDEX;
          }
        }
      }
    }
  // Check region D—bottom right area
  if (x1 > (xRight-32) && !HitResult)      // Check right side of square
    {
    mCodeX = GetWallX(mPos+1+GRID_WIDTH); // Check adjacent x wall (to right)
    mCodeY = GetWallY(mPos+1+GRID_WIDTH); // Check adjacent y wall (below)
    if (mCodeX && y1 > (yBottom-28))       // Adjacent x wall found
      {
      if (x1 > (xRight-28))
        {
```

```
        if (xp < (xRight-27))
          {
          x1 = xp;                          // Use previous x position
          HitResult = POV_SLIDEX;
          }
        else
          {
          y1 = yp;                          // Use previous y position
          HitResult = POV_SLIDEY;
          }
        }
      }
    if (mCodeY && x1 > (xRight-28))    // Adjacent y wall found
      {
      if (y1 > (yBottom-28))
        {
        if (yp < (yBottom-27))
          {
          y1 = yp;                          // Use previous y position
          HitResult = POV_SLIDEY;
          }
        else
          {
          x1 = xp;                          // Use previous x position
          HitResult = POV_SLIDEX;
          }
          }
        }
      }
    }
  }
if (AckCheckObjPosn(x1,y1,0))               // We've hit an object—not a wall
return(POV_OBJECT);
if (HitResult == POV_SLIDEX && y1 == yp)   // We've hit an x wall and we're not
sliding HitResult = POV_XWALL;
if (HitResult == POV_SLIDEY && x1 == xp)   // We've hit a y wall and we're not
sliding HitResult = POV_YWALL;
aeGlobal->xPlayer = x1;                     // Update player's new x,y position
aeGlobal->yPlayer = y1;
return(HitResult);
}


//*************************************************************************
// Moves an object based on Angle and Amount then checks for collision
// with other objects AND the POV.
//*************************************************************************
short AckMoveObjectPOV(short ObjIndex,short Angle,short Amount)
{
  short   xp,yp,x1,y1,HitResult,oNum;
  USHORT  mCodeX,mCodeY;
  short   xLeft,xRight,yTop,yBottom,mPos;
  short   MapPosn,PlayerPosn;
  NEWOBJECT **oList;
  NEWOBJECT *oPtr;
```

```
oList = &aeGlobal->ObjList[0];  // Reference the start of the object list
oPtr = oList[ObjIndex];         // Set a pointer to the object being moved
if (oPtr == NULL)               // No object is available to move; we're done
  return(0);
xp = oPtr->x;                   // Get the current x,y coordinate of the object
yp = oPtr->y;
// Calculate the new x,y, coordinates of the object (after moving)
x1 = xp + (short)((CosTable[Angle] * Amount) >> FP_SHIFT);
y1 = yp + (short)((SinTable[Angle] * Amount) >> FP_SHIFT);
xLeft = xp & 0xFFC0;            // Determine the coordinates of the grid square
xRight = xLeft + GRID_SIZE - 1; // the object is currently in
yTop = yp & 0xFFC0;
yBottom = yTop + GRID_SIZE - 1;
// Calculate the map position of the grid square the object is in
mPos = yTop + (xp >> 6);
// Calculate the map position of the grid square the objectis moving to
MapPosn = (y1 & 0xFFC0) + (x1 >> 6);
// Check to see if the object will encouner another object while moving
oNum = AckCheckObjPosn(x1,y1,ObjIndex);
if (oNum > 0)                   // Yes, return flag to indicate object found
  return(POV_OBJECT);
HitResult = POV_NOTHING;  // Nothing found yet, initialize flag
if (x1 < xp)                    // Are we moving left?
  { // We crossed the wall or we're too close
  if (GetWallX(mPos))     // Wall found in current square (left edge)
    {
    if (x1 < xLeft || abs(x1-xLeft) < 28)
      {
      x1 = xp;                  // Use the previous x position
      HitResult = POV_SLIDEX; // We're possibly sliding along the left x wall
      }
    }
  }
if (x1 > xp)                    // Are we moving right?
  {
  if (GetWallX(mPos+1))        // Wall found in current square (right edge)
    { // We crossed the wall or we're too close
    if (x1 > xRight || abs(xRight-x1) < 28)
      {
      x1 = xp;                  // Use the previous x position
      HitResult = POV_SLIDEX; // We're possibly sliding along the right x wall
      }
    }
  }
if (y1 < yp)                    // Are we moving up?
  {
  if (GetWallY(mPos))          // Wall found in current square (top edge)
    {
    if (y1 < yTop || abs(y1-yTop) < 28) // We crossed the wall or we're too close
      {
      y1 = yp;                  // Use the previous y position
      HitResult = POV_SLIDEY; // We're possibly sliding along the top wall
      }
    }
```

```
      }
    if (y1 > yp)                          // Are we moving down?
      {
      if (GetWallY(mPos+GRID_WIDTH))  // Wall found in current square (bottom edge)
        { // We crossed the wall or we're too close
        if (y1 > yBottom || abs(yBottom-y1) < 28)
          {
          y1 = yp;                    // Use the previous y position
          HitResult = POV_SLIDEY; // We're sliding along the bottom wall
          }
        }
      }
    if (!HitResult)              // Nothing hit yet, look further
      {
      if (y1 < (yTop+32))        // We are above upper half of square
        {
        if (x1 < (xLeft+32))  // and on the left half of square
          {
          mCodeX = GetWallX(mPos-GRID_WIDTH); // Check adjacent x wall (to left)
          mCodeY = GetWallY(mPos-1);          // Check adjacent y wall (above)
          if (mCodeX && y1 < (yTop+28)) // Adjacent x wall found and new y coord
            {                           // is within 28 units
            if (x1 < (xLeft+28))        // New x coord is within 28 units of edge
              {
              if (xp > (xLeft+27))      // Previous x position was outside range
                {
                x1 = xp;                // Use previous x position
                HitResult = POV_SLIDEX;
                }
              else
                {
                y1 = yp;                // Use previous y position
                HitResult = POV_SLIDEY;
                }
              }
            }
          if (mCodeY && x1 < (xLeft+28)) // Adjacent y wall found and new x coord
            {                            // is within 28 units
            if (y1 < (yTop+28))          // New y coord is within 28 units of edge
              {
              if (yp > (yTop+27))        // Previous y position was outside range
                {
                y1 = yp;                 // Use previous y position
                HitResult = POV_SLIDEY;
                }
              else
                {
                x1 = xp;                 // Use previous x position
                HitResult = POV_SLIDEX;
                }
              }
            }
          }
        if (x1 > (xRight-32) && !HitResult)    // New x is at top right
```

```
      {
      mCodeX = GetWallX(mPos+1-GRID_WIDTH); // Check adjacent x wall (to right)
      mCodeY = GetWallY(mPos+1);            // Check adjacent y wall (above)
      if (mCodeX && y1 < (yTop+28))         // Adjacent x wall found
        {
        if (x1 > (xRight-28))
          {
          if (xp < (xRight-27))
            {
            x1 = xp;                        // Use previous x position
            HitResult = POV_SLIDEX;
            }
          else
            {
            y1 = yp;                        // Use previous y position
            HitResult = POV_SLIDEY;
            }
          }
        }
      if (mCodeY && x1 > (xRight-28))        // Adjacent y wall found
        {
        if (y1 < (yTop+28))
          {
          if (yp > (yTop+27))
            {
            y1 = yp;                        // Use previous y position
            HitResult = POV_SLIDEY;
            }
          else
            {
            x1 = xp;
            HitResult = POV_SLIDEX;
            }
          }
        }
      }
    }
  if (y1 > (yTop+32) && !HitResult)          // We are below upper half of square
    {
    if (x1 < (xLeft+32))                      // and on the left half of square
      {
      mCodeX = GetWallX(mPos+GRID_WIDTH);
      mCodeY = GetWallY(mPos-1+GRID_WIDTH);
      if (mCodeX && y1 > (yBottom-28))
        {
        if (x1 < (xLeft+28))
          {
          if (xp > (xLeft+27))
            {
            x1 = xp;
            HitResult = POV_SLIDEX;
            }
          else
            {
            y1 = yp;
```

```
            HitResult = POV_SLIDEY;
            }
          }
      }
    if (mCodeY && x1 < (xLeft+28))
      {
      if (y1 > (yBottom-28))
        {
        if (yp < (yBottom-27))
          {
          y1 = yp;
          HitResult = POV_SLIDEY;
          }
        else
          {
          x1 = xp;
          HitResult = POV_SLIDEX;
          }
        }
      }
    }
  if (x1 > (xRight-32) && !HitResult)          // On right side of square
    {
    mCodeX = GetWallX(mPos+1+GRID_WIDTH);
    mCodeY = GetWallY(mPos+1+GRID_WIDTH);
    if (mCodeX && y1 > (yBottom-28))
      {
      if (x1 > (xRight-28))
        {
        if (xp < (xRight-27))
          {
          x1 = xp;
          HitResult = POV_SLIDEX;
          }
        else
          {
          y1 = yp;
          HitResult = POV_SLIDEY;
          }
        }
      }
    if (mCodeY && x1 > (xRight-28))
      {
      if (y1 > (yBottom-28))
        {
        if (yp < (yBottom-27))
          {
          y1 = yp;
          HitResult = POV_SLIDEY;
          }
        else
          {
          x1 = xp;
          HitResult = POV_SLIDEX;
          }
```

```
        }
      }
    }
  }
  }
oPtr->x = x1;            // Update the new x,y coordinates for the object
oPtr->y = y1;
oPtr->mPos = MapPosn; // Update the grid map position for the object
PlayerPosn = (aeGlobal->yPlayer & 0xFFC0) + (aeGlobal->xPlayer >> 6);
if (MapPosn == PlayerPosn)
  return(POV_PLAYER);
return(HitResult);
}


//*************************************************************************
// Checks the list of objects used in an application and sets up the current
// bitmap for each object that can be animated. Object animation is performed by
// displaying different bitmaps for an object in sequence.
//*************************************************************************
void AckCheckObjectMovement(void)
{
  short    i,maxObj;
  short    dx;
  NEWOBJECT **oList;
  NEWOBJECT *oPtr;

maxObj = aeGlobal->MaxObjects;     // Get the number of objects used
oList = &aeGlobal->ObjList[0];     // Reference the list of objects
for (i = 1; i < maxObj; i++)       // Loop to check each object in the list
  {
  oPtr = oList[i];                 // Access current object in list
  if (oPtr == NULL)                // No object here; skip
    continue;
  if (!oPtr->Active)               // Object is not active; skip
    continue;
  if (!oPtr->Speed)                // Object has no speed setting; skip
    continue;
  if (!(oPtr->Flags & OF_ANIMATE))// Object is not set up for animation
    continue;
  dx = oPtr->CurrentBm + 1;        // Use the next bitmap
  if (dx >= oPtr->Maxbm)           // We're at the end of the list of bitmaps
    {
    if (oPtr->Flags & OF_ANIMONCE)// Object should only be animated once
      {
      oPtr->Flags &= ~OF_ANIMATE; // Reset flags to indicate that we're done
      oPtr->Flags |= OF_ANIMDONE; // animating the object
      dx = oPtr->CurrentBm;        // Keep current bitmap number
      }
    else
      dx = 0;                      // Start at the beginning of the set of bitmaps
    }
  oPtr->CurrentBm = dx;            // Store the next bitmap as the current one
  }
}
// **** End of Source ****
```

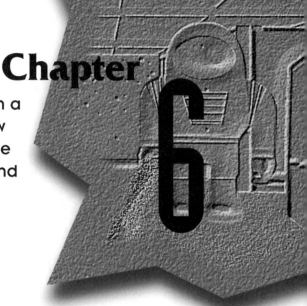

Chapter

We've been traveling around in a 2-D maze long enough! It's now time to see how we can cast the world we've been moving around in into a 3-D representation.

Casting Your Way into 3-D

hen we last saw our player in Chapter 5, he or she was moving around in a 2-D map, bumping into walls and objects. We moved the player by calling **AckMovePOV()** which in turn did the detective work of figuring out what the player would see while moving. So now that we have everything we need to navigate in a map, how do we re-create the walls and objects that are found in the map and display them fast enough to create the illusion of 3-D? I'm not going to deceive you and tell you this is an easy thing to do. In fact, this is the point where we need to pull out our clever programming tricks and even drop down to assembly language. But the head-scratching detail work is worth the effort. We'll end up with a ray-casting tool that will build your views with lightning speed.

To continue creating our adventure kit, we need to develop the code for ACKVIEW.C. This C source file provides the key high-level and low-level functions to implement the actual ray-casting engine. Some of the C functions call assembly routines in the files ACKRTN.ASM, ACKRTN1.ASM, and so on. We'll start by taking a big picture look at how the engine operates and then we'll work our way down into the different levels of code. This approach gives you the opportunity to see how the ray-casting optimization techniques outlined in Chapter 2 are actually implemented.

In this chapter we'll explore all of the code required to cast rays in both x and y planes and then build slice structures to represent a view. In the next chapter we'll look at the code required to convert the slice structures into a screen buffer. Then, in Chapters 7 and 13, I'll show you how DOS and Windows screen displays are supported.

Creating Your Worlds—Slice by Slice

A famous writer once told me that writing is like driving at night. You turn your headlights on and drive away. All you can see is what's in front of you, so you drive the road stretch-by-stretch until you get to your final destination. You don't need to see everything around you as you drive, you just need to follow the view that's ahead of you. (And if you're lucky, you end up in the right place.)

You can visualize the process of ray casting 3-D scenes the same way. For any given view that contains items such as walls, objects, a floor, and a ceiling, we'll build it piece by piece or *slice by slice*. A slice is essentially a section of a wall or other object. As each ray is cast, a slice of a wall or object is constructed and placed in a buffer. After all of the slices are built for a view, the view is displayed by copying the buffer to the screen.

The art of building a slice consists of casting out a ray, determining what the ray has hit (if anything), and drawing the section of the object or wall that the ray has hit. To do this, we'll be using the **SLICE** data structure that was introduced briefly in Chapter 4:

```
typedef struct _slicer {
  UCHAR      **bMap;         // Pointer to wall bitmap found while ray casting
  UCHAR      *mPtr;          // Grid pointer to reference multi-height wall data
  short      bNumber;        // Bitmap number of the wall found
  unsigned short  bColumn;   // Screen column location of the found slice
  short      Distance;       // Distance from the POV to the slice
  short      mPos;           // Position of the slice in the associated map
  unsigned char Type;        // Indicates if the slice is a wall or object
  void       (*Fnc)(void);   // Pointer to a function to draw wall or object
  unsigned char Active;      // Indicates last slice in list
  // The next two pointers are used if the current slice
  // is part of a transparent wall
  struct _slicer *Prev;      // References the wall slice in front of current slice
  struct _slicer *Next;      // References the wall slice behind the current slice
} SLICE;
```

If you recall from Chapters 2 and 4, the basic game plan involves casting out a ray in the x and y planes to see if something has been hit. If a section of a wall or object (slice) is found, the information about the slice is stored in a **SLICE** structure. The critical information, such as the distance from the player's POV to the slice, the actual screen column location of the slice, and the position of the slice in the map will be used to render the slice in 3-D.

DESIGN TIP

As you explore the source code presented in this chapter for creating a view, you'll find that the slice data structure is accessed by both C and assembly code. To represent the screen, an array of slice structures is defined. The array contains 320 separate slice structures, which gives us a slice structure to represent each screen column. In the ACKENG.H header file, two externals are defined so that we can easily access the **Slice** array:

```
extern SLICE    Slice[];
extern SLICE    *sPtr;
```

In the C code, we'll primarily use the ***sPtr** point to access the base of the array. Later, I'll show you how the slice array is accessed with assembly code.

Introducing ACKVIEW.C

The ACKVIEW.C module that we'll create in this chapter provides five functions (see Table 6.1), although only two of them are called by application programs—**AckRegisterStructure()** and **AckBuildView()**. The other functions are used by **AckBuildView()** to render a scene. In each scene we create, we'll need to build all of the slices that the player will see for standard height walls, multi-height walls, and objects.

Just Add Assembly

Being the speed demons that we are, we want our ray casting to be as fast as possible. Originally, I developed all of the ray casting routines in C. Unfortunately, the code didn't run fast enough to update views as quickly as you find in games like *DOOM*. So I went back to the drawing board and re-coded the critical ray-casting routines in assembly. Using assembly gave me the opportunity to optimize the code that performs time-critical calculations and table look-ups.

The only drawback with assembly code as far as we're concerned is that it is a little harder to follow and modify. To help you follow along, I'll try to explain the algorithms and logic implemented as carefully as I can. In some cases, I'll even show you how the logic is coded using an equivalent C notation. The assembly files can get rather long because of all the equates and

Table 6.1　*Functions Defined in ACKVIEW.C*

Function	Description
AckRegisterStructure()	Transfers certain variables from the interface structure to global variables so that they can be accessed faster by the assembly-language drawing functions. This approach gives us the generality of a library engine and the advantage of speed while rendering the scene.
AckBuildView()	Renders the current scene into the off-screen buffer based on the POV coordinates and angle. This function does not display the scene once it is rendered; thus, the application can overlay graphics into the buffer before it is actually displayed.
ShowNone()	Stub function for slices that do not contain walls.
BuildSlice()	Internal function to cast the x and y rays and build a slice structure for each column of the viewing window.
BuildSliceMulti()	Creates the ray cast for multi-height walls so that any wall that is taller than the walls in front of it will be displayed.
AckCheckHit()	Internal function called by AckCheckDoorOpen() to check for a possible collision between a player and a within with a specified distance. This function is actually presented in Chapter 9.

detailed "step-by-step" instructions, so I won't show you the complete listings of each of the files we reference in this chapter. I will, however, show you the complete code for the main assembly routines we discuss so that you can see what's going on under the hood.

Building a View with AckBuildView()

The main function in ACKVIEW.C that is responsible for building views is **AckBuildView()**. This function must be called by your applications to create a view. Each time your player moves around in a scene and changes his or her viewing angle or coordinate position, you must call **AckBuildView()** to update the scene. But keep in mind that **AckBuildView()** does not actually update the physical screen; it performs the background work of redrawing a scene and updating a buffer that can be accessed by your application program.

Essentially, **AckBuildView()** initializes a few important global variables and calls an assembly-language routine named **BuildUpView** from the file ACKRTN3.ASM; this routine takes over and controls the ray-casting process. Figure 6.1 shows the different C functions and assembly routines that are called once **BuildUpView** takes over the ray-casting work. The C functions that are called by **BuildUpView**, such as **BuildUpSlice()** and **BuildSliceMulti()**, are

```
AckBuildView( )

    BuildUpView                        [ACKRTN3.ASM]

            CheckDoors( )              [ACKDOOR.C]

            xRaySetup                  [ACKDOOR.C]

            yRaySetup                  [ACKRTN.ASM]

            BuildSlice( )

                    xRayCast           [ACKRTN.ASM]

                    yRayCast           [ACKRTN.ASM]

                    FindDoor( )        [ACKDOOR.C]

            BuildSliceMulti( )

                    xRayCastMulti      [ACKRTN3.ASM]

                    yRayCastMulti      [ACKRTN3.ASM]

            CheckHitMap                [ACKRTN3.ASM]

            FindObject( )              [ACKOBJ.C]

                * Call routine to draw floor and ceiling

            DrawWalls   [ACKRTN1.ASM]

                * Calls low-level routines to draw wall columns
```

Figure 6.1 *Functions used in building a view.*

actually defined in ACKVIEW.C. Table 6.2 provides a description of each of these routines.

DESIGN TIP

The only actual functions that are not listed in Figure 6.1 and Table 6.2 are the routines for drawing a floor and ceiling and actual wall columns. A number of different options are provided for drawing floors and ceilings, from drawing a solid floor and ceiling to drawing a textured floor and ceiling using special light shading effects. Some of the routines available include **AckDrawFloor**, **AckDrawFloorOnly**, **AckDrawCeiling**, and so on. The actual routine that is called is determined by the setting assigned to the **SysFlags** flag in the **ACKENG** structure. We'll explore how ceilings and floors are drawn in a later chapter.

The low-level routines needed to draw actual columns of wall slices are called by the higher-level **DrawWalls** routine. We'll be saving **DrawWalls** and the routines that it calls for the next chapter when we take a closer look at how wall slices are actually converted into a screen representation.

Table 6.2 *Key Routines Used to Create a View*

Routine	Language	File	Description
AckBuildView()	C	ACKVIEW.C	The top level function that creates a view using the player's current angle and position.
BuildUpView	Asm	ACKRTN3.ASM	The main assembly-language routine used to build a view. This routine calls all of the other C functions and assembly-language routines needed to build a view slice by slice.
CheckDoors()	C	ACKDOOR.C	C function that checks the active doors used in a view to see their state.
FindDoor()	C	ACKDOOR.C	Internal routine used to locate a door from its map coordinate and return its index position.
xRaySetup	Asm	ACKRTN.ASM	Assembly routine that sets up a ray for casting in the x plane.
yRaySetup	Asm	ACKRTN.ASM	Assembly routine that sets up a ray for casting in the y plane.
BuildSlice()	C	ACKVIEW.C	Builds up a slice data structure for a view column.
xRayCast	Asm	ACKRTN.ASM	Performs the actual ray cast by looking for intersections with walls and objects in the x plane.
yRayCast	Asm	ACKRTN.ASM	Performs the actual ray cast by looking for intersections with walls and objects in the y plane.
BuildSliceMulti()	C	ACKVIEW.C	Builds up a slice data structure for multi-height walls.
xRayCastMulti	Asm	ACKRTN3.ASM	Similar to xRayCast except this routine casts for multi-height walls in the x plane.
yRayCastMulti	Asm	ACKRTN3.ASM	Similar to yRayCast except this routine casts for multi-height walls in the y plane.
CheckHitMap	Asm	ACKRTN3.ASM	Checks to see if a movable object is in view.
FindObject()	C	ACKOBJ.C	Checks the list of objects found during the ray cast and places the object slices into the wall slices
DrawWalls	Asm	ACKRTN1.ASM	The main routine for drawing all the wall and object slices. This routine loops through the SLICE structures for the number of columns in the actual display window. To actually draw wall column slices, DrawWalls calls other low-level routines.

Coding AckBuildView()

It's now time to create the code for **AckBuildView()**. Notice how quickly this function turns over control to the fast assembly-language routine **BuildUpView**:

```
void AckBuildView(void)
{
// Set up global variables to be used with assembly language routines
  xPglobal    = aeGlobal->xPlayer;        // The player's x coordinate
  // Upper-left corner (x) of the grid square the player is in
  xBegGlobal   = xPglobal & GRID_MASK;
  // Convert x coordinate to fixed point
  xPglobalHI  = ((long)xPglobal << FP_SHIFT);
  yPglobal    = aeGlobal->yPlayer;        // The player's y coordinate
  yBegGlobal   = yPglobal & GRID_MASK;   // Upper-left corner (y) of grid square
  // Convert y coordinate to fixed point
  yPglobalHI  = ((long)yPglobal << FP_SHIFT);
  PlayerAngle = aeGlobal->PlayerAngle;  // The player's angle
  SysFlags    = aeGlobal->SysFlags;      // Ceiling and floor attributes;

  BuildUpView();  // Assembly routine defined in ACKRTN3.ASM. This routine
                  // kicks off the ray casting process.
}
```

When **AckBuildView()** is called from your application, the player's current viewing angle and position in the map is used to build up a scene. This function uses the key data stored in an **ACKENG** structure, such as the player's current angle, x,y coordinates, size of the viewport, system settings, and so on. In this case, **AckBuildView()** assumes that the global variable named **aeGlobal** references the **ACKENG** structure used by the application. (I'll show you how this global variable is set up shortly.) When you examine the assembly-language routines that perform the ray-casting operations, you'll see that global variables such as **xPglobal** and **yPglobal** are used. **xPglobal** and **yPglobal** store the player's current (x,y) position in the map. **xBegGlobal** and **yBegGlobal** store the upper-left coordinate of the grid square in which the player is located. For example, if the player is at position (100,100) in the map, the upper-left grid square coordinate would be (64,64). This position is needed so that the low-level, ray-casting routines can quickly determine where to start casting rays. Notice that these coordinates are also stored with fixed point conversion in the global variables **xPglobalHI** and **yPglobalHI**. Finally, the **SysFlags** variable stores a code to indicate the display attributes for building a scene such as "use a solid floor," "use a solid (or textured) ceiling," and so on.

DESIGN TIP

Keep in mind that **AckBuildView()** and the other C and assembly routines that are called from this function just render the current scene into an off-screen buffer based on the player's POV coordinates and angle. This function does not display the scene once the scene is rendered. This method allows your application to overlay graphics into the buffer before the view is actually displayed in either DOS or Windows. In Chapter 7 I'll show you how views are displayed with DOS, and in Chapter 13 we'll explore how scenes are displayed with Windows and WinG. The more you use the *ACK-3D* engine, the more clever ways you'll find to overlay graphics created by your application programs with the views generated by **AckBuildView()**.

Think Global, Act Local

Before we take the next step and drop down to the assembly-language level, we need to explore the C assembly language interface a little more. **AckBuildView()** sets up a few of the global variables needed for the assembly routines; however, we need to transfer more data than just the player's position and angle. To take care of all of the data transfer work, we'll use the **AckRegisterStructure()** function defined in ACKVIEW.C. This function must first be called by your application before calling **AckBuildView()** to create a new view. Once you initialize the global variables by calling **AckRegisterStructure()**, you can continue to call **AckBuildView()** to update scenes if your player is simply just moving around. If a major event occurs and you want to change one or more features in your scene, such as the light shading, the color of the floor, or the color of the ceiling, you'll need to call **AckRegisterStructure()** again before using **AckBuildView()**.

DESIGN TIP

The **ACKENG** interface structure is created and managed by your application and there can be more than one of them for different views. Each time a new view needs to be processed, the **AckRegisterStructure()** function *must* be called before calling the drawing routines.

The header for the **AckRegisterStructure()** function is defined as

```
void AckRegisterStructure(ACKENG *ae)
```

where the parameter *ae references the particular **ACKENG** structure used in your application. The first task that this function performs is setting the global variable **aeGlobal** to reference the structure:

```
aeGlobal  = ae;
```

Then, it's time to move all of the critical data to global variables:

```
AckSetupWindow(ae);             // Assign window variables to ACKENG structure
xGridGlobal = ae->xGrid;        // Map for x walls
yGridGlobal = ae->yGrid;        // Map for y walls
mxGridGlobal = ae->mxGrid;      // Wall data for multi-height walls
myGridGlobal = ae->myGrid;
WallbMaps = ae->bMaps;          // Wall bitmap data
gWinStartX  = ae->WinStartX;    // Coordinates of viewport; upper-left
gWinStartY  = ae->WinStartY;
gWinEndX   = ae->WinEndX;       // Lower-right
gWinEndY   = ae->WinEndY;
gWinHeight  = ae->WinHeight;    // Height of viewport
gWinWidth = ae->WinWidth;       // Width of viewport
gWinHalfHeight = (gWinEndY - (gWinHeight >> 1)) + 1;
gCenterRow  = ae->CenterRow;    // Center of viewport
gCenterOff  = ae->CenterOffset;
gScrnBuffer = ae->ScreenBuffer;    // Screen buffer access
gScrnBufferCenter = gScrnBuffer + gCenterOff;
gBkgdBuffer = ae->BkgdBuffer;      // Buffer for ceiling and floors
gPalTable = ae->PalTable;          // Palette of colors used
gDoor   = &ae->Door[0];            // List of moving doors
gTopColor = ae->TopColor;          // Base color of ceiling
gBottomColor = ae->BottomColor;    // Base color of floor
LightFlag = ae->LightFlag;      // Light shading on or off indicator
SysFlags   = ae->SysFlags;      // Scene display attributes (floors and ceilings)
```

You might be wondering, "Why the heck are we using so many global variables? Is this the best programming style?" The problem is that it takes a lot of information to build up a scene, and we need an efficient way to communicate with the fast assembly-language routines. By first transferring the critical data to global variables, we free up the assembly-language drawing routines so that they can perform their calculations as quickly as possible. So why not just let the application access the global variables and update them as needed? This method would work but we would not be able to support multiple views at the same time. The extra call for assigning global variables from an interface structure enhances the general nature of the engine. It provides a means of expanding the functionality of the engine while still keeping the speed at acceptable levels.

The only tricky thing about these global variables is the manner in which the viewport and screen buffer are set up. Figure 6.2 shows the layout of a viewport and buffer with labels for the key global variables that are used to access the buffer.

The first set of global variables initialized, **AckRegisterStructure()** then needs to perform a few other setup tasks including: determining how floors and ceilings should be drawn, setting a flag to process multi-height walls (if any are used), and initializing a variable to access the top of the viewport window. Let's look at each of these initialization tasks in detail.

Setting Flags to Draw Floors and Ceilings

When it comes to drawing the floors and ceilings for a view, *ACK-3D* gives you the choice of one of these four options:

- Use the same bitmap for a textured floor and ceiling.
- Use a solid color ceiling and a textured floor.
- Use a solid color floor and solid color ceiling.
- Use a solid color floor and a textured ceiling.

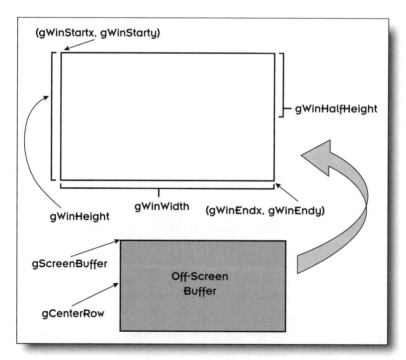

Figure 6.2　*Setting up a viewport and screen buffer.*

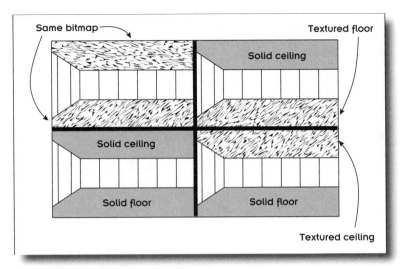

Figure 6.3 *Variations for drawing floors and ceilings in a scene.*

These variations are illustrated in Figure 6.3. In addition to selecting the floor and ceiling type, you can control how these items are displayed in your scenes by using light shading. With all of these options to support, **AckRegisterStructure()** must do some internal detective work. The **SysFlags** component in the **ACKENG** structure keeps track of the type of floor and ceilings that are used, and **LightFlag** keeps track of the current light shading setting (on or off). If you look closely at the code in **AckRegisterStructure()**, you'll see that most of it involves checking these variables and setting three global variables: **WallRtn**, **WallMaskRtn**, and **FloorCeilRtn**. As you might have guessed by now, these three variables are used in the assembly code to determine what actual routine should be called for drawing walls, ceilings, and floors. (When it comes to walls, only two choices are available: draw walls with light shading or draw walls without shading.) Don't hesitate to experiment and add your own new routines; that's what this is all about, learning how the engine works and molding it into what you want it to do. The low-level wall routines are called by the **DrawWalls** routine, which we'll explore in Chapter 7.

The options that are available for drawing floors and ceilings are listed in Table 6.3. This table also shows the assembly-language routine that is used to draw a particular floor/ceiling combination with and without light shading. The name of the routine is assigned to the **FloorCeilRtn** global variable in **AckRegisterStructure()**. As an example, here's the code that determines the setting for drawing floors and ceilings without light shading:

Table 6.3 *Setting FloorCeilRtn for Drawing Floors and Ceilings*

Option	No Light Shading	Light Shading
1	AckDrawOneFloor or AckDrawFloorHz	AckDrawFloor
2	DrawSolidCeilAndFloorNS	DrawSolidCeilAndFloor
3	DrawSolidCeilSolidFloorNS	DrawSolidCeilSolidFloor
4	DrawSolidFloorAndCeil	--

```
mode = 0;        // Draw both textured floor and ceiling
if (SysFlags & SYS_SOLID_CEIL)       // Solid ceiling is selected
  {
  mode = 1;                          // Draw floor only (ceiling will be solid)
  if (SysFlags & SYS_SOLID_FLOOR)    // Solid floor is selected
  mode = 2;                          // Draw solid floor and ceiling
  }

if (SysFlags & SYS_SOLID_FLOOR)      // Solid floor is selected
  {
  if (!mode)
    mode = 3;                        // Draw Ceiling only (floor will be solid)
  }

if (!LightFlag)                      // No light shading used
  {
  WallRtn = ShowColNS;               // Assembly routines for drawing walls
  WallMaskRtn = ShowColMaskNS;
  switch (mode)                      // Check floor and ceiling type
  {
  case 0:                            // Draw both solid floor and ceiling
    if (ae->SysFlags & SYS_SINGLE_BMP)
      FloorCeilRtn = AckDrawOneFloor; // Use the same bitmap for each
    else
      FloorCeilRtn = AckDrawFloorHz;
    break;
  case 1:                            // Draw solid ceiling and textured floor
    FloorCeilRtn = DrawSolidCeilAndFloorNS;
    break;
  case 2:                            // Draw both solid floor and solid ceiling
    FloorCeilRtn = DrawSolidCeilSolidFloor;
    break;
  case 3:                            // Draw solid floor and textured ceiling
    FloorCeilRtn = DrawSolidFloorAndCeilNS;
    break;
  default:
    break;
  }
}
```

The first part of the code contains **if** statements that check the status of the
SysFlags variable. Here we are looking for one of four conditions:

- Draw a scene with textured floor and ceiling (mode = 0).
- Draw a scene with solid ceiling and textured floor (mode = 1).
- Draw a scene with solid floor and solid ceiling (mode = 2).
- Draw a scene with solid floor and textured ceiling (mode = 3).

Once the **mode** variable has been set, a **switch** statement is used to assign
something to **FloorCeilRtn**, in this case, a pointer to a particular assembly-language routine for drawing a floor and ceiling. Notice also that the two variables
WallRtn and **WallMaskRtn** are assigned the names of the routines **ShowColNS**
and **ShowColMaskNs**, for drawing wall segments without light shading.

Finishing the Initialization

After **AckRegisterStructure()** finishes initializing the pointer variables to access the floor and wall routines, it needs to make a few adjustments to the
buffer where views are stored:

```
gWinStartOffset = ae->WinStartOffset;      // Reference start of buffer
gBottomOff = (gWinEndY * 320);             // Reference last location of buffer
gWinFullWidth = 0;                   // Set flag to indicate screen is not full width
if (gWinStartX == 0 && gWinEndX == 319)    // Viewport is full width (320)
  {
  gWinFullWidth = 1;                       // Indicates viewport is full width
  // Number of double words to access buffer
  gWinDWORDS = (gWinEndY - gWinStartY) * 80;
  }
```

First, we set a global variable (**gWinStartOffset**) to reference the starting
position of the viewport buffer. This value is actually calculated when the
ACK-3D engine is initialized by calling **AckInitialize()**. The other variable we
need is **gBottomOff**, which serves as a reference to the last location in the
viewport buffer. We calculate this reference by multiplying the position of the
last row by the number of possible pixels in the row. This calculation gives us
an offset that corresponds with the position of the lower-right corner of the
viewport where a pixel can be displayed.

The variable **gWinFullWidth** is used as a flag in the **AckDisplayScreen()**
function to determine if a fast block copy can be performed or if a slower
loop is needed to copy the scene from the buffer to the actual video screen.
We do the checking here to avoid doing it every time the screen is repainted.
If we find that the width of the view is the full width of the screen (320 pixels

in Mode 13h), we set the **gWinFullWidth** flag and calculate how many **DWORDS** (64-bit double words) are needed to actually copy the buffer, based on the height of the view. Then, **AckDisplayScreen()** simply checks this variable and jumps to the appropriate routine for copying the buffer to the screen. You'll see how this works in more detail in Chapter 7.

The final initialization task that **AckRegisterStructure()** needs to perform is a check to see if multi-height walls are used. The code checks the **xGridGlobal[ ]** and **yGridGlobal[ ]** arrays to see if any of the wall locations are set to **WALL_TYPE_MULTI**. If so, the global flag **gMultiWalls** is set to 1. This flag is later checked by the **BuildUpView** assembly routine to determine if the C function **BuildSliceMulti()** should be called to create the wall slices for multi-height walls.

```
gMultiWalls = 0;
for (i = 0; i < GRID_MAX; i++)
  {                        // Check both x and y walls
  if ((xGridGlobal[i] & WALL_TYPE_MULTI) || (yGridGlobal[i] & WALL_TYPE_MULTI))
    {
    gMultiWalls = 1;  // Indicates multi-height walls are used
    break;
    }
  }
}
```

On Our Way to Creating Slices with BuildUpView

We delayed long enough; it's now time to break out the assembly code. Our first stop is the **BuildUpView** routine defined in ACKRTN3.ASM. If you recall from our earlier discussion, this routine takes over the ray-casting process of building up each slice for an entire view. Essentially, its job is to test for certain conditions, such as the status of doors used or whether objects are found in the view. Then, it initializes registers and calls specific functions to perform the actual ray casting. The actual steps that this routine performs are as follows:

1. Check the status and update the data for the doors used in the view.
2. Clear the hit map that indicates where movable objects are located.
3. Determine the number of movable objects present and make a copy of the list of objects.
4. Check the right-most viewport x coordinate and adjust if not equal to 320.
5. Check the player's angle and adjust if necessary.
6. Sets up rays for casting in x and y planes.
7. Build each slice structure for each column of the view. This step is per-

formed by using a loop and calling the C function **BuildSlice()**. Multi-height walls are also built by calling **BuildSliceMulti()**.

8. Check to see what movable objects are present and update the slice structures.

9. Build the floor and ceiling.

10. Draw the walls.

You're probably anxious to see what some of the assembly code looks like so let's jump right in and then we'll discuss it. (If you haven't done any assembly-language programming in a while, don't panic yet. I'll walk you through the basics as we go.) Here's the complete code for **BuildUpView**:

```
ACKPROC BuildUpView
  push  ebp ; Save registers used by this routine
  push  esi
  push  edi
  push  ebx
  push  ecx
  push  edx

  ACKCALL CheckDoors       ; Determine the state of the doors used in the view

  mov   edi,offset _HitMap   ; Access the hit map
  mov   ecx,1024             ; 1/4 size of the hit map (double words)
  xor   eax,eax             ; Clear each location
  rep   stosd               ; Clear out entire hit map

; Check to see if movable objects are found in the view. If so, access the
; object list and store the objects.
  mov   [word ptr _MaxDistance],0
  movzx ecx,[word ptr _MoveObjectCount] ; Get number of movable objects
  mov   [_FoundObjectCount],cx          ; Store number of objects found in view
  jcxz  short buv010                    ; No objects are used, jump ahead
  mov   edi,offset _ObjectsSeen         ; Reference global object list
  mov   esi,offset _MoveObjectList      ; List of movable objects
  mov   ebx,ecx                         ; Number of movable objects
  sar   ecx,2                           ; Divide by 2
  rep   movsd
  mov   ecx,ebx                         ; Number of movable objects
  and   ecx,3
  rep   movsb                           ; Finish copying _ObjectSeen to
                                        ; _MoveObjectList
buv010:
  movzx esi,[_gWinEndX]     ; Get right side of viewport
  cmp   si,320             ; Is right coordinate = 320?
  jae   short buv020
  inc   esi                ; Adjust right viewport if not 320
```

```
buv020:
   movzx eax,[_PlayerAngle]     ; Get current player's angle
   sub   eax,INT_ANGLE_32       ; Check with 32 degree point
   jnc   short buv030           ; Skip if in range
   add   eax,INT_ANGLE_360      ; Add 360 degrees to angle

buv030:
   movzx ebx,[_gWinStartX]      ; Get left side of viewport
   mov   [_ViewColumn],bx       ; Save location in _ViewColumn
   add   eax,ebx                ; Add angle to left side
   cmp   eax,INT_ANGLE_360      ; Are we out of range?
   jl    short buv040           ; We're ok!
   sub   eax,INT_ANGLE_360      ; Reduce angle by 360 degrees

buv040:
   mov   [_ViewAngle],ax        ; Store updated angle

; The start of the main loop that builds individual slices for the view.
; This loop continues until the entire view has been built. Each time through
; the loop, the player's viewing angle is increased. This continues until a full
; 64 degree range is cast (assuming a full-width screen is used).
buv050:
   movzx ebx,[_ViewColumn]                  ; Get left column position
   mov   [dword ptr _WallDistTable+ebx*4],4096 ; Max distance to walls
   mov   eax,offset _Slice                  ; Access base address of Slice structure
   imul  ebx,saSize                         ; Calculate offset into actual slice
   add   eax,ebx                            ; Add offset to base address
   mov   [_sPtr],eax                        ; Set up pointer to actual column slice
   movzx edi,[_ViewAngle]                   ; Use current viewing angle
   ACKCALL xRaySetup                        ; Set up x ray to start casting

buv060:
   ACKCALL yRaySetup                        ; Set up y ray to start casting

buv070:
   mov   [word ptr _LastWallHeight],0  ; For checking multi-height walls
   ACKCALL BuildSlice                  ; Build the current slice
   cmp   [word ptr _gMultiWalls],0     ; Are multi-height walls used?
   jz    short buv080                  ; Nope, no need to check

   cmp   [word ptr _LastWallHeight],200; No need to check if > 200
   jg    short buv080

   mov   eax,[_sPtr]                   ; Get base address of column slice
   cmp   [dword ptr eax+saNext],0      ; Check for any more walls
   je    short buv080
   cmp   [word ptr eax+saDist],96      ; Distance from POV to slice is
   jle   short buv080                  ; less than or equal to 96

   ACKCALL BuildSliceMulti             ; Build the current slice for
                                       ; a multi-height wall
buv080:
   movzx eax,[_ViewColumn]                 ; Get current column
   inc   eax                               ; Advance to the next column
   inc   edi                               ; Increment the casting angle
```

```
        cmp     [word ptr _Resolution],RES_LOW  ; Check for screen resolution
        jne     short buv090
        inc     edi                     ; Increment angle and position
        inc     eax                     ; for higher resolution casting

buv090:
        cmp     edi,INT_ANGLE_360       ; Did we go past 360 degrees?
        jl      short buv100            ; We're ok!
        sub     edi,INT_ANGLE_360       ; Adjust angle for building next slice

buv100:
        mov     [_ViewAngle],di         ; Save current viewing angle
        mov     [_ViewColumn],ax        ; Save column position
        cmp     eax,esi                 ; Are we done yet?
        jl      buv050                  ; Nope; go build next slice

buv_exit:
        ACKCALL CheckHitMap
        ACKCALL FindObject                      ; Update slice structures with objects found
        call    [dword ptr _FloorCeilRtn] ; Build the floor and ceiling
        ACKCALL DrawWalls                       ; Build the walls

        pop     edx                             ; Restore the registers used
        pop     ecx
        pop     ebx
        pop     edi
        pop     esi
        pop     ebp
        ret
        endp
        end
```

First, we save the registers that we are using. Then, we call the **CheckDoors()** function to update the status of doors used in the scene. Notice how we call other routines:

```
ACKCALL CheckDoors
```

ACKCALL is a simple macro defined in the include file ACKRTN.INC for setting up our calls. You'll see it used throughout the assembly routines. The macro helps us port the assembly code so that it can be linked in by different C compilers. Some compilers require an underscore before the routine name, some require it after, some don't use it at all!

The next section of the code is needed to process movable objects. The code uses a special temporary buffer called **HitMap[ ]** to keep track of where movable objects are located. This data structure is defined in the header file ACKDATA.H as:

```
UCHAR HitMap[4096];
```

The array has 4,096 locations, where each location corresponds with one of the grid squares in the map. The technique is to store a value in each **HitMap[ ]** array location to indicate if a movable object is currently in a given grid map position. Later, you'll see how this array is used to locate objects by calling the **CheckHitMap** routine before any wall slices are drawn. For now, the code must clear out this array to initialize it. Notice that we can quickly clear it by using the **rep stosd** instruction.

The next order of business involves moving the global list of objects used in an application (**ObjectsSeen**) to an array buffer called **MoveObjectList**. These simple data structures are actually defined in ACKDATA.H as:

```
UCHAR ObjectsSeen[MAX_OBJECTS + 1];
UCHAR MoveObjectList[MAX_OBJECTS + 1];
```

This **MoveObjectList** array is used later to determine which movable objects are actually present in the view that we are currently building. If a particular object is present, we'll want to make sure that it gets added to the scene when the wall slices are built. Because this takes extra processing time, the fewer movable objects you use, the faster your views will be drawn.

The next few sections of code (**buv010** through **buv030**) perform the work of adjusting the viewport size and adjusting the player's angle to make sure that it is in range. Recall that the ray-casting process performs a sweep of 64 degrees. Before starting, we need to subtract 32 degrees from the player's angle to get the starting angle for the sweep. If the starting angle turns out to be a negative value, the value that represents the table look-up for 360 degrees is added to the starting angle to make it a positive number.

Once the starting angle has been adjusted, we're ready to start the main loop for building a view. The loop starts at label **buv050** and ends right before **buv_exit**. The logic involved here is quite simple. We take the current column for which we want to build a slice, set up variables for casting rays in the x and y planes for the column slice, and then call the C routines **BuildSlice()** and **BuildSliceMulti()** to build up the slice for standard walls and multi-height walls. After each slice is constructed, the angle and column is incremented and the loop starts again to build the next slice.

The first part of the loop reveals how the global **Slice** array is accessed:

```
mov    eax,offset _Slice    ; Access base address of Slice structure
imul   ebx,saSize           ; Calculate offset into actual slice
add    eax,ebx              ; Add offset to base address
mov    [_sPtr],eax          ; Set up pointer to actual column slice
```

The first instruction grabs the base address of the array. The next instruction multiplies the size of an individual slice structure with the current column for which we want to build a slice. (Previously, **_ViewColumn** was moved into ebx.) This process gives us an index value or offset into the memory location where the slice is stored. The offset is added to the base address of the **Slice** array. If we were coding this in C, the equivalent instruction would be something like this:

```
sPtr = Slice[ViewColumn]
```

Once **sPtr** has been set to reference the slice that represents the current view column, the other casting routines can easily do their job and build up the slice structure. In fact, you'll see this global pointer variable used quite a bit in the **BuildSlice()** function.

The remaining code in **BuildUpView** follows the steps I outlined above. Most of the tasks, such as casting rays, building slices, and checking for objects, are completed by calling other routines. As we continue in this chapter, I'll take you inside these other routines. Right now, let's see how rays are set up for casting.

Setting Up Those Rays

After the **BuildUpView** routine we just explored performs its initialization steps, it starts its loop to build up each slice. Within the loop, the **xRaySetup** and **yRaySetup** routines are called to set up rays for x plane and y plane casting for each angle that is used. Since these routines are similar, we'll only need to look at one of them to see what's involved in setting up a ray for casting. The code is actually implemented in assembly language, but let's first look at a version coded as a C function to make it easier to follow along:

```
void xRaySetup(void)
{
  // Use a look-up table to find y increment value
  // Precalculated value of BITMAP_WIDTH * Tan(angle)
  x_yNext = yNextTable[ViewAngle];
  if (ViewAngle > INT_ANGLE_270 || ViewAngle < INT_ANGLE_90)
    {
    x_xPos  = xBegGlobal + BITMAP_WIDTH; // Looking to the right
    x_xNext = BITMAP_WIDTH;              // Positive direction
    }
  else
    {
    x_xPos  = xBegGlobal;     // Looking to the left
    x_xNext = -BITMAP_WIDTH; // Negative direction
```

```
      x_yNext = -x_yNext;
    }
  // Calculate the y coordinate for the current grid intersection point
    x_yPos = (((long)x_xPos - (long)xPglobal) * LongTanTable[ViewAngle]) +
    yPglobalHI;
}
```

Now, here's the assembly-code version for **xRaySetup**:

```
ACKPROC xRaySetup
  push  esi                 ; Save registers used
  push  ebx
  push  ecx
  push  edx
  mov   dx,[_ViewAngle]     ; Get the current angle for casting
  movzx esi,dx              ; Use this angle for table look-up
  shl   esi,2               ; Hold onto ViewAngle * 4 for table access
  mov   ebx,[_yNextTable]   ; Base address of list of y increment coordinates
  mov   eax,[esi+ebx]       ; Use angle as index into table
  mov   [dword ptr _x_yNext],eax  ; Store y increment value
  cmp   dx,INT_ANGLE_270            ; Is angle > 270 degrees?
  jg      short inbetween
  cmp   dx,INT_ANGLE_90             ; Is angle >= 90 degrees?
  jge   short not_inbetween
; Set up the ray for casting to the right (270 to 90 degrees)
inbetween:
  mov   ecx,[_xBegGlobal]             ; Get left corner of grid square
  add   ecx,64                        ; Calculate right corner
  mov   [dword ptr _x_xPos],ecx       ; Store starting x position
  mov   [dword ptr _x_xNext],large 64 ; Store next x grid increment
  jmp   short xr_cont                 ; to the right (+64)
; Set up the ray for casting to the left (90 to 270 degrees)
not_inbetween:
  movzx ecx,[word ptr _xBegGlobal]  ; Get left corner of grid square
  mov   [_x_xPos],ecx                 ; Store starting x position
  mov   [dword ptr _x_xNext],large -64  ; Store next x grid increment
                                      ; to the left (-64)
  neg   [dword ptr _x_yNext]          ; Negate the second y intersection coordinate
xr_cont:
  movzx eax,[word ptr _xPglobal]      ; Get player's x coordinate
  sub   ecx,eax                       ; x Distance from player's position
                                      ; to edge of grid
  mov   ebx,[dword ptr _LongTanTable] ; Get address of tangent table
  imul  ecx,[dword ptr esi+ebx]       ; Tangent(angle) * Distance
  add   ecx,[dword ptr _yPglobalHI]
  mov   [dword ptr _x_yPos],ecx       ; Store first y coordinate where
                                      ; we hit an x boundary
  pop   edx                           ; Restore registers
  pop   ecx
  pop   ebx
  pop   esi
  ret
  endp
```

As you might have guessed, this routine performs some very important initialization tasks to start the ray-casting process. In this case, we are initializing global variables used to cast rays for the x plane. From two steps back, we can say that this routine determines the x direction that the player is moving in (right or left) and calculates the first few grid border intersection points. But what's more important to know is why we need the information that is being calculated by this initialization routine.

When we explored the optimized ray-casting techniques in Chapter 2, we determined that we don't have to check every point along a casted ray to see if it intersects with a wall or object; we only need to check the grid map borders. As shown in Figure 6.4, if a player were starting out at position 200,200 and we were casting a ray in the x plane at 0 degrees (directly to the right), we'd only need to check locations 256, 320, 384, and so on. (These are the grid borders where walls might appear.) The only problem is that we need to cast rays in different directions and when we do, we need to know both of the x,y coordinate points where the grid borders are located. This is where the **xRaySetup** and **yRaySetup** routines come in.

When **xRaySetup** is called, we are casting a ray and checking for intersections with a wall slice along the x plane. This routine locates the first intersection point (**x_xPos**, **x_yPos**) and the x and y increments to locate further intersection points (**x_xNext**, **x_yNext**). **yRaySetup** is the same except that it assumes we're checking wall slices in the y plane. These two routines assign values to the global variables listed in Table 6.4 so that the ray-casting process of checking intersection points can be completed. As you can see, two sets of variables are used: one for checking rays in the x plane and the other for the y plane.

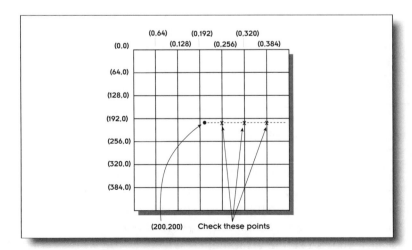

Figure 6.4   *Checking only border positions when a ray is cast.*

Table 6.4　*Coordinate Tracking Ray-Casting Variables*

Variable	Ray to Cast	Description
x_xPos	x plane	The x coordinate of the first grid border intersection point. (This is the grid in which the player starts.)
x_yPos	x plane	The y coordinate of the first grid border intersection point.
x_xNext	x plane	The x (left or right) increment needed to find the next grid intersection point as we check in the x plane. (The direction depends on the casting angle.)
x_yNext	x plane	The y increment (up or down) needed to find the next grid intersection point.
y_xPos	y plane	The x coordinate of the first grid border intersection point.
y_yPos	y plane	The y coordinate of the first grid border intersection point.
y_xNext	y plane	The x (left or right) increment needed to find the next grid intersection point as we check in the y plane. (The direction depends on the casting angle.)
y_yNext	y plane	The y increment (up or down) needed to find the next grid intersection point.

The only tricky part of the **xRaySetup** code is found in the first few instructions (or the first instruction if you are looking at the C version):

```
// C Version
x_yNext = yNextTable[ViewAngle];  // Precalc'd value of BITMAP_WIDTH * Tan(angle)

; Assembly version
mov    dx,[_ViewAngle]   ; Get the current angle for casting
movzx esi,dx             ; Use this angle for table look-up
shl    esi,2             ; Hold onto ViewAngle * 4 for table access
mov    ebx,[_yNextTable] ; Base address of list of y increment coordinates
mov    eax,[esi+ebx]     ; Use angle as index into table
mov    [dword ptr _x_yNext],eax  ; Store y increment value
```

Here we are using a look-up table (**yNextTable[ ]**) to determine a y increment value for calculating where the ray will intersect grid borders as it continues to the right or left. As shown in Figure 6.5, this table contains 1,800 entries, where each entry represents an angle increment (360 degrees / 0.5). The table contains precalculated values that represent the tan viewing angle multiplied by the width of a bitmap (64). This calculation gives us the distance to a y coordinate of a grid position as we are moving at a specified angle. You'll see how this is used in a moment.

Let's continue stepping through the assembly code for **xRaySetup** using a real example. The next major task required is to check the current casting angle to see if the ray will be cast to the left or right. If the angle is greater than 270 degrees (and less than 90 degrees), this pair of comparison/jump statements causes the code to jump to the **inbetween** section:

```
cmp     dx,INT_ANGLE_270        ; Is angle > 270 degrees?
jg      short inbetween
```

This code means that the ray will be cast to the right. If the casting angle is equal to or greater than 90 degrees (**cmp dx,INT_ANGLE_90**), the code in the **not_inbetween** section is executed and the x ray is set up for casting to the left. Let's assume our angle is 30 degrees and the player is at position 200,200. If you examine the code following the **inbetween** label, you'll see that the first thing we do is get the left x coordinate of the grid square in which the player is located (**xBegGlobal**) and add 64 to it. This step takes us to the right border of the grid square. This value is our starting x position for casting, and it is stored in the **x_xPos** variable. We store the value 64 in the x increment variable (**x_xNext**). This variable is used in the ray-casting process to determine the next grid border position as we move in the x direction. Here are the two instructions that make these assignments:

```
mov [dword ptr _x_xPos],ecx       ; Store starting x position
mov [dword ptr _x_xNext],large 64 ; Store next x grid position
```

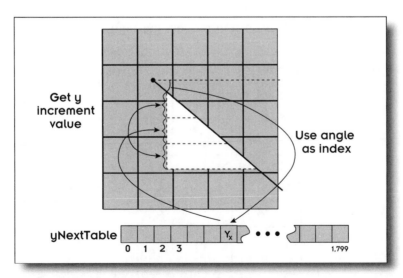

Figure 6.5 *Using the yNextTable to locate a y increment.*

We're taking advantage of a basic principle here: Once we know the starting x coordinate for a border, every other intersection point will always be 64 units to the left or right in the x direction. The y coordinate is another matter, which is why we need to use the viewing angle and calculate an increment value.

Figure 6.6 shows the path the ray is taking. Notice how the variables are labeled. What we don't know yet is the *starting* y coordinate where the ray intersects the first x grid border. The code following the **xr_cont** label performs this task. First, we use the player's actual x coordinate and calculate the distance the player is from the starting grid border:

```
movzx eax,[word ptr _xPglobal]  ; Get player's x coordinate
sub   ecx,eax                   ; x distance from player's position to edge of grid
```

Then we multiply this distance by the tangent of the angle we are casting. This gives us the y intercept as shown in Figure 6.6:

```
mov   ebx,[dword ptr _LongTanTable]  ; Get address of tangent table
imul  ecx,[dword ptr esi+ebx]        ; Tangent(angle) * Distance
```

The y coordinate of the first intersection point is then stored in the **x_yPos** global variable. Later, you'll see that each new intersection point can be calculated using a simple addition formula as shown here:

```
NewXPos = x_x_Pos + x_xNext
NewYPos = x_y_Pos + x_yNext
```

This approach makes the ray-casting process very efficient.

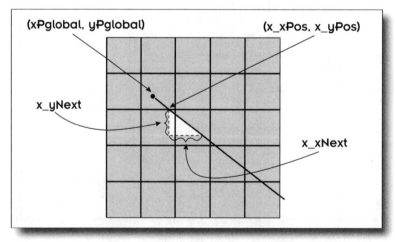

Figure 6.6 *Setting up a ray and calculating the first grid intersection points.*

The Art of Building the Slice

Now that all of the adjustments have been made and the global variables have been initialized, we're ready to build a slice. At this stage we've calculated both the starting intersection points for the x and y planes and the x and y increment values for casting. The next task is to call **BuildSlice()** to finish the work of building a slice structure for the current view column. This process extends each ray out, checking for intersection points, and returns a value to indicate what has been hit.

The first part of **BuildSlice()** is quite straightforward. First, we cast an x ray to see if an item (wall or door is found). Then, we cast a y ray. If something is encountered by casting an x or y ray, a flag (**wFound**) is set for further processing. Here's the basic code that does the checking for a ray cast in the x plane:

```
WallDistance = 3000000; // Set to a ridiculous distance
sPtr->Distance = 200;   // Initialize the distance from the POV to the slice
wFound = 0;             // Wall not found yet
sPtr->Fnc = ShowNone;   // Use the stub function for now for drawing the slice
// Call the low-level, ray-casting function and see if anything is hit
if ((BitmapNumber = xRayCast()) != 0) // Something has been hit while casting
  {                                    // in the x plane
  wFound = 1;                          // Set flag to indicate a hit
  // Use the Y intercept to determine the column of the slice
  BitmapColumn = (LastY1 >> FP_SHIFT) & (BITMAP_WIDTH-1);

  // Keep the orientation the same no matter which side we're on
  if ((short)iLastX < xPglobal)
    BitmapColumn = (BITMAP_WIDTH-1) - BitmapColumn;

  // Did we strike a door?
  if ((BitmapNumber & (DOOR_TYPE_SLIDE+DOOR_TYPE_SPLIT)))
    {
    ... <Code to check for a door>
    }

  xd = iLastX - xPglobal;         // x distance to the found slice
  mf = InvCosTable[ViewAngle];    // Get the cosine of the angle
  WallDistance = (xd * mf) >> 10; // Calculate the actual distance to the slice
  if (WallDistance > 33554432L)   // Check for out of range
    WallDistance = 1200000L;
  gPtr = xGridGlobal;             // Point to xGrid map
  mgPtr = mxGridGlobal[xMapPosn]; // Point to grid map for multi-height walls
  mPos = xMapPosn;                // Access actual map position
  }                               // End (if BitmapNumber = xRayCast() ...)

// Continue the process of casting a y ray and see if something has been hit
if ((yBitmap = yRayCast()) != 0)
  {
    <check for y intersection>
```

```
        <this code is similar to the x ray casting code>
    }

if (wFound)    //The x or y ray has hit something
    {
      <process the slice that is found>
    }
```

To cast out a ray in the x plane, **xRayCast()** is called. This is an assembly-language routine defined in ACKRTN.ASM. At this stage, all you need to know is that this routine checks to see if a ray hits an item, such as an object, wall, or door, and returns a status code. If the value returned is not equal to 0, we know the ray has hit something. (I'll present the assembly code for **xRayCast** a little later in this chapter.) Much of the code following the call to **xRayCast** is required to test if a door has been hit.

After the testing is done, we calculate the distance to the found slice. Since the x position was fixed to move 64 or -64 units, we can use it to determine the actual distance. The **InvCosTable[ ]** values are stored with a fixed point of 20 decimal places. At this time we'll knock off 14 of them, so we can later multiply with a fixed-point value of 16.

Notes on Casting y Walls

The code we just explored takes care of the operations for casting walls in the x plane. Once this work is done, we move into a second **if** block that performs the work of casting a y ray. The start of this section of code looks like this:

```
if ((yBitmap = yRayCast()) != 0)
    {
    // Use the x intercept to determine the column of the bitmap
    yBitmapColumn = (LastX1 >> FP_SHIFT) & (BITMAP_WIDTH-1);

    // Handle orientation from either side of the wall
    if ((short)iLastY > yPglobal)
      yBitmapColumn = (BITMAP_WIDTH-1) - yBitmapColumn;
    ...
```

As you can see, the algorithm used is similar to one used for casting rays in the x plane. The first step involves calling **yRayCast** to cast out the y ray. Then, we check the return code (**yBitmap**) to see if this ray has hit something. Again, we locate the grid intersection position but this time the location is a y grid border. The code continues on and checks to see if a door has been hit. If the slice found is not a door, the code drops down to this section to calculate the actual distance to the slice:

```
yd = iLastY - yPglobal; // Distance from player's position to intersection point
mf = InvSinTable[ViewAngle];  // Use look-up table
yDistance = (yd * mf) >> 8;
if (yDistance > 33554432L)    // Make sure that distance is in range
  yDistance = 1200000L;
```

If your memory serves you well, you'll notice that this code looks like the code used to calculate the distance to the slice cast in the x plane. The major difference is that we use an inverse sine lookup table to calculate the distance to the slice. The **InvSinTable** values are stored with a fixed-point representation of 20 places.

After this code has finished executing, we know that a ray has been cast in the x and y planes. The variable **Walldistance** stores the distance from the player to the slice found in the x plane (or 3,000,000 if one has not been found), and **yDistance** stores the distance from the player to the slice found in the y plane. At this point we need to check the distance to the y slice against the x slice to see which one is closer. The closer slice is the slice we'll draw at this column of the screen:

```
if (yDistance < WallDistance) // Use distance to y slice if this slice is closer
  {
  wFound = 1;                       // Indicates that a slice has been found
  WallDistance = yDistance;         // Use distance to y slice
  BitmapNumber = yBitmap;           // Transfer bitmap number
  BitmapColumn = yBitmapColumn;     // Transfer bitmap column
  gPtr = yGridGlobal;               // Store pointer to global y grid
  mPos = yMapPosn;                  // Store position of y wall in map
  mgPtr = myGridGlobal[mPos];
  }
```

If the x slice is closer, this code is skipped and the value already stored in **WallDistance** is used. If the y slice is closer, we need to transfer the data needed to process the slice into the main variables, such as **WallDistance**, **BitmapNumber**, **mPos**, and so on. These variables were previously assigned values when the x ray was cast, but since we're now using the slice found by casting the y ray, we need to change the data. These variables will be used to make calculations and fill in the slice structure. In fact, that's what we'll do next.

Back in the Fishbowl

Whenever we hit a slice, we need to check the situation and adjust our distance calculation to avoid the fishbowl effect we explored in Chapter 2. Here's the code required:

```
if (wFound) // A slice has been found
  {
  // Adjust for fishbowl effect
  UnAdjustDist = WallDistance >> 5;
  yd = ViewCosTable[ViewColumn] >> 3; // Use current column as look-up index
  WallDistance *= yd;

  // Now we strip off some more decimal points and check round-up
  xd = WallDistance >> 12;
  if (WallDistance - (xd << 12) >= 2048)
    xd++;
  // The last decimal points from the multiplication after the x and
  // y rays are stripped off and checked for round-up
  WallDistance = xd >> 5;
  if (xd - (WallDistance << 5) >= 16)
    WallDistance++;

  // This is an arbitrary minimum distance to look for
  if (WallDistance < 10)
  WallDistance = 10;

  // Don't want it to go outside our table boundaries
  if (WallDistance >= MAX_DISTANCE)
    WallDistance = MAX_DISTANCE - 1;
...
```

To avoid a fishbowl effect, we need to adjust the distance so it appears perpendicular to the center point of the display, which is relative angle 0 from the player's current angle. Our casting started at -32 degrees for the first screen column and will cycle from -32 down to 0 then back up to +32 degrees. To adjust the distance, a lookup table named **ViewCosTable[ ]** is used. This table contains pre-calculated cosine values for angles. The index into the table is the current view column for which we are building the slice.

As shown in Figure 6.7, the distance between point C and point B is not equal to the distance between C and A. Thus, we need to account for the

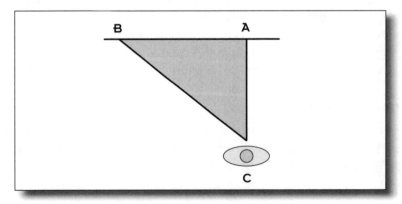

Figure 6.7 *Working with the fishbowl effect.*

current casting angle when calculating the distance from the POV to the wall. By using the cosine formula

```
cos = adj / hyp
```

we simply multiply the distance to the wall by the cosine value for the viewing angle to get the actual perpendicular distance. This approach avoids the fisheye effect seen when the cosine is not applied (try experimenting with this effect by taking out the multipication operation; the difference will be very apparent!)

Finishing Off the Slice

The last part of **BuildSlice()** involves filling in the fields for the slice structure. At this point, most of the field data has already been calculated by the different routines we've called, such as **AckRegisterStructure()**, **xRayCast**, **yRayCast**, and of course, the first part of **BuildSlice()**. The next order of business, then, is to transfer the needed data into the slice structure:

```
// Save the wall slice data to display when done with entire screen
sPtr->Distance = WallDistance;// Store the adjusted distance to the wall
sPtr->bNumber = BitmapNumber; // The bitmap number for the wall slice
sPtr->bColumn = BitmapColumn; // The screen column position to display the
bitmap
sPtr->bMap = WallbMaps;        // Pointer to the bitmap
sPtr->Active = 0;              // Indicates slice is last one
sPtr->Type = ST_WALL;          // Indicates this slice is part of a wall
sPtr->Fnc = WallRtn;           // Pointer to function to draw slice
sPtr->mPos = mPos;             // Position of the slice in the grid map
sPtr->mPtr = mgPtr;            // Grid pointer to reference multi-height wall
spNext = sPtr->Next;           // Reference wall slice behind current slice
```

The **sPtr** variable references the slice we need to build. Recall that this variable was initialized in the assembly routine **BuildUpView**. The first item stored is the distance from the player's POV to the slice. This information is accurate now because we've previously adjusted it to account for the fishbowl effect. The next three items—the bitmap number for the slice, the screen column position where the slice will be displayed, and the pointer to the bitmap—are also ready to store. We'll need this information soon to draw the actual slice.

Notice that the next field, **Active**, is set to 0 at this point. This value indicates that this is the last slice for this particular column. Recall that when we initialized the slice structure, we allocated room for up to eight levels of slices to account for multi-height walls, transparent walls, objects, and so on. What the **Active** flag tells us is that we have reached the end of the slices for this run. If we find out there is something to be displayed *behind* this slice, we set **Active** to 1 and then cast for the next obstacle in our path. The **ST_WALL** flag stored in the **Type** field indicates that the slice is part of a wall. As you'll see in a moment, this value could be changed if this slice turns out to be a transparent one. We also need to store a pointer to the function that will be used to draw the slice. Recall that in **AckRegisterStructure()** the global variable **WallRtn** was assigned a pointer to the **ShowColNS** routine if light shading was turned off and **ShowCol** if light shading was on. Next, we store the position in the grid map where the slice is located (**mPos**). We also store the grid map position for multi-height walls, in case the slice turns out to be a multi-height one. Finally, we save the next pointer in **spNext** so that we can check to see if there is another wall behind the current slice.

Before we move on and build a possible multi-height slice and then draw the slice, we need to test the slice bitmap to see if it has something behind it and whether it is above the floor level or is transparent:

```
if (((BitmapNumber & WALL_TYPE_UPPER) ||   // Wall is above the floor level
    (BitmapNumber & WALL_TYPE_TRANS)) &&    // or wall slice is transparent and it
    spNext != NULL)                         // has something behind it
    {
    BitmapColumn = gPtr[mPos];   // Get position of the multi-height wall
    gPtr[mPos]  = 0;
    sPtr->Active = 1;            // More slices to follow

    if (BitmapNumber & WALL_TYPE_TRANS) // The wall is transparent
      {
      sPtr->Type = ST_OBJECT;           // We have an object
      sPtr->Fnc = WallMaskRtn;          // Using a different drawing routine
      }
```

If one of these conditions is met, we need to reset the **Active** field to indicate that the slice has more to display behind it. If the slice turns out to be transparent, its **Type** field is changed to **ST_OBJECT**. Also notice that a different routine, **WallMaskRtn**, will then be used to draw the slice.

Since we've entered the **if** statement, we know that the current slice has a slice behind it. We're not done until we go to that slice and build it up. The slices will link to each other using the **Next** and **Prev** fields. Here's the code that comes next to get this job done:

```
sPtr     = spNext;       // Point to slice behind
spNext->Active  = 0;     // Initialize the slice behind before building it
spNext->bNumber = 0;

BuildSlice();            // Call BuildSlice() again to build the slice behind
gPtr[mPos] = BitmapColumn;
if (!sPtr->bNumber)
  {
```

```
spNext = sPtr->Prev;  // Link up slices
if (spNext != NULL)
spNext->Active = 0;
}
```

Figure 6.8 shows how the pointers are set. In this case, we have a series of two slices.

By keeping track of the minimum distance to each wall slice found, we can shorten the amount of floor and ceiling we have to draw later. Using the **UnAdjustDist** below, we maintain a table of distances for each column of the view, which is later used in the floor and ceiling draw routines:

```
else
  {
  if (UnAdjustDist < WallDistTable[ViewColumn])
    WallDistTable[ViewColumn] = UnAdjustDist;
  }
```

Casting the Ray—Getting Under the Hood

Before we finish building the basic slice structure and begin discussing the **BuildSliceMulti()** function for processing multi-height walls, we should examine the low-level, ray-casting process. To perform the casting, two assembly routines are required: **xRayCast** and **yRaycast**. Recall that both of them are called from **BuildSlice()**. The basic algorithm used loops and checks each grid intersection point along the x or y ray until something has been hit or we extend past the map grid. If we only needed to look for walls, the testing would be easy to perform and would require very little code. Unfortunately, we need to check for five types of items:

- walls
- visible doors
- invisible doors

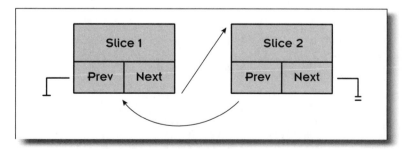

Figure 6.8 *Building slices that have slices behind them.*

- visible secret doors
- invisible secret doors

These different items are easy to spot because the grid map array stores a bitmap value that indicates the type of element that is located in the map. As you explore the code in the two ray-casting routines, you'll see how the different checks are performed. For now, let's examine the complete assembly routine for **xRayCast** and see how its basic logic is set up:

```
ACKPROC xRayCast
  push  esi     ; Save registers used
  push  edi
  push  ebx
  push  ecx
  push  edx
  mov   esi,[_x_xPos]   ; Get x,y starting position
  mov   edi,[_x_yPos]   ; (1st grid border intersection point)
  xor   ecx,ecx         ; Initialize our bitmap variable

looptop:                ; Start the ray casting loop
  mov   edx,esi         ; Get x starting position
  cmp   edx,large 0     ; If it's < 0 we're done!
  jl    short getout
  cmp   edx,large 4096      ; If it's > 4,096 we're done!
  jge   short getout
  mov   eax,edi             ; Get y starting position
  cmp   eax,large 0         ; If it's < 0 we're done!
  jl    short getout
  cmp   eax,large 010000000h  ; If it's out of range we're done!
  jl    short inbounds
getout:
  jmp   loopdone

inbounds:               ; We're in-range; continue casting
  sar   eax,16          ; Scale y starting position
  and   eax,-64
  sar   edx,6           ; Scale x starting position
  add   eax,edx         ; Calculate grid map position
  cmp   eax,4095        ; Test map position to see if it's in range
  ja    getout
  mov   [byte ptr _HitMap+eax],1  ; Record the square we cast through
  mov   ebx,[_xGridGlobal]        ; Get pointer to x wall map
  mov   cx,[ebx+eax*2]            ; Get the bitmap number there
  jcxz  next_square              ; Nothing found in square—move ahead

wall_here:                       ; We found something!
  mov   [word ptr COLOR],cx      ; Save the bitmap number
  mov   [_xMapPosn],eax          ; Save the map position
  mov   [dword ptr _iLastX],esi  ; Save the x,y position of the grid
  mov   [dword ptr _LastY1],edi  ; border where the hit was found
  test  cx,DOOR_WALL             ; Did we find a door?
  jz    short not_door           ; No match—go process a wall slice
```

```
; At this point we've found a door, so we need to process it
    mov     edx,edi                     ; Get y position
    sar     edx,16                      ; Scale position
    and     edx,large 00000FFC0h
    mov     [dword ptr YD],edx          ; YD = (yPos >> FP_SHIFT) & 0xFFC0;
                                        ; YD is the left side of door (grid corner)
    add     edx,large 64
    mov     [dword ptr XD],edx          ; XD = YD + GRID_SIZE;
                                        ; XD is the right side of door (grid corner)
    mov     eax,[dword ptr _x_yNext]    ; Get y increment
    sar     eax,1                       ; Use half of increment
    add     eax,edi                     ; Add 1/2 y increment to y position
                                        ; We need to calculate distance to door
    mov     [YTEMP],eax                 ; Store new y location
    sar     eax,16                      ; We now have actual distance to door
    cmp     eax,[dword ptr YD]          ; Is distance < YD?
    jl      short door_not_visible      ; Process invisible door
    cmp     eax,[dword ptr XD]          ; Is distance > XD?
    jle     short door_visible          ; Process visible door

door_not_visible:                       ; Door is invisible so skip to next square
    add     esi,[dword ptr _x_xNext]    ; Add x,y increment to current grid border
    add     edi,[dword ptr _x_yNext]    ; position
    jmp     looptop                     ; Cast again to check next position

door_visible:                           ; Process a visible door
    mov     eax,[dword ptr YTEMP]       ; Get y position of door
    mov     [dword ptr _LastY1],eax     ; LastY1 = yTemp;
    mov     eax,[dword ptr _x_xNext]    ; Adjust x,y position so that door
    sar     eax,1                       ; is halfway in square
    add     [dword ptr _iLastX],eax     ; iLastX += xNext >> 1;

not_door:                               ; We don't think we have a door
    test    cx,DOOR_TYPE_SECRET         ; Check bitmap type
    jz      short br_no_secret          ; Not a secret door
    cmp     [word ptr _xSecretColumn],0
    jne     short secret_door           ; We've found a secret door

br_no_secret:
    jmp     short give_color            ; Move on and get the wall's color

secret_door:                            ; Process a secret door
    movzx eax,[word ptr _xSecretColumn] ; Get secret column location
    movzx ebx,[word ptr _ViewAngle]     ; Get ViewAngle to door
    shl     ebx,2
    add     ebx,[dword ptr _LongTanTable] ; Add in address of tan table
    imul    eax,[dword ptr ebx]         ; Look up tangent of angle
    mov     [dword ptr SY],eax          ; SY = xSecretColumn * tan(ViewAngle)
    mov     ebx,edi                     ; Get x_yPos
    add     eax,ebx                     ; SY + x_yPos
    mov     [dword ptr YTEMP],eax       ; Store distance to door
    sar     eax,16                      ; eax = (x_yPos + SY) >> FP_SHIFT
                                        ; This gives us actual distance to door
    sar     ebx,16                      ; Now calculate the left side
    and     ebx,large 00000FFC0h
```

```
        mov    [dword ptr YD],ebx          ; YD = x_yPos >> FP_SHIFT & GRID_MASK
        mov    ecx,ebx                      ; Calculate the right side (XD)
        add    ecx,large 64                 ; XD = YD = BITMAP_WIDTH
        cmp    eax,ebx                       ; Is distance < YD?
        jl     short next_square
        cmp    eax,ecx                       ; Is distance <= XD?
        jle    short secret_is_visible

secret_not_visible:                          ; Process invisible secret door
        jmp    short next_square

secret_is_visible:                           ; Process visible secret door
        mov    eax,[dword ptr YTEMP]
        mov    [dword ptr _LastY1],eax
        mov    eax,[dword ptr _xSecretColumn]
        add    [dword ptr _iLastX],eax
        jmp    short give_color

next_square:                                 ; Didn't find anything—go to next square
        add    esi,[dword ptr _x_xNext]      ; Add x,y increment to current grid border
        add    edi,[dword ptr _x_yNext]      ; position
        jmp    looptop                       ; Start over again

loopdone:
        mov    [word ptr COLOR],0            ; Use bitmap value of 0 to indicate
                                             ; nothing has been found
give_color:
        movzx eax,[word ptr COLOR]           ; Get color of wall

xRayDone:
        pop    edx                           ; Restore registers
        pop    ecx
        pop    ebx
        pop    edi
        pop    esi
        ret
        endp
```

This looks like a lot of code but it's quite easy to follow, especially when you later see how doors are processed. The first thing the code does is grab the first grid intersection position (**x_xPos**, **x_yPos**). Then, it starts a loop (**looptop**) to kick off the process of casting out the ray and checking each grid intersection position. The loop starts by checking to see if the casting coordinates are in range. If the code were written in C, it would look like this:

```
while (1)
  {
  if (x_xPos < 0 || x_xPos > GRID_XMAX ||      // Are we still in range?
    x_yPos < 0 || x_yPos > GRID_YMAXLONG)
    break;                                     // Jump out of the loop
  ...
```

The ranges we are checking here are essentially 0 < **x_xPos** < 4,096 and 0 < **y_yPos** < 4,096. (The y value has been scaled using fixed-point calculations.) If everything is in range, the code jumps to the **inbounds** label and the fun begins. The goal is to cast each grid intersection point and then check the **xGridGloabl[ ]** array (the x grid map) to see if a wall or object is present. The map position is calculated using a formula you've seen before:

```
// Fixed point  Y/64 * 64 X / 64
MapPosn = ((x_yPos >> FP_SHIFT) & 0xFFC0) + (x_xPos >> 6);
```

Because the y starting coordinate has been scaled, we must first shift it by 16 bits (**sar eax,16**) before we can use it to calculate the map position. (If you forget how this works, you might want to review Chapter 4.) If the bitmap number found is 0, meaning an empty grid square, the code jumps to the **next_square** label and the next grid intersection point along the x ray is used. Because we already calculated the x and y increments in **xRaySetup**, the next intersection point is easy to locate:

```
x_xPos += x_xNext;  // Next X coordinate (fixed at 64 or -64)
x_yPos += x_yNext;  // Next calculated Y coord for a delta of X
```

or the real assembly stuff is:

```
add esi,[dword ptr _x_xNext]  ; Add x,y increment to current grid border
add edi,[dword ptr _x_yNext]  ; position
```

(I hope that showing you the C code helps you follow the assembly code; if it doesn't, just pretend you don't see it!)

After the new intersection point is calculated, the **jmp looptop** instruction takes us back to the start of the loop to begin again. This looping continues until we either read the boundaries of our grid map, or we hit something with the ray.

If the bitmap code found is not equal to 0, we know that we have hit a wall, door, or object. If a standard door is found (visible or invisible), the code continues on; otherwise the jump is taken to **not_door**. This section, which starts with the instruction,

```
test  cx,DOOR_TYPE_SECRET
```

checks to see if the object is either a secret door slice or a wall slice. If the actual item found is a visible secret door slice, visible door slice, or a wall slice, the loop is terminated and the bitmap code of the slice is returned.

Taking Care of Doors

Since we sort of glossed over the details of how door slices are checked during the ray casting process, you're probably wondering about the code in some of the sections such as **door_visible**, **secret_door**, and so on. For each type of door slice located, we'll need to process it in a special way. To help you follow along, let's work at the C level. This code shows the technique used to find and process a basic door:

```
BitMapVal = xGridGlobal[MapPosn]; // Get the bitmap # at the current map position
iLastX   = x_xPos;                // Save the first intersection position
LastY1   = x_yPos;
if ((bitMapVal & 0xFF) == DOOR_XCODE)      // We found a door slice!
  {
  yd = ((x_yPos >> FP_SHIFT) & GRID_MASK);// Get grid corner to left
  xd = yd + BITMAP_WIDTH;                  // Get grid corner to right
  ObjDist = (x_yPos + (x_yNext >> 1)) >> FP_SHIFT;// Calculate door distance
  if (ObjDist < yd || ObjDist > xd)        // Is the door visible?
    {
    x_xPos += x_xNext;     // Nope, continue casting
    x_yPos += x_yNext;     // the ray as before
    continue;
    }
  LastY1 = x_yPos + (x_yNext >> 1); // Adjust the X,Y values so
  iLastX += (x_xNext >> 1);         // the door is halfway in grid square
  }
```

Once we know we've found a door, we need to know if the player can actually see it as he or she moves from the starting point. To decide if the player can see it, we locate the x border where the wall is located and then we calculate the grid position to the left (**yd**) and right (**xd**) of the door, as shown in Figure 6.9. Notice that the position we are using in the calculation is

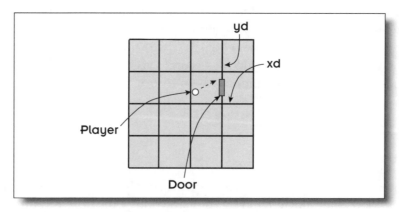

Figure 6.9 *Checking to see if a door is in view.*

based on the y position. The points **yd** and **xd** essentially tell us where the slice is positioned in relationship to the two corners of the grid square. The next thing we need to know is the y distance from the player's first intersection point (the location where the wall is) to halfway to the next intersection point. This distance is called **ObjDist**. Then, by comparing this distance to the grid square corner positions, we can determine if the player will actually see the door as he or she moves.

What is not readily apparent is how the **x_yNext >> 1** statement is used to calculate the **ObjDist** value. Recall that we want our normal doors to appear sunken in or recessed with respect to the surrounding walls. Through experimentation, I've found that sinking doors in halfway between the width of the two walls gives the best results. This depth allows us to calculate the coordinates for the door using a right shift instruction. Now we need to get the distance to the door based on it being recessed, and then see if the current ray we are casting actually hits the door or if it hits a section of wall, as shown in Figure 6.10.

The ray from A to B is cast; the intersection point with the door is recessed beyond what it would normally be if a wall were there (the dotted line). Yet the A-B ray still can see the bitmap for the door. Notice the ray from A to C however, which because of its angle, would not see the door at all, but rather should intersect with the side wall of the right wall block. This result is what the variable **ObjDist** does for us.

The other test we need to make involves checking the bitmap code to see if a secret door has been found. If the door is a secret door, a special column (or channel) is provided that the player can pass through. This column is referenced using the variable **xSecretColumn**. If the column is not equal to 0, a calculation is made using the tangent of the viewing angle. This new coordinate position is added to the y coordinate of the door to calculate the distance. The

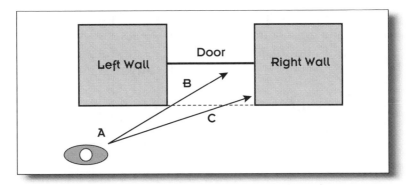

Figure 6.10 *Determining if a ray hits a sunken door or a wall slice.*

effect the player sees from all this is a portion of the wall, our secret door, sliding slowly back away, revealing the mysteries behind (or surprises!). After this point, the code follows the algorithm we just explored for checking doors. Here's the entire process involved for checking a secret door slice:

```
if (BitMapVal & DOOR_TYPE_SECRET)
  {
  if (xSecretColumn != 0)
    {
    sy = xSecretColumn * LongTanTable[ViewAngle];
    ObjDist = (x_yPos + sy) >> FP_SHIFT;
    yd = ((x_yPos >> FP_SHIFT) & GRID_MASK);  // Get the left side
    xd = yd + BITMAP_WIDTH;                    // And the right side
    if (ObjDist < yd || ObjDist > xd)          // Is door visible?
      {
      x_xPos += x_xNext;    // Nope, continue casting
      x_yPos += x_yNext;    // the ray as before
      continue;
      }
    LastY1 = x_yPos + sy;
    iLastX += xSecretColumn;
    }
```

Building the Multi-Slice Walls

We've now taken care of the work of creating slice structures. To jog your memory, the low-level routine **BuildUpView** loops and calls **BuildSlice()** to create a basic slice structure to represent each column of the view. After each call to **BuildSlice()**, a slice structure is assigned data such as the player's distance to the slice, the bitmap code for the slice, the position of the slice in the map grid, and so on. Next, **BuildUpView** checks to see if the slice found represents a multi-height wall. If it finds one, the C function **BuildUpSliceMulti()** is called to adjust the slice structure. This adjustment involves linking up the slice structure created by calling **BuildSlice()** with wall slices that are both behind the current slice and taller. The goal here is to make sure that any wall that is taller than the walls in front of it will be displayed.

Let's jump back to **BuildUpView** for a moment to see how things are set up. The following code is found right after the **buv070** label:

```
mov     [word ptr_LastWallHeight],0   ; Set height of previous wall to 0
ACKCALL BuildSlice                     ; Build the current slice
cmp     [word ptr _gMultiWalls],0      ; Are multi-height walls used?
jz      short buv080                   ; Nope, no need to check

cmp     [word ptr _LastWallHeight],200; No need to check if > 200
jg      short buv080                   ; Skip ahead
```

```
mov        eax,[_sPtr]                  ; Get base address of column slice
cmp        [dword ptr eax+saNext],0     ; Check for any more walls
je         short buv080
cmp        [word ptr eax+saDist],96     ; Distance from POV to slice is
jle        short buv080                 ; less than or equal to 96

ACKCALL BuildSliceMulti                 ; Build the current slice for
                                        ; a multi-height wall
```

The operations performed here involve calling **BuildSlice()** to create a slice structure for the current view column. Recall that we set up the global variable **gMultiWalls** in the **AckRegisterStructure()** function to indicate whether there were any multi-height walls in the map. If this variable is zero, we're finished and ready to move on. If **gMultiWalls** is not zero, we need to check further to see if our current ray will intersect with anything beyond the point where we just found a wall. We test a few additional conditions to see if **BuildSliceMulti()** should be called. First, we check the height of the slice (**LastWallHeight**) to see if it is greater than 200 units. If it is, the current wall will be too high to see anything over it so we won't need to look for multi-height walls behind it. Next, we check the current slice to see if it is linked to any other slices. This step involves checking the pointer **sPtr->Next**, which is stored in each slice structure. (Notice that in the assembly code, we access this location by using the offset **saNext**.) If this pointer is set at this stage, we know that the current slice could be a transparent wall or a door with something behind it. The other condition we check involves comparing the player's distance to the slice with the value 96. If the player's distance is within the range 0 to 96, we know that the player is too close to the wall to see over it. I'm sure you know how this works. If you're in New York and standing directly in front of the Empire State building, you certainly would not be able to see any of the buildings behind it. But, walk down the street a few blocks and you'll begin to see all of those "multi-height" buildings behind it. The different conditions that are checked by the **BuildUpView** code for multi-height walls are shown in Figure 6.11.

The code for **BuildSliceMulti()** starts like **BuildSlice()**:

```
// code from BuildSliceMulti()
WallDistance = 3000000;    // Set to a ridiculous distance
wFound = 0;                // Wall hasn't been found yet

if (ViewAngle != INT_ANGLE_90 && ViewAngle != INT_ANGLE_270)
  {
  if ((BitmapNumber = xRayCastMulti()) != 0)// Cast x ray for multi-height walls
    {
```

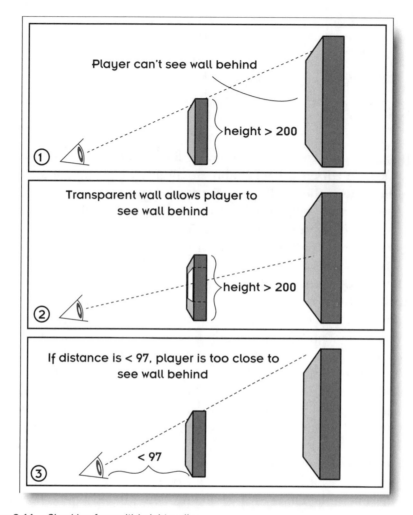

Figure 6.11 *Checking for multi-height walls.*

```
xBitmap = BitmapNumber & 0xFF;
if (((BitmapNumber & WALL_TYPE_MULTI) ||
  (BitmapNumber & WALL_TYPE_UPPER)) &&
  (xBitmap > LastWallHeight))
  {
  // LastWallHeight = xBitmap;
  wFound = 1;   // We found a multi-height slice
  // Use the y intercept to determine the wall column
  BitmapColumn = (LastY1 >> FP_SHIFT) & (BITMAP_WIDTH-1);

  // Keep the orientation the same no matter which side we're on
  if ((short)iLastX < xPglobal)
    BitmapColumn = (BITMAP_WIDTH-1) - BitmapColumn;
```

```
    xd = iLastX - xPglobal;
    mf = InvCosTable[ViewAngle];
    WallDistance = (xd * mf) >> 10; // Get distance to the slice
    if (WallDistance > 33554432L)
      WallDistance = 1200000L;
    gPtr = xGridGlobal;
    mPos = xMapPosn;
    mgPtr = mxGridGlobal[mPos];       // Store pointer to map position
    }
  }
...
```

Again, the work involves first casting a ray in the x plane and then checking to see if anything has been hit. If so, the distance to the slice is calculated and the position of the slice in the multi-height map grid (**mxGridGlobal[ ]**) is recorded.

DESIGN TIP

Notice that we don't need to check for multi-height walls when casting an x ray at 90 degree and 270 degree angles. When these angles are cast, it's impossible to intercept any multi-height x walls. This idea can also be used when we cast y walls. In this case, we won't need to check angles cast of 0 degrees or 180 degrees, as shown here:

```
// Don't cast a y ray if it's impossible to intercept any y walls
if (ViewAngle != 0 && ViewAngle != INT_ANGLE_180)
     {
     ...
```

After the ray has been cast for the x plane, it's time to cast a ray for the y plane. This task is performed by calling **yRayCastMulti()**:

```
if ((yBitmap = yRayCastMulti()) != 0) // Cast the y ray for multi-height slices
  {
  yHeight = yBitmap & 0xFF;
  if (((yBitmap & WALL_TYPE_MULTI) ||
    yBitmap & WALL_TYPE_UPPER)) &&
    (yHeight > LastWallHeight))
    {
     yWallHeight = yHeight;

     // Use the X intercept to determine the column of the bitmap
     yBitmapColumn = (LastX1 >> FP_SHIFT) & (BITMAP_WIDTH-1);
...
```

After the distance to the y slice has been calculated and its position has been recorded, we need to determine which slice is closer to the player—the x or y slice. We use essentially the same code that we used to compare the distances to x and y slices in the **BuildSlice()** function.

The last section of code involves updating the slice structure:

```
if (wFound)    // A slice has been found
  {
  LastWallHeight = xBitmap;
  yd = ViewCosTable[ViewColumn] >> 2;
  WallDistance *= yd;
  // Now we strip off some more decimal points and check round-up
  xd = WallDistance >> 12;
  if (WallDistance - (xd << 12) >= 2048)
    xd++;

//===========================================================================
// The last decimal points from the multiplication after the x and
// y rays are stripped off and checked for round-up.
//===========================================================================
  WallDistance = xd >> 5;
  if (xd - (WallDistance << 5) >= 16)
    WallDistance++;
  // Don't really need to, but put it into an integer for fast compare
  distance = WallDistance;

  // This is an arbitrary minimum distance to look for
  if (distance < 10)
    distance = 10;
  // Don't want it to go outside our table boundaries
  if (distance >= MAX_DISTANCE)
    distance = MAX_DISTANCE - 1;

  // Save the wall data to display when done with entire screen
  sPtr->Active = 1;      // Indicates walls behind
  sPtr = sPtr->Next;     // Point to wall slice behind
  if (sPtr == NULL)      // No wall found; return
    return;

    sPtr->Distance = distance;        // Store data in slice structure
    sPtr->bNumber = BitmapNumber;
    sPtr->bColumn = BitmapColumn;
    sPtr->bMap    = WallbMaps;
    sPtr->Active  = 0;                 // Indicates no walls behind
    sPtr->Type    = ST_WALL;
    sPtr->Fnc     = WallRtn;
    sPtr->mPos    = mPos;
    sPtr->mPtr    = mgPtr;             // Reference map for multi-height walls
    spNext        = sPtr->Next;        // Update pointer to next slice

  if (spNext != NULL)                  // There's a wall behind; build again
    {
    BuildSliceMulti();                 // Recursive call to build next slice
    }
  }
```

The tricky part of this code relates to the fact that multi-slice walls can have walls behind them that can also be seen by the player. The code checks for this case and makes a recursive call to **BuildSliceMulti()** if slices behind the current slice need to be processed. The idea is to keep calling **BuildSliceMulti()** until the last slice is found. Then, the recursion unwinds and the pointers (**sPtr->Next**) are updated. We end up with a doubly-linked list of slice structures that can be easily traversed during the drawing process.

On Our Way to Drawing Walls

We've now completed the work of building a view by casting rays in the x and y planes. The **BuildSlice()** function performs the work of building slice structures for standard wall slices, and the **BuildSliceMulti()** function takes care of updating the slice structures that correspond to locations in the map where multi-height walls are found.

Before we can actually draw anything (wall slices, floors, or ceilings), we need to determine where objects are stored in the map and add information about the objects found to the appropriate slice structures. When the drawing routines are called, they don't have the time to determine where stationary or movable objects are placed, so we must do this beforehand.

The first object checking routine called by **BuildUpView** is **CheckHitMap**. This assembly code routine defined in ACKRTN3.ASM checks to see if a movable object is in view in the map while the current view is being built. Earlier in the chapter when we explored **BuildUpView**, we learned that a special temporary buffer is provided to determine the positions of movable objects. This array, called **HitMap[ ]**, has 4,096 entries, where each entry corresponds with one of the locations in the grid map. The **CheckHitMap** routine spins through a loop and checks each location in the grid map and builds an array called **ObjectsSeen[ ]**. This array stores a flag in each location to indicate if a movable object is in view. Once the array has been built, the C function **FindObject()** is called, which in turn checks the list of objects found during the ray-casting process.

We won't go into the details of how objects are processed in this chapter; we'll devote an entire chapter to this topic. For now, all you need to know is that **FindObject()** checks each of the objects referenced in the **ObjectsSeen[ ]** array and places the object slices that are visible in the current view into the wall slices. The technique is to fold in objects with walls so that the drawing routines can rip through the list of slices and draw everything that needs to be displayed in one pass. This technique is another one of the clever optimization techniques that the *ACK-3D* engine uses to generate 3-D scenes as quickly as possible.

The Complete ACKVIEW.C

Here's the complete code for ACKVIEW.C. Before you move on to learn how slices are actually drawn, you might want to spend some time reviewing the main functions defined in this source file so that you are familiar with casting rays and building slices.

```c
// This file contains the declarations and functions to set up views for the
// ray casting engine.
#include <windows.h>  // Required for Windows version of engine
#include <stdlib.h>
#include <stdio.h>
#include <conio.h>
#include <dos.h>
#include <mem.h>
#include <io.h>
#include <fcntl.h>
#include <time.h>
#include <string.h>
#include <sys\stat.h>
#include <limits.h>
#include "ack3d.h"    // Main ACK-3D internal and interface data structures
#include "ackeng.h"   // Internal structures and constants
#include "ackext.h"   // Defines external (global) variables

extern  long FloorCosTable[];
void  (*FloorCeilRtn)(void);
void  (*WallRtn)(void);
void  (*WallMaskRtn)(void);
short gWinFullWidth;      // Global variables for setting up a viewport
long  gWinDWORDS;         // These are the global variables used by the
long  gWinStartOffset;    // low-level, assembly-language routines to draw slices
short gWinStartX;
short gWinStartY;
short gWinEndX;
short gWinEndY;
short gWinHeight;
short gWinHalfHeight;
short gWinWidth;
short gCenterRow;
short gCenterOff;
long  gBottomOff;
UCHAR *gScrnBufferCenter;
UCHAR *gScrnBuffer;
UCHAR *gBkgdBuffer;
UCHAR *gPalTable;
short gMultiWalls;
UCHAR **mxGridGlobal; // Global variables to reference the x and y
UCHAR **myGridGlobal; // map arrays
UCHAR gTopColor;
UCHAR gBottomColor;
UCHAR *scVid;          // Variables used in low-level routines for
```

```
UCHAR *scWall;          // building and drawing slices
UCHAR *scPal;
short scdst;
short scwht;
short scmulti;
short sctopht;
short scbotht;
short scsavwht;
short scmulcnt;
UCHAR *scsavVid;
USHORT  scbNum;
UCHAR *scMulData;
UCHAR *scColumn;
UCHAR *gPtr;
UCHAR *gmPtr;
short gBitmapNumber;
short gBitmapColumn;
short gyBitmapNumber;
short gyBitmapColumn;
long  gWallDistance;
short gmPos;
DOORS *gDoor;
DOORS *gDoorPosn;
short wFound;
UCHAR *mgPtr;
short BegX,EndX;
extern  long  x_xPos; // Variables for tracking coordinates during
extern  long  x_yPos; // the ray-casting process
extern  long  x_xNext;
extern  long  x_yNext;
extern  long  y_xPos;
extern  long  y_yPos;
extern  long  y_xNext;
extern  long  y_yNext;
short LastVht;
long  WallDistTable[VIEW_WIDTH];

// Functions used to build views and perform the ray-casting process
void AckSetupWindow(ACKENG *ae);    // Sets up variables for viewport
void BuildUpView(void);       // Main assembly-language routine for building views
void BuildSlice(void);        // Assembly-language routines for building slices
void BuildSliceMulti(void);   // Assembly-language routine for building multi-slices
void CheckDoors(void);        // Internal routines for locating and checking doors
void FindObject(void);        // and objects
short FindDoor(short MapPosn);
void FloorLoop(void);
void CeilLoop(void);
void DrawSlices(void);
short BlankSlice(USHORT col,UCHAR *bmp);
void BuildSliceAsm(void);
void xRaySetup(void);             // Routines for setting up and casting rays
USHORT xRayCast(void);
void yRaySetup(void);
USHORT yRayCast(void);
```

```
USHORT xRayCastMulti(void);
USHORT yRayCastMulti(void);
void ShowCol(void);              // Routines for drawing a slice
void ShowColMask(void);          // column by column
void ShowColNS(void);
void ShowColMaskNS(void);
void ShowColLow(void);
void ShowColMaskLow(void);
void DrawFloorCeiling(void);   // Routines for drawing floors and ceilings
void AckDrawFloor(void);
void AckDrawFloorOnly(void);
void AckDrawCeilingOnly(void);
void AckDrawFloorNS(void);
void AckDrawFloorOnlyNS(void);
void AckDrawCeilingOnlyNS(void);
void AckDrawFloorHz(void);
void AckDrawOneFloor(void);
void DrawSolidCeilAndFloor(void);
void DrawSolidCeilAndFloorNS(void);
void DrawSolidFloorAndCeil(void);
void DrawSolidFloorAndCeilNS(void);
void DrawSolidCeilSolidFloor(void);


//++++++++++++++++++++++++++++++++++++++++++++++++++++++++++++++++++++++++
// Transfers certain variables from the interface structure to global
// variables that can be accessed faster by the drawing functions. The
// interface structure is kept by the application and more than one of
// them can be used for different views. Each time a new view needs to
// be processed, this function MUST be called before calling the
// drawing routines.
//++++++++++++++++++++++++++++++++++++++++++++++++++++++++++++++++++++++++
void AckRegisterStructure(ACKENG *ae)
{
  int mode,i;

aeGlobal          = ae;             // Global variable to reference ACKENG structure
AckSetupWindow(ae);                 // Assign window variables to ACKENG structure
xGridGlobal       = ae->xGrid;      // Global map for x walls
yGridGlobal       = ae->yGrid;      // Global map for y walls
mxGridGlobal      = ae->mxGrid;     // Wall data for multi-height walls
myGridGlobal      = ae->myGrid;
WallbMaps         = ae->bMaps;      // Wall bitmap data
gWinStartX        = ae->WinStartX;  // Coordinates of viewport; upper-left
gWinStartY        = ae->WinStartY;
gWinEndX          = ae->WinEndX;    // Lower-right viewport coordinates
gWinEndY          = ae->WinEndY;
gWinHeight        = ae->WinHeight;  // Height of viewport
gWinWidth         = ae->WinWidth;   // Width of viewport
gWinHalfHeight    = (gWinEndY - (gWinHeight >> 1)) + 1;
gCenterRow        = ae->CenterRow;     // Start of center row in viewport
gCenterOff        = ae->CenterOffset;  // Offset to center of viewport
gScrnBuffer       = ae->ScreenBuffer;  // Screen buffer access
gScrnBufferCenter = gScrnBuffer + gCenterOff;
gBkgdBuffer       = ae->BkgdBuffer;  // Buffer for ceiling and floors
gPalTable         = ae->PalTable;    // Palette of colors used
```

```
gDoor         = &ae->Door[0];      // List of moving doors
gTopColor     = ae->TopColor;      // Base color of ceiling
gBottomColor  = ae->BottomColor;   // Base color of floor
LightFlag     = ae->LightFlag;     // Light shading on or off indicator
SysFlags      = ae->SysFlags;      // Scene display attributes (floors and ceilings)

mode = 0;                          // Draw both textured floor and ceiling
if (SysFlags & SYS_SOLID_CEIL)     // Soild ceiling is selected
  {
  mode = 1;                        // Draw floor only (ceiling will be solid)
  if (SysFlags & SYS_SOLID_FLOOR)  // Solid floor is selected
    mode = 2;                      // Draw solid floor and ceiling
  }
if (SysFlags & SYS_SOLID_FLOOR)    // Solid floor is selected
  {
  if (!mode)
    mode = 3;                      // Draw Ceiling only (floor will be solid)
  }

if (!LightFlag)                    // No light shading used
  {
  WallRtn = ShowColNS;             // Assembly routines for drawing slices
  WallMaskRtn = ShowColMaskNS;     // using light shading
  switch (mode)                    // Check floor and ceiling type
    {
    case 0:                        // Draw both solid floor and ceiling
      if (ae->SysFlags & SYS_SINGLE_BMP)
        FloorCeilRtn = AckDrawOneFloor; // Use same bitmap for each
      else FloorCeilRtn = AckDrawFloorHz;
      break;
    case 1:                        // Draw solid ceiling and texture floor
      FloorCeilRtn = DrawSolidCeilAndFloorNS;
      break;
    case 2:                        // Draw both solid floor and solid ceiling
      FloorCeilRtn = DrawSolidCeilSolidFloor;
      break;
    case 3:                        // Draw solid floor and texture ceiling
      FloorCeilRtn = DrawSolidFloorAndCeilNS;
      break;
    default:
      break;
    }
  }
else                               // Light shading is used
  {
  WallRtn = ShowCol;               // Assembly routines for drawing slices
  WallMaskRtn = ShowColMask;       // using light shading
  switch (mode)
    {
    case 0:   // Draw both floor and ceiling
      FloorCeilRtn = AckDrawFloor;
      break;
    case 1:   // Draw solid ceiling and textured floor
      FloorCeilRtn = DrawSolidCeilAndFloor;
      break;
```

```
      case 2:   // Draw both solid floor and solid ceiling
        FloorCeilRtn = DrawSolidCeilSolidFloor;
        break;
      case 3:   // Draw solid floor and textured ceiling
        FloorCeilRtn = DrawSolidFloorAndCeil;
        break;
      default:
        break;
      }
    }
// Test to see if viewport is full width (320 units)
gWinStartOffset = ae->WinStartOffset;   // Offset to viewport
gBottomOff  = (gWinEndY * 320);
gWinFullWidth = 0;              // Set flag to indicate viewport is not full width
if (gWinStartX == 0 && gWinEndX == 319) // Viewport is full size
  {
  gWinFullWidth = 1;                         // Indicates viewport is full size
  gWinDWORDS = (gWinEndY - gWinStartY) * 80;  // Calculate number of double
  }                                          // words to access buffer
// Test to see if multi-height walls are used
gMultiWalls = 0;
for (i = 0; i < GRID_MAX; i++)
  {
  if ((xGridGlobal[i] & WALL_TYPE_MULTI) || (yGridGlobal[i] & WALL_TYPE_MULTI))
  {
    gMultiWalls = 1;  // Indicates multi-height walls are used
    break;
    }
  }
}


//+++++++++++++++++++++++++++++++++++++++++++++++++++++++++++++++++++++++
// Render the current scene into the off-screen buffer based on the POV
// coordinates and angle. This function does NOT display the scene once
// it is rendered so the application can overlay graphics into the buffer
// before it is actually displayed.
//+++++++++++++++++++++++++++++++++++++++++++++++++++++++++++++++++++++++
void AckBuildView(void)
{
// Set up global variables to be used with assembly-language routines
xPglobal    = aeGlobal->xPlayer;            // The player's x coordinate
xBegGlobal  = xPglobal & GRID_MASK;         // Upper-left corner (x) of the
                                            // grid square the player is in
xPglobalHI  = ((long)xPglobal << FP_SHIFT);  // Convert x coordinate to
                                            // fixed point
yPglobal    = aeGlobal->yPlayer;            // The player's y coordinate
yBegGlobal  = yPglobal & GRID_MASK;         // Upper-left corner (y) of
                                            // grid square
yPglobalHI  = ((long)yPglobal << FP_SHIFT);  // Convert y coordinate to
                                            // fixed point
PlayerAngle = aeGlobal->PlayerAngle;        // The player's angle
SysFlags    = aeGlobal->SysFlags;           // Ceiling and floor attributes;
BuildUpView();  // Assembly routine defined in ACKRTN3.ASM. This routine
                // kicks off the ray-casting process.
}
```

```
//++++++++++++++++++++++++++++++++++++++++++++++++++++++++++++++++++++++++++++++
// Stub function for drawing slices that do not contain walls.
//++++++++++++++++++++++++++++++++++++++++++++++++++++++++++++++++++++++++++++++
void ShowNone(void)
{
return;
}


//++++++++++++++++++++++++++++++++++++++++++++++++++++++++++++++++++++++++++++++
// Internal function to cast the x and y rays and build a slice structure
// for each column of the viewing window.
//++++++++++++++++++++++++++++++++++++++++++++++++++++++++++++++++++++++++++++++
void BuildSlice(void)
{
  short    j,index,wFound;
  long     xBitmap,yBitmap,BitmapNumber;
  short    DoorOpenColumn;
  ULONG    xDistance,yDistance;
  ULONG    xd,yd,mf;
  long     WallDistance,UnAdjustDist;
  long     distance,LightAdj;
  USHORT   BitmapColumn,yBitmapColumn;
  long     OldMapPosn,OldMapPosn1;
  long     HoldAngle;
  long     offset;
  long     mPos;
  USHORT   *gPtr;
  UCHAR    *mgPtr;
  SLICE    *spNext;

WallDistance = 3000000;    // Set to a ridiculous distance
sPtr->Distance = 200;      // Initialize the distance from the POV to the slice
wFound = 0;                // Wall not found yet
sPtr->Fnc = ShowNone;      // Use the stub function for now for drawing the slice

// Call the low-level, ray-casting function and see if anything is hit
if ((BitmapNumber = xRayCast()) != 0) // Something has been hit while casting
  {                        // in the x plane
  wFound = 1;              // Set flag to indicate a hit
  // Use the y intercept to determine the column of the slice
  BitmapColumn = (LastY1 >> FP_SHIFT) & (BITMAP_WIDTH-1);
  // Keep the orientation the same no matter which side we're on
  if ((short)iLastX < xPglobal)
    BitmapColumn = (BITMAP_WIDTH-1) - BitmapColumn;
  // Did we strike a door?
  if ((BitmapNumber & (DOOR_TYPE_SLIDE+DOOR_TYPE_SPLIT)))
    {
    index = FindDoor(xMapPosn);        // Locate the position of the door
    if (index >= 0)                    // Is this is a valid door?
      {
      j = aeGlobal->Door[index].ColOffset;  // Get the door'scurrent pos
      offset = 0;
      if (BitmapNumber & DOOR_TYPE_SLIDE) // Is the door a slider?
        {
```

```
      DoorOpenColumn = BITMAP_WIDTH-1;
      if ((short)iLastX > xPglobal)      // Handle orientation
        j = -j;
      BitmapColumn += j;                     // Adjust column to show
      }
   if (BitmapNumber & DOOR_TYPE_SPLIT)   // Is the door a split door?
     {
     DoorOpenColumn = (BITMAP_WIDTH/2)-1;
     if (BitmapColumn < (BITMAP_WIDTH/2))
       {
       BitmapColumn += j;
       if (BitmapColumn > (BITMAP_WIDTH/2)-1) offset = 1;
       }
     else
       {
       BitmapColumn -= j;
       if (BitmapColumn < (BITMAP_WIDTH/2)) offset = 1;
       }
     }         // End processing split door

   if (offset == 1 || BitmapColumn > (BITMAP_WIDTH-1))
     {
     // Get the grid coordinates for this door
     OldMapPosn = aeGlobal->Door[index].mPos;
     OldMapPosn1 = aeGlobal->Door[index].mPos1;
     // Fake the engine into thinking no door is there
     xGridGlobal[OldMapPosn] = 0;
     xGridGlobal[OldMapPosn1] = 0;
     // Cast the ray to get walls beyond the door
     BitmapNumber = xRayCast();
     // Put back the door codes if not fully open
     if (aeGlobal->Door[index].ColOffset < DoorOpenColumn)
       {
       xGridGlobal[OldMapPosn] = aeGlobal->Door[index].mCode;
       xGridGlobal[OldMapPosn1] = aeGlobal->Door[index].mCode1;
       }
     // Calc the new bitmap column of wall behind door
     BitmapColumn = (LastY1 >> FP_SHIFT) & (BITMAP_WIDTH-1);
     if ((short)iLastX < xPglobal)
       BitmapColumn = (BITMAP_WIDTH-1) - BitmapColumn;
     }
   }
  }         // End processing doors

//=====================================================================
// Calculate the distance to the wall. Since the x position was
// fixed to move 64 or -64 we can use it to determine the actual
// wall distance. The InvCosTable values were stored with a fixed
// point of 20 decimal places. At this time we'll knock off 14 of
// them so we can later multiply with a fixed-point value of 16
//=====================================================================
  xd = iLastX - xPglobal;        // x distance to the found slice
  mf = InvCosTable[ViewAngle];    // Get the cosine of the angle
  WallDistance = (xd * mf) >> 10; // Calculate the actual distance to the slice
```

```
    if (WallDistance > 33554432L)    // Check for out of range
    WallDistance = 1200000L;
    gPtr  = xGridGlobal;              // Point to xGrid map
    mgPtr = mxGridGlobal[xMapPosn];  // Point to grid map for multi-height walls
    mPos  = xMapPosn;                 // Access actual map position
    } // End (if BitmapNumber = xRayCast() ...)

// Time to cast the ray in the y plane
if ((yBitmap = yRayCast()) != 0)  // Something has been hit while casting
  {
  // Use the X intercept to determine the column of the bitmap
  yBitmapColumn = (LastX1 >> FP_SHIFT) & (BITMAP_WIDTH-1);
  // Handle orientation from either side of the wall
  if ((short)iLastY > yPglobal)
    yBitmapColumn = (BITMAP_WIDTH-1) - yBitmapColumn;
  // Did we strike a door?
  if ((yBitmap & (DOOR_TYPE_SLIDE+DOOR_TYPE_SPLIT)))
    {
    index = FindDoor(yMapPosn);
    if (index >= 0)                // Is this is a valid door?
      {
      // Get the current door column offset
      j = aeGlobal->Door[index].ColOffset;
      offset = 0;
      // Deal with orientation
      if (yBitmap & DOOR_TYPE_SLIDE)  // Is this a sliding door?
        {
        DoorOpenColumn = BITMAP_WIDTH-1;
        if ((short)iLastY < yPglobal) j = -j;
        yBitmapColumn += j;
        }                          // End processing sliding door

      if (yBitmap & DOOR_TYPE_SPLIT)  // Is this a split door?
      {
      DoorOpenColumn = (BITMAP_WIDTH/2)-1;
      if (yBitmapColumn < (BITMAP_WIDTH/2))
        {
          yBitmapColumn += j;
          if (yBitmapColumn > (BITMAP_WIDTH/2)-1) offset = 1;
        }
      else
        {
          yBitmapColumn -= j;
          if (yBitmapColumn < (BITMAP_WIDTH/2))
            offset = 1;
        }
      }                 // End processing split door

    // If beyond width of bitmap than cast again
    if (offset == 1 || yBitmapColumn > (BITMAP_WIDTH-1))
      {
      // Get the yGrid coordinates for this door
      OldMapPosn = aeGlobal->Door[index].mPos;
      OldMapPosn1 = aeGlobal->Door[index].mPos1;
```

```
        // Fool the engine into thinking no door is there
        yGridGlobal[OldMapPosn] = 0; yGridGlobal[OldMapPosn1] = 0;
        // Cast again for walls beyond the door
        yBitmap = yRayCast();
        // Put door code back if not fully open
        if (aeGlobal->Door[index].ColOffset < DoorOpenColumn)
          {
          yGridGlobal[OldMapPosn] = aeGlobal->Door[index].mCode;
          yGridGlobal[OldMapPosn1] = aeGlobal->Door[index].mCode1;
          }
        // Get the bitmap column of wall beyond door
        yBitmapColumn = (LastX1 >> FP_SHIFT) & (BITMAP_WIDTH-1);
        if ((short)iLastY > yPglobal)
          yBitmapColumn = (BITMAP_WIDTH-1) - yBitmapColumn;
        }
      }
    }

//================================================================
// Calculate the distance to the wall. Since the y position was
// fixed to move 64 or -64 we can use it to determine the actual
// wall distance. The InvSinTable values were stored with a fixed
// point of 20 decimal places. At this time we'll knock off 14 of
// them so we can later multiply with a fixed-point value of 16
//================================================================
yd = iLastY - yPglobal;  // Distance from player's pos to intersection point
  mf = InvSinTable[ViewAngle];  // Use angle with look-up table
  yDistance = (yd * mf) >> 8;    // Calculate y distance
  if (yDistance > 33554432L)     // Distance is out of range, adjust
    yDistance = 120000L;


//================================================================
//  At this point check the distance to the y wall against the x
//  wall to see which one is closer. The closer one is the one
//  we'll draw at this column of the screen.
//================================================================
  if (yDistance < WallDistance)  // Use distance to y slice if this slice is closer
    {
    wFound = 1;                    // Indicates that a slice has been found
    WallDistance = yDistance;      // Use distance to y slice
    BitmapNumber = yBitmap;        // Transfer bitmap number
    BitmapColumn = yBitmapColumn;  // Transfer bitmap column
    gPtr = yGridGlobal;            // Store pointer to global y grid
    mPos = yMapPosn;               // Store position of y wall in map
    mgPtr = myGridGlobal[mPos];
    }
  }  // End (if yBitmap = yRayCast()) != 0)

// A slice has been found so process it
if (wFound)
  {
//================================================================
// To avoid a fishbowl effect we need to adjust the distance so
// it appears perpendicular to the center point of the display,
```

```
// which is relative angle 0 from the player's current angle. We
// started at -32 degrees for the first screen column and will
// cycle from -32 down to 0 then back up to +32 degrees. This
// cosine value was precalculated and placed in ViewCosTable.
//==============================================================
  UnAdjustDist = WallDistance >> 5;
  yd = ViewCosTable[ViewColumn] >> 3; // Use current column as lookup index
  WallDistance *= yd;
  // Now we strip off some more decimal points and check round-up
  xd = WallDistance >> 12;
  if (WallDistance - (xd << 12) >= 2048)
    xd++;
  // The last decimal points from the multiplication after the x and
  // y rays are stripped off and checked for round-up
  WallDistance = xd >> 5;
  if (xd - (WallDistance << 5) >= 16)
    WallDistance++;
  // This is an arbitrary minimum distance to look for
  if (WallDistance < 10)
    WallDistance = 10;                 // Reset distance to minimum allowed
  // Don't want it to go outside our table boundaries
  if (WallDistance >= MAX_DISTANCE)

    WallDistance  = MAX_DISTANCE - 1; // Reset distance to maximum allowed
  // Save the wall data to display when done with entire screen
  sPtr->Distance  = WallDistance;      // Store the adjusted distance to the wall
  sPtr->bNumber = BitmapNumber; // The bitmap number for the wall slice
  sPtr->bColumn = BitmapColumn; // The screen column position to display the bitmap
  sPtr->bMap    = WallbMaps;    // Pointer to the bitmap
  sPtr->Active  = 0;            // Indicates slice is not displayable yet last one
  sPtr->Type    = ST_WALL;      // Indicates this slice is part of a wall
  sPtr->Fnc     = WallRtn;      // Pointer to function to draw slice
  sPtr->mPos    = mPos;         // Position of the slice in the grid map
  sPtr->mPtr    = mgPtr;        // Grid pointer to reference multi-height wall
  spNext        = sPtr->Next;   // Reference wall slice behind current slice

  if (WallDistance > MaxDistance)
    MaxDistance = WallDistance;

  if (CeilMap[mPos])
    LastWallHeight = 9000;
    if (((BitmapNumber & WALL_TYPE_UPPER) ||  // Wall is above the floor level
    (BitmapNumber & WALL_TYPE_TRANS)) &&  // or wall slice is transparent and it
    spNext != NULL)                        // has something behind it
    {
    BitmapColumn = gPtr[mPos];  // Get position of the multi-height wall
    gPtr[mPos]  = 0;
    sPtr->Active = 1;            // More slices to follow if wall is displayable!
    if (BitmapNumber & WALL_TYPE_TRANS) // The wall is transparent
      {
      sPtr->Type = ST_OBJECT;   // We have an object
      sPtr->Fnc = WallMaskRtn;  // Using a different drawing routine
      }
    sPtr = spNext;              // Point to slice behind
```

```
      spNext->Active = 0;          // Initialize the slice behind before building it
      spNext->bNumber = 0;
      BuildSlice();                // Call BuildSlice() again to build the slice behind
      gPtr[mPos] = BitmapColumn;   // Store position of slice
      if (!sPtr->bNumber)          // Slice behind is no longer visible
        {
        spNext = sPtr->Prev;       // Link up slices
        if (spNext != NULL)
          spNext->Active = 0;
        }
      }
    else
      {   // Keep track of each distance to wall slice for drawing floor later on
      if (UnAdjustDist < WallDistTable[ViewColumn])
        WallDistTable[ViewColumn] = UnAdjustDist;
      }
    }
  }

//+++++++++++++++++++++++++++++++++++++++++++++++++++++++++++++++++++++++++++++
// Continues the ray cast for multi-height walls so that any wall that is
// taller than the walls in front of it will be displayed.
//+++++++++++++++++++++++++++++++++++++++++++++++++++++++++++++++++++++++++++++
void BuildSliceMulti(void)
{
  short   j,index,wFound;
  USHORT  yHeight;
  USHORT  xBitmap,yBitmap,BitmapNumber;
  short   DoorOpenColumn;
  short   xWallHeight,yWallHeight;
  ULONG   xDistance,yDistance;
  ULONG   xd,yd,mf;
  long    WallDistance;
  USHORT  distance,LightAdj;
  USHORT  BitmapColumn,yBitmapColumn;
  short   OldMapPosn,OldMapPosn1;
  short   HoldAngle,HoldX,HoldY,xp1,yp1;
  USHORT  offset;
  short   mPos;
  USHORT  *gPtr;
  UCHAR   *mgPtr;
  SLICE   *spNext;

WallDistance = 3000000;   // Set to a very far off distance
wFound = 0;               // Indicates a slice has not been found
// Don't cast an x ray if it's impossible to intercept any x walls
if (ViewAngle != INT_ANGLE_90 && ViewAngle != INT_ANGLE_270)
  {   // Cast the x ray and build multi-height slice
  if ((BitmapNumber = xRayCastMulti()) != 0)
    {
    xBitmap = BitmapNumber & 0xFF;          // Get the bitmap code
    // Check for multi-height or slice that is taller than one in front
    if (((BitmapNumber & WALL_TYPE_MULTI) ||
      (BitmapNumber & WALL_TYPE_UPPER)) &&
```

```
      (xBitmap > LastWallHeight))
      {
      // LastWallHeight = xBitmap;
      wFound = 1;        // Indicates a multi-slice wall has been found
      // Use the y intercept to determine the wall column
      BitmapColumn = (LastY1 >> FP_SHIFT) & (BITMAP_WIDTH-1);
      // Keep the orientation the same no matter which side we're on
      if ((short)iLastX < xPglobal)
        BitmapColumn = (BITMAP_WIDTH-1) - BitmapColumn;
      xd = iLastX - xPglobal;
      mf = InvCosTable[ViewAngle];  // Use angle to calculate distance to slice
      WallDistance = (xd * mf) >> 10;
      if (WallDistance > 33554432L) // Check for out of range
        WallDistance = 1200000L;
      gPtr = xGridGlobal;            // Reference global map grid
      mPos = xMapPosn;               // Use position of slice
      mgPtr = mxGridGlobal[mPos];    // Get pointer to multi-height slice found
      }
    }
  }

// Don't cast a y ray if it's impossible to intercept any y walls
if (ViewAngle != 0 && ViewAngle != INT_ANGLE_180)
  {
  if ((yBitmap = yRayCastMulti()) != 0) // Cast the y ray to build multi-height slice
    {
    yHeight = yBitmap & 0xFF; // Get the bitmap code of slice
    if (((yBitmap & WALL_TYPE_MULTI) ||
      (yBitmap & WALL_TYPE_UPPER)) && (yHeight > LastWallHeight))
      {
      yWallHeight = yHeight;
      // Use the x intercept to determine the column of the bitmap
      yBitmapColumn = (LastX1 >> FP_SHIFT) & (BITMAP_WIDTH-1);
      // Handle orientation from either side of the wall
      if ((short)iLastY > yPglobal)
        yBitmapColumn = (BITMAP_WIDTH-1) - yBitmapColumn;
      yd = iLastY - yPglobal;
      mf = InvSinTable[ViewAngle];  // Use angle to calculate distance to slice
      yDistance = (yd * mf) >> 8;
      if (yDistance > 33554432L)    // Is distance in range?
          yDistance = 120000L;

//================================================================
//   At this point check the distance to the y wall
//   to see which one is closer. The closer one is the one
//   we'll draw at this column of the screen.
//================================================================
      // Use distance to y slice if this slice is closer
      if (yDistance < WallDistance)
        {
        wFound = 1;                   // Indicates that a slice has been found
        WallDistance = yDistance;     // Use distance to y slice
        BitmapNumber = yBitmap;       // Transfer bitmap number
        BitmapColumn = yBitmapColumn; // Transfer bitmap column
```

```
            gPtr = yGridGlobal;            // Store pointer to global y grid
            mPos = yMapPosn;               // Store position of y wall in map
            xBitmap = yHeight;
            mgPtr = myGridGlobal[mPos];    // Store pointer to multi-height slice
            }
        }
     }
   }
if (wFound)             // A multi-wall slice has been found so process it
   {
   LastWallHeight = xBitmap;
   yd = ViewCosTable[ViewColumn] >> 2;
   WallDistance *= yd;
   // Now we strip off some more decimal points and check round-up
   xd = WallDistance >> 12;
   if (WallDistance - (xd << 12) >= 2048)
     xd++;

//================================================================
// The last decimal points from the multiplication after the x and
// y rays are stripped off and checked for round-up.
//================================================================
   WallDistance = xd >> 5;
   if (xd - (WallDistance << 5) >= 16)
     WallDistance++;
   // Don't really need to, but put it into an integer for fast compare
   distance = WallDistance;
   // This is an arbitrary minimum distance to look for
   if (distance < 10)
     distance = 10;
   // Don't want it to go outside our table boundaries if
   (distance >= MAX_DISTANCE)
     distance = MAX_DISTANCE - 1;
   // Save the wall data to display when done with entire screen
   sPtr->Active = 1;
   sPtr = sPtr->Next;
   if (sPtr == NULL)
     return;
   sPtr->Distance = distance;   // Update slice data in slice structure
   sPtr->bNumber  = BitmapNumber;
   sPtr->bColumn  = BitmapColumn;
   sPtr->bMap     = WallbMaps;
   sPtr->Active   = 0;
   sPtr->Type     = ST_WALL;
   sPtr->Fnc      = WallRtn;
   sPtr->mPos     = mPos;
   sPtr->mPtr     = mgPtr;
   spNext         = sPtr->Next;
   if (spNext != NULL)
     {
     BuildSliceMulti();            // Recursive call to build the slice behind
     }
   }
}
```

```
//********************************************************************
// Internal function called by AckCheckDoorOpen() to
// check for a collision with a wall within a certain distance.
//********************************************************************
short AckCheckHit(short xPlayer,short yPlayer,short vAngle)
{
  short BitmapNumber,yBitmap;
  short WallCode;
  ULONG WallDistance;
  ULONG xd,yd,mf,yDistance;
  long  CheckDist;

WallDistance  = 3000000;  // Set to a ridiculous value
WallCode      = POV_NOTHING;
BitmapNumber  = 0;        // (was 48) Initial minimum distance to look for
CheckDis      = 56L;      // Initialize to no bitmap found
xPglobal      = xPlayer;
xBegGlobal    = xPglobal & GRID_MASK;
xPglobalHI    = ((long)xPglobal << FP_SHIFT); yPglobal = yPlayer;
yBegGlobal    = yPglobal & GRID_MASK; yPglobalHI = ((long)yPglobal << FP_SHIFT);
ViewAngle     = vAngle;

if (MoveObjectCount)
  memmove(ObjectsSeen,MoveObjectList,MoveObjectCount);
FoundObjectCount = MoveObjectCount;
//********************************************************************
// Don't allow one of these angles, causes either the x or y ray to not be
// cast which gives a false reading about an obstacle.
//********************************************************************
if (ViewAngle == INT_ANGLE_45 ||
    ViewAngle == INT_ANGLE_135 ||
    ViewAngle == INT_ANGLE_225 ||
    ViewAngle == INT_ANGLE_315)
    {
    ViewAngle++;
    }
xRaySetup();
BitmapNumber = xRayCast();
if (BitmapNumber & (WALL_TYPE_UPPER+WALL_TYPE_PASS))
    BitmapNumber = 0;
if (BitmapNumber)
    {
    xd = iLastX - xPlayer;
    mf = InvCosTable[ViewAngle];
    WallDistance = (xd * mf) >> 10;
    if (WallDistance > 33554432L)
        WallDistance = 1200000L;
        // Set the wall struck code to an X wall
        WallCode = POV_XWALL;
        LastMapPosn = xMapPosn;
    }
yRaySetup();
yBitmap = yRayCast();
if (yBitmap & (WALL_TYPE_UPPER+WALL_TYPE_PASS))
```

```
    yBitmap = 0;
if (yBitmap)
  {
  yd = iLastY - yPlayer;
  mf = InvSinTable[ViewAngle];
  yDistance = (yd * mf) >> 8;
  if (yDistance > 33554432L)
    yDistance = 120000L;
  // If Y wall closer than X wall then use Y wall data
  if (yDistance < WallDistance)
    {
    WallDistance = yDistance;
    // Indicate the wall struck was a Y wall
    WallCode = POV_YWALL;
    BitmapNumber = yBitmap;
    LastMapPosn = yMapPosn;
    }
  }

//***********************************************************************
// Since doors appear in the middle of the wall, adjust the minimum distance
// to it. This handles walking up close to a door.
//***********************************************************************
if (BitmapNumber & (DOOR_TYPE_SLIDE+DOOR_TYPE_SPLIT))
  CheckDist += 64L;
BitmapNumber &= 0xFF;
if (WallCode)
  {
  yd = ViewCosTable[160] >> 3;
  WallDistance *= yd;
  // Now we strip off somemore decimal points and check round-up
  xd = WallDistance >> 12;
  if (WallDistance - (xd << 12) >= 2048)
    xd++;
//***********************************************************************
//  The last decimal points from the multiplication after the x and
//  y rays is stripped off and checked for round-up.
//***********************************************************************
  WallDistance = xd >> 5;
  if (xd - (WallDistance << 5) >= 16)
    WallDistance++;
//***********************************************************************
// If the wall or object is further than the minimum distance, we can
// continue moving in this direction.
//***********************************************************************
  if (WallDistance > CheckDist)
    WallCode = POV_NOTHING;
  }
return(WallCode);
}
// **** End of Source ****
```

Chapter 7

To create views from slices of wall and object bitmaps, we need a method to draw bitmaps to an off-screen buffer and then transfer buffer data to video memory.

Drawing Slices for Walls and Objects

With each step we take, we're closer to putting a 3-D view on the screen. We've already learned how to move around in a maze, run into a wall or object, and cast out x and y rays to build up a set of slice structures to represent the view that we can see. But what good is a set of slice structures if it can't be drawn on the screen? Fortunately, we're much closer to creating a 3-D representation of our view than you might think. All we need to do is put a few low-level routines together to draw a set of slice structures to an off-screen buffer. Once the off-screen buffer is created, it can be transferred to the screen by copying pixel data to video memory.

In this chapter we'll explore the **DrawWalls** routine, which manages the work of building an off-screen buffer from a set of slices to represent a view. Along the way, you'll see how viewports, buffers, and actual screen displays are supported. The video display code that we present in this chapter is DOS-related. We'll start by looking at how viewports and buffers are supported, and then we'll build some low-level routines for accessing DOS screens. This approach gives you a chance to learn how video memory is accessed, how

225

pixels are displayed, and how color palettes are loaded and changed. If you've worked with DOS low-level graphics before and modes such as Mode 13h, this chapter will serve as a good review.

In Chapter 13, we'll examine the concepts behind displaying fast graphics with Microsoft Windows using WinG.

Understanding Viewports, Screens, and Buffers

Before we get too far into the code that draws slices, we need to take a step back and explore how *ACK-3D* displays graphics on the screen. If you recall from Chapter 4 when we explored the main data structure **ACKENG**, a number of variables are stored to keep track of a region called a *viewport* or *viewport window*. The information that is required to define the viewport includes the top, bottom, left, and right position of the viewport, the height and width of the viewport, and so on. A viewport can be different sizes; it can represent a full screen or just part of a screen such as the top half. When you use the *ACK-3D* engine, you decide how much of the screen you want to use to display your 3-D scenes.

Because the viewport that you define is completely independent of the actual screen or video memory where your graphics are displayed, the code and techniques for setting up viewports can be used with both DOS and Windows. In fact, this design approach makes both the *ACK-3D* engine and the applications you develop with it easily portable to different platforms.

When any of the drawing routines is called to display graphics, the process involves looking at the size and position (left, right, bottom, and top offsets) of the viewport and then displaying data at the appropriate positions in an off-screen buffer. Later, the off-screen buffer is transferred to the actual screen (video memory) by calling a display function. In a sense, this approach gives you a sort of "virtual" screen with which to work. You can think of the drawing functions as simple translators that take data represented in one coordinate system (viewport) and transfer it to a buffer (off-screen memory) in another coordinate system.

To follow the code in the slice drawing routines that I'll present in this chapter, such as **DrawWalls** and **ShowCol**, you should be familiar with the variables used to represent a viewport window and the variables used to access the off-screen buffer. The setup work for defining a viewport is done by both your application program and the **AckInitialize()** function, which is the first *ACK-3D* function that your application must call before using the engine. The only viewport variables that your application needs to set are the viewport window's left, right, top, and bottom coordinates. As an example, here are the settings you use to create a viewport that uses the full width of the screen but only the top half:

```
ACKENG ae;          // Define an interface structure
...

ae.WinStartY = 0; // Access top half of screen
ae.WinEndY = 99;
ae.WinStartX = 0; // Access full width of screen
aeWinEndX = 319;
result = AckInitialize(&ae);  // Initialize the engine
...
```

This code takes into account the fact that the actual screen size is 320 pixels in width by 200 pixels in height. The **AckInitialize()** function calls **AckSetupWindow()**, which in turn sets up the other viewport variables that are needed to draw a scene to the off-screen buffer. These variables are set up at initialization time so that precious processing time isn't wasted when views are actually drawn.

Let's take a look at the variables that are calculated by **AckSetupWindow()**. This information will help you see how a viewport window corresponds with the off-screen buffer that is used to draw a scene.

```
// This function is defined in ACKINIT.C
void AckSetupWindow(ACKENG *ae)
{
  // Access the center row of the viewport
  ae->CenterRow      = ae->WinStartY + ((ae->WinEndY - ae->WinStartY) / 2);
  // Access a memory location for the center row
  ae->CenterOffset   = ae->CenterRow * BYTES_PER_ROW;
  // Access the starting memory location of the viewport
  ae->WinStartOffset = ae->WinStartY * BYTES_PER_ROW;
  // Calculate window length in double words
  ae->WinLength      = ((ae->WinEndY - ae->WinStartY)+1) * DWORDS_PER_ROW;
  ae->WinWidth       = (ae->WinEndX - ae->WinStartX) + 1;
  ae->WinHeight      = (ae->WinEndY - ae->WinStartY) + 1;
}
```

To draw slices in the off-screen buffer, we need an easy way to access the center row of the viewport; we'll use the **CenterRow** and **CenterOffset** variables to accomplish this. **CenterRow** stores the actual row number of the center row, and **CenterOffset** stores the memory location offset for the center row. The constant **BYTES_PER_ROW** is defined in ACKENG.H as the value 320 to indicate that it takes 320 bytes of storage space to store each row. If you create a viewport that is 100 units in height (**WinStartY** = 0 and **WinEndY** = 99), the **CenterOffset** would be calculated as

```
CenterOffset      = 0 + (99 - 0) / 2) * 320
                  = 15,680
```

which gives us the offset location to the byte in the off-screen memory buffer that represents the start of the middle row. This calculation is illustrated in Figure 7.1.

Notice that Figure 7.1 also shows how the other viewport coordinates are used to reference the off-screen buffer. The **WinStartOffset** variable gives us the offset memory location (in bytes) to the starting point in the buffer. If the top edge of the viewport is 0 (indicating that a view should be displayed starting at the top edge of the screen), the offset into the off-screen buffer will be 0. If the viewport top coordinate is set to a value such as 20, on the other hand, the offset into the beginning of the off-screen buffer will be 6,400 (20¥320). The other variable that comes in handy for accessing the off-screen buffer is **WinLength**. This variable stores the size of the buffer needed to store the viewport in double words. The constant **DWORDS_PER_ROW** is defined in ACKENG.H as:

```
#define DWORDS_PER_ROW (BYTES_PER_ROW / 4)
```

That's basically all there is to setting up a viewport. But before we examine how slices are drawn, let's take a diversion and explore how DOS VGA screens are supported.

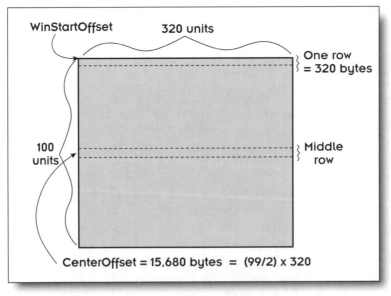

Figure 7.1 *Using viewport coordinates to calculate off-screen buffer locations.*

Supporting VGA Screens

When I first developed the code for the *ACK-3D* engine, I decided to use the popular VGA Mode X for displaying graphics under DOS. If you've written games before, or if you've heard game developers discuss their craft in public or on online forums such as GAMDEVS on CompuServe, you've probably come across this mysterious Mode X. (Rumor has it that the graphics programming wizard, Michael Abrash came up with the name "Mode X" to describe an undocumented high-resolution graphics mode on the VGA that he discovered while attempting to explain the inner workings of the VGA.) I was tempted to design the engine for Mode X because this mode supports off-screen drawing and page-flipping. My early attempts to use this mode resulted in code that worked reasonably well on fast machines but did not perform as well on slower machines. This performance issue bothered me because I wanted to create a powerful 3-D game engine that could be used to develop applications to run on most of the PCs out there in the world.

Mode X seemed like a perfect platform for DOS graphics because it supports 256 colors, a screen resolution of up to 320×240 pixels, multiple display pages, and fast copying of data to video memory. Because the *ACK-3D* engine uses different components, such as floors, ceilings, walls, and so on, to create a view, I figured I could draw each component in a separate (off-screen) display page and then quickly copy each one to video memory to draw on the screen. Unfortunately, this design meant that the *ACK-3D* engine would be dedicated to a DOS only environment and would not be easily portable to Windows or the Macintosh. This fact, coupled with a variety of algorithms for drawing into off-screen buffers, made me decide to use the more popular Mode 13h.

Mode X is a powerful VGA mode, and I encourage you to experiment with it as you build your own games and other graphics-intensive applications. In fact, I've even included some of my original Mode X switching code (it's now commented out) in the low-level source code so that you can see how Mode X is set up. If you are interested in learning more about Mode X, I suggest you go right to the source and read Michael Abrash's book, *Zen of Graphics Programming*. If you are interested in seeing how Mode X can be used to create fast-action scrolling games, check out *PC Game Programming Explorer* written by Dave Roberts. Both of these books are listed in the References section at the back of this book.

Working with VGA Mode 13h

VGA Mode 13h provides a screen resolution of 320×200 pixels with support for 256 colors. Of course, when you build a scene with the *ACK-3D* engine, you don't have to use the full screen. As shown in Figure 7.2, Mode 13h uses a linear memory organization. The starting address for display memory with Mode 13h is A000:0000. The first part of this address (A000) is called the *starting segment* or *video segment,* and the second part after the colon (0000) is called the *memory offset.* The last location of video memory in Mode 13h is referenced using the address A000:F9FF. If you're good at doing hexadecimal conversions in your head, you've probably already figured out that the entire memory area requires 64,000 bytes of storage (320×200 pixels). This screen resolution allows us to store one pixel per byte of video memory. (I'll show you how to set the video mode and access video memory shortly.)

Because the memory space for Mode 13h is linear, the first row of pixels on the screen is stored sequentially, followed by the next row of pixels, and so on. The byte value actually stored in each memory location is used to specify the color of the corresponding pixel on the screen. And because a byte of memory can store a value from 0 to 255, each pixel can be displayed in one of 256 colors. (The actual value stored is a color palette lookup index, but for now you can think of it as an actual color. I'll explain how color palettes work shortly.)

Using Mode 13h for 3-D DOS games is a good compromise, especially if you want your games to run efficiently on PCs that aren't quite as fast as a Pentium 90. The resolution of this mode is not as high as you can go with the VGA or SVGA, but if you use a higher resolution, such as 640×480, you'll have

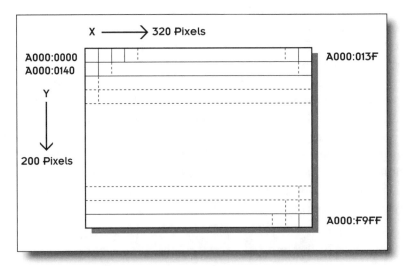

Figure 7.2   *Addressing video memory with VGA Mode 13h.*

to draw many more pixels to video memory, which will greatly increase the amount of time it takes to display a new scene. The higher-resolution modes also limit the number of colors that you can display at the same time (unless you use SVGA modes). The other two advantages of Mode 13h is that it supports 256 colors and it is easy to work with because it's accessed using a linear memory organization. Displaying a row of pixels in Mode 13h is as simple as copying a set of byte data to video memory. Displaying an entire screen is simply a block move of bytes from one buffer to the video memory. In creating 3-D type games, where screen animation is produced by displaying pre-defined bitmap images such as walls and objects, an active color palette of 256 colors provides us with enough variation to create realistic-looking light shading and texturing. If you are clever about how you create your art, you can even fool players of your games into thinking that you are using more than 256 colors at one time.

Although the color palette can contain only 256 colors, the VGA supports many more colors. In fact, the actual number of colors you can chose from is 256,000. If you can't find the color you want from a set of 256,000 colors, you probably have one heck of an eye for color.

To get the speed and flexibility needed out of Mode 13h, I've incorporated my own off-screen buffer. Thus, when the *ACK-3D* drawing routines display bitmaps, they write to the off-screen buffer instead of directly to video memory. When the buffer is full, it can be quickly copied to video memory starting at A000:0000 (assuming that you want your scenes to be displayed starting at the upper-left corner of the screen). This approach has three main benefits: It gives us the speed we need for updating views; it allows us to draw portions of the scene on top of each other, without the player seeing any flicker while graphics are erased and then redrawn; and it makes the code easily adaptable for other platforms such as Windows. A mode such as Mode X would give us the speed we need, but it would be much more difficult to translate the code that draws screens in Mode X to Windows.

Most of the functions included with the *ACK-3D* engine are designed to be portable across different platforms. However, I did provide a few screen-specific routines so that you can create DOS applications and write to the screen quickly. These routines are defined in ACKRTN.ASM; they are listed in Table 7.1. We'll be looking at two of these routines—**AckDisplayScreen** and **AckDrawPage**—later in this chapter to see how the off-screen buffer is copied to video memory. These are the only routines called by the core engine functions. The other routines are provided so that your application programs can call them and easily perform DOS screen-related tasks such as setting up the video mode or copying a block of data to video memory.

Table 7.1 *Low-Level DOS Screen Support Routines*

Routine	Description
AckDisplayScreen	Used in the DOS version to call the AckDrawPage assembly routine for displaying the off-screen buffer. This would be a good place to hook in displays to other videos without having to change your application code.
AckPutVideo	Puts a single byte into video memory.
AckGetVideo	Retrieves a single byte from video memory.
AckCopyToVideo	Copies a block from the data segment buffer to the video memory.
AckInitVideoSelector	Retrieves a selector to video memory and stores it in the VidSeg global variable. This is used with Borland's DPMI support.
AckSetPalette	Sets the 256 palette registers from a buffer of RGB values provided.
AckSetVGAmode	Switches to 320x200 256 color Mode 13h.
AckSetTextmode	Switches to 80x25 16 color Mode 3h.
AckDrawPage	Actual routine that displays a buffer onto the video screen. Called by AckDisplayScreen to provide a common interface with the application.

Getting in the Mode

When it comes to setting video modes and accessing video memory, I like to drop down to assembly language to perform these tasks as easily as possible. We're not really concerned with speed at this point; the assembly routine just clarifies what we are doing. If you've never set a VGA video mode like Mode 13h before, it might seem a little scary, but once you do it, you'll be surprised at how easy it is. The task involves making a DOS int 10h BIOS call and supplying the value for the mode you want to set as a parameter. I've provided a special function with the *ACK-3D* engine that sets the VGA Mode 13h for you. Here's the complete code for this routine, which is called **AckSetVGAmode**:

```
ACKPROC AckSetVGAmode
    push    ebx         ; Save registers used
    push    ecx
    push    edx
    mov     ax,0013h    ; AH = 0 means mode set, AL = 13h selects
    int     10h         ; IOS video interrupt
    pop     edx         ; Restore registers used
    pop     ecx
    pop     ebx
    ret
```

The register **ax** contains the function code and mode parameter value for the BIOS call that is made (int 10h). The top half of the **ax** register (**ah**) is set to 0 to tell the BIOS interrupt that we want to set a video mode; this is called the *function code*. The bottom half of the **ax** register (**al**) is assigned the value 13h, which is the video mode we want to set.

A routine like **AckSetVGAmode** could easily be coded using C. The trick is to use a built-in function for making a BIOS int 10h call, as shown here:

```
void AckSetVGAmode()
{
  union RES regs;

  regs.x.ax = 0x13;        // Use Mode 13h as parameter
  int86(0x10, &regs, &regs);  // Call BIOS int 10h and set Mode 13h
}
```

This method requires a lot less code; however it's more fun to get under the hood, get your hands dirty, and see how things are really performed when you make high-level C function calls. Right?

Accessing Video Memory

Once you set the video mode, you'll need a way to access video memory. The *ACK-3D* engine sets up a special global variable named **VidSeg** for you that references the base address of video memory. Once this variable has been initialized, routines can be called to write directly to video memory. You'll see how data is transferred to video memory later in this chapter.

Essentially what we need to do is store the base address of video memory: A000:0000. In the header file, ACKRTN.ASM, you'll find the following declarations:

```
IFDEF _BORLANDC_
VIDSEG  equ 0a0000000h
ENDIF


IFDEF _WATCOMC_
VIDSEG  equ 0a0000h
ENDIF
```

I've set it up this way so that you can see how video memory is accessed whether you are using Borland C++ or Watcom. Because Watcom sets up its memory organization so that the first megabyte is an address to the real-mode addresses, we can simply specify a 32-bit memory offset to address the video memory. The base address is the first location in video memory, which in turn is the pixel location of the left corner of the screen (first row, first column).

Since the video memory is linear, the next address A000:0001 (in real mode) is the location for the pixel at the first row, second column. If you wanted to light up the pixel at the first column of the second row, you'd write a value to location A000:0140 (offset 320). (Remember that the screen contains 320 pixels per row in Mode 13h.)

So, how can you actually write to video memory and thus display a pixel on the screen? Using assembly language, this step is a snap. All you need to do is calculate the address of video memory that corresponds to the pixel you want to light up and then write a byte value (0 to 255) that corresponds with the color you want to display. Here's an example of how the a pixel with a color value of 10 could be written to the top-left corner of the screen:

```
movzx   edi,[word ptr _VidSeg]      ; Get base address of video memory
mov     [edi],10                    ; Write pixel with color value = 10
```

To write to a location other than the base address of video memory, you simply add in the offset to video memory. For example, to light up a pixel at the first column of the second row (memory location A000:0140), here's the code required:

```
movzx   edi,[word ptr _VidSeg]
add     edi, 140h                   ; Add in offset to second row, first column
mov     [edi],10
```

Being the ultimate tool builders that we are, let's create a general-purpose routine to light up a pixel at a specific screen location. Using what we've learned about accessing video memory, this would be easy to set up, even if we want to call the routine from a C or C++ program. Let's define the routine so that it can be called as:

```
void AckPutVideo(unsigned int offset,unsigned char color);
```

This routine places a single byte value (pixel color) at a specified screen offset. Here's the code:

```
ACKPROC AckPutVideo
    push    ebp
    mov     ebp,esp                 ; Get base address of parameters
    push    es                      ; Save registers used
    push    ebx
    push    edi
    mov     bx,[word ptr _VidSeg+2] ; Pick up the video selector
    mov     es,bx                   ; and put it in es so we can access the video
```

```
movzx   edi,[word ptr _VidSeg]       ; Get base address of video memory
add     edi,[dword ptr ebp+8]        ; Add in offset
mov     edx,[ebp+12]                 ; Get pixel value to display
mov     [edi],dl                     ; Move pixel value to video memory
pop     edi                          ; Restore registers
pop     ebx
pop     es
pop     ebp
ret
endp
```

This code shows a feature we have not discussed—how to pass parameters into an assembly-language routine. Notice we use the stack pointer register (**esp**) to get the base address of where the parameters are stored. This location is moved to the **ebp** register so that we can access the parameters. The first parameter (**offset**) is stored at location **ebp+8** and the second parameter (**color**) is obtained using **ebp+12**. The instruction **mov [edi],dl** takes care of the work of sending a color value (**dl**) to the screen memory location referenced by **edi**. That's all there is to it! Well, almost. What we used for the magical value above in the **VidSeg** variable is really a protected-mode selector that was retrieved from a DPMI service call. Shown next is the routine that must be called to get the actual selector for the video. What we do is ask for the selector that corresponds to the real-mode video segment A000h. The DPMI handler, installed automatically by Borland, returns the value to use whenever we want to read or write to video memory. You will only have to be concerned with DPMI, selectors, and such, if you use Borland C++ in DOS. With Watcom and the DOS4GW library, the segments given to your application are already set up to address the first megabyte of memory. That's why I provided two different defines earlier for Borland and Watcom.

Here's the complete assembly routine, named **AckInitVideoSelector**, which retrieves a video selector:

```
ACKPROC AckInitVideoSelector
    push    ebx                         ; Save registers used
    push    ecx
    push    edx
    mov     ax,2                        ; Allocate selector for real mode address
    mov     bx,0A000h                   ; Get Video address
    int     31h
    mov     [word ptr _VidSeg+2],ax
    mov     [word ptr _VidSeg],0
    pop     edx
    pop     ecx
    pop     ebx
    ret
    endp
```

Working with the VGA Color Palette

As I mentioned earlier, the VGA in Mode 13h allows us to use up to 256 colors at one time. The color values are stored by the VGA in a special list that is called the *active color palette* or *color palette* for short. When you write your applications, it's up to you to load colors in the color palette. Of course, when the VGA is reset, a default set of colors is loaded into the palette. As an example, Table 7.2 lists the default colors for the first 16 palette entries. Notice that the colors are numbered starting with 0 instead of 1, because 0 references the first palette location.

When you send a pixel value (0 to 255) to display memory, the value actually represents an index into the color palette. For example, if you specify a value of 10, the VGA goes to the 10th location in the palette and uses the codes stored in this location to determine the actual color that should be displayed for the pixel. This arrangement provides you with a dynamic system for loading different colors and controlling how they are displayed.

What is actually stored in each palette location is a trio of values. The three values represent the red, green, and blue color components needed to create

Table 7.2 *The First 16 Palette Entries*

Palette Entry	Color Name
0	Black
1	Blue
2	Green
3	Cyan
4	Red
5	Magenta
6	Brown
7	White
8	Gray
9	Light Blue
10	Light Green
11	Light Cyan
12	Light Red
13	Light Magenta
14	Yellow
15	Bright White

the color. In color theory, these values are called the *RGB components*. Each RGB component can range from 0 to 63, where 63 represents the highest value or brightest color and 0 represents the lowest value or darkest color. Thus, to define the color bright white, you use the trio (63,63,63). For black, the RGB components are (0,0,0). These values tell the video hardware the signals to use to display colors on your PC screen. Without getting too technical, you can think of them as analog signals that control the intensity of the electron beams that strike a display tube.

So how can we change the color palette? Fortunately, the VGA provides us with a few special registers we can use to load in a new palette. This register is called the *Color Address Write Register*, which is located at address 3C8h, and the *Color Data Register*, which is located at address 3C9h. The Color Address Write Register is used to select the palette entry or index being loaded, and the Color Data Register is used to load the actual RGB components. To easily use this feature, we'll write a routine that passes the color palette we want to load and then writes to the appropriate registers to load the palette. Sounds easy? It is. Here's the format for calling our routine:

```
void AckSetPalette(UCHAR *PalBuffer);
```

The **PalBuffer** parameter must be a buffer containing 768 bytes (256 palette entries multiplied by 3 color components per entry). As shown in Figure 7.3,

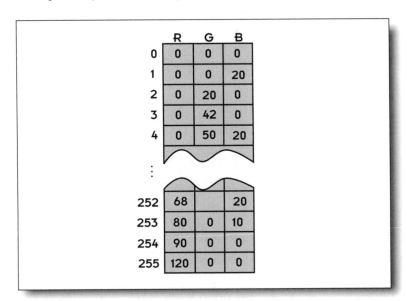

Figure 7.3 *Setting up colors in the VGA color palette.*

three values are needed to specify each color in the palette. The first three values define the RGB components (color) for the first palette entry, the next three values define the components for the second palette entry, and so on. Fortunately, setting up a buffer containing three values for each color isn't a big deal since most image formats that use 256 colors store their color information this way. All we need to do is read the RGB values from the image file and pass them into the routine shown next.

Here's the complete code for **AckSetPalette**:

```
ACKPROC AckSetPalette
    push    ebp             ; Save pointer to parameter
    mov     ebp,esp         ; Get pointer to parameters
    push    ds              ; Save Registers used
    push    ebx
    push    ecx
    push    edx
    mov     esi,[ebp+8]     ; Get address of PalBuffer parameter
    mov     ebx,0           ; Initialize with value of 0
    mov     ecx,256         ; Number of palette entries to load
    mov     dx,3c8h         ; Address of Color Address Write Register

asp_loop:
    mov     al,bl
    out     dx,al           ; Indicates which color palette to load
    inc     bx              ; Set up for loading next color palette
    inc     dx              ; Use Color Data Register (3C9h)
    lodsb
    out     dx,al           ; Write first color component—red
    lodsb
    out     dx,al           ; Write second color component—green
    lodsb
    out     dx,al           ; Write third color component—blue
    dec     dx              ; Return to address of Color Address Write Register
    loop    asp_loop        ; Repeat for next color palette entry

    pop     edx             ; Restore registers used
    pop     ecx
    pop     ebx
    pop     ds
    pop     ebp
    ret
    endp
```

To call this routine, you must make sure that the palette buffer (**PalBuffer**) has been set up properly; otherwise you'll end up with a real color mess on your screen. To help you in this respect, the *ACK-3D* engine provides a higher-level C function named **AckLoadAndSetPalette()**, which you can call from your applications to load a color palette from a data file. After loading the color palette data, this function calls the lower-level **AckSetPalette** to load the palette to the VGA. We'll explore **AckLoadAndSetPalette()** in more detail in Chapter 12 when we cover bitmaps. For now, let's get back to **AckSetPalette**.

You shouldn't have too much trouble following the assembly code for the low-level routine. First, we use **ebp** to reference the parameter **PalBuffer**. Then, we initialize the **ebx** register to reference the first palette location (0). The **dx** register contains the address of the Color Address Write Register.

The RGB components are loaded into the VGA using the loop at the label **asp_loop**. The first step involves sending the number of the palette entry to be loaded to the Color Address Write Register. This step performs the necessary initialization for writing to the color palette. Next, the three color components are loaded (one at a time) to the Color Data Register at the address 3C9h. This process continues until the three components for each of the 256 palette entries are loaded.

Drawing the Slices

It's now time to get back to the technique of drawing slices. The ray-casting routines we explored in the previous chapter performed the work of constructing an array of slices that represent 320 columns across the screen. The goal now is to make our view come to life by turning the slice information into a buffer that can in turn be sent to the screen—whether it be a DOS or Window screen

So, what does it take to turn the set of slices into a screen image? Essentially, there are six steps involved:

1. Process the key coordinates for the viewport and screen buffer (viewport height, viewport left coordinate, base address of screen buffer, and so on).

2. Determine the starting point of the array of slice structures.

3. Check the slice structure that represents the current screen column to see how it should be drawn. This step tests the slice to see if it is transparent and if there are slices behind it. We also need to test for multi-height walls.

4. Get the bitmap code of the slice and calculate a color factor to draw the slice by using the player's distance to the slice, which gives us light shading with distance.

5. Depending on the type of slice found, call a special drawing routine to place it in the buffer at the appropriate row and column position.

6. Repeat steps 2 through 5 until all slices in the array have been converted to the buffer.

The code that is responsible for controlling this process is the low-level **DrawWalls** routine found in ACKRTN1.ASM. If you recall from the previous chapter, this routine is called from **BuildUpView** after all of the slices have been constructed. Let's look at the complete source code for this routine and then we'll take it apart to see how it ticks.

DESIGN TIP

The **DrawWalls** routine actually consists of two routines in one. The first half of the routine contains the code to draw slices to a high-resolution, off-screen buffer. The labels that identify the code for this task start with the letters **stw**, which stand for "standard walls." The code found in the second half of the routine starting with the label **stw_lowres**, handles the work of drawing slices to a low-resolution buffer. The other labels in this section of code start with "**stwlr**." The process for drawing slices to either a high-resolution or low-resolution buffer is similar; however, we can speed up the code for drawing to a low-resolution buffer since we have less resolution to handle. The global flag **Resolution** is tested to determine which resolution should be used. If it is set to 1, the low-resolution code is used. The difference between high and low resolution is simply the number of pixels drawn to each column of the screen. Low resolution duplicates every column of slices, so only half the number needs to be calculated during the rendering process. This mode is useful on slower machines or video cards. Use the high resolution whenever possible for sharper images.

Here is the complete **DrawWalls** routine:

```
ACKPROC DrawWalls
    push    ebp                 ; Save registers
    push    esi
    push    edi

    mov     ax,[_gWinHeight]    ; Get height of viewport
    shr     ax,1                ; Divide the height by 2
    mov     [_Floorht],ax       ; Store as floor height
    mov     ax,[_ViewHeight]    ; ViewHeight = 31;
                                ; half-height of a bitmap
    mov     [_sctopht],ax       ; Store height of view column (bitmap)
    mov     dx,64
    sub     dx,ax                           ; Remaining half of bitmap (33)
    mov     [_scbotht],dx                   ; Store bottom reference
    movsx   ebx, [word ptr _gWinStartX]     ; Get left position of viewport
    movsx   ecx, [_gCenterOff]              ; Get buffer offset to center row
```

```
    add     ecx,ebx                     ; Add offset to left position
    add     ecx,[_gScrnBuffer]          ; Add offset to base of screen buffer
    mov     [_scVid],ecx                ; Store location of center row for
                                        ; easy off-screen buffer access
    cmp     [word ptr _Resolution],1    ; Is this low resolution mode?
    je      stw_lowres                  ; Yes, perform faster draw


                                        ; Continue on for high resolution processing
    movzx   eax,[_gWinEndX]             ; Get right position of viewport
    imul    eax,saSize                  ; Multiply by size of Slice structure (30)
    mov     [ENDPOS],eax                ; Store total storage space as ENDPOS
    imul    ebx,saSize                  ; Multiply left position of viewport by
                                        ; size of Slice structure (30 bytes)

; Top of the main loop for drawing each slice structure to the off-screen buffer.
stw010:
    mov     ebp,offset _Slice           ; Get offset to Slice array
    add     ebp,ebx                     ; Add in offset to current Slice structure

; This section of code traverses the list of slices for a column to get to
;  the last one in the list.
stw020:
    cmp     [byte ptr ebp+saActive],0   ; Is this an active slice?
    jz      short stw030                ; Nope, so it's the last one
    cmp     [dword ptr ebp+saNext],0    ; Is this the last slice?
    jz      short stw030                ; Yes, so can't go further
    mov     ebp,[dword ptr ebp+saNext]  ; Point to next slice
    jmp     short stw020                ; Go check again

stw030:
    mov     ax,[word ptr ebp+sabNumber] ; Get the bitmap number
    mov     cx,ax                       ; Save bitmap number
    and     cx,0ffh                     ; Isolate number from flags
    mov     [_scmulcnt],cx              ; Save as current multi count
    mov     [_scbNum],ax                ; and bitmap number and flags
    mov     cx,0                        ; Set multi-flag to none
    test    ax,WALL_TYPE_MULTI          ; Is the slice a multi-height one?
    jz      short stw040                ; Branch if not
    mov     esi,[dword ptr ebp+samPtr]  ; Get pointer to multi-height grid
    mov     [_scMulData],esi            ; Store pointer
    or      esi,esi                     ; Is there multi-height data?
    jz      short stw040                ; Branch if not
    mov     cx,1                        ; Set multi-height flag to yes

stw040:
    mov     [_scmulti],cx               ; Store multi-height flag (or 0)
    mov     ecx,[dword ptr ebp+sabMap]  ; Get pointer to bitmaps
    movzx   esi,al                      ; Get low byte of bitmap number
    shl     esi,2                       ; Multiply by 4
    mov     esi,[dword ptr ecx+esi]     ; Get actual bitmap pointer
    movsx   ecx,[word ptr ebp+saDist]   ; Get distance to slice
    mov     [_bmDistance],ecx           ; Save for draw routine
    shr     ecx,6                       ; Bring it down into palette range
```

```
        cmp     ecx,15                          ; Check against maximum palette number
        jbe     short stw050
        mov     ecx,15                          ; Force to maximum if above

stw050:
        shl     ecx,8                           ; Multiply by 256 for palette entry
        mov     edi,[_gPalTable]                ; Get pointer to palette table
        add     edi,ecx                         ; Add in palette entry offset
        movsx   ecx,[word ptr ebp+sabColumn]; Get column of bitmap slice
        shl     ecx,6                           ; Multiply by 64 to get correct screen col
        add     esi,ecx                         ; Adjust wall point to correct column
        mov     [_scColumn],ecx                 ; Save for multi-height walls
        mov     [_scWall],esi                   ; Pointer to top of slice bitmap
        mov     [_scPal],edi                    ; Store palette entry
                                                ; (base address of light shading zone)

        mov     eax,0
        mov     [_scsavVid],eax                 ; Null out saved video
        mov     ax,[_Floorht]                   ; Window height / 2 saved earlier
        mov     [_scwht],ax                     ; Store this height in scwht
        mov     esi,ebx                         ; Offset to SLICE structure
        call    [dword ptr ebp+saFnc]           ; Call the appropriate function for drawing
                                                ;   the slice
        mov     ebx,esi                         ; We're back save ??

stw075:
        cmp     [dword ptr ebp+saPrev],0        ; Is this the first slice?
        jz      short stw080                    ; Yes, go to next column
        mov     ebp,[dword ptr ebp+saPrev]      ; Pick up previous slice
        jmp     stw030                          ;  and start again with same column

stw080:
        inc     [dword ptr _scVid]              ; Get next video position (next column)
        add     ebx,saSize                      ; Reference next slice in array
        cmp     ebx,[ENDPOS]                    ; Did we get to the end of slices yet?
        ja      stw_getout                      ; Yes, get out
        jmp     stw010                          ; Go on to next slice

; This part of the code processes slices to be displayed in a lower-resolution mode.
stw_lowres:
        mov     eax,ebx                         ; Current column of display
        imul    eax,saSize                      ; Size of Slice structure
        mov     ebp,offset _Slice               ; Offset to slices
        add     ebp,eax

stwlr020:
        cmp     [byte ptr ebp+saActive],0       ; Is this an active slice?
        jz      short stwlr030                  ; Nope, so it's the last one
        cmp     [dword ptr ebp+saNext],0        ; Is this the last slice?
        jz      short stwlr030                  ; Yes, so can't go further
        mov     ebp,[dword ptr ebp+saNext]      ; Point to next slice
        jmp     short stwlr020
```

```
stwlr030:
  mov    ax,[word ptr ebp+sabNumber] ; Bitmap number
  mov    cx,ax
  and    cx,0ffh                      ; Isolate number from flags
  mov    [_scmulcnt],cx               ; Save as current multi count
  mov    [_scbNum],ax                 ; And bitmap number and flags
  mov    cx,0                         ; Set multi-flag to none
  test   ax,WALL_TYPE_MULTI
  jz     short stwlr040

  mov    esi,[dword ptr ebp+samPtr]
  mov    [_scMulData],esi
  or     esi,esi                      ; Is there multi-height data?
  jz     short stwlr040               ; Br if not
  mov    cx,1                         ; Set multi-flag to yes

stwlr040:
  mov    [_scmulti],cx
  mov    ecx,[dword ptr ebp+sabMap]   ; get pointer to bitmaps
  movzx  esi,al                       ; Get low byte of bitmap number
  shl    esi,2
  mov    esi,[dword ptr ecx+esi]      ; Get actual bitmap pointer
  movsx  ecx,[word ptr ebp+saDist]    ; Distance to slice
  mov    [_bmDistance],ecx            ; Save for draw routine
  shr    ecx,6                        ; Bring it down into palette range
  cmp    ecx,15                       ; Check against maximum palette number
  jbe    short stwlr050
  mov    ecx,15                       ; Force to maximum if above

stwlr050:
  shl    ecx,8                        ; X256 for palette entry
  mov    edi,[_gPalTable]             ; Pointer to palette table
  add    edi,ecx
  movsx  ecx,[byte ptr ebp+sabColumn]; Column of bitmap slice
  shl    ecx,6                        ; x64 to get correct row (column)
  add    esi,ecx                      ; Adjust wall point to correct column
  mov    [_scColumn],ecx              ; Save for multi-height walls
  mov    [_scWall],esi
  mov    [_scPal],edi
  mov    eax,0
  mov    [_scsavVid],eax              ; Null out saved video
  mov    ax,[_Floorht]                ; Window height / 2 saved earlier
  mov    [_scwht],ax

  mov    esi,ebx
  cmp    [byte ptr ebp+saType],ST_WALL ; Transparent wall?
  je     short stwlr060                 ; Nope, use solid slice routine
  ACKCALL  ShowColMaskLow
  jmp    short stwlr070

stwlr060:
  ACKCALL ShowColLow
```

```
stwlr070:
    mov     ebx,esi
    cmp     [dword ptr ebp+saPrev],0    ; Is this the first slice?
    jz      short stwlr080              ; Yes, go to next column
    mov     ebp,[dword ptr ebp+saPrev]  ; Pick up previous slice
    jmp     stwlr030                    ; And start again with same column

stwlr080:
    add     [dword ptr _scVid],2        ; Next video position
    inc     ebx                         ; Next column
    inc     ebx                         ; Next column
    cmp     bx,[word ptr _gWinEndX]     ; Are we at the end of the window?
    ja      short stw_getout            ; Yes, get out
    jmp     stw_lowres

stw_getout:
    pop     edi                         ; Restore registers
    pop     esi
    pop     ebp
    ret
    endp
    end
```

Step 1, processing the key coordinates for the viewport and screen buffer, is performed in the first section of code (everything up to the **stw010** label). The code starts by getting the height of the viewport (**gWinHeight**). (Recall that the global variable **gWinHeight** was set in the C function **AckRegisterStructure()**; it is calculated as the bottom coordinate of the viewport minus the top coordinate.) The viewport height is then divided by 2 to calculate a value for the floor height, which is stored in the variable **Floorht**. The next calculation uses **ViewHeight**, which is defined in ACKDATA.C as:

```
short ViewHeight = 31;
```

and stores this value in the variable **sctopht**. I'm using a sneaky trick here to display slices. Drawing each slice involves looking up the bitmap for the slice and then displaying the bitmap. If you recall from our earlier discussions, each bitmap is 64 pixels in height. We could display each bitmap from the bottom up or top down but I've found that this results in creating bitmaps that have too many "jaggies" for my taste. The jaggies are caused by round-off errors. When dividing the height in two based on the distance.

After some experimentation, I came up with a much better way of displaying the 64 pixel! unit bitmaps. As Figure 7.4 shows, this technique finds the midpoint of each bitmap and then draws the top half of the bitmap by starting in the middle and working up. Once this step is complete, the bottom half of the bitmap is drawn by starting in the middle and working down. This pro-

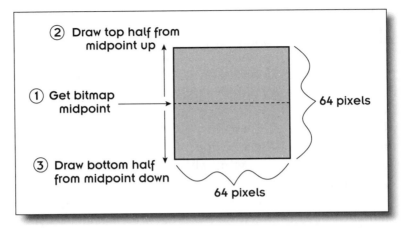

Figure 7.4 *Drawing bitmaps in two sections.*

cess is a little slower than drawing the complete bitmap from bottom to top; however, the end result—smooth bitmaps—is well worth the extra time spent. My thanks to Jaimi McEntire, who originally helped with this technique over numerous phone discussions.

With this technique in mind, the code should be easier to follow. The **sctopht** variable stores the maximum height (31) for the top part of a column (bitmap). The variable, **scbotht**, on the other hand, stores the maximum height (33) of the bottom part of a column bitmap.

The next set of instructions performs the work of calculating an offset into the off-screen buffer. This offset will be the starting address needed to write to the off-screen buffer. First, we take the coordinate of the left edge of the viewport (**gWinStartX**) and add this value to the buffer center offset (**gCenterOff**). From our earlier discussion, recall that the offset to the buffer is calculated in the **AckSetupWindow()** function as

```
CenterOffset = CenterRow * BYTES_PER_ROW
```

where **BYTES_PER_ROW** is set to 320. The result of all these calculations is to store the actual memory location that corresponds to the start of the middle viewport row in the variable **scVid**. This variable will be accessed and incremented in the drawing loop to draw slices. When we draw a scene, we'll begin by drawing at the left viewport edge of the middle of the screen.

Finally, notice how the **Resolution** flag is tested to determine if the code should branch to the low-resolution processing section (**stw_lowres**). For now, let's continue and assume we are drawing slices to the high-resolution buffer.

Step 2, determining the starting point of the array of slice structures, is an easy one to perform, as shown here:

```
stw010:
   mov    ebp,offset _Slice    ; Get offset to Slice array
   add    ebp,ebx              ; Add in offset to first Slice structure
```

The global variable **Slice** references the base address of the **Slice** array, and the register **ebx** contains the offset value to the slice structure we'll need at this point to build the view. This offset value was previously calculated by multiplying the size of a slice structure (30 bytes) by the value that represented the left position of the viewport. We did this to make sure that the starting offset into the slice array matches the left viewport offset. For example, if the left edge of the viewport is 0, the starting offset into the slices array would be 0. If the left viewport starts at 100, the starting offset into the array would be 300 (30 x 100). This system of coordinating the starting offset of the **Slice** array with the left edge of the viewport is shown in Figure 7.5. Notice that two variables are used to work with the slice array: **Slice** keeps track of the actual slice structure that is currently being drawn, and **ENDPOS** references the end of the slice array. This variable is calculated by multiplying

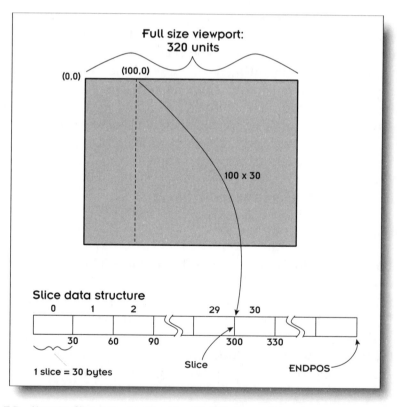

Figure 7.5   *How the Slice array corresponds with the screen viewport.*

the size of a slice structure by the coordinate representing the right edge of the viewport. This takes care of all of the setup work we need. As the code continues to loop to process each slice, we simply add in the size of the slice structure (30 bytes) to the current starting offset into the array.

The next step involves starting the code (**stw020**) that traverses the array of slice structures to build up the off-screen buffer. The first thing the loop does is to check to see if the current slice is linked to other slices. This condition is determined by checking the **Active** flag as shown:

```
cmp [byte ptr ebp+saActive],0 ; Is this an active slice? (transparent)
jz   short stw030             ; Nope, so it's the last one
```

If this flag is set, the code traverses the linked list of **Next** pointers to get to the last slice in the linked list. At this stage, we know that the slice has slices behind it, and we want to find the last one that is visible so that it can be drawn first. If we draw these slices in reverse order, they will come out just right on the screen.

Once we've located the slice to be drawn first, the code continues at label **stw030**. Here, we get the bitmap number for the slice and check it to see if it represents a multi-height wall slice. The bitmap number variable **sabNumber** actually contains both flag settings for the bitmap and the bitmap code, so we need to "and" it with the value 0ffh to separate the flags from the bitmap code. If the bitmap code indicates the slice is part of a multi-height wall, a flag is set and the pointer to the multi-height wall grid is stored. If the slice is not part of a multi-height wall, the code jumps to label **stw040**. At this point, a pointer to the slice bitmap is placed in the **esi** register, and the distance from the player to the slice is obtained and stored in the variable **bmDistance**. The code saves this distance value so that it can be used later by an actual drawing routine to draw the slice. But notice that the distance is also used as a table lookup value in the section of code at label **stw050**. This code allows us to factor in a light shading value for drawing the slice. The technique used here is to draw slices that appear further in the distance with slightly different colors from the colors used to draw slices that appear closer. Before we explore the code in **DrawWalls** any further, let's look at how the color lighting system works.

Simple Light Shading

The *ACK-3D* engine uses an array named **PalTable[ ]** to store lookup values for drawing wall slices and factoring light shading zones. This table is defined in ACK3D.H as

```
unsigned char PalTable[PAL_SIZE];
```

where **PAL_SIZE** is defined as the value 4096. The array allows us to support 256 colors using 16 zones. The idea behind the zone concept is that we divide distances from the player to a wall or object into 16 different zones. For each zone, there are 256 colors that can be used. As a player moves toward a wall or object, as shown in Figure 7.6, we use the distance to determine which zone the player is in. This is done by dividing the distance by 64, which gives us a range value from 0 to 15. (If the value is greater than 15, it is set to 15.) Once the zone value is determined, it is multiplied by 256 to calculate the actual lookup value into the **PalTable[ ]** array. This value will serve as the starting point in the array to access the color set used to draw the wall or object slice.

DESIGN TIP

Why do we use 16 lighting zones? We easily could have used more or fewer lighting zones, but 16 gives us the best results without using a lot of memory. When we calculate a zone, recall that we divide the player's distance from the POV to the slice by 64. This means that any distance over 960 units is automatically assigned to the last zone (zone 15). Thus, we are actually using 16 zones to represent 960 units. It turns out that each zone is the size of a grid square, so as the player moves from one grid to another, he or she enters a new lighting zone.

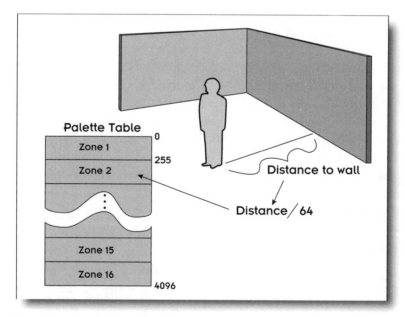

Figure 7.6   *Using zones to determine light shading.*

Getting Back to Drawing Walls

Back at the wall-drawing ranch (label **stw050**) we continue by calculating the lighting zone and determining the actual column where the slice bitmap will be displayed. The goal of these calculations is to save three global variables that will be used by the actual slice drawing routine to be called later: **scColumn**, **scWall**, and **scPal**. **scColumn** stores the correct row and column position of the slice, **scWall** stores a reference to the top of the bitmap that will be used to draw the slice, and **scPal** stores the index value into the **PalTable[ ]** array. We need to get ready to call the routine that is responsible for drawing the slice (either **ShowCol** or **ShowColNS**), so we need to initialize a few other variables (**scsavVid** and **scwht)**. And then this instruction kicks off the actual drawing routine:

```
call    [dword ptr ebp+saFnc]    ; Call the appropriate function for drawing
                                ; the slice
```

The drawing routine takes over and draws the slice at the appropriate off-screen buffer location. (I'll explain how all of this works later in the section, *Who Draws the Slice?*) All you need to know now is that one of four different routines can be called, which is the reason that the call instruction is not hard-wired to a specific routine.

After the slice has been drawn, we need to check to see if the slice is linked with other slices to indicate that the slice is part of a group of walls that need to be drawn in a certain order. The code for this testing starts with the **stw075** label. The first thing we do is test the **Prev** pointer of the slice to see if it has a slice in front of it:

```
cmp [dword ptr ebp+saPrev],0 ; Is this the first slice?
```

If the pointer is set, we know that there is a slice in front, and our next task is to get this slice and jump back to the main slice drawing loop at **stw030**. If the slice doesn't have any slices in front of it, the code jumps to label **stw080**. At this last section of code for drawing slices to a high-resolution buffer, we increment the variable that references the off-screen buffer (**scVid**) and the slice size to the register **ebx,** which is used to reference the array of slices. Then we check to see if we are at the end of the array (**ENDPOS**). If we are, we jump to the label **stw_getout**; otherwise, we branch back to **stw010** to start the drawing process all over again for the next slice in the array.

Who Draws the Slice?

The **call** instruction to draw the wall slice looks rather strange. After all, we're not providing the name of an actual routine. We're using a pointer to a function. If you recall from the previous chapter, when the slice structure was built in **BuildSlice()** or **BuildSliceMulti()**, the ***Fnc** field was assigned a pointer to a function. The variables **WallRtn** and **WallMaskRtn** keep track of the actual routine to be used to draw either a standard slice or a transparent slice, respectively. Then, one of these functions is assigned to the pointer variable as:

```
sPtr->Fnc = WallRtn;      // Use standard slice routine
```

or

```
sPtr->Fnc = WallMaskRtn;  // Use transparent slice routine
```

As Table 7.3 shows, there are two sets of routines for drawing actual slices to the off-screen buffer. **ShowColNS** and **ShowColMaskNS** are defined in the assembly source file ACKRTN4.ASM, and **ShowCol** and **ShowColNS** are defined in ACKRTN1.ASM. The **NS** functions handle the work of drawing a standard or transparent slice without using light shading. The other two functions use light shading, but keep in mind that only one of these routines is used. The decision of which routine to use is made in the C function **BuildSlice()**.

DESIGN TIP

We won't need to look at the code for all of these routines because they are similar. In fact, we'll focus on **ShowCol** since this routine is the most complex. The other routines don't perform all of the operations that **ShowCol** performs thus they are easier to follow once you know how **ShowCol** works.

Table 7.3 *Routines for Drawing Wall Slices*

Routine	Description
ShowColNS	Draws a single wall or object slice into the off-screen buffer without using light shading. This routine draws solid walls that have no transparent colors
ShowColMaskNS	Draws a transparent wall or object slice without light shading. This routine is slower than ShowColNS because every pixel drawn must be checked for transparency.
ShowCol	Draws a single wall or object slice into the off-screen buffer. This routine draws solid walls that have no transparent colors.
ShowColMask	Draws a transparent wall or object slice. This routine is slower than ShowCol because every pixel drawn must be checked for transparency.

Drawing a Standard Slice with Light Shading

Let's take a close look at one of the routines for drawing a slice in the off-screen buffer—**ShowCol**. This description will give you an idea of what's involved in transferring the slice data to the screen buffer. The **ShowCol** routine performs the work of drawing a single slice at a specified off-screen buffer position. The slice is drawn using the light shading table to adjust the actual colors of the pixels displayed. The counterpart to this routine, **ShowColNS**, is nearly identical except that the light shading table is not used to adjust pixel color values.

The **ShowCol** code is arranged into two main sections. One section draws a slice for a standard wall or object, and the other section checks and draws a multi-height slice. The process for drawing a slice involves displaying the bitmap assigned to the slice structure. But remember that we actually display the bitmap by writing the pixels for the top half of the bitmap first, and then the bottom half of the bitmap is written to the off-screen buffer.

The drawing code uses a number of special variables that were set up by the higher-level **DrawWalls** routine. I've provided a description of these key variables in Table 7.4 to help you follow the code in **ShowCol**.

Table 7.4 *Variables Used in Drawing the Slice*

Variable	Description
dmDistance	The actual distance from the player's position to the slice to be drawn.
scVid	The starting address of the off-screen buffer where the slice will be displayed.
scColumn	The actual screen column position of the slice to be drawn. This variable is used in the portion of code that draws slices for multi-height walls.
scWall	A pointer to the top of the bitmap used to display the slice.
scPal	The base address of the light shading color palette that corresponds to the light shading zone used to draw the slice.
scwht	The row mid point of the viewport. This value is calculated as window height/2.
scsavwht	Saves the location in the off-screen buffer where the previous bitmap slice was drawn.
sctopht	The height of the top part of a slice bitmap (31 pixels). This is the part of the bitmap that will be drawn first.
scbotht	The height of the bottom part of a slice bitmap (33 pixels). This is the part of the bitmap that will be drawn second.
scmulcount	The number of vertical blocks in this multi-height wall.
scMulData	Pointer to multi-height wall bitmap.

Let's examine the complete **ShowCol** routine and then we'll step through the code:

```
ACKPROC ShowCol
  push  ebp                   ; Save registers
  push  esi
  push  edi
  mov   edi,[_scVid]          ; Get off-screen buffer position for current column
  mov   ebp,[_scPal]          ; Base of the color palette for shading
  mov   ax,[_scwht]           ; Height to use (window height/2)
  mov   [_scsavwht],ax        ; Save height for later use
  movzx ecx,[_sctopht]            ; Get height of top part of bitmap (31 pixels)
  mov   ebx,[_scWall]             ; Pointer to slice bitmap
  add   ebx,ecx                   ; Move to midpoint of bitmap (pos. 31)
  mov   [_bmWall],ebx             ; Save midpoint
  mov   ch,al                     ; Get 1/2 height of window
  inc   ch                        ; ch=32 Increase height by 1
  mov   esi,[_bmDistance]         ; Get distance to slice
  mov   esi,[_LowerTable+esi*4]   ; And use for pre-scale table
  mov   [SVTABLE],esi             ; Save table start for later
  mov   eax,0
  mov   ebx,0
  test  [word ptr _scbNum],WALL_TYPE_UPPER  ; Do we have an upper wall?
  jz    short toprun                        ; Yes, time to branch
  mov   edx,[_bmDistance]                    ; Use distance to slice

zztoploop:
  dec   ch                ; Decrement loop counter
  jz    short zzdomulti ; Are we done yet?
  sub   di,320            ; Subtract 320 from buffer position
  add   bx,dx             ; Add in distance to slice
  cmp   bh,cl
  jge   short zzdomulti
  jmp   zztoploop         ; Continue looping

zzdomulti:
  mov   [_scwht],cx
  mov   [_scsavVid],edi ; Store actual buffer position for drawing
  jmp   chkmulti

; Set up to draw top part of bitmap (top 31 pixels)
toprun:
  mov   ebx,[_bmWall]   ; Get midpoint of bitmap to draw slice
; Loop to draw top part of bitmap
toploop:
  movzx edx,[word ptr esi] ; Get the scaled pixel offset into bitmap
  cmp   dl,cl              ; See if we've gone beyond halfway yet
  jg    short botrun       ; Yes, now do bottom half
  lea   esi,[esi+2]        ; Next entry into scale table
  neg   edx               ; Make negative to use upper half of bitmap
  mov   al,[ebx+edx]      ; Get the actual bitmap pixel
  mov   al,[ebp+eax]      ; Adjust for light shading
```

```
        mov     [edi],al        ; Move pixel color to off-screen buffer
        add     edi,-320        ; Go up one row
        dec     ch              ; Decrement drawing counter
        jnz     toploop         ; Continue to loop

; Set up to draw bottom part of bitmap slice (bottom 33 pixels)
botrun:
        mov     [_scwht],cx     ; Get remaining window height
        mov     [_scsavVid],edi ; Save position of last update
        mov     edi,[_scVid]    ; Get off-screen buffer position for current column
        mov     cx,[_scbotht]   ; Get size of bottom half of bitmap (33 pixels)
        mov     dx,[_scsavwht]  ; Get 1/2 window height
        mov     ch,dl
        mov     esi,[SVTABLE]   ; Get the scale table back for lower half
        inc     ebx             ; Reference next row of bitmap
        dec     cl
; Loop to draw bottom part of bitmap
botloop:
        lea     edi,[edi+320]   ; Move down one row
        movzx   edx,[word ptr esi] ; Get pixel offset from scale table
        cmp     dl,cl           ; Have we done half yet?
        jge     short chkmulti  ; Yes, done with bottom half
        lea     esi,[esi+2]     ; Next entry in table
        mov     al,[ebx+edx]    ; Get actual bitmap pixel
        mov     al,[ebp+eax]    ; Adjust for light shading
        mov     [edi],al        ; Move pixel color to off-screen buffer
        dec     ch
        jnz     botloop

chkmulti:
        mov     edi,[_scsavVid]     ; Get off-screen buffer location
        cmp     [word ptr _scmulti],0 ; Is the multi-height flag set?
        jz      alldone             ; We're done; no multi-height slice
        mov     cx,[_scmulcnt]      ; Get number of vertical blocks
        mov     ebx,[_scMulData]    ; Pointer to count and wall data
        mov     cl,[ebx]            ; Get number of walls to draw
        inc     ebx
        mov     al,[ebx]            ; Get first wall to show
        inc     ebx
        mov     [_scMulData],ebx
        movzx   ebx,al              ; Get wall number
        mov     esi,[_scColumn]     ; Current bitmap column to display x 64
        lea     esi,[esi+63]
        mov     [_scColumn],esi     ; Save column for later use
        mov     eax,[_WallbMaps]    ; Get array of bitmaps
        mov     ebx,[eax+ebx*4]     ; Get the bitmap we are using
        add     ebx,esi             ; Point to bottom of column
        mov     a x,[_scwht]        ; Get height of window
        mov     ch,ah
        cmp     ch,0            ; Is there more room to draw?
        jz      short alldone  ; br if at top of window
        mov     esi,[SVTABLE]  ; Pick up scale table for this distance
        mov     eax,0          ; Clear out all 32 bits
```

```
mulloop:
  movzx eax,[word ptr esi]  ; Get height displacement for this row
  cmp   al,64               ; Did we do the entire column?
  jge   short nextlevel     ; Yes, see if more walls
  lea   esi,[esi+2]
  neg   eax                 ; Invert so we can add it below
  movzx eax,[byte ptr ebx+eax]  ; Get the pixel from the bitmap
  mov   al,[ebp+eax]        ; Map it to the palette for shading
  mov   [edi],al            ; Place it into the video buffer
  dec   ch                  ; Bump the window height
  jz    short alldone       ; br if at the top of the window
  sub   edi,320             ; next video row
  jmp   mulloop

nextlevel:
  dec   cl                  ; Bump wall count
  jz    short alldone       ; br if no more walls
  mov   ebx,[_scMulData]    ; Get pointer to the multi-height data
  movzx eax,[byte ptr ebx]  ; next wall number
  inc   ebx                 ; Advance for next wall
  mov   [_scMulData],ebx
  mov   ebx,[_WallbMaps]    ; Get wall array
  mov   ebx,[ebx+eax*4]     ; Get wall bitmap to use
  add   ebx,[dword ptr _scColumn]  ; Add in current column
  mov   eax,0
  mov   esi,[SVTABLE]
  jmp   mulloop

alldone:
  pop   edi                 ; Restore registers
  pop   esi
  pop   ebp
  ret
  endp
```

We start by getting the off-screen buffer address that is stored in the variable **scVid**. This address will be the location where we start to display the bitmap for the slice. The other information we need includes the base address of the color zone (**scPal**) used to display the bitmap (index into the color palette), the starting height of the view window for displaying the slice (**scwht**) (calculated as one-half the height of the viewport), the size of the top part of the bitmap that will be displayed (31 pixels), and a pointer the bitmap displayed for the slice. The drawing height is calculated as one-half the height of the viewport because the floor will be displayed at the bottom half and we want our wall and object slices to be displayed on top of the floor.

By now you're probably wondering what the heck this **LowerTable** is and where it came from. The main *ACK-3D* initialization function, **AckInitialize()**, calls an internal function named **BuildWallDstTables()**, which creates the **LowerTable** array data structure. Let's discuss what that table is and how it is used.

Whenever a slice is being drawn to the off-screen buffer, a calculation must be performed to translate the distance to the slice into the height it appears on the screen. This calculation is one that either can be performed on every slice drawn or can be calculated in advance and stored in a table. I chose the latter method because I wanted to keep things fast, and every calculation that could be performed in advance, especially in a critical inner loop such as the slice drawing routine, would help the overall speed of the rendering engine.

By using a calculation where distance (divided by 256) is used to determine the pixel offset into the bitmap, I could generate a simple table to hold all of the offsets for every distance that could be found for a wall or object. A general routine for creating this table would be something like:

```
for (distance = 10; distance < 2048; distance++)
  {
  PixelOffset = 0;
  CurrentDistance = 0;
  Position = 0;
  while (PixelOffset < 64)
    {
    PixelOffset = CurrentDistance / 256;
    TempHeightTable[Position] = PixelOffset;
    Position++;
    CurrentDistance += distance;
    }
  HeightTable[distance] = malloc(Position * 2);
  memcpy(HeightTable[distance],TempHeightTable,Position * 2);
  }
```

I think an illustration is in order here. As Figure 7.7 shows, the **LowerTable** is a table of pointers to arrays that contain the actual pixel offsets to scale a bitmap based on the distance between the bitmap and the player. You can think of this as a "table of tables" so to speak.

For each distance from 10 to 2,048, a pointer to a list of offsets is used to scale the bitmap. Each of these lists varies in length, which is why the table is allocated at initialization time instead of being hard-coded into the data segment. A good example of how this works can be seen by using the distance 256 and plugging it into the generic loop above. If we plug this into our calculation

```
offset = distance / 256
```

we find the following numbers:

```
0,1,2,3,4,5,6,7 ...., 63
```

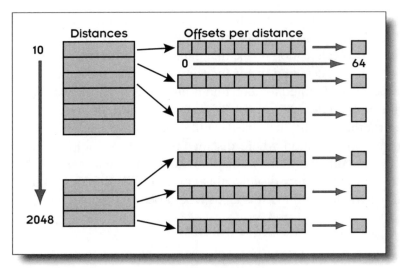

Figure 7.7 *Setting up the LowerTable as a "table of tables."*

This result tells us that every pixel of the bitmap will be drawn in the column, or more precisely, our scale factor is 1:1 for a distance of 256. It also tells us that we will need 64 values stored in the list for the distance of 256. Now let's use a distance of 512 to see what happens. As you can probably guess, we'll end up with a scale sequence that looks like this:

```
0,2,4,6,8,10,12,14,16,18,20,22,24,26,....62
```

This sequence shows us that we'll have a 2:1 scale factor when drawing, so every other pixel will be skipped as we draw the column. It also means that we only need 32 entries in our list for the distance 512. Thus, every distance from 10 to 2,048 is precalculated into the corresponding list of pixel offsets from 0 to 64 and built into the lists that are stored in the **LowerTable** array.

All well and good, but after I came up with this scheme, I felt a little guilty about using all that memory, so I decided to check the actual values the initialize function was generating. Sure enough, some distances built the exact same list of offsets as the distance before due to round-off integer values being used in the lists and how the list was generated. This fact gave me a way to optimize memory usage without sacrificing the speed gain from using tables. All I had to do was generate a table for the current distance into a temporary holding table and then compare the offsets with those from the previous distance. If they all matched, I would simply point the entry for the current distance at the list from the previous distance and voila! The same values would be used for both distances when it came time to draw the slice.

It made the initialization routine a little more cryptic, but hey, that's what this book is all about, to untangle the mess of code that you see in the engine, so you can expand and experiment to your heart's desire.

Okay, now that you know what the **LowerTable** is used for (I originally had a **LowerTable** and **UpperTable** for some experiments, but the **UpperTable** was really not needed any more), we can take a closer look at how this table is used as we draw our bitmaps from the center out. Again, let's examine how bitmaps are actually drawn to the off-screen buffer during the rendering process (see Figure 7.8).

So where do the values from 0 to 31 come from? Right from the **LowerTable** we just built. When the **ShowCol** routine begins, it first looks up the proper list based on the distance to the slice. This list (pointed to by the **esi** register) is saved in the **SVTABLE** variable so we can use it throughout the routine. The bitmap we are going to draw is placed into a pointer register (**ebx** in most cases) and is adjusted so we point to the halfway part of the bitmap. For the top-half of the bitmap, we begin by looking in our offset table (**SVTABLE**) and pulling out the actual pixel offset we want to use. But since we are already past the top half of our bitmap, we need to look in the negative direction. So we perform a **neg edx** instruction and then use that along with our bitmap pointer to get the actual pixel out of the bitmap.

For the bottom half of the bitmap, we again start with the beginning of the offset lists (**SVTABLE**). This time we can use the offsets directly because we are looking from the center down in our bitmap. Once we're finished with the

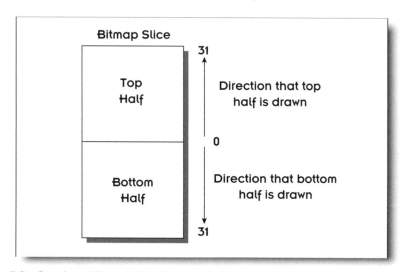

Figure 7.8 *Drawing a bitmap to the off-screen buffer.*

top and bottom half of the bitmap, we do a quick check to see if the slice is from a multi-height wall and begin drawing it if so. This is actually a two-step process since we can have different wall bitmaps for each vertical block in a multi-height wall. We need to pick up the bitmap for the section we are drawing, and then perform a complete bottom-up drawing loop until we either run out of bitmap or the top of the view is reached. And that, friends and neighbors, is why the **LowerTable** values had to be calculated from 0 to 64, instead of from 0 to 32 as you may have surmised. With the multi-height wall drawing, we are going to just blast the wall in from the bottom to the top of the bitmap, so we need all 64 pixel offsets.

Displaying the Off-Screen Buffer in DOS

Now that we have a buffer ready to go, how do we display it? A special *ACK-3D* function, **AckDisplayScreen()**, is provided to display a screen. Keep in mind that this function is designed to work with DOS screens only. In the next chapter, I'll show you how Windows screens are supported.

AckDisplayScreen() is defined in ACKRTN.ASM. It simply makes a call to a low-level assembly-language routine named **AckDrawPage**. This approach provides us with one level of an API, which eliminates the need for modifications in your application when you change the way the screen is displayed. This is a good place to hook in displays to other videos without having to change your application code. Here's the code for **AckDisplayScreen()**:

```
ACKPROC AckDisplayScreen
  push    ebp
  ACKCALL AckDrawPage           ; Call low-level display routine
  pop     ebp
  xor     eax,eax               ; Return a value of 0
  ret
  endp
```

The **AckDrawPage** routine copies the contents of the off-screen buffer to video memory so that a screen can be displayed in normal VGA mode 13h. This routine is actually divided into two parts. The first section of code executes if the viewport being displayed corresponds to the full width of the screen—320 pixels. If the viewport is less than 320 pixels, the code in the second part of the routine, which starts with the label **dp_smallscreen**, is executed.

```
ACKPROC AckDrawPage
  push  esi ; Save registers used
```

```
        push    edi
        push    ebx
        push    ecx
        push    edx
        push    es
        push    ds

        mov     edi,0
        mov     di,[word ptr _VidSeg]          ; Get address of video memory
        mov     esi,[_gScrnBuffer]             ; Get base address of off-screen buffer
        cmp     [word ptr _gWinFullWidth],0    ; Check to see if view is full width
        jz      short dp_smallscreen           ; If not, jump to process small width screen
        mov     eax,[_gWinStartOffset]         ; Get offset to viewport
        add     edi,eax                        ; Add in offset to video memory address
        add     esi,eax                        ; Add in offset to base of off-screen buffer
        mov     ecx,[_gWinDWORDS]              ; Get number of double words for screen (view)
        mov     ax,[word ptr _VidSeg+2]        ; Get address of video memory + 2
        mov     es,ax
        mov     dx,3dah                        ; Address to check for vertical retrace

fp020:
        in      al,dx           ; Wait until vertical retrace is on
        test    al,8            ; OK to draw?
        jz      fp020           ; Nope; check again

fp030:
        in      al,dx           ; Wait until vertical retrace is off
        test    al,8            ;
        jnz     fp030           ; Not ready yet; test again
        rep     movsd           ; Move buffer to screen

        pop     ds              ; Restore registers used
        pop     es
        pop     edx
        pop     ecx
        pop     ebx
        pop     edi
        pop     esi
        ret

; Screen size is not full width (< 320 units)
dp_smallscreen:
        mov     eax,[_gWinStartOffset]  ; Get offset to viewport
        add     edi,eax                 ; Add in offset to video memory address
        add     esi,eax                 ; Add in offset to base of off-screen buffer
        movzx   eax,[_gWinStartX]       ; Get starting offset of left viewport
        add     edi,eax                 ; Add left viewport offset to video memory
        add     esi,eax                 ; Add new offset to base of off-screen buffer
        mov     dx,[_gWinHeight]        ; Get height of viewport
        inc     dx                      ; Increase by 1
        movzx   ebx,[_gWinWidth]        ; Get width of viewport
        mov     ebp,320                 ; Size of full screen width
        sub     ebp,ebx                 ; Width to advance pointers
```

```
      mov    ax,[word ptr _VidSeg+2] ; Get address of video memory + 2
      mov    es,ax

; This loop will display one row of pixels at a time. The register dx contains
; the number of rows (the height of the view) + 1 and the loop decrements this
; counter each time. When dx=0, the loop terminates.
dp010:
      mov    ecx,ebx       ; Get width of viewport (screen)
      shr    ecx,1         ; Divide width by 2
      rep    movsw         ; Display row of pixels
      rcl    ecx,1         ;
      rep    movsb         ;
      add    edi,ebp       ; Add width offset to left viewport
      add    esi,ebp       ; Add width offset to base of off-screen buffer
      dec    dx            ; Check height counter
      jnz    dp010

dp090:
      pop    ds    ; Restore registers used
      pop    es
      pop    edx
      pop    ecx
      pop    ebx
      pop    edi
      pop    esi
      ret
      endp
```

Back in the **AckRegisterStructure()** (the C function that is called before a view is built), the following code initializes the global variables that are used by **AckDrawPage**:

```
gWinFullWidth = 0;                          // Set full width flag to default state
if (gWinStartX == 0 && gWinEndX == 319) // View is full width
  {
  gWinFullWidth = 1;                        // Set full width flag
  gWinDWORDS = (gWinEndY - gWinStartY) * 80; // Calculate number of double words
  }                                         // required for screen
```

Once the address of screen memory where the view will be displayed is calculated, the **AckDrawPage** routine checks until the vertical retrace is on before attempting to write to video memory using the simple loop at **fp020**. Next, the code checks to make sure the vertical retrace is off; then it sends the data in the off-screen buffer to video memory. This step is accomplished by executing the instruction **rep movsd**. The actual video address to which the data in the off-screen buffer is written is calculated by taking the base address of video memory (**VidSeg**) and adding the viewport offset (**gWinStartOffset**).

If the viewport starts at the top edge of the screen, the offset is zero, thus data is written to the base address of video memory.

The code to display data when the viewport is less than the full screen width requires a few extra steps. To calculate the starting address of video memory where data will be written, it is necessary to also add in the starting offset of the left viewport (**gWinStartX**). The width and height of the viewport, **gWinWidth** and **gWinHeight**, must also be taken into account to move data from the off-screen buffer to video memory. When the viewport is less than full width, the process for writing to video memory involves displaying one row of pixels at a time. The loop at label **dp010** performs this operation. The register **dx** is initialized before the loop to serve as a height counter, and the loop continues decrementing the counter with each iteration until this counter becomes 0.

Getting Ahead of Ourselves

In this chapter we took the *ACK-3D* engine all the way down to its lowest level and examined how views are actually displayed on the screen—at least with DOS VGA. Actually, we jumped ahead a bit because we still haven't discussed how objects, doors, floors, and ceilings are processed and added to the view during the ray-casting process. So before we start to use the *ACK-3D* functions to create applications, we'll need to spend the next three chapters discussing how the code is written to process objects, doors, floors, and ceilings.

An object, whether movable or stationary, is essentially a bitmap waiting to be displayed as wall slices are built up during the ray-casting process.

Supporting Objects in Your 3-D Worlds

One of the more powerful features of the *ACK-3D* engine is support for both movable and stationary objects. The engine handles objects a little differently from walls, but most of the processing takes place inside the engine and not in your application code. You do, however, need to call special functions to create objects and load in bitmaps for your objects. Once you do those tasks, you can easily move your objects around by calling a function like **AckMoveObjPOV()** and bring your game to life.

Objects are moved in much the same way that the POV of the player is moved. The main difference is that with objects, the code needs to check for collisions with other objects, walls, and the player as well. When we build a sample game later in the book, I'll show you how to create neat effects with movable objects, such as objects that jump out at the player and throw fireballs. For now, we need to explore some of the internal object-processing code to see how objects are actually drawn during the ray-casting process. This explanation will help you better understand what goes on behind the scenes when you create and use stationary and movable objects in your own games.

We'll primarily look at the functions in the source file ACKOBJ.C. This file contains all of the code required to process and draw objects during the ray-casting phase.

Drawing Objects

When we explored the techniques of ray casting and drawing wall slices in Chapters 6 and 7, we spent little time discussing how objects are actually handled. The assembly routine in charge of building a view, **BuildUpView**, not only casts out rays and builds slice structures for the walls that it finds, but it also folds in slices for the objects found in a view. When a view is actually produced by calling **DrawWalls**, the code that renders a scene does not care if the particular slice being displayed is an object or a wall. Therefore, what we need is a way to determine the objects that are actually seen by the player in a particular view so we can combine the object data with the wall data in the set of slice structures.

When you look at a 3-D scene created with the *ACK-3D* engine, such as the one shown in Figure 8.1, fundamentally everything displayed is created from 64¥64 pixel bitmap building blocks. The only r eal difference between objects and walls is that objects can have movable attributes and multiple views. Objects can walk around, fire weapons, and collide with one another. When we build an actual game later in this book, you'll learn how to create objects, move them around, animate them using multiple views, and perform collision detection. For now, we'll focus on how objects are incorporated into slice structures that contain wall data so that views can be displayed properly.

Figure 8.1   *A 3-D scene containing both objects and walls.*

To handle the work of combining object data with the slice data constructed during the ray-casting process, we need to create three new functions, **FindObject()**, **AckGetObjectAngle()**, and **long_sqrt()**. The code for these functions can be found in the ACKOBJ.C source file. **FindObject()** is the main internal function that checks the list of objects built up during the ray-casting process and places the object slices into the wall slices. This function is called by the **BuildUpView** routine, which in turn is called by the high-level **AckBuildUpView()** to create a new view. To fully process an object for displaying, **FindObject()** needs to call **AckGetObjectAngle()** to determine the actual angle between the player and a specified object. This angle is needed so that objects are placed in the current view position when they are drawn.

Revisiting the Object Structure

In Chapter 4 we introduced the **NEWOBJECT** structure that the *ACK-3D* engine provides to represent movable and stationary objects in an application. That was a long time ago, so let's take another look. This time around we'll discuss some of the key components that are used to process and draw objects during the ray-casting process. Here's the complete structure as defined in ACK3D.H:

```
typedef struct {
  char    Active;           // Determines object status: 0=Inactive, 1=Active
  UCHAR   Flags;            // Misc flags for this object
  char    Speed;            // Speed of object (used by application)
  short   Dir;              // Direction of object (used by application)
  short   x;               // Current x,y location in grid
  short   y;
  short   mPos;            // Current map location in grid
  UCHAR   id;              // Object id
  short   CurrentType;     // Create, Destroy, etc. is current
  UCHAR   *CurrentBitmaps; // Current bitmap list
  short   Sides;           // Number of views
  short   aFactor;         // Angle factor
  short   BitmapsPerView;  // Number of bitmaps in each view
  UCHAR   CurrentBm;        // Current bitmap number
  UCHAR   Maxbm;           // Maximum bitmap number for this view
  OBJSEQ  Create;          // Stores structures for the 5 object sequences
  OBJSEQ  Destroy;
  OBJSEQ  Walk;
  OBJSEQ  Attack;
  OBJSEQ  Interact;
  } NEWOBJECT;
```

Most of these fields are needed to draw an object during the ray-casting process, including **Active**, **Flags**, **x**, **y**, **CurrentBitmaps**, and **CurrentBm**. Some of the fields, such as **Sides**, **BitmapsPerView**, **aFactor**, and **MaxBm,** are needed solely to process and draw objects that have multiple sides. In such a case, we need these fields to determine the correct bitmap to display based on the angle between the player's POV and the object. As you examine the code in the **FindObject()** function, you'll see how these fields are used.

Combining Object Slices with Wall Slices

The **FindObject()** function might confuse you for a moment because of its name. Its job is not to search the game map and look for objects as the player moves around; that task is handled by the lower-level, ray-casting routines we explored in Chapter 6. **FindObject()** performs the last stage in the process of displaying objects: It prepares the objects that have been located for drawing. This process is accomplished by performing a number of tasks:

- Determine where the object should be displayed (the view column).
- Get the bitmap for the object.
- Determine how the bitmap should be scaled by using the player's distance and angle to the object.
- Arrange the objects in the view so that they will be displayed in the correct order. (Objects that are farther behind should be displayed first so that other objects or walls in front will appear closer to the player.)
- Check if the object has multiple sides and if so, determine which bitmap should be displayed based on the player's angle
- Update the wall slice structures by inserting the object slice structure at the correct location.

Before we look at the code for **FindObject()** to see how these tasks are performed, let's revisit the "slice system" for creating views. Imagine that you have a scene displayed on the screen as shown in Figure 8.2, then you rotate it so that it looks like a 3-D plane. From one end of the screen to the other, the display is divided into discrete columns. Each column is a slice unit. If the player only sees a wall at a particular location, the wall bitmap takes up the entire column (or at least the areas not taken up by the bitmaps for the floor and ceiling).

Now, let's introduce objects into the scene. If an object is displayed in front of a wall, the object will show up in the view column "below" the wall slice, as shown in Figure 8.3. This placement gives the appearance that it is in front of the wall. Again, if you were to rotate this scene into a 3-D plane, it would appear as shown with the scene in Figure 8.3. In this respect you can think of

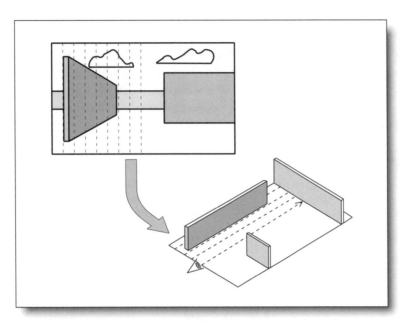

Figure 8.2   *Viewing a 3-D scene as a series of bitmap slices.*

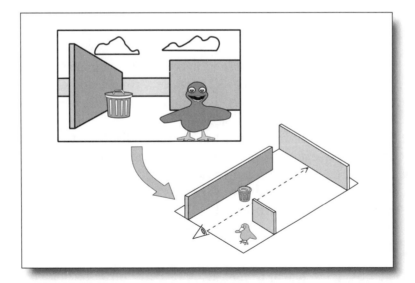

Figure 8.3   *Adding objects to a scene that is represented on the screen as a 3-D plane.*

the view column as a channel that the player sees into, while each slice structure represents the bitmap data that is displayed in one of the 320 "channels" that span the width of the screen.

Coding FindObject()

The challenging part of coding **FindObject()** is determining the most efficient way to add object slices to the already existing series of wall slices that span the view. First, we'll need to make sure that there are currently objects in the view. If so, we'll access the list of objects that may be seen and get the left and right edges of the viewport:

```
if (FoundObjectCount)    // Make sure objects were found during ray casting
  {
  oList = &aeGlobal->ObjList[0];  // Get pointer to the array of objects
  StartX = gWinStartX;            // Starting column of view
  EndX = gWinEndX;                // Ending column of view
  ...
```

The other important piece of information we need is the player's viewing angle:

```
minAngle = PlayerAngle - (INT_ANGLE_32 + 10);   // Starting angle of view
if (minAngle < 0)                   // Check for wrap-around at angle 0
  minAngle += INT_ANGLE_360;
maxAngle = PlayerAngle + (INT_ANGLE_32 + 10);   // Ending angle of view
if (maxAngle >= INT_ANGLE_360)  // Check for wrap-around at angle 360
  maxAngle -= INT_ANGLE_360;
```

Notice that we calculate a minimum and maximum view angle for generating the scene by using the **INT_ANGLE_32** as an offset. We'll add a small adjustment factor to both the start and end of the angles so we can catch those objects that may only be partially visible.

Once the viewing angle has been set up, we use a **for** loop to process all of the objects that are presently in the current view. The variable **FoundObjectCount**, which was set during the ray-casting process, provides the total number of objects found. The indexes to the actual objects seen are stored in the array **ObjectsSeen[ ]**. Objects are processed in the loop by setting up a few arrays to store the following:

- Object number
- Distance from the player to the object
- Viewing angle
- View column where the object will be displayed

The player's relative distance and angle to the object is calculated as follows:

```
dx = oPtr->x - xPglobal;  // Get the delta x,y between the
dy = oPtr->y - yPglobal;  // object and the player
```

```
// Calculate the angle the object is relative to the player
if ((objAngle = AckGetObjectAngle(dx,dy)) < 0)
  continue;   // Negative angle means it can't be seen
```

Notice that we call the **AckGetObjectAngle()** to determine the angle between two points: the location of the player and the position of the object. (We'll examine how **AckGetObjectAngle()** operates later in this chapter.) Once the angle has been determined, we need to know if the player's POV is looking toward the right or the left in a scene. We also need to calculate the actual view column where the object will be seen:

```
if (minAngle > maxAngle)
// If looking toward the right
  {
  if (objAngle >= minAngle)          // Calculate view column of object
    objColumn = objAngle - minAngle;
  else
    objColumn = (objAngle+INT_ANGLE_360) - minAngle;
  }
else
  {
  objColumn = objAngle - minAngle;  // Calculate view column of object
  }
```

The "true" distance from the player to the object is determined by using the Pythagorean theorem $a^2 + b^2 = c^2$, or $c = sqrt(a^2 + b^2)$. Our custom **long_sqrt()** function (defined in ACKOBJ.C) comes in handy here:

```
// Get the distance to the object
distance = long_sqrt((dx * dx) + (dy * dy));
// No need to check further if it's too far away
if (distance >= MaxDistance)
  continue;
```

Now we have almost everything we need to fold an object in with wall slices. The only thing missing is some code to determine if the list of objects is in the right order; that is, the objects need to be in the order that the player will see them at the current viewing angle. Let's create the code for performing this sort, and then we'll make sure the key data is saved so that new slices can be created for the objects.

Getting Objects in the Correct Order

Getting the objects in the correct viewing order involves using a **for** loop that compares the distance from the player to the current object (**distance**) with the distances to the other objects that have been processed so far. These distances are stored in the array **ObjRelDist[ ]**. If an object is found that is farther away than the current object, a second **for** loop is used to move the objects forward one position in the list. Here's the code that reorders the arrays:

```
// Place the objects in the correct order so further ones are behind
j = TotalObjects;              // Current number of objects we've found
if (j)
  {
  // Sort the objects found by distance so that further ones
  // are drawn BEFORE closer ones
  for (count = 0; count < TotalObjects; count++)
    {
    if (distance <= ObjRelDist[count])  // Current object is closer
      {
      for (j = TotalObjects; j > count; j--)
        {  // Move objects one position forward
        ObjRelDist[j] = ObjRelDist[j-1];
        ObjNumber[j]  = ObjNumber[j-1];
        ObjColumn[j]  = ObjColumn[j-1];
        ObjAngle[j]   = ObjAngle[j-1];
        }
      j = count;
      count = TotalObjects;
      }
    }
  }
```

An example of a before and after reorder is shown in Figure 8.4. Here, two objects are in the correct order in the list, then a third object is processed. The third object is closer than the other two, so it must be placed at the front of the list and the other two objects must be moved up one position. The result is that the object that is the closest to the player is at the first array position. Database aficionados will recognize this process as an "insert sort" method of adding entries to a list.

The actual object data that is stored is the distance to the object, the object number, the view column where the object is to be displayed, and the viewing angle:

```
// Hold onto relevant data for the object found
ObjNumber[j]  = i;         // Store the object number
ObjRelDist[j] = distance;  // Store the distance to the object
ObjColumn[j]  = objColumn;  // Store view column where object resides
ObjAngle[j]   = objAngle;  // Store the viewing angle
```

From Objects to Slices

The last part of **FindObject()** performs the work of building slices from the data that has been gathered into the arrays we just discussed. Again, a **for**

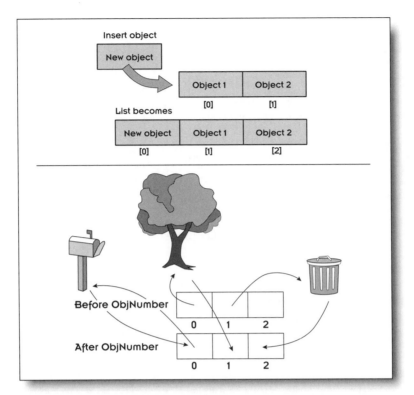

Figure 8.4   *Reordering objects to display correctly.*

loop is used to iterate through the list of objects in the view. Each time through the loop, an object in the list is selected and the object's bitmap is obtained. If the object only has one view, selecting the bitmap is easy. If the object has multiple views, the bitmap selection process requires additional code.

In addition to selecting the bitmap for the object, the loop must calculate the width and height for displaying the object's bitmap based on the player's distance to the object. Once this is done, the object slice is linked with the current array of slice structures. The main loop begins like this:

```
for (i = 0; i < TotalObjects; i++)  // Loop and process each object
  {
  ObjIndex = ObjNumber[i];           // Actual object found
  oPtr = oList[ObjIndex];            // Pointer to object structure
  if (oPtr == NULL)                  // Again check for a null object
    continue;
  // Current bitmap for the object (this number can change if the
  // object is animated)
  ObjNum = oPtr->CurrentBitmaps[oPtr->CurrentBm];
  distance = ObjRelDist[i];          // Get relative distance to object
```

```
    // Make sure distance is within a reasonable entry in our
    // precalculated table
    if (distance >= (MAX_DISTANCE - 10))
      distance = MAX_DISTANCE-11;

    // Get the width of the object
    wt = DistanceTable[distance];      // Adjust the width using the distance
    // Keep the width of the object reasonable
    if (wt > 300)          // The object is too wide
      continue;            // Skip over
    if (wt < 6) wt = 6;    // Adjust if too small

    // Get the scale factor that was precalculated based on
    // distance in AckInitialize() function
    yp = AdjustTable[distance];
    xp = 0;                    // First column of the object to display
    NewX = ObjColumn[i];  // View column where object resides
...
```

When the loop starts, the **ObjNumber[ ]** array contains the index numbers for the objects in the view. They are arranged in order of distance from the player. The **optr** variable is used to access the object that is currently being processed. Notice how it is used to fetch the bitmap number assigned to the object. The code also obtains the distance from the player to the object and uses it to determine the width for displaying the bitmap. The width calculation is performed by using the **DistanceTable[ ]** array as a look-up table. (The index into the table is the player's distance to the object.) In addition to the width, a scale factor is produced by using the distance as a lookup index into the **AdjustTable[ ]** array. Both of these lookup tables are automatically set up when the *ACK-3D* engine is initialized by calling the **AckInitialize()** function.

Handling Objects with Multiple Views

Before the last stage, inserting the object slice, we need to check if the object has multiple sides. If it does, we must determine the correct bitmap to display based on the angle between the player's POV and the object. We'll perform a trick here that breaks the problem into quadrants and uses the quadrant to determine which side we're facing. The object itself is facing a certain angle (stored in the **Dir** field of the object structure), which also needs to be taken into account.

Here's the **if** statement that processes objects with multiple sides:

```
if (oPtr->Flags & OF_MULTIVIEW)
  {
  afact = oPtr->aFactor;      // Get the angles per side of object
  numsides = oPtr->Sides;     // Get total sides for this object
  pQuad = ObjAngle[i] / afact; // Get the quadrant from POV to object
  oQuad = oPtr->Dir / afact;   // Get the quadrant it wants to face
```

```
// The difference between the POV-Object angle and the angle the
// object is facing determines the actual side of the object that
// can currently be seen
j = (pQuad - oQuad) + (numsides >> 1);

// Check for wrap-around and keep within range
if (j >= numsides)
  j -= numsides;
// Check wrap-around in both directions
if (j < 0)
  j += numsides;

// Calculate which bitmap set we should use (each side could
// have multiple bitmaps for animation)
j *= oPtr->BitmapsPerView; // Multiply index by number of bitmaps per view
j += oPtr->CurrentBm;
// Get the actual bitmap for this side and animation
ObjNum = oPtr->CurrentBitmaps[j];
}
```

The **Flags** field in the object structure is tested with the **OF_MULTIVIEW** flag to see if the object has multiple views. Then, we use the information in two fields, **aFactor** and **Sides**, to determine the quadrant representing the angle from the player to the object and the quadrant representing the angle the object wants to face.

As shown in Figure 8.5, a multi-sided object has regions surrounding it (which I have called quadrants even though there may be more or fewer than four of them). The direction the object is facing (direction A) is used to determine which side of the object will be visible. By using the angle between the POV and the object and the quadrant of the object where the POV resides, we can subtract the two to calculate the actual side we need to display. In the example above, the object has four sides, so the **aFactor** would be 360 / 4, or 90 degrees for each side. Supposing that the object is facing to the left, or 180 degrees, and the angle from the POV to the object is roughly 135 degrees, we can replace the variables in the code above with the following:

```
afact = oPtr->aFactor;      // Get the angles per side of object
  numsides = oPtr->Sides;     // Get total sides for this object
  pQuad = ObjAngle[i] / afact; // Get the quadrant from POV to object
  oQuad = oPtr->Dir / afact;   // Get the quadrant it wants to face

  // The difference between the POV-Object angle and the angle the
  // object is facing determines the actual side of the object that
  // can currently be seen
  j = (pQuad - oQuad) + (numsides >> 1);
```

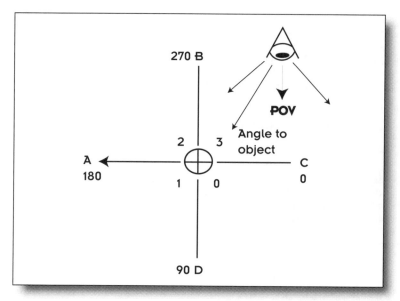

Figure 8.5 *Processing a multi-sided object.*

Here:

afact = 90 (angle per side of object)

numsides = 4 (total number of sides in the object)

pQuad = 135 / 90 = 1 (angle from POV to object divided by afact)

oQuad = 180 / 90 = 2 (direction object is facing divided by afact)

j = (1 - 2) + (4 / 2) = (-1) + 2 = 1 (side of object to use)

We need to check for wrap-around for the object sides because the above equations could produce negative numbers. The range should always fall within the minimum and maximum values for the object sides.

Finally, we end up with an index (**j**) that tells us which side of the object we are viewing and which bitmap from this side of the object should be displayed based on the viewing angle. The actual bitmap needed to display the object is obtained by multiplying the index by the number of bitmaps per side (view) and adding this result to the current bitmap number. The final bitmap number is assigned to the **ObjNum** variable.

Inserting the Object Slice

We've finished processing objects that have either single or multiple views. The final task, if you're still with me, is to fold in the object slices. To do this, we simply use the starting column of where the object bitmap should be displayed, calculate the ending column, and insert the object slice with the wall slice column at the appropriate column locations.

Earlier, we calculated the starting view column of the object slice and stored this location in the variable **NewX**. Now we need the ending column, which is calculated as

```
ColEnd = NewX + wt;
```

where **wt** is the adjusted width of the object's bitmap. The only other items we need before we insert the object slice are:

```
// Get the pointer to the actual bitmap
wall = omaps[ObjNum];
// Pick up the transparent flags at end of bitmap
bmpFlags = &wall[BITMAP_SIZE];
j = distance;
```

Then, we're ready to start the loop that continues from the starting column to the ending column and inserts slices for the object:

```
for (Column = NewX - wt; Column < ColEnd; Column++)
  {
  // Make sure column is within view width
  if (Column >= StartX && Column <= EndX)
    {
    // Scale bitmap column down from fixed point
    BmpColumn = xp >> FP_SHIFT;
    if (bmpFlags[BmpColumn])  // If transparent column
      goto keepgoing;        // Don't bother to insert slice

    j = distance;
    // Account for fisheye effect
    dy = ViewCosTable[Column] >> 2;
    dx = distance * dy;
    // Now we strip off some more decimal points and check round-up
    dy = dx >> 12;
    if (dx - (dy << 12) >= 4096)
      dy++;
    if (dy > 32L)
      j = dy;
  ...
```

Inserting the object slice is a matter of checking one of two conditions: Inserting the slice in a column already containing multiple slices or inserting the slice in a column containing a single slice. If the slice is inserted at a view column position that already contains multiple slices, we need to traverse the linked list of slices to locate the correct position to insert the object slice.

Deciding where to insert the new slice is determined by the player's distance to the slice. We check each wall slice that has already been linked in by the ray-casting process and see if the new slice we are about to link in is closer or farther away than the other slices. This insertion technique allows objects to appear between walls at various distances or behind transparent walls.

Here's the code used to insert the slice in a column containing multiple slices:

```
sa = &Slice[Column];   // Access the corresponding slice for the current column
if (sa->Active)        // Indicates multiple slices present for this column
  {
  while (sa != NULL)  // Loop until we get to end of the list
    {
    if (j <= sa->Distance)          // Object slice to insert is closer
      {
      sa2 = sa;
      while (sa2->Next != NULL)     // Go to end of slices
        sa2 = sa2->Next;
      saNext = sa2->Prev;
      while (sa2 != sa)             // Move slice down to create
        {                           // a space for new slice
        memcpy(sa2,saNext,sizeof(SLICE)-9);
        sa2->Active = saNext->Active;
        sa2 = sa2->Prev;
        saNext = saNext->Prev;
        }
      // Fill in the inserted slice structure with the
      // info about the object slice
      sa->Distance  = distance;
      sa->bNumber   = ObjNum;
      sa->bColumn   = BmpColumn;
      sa->bMap      = omaps;
      sa->Active    = 1;
      sa->Type      = ST_OBJECT;    // Indicates slice is an object
      sa->Fnc       = WallMaskRtn;
      break;
      }
    if (!sa->Active)
      break;
    sa = sa->Next;
    }
  }
```

Now, that wasn't too tricky, was it? The variable **sa** is assigned to the slice structure that corresponds to the view column where the object slice needs to be inserted. If this slice links to other slices, its **Active** field will be set to 1. The main **while** loop continues until each slice in the linked list of slices is compared with the object slice. Recall that slice structures can be linked using the **Next** and **Prev** fields, as shown in Figure 8.6. The linked slices can be traversed to determine how different slices are drawn for a specific column in a view.

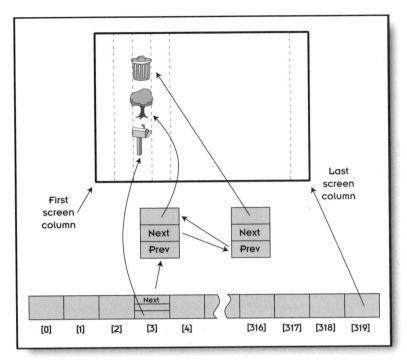

Figure 8.6 *Representing slice structures in a linked list for a specific view column.*

When a view is displayed, the slice at the end of the list is drawn first, and then the list is traversed in reverse order to draw the slices in their proper order.

When we locate a slice in the linked list of slices whose distance to the player is greater than the distance from the player to the object slice we are trying to insert, we've found the location to fold in the object slice. Once the object slice is inserted, we simply fill in the data for the slice, such as its bitmap number, its type (**ST_OBJECT**), its distance to the player, and so on.

If the object slice is inserted at a view column that only contains a single slice, the new slice is inserted at the end of the existing slice. If the player's distance to the object is less than the distance to the wall slice, we don't even bother to insert it because the player won't be able to see the object. Here's the code that puts an object slice into a single slice column:

```
else // Only one slice is used for this column (typical)
  {
  if (j <= sa->Distance)  // Only put it in if object is
    {                     // closer than current slice
    sa->Active = 1;
    saNext = sa->Next;
    memcpy(saNext,sa,sizeof(SLICE)-9);
    sa->Distance    = distance;
```

```
    sa->bColumn    = BmpColumn;
    sa->bNumber    = ObjNum;
    sa->bMap       = omaps;
    sa->Type       = ST_OBJECT;
    sa->Fnc        = WallMaskRtn;
    saNext->Active = 0;
    }
  }
```

Finding the Angle between Two Points

Before **FindObject()** can process and insert an object slice, it must calculate the distance from the player to the object. This step is accomplished by calling the **AckGetObjectAngle()** function. Although this function was designed for internal use by the engine, you can also call it from your applications to calculate the angle between two points. This function is called by providing the distance between the two points as the arguments:

```
Angle = AckGetObjectAngle(x2-x1,y2-y1);
```

This function uses a simple trig formula to calculate the angle between two sets of coordinates, as shown in Figure 8.7. The distance between x2 and x1 is called *dx*—the rate of change in the x direction or *run*. The distance between y2 and y1 is called *dy*—the rate of change in the y direction or *rise*. If we divide the rise by the run (dy/dx), we get the tangent of the angle between the two points.

What good will it do us to calculate the tangent of the angle if we actually need the angle itself? Well, recall that the *ACK-3D* engine pre-calculates tangent values of angles and loads these values into an array named **LongTanTable[ ]** when the engine is initialized by calling **AckInitialize()**. To obtain an angle once we know its tangent, all we need to do is locate the array location that contains a value that matches the angle's tangent.

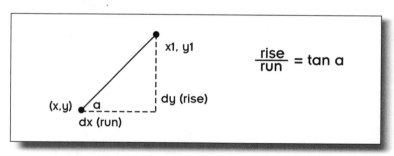

Figure 8.7   *Calculating an angle between two points.*

We want **AckGetObjectAngle()** to calculate the angle as fast as possible, so we'll use a few optimization tricks. Instead of dealing with a circular span of 360 degrees and 1,800 possible angle increments, we'll limit our calculations to a 90 degree span and then we'll transpose the results to other angles outside this range. This result is achieved by using the concept of quadrants, as shown in Figure 8.8. Quadrant 0 represents angles from 0 to 90 degrees, quadrant 1 represents angles from 90 to 180 degrees, and so on. If we need to calculate the angle between a player and an object when the object is in quadrant 2, we calculate the angle as if the object is in quadrant 0 (0 to 90 degrees) and then we add 180 degrees. If the object is in quadrants 1 or 3, we calculate the angle (from 0 to 90 degrees) and subtract either 180 or 360 from the calculated angle.

Enough math talk, let's look at some code. **AckGetObjectAngle()** first checks the two arguments passed in (**dx** and **dy**) to see if they correspond to a quadrant boundary position (0, 90, 180, and so on). If so, we're finished and one of these angles is returned:

```
if (dx == 0 || dy == 0) // Test to see if angle is 0, 90, 180, or 270
  {
  if (dx == 0)            // Distance is directly up or down
    {
    if (dy < 0)          // Distance is straight up
      return(INT_ANGLE_270);
    return(INT_ANGLE_90);
    }
```

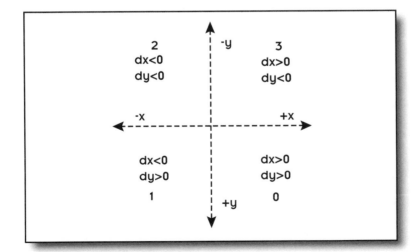

Figure 8.8 *Working with the four-quadrant system.*

```
    if (dx < 0)              // dy = 0; distance is directly left or right
      return(INT_ANGLE_180);
    return(0);
    }
```

The code that determines which quadrant we're in is shown next. You might want to compare this code with Figure 8.9 to review these calculations:

```
quadrant = 0;                // Set to quad 0 as default
if (dx < 0 && dy > 0)        // We're in quad 1
  quadrant = INT_ANGLE_180;
else
  {
  if (dx < 0 && dy < 0)      // We're in quad 2
    quadrant = INT_ANGLE_270;
  else
    {
    if (dx > 0 && dy < 0)    // We're in quad 3
      quadrant = INT_ANGLE_360;
    }
  }
```

Next, we need to convert the y distance between the two points (**dy**) into the same fixed-point representation as used in our tangent lookup table. Then, we divide **dy** by **dx** (rise/run) to get the ratio so we can determine the tangent of the angle between the two points. We use the ratio to search the tangent table; the index that is returned tells us what the actual angle is. We only need to check angles from 0 to 90 degrees. Later, the angle will be adjusted to take into account which quadrant we are in.

```
dy = dy << FP_SHIFT;    // Make the dividend the same fixed point as the table
avalue = dy / dx;       // Get our ratio to search for
                        // This ratio tells us the tangent of the angle
if (LongTanTable[INT_ANGLE_90-1] <= avalue)   // Angle is 89 degrees
  return(INT_ANGLE_90-1);
objAngle = 0;           // Initialize angle to 0

Beg = 0;                // Assume midpoint between 0 and 45 degrees
if (LongTanTable[INT_ANGLE_45] < avalue)
  {
  if (LongTanTable[360] < avalue)
    Beg = 360;          // Use angle of 360
  else
    Beg = INT_ANGLE_45; // Midpoint between 45 and 90 degrees
  }
```

```
// Loop to check the tan table and find the correct angle
for (i = Beg; i < INT_ANGLE_90; i++)
  {
  if (LongTanTable[i] > avalue)    // We've passed by the angle
    {
    objAngle = i - 1;              // Get the correct angle
    break;
    }
  }

if (objAngle < 0)                  // Adjust for angle=0
  objAngle = 0;
```

This code shows our second optimization trick at work. Here we are using a binary search method to quickly locate the correct value in the **LongTanTable[ ]**. Instead of checking each entry, we first check to see if the angle is between 0 and 45 degrees. or between 45 and 90 degrees. Then, we search the list sequentially to find the first value that is higher than our dy/dx ratio. Figure 8.9 shows how this searching method corresponds with the way the region in quadrant 0 is divided. The advantage of this approach is that we save a lot of searching time locating the angle.

Finally, we adjust the resulting angle based on the quadrant. If we are in quadrant 0, we do nothing. If we're in quadrants 1 and 3, we subtract the angle from the next higher quadrant angle (180 or 360). If we're in quadrant 2, we add the angle to the next lower quadrant angle (180) to get the actual angle between the points:

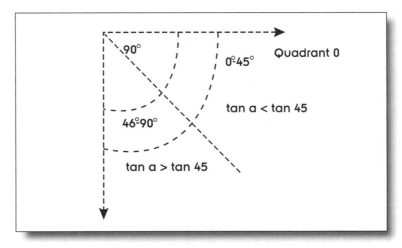

Figure 8.9 *Dividing quadrant 0 into two regions.*

```
if (quadrant)
  {
  if (quadrant != INT_ANGLE_270)
    objAngle = quadrant - objAngle;
  else
    objAngle += INT_ANGLE_180;
  }
return(objAngle);
```

The Complete ACKOBJ.C

Here's the complete ACKOBJ.C source file that we've been discussing in this chapter. This file contains the two main functions **FindObject()** and **AckGetObjectAngle()**.

```
// This source file contains the internal functions needed to add objects
// to the slice structures as a view is being built.
// (c) 1995 ACK Software (Lary Myers)
#include <windows.h>
#include <stdlib.h>
#include <stdio.h>
#include <conio.h>
#include <dos.h>
#include <mem.h>
#include <io.h>
#include <fcntl.h>
#include <time.h>
#include <string.h>
#include <sys\stat.h>
#include <limits.h>
#include "ack3d.h"          // Main ACK-3D internal and interface data structures
#include "ackeng.h"         // Internal data structures and constants
#include "ackext.h"         // Defines external (global) variables
extern  short gWinStartX; // Global variables to define the left and
extern  short gWinEndX;   // right edge of the viewport
// A function pointer to refernce the actual routine used to build a wall slice
extern  void  (*WallMaskRtn)(void);

//++++++++++++++++++++++++++++++++++++++++++++++++++++++++++++++++++++++++++++++
// Internal function called by FindObject(). Your programs may call this
// function if they need to calculate the angle between two points. dx and
// dy represent the deltas between the two points. (i.e. dx = x1 - x and
// dy = y1 - y)
//
// Quadrants
// 2 | 3    If the object is in quadrants 0 or 2, we need
//   -+-    to add the resulting angle to the quad value less
// 1 | 0    than the resulting angle. If the object is in
//          quadrants 1 or 3, we need to subtract the
//          resulting angle from the next higher quadrant
//          value. This is because quads 1 and 3 are negative
//          values returned from arctan, while 0 and 2 are
```

```
//          positive.
//
// The angle between the two points is determined by using the formula:
// tan (angle) = dy/dx. The lookup table LongTanTable[] is used to
// access tangent values of angles.
//++++++++++++++++++++++++++++++++++++++++++++++++++++++++++++++++++++++++++
short AckGetObjectAngle(long dx,long dy)
{
  short i,quadrant,objAngle;
  short Beg;
  long  avalue;

if (dx == 0 || dy == 0) // Test to see if angle is 0, 90, 180, or 270
  {
  if (dx == 0)           // Distance is directly up or down
    {
    if (dy < 0)          // Distance is straight up
      return(INT_ANGLE_270);
    return(INT_ANGLE_90);
    }
  if (dx < 0)            // dy = 0; distance is directly left or right
    return(INT_ANGLE_180);
  return(0);
  }

// Need to determine which quadrant is involved
quadrant = 0;            // Set to quad 0 as default
if (dx < 0 && dy > 0)    // We're in quad 1
  quadrant = INT_ANGLE_180;
else
  {
  if (dx < 0 && dy < 0)  // We're in quad 2
    quadrant = INT_ANGLE_270;
  else
    {
    if (dx > 0 && dy < 0)  // We're in quad 3
      quadrant = INT_ANGLE_360;
    }
  }
// Get the absolute values to use for our ratio
if (dy < 0)
  dy = -dy;
if (dx < 0)
  dx = -dx;
//======================================================================
// Next we need to convert dy into the same fixed-point representation
// as used in our tangent table. Then, we divide dy by dx (rise/run)
// to get the ratio so we can determine the tangent of the angle between
// the two pints. We use the ratio to search the tangent table
// and the index that is returned tells us what the actual angle is.
// We only need to check angles from 0 to 90 degrees. Later, the angle
// will be adjusted to take into account which quadrant we are in.
//======================================================================
dy = dy << FP_SHIFT;  // Make the dividend the same fixed point as the table
```

```
avalue = dy / dx;      // Get our ratio to search for
                       // This ratio tells us the tangent of the angle
if (LongTanTable[INT_ANGLE_90-1] <= avalue) // Angle is 89 degrees
  return(INT_ANGLE_90-1);
objAngle = 0;          // Initialize angle to 0

//=============================================================================
// Now we use a binary lookup trick to speed up the search. This invloves
// a test to see if the angle is between 0 and 45 degrees or between 45 and
// 90 degrees. Then, we search the list sequentially to find the first value
// higher than our ratio.
//=============================================================================
Beg = 0;                       // Assume midpoint between 0 and 45 degrees
if (LongTanTable[INT_ANGLE_45] < avalue)
  {
  if (LongTanTable[360] < avalue)
    Beg = 360;                 // Use angle of 360
  else
    Beg = INT_ANGLE_45;    // Midpoint between 45 and 90 degrees
  }
// Loop to check the tan table and find the correct angle
for (i = Beg; i < INT_ANGLE_90; i++)
  {
  if (LongTanTable[i] > avalue)  // We've passed by the angle
    {
    objAngle = i - 1; // Get the correct angle
    break;
    }
  }
if (objAngle < 0) // Adjust for angle=0
  objAngle = 0;
//=============================================================================
// Now we adjust the resulting angle based on the quadrant. If we are in
// quad 0 we do nothing. If we're in quads 1 and 3 we subtract the angle from
// the next higher quad angle. If we're in quad 2 we add the angle to the next
// lower quad angle to get the actual angle (0-1800) between the points.
//=============================================================================
if (quadrant)
  {
  if (quadrant != INT_ANGLE_270)
    objAngle = quadrant - objAngle;
  else
    objAngle += INT_ANGLE_180;
  }
// Returns the angle between the two points. This value is mainly used for
// determining the angle between the POV and an object, but it could
// be used for generic purposes as well.
return(objAngle);
}


//+++++++++++++++++++++++++++++++++++++++++++++++++++++++++++++++++++++++++++++
// Internal function that returns the square root of a long value.
// This function is called by FindObject().
//+++++++++++++++++++++++++++++++++++++++++++++++++++++++++++++++++++++++++++++
```

```c
short long_sqrt(long v)
{
  short    i;
  unsigned short result,tmp;
  unsigned long low,high;

if (v <= 1L) return((unsigned)v); // Value is less than 1; return value
  low = v;                         // Initialize starting variables
high = 0L;
result = 0;
for (i = 0; i < 16; i++)
   {
   result += result;
   high = (high << 2) | ((low >>30) & 0x3);
   low <<= 2;                      // Shift left by 2
   tmp = result + result + 1;
   if (high >= tmp)
     {
     result++;
     high -= tmp;
     }
   }
return(result);
}


//+++++++++++++++++++++++++++++++++++++++++++++++++++++++++++++++++++++++++++
// Internal function called by AckBuildView() which checks the list of
// objects found during the ray cast process and places the object slices
// into the wall slices.
//+++++++++++++++++++++++++++++++++++++++++++++++++++++++++++++++++++++++++++
void FindObject(void)
{
  short    i,j,StartX,EndX;
  short    oCount;
  short    minAngle,maxAngle,objAngle;
  short    objColumn;
  USHORT   distance;
  long     dx,dy;
  short    count,SaveCenter;
  short    ObjNum,oQuad,pQuad,numsides,afact;
  short    NewX,NewY,LightFlag;
  short    MaxOpp,Column,ColBeg,ColEnd;
  short    wt,ObjIndex;
  short    vidwt,vidht,hoff;
  short    MaxObjs;
  short    SliceLen;
  USHORT   BmpColumn;
  long     xp,yp;
  short    wht;
  UCHAR    *wall,*ScreenBuffer;
  UCHAR    *pTable;
  UCHAR    **omaps;
  SLICE    *sa,*sa2,*saNext;
  UCHAR    *bmpFlags;
```

```
    NEWOBJECT **oList;
    NEWOBJECT *oPtr;

  if (FoundObjectCount)    // Make sure objects were found during ray casting
    {
    oList = &aeGlobal->ObjList[0];  // Get pointer to the array of objects
    StartX = gWinStartX;            // Starting column of view
    EndX = gWinEndX;                // Ending column of view

    minAngle = PlayerAngle - (INT_ANGLE_32 + 10); // Starting angle of view
    if (minAngle < 0)                      // Check for wrap-around at angle 0
      minAngle += INT_ANGLE_360;
    maxAngle = PlayerAngle + (INT_ANGLE_32 + 10); // Ending angle of view
    if (maxAngle >= INT_ANGLE_360)         // Check for wrap-around at angle 360
      maxAngle -= INT_ANGLE_360;

    TotalObjects = 0;               // Stores number of objects in view
    SliceLen = sizeof(SLICE) - 9;   // Amount of slice we'll move later
// Loop and process each object in the view. This invloves setting up
// a few arrays to store the object number, the distance from the player
// to the object, the viewing angle, and the view column where the object
// will be displayed.
    for (oCount = 0; oCount < FoundObjectCount; oCount++)
      {
      i = ObjectsSeen[oCount];         // Get index to possible object
      oPtr = oList[i];                 // Pointer to object structure
      if (oPtr == NULL)                // Make sure it's a valid object
        continue;
      if (!oPtr->Active)               // Make sure it's visible
        continue;
      dx = oPtr->x - xPglobal;         // Get the delta x,y between the
      dy = oPtr->y - yPglobal;         // object and the player
      // Calculate the angle the object is relative to the player
      if ((objAngle = AckGetObjectAngle(dx,dy)) < 0)
        continue;                      // Negative angle means it can't be seen

      // Here we determine if the POV is looking toward the right or
      // the left and the actual column of the view (from 0 to view width)
      // where the object would be seen.
      if (minAngle > maxAngle)         // If looking towards the right
        {
        if (objAngle >= minAngle)      // Calc. view column of object
          objColumn = objAngle - minAngle;
        else
          objColumn = (objAngle+INT_ANGLE_360) - minAngle;
        }
      else
        {
        objColumn = objAngle - minAngle; // Calc. view column of object
        }
      // Get the distance to the object
      distance = long_sqrt((dx * dx) + (dy * dy));
      // No need to check further if it's too far away
```

```
      if (distance >= MaxDistance)
        continue;

      // Place the objects in the correct order so further ones are behind
      j = TotalObjects;                    // Current number of objects we've found
      if (j)
        {
        // Sort the objects found by distance so that further ones
        // are drawn BEFORE closer ones
        for (count = 0; count < TotalObjects; count++)
          {
          if (distance <= ObjRelDist[count])
            {
            for (j = TotalObjects; j > count; j--)
              {
              ObjRelDist[j] = ObjRelDist[j-1];
              ObjNumber[j]  = ObjNumber[j-1];
              ObjColumn[j]  = ObjColumn[j-1];
              ObjAngle[j]   = ObjAngle[j-1];
              }
            j = count;
            count = TotalObjects;
            }
          }
        }

      // Hold onto relevant data for the object found
      ObjNumber[j]  = i;                 // Store the object number
      ObjRelDist[j] = distance;          // Store the distance to the object
      ObjColumn[j]  = objColumn;         // Store view column where object resides
      ObjAngle[j] = objAngle;            // Store the viewing angle
      TotalObjects++;                    // Bump the count of objects in view
      ObjRelDist[TotalObjects] = 0L;     // Set to relative dist. in next object to 0
      }
    // Didn't find any objects on the above pass, so we're done
    if (!TotalObjects)
      return;
    omaps = &aeGlobal->oMaps[0];        // Bitmaps used for objects
    pQuad = PlayerAngle / INT_ANGLE_45; // Quadrant POV is facing

// Check each object in the list to be displayed and get the object's
// bitmap. Also, caluylate the width and height of the object.
// This loop also checks to see if an object has multiple sides
// and it determines which bitmap should be used to display the object.
  for (i = 0; i < TotalObjects; i++)
    {
    ObjIndex = ObjNumber[i];      // Actual object found
    oPtr = oList[ObjIndex];       // Pointer to object structure
    if (oPtr == NULL)             // Again check for a null object
        continue;
    // Current bitmap for the object (this number can change if the
    // object is animated)
    ObjNum = oPtr->CurrentBitmaps[oPtr->CurrentBm];
    distance = ObjRelDist[i];     // Get relative distance to object
```

```
// Make sure distance is within a reasonable entry in our
// precalculated table
if (distance >= (MAX_DISTANCE - 10))
  distance = MAX_DISTANCE-11;
// Get the width of the object
wt = DistanceTable[distance]; // Adjust the width using the distance
// Keep the width of the object reasonable
if (wt > 300)                  // The object is too wide
  continue;                    // Skip over
if (wt < 6) wt = 6;            // Adjust if too small
// Get the scale factor which was precalculated based on
// distance in AckInitialize() function
yp = AdjustTable[distance];
xp = 0;                        // First col of the object to display
NewX = ObjColumn[i];           // View column where object resides

// Check if object has multiple sides. If so we need to determine
// the correct bitmap to display based on the angle between the
// POV and the object. We'll perform a trick here by breaking down
// the problem into quadrants and then use the quadrant to determine
// which side we're facing. The object itself is facing a certain
// angle (stored in the Dir field of the object structure) so this
// needs to be taken into account as well.
if (oPtr->Flags & OF_MULTIVIEW)
  {
  afact = oPtr->aFactor;       // Get the angles per side of object
  numsides = oPtr->Sides;
  // Get total sides for this object
  pQuad = ObjAngle[i] / afact; // Get the quadrant from POV to object
  oQuad = oPtr->Dir / afact;   // Get the quadrant it wants to face
  // The difference between the POV-Object angle and the angle the
  // object is facing determines the actual side of the object that
  // can currently be seen
  j = (pQuad - oQuad) + (numsides >> 1);
  // Check for wrap-around and keep within range
  if (j >= numsides)
    j -= numsides;
  // Check wrap-around in both directions
  if (j < 0)
    j += numsides;
  // Calculate which bitmap set we should use (each side could
  // have multiple bitmaps for animation)
  j *= oPtr->BitmapsPerView;
  j += oPtr->CurrentBm;
  // Get the actual bitmap for this side and animation
  ObjNum = oPtr->CurrentBitmaps[j];
  }

// Done processing multiple sides. Next, find the
// ending column based on the starting column plus the scaled
// width of the object.
ColEnd = NewX + wt;
// Finally get the pointer to the actual bitmap
wall = omaps[ObjNum];
```

```
// Pick up the transparent flags at end of bitmap
bmpFlags = &wall[BITMAP_SIZE];
j = distance;

// Loop from starting column to ending column and fold in the
// object into the appropriate slice structure.
for (Column = NewX - wt; Column < ColEnd; Column++)
  {
  // Make sure column is within view width
  if (Column >= StartX && Column <= EndX)
    {
    // Scale bitmap column down from fixed point
    BmpColumn = xp >> FP_SHIFT;
    if (bmpFlags[BmpColumn])  // If transparent column
      goto keepgoing;               // Ouch! But it works

    j = distance;
    // Account for fisheye effect
    dy = ViewCosTable[Column] >> 2;
    dx = distance * dy;
    // Now we strip off somemore decimal points and check round-up
    dy = dx >> 12;
    if (dx - (dy << 12) >= 4096)
      dy++;
    if (dy > 32L)
      j = dy;

    // Now we pick up the slice for this column and insert sort
    // the object slice based on the distance. This allows objects
    // to appear between walls at various distances, behind
    // transparent walls, and so on.
    sa = &Slice[Column];  // Access the corresponding slice
    if (sa->Active)       // Multiple slices for this column?
      {
      while (sa != NULL)
        {
        if (j <= sa->Distance)
          {
          sa2 = sa;
          while (sa2->Next != NULL) // Go to end of slices
            sa2 = sa2->Next;
          saNext = sa2->Prev;
          while (sa2 != sa)           // Move slice down to create
            {                         // a space for new slice
            memcpy(sa2,saNext,sizeof(SLICE)-9);
            sa2->Active = saNext->Active;
            sa2 = sa2->Prev;
            saNext = saNext->Prev;
            }
          // Fill in the slice structure with the
          // info about the object
          sa->Distance  = distance;
          sa->bNumber   = ObjNum;
          sa->bColumn   = BmpColumn;
```

```
                sa->bMap        = omaps;
                sa->Active      = 1;
                sa->Type        = ST_OBJECT;
                sa->Fnc         = WallMaskRtn;
                break;
                }
            if (!sa->Active)
                break;
            sa = sa->Next;
            }
        }
    else // Only one slice is used for this column (typical)
        {
        if (j <= sa->Distance)  // Only put it in if object is
            {                   // closer than current slice
            sa->Active = 1;
            saNext          = sa->Next;
            memcpy(saNext,sa,sizeof(SLICE)-9);
            sa->Distance    = distance;
            sa->bColumn     = BmpColumn;
            sa->bNumber     = ObjNum;
            sa->bMap        = omaps;
            sa->Type        = ST_OBJECT;
            sa->Fnc         = WallMaskRtn;
            saNext->Active  = 0;
            }
        }
    }
keepgoing:
    xp += yp; // Advance the next column to display (scaling)
    }
  }
 }
}
// **** End of Source ****
```

As your player moves around in your world, he or she might encounter a secret or sliding door. What do you do? Do you let the player pass through? Here's your chance to find out how doors are processed in a game.

Working with Doors

magine a building without doors. How would you ever get out? Or if every entrance were simply an opening, you couldn't close a door to get any privacy.

In a game you don't need to use doors to give your player his or her own "personal space" but doors sure come in handy for creating exciting scenes. You can add secret doors to a room so that the player might feel trapped until he or she can find a way out. A situation like this could really get exciting especially if an evil creature is coming after your player. You can also liven up your games by adding sliding doors that open and close and make a big "whoosh" sound as the player passes.

In Chapter 4 we briefly introduced the basic data structure called **DOORS** used to represent doors. Now it's time for us to take a closer look at this data structure and explore how doors are actually handled during the ray-casting process. We'll also examine a handy function named **AckCheckDoorOpen()** that you can call from your applications to check on the status of doors as your player moves around in your game.

291

A World of Doors

Doors are easy to set up in *ACK-3D* because they are treated as a variation of a wall. To put in a door, you simply create the bitmaps for the door and place it into your scene using the visual map editor. In your application code, you can set attributes for the door, such as its opening and closing speed, its status (opening or closing), and its type (sliding, split, secret, or locked). Split and sliding doors open and close by either opening from the center of the door or sliding to the side as a player passes through. Secret doors, on the other hand, open by moving an entire wall block away from the player. Essentially the player slides forward until he or she hits a wall in the direction they are moving. This is the original style of the secret door introduced in *Wolfenstein 3-D*. To keep secret doors "hidden," they are displayed flush with the surrounding wall.

The main *ACK-3D* code for processing doors is provided in the source file ACKDOOR.C. This file contains two main routines, **CheckDoors()** and **AckCheckDoorOpen()**. **CheckDoors()** is called during the ray-casting process to check all of the active doors in a game to determine their state. **AckCheckDoorOpen()** can be called from your application to check if there is a door in front of the player. We'll look at each of these functions in detail to help you understand how doors are processed. But first let's review the **DOORS** structure introduced in Chapter 4; all of the door processing code uses this structure.

Recall that the **DOORS** structure is defined in ACK3D.H as:

```
typedef struct {
  short mPos;        // Stores position info for a door
  short mPos1;
  short mCode;       // Bitmap ID of the door
  short mCode1;
  UCHAR ColOffset;   // Column offset for the door
  char  Speed;       // Speed setting for opening and closing the door
  char  Type;        // Code for the door type
  UCHAR Flags;       // Door attribute settings
} DOORS;
```

All of the data needed to keep track of where a door is located in a map and the bitmaps used to display the door are stored in this structure. Each door also keeps track of its speed and the amount that it has been opened (**ColOffset**). This structure is incorporated into the **ACKENG** interface structure using the following field:

```
DOORS Door[MAX_DOORS];  // Doors moving at one time
```

Essentially, the interface structure keeps track of the list of doors used in the game. When a new view is built, the list is checked to determine the status of each door. At this stage, some of the components of each door can be changed, for example, the door's speed (**Speed**) or offset (**ColOffset**).

Secret doors are not actually stored in this structure. *ACK-3D* currently allows only one secret door at a time to be in motion, either moving in the x direction or the y direction. This approach is radically different from normal doors, because up to 10 non-secret doors can be in motion at one time (or whatever the define **MAX_DOORS** is set to in your version of the engine). You can still place secret doors all through your 3-D world; just use care that the player doesn't encounter more than one at a time. Some special global variables are used to keep track of the position the secret door is currently in as it mysteriously opens away from the player. The global variables that support secret doors are listed in Table 9.1. These variables are put into use when a secret door is activated. You'll find them used internally within the ray-casting routines and the **CheckDoors()** function mentioned earlier.

Is There a Door in View?

When you use doors that open and close as your player moves around in the game, you'll need to know when your player is close to a door so that the door can be opened at the right time. Fortunately, *ACK-3D* provides a function named **AckCheckDoorOpen()** that performs this work for you. When this function is called, it checks to see if your player is close to:

- A secret door along an x wall
- A secret door along a y wall

Table 9.1 *Global Variables Used to Support Secret Doors*

Variable	Description
xSecretColumn	Keeps track of the position of the secret door along an x wall as it opens or closes.
ySecretColumn	Keeps track of the position of the secret door along a y wall as it opens or closes.
xSecretmPos	Map position for one side of the x secret door.
xSecretmPos1	Map position for the other side of the x secret door.
ySecretmPos	Map position for one side of the y secret door.
ySecretmPos1	Map position for the other side of the y secret door.

- A sliding or split door along an x wall
- A sliding or split door along a y wall

These conditions can be tested easily by using the map grid, as shown in Figure 9.1. We just need to know how close the player is to a wall and if there is a door within the wall. **AckCheckDoorOpen()** returns one of the status codes as listed in Table 9.2 to indicate the state of the door facing the player. The **POV_DOORLOCKED** code can be combined with the other codes returned for sliding doors or secret doors to indicate that the door is currently locked and cannot be opened. This code is a good way to keep your player out of a "forbidden" room.

Here's the format for calling **AckCheckDoorOpen()**:

```
short AckCheckDoorOpen (short xPlayer, short yPlayer, short PlayerAngle)
```

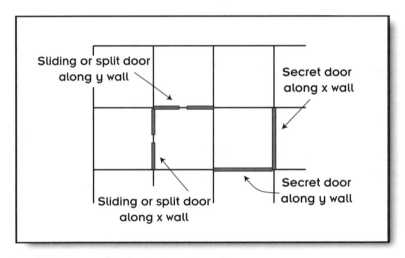

Figure 9.1 *Testing to see if a player encounters a door.*

Table 9.2 *Door Status Codes Returned by ACKCheckDoorOpen()*

Status Code	Value	Description
POV_NODOOR	0	No door is found.
POV_XSECRETDOOR	3	A secret door was found along an x wall.
POV_YSECRETDOOR	4	A secret door was found along a y wall.
POV_XDOOR	1	A sliding or split door was found along an x wall.
POV_YDOOR	2	A sliding or split door was found along a y wall.
POV_DOORLOCKED	0x80	The door is locked.

Notice that you must provide the player's position and angle. Here's a sample of how you might use this function in an application:

```
case MOUSE_UPARROW:
  j = AckMovePOV(ae,ae->PlayerAngle,16);
  if (j == POV_XWALL || j == POV_YWALL)
    AppPlaySound(SOUND_HITWALL);
  if (j == POV_OBJECT)
    CheckOurObjects();

  j = AckCheckDoorOpen(ae->xPlayer, ae->yPlayer, ae->PlayerAngle,ae);

  /* Do something if door is locked */
  if (j & POV_DOORLOCKED)
    LockedFlag = 1;
```

This is a sample handler for a mouse operation. When the player moves the mouse up, the current view is changed by calling **AckMovePOV()**. After the view has been updated, the sample code checks to see if the player has encountered a wall or an object and performs an operation such as playing a sound or updating the list of objects used in the game. Then, **AckCheckDoorOpen()** is called to see if a door is in front of the player. Notice how the sample code uses the return code to determine if the door found is locked.

In addition to returning a status code, **AckCheckDoorOpen()** updates the door that the player has encountered by setting the door's speed and other attributes, including the door's map position and status flag. This initialization allows the door to be opened automatically during the ray-casting process. If the door is a secret door, some additional testing needs to be performed to determine which side of the door the player is on. Because secret doors move in the direction the player is moving, they can only move left or right. For example, if a player is moving to the right and a secret door is encountered along an x wall, the door will move to the right. On the other hand, if the player is moving to the left and a secret door is encountered, the door will move to the left. If you keep this point in mind, you'll have a much easier time following the code that processes secret doors.

Creating AckCheckDoorOpen()

AckCheckDoorOpen() is defined in ACKDOOR.C. To determine if a door is present, the function must first find out if there is anything in front of the player. This is accomplished by calling **AckCheckHit()** as shown here:

```
i = AckCheckHit (xPlayer, yPlayer, PlayerAngle);
```

This function, which is defined in ACKVIEW.C, uses our basic ray-casting algorithm to see if one of the rays cast out from the player intersects a wall as the player is at a specific position and angle. If an intersection is found, the function returns either a value of 1 to indicate that an x wall is hit or 2 to indicate that a y wall has been hit. Once this call has been made, the code in **AckCheckDoorOpen()** simply needs to check for one of the four conditions presented earlier. But before we write the code, let's take a quick look at how the different types of doors supported are processed.

Processing Doors

At any given time in a game, a door can be in one of four states:

- Completely closed
- Completely open
- In the process of being closed
- In the process of being opened

These conditions apply to all three types of doors supported: sliding, split, and secret. When a new view is built using our ray-casting system, the code must have a way to determine which state each door is in so that it can make sure each door is displayed properly. Because there can be a large number of doors in our 3-D world, we need a way to only check those that are currently in motion. This check is accomplished by using a dynamic list of doors within the **ACKENG** interface structure. As a new door is encountered with the **AckCheckDoorOpen()** function, it is added to the **Doors[ ]** array within the interface structure. When **CheckDoors()** is called during rendering, only those doors that are active need be checked. Again, just a simple little trick to save processing time during our rendering of a full-motion, 3-D scene.

So how can we tell the state a door is in? First, let's consider split and sliding doors. We can check the **ColOffset** and **Speed** fields that are provided in the **DOORS** structure. The states represented by the different settings of these fields are listed in Table 9.3. Figure 9.2 shows the process involved in both opening and closing a sliding door.

As Table 9.3 indicates, the **ColOffset** field increases in value as the door opens wider. When this value reaches 64 (the width of a grid square), we know that the door is completely open. As the **ColOffset** decreases in value, the door begins to close until it is set to the value 0, which indicates that it is shut. You can check this field or assign values to it in your application program to control how your doors are opened and closed.

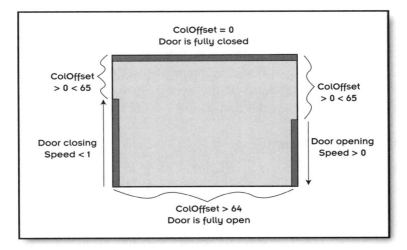

Figure 9.2 *The processes used to open and close a door.*

Table 9.3 *Settings for the ColOffset and Speed Fields to Determine the State of a Door*

ColOffset	Speed	Status
> 64	—	Door is fully open.
0	—	Door is fully closed.
> 0 and < 65	< 1	Door is in the process of being closed.
> 0 and < 65	> 0	Door is in the process of being opened.

Internally, *ACK-3D* uses the **Speed** field with **ColOffset** to open and close doors during the ray-casting process. You can initially assign a speed value for your doors by using the **DoorSpeed** field in the **ACKENG** interface structure. Here's an example:

```
ae->DoorSpeed = 10;
```

This speed setting serves as a global value for all doors. It can be assigned a value from 1 to 255 to specify the rate at which you want the door to open and close. When the **AckCheckDoorOpen()** function determines that a particular door needs to be opened, it copies this value to the corresponding data structure for the door. Each time the ray-casting code builds a new scene, the **Speed** field is added to the **ColOffset** field to make the door either open wider or close a little more. Essentially, the code will continue to open a door by adding in the speed until the door is fully opened. Then, the code reverses this procedure by negating the **Speed** value and adding the negative speed to the **ColOffset** field each time a view is built. This process continues until the door is completely closed. Now you see how the engine creates smooth transitions where the player can walk up to a door as the door is opening, then after the player walks through the doorway, the door closes behind the player.

Processing Secret Doors

Secret doors are processed a little differently from sliding and split doors. When a player comes up to a secret door and pushes on it, the door moves forward (in the direction the player is moving), instead of sliding to the side. The secret door continues to move forward until it bumps into the next grid boundary. This process is shown in Figure 9.3. Notice that the maximum distance the secret door can move is 64 units (the width or height of a grid square). Just as with sliding doors, the door speed field (**DoorSpeed**) stored in the **ACKENG** interface structure is used to control the door's rate of movement.

Remember that secret doors do not use the **DOORS** data structure. In fact, the engine only supports one secret door at a time that can move in the x and y direction. In addition to the speed component, the global variables listed back in Table 9.1 are required to keep track of the secret door's location and direction of movement in a game map.

The tricky part about processing the x or y secret door is keeping track of which side of the door the player is on. As shown in Figure 9.4, the **xSecretColumn** variable serves as a flag to help us determine the relation-

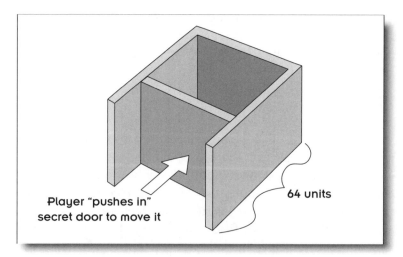

Player "pushes in" secret door to move it

64 units

Figure 9.3 *Moving a secret door.*

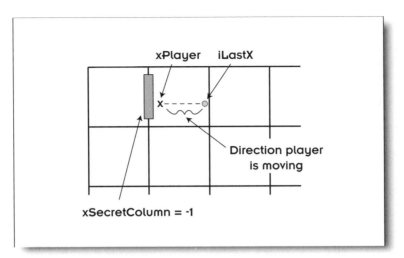

Figure 9.4 *Using variables to determine how a secret door should be moved.*

ship between the player and the door. (Here we'll be looking at the secret door that is placed along an x wall and moves in the x direction. The secret door that moves along the y direction is controlled with the **ySecretColumn** variable in the same manner.) If the secret door is to the left of the player, **xSecretColumn** is set to -1. If the secret door is to the right of the player, this variable is set to 1. If this variable is set to 0, we know that the door is closed and possibly ready to be opened. When the door is moved during the ray-casting process, **xSecretColumn** is checked to determine which direction the door should be moved. The map position variables store the locations into the **xGrid[ ]** map array that correspond with the starting and ending wall positions of the secret door.

Back to AckCheckDoorOpen()

Before we took our slight detour to discuss how the different types of doors are processed, we called **AckCheckHit()** to see if the player was close to a wall. After this call, the return value (**i**) is used to determine the type of wall the player has encountered (x or y) and the type of door. The four different conditions are tested using **if** statements. As an example, here's the code that processes the condition where the player has encountered a secret door along an x wall:

```
if (i == 1 && xGridGlobal[xMapPosn] & DOOR_TYPE_SECRET)
  {
  if (xSecretColumn == 0) // Player is on the right side of door
    {
    DoorCode = POV_XSECRETDOOR;
```

```
    // Secret door is locked; can't open
    if (xGridGlobal[xMapPosn] & DOOR_LOCKED)
      return (DoorCode | POV_DOORLOCKED);
    // Get grid map position that corresponds with the x wall
    // position of where the door starts
    xSecretmPos = xMapPosn;
    if (iLastX > xPlayer) // Door is to the right of player
      {
      xSecretmPos1 = xMapPosn + 1;
      LastMapPosn = xMapPosn;
      xSecretColumn = 1;  // Set to indicate player is on right side
      yGridGlobal[xMapPosn] = yGridGlobal[xMapPosn - GRID_WIDTH];
      }
    else
      { // Door is to the left of the player
      LastMapPosn = xSecretmPos1 = xMapPosn - 1;
      xSecretColumn = -1;
      yGridGlobal[xSecretmPos1] = yGridGlobal[xSecretmPos1 - GRID_WIDTH];
      }
    }
  }
```

Notice how values are assigned to **xSecretColumn** to record which side of the door the player is on. To determine the relationship between the door and the player, the variable **iLastX** is compared to the player's current x position. This global variable is set during the ray-casting process to the last x coordinate of the ray itself. If the ray's x position is greater than the current x position, we know that the player is moving to the left as the player encounters an x wall. This means that the door is to the right of the player.

When a secret door (or any door for that matter) is encountered, the first thing that must be determined is on which side of the wall is the player standing. Figure 9.5 shows that in the case of *POV A,* the door is to the right of the player, in other words, towards an increasing x coordinate. If the player is standing in the *POV B* position, the door would be towards a decreasing x coordinate. Recall that *ACK-3D* stores the map in separate x columns as well as separate y rows. This means that if the player is standing at the *POV A* position, the current map position of the door, as well as map position plus 1, must be accounted for when keeping track of bitmaps within the grid map. The opposite is true when the player is standing at the *POV B* position, where the current map position as well as map position *minus* 1 must be taken into account when keeping track of the bitmaps stored within the grid map.

Sliding and split doors comprise the other category of door that must be processed by **AckCheckDoorOpen()**. These doors are easy to set up for opening because they simply slide to the side.

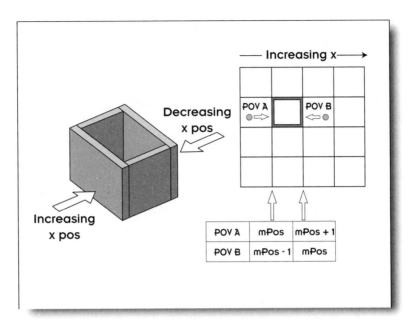

Figure 9.5 *Determining the player's position in relation to a door.*

```
if (i == 1 && (xGridGlobal[xMapPosn] & (DOOR_TYPE_SLIDE + DOOR_TYPE_SPLIT)))
  {
  j = FindDoorSlot (xMapPosn);   // Locate the door to open
  if (j >= 0)
    {
    DoorCode = POV_XDOOR;          // Found a door

    LastMapPosn = gDoor[j].mPos = xMapPosn;
    if ((short) iLastX > xPlayer)
      i = xMapPosn + 1;
    else
      LastMapPosn = i = xMapPosn - 1;
    // Can't open the door because it is locked
    if (xGridGlobal[xMapPosn] & DOOR_LOCKED)
      {
      gDoor[j].mPos = -1;
      return (DoorCode | POV_DOORLOCKED);
      }
    // Store settings for the door in the DOORS structure
    gDoor[j].mCode = xGridGlobal[xMapPosn];
    gDoor[j].mCode1 = xGridGlobal[i];
    gDoor[j].mPos1 = i;
    gDoor[j].ColOffset = 1;
    gDoor[j].Speed = aeGlobal->DoorSpeed;
    gDoor[j].Type = DOOR_XCODE;
    gDoor[j].Flags = DOOR_OPENING;
    }
  }
```

Once we know we've encountered a split or sliding door, the door's data must be updated. This data includes the door's speed, location, column offset, and flags. In this case, notice that we set the **Flags** field to **DOOR_OPENING** to indicate that the door is ready to be opened. The **Type** field is set to **DOOR_XCODE** to indicate that the door is placed along an x wall. What we also need to keep track of is the identical twin to the door we are beginning to open. When *ACK-3D* was first under construction, each map square could only indicate one wall block, with all four sides. When doors were introduced into the scheme of things, I knew a door would be on the opposite side of the door the player just encountered. That meant there are always two doors for the x direction and two doors for the y direction, both of which need to be opened at the same time. Otherwise we would see the classic scene in *Star Wars*, where Han Solo jury-rigs one door to open into the shield generator, only to have a second door close over the first! If we only handled one side of the four wall block, we would see a door open with a second "ghost" door behind it that wasn't being handled—not a good way to navigate from room to room. By recording the bitmap data from the map (using our global variable **xGridGlobal[ ]**), we can track both sides at the same time.

Processing Doors during Ray Casting

When the high-level function **AckBuildView()** is called to update the current view and kick off the ray-casting process, one other task that needs to be performed is to check all of the active doors to determine their current state. This task is easy to do by using the **Door[ ]** array field in the interface structure. If a door's column offset (**ColOffset**) is not zero, the ray caster knows that the door is either opening or closing. Thus, it can add the speed of the door to the offset and then check the door to see if it is fully opened or fully closed. This procedure is performed by the internal function **CheckDoors()** defined in ACKDOOR.C. **CheckDoors()** is called by **AckBuildView()**, and it updates the fields in each **DOORS** structure so that the ray-casting process can determine which bitmap to display and how the bitmap should be displayed.

Introducing CheckDoors()

The **CheckDoors()** function uses a **for** loop to examine each door stored in the **Door[ ]** array. However, before **CheckDoor()** is called, the list of doors stored in the **ACKENG** interface structure is assigned to a global variable named **gDoor[ ]**. Thus, one of the first things **CheckDoor()** needs to do is set a pointer to this global variable so that each door in the list can be checked

easily. This check avoids indirect addressing each time the **Door[ ]** array needs to be accessed:

```
dPtr = &gDoor[0];
```

Then, the main loop starts:

```
for (i = 0; i < MAX_DOORS; i++)
  {
  if (dPtr->ColOffset)
  ...
```

MAX_DOORS is a constant that specifies the maximum number of doors that can be opening or closing in a game at the same time. It is set to 10 in the ACK3D.H header file. You can easily change this value if you wish, but I've never come across a need to have more than 10 doors in action all at once! Each time through the loop, a set of **if** statements checks to see if a door is currently opened or if the door is a secret door that needs to be processed.

The main **if** statement shown above, **if (dPtr->CollOffset)**, is used to determine if a particular door is currently open. If this code succeeds, the speed column offset of the door is updated using the door's speed setting as shown here:

```
dPtr->ColOffset += dPtr->Speed;
mPos = dPtr->mPos;
mPos1 = dPtr->mPos1;
```

In most games an average speed setting will be 16. This setting gives you smooth motion to open and close a door. If the door slides the full width of a grid square to open or close, a speed setting of 16 results in the door being fully opened or closed in 4 cycles (16×4 = 64). Notice also that the code assigns the grid positions of the door to **mPos** and **mPos1**. These positions are needed to later determine if the player is in the same grid square as the door.

At this stage in the code, we know that the door is already open and that it is either being opened further or being closed. If the door is being opened further, most of our processing is done except for checking the door's column offset to see when we should start closing the door:

```
if (dPtr->ColOffset > 0xA0)
  {
  dPtr->Speed = -dPtr->Speed;    // Start to reduce speed
  dPtr->Flags &= ~DOOR_OPENING; // Set flag to indicate door is closing
  dPtr->Flags |= DOOR_CLOSING;
  }
```

Because we are always adding in the speed to the column offset while opening the door, at some point the column offset value will become larger than 160 (A0h). This point is when we want to reverse the situation and start to close the door. Although the maximum column offset for the door is actually 64 units, the value 160 is used to leave time for the door to stay open for a few cycles. (You wouldn't want your player to get stuck while walking through the open door.) To change the door from opening to closing, we negate the speed setting and both the **DOOR_OPENING** and **DOOR_CLOSING** flags.

So what do we do if the door is closing? We need to decrease the column offset of the door by adding in a negative speed value:

```
if (dPtr->Speed < 1 && dPtr->ColOffset < 65)
  { // Get corner of grid
  MapPosn = (yPlayer & 0xFFC0) + (xPlayer >> BITMAP_SHIFT);
  // Is player in same grid square that the door is in?
  if (MapPosn == mPos || MapPosn == mPos1)
    {
    dPtr->ColOffset -= dPtr->Speed;    // Reduce column offset
    continue;
    }
  // Is the door along an x wall?
  if (dPtr->Type == DOOR_XCODE)
    { // Store bitmap IDs for doors
    xGridGlobal[mPos] = dPtr->mCode;
    xGridGlobal[mPos1] = dPtr->mCode1;
    }
  else
    {                                  // Door is along a y wall
    yGridGlobal[mPos] = dPtr->mCode;
    yGridGlobal[mPos1] = dPtr->mCode1;
    }

  // Door is close enough to be fully closed to get rid
  // of the door from the array
  if (dPtr->ColOffset < 3)
    {
    dPtr->ColOffset = 0;               // Close door
    dPtr->mPos = -1;
    dPtr->mPos1 = -1;
    dPtr->Flags = 0;
    }
  }
```

The first thing we check for is if the player happens to be standing in the doorway! The map position of the player is calculated using our oldie but goodie formula:

```
MapPosn = (yPlayer & 0xFFC0) + (xPlayer >> BITMAP_SHIFT);
```

whereupon this position is checked against that of the current door we're processing. If the player is indeed blocking things, we skip any further processing of this door with the **continue** statement, after first removing the speed factor that we added in earlier. Should the coast be clear, the next thing checked is if the door is actually becoming visible to the player. By checking the column of the door to see if it is less than 65, we know that there is at least a partial door being displayed and the player cannot move into the same map square as the door. Earlier, when the door was being opened, we removed the door bitmap code from the map so that any checking by the ray-casting routines would not stop when a door was struck. These bitmap codes now have to be put back where they belong so all goes well within the ray cast and player movement routines. The following **if** block takes care of this process:

```
if (dPtr->Type == DOOR_XCODE)
   {  // Store bitmap IDs for doors
   xGridGlobal[mPos] = dPtr->mCode;
   xGridGlobal[mPos1] = dPtr->mCode1;
   }
else
   {  // Door is along a y wall
   yGridGlobal[mPos] = dPtr->mCode;
   yGridGlobal[mPos1] = dPtr->mCode1;
   }
```

The last thing we check is to see if the door is almost closed. By checking the column to see if it is less than 3 (an arbitrary number I pulled out of a hat), we essentially slam the door fully shut and remove it from the **Door[ ]** array. At this point, the player (should he or she be looking in the correct direction) will see a closed door just as it appeared before the opening process began.

Once the list of doors has been processed, we need to check on the secret door that can be displayed along an x wall or y wall. Recall that *ACK-3D* currently handles only one door at a time in one of these directions. Thus, we do not need to use a loop to process the secret doors. The first step in processing a secret door is to determine which side the door is on in relation to the player (right or left). For example, here's the code that accomplishes this task for the secret door that goes along an x wall:

```
if (xSecretColumn)
   {
   if (xSecretColumn > 0)  // See if the door is to the right of us
      {
      mPos = xSecretmPos1;  // Get x grid position of the door
      DeltaGrid = -1;
      xSecretColumn += aeGlobal->DoorSpeed;
```

```
      }
    else
      {
      mPos = xSecretmPos;
      DeltaGrid = 0;
      xSecretColumn -= aeGlobal->DoorSpeed;
      }
    ...
```

In either case, we calculate the x grid position of the door and add in the door speed to the **xSecretColumn** variable.

The Complete ACKDOOR.C

```
// This source file contains the functions needed to process split, sliding,
// and secret doors.
// (c) 1995 ACK Software (Lary Myers)
#include <windows.h>
#include <stdlib.h>
#include <stdio.h>
#include <dos.h>
#include <mem.h>
#include <io.h>
#include <fcntl.h>
#include <time.h>
#include <string.h>
#include <sys\stat.h>
#include "ack3d.h"    // Main ACK-3D internal and interface data structures
#include "ackeng.h"   // Internal data structures and constants
#include "ackext.h"   // Defines external (global) variables
extern DOORS *gDoor;

//+++++++++++++++++++++++++++++++++++++++++++++++++++++++++++++++++++++++++++++
// Check all the active doors to see what current state they are in. If a
// door's column offset is non-zero, it is either opening or closing,
// so the speed of the door is added in and the door is checked to
// see if it is fully opened or fully closed. This function is an internal
// function that is called during the ray-casting process.
//+++++++++++++++++++++++++++++++++++++++++++++++++++++++++++++++++++++++++++++
void CheckDoors (void)
{
  short i, MapPosn, mPos, mPos1;
  short mx, my, DeltaGrid;
  short xPlayer, yPlayer;
  DOORS *dPtr;

  xPlayer = xPglobal;
  yPlayer = yPglobal;
  dPtr = &gDoor[0];
  for (i = 0; i < MAX_DOORS; i++)
    {
    if (dPtr->ColOffset)  // Door is not closed
```

```
   {  // Add speed to door column offset
   dPtr->ColOffset += dPtr->Speed;
   mPos = dPtr->mPos;      // Get grid position of door
   mPos1 = dPtr->mPos1;
   // Door is closing and is visible; put old codes back to make non-passable
   if (dPtr->Speed < 1 && dPtr->ColOffset < 65)
     {  // Get corner of grid
     MapPosn = (yPlayer & 0xFFC0) + (xPlayer >> BITMAP_SHIFT);
     // Is player in same grid square that the door is in?
     if (MapPosn == mPos || MapPosn == mPos1)
       {
       dPtr->ColOffset -= dPtr->Speed;  // Reduce column offset continue;
       }
     // Is the door along an x wall?
     if (dPtr->Type == DOOR_XCODE)
       {  // Store bitmap IDS for doors
       xGridGlobal[mPos] = dPtr->mCode;
       xGridGlobal[mPos1] = dPtr->mCode1;
       }
     else
       {  // Door is along a y wall
       yGridGlobal[mPos] = dPtr->mCode;
       yGridGlobal[mPos1] = dPtr->mCode1;
       }
     // Door is close enough to fully closed to get rid
     // of the door from the array
     if (dPtr->ColOffset < 3)
       {
       dPtr->ColOffset = 0;        // Close door
       dPtr->mPos = -1;
       dPtr->mPos1 = -1;
       dPtr->Flags = 0;
       }
     }
   // Door is fully opened—time to start closing it
   if (dPtr->ColOffset > 0xA0)
     {
     dPtr->Speed = -dPtr->Speed;   // Start to reduce speed
     dPtr->Flags &= ~DOOR_OPENING; // Set flag to indicate door closing
     dPtr->Flags |= DOOR_CLOSING;
     }
   }
   dPtr++; // Advance to check next door
   }
//===========================================================================
// Now check for any action occuring in a secret door. This is currently
// set up to handle only one door at a time in the x and y directions, but
// it should be fairly straightforward to use a list of doors, similiar
// to normal doors, to handle more than one.
//===========================================================================
if (xSecretColumn)
   {
   if (xSecretColumn > 0)      // See if the door is to the right of us
     {
     mPos = xSecretmPos1;
```

```
      DeltaGrid = -1;
      xSecretColumn += aeGlobal->DoorSpeed;
      }
  else
    {
    mPos = xSecretmPos;
    DeltaGrid = 0;
    xSecretColumn -= aeGlobal->DoorSpeed;
    }
my = mPos & 0xFFC0;
mx = (mPos - my) << 6;
if (abs (xSecretColumn) > BITMAP_WIDTH)  // Beyond one grid square
  {
  mx += xSecretColumn;
  my = my + (mx >> BITMAP_SHIFT);
  if (xGridGlobal[my])    // No further, an obstruction
    {
    xGridGlobal[xSecretmPos] = 0;
    xGridGlobal[xSecretmPos1] = 0;
    my += DeltaGrid;
    xGridGlobal[my] = aeGlobal->NonSecretCode;
    xGridGlobal[my + 1] = aeGlobal->NonSecretCode;
    yGridGlobal[my] = aeGlobal->NonSecretCode;
    yGridGlobal[my + GRID_WIDTH] = aeGlobal->NonSecretCode;
    xSecretColumn = 0;
    }
  else
    {
    if (my != mPos)
      {
      xGridGlobal[xSecretmPos] = 0;
      xGridGlobal[xSecretmPos1] = 0;
      if (xSecretColumn > 0)
        {
        xSecretColumn -= (BITMAP_WIDTH - 1);
        xGridGlobal[my] = DOOR_TYPE_SECRET + 1;
        xSecretmPos1 = my;
        my--;
        xGridGlobal[my] = DOOR_TYPE_SECRET + 1;
        xSecretmPos = my;
        }
      else
        {
        xSecretColumn += (BITMAP_WIDTH - 1);
        xGridGlobal[my] = DOOR_TYPE_SECRET + 1;
        xGridGlobal[my + 1] = DOOR_TYPE_SECRET + 1;
        xSecretmPos = my;
        xSecretmPos = my + 1;
        }
      }
    }               // End if (xGrid[my]) ... else ...
  }                 // End if (abs(xSecretColumn) > GRID_SIZE)
}                   // End if (xSecretColumn)
```

```
//=============================================================
// Perform same process on a secret door that may be moving in the y
// direction. The same door can move either way, depending on which
// angle the player struck it at.
//=============================================================
if (ySecretColumn)
    {
    if (ySecretColumn > 0)
      {
      mPos = ySecretmPos1;
      DeltaGrid = -GRID_WIDTH;
      ySecretColumn += aeGlobal->DoorSpeed;
      }
    else
      {
      mPos = ySecretmPos;
      DeltaGrid = 0;
      ySecretColumn -= aeGlobal->DoorSpeed;
      }
    my = mPos & 0xFFC0;
    mx = (mPos - my) << 6;
    if (abs (ySecretColumn) > BITMAP_WIDTH)
      {
      my += ySecretColumn;
      my = (my & 0xFFC0) + (mx >> 6);
      if (yGridGlobal[my])
        {
        yGridGlobal[ySecretmPos] = 0;
        yGridGlobal[ySecretmPos1] = 0;
        my += DeltaGrid;
        xGridGlobal[my] = aeGlobal->NonSecretCode;
        xGridGlobal[my + 1] = aeGlobal->NonSecretCode;
        yGridGlobal[my] = aeGlobal->NonSecretCode;
        yGridGlobal[my + GRID_WIDTH] = aeGlobal->NonSecretCode;
        ySecretColumn = 0;
        }
      else
        {
        if (my != mPos)
          {
          yGridGlobal[ySecretmPos] = 0;
          yGridGlobal[ySecretmPos1] = 0;
          if (ySecretColumn > 0)
            {
            ySecretColumn -= (BITMAP_WIDTH - 1);
            yGridGlobal[my] = DOOR_TYPE_SECRET + 1;
            ySecretmPos1 = my;
            my -= GRID_WIDTH;
            yGridGlobal[my] = DOOR_TYPE_SECRET + 1;
            ySecretmPos = my;
            }
          else
            {
            ySecretColumn += (BITMAP_WIDTH - 1);
            yGridGlobal[my] = DOOR_TYPE_SECRET + 1;
```

```
            yGridGlobal[my + GRID_WIDTH] = DOOR_TYPE_SECRET + 1;
            ySecretmPos = my;
            ySecretmPos = my + GRID_WIDTH;
            }
          }
        }
      }
    }
}


//++++++++++++++++++++++++++++++++++++++++++++++++++++++++++++++++++++++
// Internal function called by FindDoorSlot(). This function
// locates a door from its map coordinate and return the index.
//++++++++++++++++++++++++++++++++++++++++++++++++++++++++++++++++++++++
short FindDoor (short MapPosn)
{
  short index;
  for (index = 0; index < MAX_DOORS; index++)
    {
    if (MapPosn == gDoor[index].mPos ||
      MapPosn == gDoor[index].mPos1)
    return (index);
    }
  return (-1);
}


//++++++++++++++++++++++++++++++++++++++++++++++++++++++++++++++++++++++
// Internal routine called by AckCheckDoorOpen() This function
// finds an empty slot for a door. If the door already occupies a slot
// and it is in a non-closed state, an error is returned.
//++++++++++++++++++++++++++++++++++++++++++++++++++++++++++++++++++++++
short FindDoorSlot (short MapPosn)
{
  short index;
  index = FindDoor (MapPosn);
  if (index >= 0 && gDoor[index].ColOffset)
    return (-1);
  for (index = 0; index < MAX_DOORS; index++)
    {
    if (gDoor[index].mPos == -1)
      return (index);
    }
  return (-1);
}


//++++++++++++++++++++++++++++++++++++++++++++++++++++++++++++++++++++++
// Checks directly in front of the POV to see if a door is there. If so,
// and the door is not locked, the door is set to begin opening.
//++++++++++++++++++++++++++++++++++++++++++++++++++++++++++++++++++++++
short AckCheckDoorOpen (short xPlayer, short yPlayer, short PlayerAngle)
{
  short i, j, DoorCode;
  DoorCode = POV_NODOOR;
```

```
// Check to see if player is close to a wall
  i = AckCheckHit (xPlayer, yPlayer, PlayerAngle);
// A secret door is found along an x wall
  if (i == 1 && xGridGlobal[xMapPosn] & DOOR_TYPE_SECRET)
    {
    if (xSecretColumn == 0) // Player is on the right side of door
      {
      DoorCode = POV_XSECRETDOOR;
      // Secret door is locked; can't open
      if (xGridGlobal[xMapPosn] & DOOR_LOCKED)
        return (DoorCode | POV_DOORLOCKED);
      // Get grid map position that corresponds with the x wall
      // position of where the door starts
      xSecretmPos = xMapPosn;
      if (iLastX > xPlayer) // Door is to the right of player
        {
        xSecretmPos1 = xMapPosn + 1;
        LastMapPosn = xMapPosn;
        xSecretColumn = 1;  // Set to indicate player is on right side
        yGridGlobal[xMapPosn] = yGridGlobal[xMapPosn - GRID_WIDTH];
        }
      else
        { // Door is to the left of the player
        LastMapPosn = xSecretmPos1 = xMapPosn - 1; xSecretColumn = -1;
        yGridGlobal[xSecretmPos1] = yGridGlobal[xSecretmPos1 - GRID_WIDTH];
        }
      }
    }
// A secret door is found along a y wall
  if (i == 2 && yGridGlobal[yMapPosn] & DOOR_TYPE_SECRET)
    {
    if (ySecretColumn == 0)
      {
      DoorCode = POV_YSECRETDOOR;
      if (yGridGlobal[yMapPosn] & DOOR_LOCKED)
        return (DoorCode | POV_DOORLOCKED);
      ySecretmPos = yMapPosn;
      if (iLastY > yPlayer)
        {
        LastMapPosn = yMapPosn;
        ySecretmPos1 = yMapPosn + GRID_WIDTH;
        xGridGlobal[yMapPosn] = xGridGlobal[yMapPosn - 1];
        ySecretColumn = 1;
        }
      else
        {
        LastMapPosn = ySecretmPos1 = yMapPosn - GRID_WIDTH;
        xGridGlobal[ySecretmPos1] = xGridGlobal[ySecretmPos1 - 1];
        ySecretColumn = -1;
        }
      }
    }
// A sliding or split door is found along an x wall
  if (i == 1 && (xGridGlobal[xMapPosn] & (DOOR_TYPE_SLIDE + DOOR_TYPE_SPLIT)))
```

```
      {
      j = FindDoorSlot (xMapPosn);
      if (j >= 0)
        {
        DoorCode = POV_XDOOR;
        LastMapPosn = gDoor[j].mPos = xMapPosn;
        if ((short) iLastX > xPlayer)
          i = xMapPosn + 1;
        else
          LastMapPosn = i = xMapPosn - 1;
        if (xGridGlobal[xMapPosn] & DOOR_LOCKED)
          {
          gDoor[j].mPos = -1;
          return (DoorCode | POV_DOORLOCKED);
          }
        // Update door data structure
        gDoor[j].mCode = xGridGlobal[xMapPosn];
        gDoor[j].mCode1 = xGridGlobal[i];
        gDoor[j].mPos1 = i;
        gDoor[j].ColOffset = 1;
        gDoor[j].Speed = aeGlobal->DoorSpeed;
        gDoor[j].Type = DOOR_XCODE;
        gDoor[j].Flags = DOOR_OPENING;
        }
      }
// A sliding or split door is found along a y wall
  if (i == 2 && (yGridGlobal[yMapPosn] & (DOOR_TYPE_SLIDE + DOOR_TYPE_SPLIT)))
    {
    j = FindDoorSlot (yMapPosn);
    if (j >= 0)
      {
      DoorCode = POV_YDOOR;
      LastMapPosn = gDoor[j].mPos = yMapPosn;
      if ((short) iLastY > yPlayer)
        i = yMapPosn + GRID_WIDTH;
      else
        LastMapPosn = i = yMapPosn - GRID_WIDTH;
      if (yGridGlobal[yMapPosn] & DOOR_LOCKED)
        {
        gDoor[j].mPos = -1;
        return (DoorCode | POV_DOORLOCKED);
        }
      gDoor[j].mCode = yGridGlobal[yMapPosn];
      gDoor[j].mCode1 = yGridGlobal[i];
      gDoor[j].mPos1 = i;
      gDoor[j].ColOffset = 1;
      gDoor[j].Speed = aeGlobal->DoorSpeed;
      gDoor[j].Type = DOOR_YCODE;
      gDoor[j].Flags = DOOR_OPENING;
      }
    }
  return (DoorCode);
}
// **** End of Source ****
```

A 3-D scene without a floor and ceiling will really look like it's missing something. Fortunately, *ACK-3D* provides a number of different ways you can add floors and ceilings to your games.

A Ceiling over Your Head and a Floor at Your Feet

Walls and objects help give your player a sense of adventure, especially if you design them so that your player encounters a surprise at every turn of the way. But to give your 3-D worlds a real sense of depth, you'll want to add floors and ceilings. When you actually walk down a hallway at home, or in the workplace, you normally see both a floor beneath your feet and a ceiling above your head. What we've used in many of our examples so far is a solid color to represent both. Wouldn't it be nice if we could enhance our 3-D world with some textures to accurately represent a tiled floor and lights in the ceiling? Well, we can because the *ACK-3D* engine has provisions for doing just that. There is a price however (oh, those dreaded words again), and that price is processing speed.

Our goal, then, is to find a way to display realistic-looking floors and ceilings without slowing down our game too much. Fortunately, we can use some of the table lookup optimization techniques we developed earlier for the ray-casting engine to efficiently display bitmapped floors and ceilings.

In this chapter, I'll show you two ways to draw floors and ceilings. The first and easiest (and also the quickest) is to display your floors and ceilings using solid color bitmaps. With this method, we don't need to perform any tricky ray-casting calculations or use table lookups to locate bitmap images to display. If you need to squeeze every ounce of speed out of your game, this is the way to go. The other technique that we'll explore takes you all the way and shows how nicely textured bitmaps can be displayed to give your player a sense of being in a real 3-D scene. You can even combine rotating background scenes with your ceilings to make your ceilings look animated.

Setting Up to Draw Floors and Ceilings

If you haven't noticed already, one of my main design goals in first designing and later expanding the *ACK-3D* engine was to create a powerful tool that offers game developers a number of choices. By setting different flags, you can turn light shading on or off, use background scenes, ray cast views in low or high resolution, and so on. This multiple-option approach is definitely available with floors and ceilings. You can easily assign flags to the **ACKENG** interface structure when the engine is initialized to select from a number of different options, for example, drawing a view with a solid ceiling and solid floor or drawing a view with a solid floor and textured ceiling.

The floor and ceiling selection flags, which are defined in ACK3D.H, are described in Table 10.1. Although there are a number of options, these flags greatly simplify the work of adding ceilings and floors to your views. For example, if you want to draw a solid color ceiling and floor, you assign these flags to the **ACKENG** interface structure when the engine is initialized, as shown here:

```
ACKENG ae;  // Declare an interface structure
ae.SysFlags = SYS_SOLID_FLOOR | SYS_SOLID_CEIL;
```

Table 10.1   *Flags that Select Floor and Ceiling Drawing Options*

Flag	Value	Description
SYS_SOLID_FLOOR	0x4000	Draw a scene with a solid color floor.
SYS_SOLID_CEIL	0x2000	Draw a scene with a solid color ceiling.
SYS_SINGLE_BMP	0x0800	Use a single bitmap for the floor and ceiling.
SYS_SOLID_BACK	0x8000	Use a solid color background instead of a bitmap image.

As we learned in Chapter 6, the **SysFlags** field is tested during the ray-casting process to determine which function should be called to actually draw the floor and ceiling.

DESIGN TIP

By default, the engine draws floors and ceilings using textured bitmaps. So, if you want to change this setting, make sure that you assign one of the flags listed in Table 10.1 to the interface structure before you build views. If you assign the **SYS_SINGLE_BMP** flag, textured floors and ceilings will be drawn; however, only one bitmap will be used to draw the floor and one bitmap for the ceiling. You can assign a different bitmap to the floor and the ceiling. This was the approach taken by the first version of *Blake Stone* (see Chapter 1) when it hit the market.

Data Structures for Drawing Floors and Ceilings

No special data structures are required to support drawing solid color floors and ceilings. *ACK-3D* simply uses color values stored in the interface structure to determine the colors for plotting the floor and ceiling pixels. Since the floor and ceiling are drawn in the off-screen buffer before the wall and object slices are drawn, you can use any color you want. As an example, if a wall appears in the line of sight path, the pixels for the wall will simply overwrite the pixels for the ceiling. The colors for the solid floor and ceiling must be assigned to the interface structure when the engine is initialized. Here's an example:

```
ae.TopColor = 30;
ae.BottomColor = 120;
```

Textured floors and ceilings are another story. To use this feature, you must create bitmap images and assign them to your game map. The bitmaps are represented as 64x64 pixel building blocks (just like walls). They are loaded by *ACK-3D* when the engine is initialized. The internal function that loads the floor and ceiling data is **AckReadMapFile()**, which is defined in ACKINIT.C. Internally, we need two separate arrays to store the bitmap data for the floor and ceiling. These arrays are defined in ACKDATA.C as:

```
unsigned int FloorMap[4096];
unsigned int CeilMap[4096];
```

Notice that these arrays are the same size as the x and y grid arrays. Recall that the game map contains 64 rows by 64 columns of grid squares. Thus, we need 4,096 locations (64×64) to store a floor and ceiling bitmap code for each grid square. Essentially, these arrays map out the floor and ceiling bitmaps that are displayed in a given game map location. You specify which bitmaps you want displayed for the floor and ceiling at the different map locations when you create your map using the visual map editor. The bitmap images you use can also be used for wall bitmaps.

As the player moves around in a scene and views are built, the ray-casting engine determines where floor and ceiling pixels should be plotted on the screen, and then uses these coordinates to index into the **FloorMap[ ]** and **CeilMap[ ]** arrays. This technique of using the floor and ceiling map arrays is shown in Figure 10.1. Because each array records which bitmap should be displayed for the floor and ceiling of a grid square, we basically have everything we need. The only real time-intensive calculation involves determining how the pixels of the floor and ceiling bitmap should be plotted on the screen so that the floor and ceiling are displayed in the correct perspective. This calculation requires some clever math tricks, which I'll explain later.

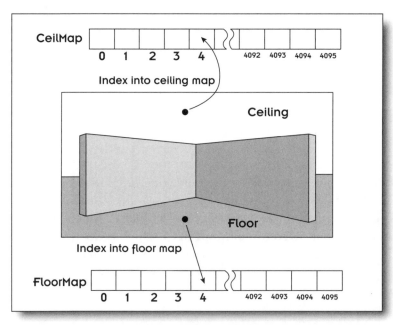

Figure 10.1 *Using floor and ceiling map arrays to locate floor and ceiling bitmaps.*

Mopping the Floor and Painting the Ceiling (the Easy Way)

Let's discuss the fast and easy way to draw a floor and ceiling, then we'll move on to the fun stuff. Drawing a solid color ceiling and floor is accomplished during the ray-casting process by using the assembly-code routine **DrawSolidCeilSolidFloor**, which is defined in ACKRTN5.ASM. This routine is automatically called if the **SysFlags** field in the interface structure is assigned to **SYS_SOLID_FLOOR** and **SYS_SOLID_CEIL**. (If only one of these flags is used, a different routine is called, such as **DrawSolidFloorAndCeil** to draw a solid floor and a textured ceiling.)

Let's take a quick look at what is involved in drawing a solid floor (and ceiling). Here's the code for **DrawSolidCeilSolidFloor**:

```
ACKPROC DrawSolidCeilSolidFloor
  mov    edi,[_gScrnBuffer]         ; Get address of off-screen buffer
  movzx  ecx,[word ptr _gCenterOff]  ; Get address of center row
  mov    al,[byte ptr _gTopColor]    ; Get color for ceiling
  mov    ah,al                       ; Copy color code to top half of buffer
  shr    cx,1
  rep    stosw
  rcl    cx,1
  rep    stosb
  ; Ceiling is done. Time to paint the floor
  mov    edi,[_gScrnBuffer]
  movzx  ecx,[word ptr _gCenterOff]
  add    edi,ecx
  mov    al,[byte ptr _gBottomColor] ; Get color for floor
  mov    ah,al ; Copy color value to bottom half of buffer
  shr    cx,1
  rep    stosw
  rcl    cx,1
  rep    stosb
  ret
  endp
```

We're back to assembly, but don't worry, because this code is very simple. As shown in Figure 10.2, we simply calculate the midpoint of the view (**gCenterOff**) and fill the top half of the buffer with the ceiling color (**gTopColor**) and the bottom half with the floor color (**gBottomColor**). These color values come from the **ACKENG** interface structure; they are assigned to the variables used in the above code during the ray casting process. The top and bottom halves of the buffer are filled with solid colors by using a fast block move before the wall slice data is added to the off-screen buffer. As you can see, this is a really fast

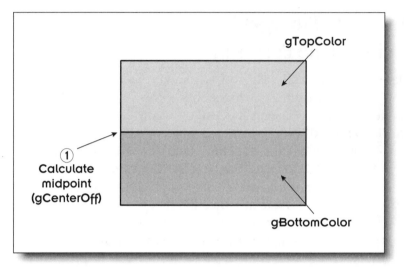

Figure 10.2 *Drawing a solid floor and ceiling.*

way to paint a floor and ceiling. The only problem is that solid ceilings and floors aren't as visually appealing as fully textured bitmaps.

Moving Up to Textured Floors and Ceilings

By adding the extra complexity of rendering both the floor and ceiling as a textured bitmap, we use many more CPU cycles than we do just drawing the walls and objects for a scene. We still end up with a fast game engine, but we hate to add too many features that might slow it down, even a little.

Let's begin our discussion of how bitmap floors and ceilings are displayed by examining the general principles involved. Fortunately, the techniques used to draw floors are similar to the ones used to draw ceilings—the algorithm is just inverted to draw the textures on top instead of on the bottom.

As a player moves in a scene, we need to be able to calculate the correct floor and ceiling bitmap to display. As shown in Figure 10.3, as the player "stands" at a given position, we can say that the player's feet are located at the player's x,y coordinate. The player's eyes would be at some point above. This height determines the intersection point of the pixel to draw for the floor (and the ceiling).

Basically, we can use the cosine and sine trig functions to calculate the x,y intersection points. For the angle, we use the player's viewing angle, and we factor in the height that the player's viewpoint is above the ground level. To speed up the process involved in calculating cosine and sine values, we can use the cosine and sine lookup tables that we used during the ray-casting process.

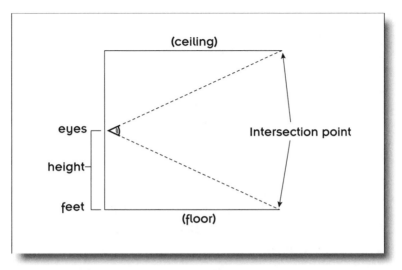

Figure 10.3 *Determining the pixel to draw for a floor intersection point.*

Here's the basic algorithm that is used to draw both textured floors and ceilings for a view. The algorithm assumes that we'll also be combining a background scene with the ceiling bitmap to give the ceiling a more realistic look:

1. Use the left edge of the viewport and the player's current angle to determine a starting view angle to display the floor and ceiling. This angle essentially tells us in which view column to start displaying the floor and ceiling bitmap.

2. Calculate the starting column for the background scene. The background scene is twice the width (640) of the normal screen (320).

3. Determine the actual starting rows to display the floor and the ceiling. These rows will be slightly offset from the middle row of the screen to speed up the process of displaying the bitmaps for the floor and ceiling.

4. Calculate a height scale value to represent the player's viewpoint from a location above the player's feet.

5. Use a nested drawing loop to plot the pixels for the floor and ceiling. The loop scans from one column of the viewport to the other and plots each row for the floor and ceiling, as shown in Figure 10.4. For each row and column position, we calculate the distance from the player to this position by using the height scale factor. Once we know the x,y location, we can look up the bitmap to display by using the **CeilMap[ ]** and **FloorMap[ ]** arrays.

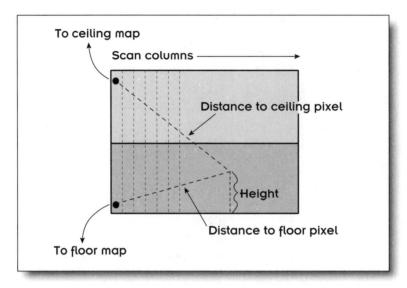

Figure 10.4   *Locating intersection points to plot floor and ceiling pixels.*

The basic math behind the algorithm to determine where pixels should be plotted is based on the intersection method I just mentioned:

```
cos (va) * height_distance = x
sin (va) * height_distance = y
```

Here *va* is the player's viewing angle and *height_distance* is the ratio between the player's viewpoint height and the position of the screen row. Because the *ACK-3D* engine keeps a table that stores cosine and sine values, these calculations can be made by using table lookup operations.

Displaying a Ceiling with a Backdrop

In the algorithm I just presented, step 2 indicates that a background scene is factored in. What is going on here? Textured floors and ceilings look nice, but we also want to have a way to display background scenes, such as some mountains or trees in the distance. With a fairly simple addition to our floor and ceiling code, such a background scene can easily be displayed. To use this feature, your application must load the background scene when the *ACK-3D* engine is initialized. The background scene will show through only when we have no ceiling over an area, giving us the ability to combine both inside and outside areas in one map!

640 Pixels

100 Pixels

Figure 10.5 *Displaying a background scene using a 640x100-pixel bitmap image.*

As shown in Figure 10.5, the background scene is created as an image 640 pixels in width and 100 pixels in height. The ceiling bitmap never takes up more than half of the screen height (100 pixels), so the background screen only needs to be 100 pixels in height. The width, on the other hand, is set to 640 pixels to provide a larger image. As a player moves in your views, different portions of the background scene can be displayed to give the player the feeling that he or she is traveling through different terrain.

The background scene should be created with a painting program. It can then be loaded by your application when the engine is initialized. After the scene is loaded, it is stored in an array named **BackArray[ ]**, which is defined in ACKDATA.C as

```
unsigned char *BackArray[INT_ANGLE_360];
```

where **INT_ANGLE_360** is defined as the value 1800. This step allows for future expansion of a background image. The current version has been geared for a 640 width image, but there's no reason that an image could not be made as large as the full 360 circle, where each column of the background would correspond to each angle increment (0.2 degrees) in the *ACK-3D* circle.

Looking at Figure 10.6, you can see that a background image is actually repeated as we spin around in our 3-D world (unless you made the background as wide as our circle, which is why **BackArray[ ]** was defined as 1,800 even though we are only using 640 of them in the current version). When a background is going to be drawn, the first thing we need to determine is

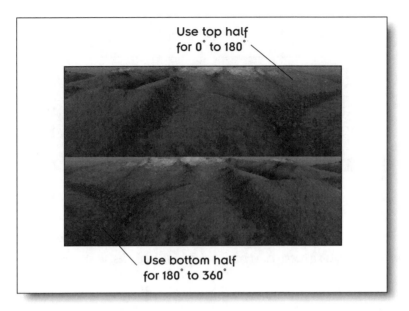

Figure 10.6 *Processing a background image.*

which column to start with in the background. If we are starting with angle 0, we begin with column 0 of the background. This 1:1 ratio holds true all the way up to angle 639. But what happens when we need to draw the background for the angles 640 up to 1,799 (the equivalent of 359.08 degrees in our *ACK-3D* universe). We just repeat the image and start drawing columns until we either reach the right side of our rendered scene, or we run out of background columns. If the latter is true, we need to wrap back around to column 0 of the background and continue. By taking the modulo of our current angle and 640, we can quickly determine the starting column of the background, thus

```
Background column = angle mod 640
```

which in C code looks something like:

```
Bcol = angle % 640;
```

Recall that taking the modulo of a number means taking the remainder of a divide. (I know, yet another time-intensive divide—maybe it's time for another lookup table, where each angle would have the correct background column assigned to it.) We then use the remainder as the starting column to begin displaying the background.

DESIGN TIP

The support code for the Windows version of the engine illustrates how background scenes are loaded and processed. In the source file, ACKSUPP.CPP, you'll find two functions, **LoadBackDrop()** and **ProcessBackDrop()**, for reading and processing a background image so that it can later be used with the ceiling display code. Your application program must call **LoadBackDrop()** to load in the background image. To use these functions with a DOS application, simply copy the code to your application. I separated these functions from the core engine library, because they perform operations that are application specific.

Exploring AckDrawFloorHz()

We don't need to look at every floor/ceiling drawing routine that *ACK-3D* provides because many of them are variations of each other. As an example, one routine draws a solid floor and a textured ceiling, whereas another routine does the reverse—draws a solid ceiling and a textured floor. We've already seen how easy it is to draw a solid floor and ceiling, so let's spend the rest of our time looking at how textured floors and ceilings are drawn.

A good way to see how the floor and ceiling drawing algorithms for textured bitmaps are applied is to examine the code in **AckDrawFloorHz()**. This function illustrates how the player's viewing angle is used to determine which bitmap data should be displayed.

The first order of business is to determine the view region where the floor and ceiling will be displayed. This step is accomplished using the following variables and calculations:

```
BegCol = gWinStartX;    // Get starting and ending position of viewport
EndCol = gWinEndX;

// Get the starting offset of the center row of the view
scr = gScrnBufferCenter + BegCol;
// Get the left side of the POV view
va = PlayerAngle - INT_ANGLE_32;
// Check for wrap-around
if (va < 0) va += INT_ANGLE_360;
```

Here **BegCol** and **EndCol** represent the left and right edges of the viewport. The variable **scr** is set to the middle row of the viewport because this middle row is the dividing point between the floor and ceiling. The viewing angle (**va**) will be needed as a table lookup index to determine which cosine or sine value to use in the floor and ceiling plotting calculations. Notice that we subtract 32 degrees from the player's current angle so that we can use a sweep of 64 degrees for the view (-32 to +32). Once we have the starting viewing angle, we need to adjust it to account for a possible viewport column offset:

```
// Adjust the viewing angle based on the starting view column
va += BegCol;
// Check for wrap-around
if (va >= INT_ANGLE_360)
    va -= INT_ANGLE_360;
```

va now is correctly set to reference the starting view column to display a floor and ceiling.

Before we start to calculate positions for the floor and ceiling bitmaps, we need to get the starting offset for the background scene. A background scene has a width of 640 pixels (twice the width of a normal view). To use the background scene, we need to factor in the starting view column:

```
bcol = va % 640;
```

By dividing the starting view column by the full width of the background screen (640), we get a remainder that gives us the starting column for the background (**bcol**).

Next, we need to locate the actual row where the ceiling will start. I mentioned before that the ceiling could start at the midpoint or horizon line. Actually, there is a little trick we can use to speed things up. Since our horizon should always have some form of wall or object, no matter how far away it is, we can optimize our ceiling drawing code a little by not drawing the first few horizon rows. We'll calculate a variable (**scrCeil**) that references our starting point—a location five rows up from the middle row:

```
// Temporarily hold onto the view height / 2
ht = gWinHalfHeight;
// Start 5 video rows above the center row
scrCeil = scr - 1600;
```

Each row is 320 pixels, so five rows is 1,600 pixels. The variable **scr** contains the location of the middle row at this point. As in the above code, we'll use the same technique to calculate the floor starting point. This time we'll move down six rows from the middle row:

```
// Start 6 video rows below the center row (6*320 = 1920)
scr += 1920;
```

```
// Initial right side of view
Rcol = 319;
wPtr = &WallDistTable[BegCol];        // Get pointers to avoid indexing
RwPtr = &WallDistTable[Rcol];
```

This code also assigns two pointers, **wPtr** and **RwPtr**, to access the wall distance array **WallDistTable[ ]**. We'll use this array to perform the actual calculation to see where the floor and ceiling pixels should be plotted during the drawing loop. Here we assign pointers to the starting column and ending column so that we can access the array quicker. Again and again, we're performing all of these steps to squeeze as much efficiency out of the code as possible.

We're almost ready to start the drawing loop, but before we do, we need to calculate a height value called **ScaleHt,** which is used to determine the distance from the player for each row of the floor and ceiling. I based the value 89 on a reasonable height above the floor on which the player is standing. By experimenting with this value, the effect of "jumping" up and down can be achieved, (as long as the walls and objects are made to "jump" by the same amount):

```
Scale_Fac = (89 - ViewHeight) * 5;
ScaleHt = 89 - ViewHeight;
ScaleHt *= Scale_Fac;
```

Creating the Drawing Loop

The best part about the drawing loop is that the floor and ceiling can be drawn at the same time. By using the same method of finding which bitmap and which pixel in the bitmap to display, we only need to change where that information is going to be displayed on the screen. This approach really helps us optimize the entire process. All we need to use is a different destination pointer in our display buffer, which we move up the display buffer row by row for ceilings instead of down the buffer column by column for floors.

The actual drawing loop needed to draw both a floor and ceiling consists of a nested **for** loop. The outer **for** statement loops through each column of the viewing window. The inner one loops through the screen rows to perform the actual drawing. To draw each row, some initial variables must be set up so that the pixel plotting calculations can be performed in the inner drawing loop. Let's take a closer look:

```
for (col = BegCol; col < EndCol; col += 2)
  {
  // Pick up the cosine and sine values for the current angle
```

```
   cv = CosTable[va];
   sv = SinTable[va];
// Point to the left side of the current floor and ceiling columns
   fscr = scr;
   cscr = scrCeil;
// Advance the columns for the next pass
   scr += 2;
   scrCeil += 2;
// Pick up the current distance to the wall that was found for the
// current column
   wdist = *wPtr;
// Advance the wall distance pointer for the next pass
   wPtr += 2;
```

The first thing you'll notice is that the loop advances in 2 unit increments (**col +=2**), which is another one of our speed-up tricks. We'll skip every other column to draw the floor and ceiling in a lower-resolution mode. The maximum number of pixels that need to be calculated then will be 160 instead of 320. Will this look as good as plotting all of the pixels? No. Will it speed up the code a lot? Yes! Is it worth it? I think so, but you can see for yourself. If you are running your game on a really fast Pentium and you want to increase the resolution, you can always change this loop to plot more pixels.

Before the inner drawing loop can start, we need to get the cosine and sine values for the current viewing angle. We also need to set up variables to point to the left side of the columns for drawing the floor and ceiling. Also, for each column that is drawn, we need to know the player's distance to the column. This value is obtained by accessing ***wPtr**. The starting distance value is stored in **wdist**.

Recall that we also need to add in a background screen when the ceiling is drawn. To set up the background scene so that it is aligned with the ceiling, we need to initialize a few variables:

```
#if DRAW_BACK
  // Pick up the pointer to the background image for the current column
    ba = BackArray[bcol++];
  // Check for wrap-around in our 640 column image
    if (bcol > 639) bcol = 0;
  // Pick up the next column as well since the floor and ceiling are
  // always done in low resolution
    ba1 = BackArray[bcol++];
    if (bcol > 639) bcol = 0;
    ba += ht;
    ba1 += ht;
#endif
```

By default, **DRAW_BACK** is set to 1 so this code will be executed. By setting this define, the rotating background and ceiling will be drawn at the same time. The variable **ba** serves as a pointer reference to the start of the bitmap data for the background image.

DESIGN TIP

I've experimented with a number of optimization methods to put in a rotating background. One technique is to draw the background *while* the ceiling is being drawn. The other method is to draw the entire background *before* drawing any parts of the ceiling or walls. The first method seems to be faster in most cases.

Now it's time to draw the floor and ceiling. The goal of the loop is to locate where each pixel needs to be plotted for the floor and ceiling, given the player's viewing angle. Since we are displaying the floor six rows down from the middle row, we can start with row 6 and scan to the midpoint. For each row and column position, we need to calculate the player's distance. Then we use this distance to look up the actual floor and ceiling bitmap that needs to be displayed. Once we have the bitmap, we can easily calculate which pixel in the bitmap to display. The basic algorithm works like this:

1. Calculate the distance to the current column and row position using this formula:

```
distance = Cosine(current column) * scale-height/current row
```

By dividing the scale height by the row, we get the relative distance from the "ground" to the row.

2. Use the distance to calculate the x,y position to plot the floor and ceiling pixel as shown:

```
x = current-xplayer-position + cosine(viewing angle) * distance
y = current-yplayer-position + sine(viewing angle) * distance
```

3. Use this x,y intersection position as a lookup index into a floor map. The floor map keeps track of which bitmap codes are assigned to floor positions:

```
mPos = (y & 0xFC0) + (x>>6)
```

4. Look up the bitmap code in the wall bitmap array to get the actual bitmap.
5. Use the x,y position to determine which pixel in the bitmap to display.

6. Store the pixel for the floor in the correct row and column position.

7. Repeat steps 3 through 6, but this time use the ceiling map array to locate the ceiling bitmap and store the correct pixel for the ceiling.

```
for (row = 6; row <= ht; row++)
  {

    scan2 = ScaleHt / row;
  // Get the distance for the current column and row position
  dist = (fcv * scan2) >> 15;

  // If we're still closer than any wall
    if (dist < wdist)
      {
  // Do some extra calculations if it's a new distance from last time
  // (Sometimes our distance works out to be the same so we can avoid
  // the next few lines)
    if (dist != LastDist)
      {
      x = xPglobal + ((cv * dist) >> 16);
      y = yPglobal + ((sv * dist) >> 16);
      LastDist = dist;
      }
    mPos = (y & 0xFC0) + (x >> 6);        // Calculate the map position
    if (mPos < 0L || mPos > 4095L)
      continue;
    bPos = (y & 63) + ((x & 63)<<6);      // Calculate the bitmap pixel

// Get the bitmap number for our floor
    bCode = FloorMap[mPos];
// And use it to pull the actual bitmap from our array of wall bitmaps
    bmp = WallbMaps[bCode];
// Make sure it's really a bitmap and then get the actual pixel to display
    if (bmp != NULL)
      ch = bmp[bPos];

// Place the pixel in this column as well as the next. Since we have a
// scattering effect, we can display in low resolution without too much
// loss in detail. This really speeds up the drawing of the floor and
// ceiling.
        *fscr = ch;                       // Put it into two locations
        fscr[1] = ch;                     // for low resolution

// Only draw a ceiling pixel if there is a ceiling tile placed in the map.
// This gives the effect of seeing the background through holes in the ceiling.
      if ((bCode = CeilMap[mPos]) != 0)
        {
        bmp = WallbMaps[bCode];
        if (bmp != NULL)
          ch = bmp[bPos];
        *cscr = ch;
        cscr[1] = ch;
```

```
        }
#if DRAW_BACK
// If no ceiling is drawn, we need to draw the background image
     else
        {
        *cscr = *ba;
        cscr[1] = *ba1;
        }
#endif
    }

    fscr += 320;        // Advance our screen position for the floor
    cscr -= 320;        // and the ceiling

#if DRAW_BACK
// Advance the pointers to the background image for the next pass
    ba--;
    ba1--;
#endif
    }
```

The Complete ACKFLOOR.C

```
// This source file contains the internal functions needed to draw
// floors and ceilings in 3-D views.
// (c) 1995 ACK Software (Lary Myers)
#include <windows.h>
#include <stdlib.h>
#include <stdio.h>
#include <conio.h>
#include <dos.h>
#include <mem.h>
#include <io.h>
#include <fcntl.h>
#include <time.h>
#include <string.h>
#include <sys\stat.h>
#include <limits.h>
#include "ack3d.h"      // Main ACK-3D internal and interface data structures
#include "ackeng.h"     // Internal data structures and constants
#include "ackext.h"     // Defines external (global) variables

#define MAX_F_VIEWHALFHEIGHT   50
extern  long FloorCosTable[];
extern  short   gWinStartX;
extern  short   gWinStartY;
extern  short   gWinEndX;
extern  short   gWinHalfHeight;
extern  UCHAR   *gScrnBufferCenter;
extern  long    WallDistTable[];
long    zdTable[VIEW_WIDTH][50];
long    mFactor;
long    dFactor;
```

```
//+++++++++++++++++++++++++++++++++++++++++++++++++++++++++++++++++++++++++
// Internal function called during the initialization process to setup the
// floor and light shading arrays.
//+++++++++++++++++++++++++++++++++++++++++++++++++++++++++++++++++++++++++
void SetupFloors(ACKENG *ae)
{
  short i,a;
  int   ht,scanline,ht1;
  int   Scale_Fac;
  long  scan1,scan2,f;
  long  x,y,dist;
  long  Lastx,Lasty;

  // Set up the light shading array; 8 zones supported
  for ( i=0; i<12;i++ ) scantables[i] = ae->PalTable + (7*256);
  for ( i=12;i<24;i++ ) scantables[i] = ae->PalTable + (6*256);
  for ( i=24;i<36;i++ ) scantables[i] = ae->PalTable + (5*256);
  for ( i=36;i<48;i++ ) scantables[i] = ae->PalTable + (4*256);
  for ( i=48;i<60;i++ ) scantables[i] = ae->PalTable + (3*256);
  for ( i=60;i<72;i++ ) scantables[i] = ae->PalTable + (2*256);
  for ( i=72;i<84;i++ ) scantables[i] = ae->PalTable + (1*256);
  for ( i=84;i<96;i++ ) scantables[i] = ae->PalTable;

Scale_Fac = (89 - ViewHeight) * 5;
ht = 89 - ViewHeight;
ht *= Scale_Fac;
for (i = 0; i < VIEW_WIDTH; i++)
  {
  f = FloorCosTable[i];
  zdTable[i][0] = 0;
  for (scanline = 1; scanline < MAX_F_VIEWHALFHEIGHT; scanline++)
    {
    scan2 = ht / scanline; zdTable[i][scanline] = (f * scan2) >> 15;
    if (zdTable[i][scanline-1] < zdTable[i][scanline])
      zdTable[i][scanline-1] = zdTable[i][scanline];
    }
  }
// Some debugging values for internal use
mFactor = 10368;
dFactor = 160;
}


// Optimization attempts were made with drawing the rotating background
// as the ceiling was being drawn and drawing the entire background before
// drawing any ceiling tiles or walls. The first approach seemed to be
// faster in most cases. The define below was used to toggle between the
// two methods. By default the first approach is set.
#define DRAW_BACK 1

//+++++++++++++++++++++++++++++++++++++++++++++++++++++++++++++++++++++++++
// Draws the floor and ceiling horizontally.
//+++++++++++++++++++++++++++++++++++++++++++++++++++++++++++++++++++++++++
void AckDrawFloorHz(void)
{
```

```
    int     i,col,row,ht,Rcol,EndCol,BegCol;
    int     Scale_Fac,ScaleHt;
    UCHAR   *scr,*fscr,*bmp,*scrCeil,*cscr;
    UCHAR   *Rscr,*Rfscr,*RscrCeil,*Rcscr;
    UCHAR   *ba,*ba1,*Rba,*Rba1;
    short   va,va1;
    long    LastDist,scan2;
    long    cv,sv,dist,x,y,bx,by,mPos,bPos,wdist,bcol;
    long    Rbcol,Rwdist,xp,yp;
    long    *zd,*wPtr,*RwPtr,*xyPtr;
    long    fcv;
    UCHAR   ch;
    USHORT  bCode;

#if !(DRAW_BACK)
DrawBackDrop(); // Draw entire background
#endif

BegCol = gWinStartX;
EndCol = gWinEndX;
// Get the starting offset of the center row of the view
scr = gScrnBufferCenter + BegCol;
// Get the left side of the POV view
va = PlayerAngle - INT_ANGLE_32;
// Check for wrap-around
if (va < 0) va += INT_ANGLE_360;
// Adjust the viewing angle based on the starting view column
va += BegCol;
// Check for wrap-around
if (va >= INT_ANGLE_360)
    va -= INT_ANGLE_360;

// Get the starting column for the background; there are 640
// columns possible, so the remainder when we divide is where
// we want to begin displaying
bcol = va % 640;
// Temporarily hold onto the view height / 2
ht = gWinHalfHeight;
// Since our horizon should always have some form of wall or object,
// no matter how far away it is, we can optimize a little here by not
// drawing the first few horizon rows (it does actually save time!).
// Start 5 video rows above the center row
scrCeil = scr - 1600;
// Start 6 video rows below the center row
scr += 1920;
// Initial right side of view
Rcol = 319;
wPtr = &WallDistTable[BegCol];      // Get pointers to avoid indexing
RwPtr = &WallDistTable[Rcol];

// The ScaleHt is used to determine the distance from the player for each
// row of the floor and ceiling. The value 89 was arrived at based on a
// reasonable height above the floor that the player is standing on. By
// experimenting with this value, the effect of jumping up and down can
```

```
// be achieved, (as long as the walls and objects are made to jump by the
// same amount).
Scale_Fac = (89 - ViewHeight) * 5;
ScaleHt = 89 - ViewHeight;
ScaleHt *= Scale_Fac;

// Here we loop through each column of the viewing window
for (col = BegCol; col < EndCol; col += 2)
  {
// Pick up the cosine and sine values for the current angle
  cv = CosTable[va];
  sv = SinTable[va];
// Point to the left side of the current floor and ceiling columns
  fscr = scr;
  cscr = scrCeil;
// Advance the columns for the next pass
  scr += 2;
  scrCeil += 2;
// Pick up the current distance to the wall that was found for the
// current column
  wdist = *wPtr;
// Advance the wall distance pointer for the next pass
  wPtr += 2;

#if DRAW_BACK
// Pick up the pointer to the background image for the current column
  ba = BackArray[bcol++];
// Check for wrap-around in our 640 column image
  if (bcol > 639) bcol = 0;
// Pick up the next column as well since the floor and ceiling are
// always done in low resolution
  ba1 = BackArray[bcol++];
  if (bcol > 639) bcol = 0;
  ba += ht;
  ba1 += ht;
#endif

// Initialize a last distance variable
  LastDist = -1;
// Our floor cosine is used to counteract a fisheye effect
  fcv = FloorCosTable[col];
  for (row = 6; row <= ht; row++)
    {
    scan2 = ScaleHt / row;
// Get the distance for the current column and row position
    dist = (fcv * scan2) >> 15;
// If we're still closer than any wall
    if (dist < wdist)
      {
// Do some extra calculations if it's a new distance from last time
// (Sometimes our distance works out to be the same so we can avoid
// the next few lines)
      if (dist != LastDist)
```

```
        {
        x = xPglobal + ((cv * dist) >> 16);
        y = yPglobal + ((sv * dist) >> 16);
        LastDist = dist;
        }
     mPos = (y & 0xFC0) + (x >> 6);      // Calc the map position
     if (mPos < 0L || mPos > 4095L)
        continue;
     bPos = (y & 63) + ((x & 63)<<6);    // Calc the bitmap pixel
// Get the bitmap number for our floor
     bCode = FloorMap[mPos];
// And use it to pull the actual bitmap from our array of wall bitmaps
     bmp = WallbMaps[bCode];
// Make sure it's really a bitmap and then get the actual pixel to display
     if (bmp != NULL)
       ch = bmp[bPos];
// Place the pixel in this column as well as the next. Since we have a
// scattering effect we can display in low resolution without too much
// loss in detail. This really speeds up the drawing of the floor and ceiling.
     *fscr = ch;                // Put it into two locations
     fscr[1] = ch;              // for low resolution
// Only draw a ceiling pixel if there is a ceiling tile placed in the map
// This gives the effect of seeing the background through holes in the ceiling
     if ((bCode = CeilMap[mPos]) != 0)
        {
        bmp = WallbMaps[bCode];
        if (bmp != NULL)
          ch = bmp[bPos];
        *cscr = ch;
        cscr[1] = ch;
        }
#if DRAW_BACK
// If no ceiling is drawn, then we need to draw the background image
     else
        {
        *cscr = *ba;
        cscr[1] = *ba1;
        }
#endif
     }
     fscr += 320;              // Advance our screen position for the floor
     cscr -= 320;              // and the ceiling
#if DRAW_BACK
// Advance the pointers to the background image for the next pass
     ba--;
     ba1--;
#endif
     }
// Advance our current viewing angle by 2 since we are in low resolution
   va += 2;
// Check for wrap-around
   if (va >= INT_ANGLE_360) va -= INT_ANGLE_360;
   }
}
```

```
//±±±±±±±±±±±±±±±±±±±±±±±±±±±±±±±±±±±±±±±±±±±±±±±±±±±±±±±±±±±±±±±±±±±±±±±±±±±±±±±±
// Draws the floor and ceiling horizontally.
//±±±±±±±±±±±±±±±±±±±±±±±±±±±±±±±±±±±±±±±±±±±±±±±±±±±±±±±±±±±±±±±±±±±±±±±±±±±±±±±±
void AckDrawCeilingOnlyNS(void)
{
  int      i,col,row,ht,Rcol,EndCol,BegCol;
  int      Scale_Fac,ScaleHt;
  UCHAR    *scr,*fscr,*bmp,*scrCeil,*cscr;
  UCHAR    *Rscr,*Rfscr,*RscrCeil,*Rcscr;
  UCHAR    *ba,*ba1,*Rba,*Rba1;
  short    va,va1;
  long     LastDist,scan2;
  long     cv,sv,dist,x,y,bx,by,mPos,bPos,wdist,bcol;
  long     Rbcol,Rwdist,xp,yp;
  long     *zd,*wPtr,*RwPtr,*xyPtr;
  long     fcv;
  UCHAR    ch;
  USHORT   bCode;

#if !(DRAW_BACK)
DrawBackDrop(); // Draw entire background
#endif

BegCol = gWinStartX;
EndCol = gWinEndX;
// Get the starting offset of the center row of the view
scr = gScrnBufferCenter + BegCol;
// Get the left side of the POV view
va = PlayerAngle - INT_ANGLE_32;
// Check for wrap-around
if (va < 0) va += INT_ANGLE_360;
// Adjust the viewing angle based on the starting view column
va += BegCol;
// and check for wrap-around
if (va >= INT_ANGLE_360)
  va -= INT_ANGLE_360;
// Get the starting column for the background, there are 640
// columns possible, so the remainder when we divide is where
// we want to begin displaying
bcol = va % 640;
// Temporarily hold onto the view height / 2
ht = gWinHalfHeight;
// Since our horizon should always have some form of wall or object,
// no matter how far away it is, we can optimize a little here by not
// drawing the first few horizon rows (it does actually save time!).
// Start 5 video rows above the center row
scrCeil = scr - 1600;
// Initial right side of view
Rcol = 319;
wPtr = &WallDistTable[BegCol];       // Get pointers to avoid indexing
RwPtr = &WallDistTable[Rcol];

// The ScaleHt is used to determine the distance from the player for each
// row of the floor and ceiling. The value 89 was arrived at based on a
```

```
// reasonable height above the floor that the player is standing on. By
// experimenting with this value, the effect of jumping up and down can
// be achieved, (as long as the walls and objects are made to jump by the
// same amount).
Scale_Fac = (89 - ViewHeight) * 5;
ScaleHt = 89 - ViewHeight;
ScaleHt *= Scale_Fac;
// Here we loop through each column of the viewing window
for (col = BegCol; col < EndCol; col += 2)
   {
// Pick up the cosine and sine values for the current angle
  cv = CosTable[va];
  sv = SinTable[va];
// Point to the left side of the current ceiling columns
  cscr = scrCeil;
// Advance the columns for the next pass
  scrCeil += 2;
// Pick up the current distance to the wall that was found for the
// current column
  wdist = *wPtr;
// Advance the wall distance pointer for the next pass
  wPtr += 2;

#if DRAW_BACK
// Pick up the pointer to the background image for the current column
  ba = BackArray[bcol++];
// Check for wrap-around in our 640 column image
  if (bcol > 639) bcol = 0;
// Pick up the next column as well since the floor and ceiling are
// always done in low resolution
  ba1 = BackArray[bcol++];
  if (bcol > 639) bcol = 0;
  ba += ht;
  ba1 += ht;
#endif

// Initialize a last distance variable
  LastDist = -1;
// Our floor cosine is used to counteract a fisheye effect
  fcv = FloorCosTable[col];
  for (row = 6; row <= ht; row++)
     {
     scan2 = ScaleHt / row;
// Get the distance for the current column and row position
     dist = (fcv * scan2) >> 15;
// If we're still closer than any wall
     if (dist < wdist)
        {
// Do some extra calculations if it's a new distance from last time
// (Sometimes our distance works out to be the same so we can avoid
// the next few lines)
        if (dist != LastDist)
          {
          x = xPglobal + ((cv * dist) >> 16);
```

```
            y = yPglobal + ((sv * dist) >> 16);
            LastDist = dist;
            }
        mPos = (y & 0xFC0) + (x >> 6);          // Calc the map position
        if (mPos < 0L || mPos > 4095L)
            continue;
        bPos = (y & 63) + ((x & 63)<<6);    // Calc the bitmap pixel
// Only draw a ceiling pixel if there is a ceiling tile placed in the map
// This gives the effect of seeing the background through holes in the ceiling
        if ((bCode = CeilMap[mPos]) != 0)
            {
            bmp = WallbMaps[bCode];
            if (bmp != NULL)
              ch = bmp[bPos];
            *cscr = ch;
            cscr[1] = ch;
            }
#if DRAW_BACK
// If no ceiling is drawn, then we need to draw the background image
        else
            {
            *cscr = *ba;
            cscr[1] = *ba1;
            }
#endif
        }
    cscr -= 320;          // and the ceiling
#if DRAW_BACK
// Advance the pointers to the background image for the next pass
    ba--;
    ba1--;
#endif
    }
// Advance our current viewing angle by 2 since we are in low resolution
  va += 2;
// Check for wrap-around
  if (va >= INT_ANGLE_360) va -= INT_ANGLE_360;
  }
}


//+++++++++++++++++++++++++++++++++++++++++++++++++++++++++++++++++++++++++++
// Draws the floor and ceiling horizontally.
//+++++++++++++++++++++++++++++++++++++++++++++++++++++++++++++++++++++++++++
void AckDrawFloorOnlyNS(void)
{
  int     i,col,row,ht,Rcol,EndCol,BegCol;
  int     Scale_Fac,ScaleHt;
  UCHAR   *scr,*fscr,*bmp,*scrCeil,*cscr;
  UCHAR   *Rscr,*Rfscr,*RscrCeil,*Rcscr;
  UCHAR   *ba,*ba1,*Rba,*Rba1;
  short   va,va1;
  long    LastDist,scan2;
  long    cv,sv,dist,x,y,bx,by,mPos,bPos,wdist,bcol;
  long    Rbcol,Rwdist,xp,yp;
```

```
    long    *zd,*wPtr,*RwPtr,*xyPtr;
    long    fcv;
    UCHAR   ch;
    USHORT  bCode;

#if !(DRAW_BACK)
DrawBackDrop(); // Draw entire background
#endif

BegCol = gWinStartX;
EndCol = gWinEndX;
// Get the starting offset of the center row of the view
scr = gScrnBufferCenter + BegCol;
// Get the left side of the POV view
va = PlayerAngle - INT_ANGLE_32;
// Check for wrap-around
if (va < 0) va += INT_ANGLE_360;
// Adjust the viewing angle based on the starting view column
va += BegCol;
// Check for wrap-around
if (va >= INT_ANGLE_360)
    va -= INT_ANGLE_360;

// Get the starting column for the background, there are 640
// columns possible, so the remainder when we divide is where
// we want to begin displaying
bcol = va % 640;
// Temporarily hold onto the view height / 2
ht = gWinHalfHeight;
// Since our horizon should always have some form of wall or object,
// no matter how far away it is, we can optimize a little here by not
// drawing the first few horizon rows (it does actually save time!).
// Start 6 video rows below the center row
scr += 1920;
// Initial right side of view
Rcol = 319;
wPtr = &WallDistTable[BegCol];        // Get pointers to avoid indexing
RwPtr = &WallDistTable[Rcol];
// The ScaleHt is used to determine the distance from the player for each
// row of the floor and ceiling. The value 89 was arrived at based on a
// reasonable height above the floor that the player is standing on. By
// experimenting with this value, the effect of jumping up and down can
// be achieved, (as long as the walls and objects are made to jump by the
// same amount).
Scale_Fac = (89 - ViewHeight) * 5;
ScaleHt = 89 - ViewHeight;
ScaleHt *= Scale_Fac;

// Here we loop through each column of the viewing window
for (col = BegCol; col < EndCol; col += 2)
    {
// Pick up the cosine and sine values for the current angle
  cv = CosTable[va];
  sv = SinTable[va];
```

```
// Point to the left side of the current floor and ceiling columns
  fscr = scr;
// Advance the columns for the next pass
  scr += 2;
// Pick up the current distance to the wall that was found for the
// current column
  wdist = *wPtr;
// Advance the wall distance pointer for the next pass
  wPtr += 2;

#if DRAW_BACK
// Pick up the pointer to the background image for the current column
  ba = BackArray[bcol++];
// Check for wrap-around in our 640 column image
  if (bcol > 639) bcol = 0;
// Pick up the next column as well since the floor and ceiling are
// always done in low resolution
  ba1 = BackArray[bcol++];
  if (bcol > 639) bcol = 0;
  ba += ht;
  ba1 += ht;
#endif
// Initialize a last distance variable
  LastDist = -1;
// Our floor cosine is used to counteract a fisheye effect
  fcv = FloorCosTable[col];
  for (row = 6; row <= ht; row++)
    {
    scan2 = ScaleHt / row;
// Get the distance for the current column and row position
    dist = (fcv * scan2) >> 15;
// If we're still closer than any wall
    if (dist < wdist)
      {
// Do some extra calculations if it's a new distance from last time
// (Sometimes our distance works out to be the same so we can avoid
// the next few lines)
      if (dist != LastDist)
        {
        x = xPglobal + ((cv * dist) >> 16);
        y = yPglobal + ((sv * dist) >> 16);
        LastDist = dist;
        }
      mPos = (y & 0xFC0) + (x >> 6);        // Calc the map position
      if (mPos < 0L || mPos > 4095L)
        continue;
      bPos = (y & 63) + ((x & 63)<<6);    // Calc the bitmap pixel
// Get the bitmap number for our floor
      bCode = FloorMap[mPos];
// And use it to pull the actual bitmap from our array of wall bitmaps
      bmp = WallbMaps[bCode];
// Make sure it's really a bitmap and then get the actual pixel to display
      if (bmp != NULL)
        ch = bmp[bPos];
```

```
// Place the pixel in this column as well as the next. Since we have a
// scattering effect we can display in low resolution without too much loss
// in detail. This really speeds up the drawing of the floor and ceiling.
        *fscr = ch;                         // Put it into two locations
        fscr[1] = ch;                       // for low resolution
        }
    fscr += 320;  // Advance our screen position for the floor
#if DRAW_BACK
// Advance the pointers to the background image for the next pass
    ba--;
    ba1--;
#endif
    }
// Advance our current viewing angle by 2 since we are in low resolution
  va += 2;
// Check for wrap-around
  if (va >= INT_ANGLE_360) va -= INT_ANGLE_360;
  }
}
//+++++++++++++++++++++++++++++++++++++++++++++++++++++++++++++++++++++++++++
// This function performs the same process as AckDrawFloorHz except
// we don't need to check for a bitmap index for every pixel since only
// one bitmap will be used for the floor and one bitmap for the ceiling.
// Draws a floor that contains only one type of bitmap. This is a much
// faster process and may be useful in some applications.
//+++++++++++++++++++++++++++++++++++++++++++++++++++++++++++++++++++++++++++
void AckDrawOneFloor(void)
{
    int     i,col,row,ht,Rcol,EndCol,BegCol;
    UCHAR   *scr,*fscr,*bmp,*scrCeil,*cscr;
    UCHAR   *ba,*ba1,*Rba,*Rba1,*cBmp;
    short   va,va1;
    long    LastDist;
    long    cv,sv,dist,x,y,bx,by,mPos,bPos,wdist,bcol;
    long    Rbcol,Rwdist,xp,yp;
    long    *zd,*wPtr,*RwPtr,*xyPtr;
    UCHAR   ch;
    USHORT  bCode;

    BegCol = gWinStartX;
    EndCol = gWinEndX;
    scr = gScrnBufferCenter + BegCol;
    va = PlayerAngle - INT_ANGLE_32;
    if (va < 0) va += INT_ANGLE_360;
    va += BegCol;
    if (va >= INT_ANGLE_360)
      va -= INT_ANGLE_360;
    bcol = va % 640;
    ht = gWinHalfHeight;
    scrCeil = scr - 1600;
    scr += 1920;
    Rcol = 319;
    wPtr = &WallDistTable[BegCol];              // Get pointers to avoid indexing
    RwPtr = &WallDistTable[Rcol];
```

```
cBmp = WallbMaps[aeGlobal->CeilBitmap];
bmp = WallbMaps[aeGlobal->FloorBitmap];
for (col = BegCol; col < EndCol; col += 2)
{
  cv = CosTable[va];
  sv = SinTable[va];
  fscr = scr;
  cscr = scrCeil;
  scr += 2;
  scrCeil += 2;
  zd = &zdTable[col][6];
  wdist = *wPtr;
  wPtr += 2;
  ba = BackArray[bcol++];
  if (bcol > 639) bcol = 0;
  ba1 = BackArray[bcol++];
  if (bcol > 639) bcol = 0;
  ba += ht;
  ba1 += ht;
  LastDist = -1;
  for (row = 6; row <= ht; row++)
    {
    dist = *zd++;
    if (dist < wdist)
      {
      if (dist != LastDist)
        {
        x = xPglobal + ((cv * dist) >> 16);
        y = yPglobal + ((sv * dist) >> 16);
        LastDist = dist;
        }
      mPos = (y & 0xFC0) + (x >> 6);       // Calc the map position
      bPos = (y & 63) + ((x & 63)<<6);     // Calc the bitmap pixel
      ch = bmp[bPos];
      *fscr = ch;                          // Put it into two locations
      fscr[1] = ch;                        //  for low resolution
      ch = cBmp[bPos];
      *cscr = ch;
      cscr[1] = ch;
      }
    fscr += 320;        // Advance our screen position for the floor
    cscr -= 320;        // and the ceiling
    ba--;
    ba1--;
    }
  va += 2;
  if (va >= INT_ANGLE_360) va -= INT_ANGLE_360;
  }
}
// **** End of Source ****
```

It's time to get down to business and explore how your applications initialize and use the *ACK-3D* engine. We'll also go behind the scenes to see what happens when the *ACK-3D* engine is initialized.

Initializing and Using the ACK-3D Engine

f you've been following along closely, you probably know quite a bit about the *ACK-3D* engine and how the powerful world of ray casting operates. But we haven't spent much time discussing how the main *ACK-3D* functions are used in an application. For the most part, creating an application with the engine is not overly complicated, but there are a few important initialization steps that you must follow. For example, if you don't set up your screen viewport properly, you'll end up with either a blank screen or a scene that won't look anything like the one you designed. Most of the initialization work is performed by a function named **AckInitialize()**, which we'll explore in this chapter. I'll show you how this function is called, then we'll discuss the background tasks that need to be performed, including setting up the viewport, building lookup tables, setting up the map grid, and so on. The main source file that I'll cover in this chapter is ACKINIT.C.

Talking to the Engine

When I started along the winding road to create the *ACK-3D* engine, I wanted to keep the actual engine code as separate from the application code as possible to make the engine as portable and flexible as I could. As you've seen, the engine provides an interface structure (**ACKENG**) that needs to be maintained by your applications and passed into the engine functions using C pointers. Every application that wants to call the *ACK-3D* functions must first create an interface structure and use the components of the structure, such as the player's position and view angle, to "talk" to the 3-D engine.

Your applications can either declare an interface structure as part of their data segment, or allocate the size of the structure at run-time. I prefer to use the latter approach. In this case, the first thing your application should do is to perform the following operations:

```
int main()
{
  ACKENG  ae;
  // Declare all of the other variables for your application here
  ...
  // Dynamically create an interface structure
  ae = (ACKENG *)malloc(sizeof(ACKENG));
  if (ae == NULL)       // Make sure the structure was created
    return(ERROR);      // Return an error code if not
  // Continue with your application code
  // Initialize fields in the interface structure
  // Call AckInitialize() to initialize the system
  // Call AckReadMapFile() to read in the grid map in which the player moves around
  // Call other ACK-3D functions to display and process views
  ...
}
```

These operations serve as a handy template that you can use to set up your own applications. I'll expand on the template later to include some actual data for setting up a viewport and performing error checking.

This simple shell allocates a structure that can then be filled in by your application. Notice that it is a good idea to make sure that the interface structure is allocated correctly. If the memory allocation operation fails, you'll want to return an error message and quit the program. The fields that make up the interface structure are used by both your application and the *ACK-3D* functions. They have evolved over time to provide as much flexibility as possible and to better optimize the speed of the 3-D rendering techniques used. A few of the fields *must* be initialized by your application before you can call any of the engine functions. These fields include:

WinStartX   The leftmost x coordinate of the viewport

WinEndX   The rightmost x coordinate of the viewport

WinStartY   The upper row of the viewport

WinEndY   The lower row of the viewport

Don't forget to set these fields; otherwise you'll get yourself into big trouble! Here's an example of how these variables can be set to create a viewport size that is commonly used for games:

```
ae = (ACKENG *)malloc(sizeof(ACKENG));   // Allocate memory for the structure
ae->WinStartX = 0;                       // Set to full screen width
ae->WinEndX = 319;
ae->WinStartY = 0;                       // Set to partial screen height
ae->WinEndY = 160;
```

This creates a viewing window that fills the width of the screen (320 pixels). The height of the screen is 160 pixels. The viewing area starts at the top of the screen and extends to row 160. This area leaves you with 40 rows at the bottom of the screen to display statistics for your game. After all, you'll want to leave room to tell your player how many bad guys he or she has wiped out so far! Once these fields are initialized, we're ready to start firing up the engine.

Say Hello to the Engine

Okay, we've allocated our structure and set up the size of the viewport we wish to display; now what? The first thing we want to do is pass our interface structure to the engine so that the engine can set up the tables and global variables it needs to use. We accomplish this task by making the following function call:

```
result= AckInitialize(ae);
// Perform error checking next
```

By passing a pointer to the interface structure as the parameter, we maintain the engine as a separate entity from the application. The **AckInitialize()** function now goes on to perform the following tasks:

- Checks the viewport coordinates to make sure that they are set up properly.
- Allocates memory for all of the look-up tables that are required for the engine. These tables include the cosine table, sin table, tangent table, the map grid, and so on.
- Allocates memory for the off-screen buffers.

- Reads in the trig data that is required for the lookup tables.
- Sets up internal viewport variables that are needed to draw scenes.
- Sets up floors for drawing.
- Constructs the height and adjustment tables used to draw slices.
- Creates an array called **BackArray[ ]** that is used to display rotating backgrounds such as mountains.

For now, we won't worry about these internal details, but we'll come back to some of them when we explore the code required for **AckInitialize()** later in this chapter.

DESIGN TIP

Notice that in the sample call to **AckInitialize()** I've used the variable **result** to grab the return value. After the call, I use the return value to check the status of the functions. Many of the *ACK-3D* functions like this one return values that serve as error detection codes. If the value returned is 0, you know that the function did its job without running into any problems. If a different value is returned, you know that an error has occurred. In such a case, you should take some action, such as quitting your application and displaying an error message. Try to get in the habit of checking the error codes returned by the *ACK-3D* functions and processing them accordingly. Many of the functions allocate memory dynamically for critical data structures and if something goes wrong and you don't catch it, your user will and your tech support lines will be ringing off the hook!

A World of Data

After calling **AckInitialize ()**, the setup work is done; we're ready to get to work and create a map for our 3-D creation. After all, we haven't told the engine about any map data yet. The map represents the world we are going to be walking around in and indicates which bitmaps are used to draw walls and objects. Recall from our earlier discussions in this book that we represent our worlds with a two-dimensional map that contains the placement of all walls and objects. We need to load this map into memory and let the engine know about it. The following function does this for us:

```
result = AckReadMapFile(ae,MapFileName);
```

As you can see, the interface structure is passed into this function so the engine can set up the necessary fields within the structure for later use. The second parameter is the actual filename of the map we want to use. This map is created with the DOS version of the map editor that we'll present in Chapter 15, and is included on the accompanying CD-ROM. The interactive editor allows you to place the walls where you want them and assign different bitmaps to each wall. When you finish designing a map, you can save it to a file so that it can be read by the **AckReadMapFile()** function.

This method is the way that games should be developed! You use powerful off-line tools to design the components of your game and then you make function calls to load all of the components of your game. Once a map has been loaded by your application, you'll need to call a special function to assign specific bitmaps to the walls placed in your map. These are the bitmap images that will be displayed when a player encounters walls in a 3-D world. The function used for assigning bitmap images to walls is:

```
result = AckLoadWall(ae,WallNumber,WallFileName);
```

Note that our old friend the interface structure is passed as the first parameter. The second parameter specifies the wall number that is being assigned a specific bitmap image. You can use up to 255 possible wall numbers to set up your 3-D worlds, beginning with number 1 and ending with 255. (The value 0 is reserved to indicate that no wall is present.) Although this may not seem like a lot of walls, the possible combinations and uses provide quite a bit of flexibility for any type of scene that you'll want to create. There are also a few tricks you can perform to make this number even less of a limitation.

The final parameter is the filename of the graphic bitmap you want to assign to the specified wall number. The engine allows you to load in .PCX or .BBM files.

Opening Your Eyes

It's time to see some results for the effort we've put forth. So far, the application has performed the following calls:

```
result = AckInitialize(ae);
// Perform error checking
result = AckReadMapFile(ae,MapFileName);
// Perform error checking
```

And for each wall loaded:

```
AckLoadWall(ae,WallNumber,WallFileName);
```

Now we're ready to do one last piece of housekeeping before we actually draw something:

```
AckRegisterStructure(ae);
```

My main goal in designing the *ACK-3D* engine was to make it fast, and the **AckRegisterStructure()** function is used to help achieve that goal. Your application is responsible for owning the interface structure, but a lot of the data within the structure is fairly static once it has been initialized. For this reason, I decided to have the structure registered with the engine so that certain variables could be set up to enhance the overall performance of the rendering process. In most cases, your application need only make this function call once during a particular session. Later, we'll discuss when your application might need to call the function again.

Setting Up Your Screen for DOS Applications

If you're planning to have your application run under DOS, you'll need to switch into a special graphics mode. The *ACK-3D* engine was designed to support the common VGA mode where you have 256 colors with a screen resolution of 320 columns by 200 rows. This is Mode 13h, which we explored in Chapter 7. To help you select this graphics mode, I have provided a special *ACK-3D* function:

```
AckSetVGAmode();
```

This function switches your screen to graphics mode and clears the screen. It passes the value that needs to be passed to the video BIOS using Interrupt 10h (or 16 decimal). If you are creating a DOS application, don't forget to call this function before you attempt to display anything on the screen or call any of the *ACK-3D* engine functions that display views, such as **AckDisplayScreen()**.

If you need to have your application switch to text mode at any time, you can call the function **AckSetTextmode()**. This function puts the screen into the standard 80x25 text color mode (mode 3). The function is especially useful if your application is in the VGA graphics mode and an error occurs; you'll want to display an error message and exit. For example, this code shows an error routine used to determine if a new object structure was created successfully:

```
result = AckCreateObject(&ae, ObjNum);// Try to create a new object
if (result)                           // Perform error checking
```

```
{
AckSetTextmode();                        // Switch to text mode
printf("Error creating object - Code: %d\n",result);
exit(1);
}
```

Setting Up for Windows

Initializing the system for Windows is a little bit more involved than setting up an application to display views in DOS. To help automate the work involved, I've provided a special function called **InitACKEngine()**, which is defined in the source file ACKWIN.CPP. This function performs a number of tasks including:

- Allocating memory for the *ACK-3D* interface structure.
- Setting the coordinates for the viewport.
- Setting some of the key fields in the interface structure to default values.
- Opening the resource file KIT.OVL (I'll describe this file later in this chapter).
- Calling the main functions **AckInitialize()** and **AckRegister()** to set up and register the interface structure.
- Reading a game resource file. (User-definable game resource files are explained in detail in Chapter 15 and Appendix A.)

This function really streamlines the process of getting all of the internal data set up for a Windows application that uses the engine.

The **InitACKEngine()** function, however, does not create an actual window to display the rendered views created by the engine. The engine relies on the WinG bitmap processing functions to display images. The code for setting up all of the necessary Windows-related bitmap processing must be placed in your application. However, the ACKWIN.CPP file does provide some Windows support functions to help you process and display bitmaps with WinG. I'll show you in detail how WinG works in Chapter 13, and then in Chapter 14 we'll explore the ACKWIN.CPP file and create a sample Windows application so that you can see how easy the engine is to use with Windows.

Drawing Scenes

Once the interface structure is registered and your screen has been set up for DOS or Windows, the next thing to do is to tell the engine to draw something! Now we begin to get into the fun stuff. We'll start by building the current view as seen from the player's POV. This function is really the meat and potatoes of the *ACK-3D* engine. The function called to build a view is:

```
AckBuildView();
```

Hey! No interface structure! What gives? By previously calling **AckRegister()** and forcing the application to register the structure, the engine already knows about the structure itself. We no longer need to pass in the interface structure when *ACK-3D* routines are called. This approach helps speed up the dynamic rendering process.

DESIGN TIP You might wonder why the **AckRegister()** function needs to be passed the interface structure in the first place. After all, why not just perform all of the initialization in **AckInitialize()**? By providing a second level of initialization, the engine allows us to use multiple interface structures to represent multiple views on the same screen. You can use this feature to create multi-player games or create all kinds of interesting effects. To support another view, you simply create another interface structure by allocating memory for it and registering it by calling **AckRegister()**.

The best place to put the **AckBuildView()** function in your application is in a main loop that continues to test to see if the player's POV changes. If the POV has changed, the loop can make calls to update the view. Here's an example:

```
for (;;)                 // Repeat loop until game is terminated
  {
...
  if ( ae.PlayerAngle != newangle
    || ae.xPlayer != newx || ae.yPlayer != newy)
    {
    PlayerAngle = newangle;
    PlayerX = newx;
    PlayerY = newy;
...                       // Call function to move the player
    AckBuildView();    // Build new view
    result = AckDisplayScreen() // Call functions to draw view
    // Put error checking code here
    }
...                       // Check to see if game has terminated
  }
```

This is a very simple shell but it should give you an idea how you can control the way that views are built. The **if** statement checks to see if the player's angle, x position, or y position has changed. If so, the player's POV data is updated and **AckBuildView()** is called to create the new view. If you don't update one of the key POV components (angle, x position, or y position) in the interface structure before calling **AckBuildView()**, your view will not change. You'll get the best results by having the player move a little bit at a time and then calling **AckBuildView()** to create the new scene. (I'll show you how to actually move the player around in the map in the next section.)

Keep in mind that **AckBuildView()** doesn't actually display anything on the screen. Thus, the screen is not updated even though the player's POV data has changed and **AckBuildView()** has been called. But, we do have the current view represented right there in the interface structure, begging to be displayed. All we need to do is call the function:

```
result = AckDisplayScreen();
```

If everything has gone correctly and all the necessary data has been read in, you should see your first view of the 3-D world. Congratulations! Now the sky's the limit. Only your imagination can hold you back from creating some exciting games and applications. After the initial excitement of seeing 3-D walls on the screen, you may want to walk around a bit and stretch your legs, both in a literal and a virtual sense. So let's explore how we can put real motion into our world.

Your First Steps

In our previous example, we updated the view by changing one of the POV attributes and calling **AckBuildView()**. But completing these steps doesn't actually move the player around in the map or maze. Recall that the process of creating animated 3-D worlds involves moving a player around in a maze to see what he or she encounters—a wall, door, stationary object, or movable object—then rendering what the player sees on the screen by casting rays. **AckBuildView()** takes care of the scene-rendering process but we still need to call a function to move the player around in a maze. The function that actually moves the player around is **AckMovePOV()**.

The way we determine how the player moves is entirely up to the application. A player's movement can be controlled by the keyboard, mouse, joystick, or a cybernetic device. Your application will read data from an input device and then use the data to calculate new coordinate positions. Once you have new input data, all you need to do is change the POV attributes to create the effect of moving within the 3-D world. Recall from Chapter 1 and our previous discussion that the POV was made up of the following attributes:

xPlayer   The x coordinate
yPlayer   The y coordinate
PlayerAngle   The angle the POV is facing

By changing any or all of these attributes, we can alter the way the world around us is viewed. The easiest thing to do would be to spin the POV around in a circle while standing in one place. Let's start with that. How fast you spin is up to the application, but for our example purposes, let's use one of the pre-defined constants defined in the ACK3D.H header file. You'll notice that near the top of this header file there are several **#define**s describing the angles used by the *ACK-3D* engine. The most common one used for turning is the **INT_ANGLE_2** define, which represents an increment of 2 degrees. Here's the basic code to start a 2 degree turn:

```
ae->PlayerAngle += INT_ANGLE_2;
if (ae->PlayerAngle >= INT_ANGLE_360)
  ae->PlayerAngle -= INT_ANGLE_360;
```

This code spins the POV to the right 2 degrees. So far so good, but now we need to let the engine build a new view with this change, so we make the following call again:

```
AckBuildView();
```

Once built, we can display the new view on the screen with:

```
result = AckDisplayScreen();
```

Voila! We have now made a small turn in our 3-D world! Notice how the walls are slightly different from the way they were in the earlier view? We can continue this 3-step process as many times as we wish. We can go full circle if we want to! Note the check above to make sure the angle we're facing does not go beyond 360 degrees. The test and subtraction forces the player angle to always stay in the range zero to **INT_ANGLE_360 - 1**.

Turning left instead of right is simply a matter of subtracting a value from the **PlayerAngle**:

```
ae->PlayerAngle -= INT_ANGLE_2;
if (ae->PlayerAngle < 0)
  ae->PlayerAngle += INT_ANGLE_360;
```

Again, checking to make sure we don't go below zero keeps us in the valid range of angles. Then we make our build and display function calls and we are now turning to the left while standing in one spot.

Moving forward or backwards is a little trickier, but the engine makes it easier by providing the **AckMovePOV()**. All it needs to know is what angle you wish to move (normally the one you are facing) and how big a step you wish to take:

```
result = AckMovePOV(Angle,Amount);
```

The first parameter is usually passed as the current angle the POV is facing. This tells the engine to move the POV forward by the value given in the second parameter, the amount. Smaller amounts will move the POV in baby steps, larger amounts will jump the POV from one location to another. Keep in mind that each square of the map is 64 units across by 64 units down, so any amount greater than 64 will jump the POV completely over squares and could invalidate some of the collision checking that the engine performs.

Do you want to move backwards? Change the angle parameter to be 180 degrees from the current angle the POV is facing as shown here and then call **AckMovePOV()**:

```
NewAngle = ae->PlayerAngle + INT_ANGLE_180;
if (NewAngle >= INT_ANGLE_360)
  NewAngle -= INT_ANGLE_360;

result = AckMovePOV(NewAngle,Amount);
```

This code causes the POV to take a step backwards while still facing the same way it was before. Moving diagonally would be a matter of using something other than **INT_ANGLE_180** in the above example.

Building an Initialization Template

I presented a basic initialization shell at the beginning of this chapter to show you the order of function calls and the flow of logic involved in initializing the *ACK-3D* engine. Let's now expand the shell and make a simple template that you can use to start creating your own applications. This template is set up for DOS applications, since it includes **printf** statements to write to the screen. But you can easily change it to work with Windows. Here's the template:

```
ACKENG ae;      // Create interface structure in global memory
```

```
int main()
{
    int result;    // Used for error checking
    ...            // Add other variable declarations here

memset(&ae,0,sizeof(ACKENG));    // Make sure structure is zeroed
ae.WinStartY = 0;                // Set up viewport coordinates
ae.WinEndY = 104;                // This viewport is full-screen width
ae.WinStartX = 0;                // but not full height
ae.WinEndX  = 319;

ae.xPlayer = 100;                // Put the player at an initial starting
ae.yPlayer = 100;                // position
ae.PlayerAngle = 0;

result = AckInitialize(&ae);     // Initialize the engine
if (result)                      // Perform error checking
  {
  printf("Error initializing - Code: %d\n",result);
  exit(1);
  }

result = AckReadMapFile(&ae,"DEMOMAP.L01");  // Read map file

if (result)                      // Perform error checking for map
  {
  printf("Error reading map - Code: %d\n",result);
  exit(1);
  }

AckRegisterStructure(&ae);       // Register the structure before building views

...

// Ready to move ahead and load in bitmaps and objects
// The functions used here include: AckLoadWall(), AckLoadObject(),
// AckCreateObject(), and AckLoadBitmap()

// Then, go forward and move the player and objects around and build views
// The functions used here include AckMovePOV(), AckBuildView(),
// AckMoveObjectPOV(), AckCheckObjectMovement(), and AckDisplayScreen() (DOS)

result = AckWrapUp(&ae)          // Make sure you call this function before
                                 // you terminate your application
}
```

All the basics are taken care of by this code. The interface structure is set up in global memory. Before the interface structure is actually used, its fields are zeroed out by calling the standard C function **memset()**. Then, the coordinates for the viewport are set up. Last but not least, we assign values to the POV fields to give the player an initial starting position and angle. Here we've put the player at location (100,100) in the map, and the player is headed to the right as shown in Figure 11.1.

Of course, what the player will encounter at this position depends on how you've set up your map using the 3-D game editor.

The first engine function called is **AckInitialize()**. Notice that the address of the structure (**&ae**) is passed as the parameter. This is important because the initialization routines modify the structure. If you called **AckInitialize()** using the call

```
result = AckInitialize(ae);    // This function call won't work.
```

the code would not work because the initialization function expects to be passed a pointer to the interface structure. As an alternative, you can declare the interface structure using a pointer, such as

```
ACKENG *ae;    // Create interface structure and set up pointer
```

and then you can call the engine functions using the format:

```
result = AckInitialize(ae);    // This will work now
```

Notice that the **AckInitialize()** function returns a value (**result**) and the value is tested before any other function calls are made. Throughout the internal *ACK-3D* initialization functions, you'll find error-checking return statements such as:

```
return(ERR_BADWINDOWSIZE);    // Return error code for invalid viewport
```

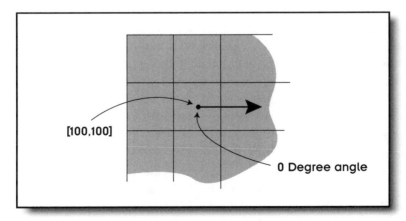

Figure 11.1 *Setting initial coordinates and angle for a player.*

In this case, this **return()** statement tells the engine that the viewport is not a valid size. The parameter inside the return statement is defined in ACK3D.H. This header file contains a complete set of error-code definitions that you can check in your main application to display error messages if something goes wrong while the engine is being initialized. Thus, the code in our template

```
result = AckInitialize(&ae);    // Initialize the engine
if (result)       // Perform error checking
  {
  printf("Error initializing - Code: %d\n",result);
  exit(1);
  }
```

checks to see if an error code has been returned and if so, it displays a message and terminates. I cannot overemphasize how important it is to include good error checking code in your applications. Whenever you call one of the critical engine functions that returns an error code, make sure you check the error code and display an appropriate message so you don't leave the player of your game wondering what's gone wrong. The error messages used in this template are quite simple; however you can easily expand them to make them more meaningful.

Once the engine has been initialized with **AckInitialize()**, it's time to load the map file. The template code loads in a file named DEMOMAP.L01 by calling **AckReadMapFile()**. This file is generated by the 3-D game editor. (Of course, I'm using a sample name here; you should include the actual name of the file you create for your game by using the 3-D editor.) The map file contains all of the data, such as wall and object positions, that the engine needs to store the map as a set of internal data structures. Notice that error checking code is provided once again to make sure that the map file is properly loaded.

After the map file is loaded, **AckRegisterStructure()** is called to set up the **ACKENG** interface structure and initialize the global variables that are required by the internal engine routines. Once this is done, you're almost ready to move the player around and build views. But before anything can be displayed, you'll need to load in bitmaps and objects. We've already discussed the basics of how the **AckLoadWall()** function is called to assign bitmap IDs with bitmap image files. Recall that every wall ID that is used in your map must be assigned a bitmap file so that the engine will know which bitmap to display. You can also load in your bitmaps using the lower-level **AckLoadBitmap()** function we explored in Chapter 10.

As you know, objects can be either stationary or movable. To create and load in an object, we'll follow a simple three-step process:

1. Load any bitmaps associated with the object by calling the **AckLoadBitmap()** or **AckLoadObject()** functions.
2. Call **AckCreateObject()** to create a data structure for the object.
3. Specify attributes for the object, such as its speed and any flags (**OF_PASSABLE** or **OF_ANIMATE**).

As an example, this code creates and initializes an object as an animated object:

```
result = AckLoadObject(&ae,1,"object1.bbm");  // Load in a bitmap for object

ae.ObjList[1].Flags |= OF_ANIMATE;            // Stay in place and animate
ae.ObjList[1].Speed = 1;                       // Speed is non-zero to activate
result = AckCreateObject(&ae,1,1,nums);
```

Recall that the interface structure uses the **ObjList[ ]** field to keep track of the objects that are used in a view. Here an array of unsigned chars called **nums[ ]** is used to specify the different views for the object. In this case there is only one, so the number of views is also passed as 1. There can be as many as **MAX_VIEWS** (currently defined in ACK3D.H as 47) different bitmaps assigned to one object for use as animation. In the next chapter I'll present more techniques for loading bitmaps and creating stationary and movable objects.

For the final work of moving the player around and displaying views, I'd be hard pressed to create a template for such code because there are so many ways to process user input and move a player around. I suggest that you take a close look at the sample programs that are provided on the CD-ROM to see different examples how motion is controlled and views are built in an actual game. If you initialize everything properly, you shouldn't have too much trouble moving your player around.

Alternatives for Initialization

The code in the template we just explored allows **AckInitialize()** to perform all of the "behind the scenes" work of setting up the engine. Essentially, it sets up a few of the fields in the **ACKENG** structure, loads in the data configuration file TRIG.DAT, and transfers the data in this file to various lookup tables. TRIG.DAT contains all of the precalculated trig data (cosine, sine, and tangent values of angles from 0 to 360) that the engine needs to perform ray casting. You don't have to change this special file, you just have to make sure that it is in a directory that your application can find.

If you don't want to go this route, I've provided another alternative for initializing the engine. You can use the pre-compiled engine resource file named KIT.OVL, which contains the file TRIG.DAT within it. The following example demonstrates this approach:

```
// First we open up the resource that contains TRIG.DAT
result = AckOpenResource("KIT.OVL");
// If an error occurs don't go any further
if (result)
   {
   printf("Unable to load resource file KIT.OVL\n");
   exit(1);
   }
// Now we perform the normal initialization of the engine
result = AckInitialize(&ae);
// Again check for an error and exit if one occurs
if (result)
   {
   printf("Error initializing.\n");
   exit(1);
   }
// After initializing we can close this resource
AckCloseResource();
```

Here the **AckOpenResource()** function is called to load in the resource file KIT.OVL. Once the resource file has been opened, you can continue to initialize the engine by calling **AckInitialize()**. When **AckInitialize()** executes, it checks to see if a resource has already been opened, and if so, it does not open the TRIG.DAT file. Once the engine has been initialized, you'll need to close the resource file by calling **AckCloseResource()**.

In addition to the engine resource file KIT.OVL, you can use other resource files to create your games. These files are called *user-definable resource files* and they are created using the Windows-based map editor or a utility program that comes with the *ACK-3D* engine. Basically, a user-definable resource file is a binary file that contains all of the unique game-specific data needed to create a game. This data includes the game map file, wall bitmap files, object bitmap files, background screen bitmap files, and so on. The resource file also contains a set of configuration commands that tell the engine how to process the user-definable resource file. The instructions for creating a resource file are presented in Appendix A. In Chapter 14, I'll show you how to build an application that uses a resource file to automate the process of setting up a game.

DESIGN TIP

The main advantage of using resource files is that you can combine several small files into one larger file, thus making it easier to keep all the needed files in one place. The KIT.OVL file actually contains the TRIG.DAT file mentioned previously and another precalculated table for earlier renderings of floors and ceilings, which are not used in the current engine. By keeping the math tables separate from your game files, you can have many levels in different resource files, and only one copy of the math tables used by the engine. In most cases you will only need the following files for your application:

- Your application .EXE file
- KIT.OVL for the math tables
- One or more user-definable resource files containing game maps, bitmaps, and so on

Initializing Other View Attributes

We've explored how to set up some of the basic viewing attributes, such as the player's angle and coordinates, that *must* be initialized before calling the *ACK-3D* functions to build a view and display it. However, you can set other fields in the **ACKENG** structure to control how your initial views will appear. As an example, here's some code taken from *Station Escape*, an early game I built for DOS. This code appears before **AckInitialize()** is called:

```
// ─────────────────────────────────
// Set up the structure for this particular application. The most important
// fields before initializing are the viewport (or Win...) fields.
// ─────────────────────────────────
ViewNum = 0;                          // Start with first view
ae->WinStartY = VP_STARTY;            // Set up viewport coordinates
ae->WinEndY = VP_ENDY;
ae->WinStartX = VP_STARTX;
ae->WinEndX = VP_ENDX;
ae->LightFlag = SHADING_ON;           // Use light shading
ae->xPlayer = Views[ViewNum].xP;      // Set initial coordinates
ae->yPlayer = Views[ViewNum].yP;
ae->PlayerAngle = Views[ViewNum].Angle; // Set viewing angle
ae->TopColor = 28;
ae->BottomColor = 28;
ae->DoorSpeed = 4;                    // Set door speed for doors that open
ae->NonSecretCode = 1;               // Bitmap for non-secret doors
```

When the first view for the game is displayed, it appears as shown in Figure 11.2. In this case, I defined the interface structure (**ae**) in the application as a global pointer. Thus, the notation **ae->** is used to access each field. In addition to setting the viewport coordinates, the code sets a light shading flag to indicate that light shading should be used to draw the views. Values are specified for the **TopColor** and **BottomColor** fields. When the game first appeared, the *ACK-3D* engine did not have the capability to render textured floors and ceilings, so a solid color was used to represent each. By dynamically changing the value for **TopColor** and **BottomColor,** some interesting effects, such as lightning flashes, can be achieved. The engine has since matured and now supports fully textured floors and ceilings (but those lightning strikes were pretty awesome in their day!) The code also provides a speed setting for the doors that open in the game. Because secret doors are a special type of door, I needed a way to tell the engine which bitmap to display once a secret door was opened; I accomplished this by using the **NonSecretCode** field in the interface structure. This is kind of a brute force approach, but it works well. When the player runs into a door, the door will open at the rate of the speed setting assigned to the **DoorSpeed** field. After the player passes through the door way, the door will close.

This example should give you an idea of some of the fields that you can set in the **ACKENG** structure before calling **AckInitialize()**. Of course, you can also change fields in the structure at any time in your application. For example, if your player moves into a secret chamber, you could increase the door open and close speed to make the action in the game more intriguing. As you build your games, try experimenting with different settings.

DESIGN TIP

In looking over this initialization code, you probably noticed the **Views[ ]** array and wondered, what is this? I used this array so that I could keep track of pre-defined view positions, that is, locations in the game map. Each location in the array corresponds with a location and angle for movement that I've pre-selected in the map for certain conditions. For example, when the game is first started, I put the player at location **Views[0]**. The simple structure at this array

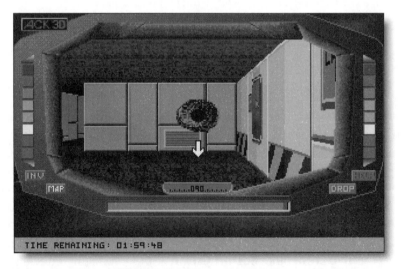

Figure 11.2　*The first view displayed in the DOS version of the* Station Escape *game.*

location stores the POV data need to position the player at the correct starting location. If a special event occurs in the game, I can easily move the player to a new position by indexing into the **Views[ ]** array and assigning the values stored there to the appropriate fields in the **ACKENG** structure. Adding coding tricks like this to your applications will help you to organize your code and maintain it. The **Views[ ]** array also provides a hook for designing a multi-player game via a network or modem. By having a player log into the game, each player could be assigned a different index into the **Views[ ]** array. Then when it comes time to display and keep track of the various players, we just need to look through the array and build the scene for any one of the players we want to see.

Tips for Moving Your Player Around

You can easily move your player around manually by assigning specific values to the **xPlayer** and **yPlayer** fields as well as updating the **Angle** field. But to get smooth motion from your games, you'll want to find ways to tie in these fields to the keyboard and the mouse activity. For example, every time the user presses the right-arrow key or moves the mouse to the right, you'll need a way to move the player to the right. There are many different coding techniques you can use to coordinate motion, but let me show you a few I've come up with to create smooth animation. The code we'll explore here will also give you some ideas on how you can set up your own game control loop.

I like to put all of the game action code inside a **while** loop that repeats until a flag is set. Before the loop, I initialize a few variables to help control how the mouse and keyboard tie in with the player's movement:

```
Spin = 0;          // A scale factor used to "spin" the player
SpinAngle = 0;     // Angle used to spin or move the player
done = 0;          // Flag to control the main game loop

//
// This is our main loop for processing until the player exits or the
// game is completed (win or lose).
//
while (!done)
  {
  if (LastSeconds != tmSeconds)    // Include a timer to check the game
    {                              // playing time
    ShowTime();
    LastSeconds = tmSeconds;
    if (tmHours == 0 && tmMinutes == 0 && tmSeconds == 0)
      {
```

```
        LostFlag = 1;
        break;
        }
    }

...
// Call the engine to animate objects and then build the scene
  AckCheckObjectMovement(ae);
  AckBuildView(ae);
  AckDrawOverlay(ae->ScreenBuffer,ae->OverlayBuffer);
...
  result = AckDisplayScreen(ae);     // Actually displays the current view
```

This code greases the skids and gets everything set up to start moving the player around. Notice that I've included some timer code to see if the loop should continue. Heck, you can't let your player keep going forever. The old "race against the clock" is always a good technique to keep the player on his or her toes.

Once a view has been displayed, we can begin to process how the player should move around. This is the main control code I like to use:

```
if (Spin)
  {
  Spin >>= 1;                        // Turn flag off
  ae->PlayerAngle += SpinAngle;
  if (ae->PlayerAngle >= INT_ANGLE_360) // Angle is out of range
    ae->PlayerAngle -= INT_ANGLE_360;
  if (ae->PlayerAngle < 0)           // Angle is less than 0
    ae->PlayerAngle += INT_ANGLE_360;
  }
```

The variables **Spin** and **SpinAngle** are used together to determine the angle the player should move next. These variables are always updated whenever the player moves the mouse or presses one of the arrow keys. (We'll explore this in a moment). Recall that a player can only move in a circle from 0 to 360 degrees. Thus, we always need to check to make sure that the calculated angle of movement is in this range. If a **Spin** value is set, the player's angle is adjusted by adding the **SpinAngle** to the current angle. This helps give the feeling of inertia to the player's movements, instead of an abrupt starting and stopping of motion when the mouse or keyboard is used. With this approach, the player will seem to gradually speed up and slow down while turning. The same effect can be used to move the player forward and backwards.

So how are **Spin** and **SpinAngle** calculated? For processing mouse inputs, you might want to add icon buttons to your game that the user can click on to move the player, as shown in Figure 11.3. Notice that buttons are provided to

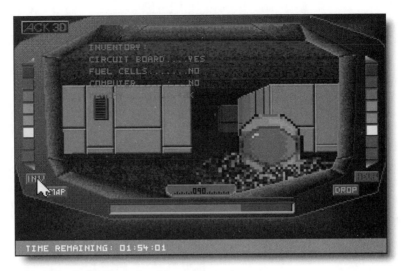

Figure 11.3 *Using button icons for player movement.*

move the player left, right, up, and down. The idea here is that each time the player clicks on one of the buttons, the new angle is calculated. Here's some sample code that shows the general idea:

```
switch (Mouse_Select_Code)     // Use switch statement like this
  {                            // to process the player movement button
  case MOUSE_LTARROW:          // Process select left arrow button
    SpinAngle = -INT_ANGLE_4;  // Reduce by 4 degree increment
    Spin = 1;                  // Set spin multiplier
    break;

  case MOUSE_RTARROW:          // Process select right arrow
    SpinAngle = INT_ANGLE_4;   // Increase by 4 degree increment
    Spin = 1;                  // Set spin multiplier
    break;

  case MOUSE_UPARROW:                        // Process select up arrow
    j = AckMovePOV(ae,ae->PlayerAngle,16);   // Move the player current angle
                                             // and 16 units
    ...                                      // Check walls and objects
    break;

  case MOUSE_DNARROW:                        // Process select down arrow
    j = ae->PlayerAngle + INT_ANGLE_180;     // Add 180 to current angle
    if (j >= INT_ANGLE_360)                  // Out of range, so adjust
      j -= INT_ANGLE_360;
    i = AckMovePOV(ae,j,16);                 // Move the player 16 units
    break;

  default:
    break;
  }
```

Each time a button is clicked, the player moves by a fixed increment. If the player clicks on a left- or right-arrow button, the "spin" angle is increased or decreased by four degrees. This adjustment takes care of moving the player a fixed angle at a time, but how do we support freeform movement? That is, how can we tie in the player's movement with the freeform movement of the mouse?

The basic approach is to track the movement of the mouse and then calculate a new angle and distance based on the distance the mouse has moved. Here's some sample code that checks each of the directions that the mouse can move. The **mouse.mdx** field stores the horizontal movement of the mouse, and **mouse.mdy** stores the vertical movement:

```
if (mouse.mdx < 0)     // Moving to the left
  {
  Spin = -mouse.mdx;   // Moving to the left; make positive
  Spin >>= 3;          // Convert coordinates to a scale factor
  SpinAngle = -INT_ANGLE_2 * Spin;  // Multiply scale factor by 2 degrees
  Spin = 1;            // Set flag
  }

if (mouse.mdx > 0)     // Moving to the right
  {
  Spin = mouse.mdx;    // Use distance mouse has moved right
  Spin >>= 3;          // Convert to scale factor
  SpinAngle = INT_ANGLE_2 * Spin;
  Spin = 1;
  }

if (mouse.mdy < 0)     // Moving up
  {
  i = -mouse.mdy;      // Make positive
  i >>= 2;
  i += 16;
  j = AckMovePOV(ae,ae->PlayerAngle,i);   // Move the player up
  ...
  }

if (mouse.mdy > 0)     // Moving down
  {
  i = mouse.mdy;       // Distance moving down
  i >>= 2;
  i += 16;
  j = ae->PlayerAngle + INT_ANGLE_180;   // Reverse direction
  if (j >= INT_ANGLE_360)                // Make sure new angle is in range
    j -= INT_ANGLE_360;
  i = AckMovePOV(ae,j,i);                // Move the player down
  ...
  }
```

This takes care of the mouse. The keyboard can be set up in the same manner. If the user presses a right or left arrow, the **SpinAngle** can be calculated. But since only one key can be pressed at a time, we can use a fixed amount to move the player left or right. Whenever the user presses the up- or down-arrow key, the player is moved in the map by calling the **AckMovePOV()** function:

```
//————————————————————
// The keyboard is now checked.
//————————————————————
if(Keys[ESCAPE_KEY])
  break;

if(Keys[RIGHT_ARROW_KEY])    // Move right
  {
  Spin += 2;                  // Add 2 units to the spin scale factor
  SpinAngle = INT_ANGLE_2 * Spin;
  }

if(Keys[LEFT_ARROW_KEY])     // Move left
  {
  Spin += 2;
  SpinAngle = -INT_ANGLE_2 * Spin;
  }

if(Keys[UP_ARROW_KEY])        // Move up
  {
  j = AckMovePOV(ae,ae->PlayerAngle,16);  // Move up 16 units
  ...      // Player has moved; check for collisions
  }

if(Keys[DOWN_ARROW_KEY])      // Move down
  {
  j = ae->PlayerAngle + INT_ANGLE_180;    // Reverse by 180 degrees
  ...      // Player has moved; check for collisions
  }

if ...    // Continue to process other keys supported
```

This sample code should provide you with enough ideas to help you get started moving your player around. When we create actual applications with the *ACK-3D* engine later in the book, you'll find some other techniques for moving a player. Now it's time to move on and take a closer look at some of the actual code in the initialization routines. The more you know abut the initialization functions, the better you'll understand how they should be used and how you can change them to add additional features to the engine.

Getting Inside AckInitialize()

We've discussed how the *ACK-3D* system must be initialized and how the basic functions are called for using the 3-D engine. Let's now move down a level and take a closer look at what goes on behind the scenes. Here is the complete code for **AckInitialize()**:

```
short AckInitialize(ACKENG *ae)
{
  short    i,result = 0;
  short    j;
  UCHAR    topcolor;

#ifdef __BORLANDC__       // Conditional for Borland C++
OurDataSeg = _DS;
#endif

AckKeyboardSetup = 0;    // Indicates keyboard interrupt has not been set up
AckTimerSetup = 0;       // Indicates timer has not been set up

// Check to see if viewport coordinates are set up properly
if (!ae->WinEndY || !ae->WinEndX ||
  (ae->WinEndY - ae->WinStartY) < 10 ||    // Height is less than 10 pixels
  (ae->WinEndX - ae->WinStartX) < 10)      // Width is less than 10 pixels
  {
  return(ERR_BADWINDOWSIZE);  // Return error code for invalid viewport
  }

result = AckBuildTables(ae);  // Read in TRIG.DAT and allocate tables
if (result)
  return(result);

AckSetupWindow(ae);    // Set up the internal coordinates for the viewport
SetupFloors(ae);       // Set up the floors

AckBuildHeightTables(ae);   // Build height and adjustment tables

topcolor = ae->TopColor;
BackDropRows = 100;

for (i = 0; i < 640; I++)    // Create the rotating background array
  {
  BackArray[i] = AckMalloc(BackDropRows+1);   // Allocate storage for the array
  if (BackArray[i] == NULL)
    return(ERR_NOMEMORY);
  memset(BackArray[i],topcolor,BackDropRows); // Set to top color
  }
return(result);
}
```

The first major task this function performs is to check the coordinates of the viewport to make sure that they are in range. If they are not in range, an error message is returned and the engine is shut down. The error code returned is:

```
return(ERR_BADWINDOWSIZE);    // Return error code for invalid viewport
```

In this case, the **return()** statement tells the engine that the viewport is not a valid size. Recall that the error codes such as **ERR_BADWINDOWSIZE** are defined in ACK3D.H. Once the viewport coordinates have been checked, the internal function **AckBuildTables()** is called. Referring to this function as a workhorse is something of an understatement. Behind the scenes it reads in all of the critical data that makes the engine tick. Some of this data includes the distance tables and the trig tables such as **CosTable[]**, **SinTable[]**, **LongTanTable[]**, and so on. Because all of these tables are created dynamically, **AckBuildTables()** must allocate the memory and make sure that no memory allocation errors occur. Memory is allocated by calling the internal routine **AckMalloc()**. For example, here's how memory is allocated for the **CosTable[]** and **SinTable[]** arrays:

```
CosTable = (long *)AckMalloc(sizeof(long) * INT_ANGLE_360);
SinTable = (long *)AckMalloc(sizeof(long) * INT_ANGLE_360);
```

Here **INT_ANGLE_360** is the constant that specifies the size of memory needed for the array (1800). In addition to the trig tables, **AckBuildTables()** also allocates memory for the map grid and object grid, as shown here:

```
Grid = (unsigned short *)AckMalloc((GRID_MAX * 2)+1);
ObjGrid = (unsigned short *)AckMalloc((GRID_MAX * 2)+1);
```

The other important data structures that this function must set up are the buffers for the screen and background:

```
ae->ScreenBuffer = (UCHAR *)AckMalloc(SCREEN_SIZE+640);
ae->BkgdBuffer = (UCHAR *)AckMalloc(SCREEN_SIZE+640);
```

In this case, notice that the pointers to the buffers allocated are directly assigned to the **ACKENG** interface structure. After **AckBuildTables()** finishes allocating memory, it must check to make sure that all of the tables and buffers are set up properly. If one of them is set to NULL, the error code **ERR_NOMEMORY** is returned to the calling function **AckInitialize()**.

Once the tables have been allocated and the trig data has been read in, **AckInitialize()** calls **AckSetupWindow()** to set up the internal coordinates and dimensions for the viewport. If you recall from Chapter 7, these are the fields such as **CenterOffset** and **WinLength** that are used by the low-level drawing routines. Next, the internal routine **SetupFloors()** is called to set up the floors used for the view.

The last function called by **AckInitialize()** is **AckBuildHeightTables()**. This function creates two arrays, **DistanceTable[ ]** and **AdjustTable[ ]**, which are used by the internal ray-casting routines to determine how high a wall should be when it is displayed. The height of a wall is determined by using the player's distance to the wall as a table lookup value into the **DistanceTable[ ]** array. Figure 11.4 shows some of the values that are stored in the **DistanceTable[ ]** array. If a player is 8 pixels or less away from a wall, the maximum height value is used (960 pixels). The maximum distance the player can be from a wall is 2,047 pixels, but as Figure 11.4 shows, any

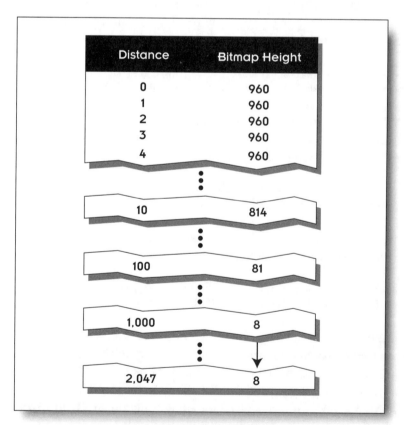

Distance	Bitmap Height
0	960
1	960
2	960
3	960
4	960
10	814
100	81
1,000	8
2,047	8

Figure 11.4　*Some of the values stored in the DistanceTable[] array.*

distance over 1,000 pixels would result in the minimum wall height being used, which is 8 pixels.

The **AdjustTable[ ]** array is used to determine how wide an object should appear at different distances. This value helps us later on in the **FindObject()** function when we need to insert object slices into our list of wall slices.

The last thing we want to do is pre-allocate an array used to display a neat rotating background should we decide to have an outside scene rendered. I picked twice the maximum screen wide columns (320×2, or 640) for this array to give the player the feeling that he or she is looking out onto a wide expanse of mountain ranges, stars, or whatever you wish for a great looking background to your application. Figure 11.5 shows how this array is set up.

Each entry in the **BackArray** is 200 pixels in length to correspond to the height of the VGA screen. To draw the rotating background, the player's angle is first divided by 640 (our total number of elements in the array) and the remainder from the division is used as the starting column in the array. As each column of the scene is rendered, the **BackArray[ ]** column (**bcol** is the variable in the floor drawing routine) is advanced. When the maximum column of 639 (base 0) is reached, the column value is wrapped back to zero to provide a continuous loop no matter what angle the player may be facing.

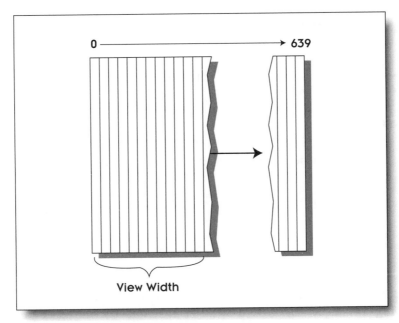

Figure 11.5 *Using the BackArray[] to set up a rotating background.*

DESIGN TIP

You might want to expand on this neat technique of displaying backgrounds. If you know that the application you are creating is going to be fully inside (a textured ceiling in every block), you might want to set some kind of switch that tells the initialization process not to allocate the memory for the rotating background. This approach cuts down on memory usage if you find you are running short on free memory. I've included it as always allocated to be more generic in nature.

Processing Resources

Before we get too far into the process of reading in a map file, we need to discuss the concept of resource files in a little more detail. If you recall from earlier discussions, ACKINIT.C provides two functions for opening and closing resources—**AckOpenResource()** and **AckCloseResource()**. These functions allow you to streamline the way the *ACK-3D* engine gets the data that it needs to initialize the system. Instead of opening separate files such as TRIG.DAT and the map files for a game, you can combine all of these data files into one file, then use the two resource processing functions to open and close the resource. But if you use resource files, keep in mind that only one can be opened at a time.

When **AckOpenResource()** is called to open a resource file, it first checks to see if a resource is currently open:

```
if (rsHandle)          // Is a resource file currently opened?
  _lclose(rsHandle);   // Close it before opening a new one
```

Here, **rsHandle** serves as a flag, as well as a file handle, to indicate if a resource file is currently open. If a resource file is open, it is closed. Next, the new resource file is opened and the operation is tested:

```
rsHandle = _lopen(fName,OF_READ); // Open new resource file
if (rsHandle < 1)                 // Check to see if file is opened properly
  {
  rsHandle = 0;                   // Reset file handle
  return(ERR_BADFILE);            // Return error code for failure
  }
```

The next task is to read in the resource data and store it in an array called **rbaTable[]**. This array will be used by other functions, such as **AckReadMap()**, to read in map data if a resource file is used instead of a map file. First, we need to allocate memory for the array:

```
hLen = MAX_RBA * sizeof(long);          // Get size of file
if (rbaTable == NULL)
  rbaTable = (ULONG *)AckMalloc(hLen);  // Allocate buffer for file
```

Next we read in the data from the file:

```
// Read in the file and check for byte count error
if (_lread(rsHandle,(ULONG *)rbaTable,hLen) != hLen)
  {
  _lclose(rsHandle);        // Close file
  rsHandle = 0;             // Reset file handle
  AckFree(rbaTable);        // Free up buffer
  return(ERR_BADFILE);      // Return file error code
  }
```

Now the resource data is ready to be used.

Reading the Map File with AckReadMapFile()

Earlier we saw that the function that loads in a map file is **AckReadMapFile()**. This function takes two parameters

```
short AckReadMapFile(ACKENG *ae,char *fName)
```

which are a pointer to the interface structure and the name of the map file to be read in. The map file is created by the 3-D map editor. It contains information about the walls, floors, and ceilings, as well as the initial placement for non-moving objects. This file can be a standalone file, or it can be combined with a resource file.

DESIGN TIP

The loading of a map is kept separate from the **AckInitialize()** function to allow multiple levels of maps to be used without having to re-initialize the engine each time. In fact, you could easily use the same bitmaps for walls and objects over and over again in different maps just by loading each map with the **AckReadMapFile()** function and including a different map filename. The trig tables are kept in a separate file, called KIT.OVL, for the same reason: so that multiple resource files can be used without needing to place each math table in a separate file.

AckReadMapFile() begins by opening the map file specified by the ***fName** parameter. If the file cannot be opened, an error code is returned; otherwise, the file is assigned to a variable named **handle** for easy access:

```
if (!rsHandle)          // Check to see if resource file is open already
   { // No resource file so open new one
   handle = _lopen(fName,OF_READ); // Open the specified resource
   if (handle < 1)
       return(ERR_BADMAPFILE);     // File was not opened; return error code
   }
else
   {
   handle = rsHandle;   // Get handle to open resource
   _llseek(handle,rbaTable[(ULONG)fName],SEEK_SET);  // Access opened resource file
   }
```

Recall that the variable **rsHandle** is used as a flag to indicate if a resource is currently opened. Because only one resource file can be opened at a time, we need to check the status of this flag. If it is not set, the map file is opened and a test is made to make sure the file is opened properly. If a resource file is already opened, the code at the **else** clause is executed. In this case, the file's name, **fName**, is used as an index into the **rbaTable[]** array. This array serves as a resource table that stores the data in the opened resource file.

In fact, every *ACK-3D* function that takes a filename as a parameter (with the exception of **AckOpenResource()**), can use an index value instead of a filename string. Just typecast the call with a (char *) before passing in the numeric value to use as an index. For example the function call

```
AckReadMapFile("demo.map")
```

would open and use the filename DEMO.MAP if no resource was currently open, while the function call

```
AckReadMapFile((char *)1)
```

would read a map from index 1 in the currently open resource file.

Once the map file has been opened or the appropriate location in the resource file has been located, **AckReadMapFile()** continues on and reads in the map data. The order of the data read in includes the grid map data, object map data, x grid and y grid map data, floor and ceiling map data, and multi-height wall data.

If you look at the code, you'll see a number of **if** statements such as:

```
if (_lread(handle,ae->xGrid,aLen) != aLen)  // Read in x grid data
  {
  if (!rsHandle)                            // Error occurred; close file
    _lclose(handle);
  return(ERR_READINGMAP);
  }
```

The **_lread()** function reads in the data referenced by **handle**. The data can come from a map file that has just been opened in **AckReadMapFile()** or from a resource file that has been opened by a previous call to **AckOpenResource()**. The data is read in and stored in a variable—in this case the **xGrid[]** array.

The last task that **AckReadMap()** performs is to call **AckBuildGrid()** to process the doors and objects used in a map. This step involves initializing the list of doors by setting their column offset to 0 and map positions to -1. The objects processed are the stationary ones. To process them, we use a nested **for** loop to check each location of the map grid to see if an object is present. If an object is detected in a map location, memory is allocated for the object and the object's coordinates and map position are stored in an object list assigned to the interface structure.

The Complete ACKINIT.C

```
// This file contains the key initialization functions for the ACK-3D engine.
// The main function AckInitialize() must be called first before any of the
// other ACK-3D functions are called. The internal functions defined in this file
// perform all of the setup work of loading tables and resource files.
#include  <windows.h>
#include  <stdlib.h>
#include  <stdio.h>
#include  <dos.h>
#include  <mem.h>
#include  <io.h>
#include  <fcntl.h>
#include  <time.h>
#include  <string.h>
#include  <sys\stat.h>
#include  "ack3d.h"
#include  "ackeng.h"
#include  "ackext.h"

extern  char AckKeyboardSetup;
extern  char AckTimerSetup;
short   *LowerTable[2048];
short   tmpLowerValue[400];
short   LowerLen[2048];
short   OurDataSeg;
char    rsName[128];
long FloorCosTable[VIEW_WIDTH+1];
short AckBuildTables(ACKENG *ae);
void AckBuildHeightTables(ACKENG *ae);
void AckBuildGrid(ACKENG *ae);
void SetupFloors(ACKENG *ae);
```

```
//**********************************************************************
// Internal function called by AckInitialize(). This function sets up the
// internal variables that are required to support the off-screen buffer.
//**********************************************************************
void AckSetupWindow(ACKENG *ae)
{
// Access the center row of the viewport
ae->CenterRow   = ae->WinStartY + ((ae->WinEndY - ae->WinStartY) / 2);
// Access a memory location for the center row
ae->CenterOffset   = ae->CenterRow * BYTES_PER_ROW;
// Access the starting memory location of the viewport
ae->WinStartOffset = ae->WinStartY * BYTES_PER_ROW;
// Calculate the window length in double words
ae->WinLength   = ((ae->WinEndY - ae->WinStartY)+1) * DWORDS_PER_ROW;
// Calculate the viewport window width and height
ae->WinWidth    = (ae->WinEndX - ae->WinStartX) + 1;
ae->WinHeight   = (ae->WinEndY - ae->WinStartY) + 1;
}


//**********************************************************************
// Initializes the ACK interface structure and reads in the TRIG tables
// from either the stand alone file TRIG.DAT or from a resource file that
// was opened previous to this call.
// This function MUST be called before AckBuildView() and AckDisplayScreen().
//**********************************************************************
short AckInitialize(ACKENG *ae)
{
  short  i,result = 0;
  short  j;
  UCHAR  topcolor;

#ifdef __BORLANDC__    // Conditional for Borland C++
OurDataSeg = _DS;
#endif

AckKeyboardSetup = 0; // Indicates keyboard interrupt has not been set up
AckTimerSetup = 0;    // Indicates timer has not been set up

// Check to see if viewport coordinates are set up properly
if (!ae->WinEndY || !ae->WinEndX ||
(ae->WinEndY - ae->WinStartY) < 10 ||  // Height is less than 10 pixels
(ae->WinEndX - ae->WinStartX) < 10)    // Width is less than 10 pixels
  {
  return(ERR_BADWINDOWSIZE);      // Return error code for invalid viewport
  }
result = AckBuildTables(ae);    // Read in TRIG.DAT and allocate tables
if (result) return(result);
AckSetupWindow(ae);             // Set up the internal coordinates for the viewport
SetupFloors(ae);                // Set up the floors
AckBuildHeightTables(ae);       // Build height and adjustment tables
topcolor = ae->TopColor;

BackDropRows = 100;
for (i = 0; i < 640; i++)
```

```
  {
  BackArray[i] = AckMalloc(BackDropRows+1);
  if (BackArray[i] == NULL)
    return(ERR_NOMEMORY);
  memset(BackArray[i],topcolor,BackDropRows);
  }
return(result);
}


//***************************************************************
// Opens a resource file for use by any ACK routine that requires a
// filename. Only one resource file can be opened at a time.
//***************************************************************
short AckOpenResource(char *fName)
{
  ULONG hLen;
if (rsHandle)          // Is a resource file currently opened?
  _lclose(rsHandle);   // Close it before opening a new one
rsHandle = _lopen(fName,OF_READ); // Open new resource file

if (rsHandle < 1)                  // Check to see if file is opened properly
  {
  rsHandle = 0;        // Reset file handle
  return(ERR_BADFILE); // Return error code for failure
  }

hLen = MAX_RBA * sizeof(long);     // Get size of file
if (rbaTable == NULL)
  rbaTable = (ULONG *)AckMalloc(hLen);  // Allocate buffer for file
if (rbaTable == NULL)                    // Was memory available?
  {
  _lclose(rsHandle);                // Close file
  rsHandle = 0;                     // Reset file handle
  return(ERR_NOMEMORY);             // Return error code
  }
// Read in the file and check for byte count error
if (_lread(rsHandle,(ULONG *)rbaTable,hLen) != hLen)
  {
  _lclose(rsHandle);      // Close file
  rsHandle = 0;           // Reset file handle
  AckFree(rbaTable);      // Free up buffer
  return(ERR_BADFILE);    // Return file error code
  }
strcpy(rsName,fName);      // Store resource filename
return(0);
}


//***************************************************************
// Closes a resource file if one is opened.
//***************************************************************
void AckCloseResource(void)
{
if (rsHandle)            // Check to make sure resource file is opened
  _lclose(rsHandle);     // Close the resource
if (rbaTable != NULL)  // Do we need to free the memory for the file buffer?
```

```
   {
   AckFree(rbaTable);   // Free up the file buffer
   rbaTable = NULL;
   }
rsHandle = 0;            // Reset the file handle
}


//************************************************************************
// Internal function used to pre-define height tables for the wall
// drawing code.
//************************************************************************
void BuildWallDstTables(void)
{
   short i,j,dst,row,HiValue;
   long  ldst,value,LowValue,len;
   short *lp;

for (ldst = 10;ldst < 2048; ldst++)
   {
   HiValue = value = 0;
   row = 0;
   while (HiValue < 64 && row < 100)
      {
      HiValue = (value >> 8) & 0xFF;
      tmpLowerValue[row] = HiValue; row++;
      value += ldst;
      }
   LowerLen[ldst] = row;
   len = row * 2;
   j = 1;
   if (row == LowerLen[ldst-1])
      {
      j = 0;
      lp = LowerTable[ldst-1];
      for (i = 0; i < row; i++)
         {
         if (tmpLowerValue[i] != lp[i])
            {
            j = 1;
            break;
            }
         }
      }
   if (j)
      {
      lp = AckMalloc(len);
      if (lp == NULL)
         {
         return;
         }
      LowerTable[ldst] = lp;
      for (i = 0; i < row; i++)
         lp[i] = tmpLowerValue[i];
      }
```

```
  else
    {
    LowerTable[ldst] = LowerTable[ldst-1];
    }
  }
}


//*************************************************************************
// Internal function called from AckInitialize() to read in the trig tables
// and allocate memory for the various buffers.
//*************************************************************************
short AckBuildTables(ACKENG *ae)
{
  short handle,len,ca,na;
  int   c,s,ang;
  long  fAng,tu,tv;
  SLICE *sa,*saNext;

BuildWallDstTables();          // Create the distance tables
if (!rsHandle)                 // Check to make sure resource file is not opened
  {
  handle = _lopen("trig.dat",OF_READ);// Open trig data file
  if (handle < 1)
    return(ERR_BADFILE);               // File can't be opened; return error code
  }
else
  {
  handle = rsHandle;                    // Get handle for resource file
  _llseek(handle,rbaTable[0],SEEK_SET);
  }

// Allocate memory for trig and coordinate tables
LongTanTable    = (long *)AckMalloc(sizeof(long) * INT_ANGLE_360);
LongInvTanTable = (long *)AckMalloc(sizeof(long) * INT_ANGLE_360);
CosTable        = (long *)AckMalloc(sizeof(long) * INT_ANGLE_360);
SinTable        = (long *)AckMalloc(sizeof(long) * INT_ANGLE_360);
LongCosTable    = (long *)AckMalloc(sizeof(long) * INT_ANGLE_360);
xNextTable      = (long *)AckMalloc(sizeof(long) * INT_ANGLE_360);
yNextTable      = (long *)AckMalloc(sizeof(long) * INT_ANGLE_360);
ViewCosTable    = (long *)AckMalloc(sizeof(long) * VIEW_WIDTH);
// Allocate memory for map grid and object grid
Grid = (unsigned short *)AckMalloc((GRID_MAX * 2)+1);
ObjGrid = (unsigned short *)AckMalloc((GRID_MAX * 2)+1);
// Allocate memory for height adjustment table
AdjustTable = (long *)AckMalloc((MAX_DISTANCE+1) * sizeof(long));
// Allocate memory for screen buffers
ae->ScreenBuffer = (UCHAR *)AckMalloc(SCREEN_SIZE+640);
ae->BkgdBuffer = (UCHAR *)AckMalloc(SCREEN_SIZE+640);

if (LongTanTable     == NULL ||        // Make sure memory is allocated for tables
  LongInvTanTable    == NULL ||
  CosTable           == NULL ||
  SinTable           == NULL ||
  LongCosTable       == NULL ||
```

```
         xNextTable        == NULL ||
         yNextTable        == NULL ||
         Grid              == NULL ||
         ObjGrid           == NULL ||
         AdjustTable       == NULL ||
         ae->ScreenBuffer  == NULL ||
         ae->BkgdBuffer    == NULL ||
         ViewCosTable      == NULL)
         {
         if (!rsHandle)
           _lclose(handle);
           return(ERR_NOMEMORY);                   // Return memory allocation error code
         }
len = sizeof(long) * INT_ANGLE_360;    // Calculate size for each trig table
_lread(handle,SinTable,len);    // Read in trig data and place in appropriate tables
_lread(handle,CosTable,len);
_lread(handle,LongTanTable,len);
_lread(handle,LongInvTanTable,len);
_lread(handle,InvCosTable,len);
_lread(handle,InvSinTable,len);
_lread(handle,LongCosTable,len);
if (!rsHandle)
  _lclose(handle);              // Done reading, close TRIG.DAT
ca = INT_ANGLE_32;
na = -1;

// Set up viewing tables for 32 to -32 angle sweep
for (len = 0; len < VIEW_WIDTH; len++)
  {
  ViewCosTable[len] = LongCosTable[ca];
  FloorCosTable[len] = InvCosTable[ca] >> 6;
  ca += na;
  if (ca <= 0)      // Index is less than 0 so switch
    {
    ca = -ca;
    na = -na;
    }
  }
// Adjust tables for 90, 180, and 270 degree angles
LongTanTable[INT_ANGLE_90] = LongTanTable[INT_ANGLE_90+1];
LongInvTanTable[INT_ANGLE_90] = LongInvTanTable[INT_ANGLE_90+1];
LongTanTable[INT_ANGLE_180] = LongTanTable[INT_ANGLE_180+1];
LongInvTanTable[INT_ANGLE_180] = LongInvTanTable[INT_ANGLE_180+1];
LongTanTable[INT_ANGLE_270] = LongTanTable[INT_ANGLE_270+1];
LongInvTanTable[INT_ANGLE_270] = LongInvTanTable[INT_ANGLE_270+1];
for (len = 0; len < INT_ANGLE_360; len++)
  {
  // Calculate y intercept increments
  yNextTable[len] = (long)BITMAP_WIDTH * LongTanTable[len];
  // Calculate x intercept increments
  xNextTable[len] = (long)BITMAP_WIDTH * LongInvTanTable[len];
  InvCosTable[len] = InvCosTable[len] >> 4;    // Scale inverse tables
  InvSinTable[len] = InvSinTable[len] >> 6;
  }
// Set up the array of slice structures to represent the full width of the view
```

```
// Each slice structure is initialized by setting its data fields to 0s
// Each slice in the array is also linked to a second slice to reference a slice
// that could be visually behind the current slice
for (len = 0; len < VIEW_WIDTH; len++)
  {
  sa = &Slice[len];                     // Initialize array of slice structures
  memset(sa,0,sizeof(SLICE));           // Set all data to 0
  for (ca = 0; ca < 8; ca++)
    {
    saNext = AckMalloc(sizeof(SLICE));  // Create a slice structure to link in
    if (saNext == NULL)
      return(ERR_NOMEMORY);             // Check for memory allocation
    memset(saNext,0,sizeof(SLICE));     // Initialize all data to 0
    sa->Next = saNext;                  // Link in slice
    saNext->Prev = sa;
    sa = saNext;
    }
  }
return(0);
}


//***********************************************************************
// Reads a map file and processes any multi-height walls.
//***********************************************************************
short AckReadMapFile(ACKENG *ae,char *fName)
{
  short len,handle,rdlen,count,i,pos;
  int   mLen,aLen;
  UCHAR buf[MAX_MULTI+2];
  UCHAR *mPtr;

if (!rsHandle)    // Check to see if resource file is open already
  {               // No resource file so open new one
  handle = _lopen(fName,OF_READ);      // Open the specified resource
  if (handle < 1)
    return(ERR_BADMAPFILE);            // File was not opened; return error code
  }
else
  {
  handle = rsHandle;                   // Get handle to open resource
  _llseek(handle,rbaTable[(ULONG)fName],SEEK_SET);// Access opened resource file
  }
aLen = GRID_ARRAY * 2;
mLen = GRID_MAX * 2;
if (_lread(handle,Grid,mLen) != mLen) // Read in grid map data
  {
  if (!rsHandle)
    _lclose(handle);
  return(ERR_READINGMAP);             // Return file read error code
  }
if (_lread(handle,ObjGrid,mLen) != mLen)  // Read in object map data
  {
  if (!rsHandle)
    _lclose(handle);
  return(ERR_READINGMAP);
```

```
    }
  if (_lread(handle,ae->xGrid,aLen) != aLen)    // Read in x grid data
    {
    if (!rsHandle)
      _lclose(handle);
    return(ERR_READINGMAP);
    }
  if (_lread(handle,ae->yGrid,aLen) != aLen)    // Read in y grid data
    {
    if (!rsHandle)
      _lclose(handle);
    return(ERR_READINGMAP);
    }
  if (_lread(handle,FloorMap,mLen) != mLen)    // Read in floor map data
    {
    if (!rsHandle)
      _lclose(handle);
    return(ERR_READINGMAP);
    }
  if (_lread(handle,CeilMap,mLen) != mLen)   // Read in ceiling map data
    {
    if (!rsHandle)
      _lclose(handle);
    return(ERR_READINGMAP);
    }
  _lread(handle,&count,2);              // Check counter for multi-height walls
  if (count)
    {
    for (i = 0; i < count;i++)         // Read in multi-height wall data
      {
      _lread(handle,&pos,2);   // Get grid position for this multi-height wall
      // Allocate memory for multi-height wall data
      mPtr = (UCHAR *)AckMalloc(MAX_MULTI+1);
      if (mPtr == NULL)
        {
        if (!rsHandle)
          _lclose(handle);
        return(ERR_NOMEMORY);
        }
      ae->mxGrid[pos] = mPtr;    // Store pointer to multi-height wall
      ae->myGrid[pos] = mPtr;
      ae->mxGrid[pos+1] = mPtr;
      ae->myGrid[pos+GRID_WIDTH] = mPtr;
      _lread(handle,buf,MAX_MULTI);
      buf[MAX_MULTI] = '\0';
      len = strlen(buf);
      if (len > MAX_MULTI) len = MAX_MULTI;
      *mPtr = len;
      if (len)
        memmove(&mPtr[1],buf,len);
      }
    }
  if (!rsHandle)                // Close handle
    _lclose(handle);
  AckBuildGrid(ae);             // Build object lists
```

```
return(0);
}


//**********************************************************************
// Internal function to create height and distance tables for objects. In
// the DistanceTable[] each entry represents the distance from the player
// to a wall. The value stored in the array is the height of the wall at
// the corresponding distance. For example, DistanceTable[100] indicates
// that the distance to the wall is 100 units. The value stored at this
// location is 81—the pixel height of the wall.
//**********************************************************************
void AckBuildHeightTables(ACKENG *ae)
{

  short i,x;
  short result;
  long  height;

height = BITMAP_WIDTH * 128L; // Calculate distance to height conversion factor
DistanceTable[0] = MAX_HEIGHT;  // First entry = max. height (960)
//************ 64 * 65536 ********
AdjustTable[0] = 4194304L / height;
for (i = 1; i < MAX_DISTANCE; i++)   // Loop to calculate each entry for the arrays
  {
  DistanceTable[i] = height / i;
  if (height - (DistanceTable[i] * i) > (i / 2))
    DistanceTable[i]++;               // Add 1 to height value
  if (DistanceTable[i] < MIN_HEIGHT)  // Adjust for min. height (8)
    DistanceTable[i] = MIN_HEIGHT;
  if (DistanceTable[i] > MAX_HEIGHT)  // Adjust for max. height (960)
    DistanceTable[i] = MAX_HEIGHT;
  AdjustTable[i] = 2097152L / DistanceTable[i];
  }
}


//**********************************************************************
// Internal function called by AckReadMapFile() to process the objects
// in the map. Movable vs stationary objects are processed here.
//**********************************************************************
void AckBuildGrid(ACKENG *ae)
{
short  i,j,CurIndex,pos,x1,y1;
USHORT MapCode,MapHiCode;

// Initialize doors
for (i = 0; i < MAX_DOORS; i++)
  {
  ae->Door[i].ColOffset = 0;
  ae->Door[i].mPos = ae->Door[i].mPos1 = -1;
  }
ae->SysFlags |= SYS_NO_WALLS; // Assume no floating walls
CurIndex    = 1;
TotalSpecial = 0;
TotalSecret  = 0;
```

```
for (i = 0; i < GRID_HEIGHT; i++)        // Loop until entire grid has been checked
  {
  for (j = 0; j < GRID_WIDTH; j++)
    {
    pos = (i * GRID_WIDTH) + j;
    MapCode = ObjGrid[pos];   // Check object at current grid position
    if (MapCode)                   // Is there an object here?
      {
      CurIndex = MapCode & 0xFF;
      if (CurIndex < MAX_OBJECTS)    // Get the index of the object
        {
        if (ae->ObjList[CurIndex] == NULL)  // No object allocated yet
          {
          // Allocate memory for object
          ae->ObjList[CurIndex] = (NEWOBJECT *)AckMalloc(sizeof(NEWOBJECT));
          if (ae->ObjList[CurIndex] != NULL)
          memset(ae->ObjList[CurIndex],0,sizeof(NEWOBJECT));
          }
        // If memory has been allocated calculate coordinates for object
        if (ae->ObjList[CurIndex] != NULL)
          {
          x1 = (j * BITMAP_WIDTH) + (BITMAP_WIDTH/2);
          y1 = (i * BITMAP_WIDTH) + (BITMAP_WIDTH/2);
          ae->ObjList[CurIndex]->x = x1;      // Store x,y position
          ae->ObjList[CurIndex]->y = y1;
          ae->ObjList[CurIndex]->mPos = pos;  // Store map position
          ae->ObjList[CurIndex]->Active = 1;  // Indicates object is active
          }
        }
      }
    }
  }
}
// **** End of Source ****
```

12

Without bitmaps there would be no 3-D games or an *ACK-3D* engine. In this chapter, you'll find out how the basic bitmap graphical building blocks of our games are created, loaded, and processed.

Working with Bitmaps

W hen you first encounter a game like *DOOM* or *Slob Zone*, what catches your eye are the stunning graphics. In its basic form, a 3-D engine like *ACK-3D* is simply a tool to load and process bitmap building blocks to create dynamic 3-D views. Using the same engine, you can create games that look completely different from each other, even though they are all based on the same underlying technology. The trick, then, is learning how to master the art of designing and working with bitmaps.

In this chapter we'll explore the concepts and techniques of how bitmaps are created for 3-D games—primarily walls and objects. First, we'll explore some important design issues to help you get started. Next, we'll examine the *ACK-3D* engine functions provided for loading and processing bitmaps. Along the way you'll learn about the techniques of reading bitmap files. In the last part of the chapter, we'll discuss some additional techniques for creating objects with bitmaps.

The more you work with *ACK-3D*, the more you'll discover that the essence of creating walls and objects is simply a matter of drawing bitmap building blocks and then assigning these bitmaps to wall and object structures. Thanks to the high-level, easy-to-use *ACK-3D* functions, you'll find that creating wall and object components for your games is easy to master.

The Art of Creating Bitmaps

When you create the bitmaps for your game, you don't build entire scenes or objects as a single bitmap. Instead, you draw each bitmap as a 64×64 pixel building block, as shown in Figure 12.1. You can use any type of painting program to create and modify your bitmaps, as long as the program can save them in a .PCX or .BBM (Deluxe Paint II) format. You can use a program that saves your files in a different format if you have a way to eventually convert your bitmap files to .PCX or .BBM. (The *ACK-3D* engine is also internally designed to support .GIF files; however, the code to read in files of this format is not included because of the pending GIF file legal woes—I'll have more to say on this topic shortly.)

DESIGN TIP

With Deluxe Paint II, .LBM files are the main bitmap files created. These files usually represent full-screen bitmaps. The .BBM files, on the other hand, are smaller images used as brushes to draw special effects and such. See the next section for more information about these file types. The *ACK-3D* function for reading Deluxe Paint II files, **AckReadiff()**, can read either .LBM files or .BBM files, although I typically use .BBM files to store wall and object bitmaps.

The companion CD-ROM provides a useful shareware image processing program called Paint Shop Pro to help you convert your bitmap images from one format to another. This program provides support for all of the major bitmap file formats, including .GIF, .TIF, .PCX, .TGA, .LBM, .BMP, and so on. This utility gives you much greater flexibility for creating your bitmaps and converting them to a format that the *ACK-3D* engine supports.

Notes on Graphic (Bitmap) File Formats

There are probably more graphics file formats out there than anyone could ever imagine. In fact, recently I received a book entitled *Encyclopedia of Graphics File Formats* (O'Reilly and Associates) that contained over 800 pages of information about graphics file formats. Of all the more popular formats

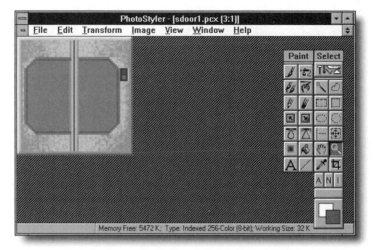

Figure 12.1 *Creating an* ACK-3D *bitmap as a 64x64 building block.*

like .TIF, .GIF, and .TGA, .PCX files are probably the most widely used by PC game designers and graphic artists. If you hire an artist to help you create the bitmap images for your game and the artist cannot work with .PCX files, you probably have the wrong artist!

The .PCX format was developed for Zsoft's *PC Paintbrush* program in the early days of the PC. It provides a simplistic data compression scheme to squeeze some of the fat out of bitmap images—especially images that contain a high percentage of adjacent colors. The two main reasons that game developers like to use .PCX files is that they are widely used by developers and graphics designers alike and they are very easy to work with.

The other graphics format supported by *ACK-3D* is .BBM files—a format used by the Deluxe Paint II program. This program, published by Electronic Arts, has not caught on in a big way with mainstream PC graphics designers, but many game artists use it quite often because it provides powerful tools for creating textured bitmaps. It also sports a nice interface and a wide variety of SVGA formats (which is quite outdated now). Alas, Deluxe Paint II became more of a cult program to game designers than an everyday utility like the more popular PC Paintbrush. The .BBM format is an internal format used by Deluxe Paint II to save its files. The .BBM format differs from the .LBM format in that .BBM files are considered brushes by Deluxe Paint II, while .LBM files are treated as full-screen images. Other than that, the differences are minor. *ACK-3D* makes use of the .BBM format for images saved as 64x64 sized bitmaps. Not many other programs read these files; however, there are graphics file conversion programs that can convert this format to other formats, such as .PCX or .GIF.

.GIF files are hot these days. You can find them everywhere—especially if you use online services like CompuServe. And if you are a cyberspace explorer who is connected to the Internet (or the World Wide Web), you can't go anywhere without encountering a plethora of .GIF files.

.GIF stands for *graphics interchange file*. When it comes to data compression, they beat the pants off .PCX files. That's why they are so widely used in the online world. (The smaller the file, the faster it will download, and the less money you'll spend for online time.) Although .GIF files were originally designed to be just viewed by computers from different platforms—PCs, Macs, Amigas, UNIX machines, and so on—they have caught on with game developers, and many game development tools and engines now support them.

The big problem with using .GIF files in the game industry is the looming file format patent issues. It seems that the company that developed the encoding technology used in .GIF files received a patent years ago, and now they are coming after companies or individuals who include code in their applications that reads and processes .GIF files. The unfortunate thing is that many programs were written before any of the developers had knowledge of the patent, so they did not obtain proper permission or expect to have to pay royalties. As you might guess, this situation is creating a lot of confusion in the game market especially because a lot of games are distributed as shareware programs. In fact, the original version of *DOOM* was distributed as shareware—at least the first few episodes were. It makes no sense for shareware authors to have to pay royalties or license fees for programs that they give away.

My advice is to take the high road and be careful. I originally included a function in the *ACK-3D* engine to read .GIF files and convert them to the proper bitmap format that the engine requires. I've omitted this function with the code distributed with this book; however, all of the hooks are in the engine if you want to add this feature yourself. In the meantime, let's hope not too many lawyers get rich over this .GIF patent battle.

3-D Bitmap Creation 101

Here's the good news: you don't need to be a professional 3-D artist to create nice-looking animated scenes. You also don't need to be a 3-D animation expert. Your mission as a 3-D game designer is to create the 2-D bitmap building blocks that give the appearance of a 3-D scene when the building blocks are combined. Whether you are creating realistic looking walls with exotic textures or life-like animated objects that contain multiple sides for viewing, everything needs to be represented with little bitmap images that are only 64×64 pixels in size.

So how do you approach the craft of creating 3-D game components like walls and objects? There are many methods. In fact, every experienced game designer you ask will give you different advice. Some will tell you to build 3-D models, others will tell you to use animation software, and still others will tell you to play games like *DOOM* and copy everything they do because it's the latest craze. The best advice I can give is to experiment and be original. The hardest thing to do is be able to visualize an animated scene in 3-D and then represent it in two dimensions. Like playing the piano or mountain climbing, this is one of those activities you have to practice frequently to get good at it.

One way to start as a 3-D game designer is to build a 3-D model out of cardboard or other material you have laying around. This task will help you better visualize the 3-D world you want to create inside the computer. Once you have your model, draw little squares on the surfaces you've built. An example of this process is illustrated in Figure 12.2. The squares represent the places where bitmap images will be displayed. Once you have your model divided into bitmap sections, try to image what shapes and textures you'd like to display in each square. (If you are feeling really creative, you might even want to draw some of the bitmap patterns on your model.) One section of wall might be textured as if it were made out of bricks, while another wall might have a metal finish as if it were the side of a spaceship. You might even want to place a few windows in your walls. The goal at this stage is not to work out

Figure 12.2 *Building a model and dividing it into bitmap regions.*

every detail for your game map, but to help you conceptualize the relationship between bitmap images and textures and actual wall surfaces. Once you have bitmap images roughed out, you'll be ready to begin the drawing process. Well, almost ready—you still need to design the objects for your 3-D world.

Many game artists also like to use 3-D models to help them design their objects. For example, here's some advice I received recently from noted game designer Andrew Hunter. Andrew created the art for the *Slob Zone* game distributed with this book, and he's developed quite a reputation for creating characters in games that really have a unique look and interact with the player in very creative ways.

"The characters in *Slob Zone* weren't actually drawn by hand. They were sculpted and animated in clay and then digitized and colorized. Clay! Can you believe it? In this age of desktop super computing. By making them in clay I could easily grab all of the different views to help the player better experience the character. Not only did this approach make it easier for me to draw some eight different views of each pose but I had the coolest cast of characters hanging out on my desk for a couple of months. As you might guess, I was a hit with the local kids who come by our offices while I was building my models.

But as you are designing your game objects, keep in mind that clay isn't appropriate for all, or even most games. Early on, I created concept sketches of the characters I wanted to see in our game; they were quirky, kind of like Warner Bros. characters. If you took one look at them, you'd cringe at the thought of having to model them in 3-D. The look that we got from our characters by modeling them in clay was distinctive and fun. (I even tried putting a 3-D rendered robot vacuum cleaner in the game using the "clay" technique but he looked so out of place I ended up taking him out.)"

Clay is not the best medium for all situations because it does not lend itself to creating objects that look super clean with sharp edges. In many cases, you can get better results using an animation program like 3-D Studio. The one thing I missed from not animating our characters digitally was that after four or five frames of animation, the characters had to be pretty much resculpted. The distinctive "clay" look worked for *Slob Zone*, but if you are after a different look, you should experiment with other techniques, such as digital animation."

If you haven't taken the time to play the *Slob Zone* game included on the companion CD-ROM, I suggest you do so now. Take a close look at how the objects are drawn and how they interact with the player. In some cases, it's hard to believe that they were created with simple 64x64 pixel building blocks. Andrew Hunter and Ken Lemieux, the chief software designer of *Slob Zone*, went through some artistic and programming loops to bring *this game to life*. If this game doesn't inspire your creative juices, I don't know what will!

The biggest challenge in creating bitmaps for objects is deciding how you want the object to look as the player moves around the object. If your object is complex, you could need a number of separate bitmap images to represent the object. The best way I've found to create objects is to keep them very simple in the beginning; draw only the basic bitmaps you need, and then test the objects in your game. You'll often know right away if they'll work. Once you've tested them, you can always invest more time and draw more bitmaps and add more views to perfect them. Think of this approach as if you're writing code—get the basic algorithm working and then go in and optimize and refine everything.

Drawing Bitmap Images

To create the actual bitmap images for your walls and objects, you'll need a painting program that creates .PCX or .BBM files. Whatever painting program you use, you must define the size of each bitmap image to be 64¥64 pixels. Most painting programs provide a menu command for setting image size attributes. Even a simple painting program like Windows Paintbrush allows you to define the size of your images by using the Image Attributes dialog box as shown in Figure 12.3.

One approach you might want to adopt for creating bitmaps that will be used together as a group (such is in a wall) is to draw all of the bitmaps together, side-by-side. As an example, Figure 12.4 shows the set of bitmaps I

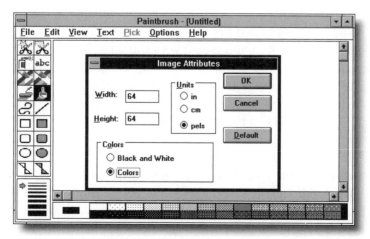

Figure 12.3 *Using Windows Paintbrush to define a 64x64 pixel image.*

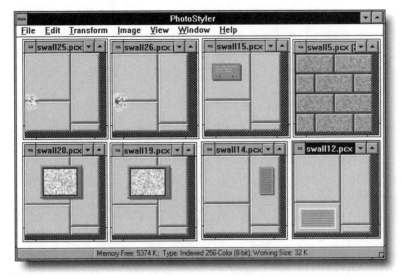

Figure 12.4 *The bitmap set used to define some of the walls in* Station Escape.

used to create the walls in an early version of my *Station Escape* game. Notice that many of the wall bitmaps are similar to each other. By drawing them together, you can create a master bitmap, cut and paste it, and then edit it slightly to create a variation. This technique can save you a lot of time. In addition, it will help you to create bitmaps for wall sections that should look like they are all part of one family. Once you have finished with a group of bitmaps, you can copy and paste each one to a new window that is set up to represent a 64×64 pixel bitmap and save it.

When you draw bitmaps as 64×64 pixel building blocks, you are dealing with very small images. When they are displayed in your game, on the other hand, they will appear much larger, especially whenever a player gets close to an object or wall that is created from the bitmap. You should always keep this sense of scale in mind when you create your bitmaps. In fact, I find this issue one of the hardest things to get used to when I design my games.

When a designer creates a bitmap as a 64×64 pixel image like the ones shown in Figure 12.5, he or she typically tries to put in as much detail as possible. Of course, this is difficult to do because of the few pixels available to work with. But what is important isn't just how the bitmap looks at its 1:1 scale, but how it will look when it is magnified. As you draw your bitmap, you should zoom in on it to make sure that it still looks good. If you don't have enough detail in the bitmap, it may look very "grainy" when it is rescaled. On the other hand, if you have too much detail, some of the detail will be lost when the player is far away from the wall or object created from the bitmap.

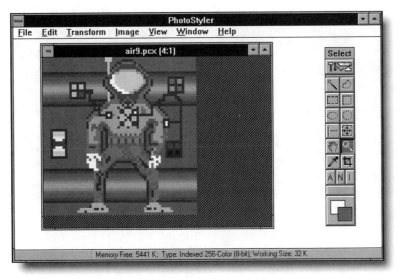

Figure 12.5 *Viewing a bitmap by zooming in.*

But no matter how much designing, scaling, and editing you do with your bitmap drawing program, there's no substitute for spending a lot of time testing your objects in an actual game. As you design your objects, it's difficult to visualize and anticipate all of the interactions that may occur.

Tips on Designing Your Own Bitmaps

When it comes to designing bitmaps for your game, you can really let your creativity go wild. Don't just settle for the same old bitmap images you see in every other 3-D, maze-type game. Here are some tips to help you start designing your own bitmaps. First, we'll discuss some ideas for drawing wall bitmaps and then we'll explore object bitmaps.

- **Design your wall bitmaps to be as modular as possible.** Remember that each wall bitmap you create is a 64x64 pixel building block that will be used to create entire walls. By taking a modular design approach, you'll be able to use your wall building blocks over and over to create nice-looking walls. You'll be surprised at the number of wall variations you can make with just a few bitmaps.

  One way to help you get in the modular wall building block mindset is to use your painting program to draw an entire wall section that is much larger than a 64x64 bitmap. An example is shown in Figure 12.6. Next, look at the image and see if you can find ways to arrange it with as few 64x64 squares as possible. This approach will help you see how

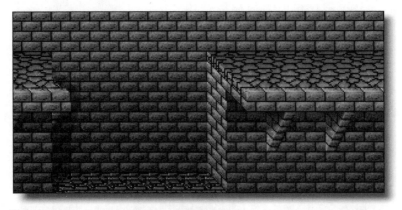

Figure 12.6   *Drawing a wall section as a larger bitmap.*

bitmap sections come together to create a complete wall in the micro world. That's how the shuttle bay was designed in *Station Escape*. By tying three bitmaps together, I was able to create a very wide-looking shuttle bay door, complete with animated stars!

- **Use textures—they're cheap.** One way to create attractive-looking walls is to use textures in your walls. Textures can really help to give your games a 3-D look. Standard fare here includes stone, brick, marble, metal, glass, wood, and so on. Many of the newer painting programs provide libraries or tools to help you create textures even if you are not an experienced artist.

  Try to experiment with different textures. Don't just make all of your walls like brick walls. For example, you can create walls that look like chain link fences, as shown in Figure 12.7. You can also design wall bitmaps to look like embedded objects such as paintings or bookshelves so that your walls will have some variation. The nice thing about textures is that they don't require any more storage space. A highly textured bitmap is still 64×64 pixels—the same size as a flat looking bitmap.

- **Be a trend setter.** Many of the 3-D games on the market look the same. They are dark and the graphics (walls) are very predictable—typically bricks or stone. Some of this has to do with the fact that most game designers are caught up in the trap of trying to make their games look and feel like *DOOM* because of its popularity. Don't get me wrong, I think *DOOM* is a great game and has a great design. But *DOOM* is *DOOM* and you want to strive to develop your own style.

  If you really let your imagination soar, you can come up with many unique ways of representing walls. One of my all-time favorites is shown in Figure 12.8. Here the designers of *Slob Zone* created wall bitmaps that

Figure 12.7 *Creating a wall that looks like a chain link fence.*

Figure 12.8 *Creating walls that look like the sides of a bus.*

look like the sides of a bus. They came up with an ingenious method of representing certain types of objects that were much larger than the 64×64 objects supported by *ACK-3D*. This method gives players the feeling that they are outdoors walking around in a true 3-D world. Because the *ACK-3D* engine easily lets you create transparent walls, you can represent all kinds of real-world objects as wall bitmaps that the player can move around. Here are some examples:

- An tunnel entrance
- A banner that goes across a street
- A window in a building
- Any type of fence (rope, wood, cable, chain-link)
- Bars for a cage or prison cell
- A mesh screen

- **Don't skimp on colors.** You don't have to make your bitmaps look like scenes from yet another dungeon or cave. You can create wall bitmaps to take your player into other settings such as outdoors, a building with lots of windows, or an art gallery. Experiment by varying the colors that you use to draw your bitmaps. Although only 256 colors can be used at one time, you can move your player into different settings and change the color palette before displaying new bitmaps. By using different colors, you'll give your games a more real-world look and feel.

- **Get an artist to help when you need one.** If you were building a house for your family, you probably wouldn't try to do everything yourself. You might try to design the house on your own, or if you are handy with woodwork, you might build some of the cabinets or the redwood deck in the back yard. However, unless you are a trained builder with lots of experience, you probably wouldn't have all the skills you'd need and you're bound to mess some things up; I know I would!

  This advice also goes for designing games. You don't need to be an artist to create bitmaps, especially if you have one of the powerful painting programs to work with like Deluxe Paint II. However, good artists have that unique way of seeing and drawing things so that they really come to life. One way I like to work is to create my own rough bitmaps and then show them to an artist to get some feedback. Usually, the artist will come back with a few ideas that really make the bitmaps pop out. And sometimes, the artist will come up with an idea that is so much better than my own that I find myself going back to the drawing board. If you want your game to look great, always be on the look-out for design tips from good artists.

- **Design some bitmaps with animation in mind.** Don't hesitate to put a little action in your bitmaps. As you walk around in the *Station Escape* game, supplied on the CD-ROM, notice the portholes and computer screens along the walls. They are constantly animating, either by showing different star patterns or screens full of static. These details were added to give a more realistic effect. When you draw multiple bitmaps, each just slightly different from the other, you can create all kinds of exciting animation effects, at a very small cost in programming and performance.

We've been discussing design tips for creating wall bitmaps, but what about objects? In general, most of the ideas we discussed apply to object bitmaps as well. But there are some specific design tips you'll want to keep in mind as you design the objects for your game:

- **Design your object bitmaps for maximum contrast.** You don't want your objects to simply fade into your walls. If your walls are dark, you can use a brightly colored object to make it stand out.

- **Use objects that fit into your scenes.** Don't put in objects just to dazzle your player. Make sure that they are there for a reason or that they are relevant to the scene the player is in. For example, if your players are moving around in an ancient castle, it's unlikely that they would run into a modern looking computer table.

- **Give your objects realism by using multiple views.** Take advantage of the support that *ACK-3D* provides for defining objects with multiple views. As you design an object, try to model it in some way to help you visualize what the object will look like as a player moves around it. Make drawings of each of the views and then turn your drawings into bitmaps.

Loading and Processing Bitmaps—Getting under the Hood

The *ACK-3D* code that performs the work of loading and processing bitmaps is found in ACKLDBMP.C. Most of the functions in this file, such as **AckLoadBitmap()**, **AckLoadWall()**, and **AckLoadObject()**, can be called from your applications. The two other files needed to perform the actual work of reading bitmap data from a file are ACKGIFF.C and ACKPCX.C. These files contain the functions for reading .BBM and .PCX files, respectively. We'll look at how some of this code operates shortly, but first let's revisit how bitmap data is stored and processed.

Bitmap Data In—Bitmap Data Out

If you read a .PCX or .BMP file into a editor that allows you to view the actual data that is stored, you'd find a series of numeric values or bitmap codes. Each value in the file represents a pixel color to light up the image on the screen. The file would also contain color palette information for the pixel data to be displayed. In this sense, a bitmap file is a self-contained unit.

To process and display bitmaps, *ACK-3D* needs to read in the raw data and store it in special data structures. Eventually the bitmap data for walls is assigned to the array

```
unsigned char *bMaps[MAX_WALLBMPS]
```

in the **ACKENG** interface structure. The bitmap data for objects is assigned to:

```
unsigned char *oMaps[MAX_OBJBMPS];
```

Both of these data structures are actually simple arrays that store pointers to the bitmap data. Each array may contain up to 256 pointers. The bitmap data itself is stored in memory as a sequence of bytes. But as it is read from a bitmap file, some special processing needs to be performed to make the bitmap data easily accessible.

The bitmap data read is represented in a row-order format. As shown in Figure 12.9, the first set of bitmap codes represents the first row of pixels on the screen, the next set of codes represents the second pixel row, and so on. This format is ideal for programs that display images for viewing or editing, but it is not well suited for the processing that needs to be done with the engine. A better representation is to convert the data so that it is in a column-order format as shown in Figure 12.10. Internally, the image would appear as if it has been rotated 90 degrees. But when the image is displayed, it does not appear rotated. (If it were, your player would really think he or she is in a funhouse.) This column-order format just makes it much easier for us to per-

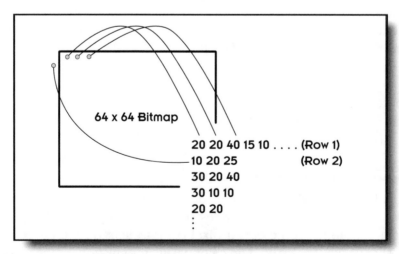

Figure 12.9   *The row-order format of data stored in a bitmap file.*

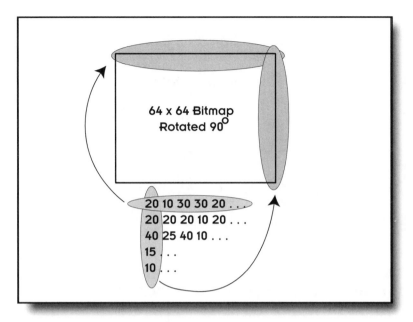

Figure 12.10 *Representing bitmap data in a column-order format.*

form ray casting and build up slice structures. Keep in mind that when the bitmap data is eventually displayed, some bitmaps, such as wall bitmaps, need to be combined with other bitmaps, such as object bitmaps, to give the player the sense that an object is in front of a wall.

Internal Representation of Bitmap Data

You now know that bitmap data is stored internally in a column order format. Is there any other processing that is done? After the bitmap data is read, some additional information is added to the bitmap data. Let's take a look.

Figure 12.11 shows exactly what is stored in memory. The majority of the data consists of values from 0 to 255 to represent one pixel color. Notice that it takes 4,096 bytes to store the bitmap codes (64 columns × 64 rows). But if you look closely at Figure 12.11, you'll see that we've added another row of data. This data stores flags to indicate if a particular column of the bitmap contains all transparent colors. If all of the colors in a column are transparent, the flag is set to a value of 1; otherwise it is set to 0.

By storing these flags, we'll be able to draw the bitmap much quicker. As the bitmap is loaded, each column is tested and the flag is set accordingly. When the bitmap is drawn, a column is skipped if its associated transparent flag is set.

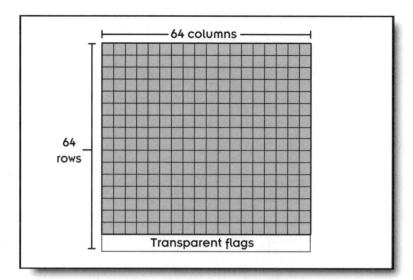

Figure 12.11 *How bitmap data is stored internally with* ACK-3D.

DESIGN TIP

Using the transparent flags with the bitmap is another one of those optimization tricks that can really help to speed up the drawing of your 3-D views. The idea is to off-load time-intensive processing tasks during the initialization stage, so that data can be processed and displayed as quickly as possible when scenes are updated and displayed. The real art of creating a powerful engine like *ACK-3D* is to constantly be on the look-out for ways to optimize your techniques. When you display your bitmaps, you'll need every spare processing cycle you can get your hands on!

The Art of Loading Bitmaps

Now that you know how bitmaps are stored by the engine, let's look at how they are loaded. *ACK-3D* provides two main functions for loading bitmaps: **AckLoadWall()** and **AckLoadObject()**. As their names suggest, one loads a bitmap for a wall section and the other loads a bitmap for an object section. They are both high-level functions that you can call from your applications. As shown here, they simply set up parameters and call **AckLoadBitmap()**, which is the real bitmap loading workhorse:

```
short AckLoadWall(ACKENG *ae,short WallNumber,char *bmFileName)
{
return( AckLoadBitmap(ae,WallNumber,TYPE_WALL,bmFileName) );
}
```

```
short AckLoadObject(ACKENG *ae,short BmpNumber,char *bmFileName)
{
return( AckLoadBitmap(ae,BmpNumber,TYPE_OBJECT,bmFileName) );
}
```

Both of these functions take the following parameters:

ae	Interface structure
BitmapNumber	A value from 1 to 255 that specifies the bitmap number
bmFileName	Name of bitmap file to read or the index into the opened resource file

Essentially, these functions make sure that **AckLoadBitmap()** is called with the correct flag setting—**TYPE_WALL** or **TYPE_OBJECT**. If you want, you can also call **AckLoadBitmap()** directly from your applications.

DESIGN TIP

In order for the *ACK-3D* engine to know the type of bitmap files you want to load, you can set the **bmLoadType** field in the **ACKENG** interface structure. This field can be set to one of two flags: **BMLOAD_BBM** or **BMLOAD_PCX**. As an example, here's how you tell the engine you want to load .PCX files:

```
ACKENG ae;
ae.bmLoadType = BMLOAD_PCX;
```

When a function such as **AckLoadWall()** is called the engine checks the setting of the **bmLoadType** field to determine the type of bitmap data that needs to be processed.

Inside AckLoadBitmap()

Let's take a closer look at **AckLoadBitmap()** so that you can see what tasks are performed to load in a bitmap. If a bitmap file is passed as a parameter, the function checks the file extension to determine which type of file needs to be read. This operation is performed by calling the **GetExtent()** function, which is defined in ACKLDBMP.C. If the file has a .BBM extension, **AckReadiff()** is called to read in a Deluxe Paint II image. If the file has a .PCX extension, **AckReadPCX()** is called. Each of these functions reads in the bitmap file and stores the raw data in a buffer, where the first two bytes of the buffer include the size information for the width and height of the bitmap. Here's an example of how one of these calls is made within **AckLoadBitmap()**:

```
if (ae->bmLoadType == BMLOAD_PCX) // Read in PCX bitmap
  buf = AckReadPCX(BitmapName);
```

The bitmap data read is stored in a temporary buffer called **buf**. After the data has been read, the buffer needs to be checked to make sure that it is the correct size. If it isn't, an error is returned.

At this stage, the buffer stores the bitmap's width and height information in its first two bytes if the bitmap data is read by calling **AckReadiff()** or **AckReadPCX()**. What we need to do is allocate memory for the actual bitmap data buffer and then transfer one buffer to the other, skipping over the width and height information. The new buffer is allocated with this code:

```
bmp = AckMalloc(bLen);  // Allocate memory for bitmap
if (bmp == NULL)
  {
  AckFree(buf);
  return(ERR_NOMEMORY);
  }
```

Notice that I've included critical error checking code whenever memory is allocated. If the test fails, any buffers that are currently allocated are released and an error code is returned. The memory allocated for the actual bitmap buffer, **bmp**, is calculated as:

```
bLen = BITMAP_SIZE + BITMAP_WIDTH;
```

This calculation gives us room for an extra row of data so that the transparent flags can be stored. Once the memory has been allocated, the bitmap buffer is assigned to the **ACKENG** interface structure:

```
if (BitmapType == TYPE_WALL)// Process a wall bitmap
  { // Store the wall bitmap in the interface structure
  ae->bMaps[BitmapNumber] = bmp;
  }

if (BitmapType == TYPE_OBJECT)// Process an object bitmap
  { // Store the object bitmap in the interface structure
  ae->oMaps[BitmapNumber] = bmp;
  }
```

Recall that **BitmapNumber** is the parameter passed into **AckLoadBitmap()**, which specifies the number for the bitmap. This is how we assign bitmap data to a bitmap ID.

The last two steps involve rotating the data 90 degrees and adding the transparent flags. The bitmap data is easy to rotate by using a nested **for** loop:

```
// Convert format of bitmap by rotating it 90 degrees
for (y = 0; y < BITMAP_HEIGHT; y++)
```

```
{
sPos = y;
dPos = y * BITMAP_WIDTH;
for (x = 0; x < BITMAP_WIDTH; x++)
  {
  ch = buf[sPos];
  bmp[dPos++] = ch;
  sPos += BITMAP_WIDTH;
  }
}
```

The outer loop counts through the columns and the inner loop counts through the rows. Now you can see why we need the temporary buffer, **buf**. With each iteration of the loop, pixel data is transferred from **buf** to **bmp**. Again, we're not that concerned with speed at this stage, so the above routine was not optimized. I just coded it as one of those utility type routines to get the job done.

Once the data has been rotated, it's time to add in the transparent flags, which is accomplished by using another **for** loop. But first, we need to get access to the location where the flags are to be stored and then set the memory area to all 0s:

```
bmpFlags = &bmp[BITMAP_SIZE];    // Get address of end of bitmap
memset(bmpFlags,0,BITMAP_WIDTH);// Clear one row with 0s

// Check each column of pixels in the bitmap to see
// if it is transparent
for (x = 0; x < BITMAP_WIDTH; x++)
  {
  if (!BlankSlice(x,bmp)) // Transparent column is found
    bmpFlags[x] = 1;    // Mark transparent columns
  }
```

The loop checks each column of the bitmap by calling **BlankSlice()**. This function checks to see if the column contains all 0s. If it does, it returns 0. Whenever this happens, the loop sets the transparent data flag to 1.

And there you have it—everything you want to know about loading bitmaps, well, almost everything. To see what really goes on behind the curtain, we need to drop down a level and explore how a bitmap file is read. Let's focus on .PCX files since they are the most popular.

PCX File Support

In the world of PC bitmap graphics and graphics file formats, you won't find another file format that is as popular as .PCX. Just about every painting program on the market supports .PCX files, and game programmers cannot seem to live without them. As I mentioned earlier, one of the reasons that .PCX files are so popular is that they are really easy to work with.

To help you read in bitmaps from .PCX files, the *ACK-3D* engine provides the function **AckReadPCX()**, which is defined in the file ACKPCX.C. This function reads in image data from a specified file or from an opened resource file. For example, if you call this function from your application

```
pcxbuf = AckReadPCX("REDWALL.PCX");
```

the file REDWALL.PCX will be read in and the bitmap data will be returned to the variable **pcxbuf**. **AckReadPCX()** performs some special processing to put the bitmap data found in the .PCX file into a format that can be used by the engine. You'll see what needs to be done shortly. But first let's take a close look at what is inside a .PCX file.

Getting Inside .PCX Files

How is data stored in a .PCX file and how do we read one? As shown in Figure 12.12, a .PCX file is arranged in three sections: a *header block*, an *image data block*, and a *color palette data block*. The header block is always 128 bytes, no matter if the .PCX image data is large or small. The header block contains

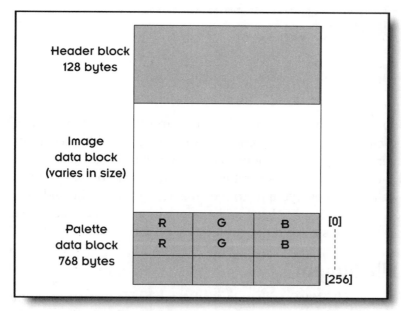

Figure 12.12   *The structure of a .PCX file.*

information such as the number of bits used per pixel to represent the image data, the width and height of the image, the resolution of the image, and so on.

The image data block contains the raw data for the bitmap. The size of this section varies depending on the resolution, size, and compression of the image. The nice feature about .PCX images is that image data can be compressed somewhat by using an encoding scheme, which we'll explore in the next section. No matter how the image data is encoded, however, the data is stored in standard row order. That is, the first set of pixels stored corresponds to the first row of pixels to be displayed on the screen, and so on. (As we learned earlier, the *ACK-3D* engine always needs to rotate this image data to be in a column-first order instead of a row-first order to quickly display the pixel data.)

The last section, the palette data block, is 768 bytes. This section is optional, although .PCX files created for 256-color Mode 13h always contain a color palette. Here you'll find the data for the red, green, and blue components for each color in the 256 color palette that is used to display the image.

PCX Data Encoding

Like other graphics file formats, .PCX files use a system of data encoding to keep stored information as compact as possible. Think about it. If you have a .PCX file that contains data for a full-screen image in VGA Mode 13h, the file would need to store 64,000 pixels for an image that has a resolution of 320×200 pixels. Each pixel can be set to a value from 0 to 255, so 64,000 bytes would be required to store the file. That's one big file! And when it comes to bitmap images and 3-D games, bigger is definitely not better.

To reduce the overhead of storing bitmaps, the designers of the PCX format incorporated an encoding scheme called *run-length encoding* or *RLE* that takes into account that many images contain similar image data. At the extreme, a bitmap image could be one solid color, which means that every pixel stored in the file would have the same value. So why store every pixel in such a case?

RLE comes to the rescue and reduces the overhead of storing adjacent pixels that have the same color value by combining them, as shown in Figure 12.13. The trick here involves grouping the pixels of the same color and then including a counter. For example, the image in Figure 12.13 contains a band of a red color of value 30. Instead of storing the color as a stream of 30s, two values are stored:

```
10 30
```

Here, the first value (10) indicates the number of adjacent pixels in a row having the same color—in this case the color value 30.

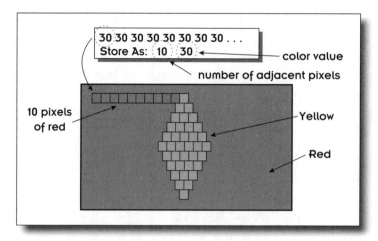

Figure 12.13   *Using run-length encoding to store a .PCX image.*

When a .PCX file is stored using run-length encoding, every row of pixels must be stored using pairs (*counter, color value*). The big drawback with this scheme is that images that do not have many adjacent colors could actually get bigger because the counter data must be stored even if two adjacent pixels are not the same color. For example, if an image had a row of pixels that started with color values

```
20 24 27 23 20 21 23 24 24
```

the data would actually be stored as

```
1 20 1 24 1 27 1 23 1 20 1 21 1 23 2 24
```

where a counter value of 1 is needed for adjacent pixels having different color values.

As you are reading the description of how the RLE scheme works, you're probably wondering how the code that reads in the image data can decipher the difference between a counter value and a color value. After all, color values can be stored in the range 0 to 255. The trick is to encode counter values so that they can be detected. This encoding scheme works as follows:

- Any value read in from 0 to 191 is treated as a color value.
- The value 192 is added to counter values so that we know that any value in the range 192 to 255 is an RLE counter. To get the counter, we subtract 192 from the value (or "**and**" the value with 3Fh). For example, a value of 200 specifies a counter of 8 (200-192).

Reading .PCX Files

Now that we know how .PCX files are arranged, let's create the function to read them. First, we need a data structure to store the .PCX data. Our structure has components to hold each of the three sections of the .PCX file. In addition, a few fields are added to store image size information:

```
typedef struct
{
  PcxHeader hdr;      // Header information
  UCHAR *bitmap;      // The bitmap data
  UCHAR pal[768];     // Color palette for the bitmap data
  unsigned short imagebytes,width,height; // Size of the bitmap
} PcxFile;
```

The image size information, **width**, **height**, and **imagebytes** (total number of bytes to store the bitmap image) will be used after the image data is read in and needs to be processed.

To store the header data, we'll need another structure named **PcxHeader**:

```
typedef struct
{
  char  manufacturer;   // Always set to 0
  char  version;        // Always 5 for 256-color files
  char  encoding;       // Always set to 1
  char  bits_per_pixel; // Should be 8 for 256-color files
  short xmin,ymin;      // Coordinates for top-left corner
  short xmax,ymax;      // Width and height of image
  short hres;           // Horizontal resolution of image
  short vres;           // Vertical resolution of image
  char  palette16[48];  // EGA palette; not used for 256-color files
  char  reserved;       // Reserved for future use
  char  color_planes;   // Color planes
  short bytes_per_line; // Number of bytes in one line of pixels
  short palette_type;   // Should be 2 for color palette
  char  filler[58];     // Reserved
} PcxHeader;
```

The process for reading in a .PCX file with **AckReadPCX()** involves the following steps:

1. Open the .PCX file or use the .PCX filename to access the opened resource file. (.PCX files can be combined with the resource file we introduced in the previous chapter.)

2. Read in the header data and store it in the **PcxHeader** structure.

3. Calculate the **width**, **height**, and **imagebytes** fields using the header information that was read in.

4. Make sure that the size of the image data does not exceed the maximum size allowed. The maximum number of pixels required for a 320×200 256-color bitmap is 64,000 bytes.

5. Read in the image data and store it in a buffer. This is where the RLE decompression is performed.

6. Read in the color palette data and store it in the **colordat[]** array. This array is used internally by the *ACK-3D* engine; however, it can also be treated as a *global* variable for use by the application.

7. Close the opened .PCX file if a file is used instead of a resource.

8. Add the width and height values to the beginning of the bitmap buffer. These values are used by the **AckLoadBitmap()** function to determine the size of a bitmap.

9. Return the buffer that contains the bitmap data.

As you can see, most of the processing that is done is standard fare for reading in a .PCX file. However, a few tasks are needed to prepare the bitmap data read in for the *ACK-3D* engine. For example, the bitmap buffer returned contains four bytes at the beginning to indicate the width and height of the bitmap. Recall that this data is used by **AckLoadBitmap()** to rotate the bitmap 90 degrees. The **width**, **height**, and **imagesize** components are calculated by first reading in the header data and then using a few of the fields, as shown here:

```
fread(&pcx->hdr,sizeof(PcxHeader),1,f);   // Read in the header data
pcx->width=1+pcx->hdr.xmax-pcx->hdr.xmin; // Store width and height
pcx->height=1+pcx->hdr.ymax-pcx->hdr.ymin;
// Store number of bytes used for image
pcx->imagebytes=(unsigned int)(pcx->width*pcx->height);
```

The other noteworthy part of the code is the loop used to read in the image data. This is the place where .PCX bitmap data is read in, decompressed using RLE, and stored in a buffer. By using a system of toggling between two modes, **NORMAL** and **RLE**, the code can uncompress the data using only one loop. (This is the kind of programming I like—fast, clean, and clever.) Here's the entire loop:

```
for (i=0;i<pcx->imagebytes;i++)
  {
  if(mode == NORMAL)  // Normal color read mode
    {
    abyte=fgetc(f);                    // Read in pixel value from file
    if ((unsigned char)abyte > 0xbf)   // Value read > 191
      {
```

```
      nbytes=abyte & 0x3f;   // Get the RLE counter
      abyte=fgetc(f);
      if (-nbytes > 0)       // Is counter is greater than 1?
        mode=RLE;            // Yes, we're in RLE mode
      }
    }
  else if (-nbytes == 0)     // Counter is down to 0
    mode=NORMAL;             // Return to color read mode
  *p++=abyte;                // Store pixel value
  }
```

When **mode** is set to **NORMAL**, the code reads the .PCX data stream and
checks to see if the value read in is greater than 191. If so, we could have a
counter on our hands. The counter value is stored in **nbytes** and then the
color value is read. If the counter read is greater than 1, the **mode** flag is set
to **RLE**. Next time around, the **if** clause of the loop is skipped and the pixel
data is placed in the buffer, which is referenced by ***p**. The counter continues
to count down until the particular run is completed.

Here's the complete source file for ACKPCX.C:

```
// This source file contains the functions needed to read in .PCX files.
// (c) 1995 ACK Software (Lary Myers)
#include <windows.h>
#include <stdio.h>
#include <stdlib.h>
#include <string.h>
#include <time.h>
#include <dos.h>
//typedef unsigned short USHORT;
#include "ack3d.h"      // Main ACK-3D internal and interface data structures
#include "ackeng.h"     // Internal data structures and constants
#include "ackext.h"     // Defines external (global) variables

typedef struct
{
  char  manufacturer;   // Always set to 0
  char  version;        // Always 5 for 256-color files
  char  encoding;       // Always set to 1
  char  bits_per_pixel; // Should be 8 for 256-color files
  short xmin,ymin;      // Coordinates for top-left corner
  short xmax,ymax;      // Width and height of image
  short hres;           // Horizontal resolution of image
  short vres;           // Vertical resolution of image
  char  palette16[48];  // EGA palette; not used for 256-color files
  char  reserved;       // Reserved for future use
  char  color_planes;   // Color planes
  short bytes_per_line; // Number of bytes in 1 line of pixels
  short palette_type;   // Should be 2 for color palette
  char  filler[58];     // Reserved
} PcxHeader;
```

```
typedef struct
{
    PcxHeader hdr;          // Header information
    UCHAR *bitmap;          // The bitmap data
    UCHAR pal[768];         // Color palette for the bitmap data
    unsigned short imagebytes,width,height; // Size of the bitmap
} PcxFile;

#define PCX_MAX_SIZE 64000L
enum {PCX_OK,PCX_NOMEM,PCX_TOOBIG,PCX_NOFILE};
enum {NORMAL,RLE};
//enum {FALSE,TRUE};
PcxFile pcxGlobal;     // Data structure for reading PCX files
extern unsigned char colordat[];


//=============================================================================
//  This routine loads a 256 color .PCX file. The file can be a standalone
// .PCX file or it can be combined with a resource. If the data is part
// of a resource, the rshandle flag will be set. The bitmap data is read
// into a buffer that is the size of the bitmap + 4 bytes. The first 4
// bytes in the buffer contain the width and height of the bitmap.
//=============================================================================
unsigned char *AckReadPCX(char *filename)
{
    long i;
    int mode=NORMAL,nbytes;
    char abyte,*p;
    FILE *f;
    PcxFile *pcx;

pcx = &pcxGlobal;
// Open the file since no resource is open
if (!rsHandle)
  {
  f=fopen(filename,"rb"); // Open the file for reading
  if (f==NULL)  // Make sure file is opened
    {
    ErrorCode = ERR_BADFILE;
    return NULL;
    }
  }
else  // Use the resource instead
  {
  f = fdopen (rsHandle, "rb");
  if (f == NULL)  // Make sure the resource is opened
    {
    ErrorCode = ERR_BADPICNAME;
    return (0L);
    }
  // Move to the location in the resource where the data is stored
  fseek (f, rbaTable[(ULONG) filename], SEEK_SET);
  }
fread(&pcx->hdr,sizeof(PcxHeader),1,f);   // Read in the header data
pcx->width=1+pcx->hdr.xmax-pcx->hdr.xmin; // Store width and height
```

```
pcx->height=1+pcx->hdr.ymax-pcx->hdr.ymin;
// Store number of bytes used for image
pcx->imagebytes=(unsigned int)(pcx->width*pcx->height);
// Make sure bitmap is correct size
if (pcx->imagebytes > PCX_MAX_SIZE)
  {
  if (!rsHandle)
    fclose(f);
  ErrorCode = ERR_INVALIDFORM;
  return(NULL);
  }
// Allocate size for bitmap; four extra bytes are included to give
// room to store bitmap width and height info
pcx->bitmap=(char*)AckMalloc(pcx->imagebytes+4);
if (pcx->bitmap == NULL)  // Make sure memory is allocated
  {
  if (!rsHandle)
    fclose(f);
  ErrorCode = ERR_NOMEMORY;
  return(NULL);
  }
p=&pcx->bitmap[4];    // Get address of data area
// Loop and read in pixel data for bitmap
// Uses RLE decompression
for (i=0;i<pcx->imagebytes;i++)
  {
  if(mode == NORMAL)  // Normal color read mode
    {
    abyte=fgetc(f);   // Read in pixel value from file
    if ((unsigned char)abyte > 0xbf)// Value read > 191
      {
      nbytes=abyte & 0x3f;  // Get the RLE counter abyte=fgetc(f);
      if (-nbytes > 0)      // Is counter is greate than 1?
        mode=RLE;          // Yes, we're in RLE mode
      }
    }
  else if (-nbytes == 0)   // Counter is down to 0
      mode=NORMAL;         // Return to color read mode
  *p++=abyte;              // Store pixel value
  }
fseek(f,-768L,SEEK_END); // Get palette from .PCX file
fread(colordat,768,1,f); // Read in palette data and store in colordat[]
p=colordat;
for (i=0;i<768;i++) // Bit shift palette
  *p++=*p >>2;
if (!rsHandle)  // Close .PCX file if one is opened
  fclose(f);
// Add in bitmap width and height to first 4 bytes of buffer
p = pcx->bitmap;
(*(short *)p) = pcx->width;
p += sizeof(short);
(*(short *)p) = pcx->height;
return(pcx->bitmap);   // Return bitmap buffer }
// **** End of Source ****
```

.GIF File Support

Because of the popularity of .GIF files, many game developers use this file format for creating bitmap images, and as I mentioned earlier in this chapter, I originally included a function to read .GIF files. The function operates like the **AckReadPCX()** function we just explored. To read in a .GIF file, you could call the GIF-specific function from your application as:

```
gifbuf = AckReadgif("REDWALL.GIF");
```

This function *is not* included with the *ACK-3D* engine provided with this book. If you want to have support for .GIF files, you can code your own version of **AckReadgif()**. I suggest that you put this function in a file named ACKGIF.C (this is how I had it set up). All of the other hooks are in place so that you can use .GIF files with the *ACK-3D* engine. Good luck, and once again, let's hope the patent issue gets resolved soon.

.BBM File Support

The original version of the *ACK-3D* engine supported Deluxe Paint II enhanced brush files (.BBM). Many game designers still use this program to create their artwork, so I've continued to support it. The function provided for loading in a Deluxe Paint II image from your applications is **AckReadiff()**. Here's an example of how you can use it:

```
bbmbuf = AckReadiff("REDWALL.BBM");
```

The code for this function is found in the source file ACKIFF.C. I won't cover the format of the Deluxe Paint II files in this book, but you can look over the code if you want to see how .BBM files are read and processed.

Setting Up Objects

AckCreateObject(), **AckSetObjectType()**, and **AckSetupObject()**—the remaining functions in ACKLDBMP.C—are needed to allocate memory for objects and set them up by initializing data fields in the **NEWOBJECT** structure.

Recall that objects in *ACK-3D* can be either stationary or movable depending on your needs. Both object types are handled exactly the same; stationary ones just never change location. Objects can share bitmaps if needed and can have more than one bitmap to accomplish different tasks. If the object has multiple bitmaps, it can either stay in one spot and display the bitmaps in sequence (this animates the object) or it can use multiple bitmaps to show the player different views of the object as the player moves around it.

Here are the basic steps you need to follow to create an object:

1. Load any bitmaps associated with the object by calling **AckLoadBitmap()** or **AckLoadObject()**.
2. Call **AckCreateObject()** to allocate memory for a **NEWOBJECT** data structure for the object being created. This function allocates memory for the object and assigns the object to the list of objects (**ObjList**) kept by the **ACKENG** interface structure.
3. Specify the object attributes such as object speed and any flags such as **OF_PASSABLE** or **OF_ANIMATE**.

To show you how these steps are performed, here's a simple function that defines a few objects:

```
int AppSetupObjects(void)
{
  int result;
  OBJSEQ  os;

result = 0;

result = AckCreateObject(ae,1); // Create first object
if (result)
  return(result);
ae->ObjList[1]->Dir = 0;
ae->ObjList[1]->Speed = 0;

result = AckCreateObject(ae,2); // Create second object
if (result)
  return(result);
ae->ObjList[2]->Dir = 0;
ae->ObjList[2]->Speed = 0;

// Set up object sequence for object #1
os.bmBitmapsPerView = 1;
os.flags = 0;
os.MaxBitmaps = 1;
os.bmSides = 1;
os.bitmaps[0] = 1;
result = AckSetupObject(ae,1,NO_WALK,&os);
if (result)
  return(result);

// Set up object sequence for object #2
os.bitmaps[0] = 2;
result = AckSetupObject(ae,2,NO_WALK,&os);
return(result);
}
```

Defining Object Sequences

The sample code in **AppSetupObject()** also performs a task we haven't discussed yet—it sets up an object sequence for each object. Recall that each object you create with *ACK-3D* can have five different sequences. The sequences are listed in Table 12.1 along with the labels that are used to define the sequence.

The way you actually use these sequences is completely up to your application. They are provided so that you easily toggle an object between different states. Essentially, the sequence consists of a data structure that stores bitmaps for the particular sequence, as well as information concerning the number of views the object has for the sequence and the number of bitmaps used to display each view.

To set up a sequence, you need to declare a sequence structure in your program as shown here:

```
OBJSEQ  os;
```

Then assign values to the sequence structure and call the **AckSetupObject()** function to set up the sequence. The format for calling this function is:

```
short AckSetupObject(ACKENG *ae,short oNum,short oType,OBJSEQ *os)
```

Here **ae* is a pointer to the interface structure, **oNum** specifies the object number being set up, **oType** specifies the sequence type (**NO_WALK**, **NO_CREATE**, and so on), and ***os** specifies the pointer to the object sequence structure. This function essentially copies the data stored in the object sequence into the main object structure so that this data will be used when the object is displayed. For example, here's the code used within **AckSetupObject()** to process a sequence of type **NO_CREATE**:

Table 12.1 *Object Sequences Supported in* ACK-3D

Sequence	Label	Description
Create	NO_CREATE	Typically used to display an object when an object is first created.
Destroy	NO_DESTROY	Used to display an object when an object is wiped out.
Walk	NO_WALK	Used to have the object "walk" around in the game.
Attack	NO_ATTACK	Used to have the object attack the player or other objects.
Interact	NO_INTERACT	Used to have the object interact with the player or other objects.

```
case NO_CREATE:
  memmove(&ae->ObjList[oNum]->Create,os,sizeof(OBJSEQ));
  break;
...
```

You can think of the object sequence feature as a sort of object manager. For each object you define, you can set up five different sequences with each sequence having its own set of views and bitmaps. At any time during the course of your game, you can load in a different sequence by calling **AckSetupObject()**.

The Complete ACKLDBMP.C

```
// This source file contains the functions needed to process bitmaps
// and objects.
// (c) 1995 ACK Software (Lary Myers)
#include <windows.h>
#include <stdlib.h>
#include <stdio.h>
#include <dos.h>
#include <mem.h>
#include <io.h>
#include <fcntl.h>
#include <time.h>
#include <string.h>
#include <sys\stat.h>
#include "ack3d.h"    // Main ACK-3D internal and interface data structures
#include "ackeng.h"   // Internal data structures and constants
#include "ackext.h"   // Defines external (global) variables
char *GetExtent(char *s);
UCHAR *AckReadiff(char *s);
UCHAR *AckReadPCX(char *s);
short BlankSlice(short,UCHAR *);

//++++++++++++++++++++++++++++++++++++++++++++++++++++++++++++++++++++++++
// Determines if the column of the specified bitmap contains all transparent
// colors or not. If so, it is marked to be skipped during the draw phase.
// This function is called by AckLoadBitmap().
//++++++++++++++++++++++++++++++++++++++++++++++++++++++++++++++++++++++++
short BlankSlice(short col,UCHAR *bmp)
{
  short i,pos;
pos = col * 64;          // Move to the specified column
for (i = 0; i < 64; I++)  // Check each pixel in this column
  {
  if (bmp[pos++])        // Look for a value other than 0
    return(1);
  }
return(0);               // Indicates the column is transparent
}

//++++++++++++++++++++++++++++++++++++++++++++++++++++++++++++++++++++++++
// Loads a bitmap of different formats based on the setting of bmLoadType
```

```
// in the ACKENG interface structure. The bitmap loaded is placed into
// either the wall bitmap array or the object array based on the value
// of BitmapType passed to this function.
// BitmapName can be either a filename or an index into the currently
// opened resource file.
//
// To read in the bitmap, two buffers are required. The first buffer (buf)
// is used to read in the bitmap in its normal order and the other buufer
// is used to rotate the bitmap 90 degrees for storing it with the ACK
// interface structure.
//±±±±±±±±±±±±±±±±±±±±±±±±±±±±±±±±±±±±±±±±±±±±±±±±±±±±±±±±±±±±±±±±±±±±±±±±±±±±

short AckLoadBitmap(ACKENG *ae,short BitmapNumber, short BitmapType,char *BitmapName)
{
  short handle,bFlag;
  short x,y,bLen;
  short sPos,dPos;
  UCHAR ch;
  UCHAR *buf;    // Buffer to store read in bitmap
  UCHAR *bmp;    // Buffer to store bitmap after rotating it
  UCHAR *bmpFlags;

bFlag = 0;
// Size of a bitmap to load in. One extra row is added to include
// status information about the bitmap.
bLen = BITMAP_SIZE + BITMAP_WIDTH;
buf = NULL;
// Read in bitmap from a resource file or a .BBM file
if (rsHandle || !(stricmp(GetExtent(BitmapName),"BBM")))
  { // Read in a bitmap file
  if (ae->bmLoadType == BMLOAD_BBM)   // Read in .BBM bitmap
    buf = AckReadiff(BitmapName);
// This feature is disabled for now pending patent resolution
// To use it uncomment out the code and make sure you create your own
// AckReadgif() function.
//   if (ae->bmLoadType == BMLOAD_GIF)
//       buf = AckReadgif(BitmapName);
// Read in bitmap from a .PCX file
  if (ae->bmLoadType == BMLOAD_PCX)   // Read in .PCX bitmap
    buf = AckReadPCX(BitmapName);
  if (buf == NULL)                    // Nothing to load in
    return(ERR_LOADINGBITMAP);        // Return error
// Make sure buffer is correct size
  x = (*(short *)buf);
  y = (*(short *)&buf[2]);
  if ((x*y) != BITMAP_SIZE)
    {
    AckFree(buf);                     // Deallocate the memory
    return(ERR_INVALIDFORM);          // Return error message
    }
  memmove(buf,&buf[4],BITMAP_SIZE);   // Skip width and height
  bFlag = 1;                          // Indicates bitmap has been read in
  }
// Allocate memory for the temp bitmap buffer
```

```
else
  {
  buf = AckMalloc(BITMAP_SIZE);
  if (buf == NULL)
    return(ERR_NOMEMORY);
  }
bmp = AckMalloc(bLen);              // Allocate memory for bitmap
if (bmp == NULL)
  {
  AckFree(buf);
  return(ERR_NOMEMORY);
  }
if (BitmapType == TYPE_WALL)    // Process a wall bitmap
  { // Store the wall bitmap in the interface structure
  ae->bMaps[BitmapNumber] = bmp;
  }
if (BitmapType == TYPE_OBJECT)  // Process an object bitmap
  { // Store the object bitmap in the interface structure
  ae->oMaps[BitmapNumber] = bmp;
  }
if (!bFlag) // Haven't read in the bitmap yet
  {
  handle = _lopen(BitmapName,OF_READ);// Open bitmap file
  if (handle < 1)   // Error Opening file
    {
    AckFree(buf);                // Free buffers
    AckFree(bmp);
    return(ERR_BADFILE);         // Return error code
    }
    read(handle,buf,4);          // Skip width and height for now
    read(handle,buf,BITMAP_SIZE);
  _lclose(handle);
  }
// Convert format of bitmap by rotating it 90 degrees
for (y = 0; y < BITMAP_HEIGHT; y++)
  {
  sPos = y;
  dPos = y * BITMAP_WIDTH;
  for (x = 0; x < BITMAP_WIDTH; x++)
    {
    ch = buf[sPos];
    bmp[dPos++] = ch;
    sPos += BITMAP_WIDTH;
    }
  }
bmpFlags = &bmp[BITMAP_SIZE];      // Get address of end of bitmap
memset(bmpFlags,0,BITMAP_WIDTH);  // Clear one row with 0s
// Check each column of pixels in the bitmap to see
// if it is transparent
for (x = 0; x < BITMAP_WIDTH; x++)
  {
  if (!BlankSlice(x,bmp))          // Transparent column is found
    bmpFlags[x] = 1;               // Mark transparent columns
  }
```

```
AckFree(buf);                        // Free the temporary buffer
return(0);
}
//++++++++++++++++++++++++++++++++++++++++++++++++++++++++++++++++++++++++++
// Returns a pointer to a file extentension.
//++++++++++++++++++++++++++++++++++++++++++++++++++++++++++++++++++++++++++
char *GetExtent(char *s)
{
  char  *e;
e = strchr(s,'.');
if (e == NULL)
  return(s);
e++;
return(e);
}


//++++++++++++++++++++++++++++++++++++++++++++++++++++++++++++++++++++++++++
// Calls AckLoadBitmap with the TYPE_WALL flag set so the bitmap is placed
// in the wall array.
//++++++++++++++++++++++++++++++++++++++++++++++++++++++++++++++++++++++++++
short AckLoadWall(ACKENG *ae,short WallNumber,char *bmFileName)
{
return( AckLoadBitmap(ae,WallNumber,TYPE_WALL,bmFileName) );
}
//++++++++++++++++++++++++++++++++++++++++++++++++++++++++++++++++++++++++++
// Calls AckLoadBitmap with the TYPE_OBJECT flag set so the bitmap is
// placed in the object array.
//++++++++++++++++++++++++++++++++++++++++++++++++++++++++++++++++++++++++++
short AckLoadObject(ACKENG *ae,short BmpNumber,char *bmFileName)
{
return( AckLoadBitmap(ae,BmpNumber,TYPE_OBJECT,bmFileName) );
}


//++++++++++++++++++++++++++++++++++++++++++++++++++++++++++++++++++++++++++
// Creates an object structure. This function MUST be called before the
// object data can be initialized in the NEWOBJECT structure.
//++++++++++++++++++++++++++++++++++++++++++++++++++++++++++++++++++++++++++
short AckCreateObject(ACKENG *ae,short ObjNumber)
{
// Check to see if this object already exists
if (ae->ObjList[ObjNumber] == NULL)
  {
  ae->ObjList[ObjNumber] = (NEWOBJECT *)AckMalloc(sizeof(NEWOBJECT));
  if (ae->ObjList[ObjNumber] == NULL)
    return(ERR_NOMEMORY);  // Error allocating memory for the object
  memset(ae->ObjList[ObjNumber],0,sizeof(NEWOBJECT));
  }
if (ObjNumber >= ae->MaxObjects)
  ae->MaxObjects = ObjNumber + 1; // Increment max object counter
return(0);
}


//++++++++++++++++++++++++++++++++++++++++++++++++++++++++++++++++++++++++++
// Sets an object up into one of the pre-defined sequence types (CREATE,DESTROY,
```

```c
// etc.). Moveable objects are placed into a special list that is used
// later in the drawing phase.
//+++++++++++++++++++++++++++++++++++++++++++++++++++++++++++++++++++++++++++

short AckSetObjectType(ACKENG *ae,short oNum,short oType)
{
  short i,j,result = 0;
  OBJSEQ  *os;

switch (oType)
  {
  case NO_CREATE:
    os = &ae->ObjList[oNum]->Create;
    break;
  case NO_DESTROY:
    os = &ae->ObjList[oNum]->Destroy;
    break;
  case NO_WALK:
    os = &ae->ObjList[oNum]->Walk;
    break;
  case NO_ATTACK:
    os = &ae->ObjList[oNum]->Attack;
    break;
  case NO_INTERACT:
    os = &ae->ObjList[oNum]->Interact;
    break;
  default:
    result = ERR_BADOBJTYPE;
    break;
  }
if (!result)  // Transfer object attributes
  {
  ae->ObjList[oNum]->CurrentBitmaps = (UCHAR *)&os->bitmaps;
  ae->ObjList[oNum]->Flags = os->flags;
  ae->ObjList[oNum]->Sides = os->bmSides;
  ae->ObjList[oNum]->BitmapsPerView = os->bmBitmapsPerView;
  ae->ObjList[oNum]->CurrentBm = 0;
  ae->ObjList[oNum]->Maxbm = os->MaxBitmaps;
  ae->ObjList[oNum]->CurrentType = oType;
  ae->ObjList[oNum]->aFactor = os->AngleFactor;
  }
// Object is a moveable object
if (ae->ObjList[oNum]->Flags & OF_MOVEABLE)
  {
  j = 0;
  for (i = 0; i < MoveObjectCount; i++)
    {
    if (MoveObjectList[i] == oNum)
      {
      j = 1;
      break;
      }
    }
  if (!j)
```

```
      MoveObjectList[MoveObjectCount++] = oNum;
   i = (ae->ObjList[oNum]->y & 0xFFC0) + (ae->ObjList[oNum]->x >> 6);
   ObjGrid[i] = 0; // Store map position of object
   }
return(result);
}


//±±±±±±±±±±±±±±±±±±±±±±±±±±±±±±±±±±±±±±±±±±±±±±±±±±±±±±±±±±±±±±±±±±±±±±±±±±±±±±±±±
// Fills in the object structure with a communication structure passed
// by the application. This allows the application to setup the fields
// such as number of sides to an object, what bitmaps are displayed for
// each side, etc. The object structures are defined in ACK3D.H
//±±±±±±±±±±±±±±±±±±±±±±±±±±±±±±±±±±±±±±±±±±±±±±±±±±±±±±±±±±±±±±±±±±±±±±±±±±±±±±±±±
short AckSetupObject(ACKENG *ae,short oNum,short oType,OBJSEQ *os)
{
  short result = 0;

if (ae->ObjList[oNum] == NULL)
  return(ERR_BADOBJECTNUM);
if (os->flags & OF_MULTIVIEW)
  {
  os->AngleFactor = INT_ANGLE_360 / os->bmSides;
  }
switch (oType)
  {
  case NO_CREATE:
    memmove(&ae->ObjList[oNum]->Create,os,sizeof(OBJSEQ));
    break;
  case NO_DESTROY:
    memmove(&ae->ObjList[oNum]->Destroy,os,sizeof(OBJSEQ));
    break;
  case NO_WALK:
    memmove(&ae->ObjList[oNum]->Walk,os,sizeof(OBJSEQ));
    break;
  case NO_ATTACK:
    memmove(&ae->ObjList[oNum]->Attack,os,sizeof(OBJSEQ));
    break;
  case NO_INTERACT:
    memmove(&ae->ObjList[oNum]->Interact,os,sizeof(OBJSEQ));
    break;
  default:
    result = ERR_BADOBJTYPE;
    break;
  }
if (!result && ae->ObjList[oNum]->CurrentBitmaps == NULL)
    result = AckSetObjectType(ae,oNum,oType);
return(result);
}
// **** End of Source ****
```

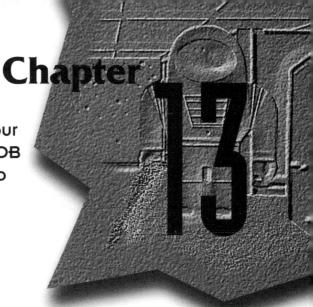

Chapter 13

The WinG API can make your Windows games faster than your DOS-based games that use DDB bitmaps! Here's your chance to learn how WinG operates.

The WinG Connection

We've now seen how the *ACK-3D* engine is constructed and how the major functions are used to set up an application. One of the key design issues I've emphasized throughout this book is that the engine works with different platforms including DOS and Windows. We've already explored how some of the low-level DOS specific routines, such as **AckSetVGAmode()** and **AckDisplayScreen()**, are used to support DOS VGA screens, but what about Windows? How do we take the core engine and adapt it so that Windows applications can be built?

Fortunately, we don't need to rewrite the engine. In fact, we can use most of the C functions and assembly-language routines that we've developed so far. What we need to do is add a Windows interface level to the engine so that we can display 3-D views in a window. The secret weapon that we'll use to build the Windows interface is called *WinG*—Microsoft's latest API for game developers and other programmers who need to quickly process and update bitmaps in their programs.

In this chapter you'll learn what WinG is about and how you can use it to display lightning-fast bitmaps in Windows. Along the way you'll be introduced to the ten functions that the WinG API provides and how Windows bitmaps are created, processed, and displayed. We'll finish by creating a sample Windows game that scrolls on the screen. At this stage, we won't tie the WinG API into the *ACK-3D* engine, but in the next chapter we'll plug WinG support into our 3-D engine. Before we get too far into WinG programming, I'd like to thank Windows game wizard Bob Provencher for providing most of the text in this chapter on WinG, as well as the sample scrolling game.

The Need for WinG

If you have ever written a Windows-based game or multimedia application that uses animation, you already know how difficult it can be to produce the type of fast animation for which DOS games are famous. What gives? With a user base of over 30 million, you'd think that game developers would be finding ways to perform fast animation and rushing to create games for Windows. Once you have passed the initial learning curve, the Windows API has much to offer; a consistent, ready-to-use user interface, device independence, great screen fonts, and handy interface components such as dialog boxes. For the user, the benefits are obvious. Windows-based applications are consistently outselling DOS applications in all categories but one—games!

Despite its ease of use and user interface, the Windows API has little to offer game programmers. The *Graphics Device Interface*, or GDI, is the Windows API for all graphics operations. It provides a set of general-purpose graphics functions, but no direct access to the screen display or bits of a bitmap. Without this access, it's very difficult to achieve the performance required of an action game. How can we perform some of the low-level screen operations, such as writing pixel color values to display memory, that we performed with the DOS code we created for the *ACK-3D* library? Fortunately, there is a new tool available to help us bring our Windows applications into the fast lane—WinG.

WinG is Microsoft's SDK designed to assist Windows programmers, mostly game programmers, in meeting their graphics performance goals. How does WinG do this? It provides two key features not available with the standard Windows GDI. The first is direct access to the bits of a special type of bitmap, called a *WinG bitmap*, which is almost as good as accessing the display itself. The second is a WinG API function for copying a WinG bitmap to the screen. Now doesn't this sound a lot like the technique we used earlier with the *ACK-3D* engine to create a special off-screen buffer, write data to the off-screen buffer, and then send the off-screen buffer to video memory? In principle it is; we just need to develop a new set of programming techniques to incorporate WinG bitmaps into our applications.

DESIGN TIP

When Microsoft first introduced WinG, they distributed it with a document that marketed WinG as a tool for creating "hot" games. Many developers get confused when they hear about WinG and refer to it as a game-development engine. This is not what it is at all. Essentially, WinG is a replacement for the **CreateDibSection()** function, which is found in the Win32 API. The goal of WinG is to give graphics programmers a way to have more control over bitmaps and of course to speed bitmap processing up quite a bit. As you'll discover in this chapter and the next, the WinG bitmap approach does provide enough speed to create fast-action games that must constantly update the screen.

Introducing the WinG API

WinG defines a new type of device context (DC). This device context is known as the WinG DC. (If you are relatively new to Windows programming, it helps to think of a device context as a link to send output to a device such as a screen or printer.) WinG also provides a new specialized type of bitmap called the *WinG bitmap*. The WinG API itself consists of ten functions, which are listed in Table 13.1. Notice that functions are provided to manipulate the WinG DC and the bits of a WinG bitmap. We'll take a look at each of the WinG functions when we discuss the important parts of the WinG API.

WinG Device Context

At the core of WinG is the new WinG DC. This is a special kind of DC that can be used just like a regular DC, but has some extended capabilities. Using a WinG DC, you can retrieve a pointer to the bits of the WinG bitmap currently selected into the WinG DC. The neat thing about WinG DCs is that you can retrieve a special pointer called a *DIB pointer* to draw on the DC directly. You still can use GDI functions to draw and manipulate the bitmap. This flexibility gives you the benefit of both worlds—low-level bitmap support and access to high-level drawing functions if you care to use them. Even though you might be tempted to write your own efficient high-level drawing functions, don't discount the built-in power of the GDI. After all, imagine trying to create your own routines to create font output that looks as nice as TrueType. Well, now

Table 13.1 *WinG API Functions*

```
HDC WINGAPI WinGCreateDC( void );
```
Creates a WinG device context for displaying a bitmap.

```
BOOL WINGAPI WinGRecommendDIBFormat( BITMAPINFO FAR *pFormat );
```
Recommends the most efficient display independent bitmap (DIB) for the active display.

```
HBITMAP WINGAPI WinGCreateBitmap( HDC WinGDC, BITMAPINFO const FAR
                              pHeader, void FAR *FAR *ppBits );
```
Creates a WinG bitmap.

```
void FAR* WINGAPI WinGGetDIBPointer( HBITMAP WinGBitmap, BITMAPINFO FAR* pHeader );
```
Retrieves a pointer to a WinG bitmap surface and its attributes.

```
UINT WINGAPI WinGGetDIBColorTable( HDC WinGDC, UINT StartIndex,
                              UINT NumberOfEntries, RGBQUAD FAR* pColors );
```
Retrieves a color table for the WinG bitmap.

```
UINT WINGAPI WinGSetDIBColorTable( HDC WinGDC, UINT StartIndex,
                              UINT NumberOfEntries, RGBQUAD const FAR* pColors );
```
Sets the color table for a WinG bitmap.

```
BOOL WINGAPI WinGBitBlt( HDC hdcDest, int nXOriginDest,
     int nYOriginDest, int nWidthDest,
     int nHeightDest, HDC hdcSrc, int nXOriginSrc,
     int nYOriginSrc );
```
Displays a WinG bitmap on the screen by bliting it.

```
BOOL WINGAPI WinGStretchBlt( HDC hdcDest, int nXOriginDest,
     int nYOriginDest, int nWidthDest,
     int nHeightDest, HDC hdcSrc, int nXOriginSrc,
     int nYOriginSrc, int nWidthSrc, int nHeightSrc );
```
Displays a WinG bitmap and performs scaling of the bitmap.

```
HPALETTE WINGAPI WinGCreateHalftonePalette( void )
```
Creates a palette that contains 20 static colors and 236 other colors for true-color simulation on an 8-bit display.

```
HBRUSH WINGAPI WinGCreateHalftoneBrush( HDC context, COLORREF crColor,
                              WING_DITHER_TYPE DitherType )
```
Creates a brush to paint with the halftone palette colors.

you don't have to. On the other hand, you can handle the drawing yourself whenever you can do a better or faster job than the GDI.

To create a WinG DC, you simply call the **WinGCreateDC()** function as shown here:

```
Buffer = WinGCreateDC();
```

This function takes no parameters and returns a handle to a device context (HDC) for the WinG DC. This handle can then be used by the other WinG functions to access the device context. The WinG DC that is created must be destroyed with the regular Windows API function **DeleteDC()**; WinG does not have a special **DeleteDC()** function for deleting WinG DCs. Now that we've got a WinG DC, let's explore how we can create a WinG bitmap and access the bitmap using the device context we've set up.

Working with WinG Bitmaps

A WinG bitmap is a special type of Device Independent Bitmap, commonly called a *DIB* in the world of Windows programming. This DIB can be "selected" into a WinG DC so that the bitmap can be accessed. A WinG bitmap is created by calling the WinG API function **WinGCreateBitmap()**. This function takes three parameters, as shown here:

```
HBITMAP WINGAPI WinGCreateBitmap( HDC WinGDC, BITMAPINFO const FAR *pHeader,
                                  void FAR *FAR *ppBits );
```

The first parameter, **WinGDC**, is an HDC (handle to a device context in case you've forgotten already), which specifies a WinG DC. The second parameter, ***pHeader**, is a long pointer to a **BITMAPINFO** structure that stores the attributes of the bitmap. The third parameter, ***ppBits**, is a pointer to an **LPVOID**, which will receive the address of the surface of the WinG bitmap. A pointer to the WinG bitmap surface and its attributes can also be retrieved at any time by calling the **WinGGetDIBPointer()** function.

Both the attributes of a WinG bitmap and the attributes of a DIB are specified in a **BITMAPINFO** structure. The **BITMAPINFO** structure contains two members, as shown here:

```
typedef struct tagBITMAPINFO
{
    BITMAPINFOHEADER  bmiHeader;
    RGBQUAD           bmiColors[1];
} BITMAPINFO;
```

The first member is the **BITMAPINFOHEADER** structure. This structure specifies the key attributes of a DIB, such as the size of the bitmap and the number of bytes used to represent a pixel. The second member is an array of **RGBQUAD** structures that is used to specify the color table for the WinG bitmap or DIB.

BITMAPINFO Structure

It's worth taking a detailed look at the important members of the **BITMAPINFO** structure, because it's the basic structure used to define DIBs and their cousins—WinG bitmaps. After all, the more you know about how DIBs are set up, the better you'll be at using the WinG API.

The **BITMAPINFOHEADER** specifies the attributes of the DIB as follows:

```
typedef struct tagBITMAPINFOHEADER
{
    DWORD   biSize;          // Size of the bitmap header
    LONG    biWidth;         // The size of the DIB
    LONG    biHeight;
    WORD    biPlanes;        // Number of bit planes (should be 1)
    WORD    biBitCount;      // Number of bits per pixel
    DWORD   biCompression;   // Type of compression
    DWORD   biSizeImage;
    LONG    biXPelsPerMeter;
    LONG    biYPelsPerMeter;
    DWORD   biClrUsed;       // Used to calculate number of colors
    DWORD   biClrImportant;  // in the bitmap
} BITMAPINFOHEADER;
```

The **biSize** member specifies the size of the **BITMAPINFOHEADER**, currently 28h. The **biWidth** and **biHeight** members, as you've probably guessed, specify the size of the DIB. The bits are packed into array of scan lines, where each scan line is double word aligned. WinG interprets the **biHeight** value as the orientation of the DIB. If **biSize** is positive, the DIB orientation is the normal (for a DIB at least) bottom-up orientation. If the sign is negative, the orientation is top-down, what most of us think of as the normal orientation. The **biPlanes** member specifies the number of planes for the *target device*. DIBs are always single-plane devices, so this member will always be 1.

The number of bits per pixel for the DIB is specified by the **biBitCount** member. This member, in combination with the **biClrUsed** and **biClrImportant** members, specifies the number of colors in the bitmap. If this member is zero, the number of colors in the bitmap is the maximum number of colors that can be specified by **biBitCount** or **1 << biClrUsed**. Currently, WinG only supports 256-color DIBs, so our DIBs and the **BITMAPINFO** structures that we pass to WinG will have **biClrUsed** = 0 and **biBitCount** = 8. Finally, the **biCompression** member specifies the type of compression the DIB uses. WinG requires that DIBs be uncompressed by setting **biCompression** equal to **BI_RGB**.

The WinG SDK comes with some sample utility macros and functions for handling DIBs. These can be found in the WinG SAMPLES\UTILS directory.

We won't use the sample macros, but they cover just about everything you'd need to do with DIBs, for example, reading them from disk or as a resource from an .EXE or getting a DIB's width or height.

DIBs can be stored as resources in an .EXE or as .BMP files on disk. To store a DIB as a resource, specify resource type **BITMAP** in the .RC file, the same as you would for a normal Device Dependent Bitmap (DDB). This step causes the DIB to be stored as a resource in packed format, that is, the **BITMAPINFO** structure will be followed immediately by the bits of the bitmap. Loading a DIB is not the same, however, as loading a DDB. The **LoadBitmap()** API function assumes a 16-color DDB; it will not recognize the color-table in the packed DIB, so you can't use the **LoadBitmap()** function. To load a DIB, you must use the **FindResource()**, **LoadResource()**, and **LockResource()** series of calls, as shown in this code sample:

```
LPVOID LoadDIBitmap( HINSTANCE hInst, LPCSTR lpszResName )
{

    HRSRC    hRsrc;
    HGLOBAL  hGlobal;
    LPVOID   lpDIB = 0;

    if ( ( hRsrc = FindResource( hInst, lpszResName, BITMAP ) ) != 0 )
        if ( ( hGlobal = LoadResource( hInst, hRsrc ) ) != 0 )
            lpDIB = LockResource( hGlobal );
    return lpDIB;
}

void FreeDIBitmapRes( LPVOID lpDIB )
{
    HGLOBAL hGlobal = LOWORD( GetHandle( SELECTOROF( lpDIB ) ) );
    UnlockResource( hGlobal );
    FreeResource( hGlobal );
}
```

We'll use this approach for the sample game presented later in this chapter. The final thing that a **BITMAPINFO** structure contains that we haven't explored is the array of **RGBQUAD** structures, which specifies the colors of the bitmap itself, also known as the *color table* :

```
typedef struct tagRGBQUAD
{
    BYTE     rgbBlue;
    BYTE     rgbGreen;
    BYTE     rgbRed;
    BYTE     rgbReserved;
} RGBQUAD, FAR* LPRGBQUAD;
```

Notice that each pixel of the bitmap is represented by red, green, and blue components. These components determine the actual color of the pixel when it is displayed.

Before we talk about how to draw on a DIB, let's take a look at the last Windows data structure that's required to use WinG, the *palette*.

Introducing the Windows Palette

The Windows Palette and the Palette Manager are pretty complex topics. We don't have the space or time to cover everything that you might want to eventually know about these topics. However, to use WinG, you do need a basic understanding of how they operate. To help you get started, we'll cover the basics in this chapter. If you want to learn more about the Palette Manager, you should check out Ron Gery's article, "The Palette Manager: How and Why," which is provided on the Microsoft Developer's Network CD-ROM. Gery covers the topic thoroughly.

As you know, bitmaps are made up of pixels, and pixels are displayed by using selected colors. A pixel's color on an 8-bit color display is determined by looking up its 8-bit pixel value in a color table or *palette*, as shown in Figure 13.1. A palette contains a set of 256 24-bit RGB (red, green, blue) color values. The maximum number of color entries in a palette is 256, numbered from 0 through 255. A palette need not contain all 256 entries. In the display memory, each pixel entry contains a value from 0 through 255. This pixel value indicates which palette entry to use to color the pixel. To change the color of a pixel, you have two options: You can either change the index value of the pixel to another palette entry, or you can change the RGB value of the palette entry itself, which will change the color of all pixels on the screen that reference that palette entry.

Palettized color certainly imposes limitations—the 256 color limitation applies to the entire screen, not just to each window or application—but it also offers two important advantages. First, it keeps your uncompressed image files relatively small, and second, you can use built-in Windows palette manipulation functions to perform two popular (and economical) forms of animation: *palette animation* and *color cycling*.

Inside the Palette Manager

Each image you display can carry its own color palette. In addition, each active window can manipulate the current palette for its own purposes. But remember, the 256 colors of the current palette apply to the entire screen, not just to each window or application. With such limited seating, someone has to

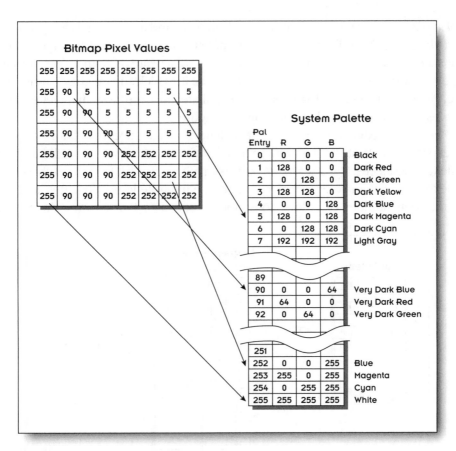

Figure 13.1 *Using a color palette to locate a pixel's color.*

play the role of the bouncer. And that's where the Windows Palette Manager comes in.

Windows uses the Palette Manager to determine which window has control of the palette at any given time. The active window, the one in the foreground, always has priority. If that window doesn't use the palette, the priority goes to the next window in the *z-order* (the order in which windows are stacked on the desktop). Once the window with the highest priority "realizes" its palette as the *foreground palette*, the other windows are signaled in order by the Palette Manager to "realize" their palettes as *background palettes*.

But what does it mean to *realize* a palette? Each image you display could have its own color palette (several palettes can be kept in memory simultaneously). A palette stored in memory is called a *logical palette*. The palette in your display system that determines which colors actually appear on the screen is called the *hardware*, or *system palette*. In the system palette, palette indexes

0-9 and 246-255 are reserved for use by Windows and are referred to as *static* or *system* colors. There is only one system palette, and the Palette Manager maintains a copy of it. When an application wants to activate its own colors, it must select its logical palette into a DC and *realize* it, which means that it must ask the Palette Manager to load its logical palette into the system palette. This process of realizing a palette is shown in Figure 13.2.

Because palettes vary in size, the Palette Manager doesn't blindly copy a fixed-sized block of 256 color elements from the logical palette to the system palette. The Palette Manager loads only as many colors as it finds in each logical palette. The system palette can accommodate multiple logical palettes, as long as the total number of colors does not exceed 256. Furthermore, Windows

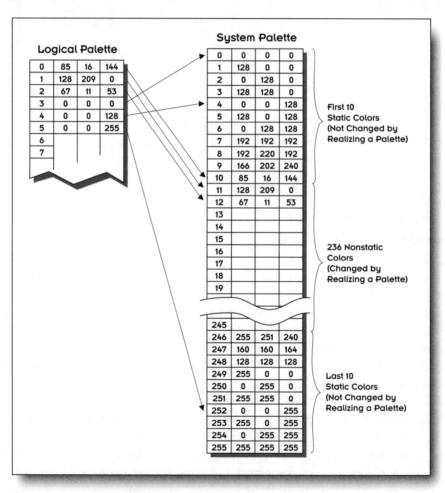

Figure 13.2 *The process of realizing a palette.*

reserves 20 of the palette entries for its *static colors*—the colors it uses to draw buttons, borders, text, icons, and so on. So we're left with only 236 changeable color slots. But this doesn't mean a palette should include only the 236 colors it needs to support its bitmap. It's wise to convert the palette of any 8-bit image into a Windows *identity palette*, which is a palette that includes the 20 reserved colors, especially if you plan to draw with the palette. I'll review identity palettes shortly. Otherwise, you won't be able to use the reserved colors. If you wish, you *can* tamper with the system static colors to extend the range of definable colors up to 256; the GDI provides special functions just for that purpose. But that would violate the Windows prime directive of not interfering with other active applications since it could dramatically alter their appearance.

The colors in a logical palette often do not occupy the same positions in the system palette that they do in the logical palette. So the Palette Manager must build a cross-reference table, called a *palette mapping*, as it loads a logical palette into the system palette. This table is used by GDI drawing functions to translate pixel values from logical palette indexes into system palette indexes. Keep in mind that a pixel's color is determined by looking up its value in a color table. In the case of a DIB, which is the most common form of 256-color bitmap file, the bytes that make up the bitmap pixel data contain values that reference the entries in the color table contained within the file. As the GDI transfers the image from the file to the screen, that is, from a device *independent* bitmap into a device *dependent* bitmap, it uses the palette mapping to change the pixel values so they reference the correct colors in the system palette. The palette mapping that's created for a logical palette is called the *foreground mapping*.

If the active window does not hog all the palette entries, the remaining slots are filled with colors from the inactive windows until either all the slots are occupied or no other windows ask to realize their own palettes. If the foreground window requires all 236 free color slots, all the inactive windows must conform to the active foreground palette. The Palette Manager can also perform this service automatically by mapping colors in the inactive windows to the closest matching colors in the currently realized palette, which occasionally produces amusing (or ugly) results. This is called a *background mapping*. Each time the focus changes from one palette-based application to another, the entire realization process starts over.

The difference between device independent and device dependent bitmaps is worth repeating: The pixels in a DIB contain the indexes of the colors in the logical palette that accompanies the bitmap, usually a color table stored in the DIB file. The pixels in a DDB contain the indexes of the colors in the

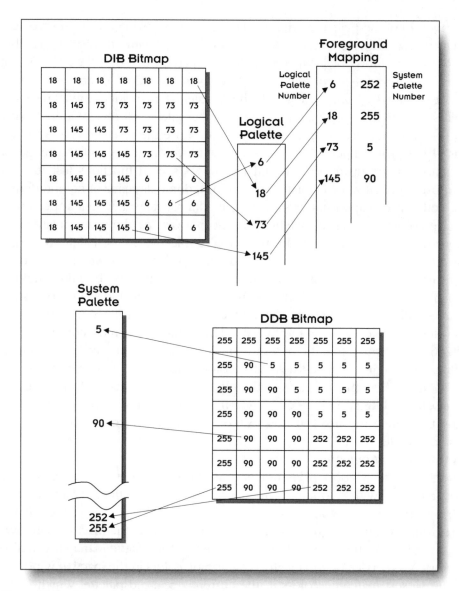

Figure 13.3 *Comparing a DIB to a DDB.*

system palette. Figure 13.3 illustrates the difference between the two structures. A DIB does not exist in a DC. It must be translated into a DDB either before it's selected into a DC or as it is painted into the device context. The foreground and background palette mappings are the tables used to translate DIBs into DDBs.

Using Messages for Palette Control

When an application window is brought to the foreground, the window can request that the Palette Manager give its colors priority by selecting and realizing a logical palette. The act of realizing a palette essentially requests that the Palette Manager match the colors in the logical palette to the system palette, either by matching to existing colors, or by creating new entries. After a foreground window realizes a palette, the Palette Manager sends the **WM_PALETTECHANGED** message to all top-level windows. When a background window receives the **WM_PALLETTECHANGED** message, it should compare its window handle to **wParam** to check whether it is the window that changed the palette. If it is not, it should re-realize its palette. During the life of a window, Windows will send it the **WM_QUERYNEWPALETTE** message whenever a window is activated. This is a good point to realize a palette. Here's some sample code to show how this process can be set up:

```
case WM_PALETTECHANGED:
    if ( hWnd == (HWND)wParam )
        break;

// If not this window, fall through to WM_QUERYNEWPALETTE
case WM_QUERYNEWPALETTE:
    hDC = GetDC( hWnd );
    if ( hPal )
        SelectPalette( hDC, hPal, FALSE );
    u = RealizePalette( hDC );
    ReleaseDC( hWnd, hDC );

    //If any colors were remapped, force repaint
    if ( u )
        InvalidateRect( hWnd, NULL, TRUE );
    return f;
```

Now we know something about handling a palette, but how do we get one? You create a palette by calling the Windows API function **CreatePalette()**. **CreatePalette()** takes a long pointer to a **LOGPALETTE** structure, and returns an **HPALETTE**.

LOGPALETTE and PALETTEENTRY Structures

The **LOGPALETTE** structure defines the attributes of a logical palette as shown here:

```
typedef struct tagLOGPALETTE
{
```

```
    WORD          palVersion;      // Version number for the structure
    WORD          palNumEntries;   // Number of palette entries
    PALETTEENTRY  palPalEntry[1];  // Defines colors for the palette
} LOGPALETTE, FAR* LPLOGPALETTE;
```

As we just discovered, this structure is passed as input to **CreatePalette()**, which returns a handle to a GDI palette object. The logical palette consists of a **WORD** defining the Windows version number for the structure (**palVersion**), and a **WORD** for the number of entries in the structure (**palNumEntries**). These are followed by an array of **PALETTEENTRY** structures defining the colors of the palette. Sound familiar? It should. It's very similar to the **BITMAPINFO** structure used to define a DIB. Unfortunately, the two color table arrays are not compatible, but it's easy enough to copy one into the other. That's what we'll do using a **BITMAPINFO** structure: copy the colors into a **LOGPALETTE** structure and create our custom palette.

Here's the definition of the **PALETTEENTRY** structure:

```
typedef struct tagPALETTEENTRY
{
    BYTE    peRed;      // Red, green, and blue color components
    BYTE    peGreen;    // for the particular palette entry
    BYTE    peBlue;
    BYTE    peFlags;    // Flag for determining how the palette entry
                        // is handled
} PALETTEENTRY, FAR* LPPALETTEENTRY;
```

The members of this structure should be fairly self-explanatory, with the exception of **peFlags**. The **peFlags** member specifies special flags for the palette entry. This member's value can be 0, **PC_EXPLICIT**, **PC_RESERVED**, or **PC_NOCOLLAPSE**. A **peFlags** = 0 entry specifies a normal palette entry, which can be matched to another entry. **PC_EXPLICIT** maps directly to the corresponding system palette entry. **PC_NOCOLLAPSE** and **PC_RESERVED** both use unused entries in the system palette. **PC_NOCOLLAPSE** matches to an existing color if none is available, and it can be matched to by other entries. A **PC_RESERVED** entry does not match to other colors, and cannot be matched to by other colors. It is normally used for palette animation in conjunction with the **AnimatePalette()** API function.

If we are careful about how we copy the colors and which system colors we use, we can create something called an *identity palette*. An identity palette is a logical palette that *exactly* matches the system palette. Using an identity palette, we can drastically improve the drawing speed. To create an identity palette, do the following:

1. Retrieve the system colors for palette entries 0-9 and 246-255 using the **GetSystemPaletteEntries()** API call.
2. Set palette entries 10-245 to your custom colors, with **peFlags** set to **PC_NOCOLLAPSE** or **PC_RESERVED**.

For applications where you know you've got a palette of 236 unique entries that do not duplicate any system entries, use **PC_NOCOLLAPSE**. If you are animating, or if you aren't sure about your palette, go with **PC_RESERVED**.

Halftone Palettes

Two other functions supplied with WinG involve the use of *halftone palettes*. The function **WinGCreateHalftonePalette()** creates a palette that contains the 20 static colors and 236 colors that are selected to permit true color simulation on an 8-bit display device. The halftone colors are laid out in the palette in such a way that each one can be **XOR**ed with its complementary color. The halftone palette can then be used by the **WinGCreateHalftoneBrush()** function or the standard **PALETTEGRAB** GDI function. We will not use any halftone palettes in the sample game, but it's nice to know that they are there.

We've talked a lot about the various structures and functions required to use WinG. We've got enough basics behind us to actually use WinG—it's about time we put it all together!

Drawing on a DIB

Drawing on a DIB is simple; it is similar to assigning a value to a 2-dimensional array, especially if you are using 256-color (one byte per pixel) DIBs. When we get to the sample game later in this chapter, we'll use more specialized drawing routines, but for now let's imagine we want to create a general-purpose function to set a pixel in a 256-color DIB. I'll name this function **SetDIBPixel()** and code it as follows:

```
void SetDIBPixel( LPBITMAPINFOHEADER pHeader, LPVOID pBits, WORD x, WORD y,
            BYTE color )
{
    WORD width = ( ( pHeader->bmiHeader.biWidth - 1 ) | 0x0003 ) + 1;
    WORD height = pHeader->bmiHeader.biHeight;
    if ( height > 0 )          // Bottom-up DIB
        y = height - y - 1;
    pPixel = (LPBYTE)pBits + ( y * width ) + x;
    *pPixel = color;
}
```

The first thing we do is calculate the double word aligned width of the bitmap. The method shown assumes an 8-bit per pixel bitmap. Notice that the width of the bitmap is retrieved using the **biWidth** field from the **BITMAPINFOHEADER** structure. Next, we retrieve the height of the bitmap using the **biHeight** field. The y coordinate of the pixel is normalized for a bottom-up DIB by calculating its offset from the bottom of the bitmap. The offset to the scan line is computed by multiplying y by the DIB width. Finally, the x position on the scan line is added, and the pixel is set to the desired color.

Comparing Top-Down DIBs to Bottom-Up DIBs

I mentioned top-down and bottom-up bitmaps in passing, without really defining them, so an explanation is in order. DIBs are normally stored as *bottom-up*. This method refers to the lowest y coordinate of the bitmap starting at the bottom and progressing upward. In other words, x,y coordinate (0, 0) of the DIB is in the lower-left corner. As you've probably noticed, this approach is exactly the opposite of the default **MM_TEXT** mapping mode for a window. This discrepancy can sometimes be confusing, so the developers of WinG decided to provide for top-down DIBs, or DIBs where the point (0,0) is the top-left corner in the DIB.

The reason for DIBs being *bottom up* is mostly historical (hysterical?) in Windows. The DIB format was originally defined in OS/2. The Windows 3.0 developers borrowed the specification without changing the bottom-up orientation. OS/2 DIBs, in turn, were specified as bottom-up to make them compatible with IBM's mainframe graphics package, GDDM.

You may be saying to yourself "Why bother handling bottom-up DIBs? If WinG allows for top-down DIBs, that's what I'll use." Well, the answer is that in some cases, WinG will have determined that it can blit bottom-up DIBs faster. Fast, after all, is good.

Using the WinG Recommended DIB Format

The **WinGRecommendDIBFormat()** function, as the name might imply, is a WinG API function that recommends the most efficient DIB format for the current platform. It fills in a **BITMAPINFO** structure with values for the best DIB configuration for 1:1, memory-to-screen blits. Currently, for version 1.0, WinG only supports 8-bit per pixel DIBs and will always return 256 colors as the optimal bitmap. But in the future, WinG may determine that it can perform better with a 24-bit bitmap. Huh? Yup, and if you think about it, it makes sense. Certain graphics accelerators may be highly optimized for true color, and actually perform better than 8-bit per pixel DIBs. It all depends on the

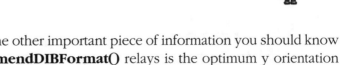

hardware. Anyway, the other important piece of information you should know is that **WinGRecommendDIBFormat()** relays is the optimum y orientation for the DIB. The API will return 1 for the "normal" bottom-up, or -1 for top-down. It's a good idea to use the recommended DIB layout.

If you haven't run any of the sample apps that come with the WinG SDK yet, start one. These applications are provided on the companion CD-ROM in the directory \TOOLS\WING. The first time you start a WinG application under a display driver, WinG profiles the current display/driver combination and saves the results in WIN.INI. This procedure is probably the only complaint I have with WinG. It does a lot of profiling just to tell me that it can handle top-down DIBs faster than bottom-up DIBs. I don't buy it. I think there's a lot of useful profiling information there, and I'd like WinG to have a function that allows you to decode the WinG WIN.INI strings.

Creating a Sample Game with WinG

Let's create a sample game that uses everything we've learned about WinG. We want the project to be simple enough to cover in the remainder of this chapter, but not so simple as to be worthless. In the next chapter, we'll create some interface classes for the WinG API so that we can drop WinG support right into the *ACK-3D* engine. Is this plug-and-play programming at its best or what?

The Windows application we'll build is a simple tiled game, as shown in Figure 13.4. The game supports a tiled-overhead view scrolling map of one level. The map itself will consist of either spaces or walls, and the spaces may contain our character, a monster, or some gold. You can move around in the game by pressing one of the arrow keys. Before you get too far into the code, you might want to start the game and take it for a test drive to see how it works. The game is stored on the companion CD-ROM in the directory \CHAP_13. The name of the program file is WINGTD.EXE.

Note: Before you run the game, make sure that you have installed the WinG DLLs in your Windows directory. You'll also need to install these DLLs to use the *ACK-3D* engine with Windows.

The game is based on a map that is read in when the game starts. You can create maps for the scrolling game engine by using a text editor. As an example, Figure 13.5 shows a sample of some of the contents of the text file WINGTD.TMA, which creates the map for our game. Notice that you can add comments to this file by placing the comment on a line like this:

```
;   Comments are preceded by a semi-colon
```

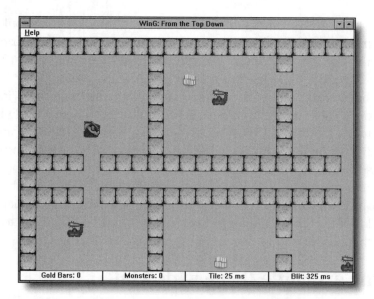

Figure 13.4 *The sample scrolling Windows game created with WinG.*

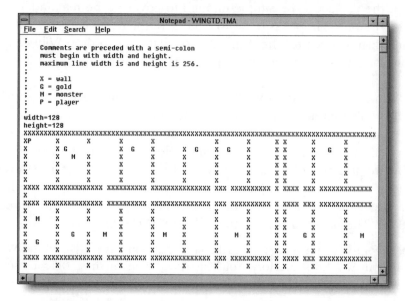

Figure 13.5 *The sample game map file WINGTD.TMA.*

The first two instructions in the file must specify the width and height for the game as shown here:

```
width=128
height=128
```

These values are read in when the game first starts, and the engine uses them to determine the size of the game map that is used. The maximum width and height supported is 256. The map itself is created by inserting one of four characters where the character *X* indicates a wall, *G* is a gold bar, *M* is a monster, and *P* is the player. Essentially, the game engine places bitmap images at the locations in the map wherever one of these characters occurs. The bitmap images are read in from the files FLOOR.BMP, GOLD.BMP, MONSTER.BMP, PLAYER.BMP, and WALL.BMP.

The game engine does not directly read in the map text file. To use it, you must convert the file to a compiled format using the TMACOMP program that is provided on the companion CD-ROM. You must run this program from DOS, and the format for using it is:

```
TMACOMP inputfile.tma outputfile.cma
```

For example, the command

```
TMACOMP WINGTD.TMA WINGTD.CMA
```

creates the resource file WINGTD.CMA from the text map file WINGTD.TMA. (This is the resource file that the sample game is set up to read.)

Supporting Animation

Because our sample game features a scrolling overhead view of a dungeon, there are certain assumptions we can make. If we always want to try to maintain the character at the center of the screen, we can assume that whenever the screen changes, the entire screen has changed. This assumption is important because it allows us to easily decide on the type of animation we'll use for the sample game: *dirty rectangle animation* or *double buffered animation.*

Dirty rectangle animation is an animation technique that keeps track of the region that has changed on the screen, and only updates that region when necessary. For example, if a character moves two spaces to the right in a board game, only those two rectangles are updated. For the movement to be flicker-free, the update is normally done in an off-screen memory copy of the screen, and then either the exact changed region or the union of all changed regions is copied to the screen. By the exact changed region, I'm referring to *only* the changed areas of the screen. In Figure 13.6, the tank figure has moved towards the northeast, and the update region is specified by the two rectangles.

If the update region is complex, the various updates required to redraw the entire region may be too lengthy to accomplish. In that case it's easier to

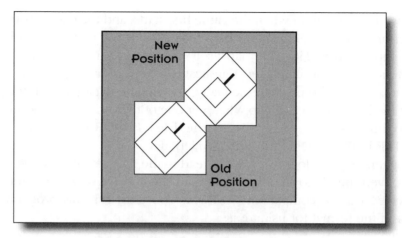

Figure 13.6 *Specifying an update region using two rectangles.*

update the union of the updated region, or the largest rectangle that covers all of the updates, as shown in Figure 13.7. Another case is where the union of all the updated regions is guaranteed to be the entire screen, such as in a tiled scrolling game. In that case it's just quicker to always copy the entire off-screen buffer to the screen on every update, or at specific intervals. This technique is known as *double buffering*.

In Windows, an application's window may be overlaid at any time. When the overlaid region is exposed, Windows automatically sends a **WM_PAINT** message. If we're using double buffering, responding to this message is simply a matter of copying the invalid region back to the screen. If you're only

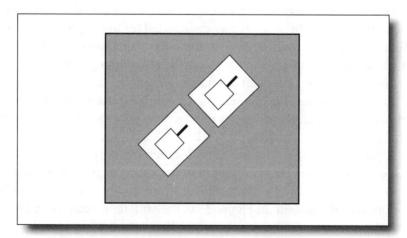

Figure 13.7 *Using one rectangle to represent an entire image area.*

updating dirty rectangles, you'll have to recompose the screen in the same way you do for any other dirty rectangle. For this reason, even for dirty-rectangle animation, it may be a good idea to keep an entire copy off-screen as with double buffering. If you do keep an entire copy, the difference between the two processes boils down to whether you're always copying the entire screen, or just the updated area.

A tiled scrolling game will, by its nature, update every tile on the screen when it scrolls. So it's only natural to always update the entire screen. For a sprite-based game, the various approaches should be timed. If an off-screen buffer is always supported, it's trivial to switch between the two, or to support both. Our approach will be to support both, just in case we have some circumstances where we wish to update only a dirty rectangle. Since we never know when we may have to update the screen in response to a **WM_PAINT** message, it's a good idea to support both.

Okay, enough about animation techniques. We've discussed some of the basic Windows data structures and operations that are important to us as WinG programmers. It's now time to start developing the code for the game.

C++ Classes for the Scrolling Game

Instead of jumping in and throwing a few functions together to create the game, let's stand back a moment and try to generalize some of the basic support routines that we'll need. We could easily encapsulate the data and code for processing WinG bitmaps, WinG DCs, logical color palettes, and so on. This technique will provide us with powerful classes that can easily be adapted to implement other games. The classes will take care of all of the background work that is required to display graphics with WinG.

The files used to define the support classes for the sample scrolling game are listed in Table 13.2. Notice that all of the major support areas are covered, from WinG bitmaps to WinG DCs. The classes are designed to be as flexible as possible so that they can easily be extended.

The starting point is to create a class to support the **BITMAPINFO** structure. As we've seen, this structure is used both by WinG bitmaps and Windows DIBs. I've encapsulated the basic data and operations of the **BITMAPINFO** structure in the **BitmapInfo** class, whose definition can be found in the header file BMPINFO.H. This class encompasses many of the same operations that the WinG sample UTILS directory handles. It includes member functions for querying the **BITMAPINFO** structure. It also includes functions for handling color tables of various sizes. For the current release, WinG only supports 256-color DIBs, but in the future it will support more.

Table 13.2   *Files Used to Define the Support Classes*

File	Description
BMPINFO.H	Defines the BitmapInfo class to encapsulate the data and operations of the BITMAPINFO structure.
BMPINFO.CPP	Implements the methods for the BitmapInfo class.
WINGBMP.H	Defines the WinGBitmap class to encapsulate the basic operations for a WinG bitmap.
WINGBMP.CPP	Implements the methods for the WinGBitmap class.
DIBITMAP.H	Defines the DIBitmap class to encapsulate the basic operations of a DIB).
DIBITMAP.CPP	Implements the methods of the DIBitmap class.
RES.H	Defines the Resource class for loading in any user-defined resources.
RES.CPP	Code to initialize the Resource class. Only one method is required.
LOGPAL.H	Defines the LogPalette class for managing logical color palette operations.
LOGPAL.CPP	Implements the methods for the LogPalette class.
WINGDC.H	Defines the WinGDC class to encapsulate the operations that can be performed on a WinG device context.
WINGDC.CPP	Implements the methods for the WinGDC class.
MAP.H	Defines the Map class that handles the work of loading a map from a Windows resource.
MAP.CPP	Implements the methods for the Map class.

I've also created a **WinGBitmap** class, which encapsulates the basic operations of a WinG bitmap, and a **DIBitmap** class that does the same for a DIB. These classes both contain a **BitmapInfo** object. They can be found in WINGBMP.H and DIBITMAP.H, respectively. The **WinGBitmap** class is primarily an interface object to the WinG SDK bitmap functions. It also includes the specialized tile routines for the sample game.

The **DIBitmap** class manages its contained **BitmapInfo** object and the bitmap bits for the DIB. The **DIBitmap** class can return a pointer to the DIB bits for use by the application. It also contains methods for copying a DIB, as well as loading a DIB from a resource.

As we've seen, loading a resource involves several layers of function calls, any of which might fail. To streamline this process, I've encapsulated this functionality in a **Resource** class, which is defined in the header file RES.H. The **Resource** class can be used to load any user-defined resources. It breaks down the operations of finding, loading, and locking a resource into atomic units, and it contains member functions for querying the state of a **Resource** object.

I've also encapsulated the various functions for a logical palette in the **LogPalette** class, which is defined in LOGPAL.H. Its primary purpose is to manage resizing the color table of a palette, copying the color table of a **BitmapInfo** object, getting system palette entries, and setting the **peFlags** member of an individual or a range of **PALETTEENTRY**s in a **LogPalette** object.

The **WinGDC** class encompasses the basic operations that can be performed on a WinG DC. This class is defined in the header file WINGDC.H. The methods for this class are implemented in the file WINGDC.CPP. The **WinGDC::Create()** member function is a wrapper for the WinG API **WinGCreateDC()**. **WinGDC::Delete()** checks for a currently selected WinG bitmap, deselecting it if necessary, and deletes the WinG DC by calling the standard Windows **DeleteDC()** API function. **WinGDC::BitBlt()** is an encapsulation of the WinG API function to copy a WinG DC to a display DC. Finally, the **WinGDC::SetDIBColorTable()** member function encapsulates the functionality of the **WinGSetDIBColorTable()** API function. This method takes a constant reference to a **BitmapInfo** object. Internally, it passes the pointer to the **BitmapInfo** color table, the array of **RGBQUAD**s, to **WinGSetDIBColorTable()**.

I've also created a simple map class that manages loading the map from a Windows resource, querying a position on the map, and tracking the position of the player on the map. Its implementation can be found in MAP.H and MAP.CPP. That's about it for the support classes; now let's get to the sample game.

Creating the Sample Game Files

We've developed a basic understanding of the various data structures and objects required to use WinG, **BITMAPINFO**s, and **PALETTE**s, as well as the new WinG DCs and bitmaps. We've also put together some basic classes to handle the various objects. Let's now put them to work. The main files for the game are listed in Table 13.3. Note that the first set of these files ends with the letters "TD" before the file extension. These files, along with WINGWND.H and WINGWND.CPP, implement the main code for the game. The other files provide definitions and functions for support operations, such as displaying debugging information, popping up an About dialog, and so on.

The WINGTD.CPP source file contains the functions **WinMain()**, **AppIdle()**, **InitApplication()**, **InitInstance()**, and **MainWndProc()**. The **WinMain()** function performs the initialization work and sets up the main loop for the game. The main loop is quite simple. We just continue to process messages until the

Table 13.3   *Files Used to Implement the Main Game Code*

File	Description
WINGTD.DEF	The Windows definition file needed to create the game.
WINGTD.RC	The Windows resource file needed.
WINGTD.RH	Defines the resource IDs.
WINGTD.H	The header file for the main module WINGTD.CPP.
WINGTD.CPP	Defines the main functions for controlling the game loop, initializing the game window, and processing messages.
WINGWND.H	The WinG window module header file.
WINGWND.CPP	The main WinG window processing functions.
WINGBMP2.ASM	The low-level, assembly-language module that implements the Tile() routine for fast bitmap processing.
ABOUT.H	The header file for the About() dialog box function.
ABOUT.CPP	The code for the About() function, which displays an About dialog box.
DEBUG.H	The header file that defines the debugstream class that is used to help debug the application.
DEBUG.CPP	The methods for the debugstream class.
PALETTE.H	The header file that defines the Palette class.
PRECOMP.H	Provides the list of precompiled header files for the sample game.
GEN.H/GEN.CPP	Defines prototypes for the general-purpose functions that are used with the game.

WM_QUIT message is received. This message is triggered when the user selects the Quit command from the menu bar. Here's the code for the main loop:

```
do    // Main control loop for the game
{
    if ( PeekMessage( &msg, NULL, 0, 0, PM_REMOVE ) )
    {
        if ( msg.message != WM_QUIT )  // Skip over the quit message
        {
            TranslateMessage( &msg );  // Message received
            DispatchMessage( &msg );   // Process it
        }
    }
    else
    {
        if ( AppIdle() )  // Application is idle so wait around
        WaitMessage();    // for a message to come in
    }
}
while ( msg.message != WM_QUIT );  // We're done!
```

The **PeekMessage()** function gets the message and then **TranslateMessage()** and **DispatchMessage()** are called to set up the message and dispatch it. If no message is found, **WaitMessage()** is called to wait until an event occurs, such as the user trying to resize the window or quitting the application.

The initialization code in **WinMain()** is all generic startup stuff, and not particularly interesting except for the registration of the windows to be used for destination of WinG blits. One of the topics in the WinG help file recommends aligning the destination rectangle of a blit on a double word boundary. To ensure that the upper-left corner of the rectangle is double word aligned, we create the window where animation will occur with the **CS_BYTEALIGNCLIENT** style bit set:

```
WNDCLASS  wc;
wc.xtyle = CS_BYTEALIGNCLIENT;
```

This initialization work is performed in **InitApplication()**.

The **InitInstance()** function defined in WINGTD.CPP creates the main window for the sample game, as shown here:

```
hWndMain = CreateWindow( lpszMainWndClass, lpszWinGTopDown,
        WS_OVERLAPPEDWINDOW,
        CW_USEDEFAULT, CW_USEDEFAULT,
        CW_USEDEFAULT, CW_USEDEFAULT,
        NULL, NULL, hInstance, NULL );
```

Its only job is to create and update four static text windows at the bottom of the screen (which contain some application information) and to create the game window.

The last function, **MainWndProc()**, is your typical main Windows processing function. It consists of one big **switch** statement that processes the Windows messages **WM_CREATE**, **WM_ACTIVATEAPP**, **WM_COMMAND**, **WM_SETFOCUS**, and **WM_DESTROY**.

Adding the WinG Support Files

We created classes earlier to wire in WinG bitmaps and DCs, but we still need WinG code to control tasks such as sizing a window, setting up a view, tiling a window, moving the player, and so on. The functions that perform this work are defined in WINGWND.CPP and its header file WINGWND.H.

WINGWND.CPP actually contains most of the WinG-specific code for the sample game. It also contains static objects used in the game window, a **BitmapInfo** object that is used to create the WinG bitmap, the WinG DC and bitmap, the palette and logical palette, and the various DIB tiles. The main function defined in this file, **WinGWndProc()**, is a window processing procedure that contains the code to handle the window where WinG animation takes place.

WinGWndProc() sets up the various static objects in response to the **WM_CREATE** message. First, it gets a handle to the desktop DC, which will be used for palette creation. Then it does the equivalent of the **ClearSystemPalette()** routine found in the WinG SAMPLES\UTILS directory.

The logical palette **logPalClear** object's color table is initialized to 256 entries. The entry flags for these entries are set to **PC_NOCOLLAPSE**. A **Palette** object is then created from the **logPalClear** object. This blank palette is selected into the screen DC, selected out of it, and deleted. This process supposedly clears the system palette. The screen DC is then released.

Next, the **WM_CREATE** handler loads the various DIBs used for tiling. Each DIB is stored as a Windows resource. The **DIBitmap::Load()** method defined in BIBITMAP.CPP handles the work of loading them.

Each of these DIBs must use the same palette. Because we want to create an identity palette, these DIBs must not use any colors in the 0-9 or 246-255 ranges. The DIBs, however, may specify any colors for these ranges in their palettes, since these colors will be overwritten by system palette entries when loaded. The palette from one of the DIBs is copied into the **logPalGame** object by calling the **CopyColors()** method. The **logPalGame** object retrieves the system palette entries, and sets the entry flags of the middle range to **PC_NOCOLLAPSE**. Finally, a palette is created from the logical palette, and if we did everything correctly, we should have an identity palette. We can verify this step by setting the **Debug** and **DebugPalette** entries of the WIN.INI [WinG] section to 1. WinG will detect if we have an identity palette when we attempt to use it, and send a debug string to the auxiliary device.

The next thing we've got to do is initialize the WinG bitmap. First, we resize the **recInfo** object's color table to 256, and ask WinG to recommend a DIB format through our **bitmapInfo** wrapper function, **WinGRecommendFormat()**. To complete the initialization of our **bitmapInfo** object, we copy the color table from our prepared logical palette.

Next, we initialize a full-screen WinG bitmap. I took this approach to minimize re-creating WinG bitmaps, but you may want to re-create the bitmap each time a **WM_SIZE** message is received. At any rate, the bitmap size is rounded up to be 32-byte aligned, the width of my tiles, to minimize the amount of coding needed to clip the bitmap edges. The width and the height are then set into the **recInfo** object, being careful to preserve the existing sign of the DIB's height, for the recommended DIB orientation. Finally, the

WinG bitmap is created by passing it the WinG DC and the **BitmapInfo** object; it's selected into the WinG DC and the window is tiled.

Tiling the window also occurs when the player moves. When this happens, the player position is updated, the new window is tiled, the previous window is invalidated, and **UpdateWindow** causes a **WM_PAINT** message to be sent, updating the window on the screen.

How Fast Is It?

I admit it; when I first heard about WinG, I was skeptical. How can something that's based on DIBs be faster than DDBs? I thought, "For something like the tile sample game we're doing, we're probably better off using the standard Windows API function **BitBlt()** with DDBs." How can **WinGBitBlit()** on a DIB beat **BitBlt()** on a DDB in performance? Well, the answer is that it may be able to, but it doesn't matter. Comparing the two is like comparing apples to oranges: You may be able to write a tiled game with DDBs, but it's faster to write directly to the bitmap, which you cannot do with a DDB.

My first attempt at creating a function to tile the window was a dismal failure. Actually, I knew it was going to be, but I wanted to see just how slow it was. I wrote a **BitBlt()** function for my WinG bitmap that looped through the scan lines and did a **memcpy()** for each one. The time to tile a 640×480 screen was approximately 3,600 milliseconds, pretty much what I expected. If I wanted to continue with my **BitBlt()** function, I'd probably optimize it by eliminating function calls and doing it entirely in assembly—but that's not the point.

Even if I could write a **BitBlt()** function that's as fast as the Windows **BitBlt()** for DDBs, it would still be too slow to call it for each and every tile on the screen and then copy it to the window. A better approach is to write a specialized function that tiles across the WinG bitmap. So I went about writing a C function to tile the window. This was a little better, since it did have an internal call to **memcpy()**, and now it "only" took 740 milliseconds to tile the window. By rewriting the inner loop in inline assembly and rearranging the number of accesses to tiles, I was able to get this down to about 48 milliseconds. Not bad—but still not what we need.

By rewriting the entire **Tile()** routine in assembly (WINGBMP2.16), I was able to get that down to about 20 milliseconds. The final version (WINGBMP2.ASM), which was written in 32-bit assembly with the help of Microsoft's CMACRO32.INC, brings it down to 10 milliseconds. Time and space don't permit me to explain how to use 32-bit assembler instructions in a Win16 application in detail. For more information on how this is done, check out the bibliography at the back of this book for more information. (Thanks to Gary Blaine of Borland Team B for his help in getting CMACRO32.INC to work with BC++ 4.5.)

I was pretty happy with 10 milliseconds, but I have no doubt that if I further pursued the optimization, I could have gotten that time down even lower. So, the point of all this is that even though **WinGBitBlt()** may not be as fast as **BitBlt()**, it doesn't have to be. The boost in performance you can get by bypassing GDI is well worth it. Factor in the video cards that are specifically designed to speed up Windows, and you'll realize that WinG may actually make games play *faster* if you have the time and knowledge to code them well.

To sum it all up, WinG gives you access to the drawing surface of a DIB, where in Microsoft parlance, you can "party on the bitmap" as much as you want. You have to be aware that you're still in Windows, and you've got to deal with the Palette, DIBs, windows, and all the other Windows objects, but that's a small price to pay to finally be able to write a fast animated game in Windows!

Building the Game

The game program, WINGTD.EXE, can be created using Borland C++ 4.5, but you'll need TASM if you want to rebuild (compile and link) everything from scratch. All of the source files are included on the companion CD-ROM in the subdirectory \CHAP_13.

To help you experiment with and recompile the game program, I've provided a MAKE file named WINGTD.MAK. This file was generated by Borland C++ 4.5.

Before you build the project, you must do two things:

1. Generate a .LIB file for WING.DLL with Borland's IMPLIB utility. Then, place the .LIB file in a directory in the project's LIB path. (The WING.LIB provided with WinG is not compatible with Borland C++.)

2. Copy the CMACRO32.INC assembler include file into the project directory from the WING\SAMPLES\DOGGIE directory. CMACRO32.INC is a Microsoft file that is distributed with the WinG SDK. The final version of the WINGBMP2.ASM module that I've included is a 32-bit assembler module that can be called from a 16-bit Windows .EXE via the special **cProc** macros in CMACRO32.INC.

WinG and the *ACK-3D* engine are perfect companions. Find out how you can combine these two powerful tools to create fast-action 3-D games for Windows.

Creating a Windows App with ACK-3D

Now that you've seen what WinG can do, you're probably anxious to see how the *ACK-3D* engine can be used with a Windows application. Windows provides a number of benefits that are not readily supported in DOS. Mouse and keyboard game input is relatively easy to process, thanks to the built-in Windows API functions. In addition, Windows allows you to create games that have a consistent interface and features like resizeable windows. If you are really industrious, you can even create games that use multiple windows to display different views as a player moves around in a game map.

In this chapter I'll show you how to use the *ACK-3D* engine with Windows applications. To get there, we'll need to develop some Windows-related support functions. We'll also extend the standard WinG interface a little by encapsulating the WinG structures and functions in a C++ class. This approach will give you new ideas on how you can use WinG bitmaps with Windows applications. You'll also get a chance to expand your knowledge of both C++ and object-oriented programming. Before we finish the chapter, we'll build a complete Windows application that uses WinG to display 3-D scenes in which the player is able to move around and bump into walls using the keyboard and the mouse. The program presented makes a useful template to help you start building your own 3-D games.

Connecting *ACK-3D* to Windows

To set up the engine so that it works with WinG, we need a way to link a WinG bitmap with the **ACKENG** interface structure. As it turns out, this is easy to do and does not require much code. But as we move into Windows, we'll want to add features that help to automate the work of creating 3-D games that run in Windows. Essentially, we'll create a *wrapper* for Windows that provides a number of useful features including:

- A flexible class to access WinG bitmaps
- A high-level function to initialize the 3-D engine in Windows applications
- Support for processing mouse and keyboard input
- Support for creating and processing the system palette and identity palettes
- Routines to draw (paint) 3-D scenes in a window and resize a window as appropriate messages are received
- An auto-configuration feature to help you read in a specification file and easily set up the components of a game, including wall and object bitmaps, the game map file, the player's starting position and angle, background screen, and so on

The Windows-specific source files used to implement the Windows wrapper for the *ACK-3D* engine are listed in Table 14.1. These files are provided to help simplify the complexity of using WinG and writing Windows applications. Using the wrapper functions, you'll find that you can easily get your Windows-based game up and running very quickly. If you do not have much experience writing Windows games or other Windows applications, you'll especially appreciate the higher-level of support that the wrapper functions provide.

Creating a WinG Interface Class

In Chapter 13 you learned how the WinG functions are accessed in a Windows application to set up a WinG bitmap and blit it to the screen. We could use the standard WinG functions just as they are and call them from a Windows application that also makes calls to the *ACK-3D* engine functions. But we want to build a higher-level wrapper for Windows, so we're better off

Table 14.1 *Windows Specific Source Files*

File	Description
WINGDLL.H	Header file for the WinG interface class, WinGdll. This class is used to set up WinG bitmaps and make calls to the standard WinG functions.
WINGDLL.CPP	Defines the methods for the WinGdll interface class. The goal here is to package the standard WinG functions as C++ methods.
WINPALL.CPP	Defines functions to create and process system and identity palettes with WinG.
ACKINFO.CPP	Defines the configuration support functions to build Windows applications.
ACKSUP.H	Header file for the functions defined in ACKSUP.CPP.
ACKSUP.CPP	Defines Windows support functions.
ACKWIN.H	Header file for the functions defined in ACKWIN.CPP.
ACKWIN.CPP	Wrapper functions for calling the standard *ACK-3D* functions from Windows. These functions initialize the engine in a Windows application, process inputs (mouse and keyboard), control how windows are drawn, set up WinG bitmaps, and so on.

creating a WinG C++ class and implementing some methods to encapsulate the calls to the standard WinG functions. The class approach will help us simplify the process of creating and displaying WinG bitmaps.

The class we'll define is named **WinGdll**. You can find the code for this class definition in the header file WINGDLL.H:

```
class WinGdll {  // Interface class for accessing the WinG functions

public:
  WinGdll();    // Constructor
  ~WinGdll();   // Destructor

  BOOL Load();  // Loads a WinG bitmap
  BOOL Free();  // Frees memory for a WinG bitmap

  HINSTANCE m_hLib;
  BOOL m_bLoaded;

// Set up methods for the main WinG functions
  wingCreateDC              pCreateDC;
  wingRecommendDIBFormat    pRecommendDIBFormat;
  wingCreateBitmap          pCreateBitmap;
  wingGetDIBPointer         pGetDIBPointer;
  wingGetDIBColorTable      pGetDIBColorTable;
  wingSetDIBColorTable      pSetDIBColorTable;
  wingCreateHalftonePalette pCreateHalftonePalette;
  wingCreateHalftoneBrush   pCreateHalftoneBrush;
```

```
   wingBitBlt          pBitBlt;
   wingStretchBlt      pStretchBlt;
} ;
```

This class is quite simple; it primarily encapsulates the ten functions that create and process WinG bitmaps. In addition, a few support methods are added: The **WinGdll()** method is automatically called whenever a **WinGdll** object is first created in a program. This method is called a *constructor* in the world of C++ programming. Its counterpart, **~WinGdll()**, is called when a **WinGdll** object is deallocated in a program. This method is called a *destructor.* I'll show you the code for these methods in a moment.

The other two new methods are **Load()** and **Free()**. **Load()** handles the work of loading one of the WinG DLL files—WING32.DLL or WING.DLL—and setting up a WinG bitmap. When you use WinG functions in a Windows application, you must first make sure that one of these DLLs is loaded; otherwise, you won't be able to call any of the WinG functions. In addition to loading one of the DLLs, **Load()** links the WinG DLL's functions to the names used in the class. The **Free()** function simply frees the WinG DLL that was loaded by the **Load()** function.

Just Add Methods

The methods for the **WinGdll** class are implemented in WINGDLL.CPP. A Windows application that uses this class must first define an object using a declaration like this:

```
WinGdll WinG;
```

Then, the object can be used to call any of the WinG methods. For example, here's how the **Load()** method is called using the WinG object we just defined:

```
WinG.Load();
```

Most of the methods implemented in WINGDLL.CPP simply create a wrapper for a corresponding WinG function. For example, the **pCreateBitmap()** method is primarily a device for calling the **WinGCreateBitmap()** function. The methods, however, do check to see if memory is allocated for a bitmap or device context and return a value of FALSE if an error occurs.

Here's the complete set of methods implemented in WINGDLL.CPP. You'll see how these methods are used when we create the Windows support functions and build a sample application. So stay tuned.

```
/////////////////////////////////////////////////////////////////////////
// WINGDLL.CPP
//
// Interface class for WinG.
//
// Uses LoadLibrary() and GetProcAddress() to populate the class.
//
/////////////////////////////////////////////////////////////////////////
#include <windows.h>
#include <wing.h>
#include "wingdll.h"

WinGdll::WinGdll()          // WinGdll constructor
{
  m_bLoaded = FALSE;
}


WinGdll::~WinGdll()         // WinGdll destructor
{
  if (m_bLoaded)
    FreeLibrary (m_hLib); // Free WinG DLL if loaded
  m_bLoaded = FALSE;
}

BOOL WinGdll::Load()
{
#if defined (WIN32) || defined (_WIN32)   // Load 32-bit version of the DLL
  m_hLib = LoadLibrary("wing32.dll");
  if ( m_hLib == NULL ) {
    return FALSE;
  }
#else
  m_hLib = LoadLibrary("wing.dll");      // Load 16-bit version of the DLL
  if ( m_hLib < HINSTANCE_ERROR ) {
    return FALSE;
  }
#endif

  // Link the DLL's functions to our function pointers
  pCreateDC = (wingCreateDC) GetProcAddress (m_hLib, "WinGCreateDC");
  if (pCreateDC == NULL) {
    FreeLibrary (m_hLib);
    return FALSE;
  }

  pRecommendDIBFormat = (wingRecommendDIBFormat)
  GetProcAddress (m_hLib, "WinGRecommendDIBFormat");
  if (pRecommendDIBFormat == NULL) {
    FreeLibrary (m_hLib);
    return FALSE;
  }

  pCreateBitmap = (wingCreateBitmap)
  GetProcAddress (m_hLib, "WinGCreateBitmap");
```

```
if (pCreateBitmap == NULL) {
  FreeLibrary (m_hLib);
  return FALSE;
}

pGetDIBPointer = (wingGetDIBPointer)
GetProcAddress (m_hLib, "WinGGetDIBPointer");
if (pGetDIBPointer == NULL) {
  FreeLibrary (m_hLib);
  return FALSE;
}

pGetDIBColorTable = (wingGetDIBColorTable)
GetProcAddress (m_hLib, "WinGGetDIBColorTable");
if (pGetDIBColorTable == NULL) {
  FreeLibrary (m_hLib);
  return FALSE;
}

pSetDIBColorTable = (wingSetDIBColorTable)
GetProcAddress (m_hLib, "WinGSetDIBColorTable");
if (pSetDIBColorTable == NULL) {
  FreeLibrary (m_hLib);
  return FALSE;
}

pCreateHalftonePalette = (wingCreateHalftonePalette)
GetProcAddress (m_hLib, "WinGCreateHalftonePalette");
if (pCreateHalftonePalette == NULL) {
  FreeLibrary (m_hLib);
  return FALSE;
}

pCreateHalftoneBrush = (wingCreateHalftoneBrush)
GetProcAddress (m_hLib, "WinGCreateHalftoneBrush");
if (pCreateHalftoneBrush == NULL) {
  FreeLibrary (m_hLib);
  return FALSE;
}

pBitBlt = (wingBitBlt) GetProcAddress (m_hLib, "WinGBitBlt");
if (pBitBlt == NULL) {
  FreeLibrary (m_hLib);
  return FALSE;
}

pStretchBlt = (wingStretchBlt) GetProcAddress (m_hLib, "WinGStretchBlt");
if (pStretchBlt == NULL) {
  FreeLibrary (m_hLib);
  return FALSE;
}

m_bLoaded = TRUE;    // DLL is loaded; ready for business!
return TRUE;
}
```

```
BOOL WinGdll::Free()  // Free the memory allocated for the WinG DLL
{
  if (m_bLoaded)
    FreeLibrary (m_hLib); // Free WinG DLL
  m_bLoaded = FALSE;
  return TRUE;
}
```

Creating ACKWIN.CPP

Now that we have an interface class for the WinG DLL, we're ready to move on and create a set of functions to tie the WinG features to the *ACK-3D* engine. The functions we'll need are defined in ACKWIN.CPP. Table 14.2 describes each of these six functions.

To initialize the engine from a Windows application, you call **InitACKEngine()**. This function takes care of the initialization details needed to get the engine up and running. It starts by allocating memory for an **ACKENG** interface structure:

```
ae = (ACKENG *)AckMalloc(sizeof(ACKENG));  // Allocate memory for interface
                                           // structure
if (ae == NULL)
  {
  MessageBox(NULL,"Unable to allocate memory","ACK Error",MB_OK);
  return(-1);
  }
memset(ae,0,sizeof(ACKENG));               // Initialize to all zeroes
```

Table 14.2 *Functions Defined in ACKWIN.CPP*

Function	Description
InitACKEngine()	Generic Windows *ACK-3D* initialization function that creates an ACKENG interface structure and opens the resource file KIT.OVL.
CreateAckPalette()	Creates the screen color palette that the engine needs to display views in Windows.
AckDoSize()	Changes the size of a window when the standard WM_SIZE message is received.
DoCycle()	Processes a drawing cycle for the engine.
ProcessKeys()	Processes the Windows messages WM_KEYDOWN and WM_KEYUP as they are received.
ProcessMouse()	Processes the location of the mouse within the 3-D window.

Because this code runs in Windows now, we need to call the Windows function **MessageBox()** to display an error message if something goes wrong. In this case, memory may not be available to allocate the interface structure, so we'll need to display an appropriate error message if **ae==NULL**. After the interface structure has been allocated and set to all zeroes, the basic components of the interface structure are initialized:

```
ae->WinStartX = 0;          // Set coordinates to full viewport
ae->WinStartY = 0;
ae->WinEndX = 319;
ae->WinEndY = 199;
ae->LightFlag = SHADING_OFF; // Light shading is turned off
ae->xPlayer = 192;          // Set starting coordinates and angle
ae->yPlayer = 640;
ae->PlayerAngle = 0;
ae->TopColor = 0;
ae->BottomColor = 24;
ae->DoorSpeed = 6;          // Set initial door speed
ae->NonSecretCode = 1;      // Set to non-secret doors
```

The top-left corner of the viewport is set to (0,0) and the bottom-right corner is set to (319,199). I've also included a starting position and angle for the player as well as a default setting for light shading and door speed. Keep in mind that these settings are defaults. You can change any of them in your own application; all you need to do is modify the appropriate assignment statements in this function. Of course, you can also override these values by changing them in your application after you call **InitACKEngine()**.

The next initialization task in **InitACKEngine()** opens a game resource file. The file used by default is the standard KIT.OVL, as shown here:

```
result = AckOpenResource("KIT.OVL"); // Open resource file KIT.OVL
if (result)
  {
  MessageBox(NULL,"Error Opening KIT.OVL","ACK Error",MB_OK);
  return(-1);
  }
```

Recall that KIT.OVL contains the data for the trig tables that the engine requires. Again, notice that error-checking code is provided—this time to make sure the resource file is opened properly. Next, the engine is initialized by calling the standard **AckInitialize()** function. After that, the resource file is closed and the interface structure is registered by calling **AckRegisterStructure()**:

```
result = AckInitialize(ae); // Call the main ACK initialization function
if (result)
```

```
{
MessageBox(NULL,"Error Initializing","ACK Error",MB_OK);
return(-1);
}
AckCloseResource();        // Close the resource file
AckRegisterStructure(ae); // Register the interface structure
```

After seeing how all of the initialization routines operate in Chapter 11, most of the code in **InitACKEngine()** should look familiar to you. If you find yourself getting lost in all of these set-up details, you might want to go back and review Chapter 11. The Windows version of the initialization function does not actually perform any Windows-specific operations (except for calling **MessageBox()** to display error messages). It completely sets up the engine so that a Windows application can move on and perform other important operations, such as creating a window to display views and kicking off a message loop to process inputs for a game. I'll show you how easy the Windows-specific tasks are to perform after we discuss how the engine is connected to WinG.

DESIGN TIP

The **InitACKEngine()** function defined in ACKWIN.CPP is provided as a template so that you can see the steps involved in initializing the engine. Feel free to modify this function and add your own initialization code. You can also override any of the assignments made to the **ACKENG** structure by resetting fields in your own application code. But if you make changes to the interface structure, remember to call **AckRegisterStructure()** to reload the structure.

Connecting to WinG

Now that you know how to initialize the *ACK-3D* interface structure in a Windows app, you're probably wondering how we can wire in a WinG bitmap to display views. Recall that the engine itself updates views by writing to an off-screen buffer. Then, the buffer is transferred to video memory. When I showed you how the engine writes to the screen with DOS applications, I presented the **AckDisplayScreen()** function in Chapter 7. The problem is that we're not in Kansas, I mean DOS, anymore.

In a Windows application, we cannot write directly to video memory. We need to change our approach a little. Instead of writing to an off-screen buffer, we'll update views by writing to a WinG bitmap and then we'll use a WinG function to blit the bitmap in a Window. I told you that it would be relatively easy! Figure 14.1 shows the differences between the DOS and Windows approaches.

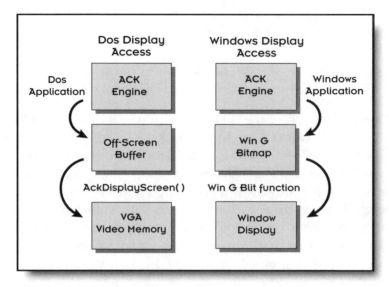

Figure 14.1 *Comparing display access in DOS with WinG access in Windows.*

DESIGN TIP

If you want to port the *ACK-3D* engine to another platform, such as OS/2, you can take the same approach that I did in moving the engine from DOS to Windows. The major work involves transferring view data generated by the engine and stored in an off-screen buffer to a video display. The core engine code that performs the ray casting process is designed to be easily adaptable. Of course, if you port the engine to a machine that uses a processor other than the 80x86 family, you'll need to rewrite some of the low-level assembly code.

The support function that sets up a WinG bitmap and assigns the bitmap to the **ACKENG** interface structure is **AckDoSize()**. This function is really important, so let's take a close look at the entire function now:

```
void AckDoSize(HWND hWnd,LPARAM lParam)
{
  HBITMAP hbm;
  int Counter;

//nBitmapW = LOWORD(lParam);
//nBitmapH = HIWORD(lParam);
nBitmapW = 319; // We'll hard-code the size for now since the map editor
nBitmapH = 199; // is a non-sizeable window
// Make sure the width is on an even boundary for the size it is set to
nBitmapW = ((nBitmapW+3)/4)*4;
```

```
if (AckBuffer)  // Buffer has already been created—use existing one
  {
  BufferHeader.Header.biWidth = nBitmapW;   // Store the width of the bitmap
  BufferHeader.Header.biHeight = -nBitmapH; // Use height for top-down display

  hbm = WinG.pCreateBitmap(AckBuffer,        // Create the bitmap
     (BITMAPINFO *)&BufferHeader, &pAckBuffer);

  hbm = (HBITMAP)SelectObject(AckBuffer, hbm);      // Set up selector to bitmap
  DeleteObject(hbm);
  PatBlt(AckBuffer, 0,0,nBitmapW,nBitmapH, BLACKNESS);  // Set to all black

  if (ae != NULL)  // Check for allocated ACK interface structure
    {
    ae->ScreenBuffer = (UCHAR *)pAckBuffer; // Store pointer to bitmap
    ae->WinEndX = (short)nBitmapW;          // Store end coordinates of viewport
    ae->WinEndY = (short)nBitmapH;
    if (ae->WinEndX > 319)                  // Set to maximum size if over
      ae->WinEndX = 319;
    if (ae->WinEndY > 199)
      ae->WinEndY = 199;
    AckRegisterStructure(ae);               // Register structure
    }
  }
else
  { // Need to create new buffer
    // Create the BITMAPINFO structure
  if (WinG.pRecommendDIBFormat((BITMAPINFO *)&BufferHeader))
    {
    BufferHeader.Header.biBitCount = 8;
    BufferHeader.Header.biCompression = BI_RGB;
    }
  else
    {
    BufferHeader.Header.biSize = sizeof(BITMAPINFOHEADER);
    BufferHeader.Header.biPlanes = 1;
    BufferHeader.Header.biBitCount = 8;
    BufferHeader.Header.biCompression = BI_RGB;
    BufferHeader.Header.biSizeImage = 0;
    BufferHeader.Header.biClrUsed = 0;
    BufferHeader.Header.biClrImportant = 0;
    }

  BufferHeader.Header.biWidth = nBitmapW; // Store width and height of bitmap
  BufferHeader.Header.biHeight = -nBitmapH;

  CreateAckPalette();              // Set up the color palette
  for (Counter = 0;Counter < 256;Counter++) // Store colors in bitmap structure
    {
    BufferHeader.aColors[Counter].rgbRed= ColorTable[Counter].rgbRed;
    BufferHeader.aColors[Counter].rgbGreen = ColorTable[Counter].rgbGreen;
    BufferHeader.aColors[Counter].rgbBlue = ColorTable[Counter].rgbBlue;
    BufferHeader.aColors[Counter].rgbReserved = 0;
    }
```

```
AckBuffer = WinG.pCreateDC();    // Create device context (DC) for bitmap
hbm = WinG.pCreateBitmap(AckBuffer,
              (BITMAPINFO *)&BufferHeader, &pAckBuffer);

SelectObject(AckBuffer, hbm);

PatBlt(AckBuffer, 0,0,nBitmapW,nBitmapH, BLACKNESS);  // Initialize to black
if (ae != NULL)
  {
  ae->ScreenBuffer = (UCHAR *)pAckBuffer;
  AckRegisterStructure(ae);
  }
 }
}
```

AckDoSize() starts by defining the size of the bitmap to be used. I've hardcoded the size to be 320x200. Once the size is determined, the code checks to see if a bitmap has already been set up (**if (AckBuffer)**). **AckBuffer** is the WinG bitmap, and **pAckBuffer** serves as the pointer to reference the bitmap.

The processing work in **AckDoSize()** is split down the middle: Half of the code sets up a WinG bitmap (if one has been previously created) and assigns a pointer to the bitmap to the **ACKENG** interface structure. The other half of the code creates a **BITMAPINFO** structure the first time it's needed and sets up a Windows color palette. Let's explore both sections of the code in a little more detail. We'll start with the second half first since it is responsible for creating the bitmap structure. Then, we'll look at the first half, which sets up the structure.

If a bitmap structure has not been created, the main **else** clause is executed. Here, the first order of business is to call **WinGRecommendDIBFormat()** to create a new **BITMAPINFO** structure:

```
if (WinG.pRecommendDIBFormat((BITMAPINFO *)&BufferHeader))
```

DESIGN TIP

Notice that we don't call the **WinGRecommendDIBFormat()** directly. Here, the object **WinG** calls the method **pRecommendDIBFormat()**. The **WinG** object is defined in the global declarations section of the ACKWIN.CPP file, as shown here:

```
WinGdll WinG;
```

This approach allows us to access the WinG methods that were defined in the WINGDLL.CPP source file. As you explore the code in ACKWIN.CPP and the sample Windows application presented later, you'll see that this technique is used throughout to access all of the WinG functions.

After the bitmap structure is created, the width and height fields are assigned values to reflect the size of the WinG bitmap:

```
BufferHeader.Header.biWidth = nBitmapW; // Store width and height of bitmap
BufferHeader.Header.biHeight = -nBitmapH;
```

Next, the internal **CreatePalette()** function is called to set up the screen palette. (I'll show you how this function works in the next section.) Essentially, **CreatePalette()** assigns red, green, and blue color components to the **ColorTable[ ]** array. After the function call, **AckDoSize()** transfers the color components in the array to the bitmap structure.

Once the bitmap structure is set up, it's time to create a WinG bitmap device context (DC) and create the memory for the bitmap:

```
AckBuffer = WinG.pCreateDC();    // Create device context (DC) for bitmap
hbm = WinG.pCreateBitmap (AckBuffer,
          (BITMAPINFO *)&BufferHeader, &pAckBuffer);
```

Now you see how **AckBuffer** and **pAckBuffer** are set up. **AckBuffer** serves as the WinG DC and **pAckBuffer** is the pointer that references the bitmap in memory. All that remains is to initialize the buffer to the color black and assign the bitmap to the **ACKENG** interface structure:

```
PatBlt(AckBuffer, 0,0,nBitmapW,nBitmapH, BLACKNESS);  // Initialize to black
if (ae != NULL) // An interface structure is available
  {
  ae->ScreenBuffer = (UCHAR *)pAckBuffer;
  AckRegisterStructure(ae); // Register the updated structure
  }
```

Now when an *ACK-3D* function, such as **AckBuildView()**, is used to update a view and write to the off-screen buffer, the code actually builds a view and fills up the WinG bitmap instead of an off-screen buffer.

Okay, we discussed the second half of **AckDoSize()** and saw how a new WinG bitmap is created and initialized. Let's return to the first part of the function. If a bitmap structure already exists, we only need to set up the bitmap by calling the **pCreateBitmap()** method as shown:

```
hbm = WinG.pCreateBitmap (AckBuffer,     // Create the bitmap
          (BITMAPINFO *)&BufferHeader, &pAckBuffer);
```

Then, the bitmap is initialized to all black:

```
PatBlt(AckBuffer, 0,0,nBitmapW,nBitmapH, BLACKNESS);// Set to all black
```

Lastly, the WinG bitmap is assigned to the interface structure, as shown here:

```
if (ae != NULL)  // Check for allocated ACK interface structure
  {
  ae->ScreenBuffer = (UCHAR *)pAckBuffer; // Store pointer to bitmap
  ae->WinEndX = (short)nBitmapW;// Store end coordinates of viewport
  ae->WinEndY = (short)nBitmapH;
  ...
```

Notice that this time around we need to update the lower-right coordinates of the viewport because the window size for viewing a scene may have changed. You now know how to link up a WinG bitmap with the **ACKENG** structure!

Color Palette Support

Part of the process of initializing the *ACK-3D* engine involves setting up a color palette for the engine to draw views. When the engine is initialized in a DOS application, the program must define the set of colors used and the colors are stored in the **colordat[ ]** array. In Windows we have a choice; we can use the colors already stored in the system palette, or we can load in the colors assigned to the **colordat[ ]** array. The support function **CreateAckPalette()** sets up a Windows palette.

At this point you might be wondering where the palette color data is stored. The colors are assigned to the bitmap structure itself. Thus, each WinG bitmap can have its own color set. The **header** structure used to store bitmap and color palette information is defined in ACKWIN.H as:

```
typedef struct header
{
  BITMAPINFOHEADER Header;
  RGBQUAD aColors[256];
} header;
```

This is similar to the structure used in the previous chapter to call the WinG functions. The **RGBQUAD** field consists of an array of structures; each structure stores the red, green, and blue component for a color.

The **CreateAckPalette()** function must determine which palette should be used (the Windows system palette or a user-defined palette) and then load in the palette into the **header** structure. The decision of which palette to use is controlled by a flag named **_USE_SYSTEM_PALETTE**. This flag is set to 0 by default. If it is set to 1, the system palette is loaded.

Processing a Drawing Cycle

When we create a Windows application that uses the *ACK-3D* engine, we need to set up some sort of drawing cycle to continue to update views as the player moves around. Basically, you need a main loop that looks something like this:

```
for (;;)
  {
  if (windows_event)
    {
      <check for windows messages and process them>
    ...
    }
  else
    {
    DoCycle();
    ...
    }
  }
```

The loop continues until the player quits the program. Inside the loop, Windows events are processed, such as a mouse click or keyboard press. If there is no pending event, the function **DoCycle()** is called to update a view.

DoCycle() is a custom function I've placed in ACKWIN.CPP to give you an idea of how a drawing cycle should be processed in Windows. Of course, this code is not cast in stone—you might even find a number of ways to improve it! The basic processing steps include:

1. Test a global flag to make sure that it's okay to display a new view.
2. Set up some internal variables to determine the increments to move a player.
3. Test to see if one of the arrow keys has been pressed and if so, update the player's angle. This step also checks mouse activity.
4. Get a device context to update the window and call a painting function, **AckPaint()**, to update the view.
5. Update the player's moving and turning speeds.

Because some of these operations are application-specific, it's difficult to come up with a completely general drawing cycle function that will fit all situations. But by having this template, you'll have a head start. Let's look at some of the code in **DoCycle()**.

The first step is accomplished with the simple **if** statement:

```
if (bNoShow)
  return;
```

This flag, **bNoShow**, should be set to false in your application. It controls whether or not views will be updated. Next, the function must set up some internal variables to determine the increments used to move the player around:

```
Amt = 16;        // Default amount to move the player
if (kbPressed[kbCtrl]) // A Ctrl key press doubles this rate
  Amt = 32;
// Add the increment to the player's current speed
Amt += nMoveSpeed;
// Calculate the angle increment to turn the player
TurnAmt = (short)(INT_ANGLE_6 + nTurnSpeed);
```

The variables **nMoveSpeed** and **nTurnSpeed** are global variables that must be defined in your application program. They are used to keep track of the player's speed for moving forward and angle increment for turning. By continuing to increment or decrement them in a game, your player will get a sense of acceleration and deceleration. The **if** statement in the above code checks to see if the Ctrl key has been pressed. If it has, the increment variable **Amt** is set to double its default value to increase the rate at which the player moves through a view. (You can think of the Ctrl key as the "turbo" accelerator.)

To move a player, we need to know if an arrow key has been pressed (or if the mouse has been moved). This text is moved by using **if** statements as shown here:

```
if (kbPressed[kbLeftArrow])
  {
  ae->PlayerAngle -= TurnAmt; // Add in the turn amount
  if (ae->PlayerAngle < 0)
    ae->PlayerAngle += (short)INT_ANGLE_360;
  }

if (kbPressed[kbRightArrow])
  {
  ae->PlayerAngle += TurnAmt;
  if (ae->PlayerAngle >= INT_ANGLE_360)
    ae->PlayerAngle -= (short)INT_ANGLE_360;
  }
```

The array **kbPressed[ ]** keeps track of the state of the mouse and keyboard. I'll show you how this works shortly. For now, all you need to know is that if one of these conditions is met, the player wants to turn. Turning is easily accomplished by factoring in the **TurnAmt** to the **PlayerAngle**, the field in the interface structure that stores the player's current viewing angle. If the player presses a key or moves the mouse to indicate he or she wants to move up or down, the player's angle is adjusted again. But it is also necessary to call **AckMovePOV()** because of the major change in the viewing angle. Here's an example of the code used to move the player around:

```
if (kbPressed[kbDownArrow])
  { // Turn the player around
  MoveAngle = (short)(ae->PlayerAngle + INT_ANGLE_180);
  if (MoveAngle >= INT_ANGLE_360)
    MoveAngle -= (short)INT_ANGLE_360;
  AckMovePOV(MoveAngle,Amt);
  }
```

After the player's angle and position have been updated, it's time to get a device context for the view and display it by calling **AckPaint()**, as shown here:

```
HDC hdc = GetDC(hwndApp);
AckPaint(hwndApp, hdc);
ReleaseDC(hwndApp, hdc);
```

But don't look for **AckPaint()** in the ACKWIN.CPP file because it's not there. This function must be custom written for your application program. I'll show you how to write one when we explore the sample application later in this chapter. Basically, this function builds a new view by calling **AckBuildView()**, and then displays the new view by using one of the WinG bitblt functions.

Before **DoCycle()** finishes, it updates the player's moving and turning speeds. The goal here is to create the effect of acceleration and deceleration as the player moves:

```
nMoveSpeed -= (short)3;
// Keep the movement within reasonable bounds. This process
// will simulate acceleration and deceleration of the POV.
if (nMoveSpeed < 0) nMoveSpeed = 0;
if (nMoveSpeed > 16) nMoveSpeed = 16;
nTurnSpeed -= (short)3;
// Do the same thing with turn speed. By experimenting with
// the number above, various acceleration and deceleration
// levels can be achieved.
if (nTurnSpeed < 0) nTurnSpeed = 0;
if (nTurnSpeed > 90) nTurnSpeed = 90;
```

Notice that whenever we update **nMoveSpeed** or **nTurnSpeed**, we need to ensure that the new setting is in range. This check keeps the player from taking too big a step or moving at too wide an angle. Code like this should provide you with some ideas for adding "intelligence" to the way a player can move around in a game.

Processing Mouse and Keyboard Inputs

The ACKWIN.CPP file provides two functions for processing the keyboard and the mouse: **ProcessKeys()** and **ProcessMouse()**. Each of these functions uses a global array named **kbPressed[ ]**, which must be declared in the global definitions of your Windows application as:

```
UCHAR kbPressed[128];
```

This array is used in connection with index variables that are defined in the header file KEYS.H. As an example, here are some of the settings for keys that are supported:

```
kbDownArrow = 0x50,
kbLeftArrow = 0x4B,
kbRightArrow = 0x4D,
kbUpArrow = 0x48,
```

To indicate that one of these keys was pressed, a value of 1 is assigned to the corresponding location in the **kbPressed[ ]** array. For example, if the left arrow key is pressed, the following assignment is made:

```
kbPressed[kbLeftArrow] = 1;
```

As you can see, this is a very useful technique to keep track of the state of the keyboard.

When you write a Windows application, your program can call **ProcessKeys()** or **ProcessMouse()** whenever a Windows message such as **WM_KEYDOWN** or **WM_MOUSEMOVE** is received. Either of these functions will detect which event has occurred and update the **kbPressed[ ]** array. You might be wondering what mouse events have to do with a keyboard status array. Well, mouse events such as moving the mouse to the right or left can be represented as pressing the right or left arrow key. With this approach, we only need to use one status array to keep track of keyboard and mouse activity. To see how this works, let's walk through an example.

Assume that your player, navigating in your Windows game, slides the mouse to the right. Your program will generate a **WM_MOUSEMOVE** message that in turn would cause the **ProcessMouse()** function to be called. This function is defined with the parameters:

```
void ProcessMouse(HWND hWnd,short nType,short xPos,short yPos)
```

where **hWnd** is the handle to the current window, **nType** is the status code, and **xPos** and **yPos** are the x and y position of the mouse. As long as the **nType** status code is set to 1, the mouse activity will be processed. If you take a peek at the code in **ProcessMouse()**, you'll find the following set of **if** statements that determine how the **kbPressed[ ]** array should be updated:

```
if (yPos < 60)   // Simulate an up arrow if near the top of the window
   {
   kbPressed[kbUpArrow] = 1;
   nMoveSpeed += (short)SPEED_AMOUNT;
   }
if (yPos > (yMax-60)) // Simulate down arrow if near the bottom
   {
   kbPressed[kbDownArrow] = 1;
   nMoveSpeed += (short)SPEED_AMOUNT;
   }
if (xPos < 60)        // Simulate left arrow if near left edge
   {
   kbPressed[kbLeftArrow] = 1;
   nTurnSpeed += (short)SPEED_AMOUNT;
   }
...
```

Notice that the (x,y) position of the mouse is examined and one of the locations in the keyboard array is set to 1 to emulate a keyboard position key. We also need to update the moving speed and turning speed so that the player will later be moved or turned as the mouse is moved around.

The ACKWIN.CPP File

Before we move on and create the other Windows support file, here is the complete code for ACKWIN.CPP. You might want to spend some time looking over this code.

```
// Assorted routines that can be used in Windows based ACK applications
// These routines are not necessarily tied to the ACK map editor and they are
// more generic in nature.
// (c) 1995 ACK Software (Lary Myers)
#define STRICT
#include <windows.h>
#pragma hdrstop
#include <stdlib.h>
```

```c
#include <string.h>
#include <wing.h>
#include "wingdll.h"
#include "ackwin.h"
#ifndef SPEED_AMOUNT
  #define SPEED_AMOUNT 5
#endif

extern "C" {
#include "keys.h"
#include "ack3d.h"
extern   short rsHandle;
extern   ULONG *rbaTable;
extern   short Resolution;
extern   UCHAR colordat[];
extern   UCHAR *BackArray[];
extern   unsigned short FloorMap[];
extern   unsigned short CeilMap[];
extern   unsigned short *ObjGrid;
};

extern   ACKENG  *ae;           // Interface structure
extern   short nMoveSpeed;
extern   short nTurnSpeed;
extern   HINSTANCE hInstGlobal;
extern   BOOL bNoShow;          // Do not display if TRUE
extern   short nViewType;       // Current view in grid window
extern   short nEditType;       // Editing walls or objects
extern   HWND hwndApp;
extern   UCHAR kbPressed[];
extern   WinGdll WinG;
extern   header BufferHeader;
extern   void *pBuffer;
extern   HDC Buffer;
extern   void *pAckBuffer;
extern   HDC AckBuffer;
extern   void *pMapBuffer;
extern   HDC MapBuffer;
extern   HPALETTE  hpalApp;
extern   int nBitmapW;
extern   int nBitmapH;          // WinG bitmap dimensions
extern   RGBQUAD ColorTable[];
extern   pal   LogicalPalette;

//****************************************************************************
// Here is a generic ACK Initialization proceedure, with Windows modifications
// for error reporting, etc. Replace the initial values below with your own
// starting values.
//****************************************************************************
short InitACKEngine(void)
{
    short result;
ae = (ACKENG *)AckMalloc(sizeof(ACKENG)); // Allocate memory for interface
                                          // structure
```

```
if (ae == NULL)
  {
  MessageBox(NULL,"Unable to allocate memory","ACK Error",MB_OK);
  return(-1);
  }
memset(ae,0,sizeof(ACKENG));        // Initialize to all zeroes
ae->WinStartX      = 0;             // Set coordinates to full viewport
ae->WinStartY      = 0;
ae->WinEndX        = 319;
ae->WinEndY        = 199;
ae->LightFlag      = SHADING_OFF;   // Light shading is turned off
ae->xPlayer        = 192;           // Set starting coordinates and angle
ae->yPlayer        = 640;
ae->PlayerAngle    = 0;
ae->TopColor       = 0;
ae->BottomColor    = 24;
ae->DoorSpeed      = 6;             // Set initial door speed
ae->NonSecretCode  = 1;             // Set to non secret doors
result             = AckOpenResource("KIT.OVL");   // Open resource file KIT.OVL
if (result)
  {
  MessageBox(NULL,"Error Opening KIT.OVL","ACK Error",MB_OK);
  return(-1);
  }
result = AckInitialize(ae); // Call the main ACK initialization function
if (result)
  {
  MessageBox(NULL,"Error Initializing","ACK Error",MB_OK);
  return(-1);
  }
AckCloseResource();         // Close the resource file
AckRegisterStructure(ae); // Register the interface structure
return(0);
}


//****************************************************************************
// Use this routine to create the screen palette based on the RGB contents
// of the colordat[] array used by the ACK engine. The global LogicalPalette
// array is assumed to contain the entries for setting the palette if the
// Windows system palette is used.
//****************************************************************************
void CreateAckPalette(void)
{
    int i;
    int nColors;
    UCHAR col;

#ifdef _USE_SYSTEM_PALETTE    // Use built-in system palette
    HDC Screen;               // If flag set
    RGBQUAD *pColorTable;

Screen = GetDC(0);            // Get system color palette
GetSystemPaletteEntries(Screen,0,256,LogicalPalette.aEntries);
ReleaseDC(0,Screen);
for (i=0; i<256; i++)         // Load colors in ACK-3D ColorTable[]
```

```
      {
        ColorTable[i].rgbRed = LogicalPalette.aEntries[i].peRed;
        ColorTable[i].rgbGreen = LogicalPalette.aEntries[i].peGreen;
        ColorTable[i].rgbBlue = LogicalPalette.aEntries[i].peBlue;
        ColorTable[i].rgbReserved = 0;
      }
#else // Use user-defined colors
    ClearSystemPalette();                 // Clear the system palette
    nColors = 0;
    for (i=0; i<256; I++)                  // Loop to load in pre-defined colors
      {
      col = colordat[nColors++];          // Get color from list
      col <<= 2;  // Scale for storage
      ColorTable[i].rgbRed = col;         // Store red component
      col = colordat[nColors++];          // Get next color
      col <<= 2;
      ColorTable[i].rgbGreen = col;       // Store green component
      col = colordat[nColors++];
      col <<= 2;
      ColorTable[i].rgbBlue = col;        // Store blue component
      ColorTable[i].rgbReserved = 0;
      }
#endif
if (hpalApp)
  DeleteObject(hpalApp);
hpalApp = CreateIdentityPalette(ColorTable, 256); // Use ColorTable values to
                                                  // create an indentity palette

}


//********************************************************************************
// Use this routine when a window WM_SIZE message is received. Pass the new
// size of the window in the lParam variable. As you can see below, the current
// size is hard-coded to a 320x200 size window to support the Map Editor.
// The current ACK engine only supports sizes up to 320x200.
//*******************************************
#pragma argused
void AckDoSize(HWND, hWnd, LPARAM lParam)
{
  HBITMAP hbm;
  int Counter;

nBitmapW = 319; //We'll hard-code the size for now since the map editor
nBitmap = 199;  //is a non-sizable window.
//Make sure the width is on an even boundary for the size it is set to
nBitmap = ((nBitmapW+3)/4)*4;
if (AckBuffer)  // Buffer has already been created—use existing one
  {
  BufferHeader.Header.biWidth = nBitmapW;   // Store the width of the bitmap
  BufferHeader.Header.biHeight = -nBitmapH; // Use height for top-down display
  hbm = WinG.pCreateBitmap(AckBuffer,           // Create the bitmap
  (BITMAPINFO *)&BufferHeader, &pAckBuffer);
  hbm = (HBITMAP)SelectObject(AckBuffer, hbm);       // Set up selector to bitmap
  DeleteObject(hbm);
  PatBlt(AckBuffer, 0,0,nBitmapW,nBitmapH, BLACKNESS);  // Set to all black
  if (ae != NULL) // Check for allocated ACK interface structure
```

```
      {
      ae->ScreenBuffer = (UCHAR *)pAckBuffer;  // Store pointer to bitmap
      ae->WinEndX = (short)nBitmapW;           // Store end coordinates of viewport
      ae->WinEndY = (short)nBitmapH;
      if (ae->WinEndX > 319)                   // Set to maximum size if over
        ae->WinEndX = 319;
      if (ae->WinEndY > 199)
        ae->WinEndY = 199;
      AckRegisterStructure(ae);                // Register structure
      }
    }
  else
    { // Need to create new buffer
    // Create the BITMAPINFO structure
    if (WinG.pRecommendDIBFormat((BITMAPINFO *)&BufferHeader))
      {
      BufferHeader.Header.biBitCount = 8;
      BufferHeader.Header.biCompression = BI_RGB;
      }
    else
      {
      BufferHeader.Header.biSize = sizeof(BITMAPINFOHEADER);
      BufferHeader.Header.biPlanes = 1;
      BufferHeader.Header.biBitCount = 8;
      BufferHeader.Header.biCompression = BI_RGB;
      BufferHeader.Header.biSizeImage = 0;
      BufferHeader.Header.biClrUsed = 0;
      BufferHeader.Header.biClrImportant = 0;
      }
    BufferHeader.Header.biWidth = nBitmapW;    // Store width and height of bitmap
    BufferHeader.Header.biHeight = -nBitmapH;
    CreateAckPalette();                        // Set up the color palette
    for (Counter = 0;Counter < 256;Counter++)  // Store colors in bitmap structure
      {
      BufferHeader.aColors[Counter].rgbRed= ColorTable[Counter].rgbRed;
      BufferHeader.aColors[Counter].rgbGreen = ColorTable[Counter].rgbGreen;
      BufferHeader.aColors[Counter].rgbBlue = ColorTable[Counter].rgbBlue;
      BufferHeader.aColors[Counter].rgbReserved = 0;
      }
    AckBuffer = WinG.pCreateDC();     // Create device context (DC) for bitmap
    hbm = WinG.pCreateBitmap(AckBuffer,
                      (BITMAPINFO *)&BufferHeader, &pAckBuffer);
    SelectObject(AckBuffer, hbm);
    PatBlt(AckBuffer, 0,0,nBitmapW,nBitmapH, BLACKNESS);// Initialize to black
    if (ae != NULL)
      {
      ae->ScreenBuffer = (UCHAR *)pAckBuffer;
      AckRegisterStructure(ae);
      }
    }
  }
//***************************************************************************
// Use this routine to process a drawing cycle of the engine. The best place
// to call this is within the message loop handler itself (see ACKEXAM.CPP for
```

```
// and example). The routine will check the current status of the keyboard
// (and mouse) and then move the POV accordingly.
//***************************************************************************
void DoCycle(void)
{
  short Amt,TurnAmt,MoveAngle;

  if (bNoShow)              // Check display flag set in main application
    return;

  Amt = 16;                // Default amount to move the player
  if (kbPressed[kbCtrl])   // A Ctrl key press doubles this rate
    Amt = 32;
  // Add the increment to the player's current speed
  Amt += nMoveSpeed;
  // Calculate the angle increment to turn the player
  TurnAmt = (short)(INT_ANGLE_6 + nTurnSpeed);
  if (kbPressed[kbLeftArrow])
    {
    ae->PlayerAngle -= TurnAmt; // Add in the turn amount
    if (ae->PlayerAngle < 0)
      ae->PlayerAngle += (short)INT_ANGLE_360;
    }
  if (kbPressed[kbRightArrow])
    {
    ae->PlayerAngle += TurnAmt;
    if (ae->PlayerAngle >= INT_ANGLE_360)
      ae->PlayerAngle -= (short)INT_ANGLE_360;
    }
  if (kbPressed[kbDownArrow])
    { // Turn the player around
    MoveAngle = (short)(ae->PlayerAngle + INT_ANGLE_180);
    if (MoveAngle >= INT_ANGLE_360)
      MoveAngle -= (short)INT_ANGLE_360;
    AckMovePOV(MoveAngle,Amt);
    }
  if (kbPressed[kbUpArrow])
    AckMovePOV(ae->PlayerAngle,Amt);

  HDC hdc = GetDC(hwndApp); // Get the device context to paint the view
  AckPaint(hwndApp, hdc);   // Paint it using function in main application
  ReleaseDC(hwndApp, hdc);
  nMoveSpeed -= (short)3;

  // Keep the movement within reasonable bounds. This process
  // will simulate acceleration and deceleration of the POV.
  if (nMoveSpeed < 0)
    nMoveSpeed = 0;
  if (nMoveSpeed > 16)
    nMoveSpeed = 16;
  nTurnSpeed -= (short)3;
  // Do the same thing with turn speed. By experimenting with
  // the number above, various acceleration and deceleration
  // levels can be achieved.
```

```
if (nTurnSpeed < 0)
  nTurnSpeed = 0;
if (nTurnSpeed > 90)
  nTurnSpeed = 90;
}


//***************************************************************************
// Use this routine to process the windows messages WM_KEYDOWN and WM_KEYUP
// as they are received. It will set a global array of virtual keyboard elements
// to correspond to the key being pressed or released. The routine DoCycle will
// then look at this keyboard array to determine if the POV should be moved
// or rotated.
//***************************************************************************
void ProcessKeys(UINT iMessage,WPARAM wParam)
{
switch (iMessage)
{
  case WM_KEYDOWN:
    switch (wParam)
    {
    case VK_UP:
        kbPressed[kbUpArrow] = 1;
        nMoveSpeed += (short)SPEED_AMOUNT;
        break;
      case VK_DOWN:
        kbPressed[kbDownArrow] = 1;
        nMoveSpeed += (short)SPEED_AMOUNT;
        break;
      case VK_LEFT:
        kbPressed[kbLeftArrow] = 1;
        nTurnSpeed += (short)SPEED_AMOUNT;
        break;
      case VK_RIGHT:
        kbPressed[kbRightArrow] = 1;
        nTurnSpeed += (short)SPEED_AMOUNT;
        break;
      case VK_CONTROL:
        kbPressed[kbCtrl] = 1;
        break;
      case VK_ESCAPE:
        kbPressed[kbEsc] = 1;
        break;
      case VK_SPACE:
        AckCheckDoorOpen(ae->xPlayer,ae->yPlayer,ae->PlayerAngle);
        break;
      case VK_SHIFT:
        kbPressed[kbLeftShift] = 1; break;
      case VK_TAB:
        kbPressed[kbAlt] = 1; break;
      }
    DoCycle();
    break;
  case WM_KEYUP:
    switch (wParam)
```

```
       {
         case VK_UP:
           nMoveSpeed = 0;
           kbPressed[kbUpArrow] = 0;
           break;
         case VK_DOWN:
           nMoveSpeed = 0;
           kbPressed[kbDownArrow] = 0;
           break;
         case VK_LEFT:
           nTurnSpeed = 0;
           kbPressed[kbLeftArrow] = 0;
           break;
         case VK_RIGHT:
           nTurnSpeed = 0;
           kbPressed[kbRightArrow] = 0;
           break;
         case VK_CONTROL:
           kbPressed[kbCtrl] = 0;
           break;
         case VK_ESCAPE:
           kbPressed[kbEsc] = 0;
           break;
         case VK_SPACE:
           kbPressed[kbSpace] = 0;
           break;
         case VK_SHIFT:
           kbPressed[kbLeftShift] = 0;
           break;
         case VK_TAB:
           kbPressed[kbAlt] = 0;
           break;
         }
     DoCycle();
     break;
   }
}


//****************************************************************************
// Use this routine to process the location of the mouse within the 3D window.
// It will check the mouse position to determine if the left button is being
// pressed near the edges of the window and then will emulate a key being
// pressed accordingly. The DoCycle() function will then handle the emulated
// key as if the keyboard were actually pressed.
//****************************************************************************
void ProcessMouse(HWND hWnd,short nType,short xPos,short yPos)
{
  short xMax,yMax;
  RECT  rect;

memset(kbPressed,0,128);  // Clear out all previous key presses
if (!nType)      // For now, a mouse released will just return
  {
  nMoveSpeed = nTurnSpeed = 0;
```

```
  return;
  }
GetClientRect(hWnd,&rect);
xMax = (short)rect.right;
yMax = (short)rect.bottom;
if (yPos < 60)        // Simulate an up arrow if near the top of the window
  {
  kbPressed[kbUpArrow] = 1;
  nMoveSpeed += (short)SPEED_AMOUNT;
  }
if (yPos > (yMax-60)) // Simulate down arrow if near the bottom
  {
  kbPressed[kbDownArrow] = 1;
  nMoveSpeed += (short)SPEED_AMOUNT;
  }
if (xPos < 60)        // Simulate left arrow if near left edge
  {
  kbPressed[kbLeftArrow] = 1;
  nTurnSpeed += (short)SPEED_AMOUNT;
  }
if (xPos > (xMax-60)) // Simulate right arrow if near right edge
  {
  kbPressed[kbRightArrow] = 1;
  nTurnSpeed += (short)SPEED_AMOUNT;
  }
DoCycle();                // Update the 3-D window
}
```

Providing Auto-Configuration Support with ACKINFO.CPP

When you look at the sample program that is created in the last part of this chapter, you'll first notice that the program seems to be missing most of the initialization calls, such as **AckLoadMap()**, **AckLoadWall()**, **AckLoadObject()**, and so on. Recall that these were the functions we introduced in Chapter 11 to load in game components during the initialization phase. The program presented in this chapter takes a different approach, however. For example, here are all of the function calls required to load in and process the user-definable components for the game:

```
AckOpenResource("PICS.DTF");
ProcessInfoFile();
AckCloseResource();
```

What gives? How does the engine know how to load in and process all of the bitmap files and map files that are needed to create the game map and set up walls and objects?

The **ProcessInfoFile()** function performs this work for us. Essentially, this function loads in a special user-definable resource file and initializes the game based on the contents of the resource file. The technique of using resource files can really help you automate the process of creating your own games with the *ACK-3D* engine. To learn how to do this, read Chapter 15 and Appendix A, *A Better System for Building Games.* For now, let's focus on creating the Windows support code that we need to implement the auto-configuration system.

The **ProcessInfoFile()** function is defined in the Windows support file ACKINFO.CPP. Listed in Table 14.3, this file also contains all the internal support functions called by **ProcessInfoFile()** to read in and process a game resource file.

To use **ProcessInfoFile()** you need to create a user-definable resource file for your game by using the Windows-based map editor. You can also create one by following the techniques outlined in Appendix A. Then, you can call **AckOpenResource()** to open the file for reading. When **ProcessInfoFile()** is called, it performs these tasks:

- Reads the section of the resource file that contains set-up commands
- Processes each command read by calling internal functions like **LoadWall()** and **LoadObject()**, which in turn call *ACK-3D* functions like **AckLoadWall()** and **AckLoadObject()**.
- Stores initialization data in the **ACKENG** interface structure. Some of this configuration data includes the player's starting angle, x,y map position, the light shading flag, and so on.

Table 14.3 *Functions Defined in ACKINFO.CPP and ACKSUP.CPP*

Function	Description
ProcessBackDrop()	Creates the correct arrays to display a rotating background.
LoadBackDrop()	Loads a background image and processes the image into separate slices for use at display time.
ReadLine()	Internal function called by ProcessInfoFile() to read in a text line from the opened configuration file.
GetNextParm()	Internal function called by ProcessInfoFile() to skip to the next parameter in a configuration file.
LoadWall()	Loads a wall bitmap specified in a configuration file.
LoadObject()	Loads an object bitmap specified in a configuration file.
SkipSpaces()	Removes any leading spaces from a command string.
CreateObject()	Creates an object of a specified style.
ProcessInfoFile()	Reads in an ASCII configuration file one line at a time and processes the commands stored in the file.

- Creates data structures for new objects if objects are specified in the resource file.

We'll examine how **ProcessInfoFile()** operates. But before we explore this function, let's take a few moments to discuss resource files.

ACK-3D User-Definable Resource Files

If you've done any game programming in the past or if you've built applications that require numerous support files, you're probably familiar with the concept of resource files. In *ACK-3D* a user-definable resource file is simply a binary file that combines all of the different files used to create a game. These files include a game configuration script, map file, wall bitmap files, object bitmap files, and so on. An example of how the resource file can be arranged is shown in Figure 14.2. Resource files are created by using the Windows-based map editor or a utility program provided with the *ACK-3D* engine called BPIC.EXE. The order of how data is arranged in any given resource file is determined by the order in which game files are listed when the BPIC program is used. (Appendix A provides instructions for using the BPIC.EXE program to build a resource file.)

Don't confuse the user-definable game resource file with the built-in system resource KIT.OVL. These are two different kinds of resource files. The KIT.OVL system resource file contains the trig data that the engine needs to build its internal lookup tables. The user-definable resource file contains data files that are unique to your game.

DESIGN TIP

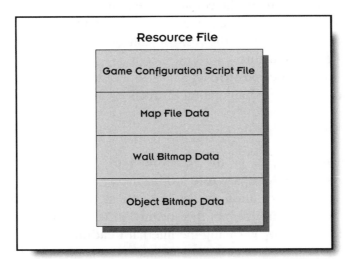

Figure 14.2 *The structure of a user-definable resource file.*

As Figure 14.2 indicates, one section of the compiled resource file contains game configuration instructions. You can think of these instructions as a script that tells the engine how to build the resources for your game. These instructions are placed in a separate text file and combined into the user-definable resource file by the BPIC.EXE program.

What do these configuration instructions look like? Basically, they come in the form:

```
INSTRUCTION: value
```

An exception to this form are instructions that serve as labels to define sections within the configuration file. Here are a few examples that show how some of the instructions are used:

```
XPLAYER: 100
YPLAYER: 500
PLAYERANGLE: 0
```

The complete set of instructions supported and the techniques for using these instructions are provided in Appendix A. You might find it helpful to read these instructions before you look at the code in **ProcessInfoFile()**.

Inside ACKINFO.CPP and ProcessInfoFile()

Most of these functions in ACKINFO.CPP are required to support the configuration setup function **ProcessInfoFile()**. When **ProcessInfoFile()** is called by your application, it reads the command section of the opened resource file and processes one command at a time. Depending on the command found, it either eventually calls one of the *ACK-3D* functions, or it assigns data to the **ACKENG** interface structure.

The first thing **ProcessInfoFile()** must do is access the location in the resource file where the configuration instructions are stored:

```
_llseek(rsHandle,rbaTable[0],SEEK_SET);
```

As we learned in Chapter 11, the **rbaTable[ ]** array is used to reference the opened resource file. Next, a **while** loop is used to read in each instruction. The configuration script must always be terminated with the **END:** instruction, so the loop continues until this instruction is read. **ProcessInfoFile()** reads one line at a time by calling the internal **ReadLine()** function.

After an instruction line has been read, the instruction is processed by using a **switch** statement. The **default** section of the **switch** statement actually determines which instruction has been read:

```
default:
   if (!strnicmp(LineBuffer,"WALLS:",6))
      {
      mode = 4;
      break;
      }

   if (!strnicmp(LineBuffer,"OBJECTS:",8))
      {
      mode = 5;
      break;
      }

   if (!strnicmp(LineBuffer,"MAPFILE:",8))
      {
      MapResource = atoi(&LineBuffer[8]);
      pos = _llseek(rsHandle,0L,SEEK_CUR);
      result = AckReadMapFile(ae,(char *)MapResource);
      _llseek(rsHandle,pos,SEEK_SET);
      break;
      }

   if (!strnicmp(LineBuffer,"PALFILE:",8))
      {
      PalResource = atoi(&LineBuffer[8]);
      break;
      }

   if (!strnicmp(LineBuffer,"XPLAYER:",8))
      {
      ae->xPlayer = (short)atoi(&LineBuffer[8]);
      break;
      }
```

If an instruction such as **WALLS:** or **OBJECTS:** is read, a mode flag is set so that next time around in the **while** loop, a walls or objects section is processed. If a command like **MAPFILE:** is read, the code then reads in the parameter to this command and uses the parameter to read in the data at a specified location in the resource file. In this case, the variable **MapResource** serves as an index into the resource file where the game map data is stored. The **AckReadMapFile()** can then be called with **MapResource** as a parameter to allow access to the actual map data.

Commands such as **XPLAYER:** are easy to process. The only extra step required involves reading in the data for the command (in this case the player's starting x position) and storing the data in the interface structure.

The code for **ProcessInfoFile()** and its support functions such as **LoadObject()** and **LoadWall()** are provided in the Windows support file ACKINFO.C since we'll be using these routines in the Windows applications that we build in this chapter and Chapter 6. These functions are also needed by the Windows version of the map editor. You can, however, also use these functions with DOS applications. You'll just need to put the code for these functions in a .C source file and link the compiled code to the core engine library.

If you extend the engine and add additional features, you'll want to update **ProcessInfoFile()** to support the new features you add. The easiest way to do this is to add a new command to the configuration command set and then add the processing code for this command to the switch statement in **ProcessInfoFile()**. This is the way good software should be designed—easily extendible!

Creating a Windows Application

Now that we have all of the Windows support functions needed, let's put together a simple demonstration program. The program is named ACKEXAM.EXE, and the source files for the program are ACKEXAM.CPP and ACKEXAM.H. Figure 14.3 shows a view created by the program. You'll need to make sure that you have the files KIT.OVL and PICS.DTF in the same directory from which you are running the program. The file PICS.DTF is the game resource file that contains the specifications for the walls, objects, game map, bitmaps, and the player's starting position and angle, as well as all of the bitmaps needed for the game's walls and objects. The resource file was created using the Windows-based map editor presented in the next chapter.

To run the application, you'll also need to make sure that you have one of the Windows WinG DLL files (WING32.DLL or WING.DLL) in your \WINDOWS directory. The instructions for installing WinG are presented in Chapter 15.

When you examine the source file ACKEXAM.CPP, you may be surprised at how few lines of code are needed to create a basic 3-D Windows application. In fact, only the following six functions are required:

WinMain()	Main setup function
Register()	Registers the window class used
CreateAll()	Creates a display window for the application

Figure 14.3   *A view created by the Windows application ACKEXAM.EXE.*

MessageLoop()   Main control loop (message dispatcher)
AckPaint()   Displays the current view in a window
AckWndProc()   Main message handler

Here's the abbreviated version of how the program operates. First, it initializes the *ACK-3D* engine, loads in the game resources, and creates the display window. Then, it starts a message loop that continues to process messages until the player quits the program. Whenever the player performs an action, such as moving the mouse, clicking a mouse button, or pressing an arrow key, a message is sent for processing and an action takes place, such as changing the current view. That's all there is to it!

So are you ready to get under the hood? Let's start with **WinMain()**. This function controls the program. It starts by registering the Window class and initializing the *ACK-3D* engine:

```
// Register our Window class if this is the first time in
if (!hPrevInstance)
  if (!Register(hInstance))
    return(-1);

// Prime the ACK-3D engine with our startup parameters
if (InitACKEngine())
  return(-1);
```

Notice that **InitACKEngine()** is called to perform the initialization. This is the function defined in ACKWIN.CPP that we explored earlier. Next, **WinMain()** opens and processes the default resource file PICS.DTF:

```
AckOpenResource("pics.dtf");        // Open the resource file
ProcessInfoFile(1);        // Read in the resource file and process
                           // the components of the game—objects, walls, and so on
LoadBackDrop();            // Load in a background screen
AckCloseResource();        // Close the configuration file
```

We're almost ready to start displaying the game, but first we need to create the application window. Here's the function call that performs this job:

```
if (!CreateAll(hInstance))
  return(-1);
```

After the display window has been created, the message loop starts and continues until the player quits the program.

```
// Here we loop until the application closes
result = MessageLoop();
```

MessageLoop() takes over at this stage, but once the loop finishes, we're back to **WinMain()**, and the clean-up code is executed to close the *ACK-3D* engine and the WinG DLL:

```
// Free up buffers we used from WinG
if (AckBuffer)
  {
  hbm = (HBITMAP)SelectObject(AckBuffer, gbmOldMonoBitmap);
  DeleteObject(hbm);
  DeleteDC(AckBuffer);
  }

if(hpalApp)
  DeleteObject(hpalApp);

// Shutdown WinG DLL
WinG.Free();
```

Creating the Display Window

The **CreateAll()** function must be called to set up the display window before the 3-D engine attempts to display any views. This process first involves calling the **WinG.Load()** method to load in one of the WinG DLL files, WING32.DLL:

```
if (!WinG.Load()) // Load the WinG DLL
  {
  MessageBox(0,"Can't find WING32.DLL","Error!",MB_OK);
  return(FALSE);
  }
```

Notice how we are using the object **WinG** to call the method **Load()**. The **WinG** object is defined in the global declarations section of the ACKEXAM.CPP file, as shown here:

```
WinGdll WinG;
```

This step allows us to access the WinG methods that were defined in the WINGDLL.CPP source file.

The **if** statement shown above calls the **Load()** method. If the DLL cannot be found, a message box is displayed to warn you that you need the DLL to run the program. Next, some variables are set up to store the actual size of the window that is to be created. The window is configured to be 320×200 pixels:

```
nBitmapW = 319;   // Default size (window client size to use).
nBitmapH = 199;

windx = windy = GetSystemMetrics(SM_CXBORDER)*2;  // Get actual size for window
windx += nBitmapW;
windy += nBitmapH + GetSystemMetrics(SM_CYCAPTION) - 1;
```

The actual work of creating the display window is handled by calling the Windows API function **CreateWindow()**. Here's the function call with the required parameters:

```
hwndApp = CreateWindow ("ACK3DVIEW",     // Class name
    "ACK-3D Example",   // Caption
    WS_POPUP|WS_BORDER|WS_CAPTION|WS_VISIBLE|WS_SYSMENU,
    CW_USEDEFAULT,      // Position
    CW_USEDEFAULT,
    windx,windy,        // Size
    (HWND)NULL,         // Parent window
    (HMENU)NULL,        // Use class menu
    hInst,              // Handle to window instance
    (LPSTR)NULL );      // No parameters to pass on
```

As you can see, the title bar for the window is set to "ACK-3D Example." The window is created as a visible pop-up window having a border, system menu, and a caption. The size of the window is specified by the parameters **windx** and **windy** we just calculated. After the **CreateWindow()** function is called, we need to test the outcome to make sure the window was created properly:

```
if (!hwndApp)
  {
  MessageBox(NULL,"Unable to create 3D window","ERROR",MB_OK);
  return(FALSE);
  }
```

If all goes well, this code is skipped and it's time to set up the window so that it can be displayed. This step is achieved by calling the API function **ShowWindow()** as shown here:

```
ShowWindow(hwndApp,SW_NORMAL);
```

The handle **hwndApp** is used to reference the window. By calling this function, we are setting up Windows to generate a **WM_SIZE** message, which in turn causes the support function **AckDoSize()** to be called. As we learned earlier, **AckDoSize()** handles the work of setting up a WinG bitmap and assigning the bitmap to the interface structure. When graphics are displayed in the window, the data that is stored in the WinG bitmap, which is referenced by the global variable **AckBuffer**, is displayed by using the standard WinG blit function. I'll show you how this is done after we explore the message loop in the program.

Creating the Message Loop

Like all good Windows applications, our game is controlled by a basic message loop. The loop's job is to keep an eye out for a message and then dispatch a message when it comes. The best way to implement this type of message handler is to set up a continuous **for** loop:

```
int MessageLoop(void)
{
  MSG msg;

for (;;)  // Repeat until terminated by the WM_QUIT message
  {
  if (PeekMessage(&msg, NULL, 0, 0,PM_REMOVE))  // Look for a message
    {
    if (msg.message == WM_QUIT) // We're done
      break;
    TranslateMessage(&msg);      // Translate and send off the message
    DispatchMessage(&msg);
    }
  else
    {
    DoCycle();   // Display the 3-D window
    }
  }
return msg.wParam;
}
```

PeekMessage() will tell us if there is a message or not. If there is a message, it is processed. If there is no message, **DoCycle()** is called to process a drawing cycle of the engine.

So how is a message actually processed? If you take a close look at the code that registers the application window (**Register()** function), you'll find the following initialization statement:

```
wndclass.lpfnWndProc  = AckWndProc;
```

This statement assigns the function **AckWndProc()** as the main message handler for the application window. Thus, when a message is received by the message loop, **AckWndProc()** is called. This function is one big switch statement with cases to handle Windows messages such as **WM_CREATE**, **WM_SIZE**, **WM_PAINT**, and so on. For example, when the **WM_PAINT** message is received, this section of code is executed:

```
case WM_PAINT:           // Draw the window
  BeginPaint(hWnd,&ps);
  AckPaint(hWnd,ps.hdc); // Call the ACK painting function
  EndPaint(hWnd,&ps);
  break;
```

Painting the Window with WinG

When a **WM_PAINT** message is received by the application, **AckPaint()** is called. First, this function checks to see if a scene needs to be updated before it is displayed:

```
if (ae != NULL) // Does an ACK interface structure exist?
  {
  AckCheckObjectMovement(); // Check object animation
  AckBuildView();           // Render the 3-D view
  }
```

We need to test whether an interface structure exists before calling **AckCheckObjectMovement()** and **AckBuildView()** to update the objects in the view and build up the new view. When the view is built, the off-screen buffer is updated. This off-screen buffer is set up as a WinG bitmap.

Second, **AckPaint()** uses the WinG bitmap created earlier to display the bitmap by either calling **WinGBitBlt()** or **WinGStretchBlt()**. A flag named **StretchFactor** determines which function should be called, as shown here:

```
// Let WinG display the buffer into our window. We can use a StretchFactor
// to display larger windows if so desired, at the cost of speed. The
```

```
// fastest way is to simply BitBlt the buffer into our window.
if (StretchFactor != 1)
  WinG.pStretchBlt(hdc,0,0,StretchFactor*nBitmapW,StretchFactor*nBitmapH,
              AckBuffer,0,0,nBitmapW,nBitmapH);
else
  WinG.pBitBlt(hdc,0,0,nBitmapW,nBitmapH,AckBuffer,0,0);
```

By default, **StretchFactor** is set to 1 at the beginning of the program, causing the **else** clause to be executed and the method **WinG.pBitBlt()** to be used. This default results in calling the WinG function **WinGBitBlt()**. Notice that the global variable **AckBuffer** is used to specify the bitmap to be displayed. To refresh your memory, this buffer is created and assigned to the *ACK-3D* interface structure in the support function **AckDoSize()**, as shown here:

```
hbm = WinG.pCreateBitmap(AckBuffer,      // Create the bitmap
      (BITMAPINFO *)&BufferHeader, &pAckBuffer);
...
if (ae != NULL)  // Check for allocated ACK interface structure
    {
    ae->ScreenBuffer = (UCHAR *)pAckBuffer; // Store pointer to bitmap
    ...
```

Calling **WinGBitBlt()** is the fastest way to display the buffer in the window. But you can also use a stretch factor and call **WinGStretchBlt()**, as the code shows. In this case, the stretch factor is multiplied by the buffer width and height (**nBitmapW** and **nBitmapH**) to determine the size of the actual bitmap to display. You might want to experiment with this feature by setting **StretchFactor** to a value other than 1, but remember, it'll slow down your program.

The Complete Windows Application Code

We have now covered the highlights of our sample Windows application. To compile the program with Borland C++, make sure you follow the steps listed at the end of the source code listings.

```
//WINEXAM.H
// Header file for example program
BOOL Register(HINSTANCE hInst);
BOOL CreateAll(HINSTANCE hInst);
int MessageLoop(void);
LRESULT CALLBACK _export AckWndProc( HWND hWnd, UINT iMessage,
    WPARAM wParam, LPARAM lParam );

int LoadBackDrop(void);
int ProcessInfoFile(short qFlag);
```

```
// WINEXAM.CPP
// Example program for using ACK-3D in Windows
// (c) 1995 ACK Software (Lary Myers)
#define STRICT
#include <windows.h>
#pragma hdrstop
#include <stdlib.h>
#include <string.h>
#include <wing.h>
#include "wingdll.h"
#include "ackwin.h"
#include "ackexam.h"

extern "C" {
#include "keys.h"
#include "ack3d.h"
};

// Some globals to use for the Windows application
  ACKENG      *ae = 0;                // Interface structure
  HWND        hwndApp;
  UCHAR       kbPressed[128];         // Stores state of keyspressed and mouse
  WinGdll     WinG;                   // Create a global WinG object
  header      BufferHeader;
  void        *pAckBuffer = 0;        // Pointer to the off-screem buffer
  HDC         AckBuffer = 0;          // Buffer to be set up as a WinG bitmap
  HPALETTE    hpalApp;
  RGBQUAD     ColorTable[256];
  pal         LogicalPalette = {0x300,256};
  HBITMAP     gbmOldMonoBitmap = 0;
  int         StretchFactor = 1;      // Determines if bitmaps will be scaled
  int         nBitmapW;               // WinG bitmap dimensions (width and height)
  int         nBitmapH;
  short       nMoveSpeed;             // Players cuurent moving and turning speed
  short       nTurnSpeed;
  HINSTANCE   hInstGlobal;
  BOOL        bNoShow;                // Do not display if TRUE

//*********************************************************************
// The main demonstration window
//*********************************************************************
#pragma argsused
int PASCAL WinMain( HINSTANCE hInstance, HINSTANCE hPrevInstance,
                    LPSTR lpszCmdLine, int nCmdShow )
{
  int  result;
  HBITMAP hbm;

// Register our Window class if this is the first time in
if (!hPrevInstance)
  if (!Register(hInstance))
    return(-1);
// Prime the ACK-3D engine with our startup parameters
if (InitACKEngine())
```

```
  return(-1);
// Open our default resource file and load bitmaps, etc.
AckOpenResource("pics.dtf");  // Open the configuration file
ProcessInfoFile(1);           // Read in the configuration file and process
                              // the components of the game-objects, walls, etc.
LoadBackDrop();               // Loads in a background screen
AckCloseResource();           // Close the configuration file
// Create the actual window to display the rendered view
if (!CreateAll(hInstance))
  return(-1);
// Here we loop until the application closes
result = MessageLoop();
// Free up our buffers we used from WinG
if (AckBuffer)
  {
  hbm = (HBITMAP)SelectObject(AckBuffer, gbmOldMonoBitmap); DeleteObject(hbm);
  DeleteDC(AckBuffer);
  }
if(hpalApp)
  DeleteObject(hpalApp);
// Shutdown WinG DLL
WinG.Free();
return(result);
}

//**********************************************************************
// Registers the window class.
//**********************************************************************
BOOL Register(HINSTANCE hInst)
{
  WNDCLASS wndclass;
wndclass.style         = CS_HREDRAW | CS_VREDRAW | CS_OWNDC;
wndclass.lpfnWndProc   = AckWndProc;
wndclass.cbClsExtra    = 0;
wndclass.cbWndExtra    = 0;
wndclass.hInstance     = hInst;
wndclass.hIcon         = LoadIcon(hInst,"ackicon");
wndclass.hCursor       = LoadCursor( NULL, IDC_ARROW );
wndclass.hbrBackground = (HBRUSH)GetStockObject( WHITE_BRUSH );
wndclass.lpszMenuName  = NULL;
wndclass.lpszClassName = "ACK3DVIEW";
if (!RegisterClass(&wndclass))  // Register the window class
  return(FALSE);
return(TRUE);
}

//**********************************************************************
// Loads the WinG DLL and creates the display window for the application.
//**********************************************************************
BOOL CreateAll(HINSTANCE hInst)
{
  int  windx, windy;
```

```
if (!WinG.Load()) // Load the WinG DLL
  {
  MessageBox(0,"Can't find WING32.DLL","Error!",MB_OK);
  return(FALSE);
  }

nBitmapW = 319; // Default size (window client size to use).
nBitmapH = 199;
windx = windy = GetSystemMetrics(SM_CXBORDER)*2;  // Get actual size for window
windx += nBitmapW;
windy += nBitmapH + GetSystemMetrics(SM_CYCAPTION) - 1;
// Note that in this example we're not allowing any resizing borders
// This helps to keep things a little more constrained with the current
// ACK-3D engine.
    hwndApp = CreateWindow ("ACK3DVIEW",// Class name
    "ACK-3D Example",                   // Caption
    WS_POPUP|WS_BORDER|WS_CAPTION|WS_VISIBLE|WS_SYSMENU,
    CW_USEDEFAULT,  // Position
    CW_USEDEFAULT,
    windx,windy,    // Size
    (HWND)NULL,     // Parent window
    (HMENU)NULL,    // Use class menu
    hInst,          // Handle to window instance
    (LPSTR)NULL );  // No paramaters to pass on
if (!hwndApp)
  {
  MessageBox(NULL,"Unable to create 3D window","ERROR",MB_OK);
  return(FALSE);
  }
// Now we'll display the window and setup the WinG buffer when we
// receive the WM_SIZE message
ShowWindow(hwndApp,SW_NORMAL);
return(TRUE);
}


//**********************************************************************
// Main messsage loop that continues until game is terminated.
//**********************************************************************
int MessageLoop(void)
{
  MSG msg;

for (;;)  // Repeat until terminated by the WM_QUIT message
  {
  if (PeekMessage(&msg, NULL, 0, 0,PM_REMOVE))  // Look for a message
    {
    if (msg.message == WM_QUIT) // We're done
        break;
    TranslateMessage(&msg);  // Translae and send off the message
    DispatchMessage(&msg);
    }
  else
    {
    DoCycle();    // Display the 3D window
```

```
      }
    }
  return msg.wParam;
  }


//*************************************************************************
// Displays the current scene in the opened window. This function displays
// the scene by using WinG.
//*************************************************************************
#pragma argsused
void AckPaint(HWND hWnd,HDC hdc)
{
if (ae != NULL)
  {
  AckCheckObjectMovement(); // Check object animation
  AckBuildView();           // Render the 3-D view
  }
// Let WinG display the buffer into our window. We can use a StretchFactor
// to display larger windows if so desired, at the cost of speed. The
// fastest way is to simply BitBlt the buffer into our window.
if (StretchFactor != 1)
WinG.pStretchBlt(hdc,0,0,StretchFactor*nBitmapW,StretchFactor*nBitmapH,
AckBuffer,0,0,nBitmapW,nBitmapH);
else
  WinG.pBitBlt(hdc,0,0,nBitmapW,nBitmapH,AckBuffer,0,0);
}


//*************************************************************************
// The main Windows application processing function. This function checks the
// current message received and performs an appropriate action.
//*************************************************************************
LRESULT CALLBACK _export AckWndProc(HWND hWnd,UINT iMessage,
                                    WPARAM wParam,LPARAM lParam)
{
  HDC hDC;
  PAINTSTRUCT ps;

switch (iMessage)            // Processs the current message
  {
  case WM_CREATE:            // Create a new window
    break;                   // Doesn't do anything for now
  case WM_DESTROY:           // Remove the window
    PostQuitMessage( 0 );    // Display the quit warning message
    break;
  case WM_SIZE:              // Resize the window
    AckDoSize(hWnd,lParam);
    break;
  case WM_PAINT:             // Draw the window
    BeginPaint(hWnd,&ps);
    AckPaint(hWnd,ps.hdc);   // Call the ACK painting function
    EndPaint(hWnd,&ps);
    break;
  case WM_KEYDOWN:           // Call internal function to process up
  case WM_KEYUP:             // or down arrow keys
    ProcessKeys(iMessage,wParam);
```

```
    break;
  case WM_RBUTTONDOWN:        // Process a right mouse button press
    AckCheckDoorOpen(ae->xPlayer,ae->yPlayer,ae->PlayerAngle);
    break;
  case WM_LBUTTONDOWN:        // Process a left mouse button press
    ProcessMouse(hWnd,1,LOWORD(lParam),HIWORD(lParam));
    SetCapture(hWnd);
    break;
  case WM_MOUSEMOVE:          // Process moving the mouse
    if (wParam & MK_LBUTTON)
      ProcessMouse(hWnd,1,LOWORD(lParam),HIWORD(lParam));
    break;
  case WM_LBUTTONUP:          // Process a left mouse button release
    ProcessMouse(hWnd,0,LOWORD(lParam),HIWORD(lParam));
    ReleaseCapture();
    break;
  case WM_PALETTECHANGED:     // Process a change in the palette
  if (hWnd == (HWND)wParam)
      break;
    // Fall through here
  case WM_QUERYNEWPALETTE:
    hDC = GetDC(hWnd);
    if (hpalApp)
      SelectPalette(hDC,hpalApp,FALSE); // Select a new palette
    RealizePalette(hDC);      // Realize a palette ReleaseDC(hWnd,hDC);
    return FALSE;
  default:
    return DefWindowProc( hWnd, iMessage, wParam, lParam );
  }
return 0;
}
```

Running the Windows Example

To run the Windows example program presented in this chapter, you'll need to make sure the following software is installed on your computer:

- WinG DLLs
- Win32s DLL
- Borland 32-bit DLLs

The step-by-step instructions for installing this software is presented in Chapter 15. If you already have the WinG DLLs installed on your system, you won't need to install the WinG DLLs. Also, if you are currently running Windows 95 or Windows NT, you won't need to install Win32s.

Once the required DLLs have been installed, you can run the program by selecting the WINEXAM.EXE program in the directory \ACK\WIN\WIN_EXAM. When the program starts, it loads in the internal resource file, KIT.OVL and the user-defined resource file PICS.DTF. If you want to run the sample program from your hard drive, make sure you copy the files KIT.OVL and PICS.DTF to the subdirectory where you've copied WINEXAM.EXE.

Compiling WINEXAM

All the source code for the WINEXAM.EXE program is stored in the directory \ACK\WIN\WIN_EXAM\SOURCE. You'll probably want to experiment with the program by making changes to the source files, recompiling them, and then testing your changes. I've included project files for rebuilding the program with Borland 4.0 and 4.5. The project files are:

ACKEXAM4.IDE   Project file for Borland 4.0
ACKEXAM.IDE   Project file for Borland 4.5

To rebuild the program, you'll need to copy all of the source and header files that the program requires to a working together on your hard drive. Your also need to copy the compiled *ACK-3D* engine library ACKLIB.LIB. After you start up the Borland compiler and load in the appropriate project file, make sure the directories referenced in the project file are updated to reflect the directories in which you have placed program files.

Keep in mind that the ACKEXAM program is basically a template that allows you to move around in a 3-D world set up by the *ACK-3D* map editor. If you want to change the game layout by adding or removing walls or objects, you'll need to use the map editor, which is discussed in the next chapter. You can also test out this template program with other game resource files (PICS.DTF) included on the companion CD-ROM.

Creating a map for your game
populated with walls, doors,
and objects is as simple as
using the Windows-based interactive map editor and pointing and
clicking with the mouse.

Mapping Your Worlds

The *ACK-3D* engine we've explored so far gives you just about everything you need to build your own amazing 3-D creations. The only thing missing is a tool to help you create the game maps and resource file for use in your applications. Such a tool allows you to interactively specify where you want to place the walls and objects in your game without writing any code. You can even set up the layout and attributes for your floor and ceiling. This is visual programming at its best!

Many game developers create tools like my map editor to help automate the process of writing games. Some of these tools perform very specific operations and some are very difficult to use (unless you are the one who wrote the tool). My goal in creating a Windows-based map editor was to make it as general purpose and powerful as possible and at the same time make it easy to use. To create your game layouts, you don't need to know any tricky commands or write any scripts. You simply design your game by using the mouse and placing walls and objects in your world.

What's most unique about the visual *ACK-3D* map editor presented with this book is that it not only allows you to create layouts for your games, but it lets you interactively "walk through" your games in three dimensions as you build them. This design feature came as a by-product of Windows and WinG. Instead of providing one main editing window, I use multiple windows to give you different views. The map editor uses the same basic navigation code that the *ACK-3D* engine uses, so you can explore all of the features of your game, such as floors, ceilings, secret doors, sliding doors, standard walls, multi-height walls, and so on in a 3-D view while you design your games. This feature alone can save you a lot of development time.

In this chapter, I'll show you how to use the visual map editor. You'll learn how to use all of the key features so that you can create maps for your games. The map I'll use as an example in this chapter will serve as the map for the *Station Escape* game that we'll create in the next chapter. Feel free to make a backup copy of the sample game resource file provided with the map editor so you can change it to your heart's delight.

A Map Making Utility

The nice feature about building games with the *ACK-3D* engine and visual map editor is that you can design your games interactively. Using the full working version of the map editor provided on the accompanying CD-ROM, you can "draw" your game maps and get your 3-D creations up and running in no time at all. The editor was designed with a mouse-driven interface, and it contains handy features including dialog boxes, menus, display windows, and both a 2-D and 3-D view of the current map you are designing.

The 3-D view is something I'm particularly proud of because it allows you to test the actual 3-D view that the *ACK 3-D* engine displays when you are running your game. My goal is to make the game design process as close as possible to the experience of actually playing the game. This feature is also useful for game designers who lack programming experience but still want to be able to test their designs and ideas.

Installing and Running the *ACK-3D* Map Editor

To run the Windows-based visual map editor provided on the companion CD-ROM, you'll need the following hardware and software:

- 386 (or 486) CPU with at least 8M of RAM
- SVGA card

- Windows 3.1 or later
- The WinG DLLs installed (WinG32.DLL, WinGDE.DLL, and so on)
- Win32s installed (WIN32S16.DLL)
- Borland v4.5 32-Bit DLLs (CW3215.DLL and CW3215MT.DLL); or
- Borland v4.0 32-Bit DLLs (CW3211.DLL and CW3211MT.DLL)

Installing the Map Editor

Before running the *ACK-3D* map editor, you first must install the support DLLs needed by the map editor. This step includes installing WinG, Win32s, and Borland's 32-bit DLLs. If you have all of this software installed on your PC, you're all set; otherwise, you need to run a few installation programs and copy a few files from the companion CD-ROM to your hard drive. Here are the steps to follow:

1. Install the WinG DLLs.
The setup program for installing WinG is SETUP.EXE; it is located in the \TOOLS\WING subdirectory on the companion CD-ROM. Run Windows, select File | Run and then browse. Select the drive where your CD is located and double click on the WING subdirectory. Then, double-click on SETUP.EXE to start it. The WinG installation program will copy the required WinG DLLs to your \WINDOWS\SYSTEM directory on your hard disk. These DLLs are needed so that you can run the *ACK-3D* map editor or any of the Windows examples provided on the companion CD-ROM.

Note: The first time you run a program on your PC that uses the WinG DLL, such as the *ACK-3D* map editor, WinG will perform some screen setup operations to optimize how bitmaps will display on your system.

2. Install the Win32s DLL.
The *ACK-3D* map editor is compiled as a 32-bit Windows application. To run it with Windows 3.1 or Windows for Workgroups, you'll need to install Microsoft's Win32s compatibility module. This module is essentially a special DLL that allows you to run 32-bit applications under a 16-bit version of Windows. If you are already using one or more 32-bit applications with Windows, Win32s should already be installed on your system. If your Windows system files are on your C: drive, check to see if you have a path such as:

```
C:\WINDOWS\SYSTEM\WIN32S
```

If you do, you do not need to install the Win32s software. Of course, if you are running a 32-bit version of Windows, such as Windows NT or Windows 95, you also don't need to install Win32s.

The set-up program for Win32s is SETUP.EXE, which is located in the directory \TOOLS\WIN32S on the companion CD-ROM. To use this program, run Windows, select File|Run and click on the Browse button. Select the drive where your CD is located and switch to the WIN32S subdirectory. Then, double-click on SETUP.EXE. The Win32s installation program will take over and install the necessary files in your \WINDOWS\SYSTEM directory. After the files have been installed, you'll need to reboot your computer.

Note: The Win32s installation program gives you the option of installing a sample game called Freecell. I suggest that you install this game and run it to verify that Win32s has been installed properly on your computer before you attempt to run any of the *ACK-3D* Windows programs.

3. Install the Borland 32-Bit DLLs.

If you don't have Borland 4.5 installed on your system, you'll need to copy the two DLL files in the \BORLAND directory on the companion CD-ROM to your \WINDOWS\SYSTEM directory on your hard drive. The two files to copy are CW3215.DLL and CW3215MT.DLL. The Windows version of the *ACK-3D* map editor has been compiled with Borland 4.5, and these two DLLs are needed to run the editor.

Note: Files stored on a CD-ROM are assigned the read-only attribute because of the read-only nature of CD-ROMs. After you copy files from the companion CD-ROM to your hard drive, you'll want to change the file attributes to remove the read-only setting. You can easily do this from Windows by using the File Manager. Here are the steps to follow:

a. Select the files to change from the File Manager.
b. Choose the Properties command from the File Manager's File menu.
c. Deselect the Read Only check box in the Properties dialog box.
d. Click OK.

4. Copy the files for the *ACK-3D* map editor to your hard drive.

The *ACK-3D* map editor files are located in the directory \ACK\WIN\ACK_EDIT on the companion CD-ROM. Create a directory on your hard drive, such as ACKEDIT, and copy the files from the CD-ROM to this directory. The files required are ACKEDIT.EXE, KIT.OVL, and PICS.DTF. (The PICS.DTF file contains the resource data for a sample game that you can fool around with while running the game editor.) After you've copied these files to your hard disk, make sure that you change their attributes from the "read-only" settings. (See the steps described above.)

Running the Editor

Once you have all of the files installed correctly, running the map editor is easy. Go to the directory where the map editor files are stored and double click on the ACKEDIT.EXE program. The start up windows that should appear are shown in Figure 15.1. Notice that there are three windows associated with the editor: *Map Editor*, *Wall*, and *3D View*. The main window, Map Editor, displays the 2-D map layout for your game. You can select menu options and display either the layout for walls (and objects), floor, or ceiling. You use this window to design and change the layout for your games.

The next window, which is entitled Wall in Figure 15.1, is the window that displays either the set of wall or object bitmaps available to you as you are designing your game. The contents of this window change depending on which mode you are in (Edit | Map or Edit | Objects).

The final window displays the 3-D view for your map layout. This window shows exactly how the *ACK-3D* engine displays your game map in a 3-D view. To see how this works, slide the window so that it is in full view. Then, press one of the arrow keys to move around in the 3-D scene that is displayed. As you change your game layout using the Map Editor window, the 3D View window will be updated.

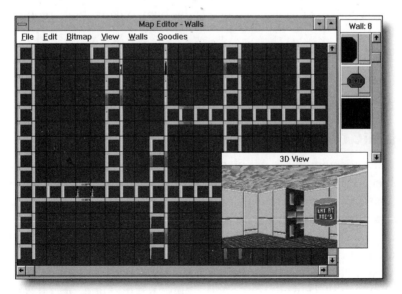

Figure 15.1 *Running the* ACK-3D *map editor.*

Map Editor Functions

Before we get too far into the details of using the map editor, you'll want to know exactly what the map editor does. It takes the map layout that you design and the configuration information you select with the editor and outputs a resource file. This resource file contains all of the data needed to create a game, including wall bitmaps, object bitmaps, game layout information, and a configuration script. If you recall from the previous chapter when we created a sample Windows application, the **ProcessInfoFile()** function was called to process the game resource and configuration file. The actual data processed by this function is produced behind the scenes by the map editor. This flexible auto-configuration feature helps you build applications with the *ACK-3D* engine in such a way that you can spend more time designing your games and creating neat effects instead of coding function calls to load in your game components.

Although you don't need to know how resource files and game configuration scripts are produced to use the editor, I've provided a detailed guide to working with resource files in Appendix A. If you want to add new features to the game engine or map editor, you'll find this information to be very valuable. Also, if you use the older DOS-based version of the map editor, you'll need to know how to create your own resource files.

The Windows-based map editor is designed to display your wall, door, object, floor, ceiling, and background bitmaps and enable you to place these components in a 64×64 grid map. You can think of it as you would a painting program, except that your set of tools or palette is the bitmap game building blocks.

Using the Menu System

Most of the main map editor setup commands and editing operations can be selected from the menu bar. The menus provided are listed in Table 15.1.

Using the Map Editor Window

The Map Editor window is the place where you interactively place the wall, door, object, floor, and ceiling components for your game. This window provides a basic overhead 2-D map of your game layout. Let's take a look at a sample configuration so that you can see how this window is used.

Figure 15.2 shows a game map that is under construction. This illustration is actually part of the map for the *Station Escape* game that we'll create in the next chapter. Notice that the map provides grid lines to indicate each grid square. You can place walls (or doors) along each grid line, or you can assign an object to a grid square. By default, the game editor operates in the "Walls"

Table 15.1 *Main Menus Provided with the Map Editor*

Menu	Description
File	Commands to open and save resource files.
Edit	Commands to specify a game map editing mode (walls or objects) and commands to clear the current map and set global attributes, such as solid colors for a floor and ceiling.
Bitmap	Commands to load in wall and object bitmaps as well as to delete bitmaps that have been previously loaded.
View	Commands to display different views in the main Map Editor window (supported views include walls and objects, floor, and ceiling); also provides a command to view the game configuration script.
Walls	Commands to set attributes for walls and doors.
Goodies	Commands to set attributes for walls, objects, floors, ceilings, and light shading.

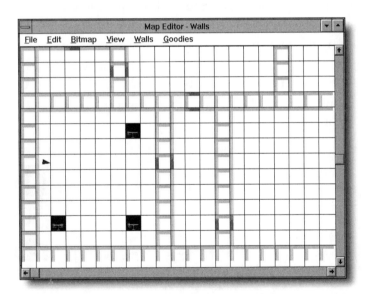

Figure 15.2 *Creating a game map with the Map Editor window.*

mode so that you can select walls from the Wall window and place them in the Map Editor window.

If you look closely at the grid map, you'll see that one of the squares contains a triangle symbol. This symbol indicates the player's current position and angle with respect to the grid map. As you move around in the 3-D view, this position is updated if the Track Player option is selected in the Goodies menu. If you are having trouble relating your movement in the 3-D view to the grid map, just look for the triangle symbol. Once you get some experience moving around, you won't get lost.

To change the editing mode so that you can place objects in the game map, you first select the Objects command from the File menu. The editor's configuration will change as shown in Figure 15.3. Notice that the Obj window is now displayed to the right of the Map Editor window. (You can return to the walls editing mode by selecting the Map command from the Edit menu.)

Once you've selected either the wall or object editing mode, you can make changes to your game map by choosing a wall or object bitmap from the displayed Wall or Obj window and clicking the mouse at a desired location inside the Map Editor window. The types of operations supported include:

- Left mouse button click: Places the currently selected wall or object bitmap at one of the grid borders (a side-wall) or the entire square.

- Left mouse button click + Shift key: Relocates the POV to the square selected by the mouse pointer; the viewing angle does not change.

- Left mouse button click + Ctrl key: Grabs the wall or object bitmap selected by the mouse pointer and makes it the currently selected one.

- Right mouse button click: Removes the wall or object selected by the mouse pointer.

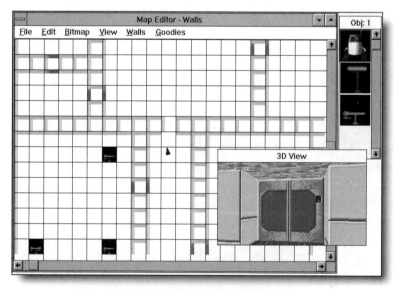

Figure 15.3 *Setting up the editor for the object editing mode.*

DESIGN TIP

Because bitmaps are represented by color shading within the Map Editor window, you may find it hard to see some of them with the default background color (dark blue is the default). With the Map Editor window active, press the PgUp or PgDn keys to cycle through various background colors until you find one you like. The background color you select is only used in the map editor itself, not in the resource file created by the map editor. It is not saved anywhere so the default color will be used the next time you run the map editor.

If you are placing a wall bitmap and click inside a grid square, all four sides of the grid will be assigned the bitmap. If you only want to place the bitmap on one side, point to the desired grid line and click the left mouse button. This technique might take a little practice to get your positioning just right. But don't worry, if you make a mistake and place a wall bitmap in the wrong place, you can easily erase it by pointing to it with the mouse and clicking the right button.

To see how the different operations are used, go to the Wall window and select one of the wall bitmaps shown by pointing at the bitmap and clicking the left mouse button. You can scroll through the window using the scroll arrows or scroll bar. When you click on a bitmap, a red border will be displayed around the bitmap to indicate that it has been selected. Then, return to the Map Editor window and click the left mouse button in one of the empty grid squares. Notice that walls are placed for all four edges of the grid square using the bitmap you've selected.

Now erase one of the walls by pointing at it and clicking the right mouse button. (If you point inside the grid square, all four walls will be erased.) After you've put in a few walls, check out the changes you've made by pressing the Shift key, positioning the mouse pointer in front of one of the walls you've added, and clicking the left mouse button. The 3-D View window is updated so that you can see your changes to the game map in the 3-D view your player will see.

Working with Walls

The map editor allows you to place all of the different types of walls that *ACK-3D* supports, including normal, transparent, passable, split doors, and sliding doors. Different types of walls are created by setting attributes for a wall bitmap. To do this, you first select the wall bitmap in the Wall window and then choose the Wall Attributes command from the Goodies menu. Figure 15.4 shows the Attributes dialog box that is displayed.

Here you can decide to make the wall a normal wall or a door (split or sliding) by selecting one of the radio buttons. In addition, you can make the

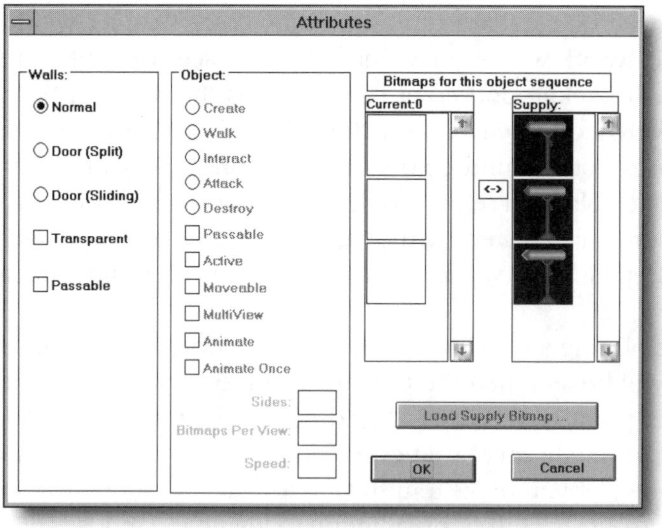

Figure 15.4 *The Attributes dialog box used to set wall attributes.*

wall (or door) passable or transparent by selecting one of the two check boxes provided. Let's practice by adding a sliding door to the map. Scroll through the Wall window until you find the split door bitmap, as shown in Figure 15.5. Next, click on the bitmap and choose the Wall Attributes command from the Goodies menu. When the Attributes dialog appears, click on the Door (Split)

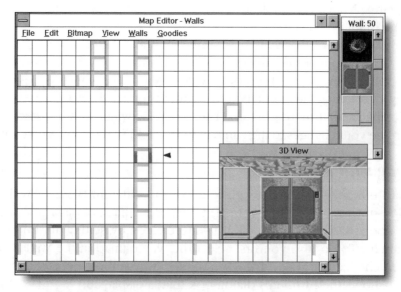

Figure 15.5 *Adding a split door to the game map.*

radio button. Now you are ready to put in the door. Go to the Map Editor window and click the left mouse button on one of the grid borders that currently does not contain a bitmap. To see your change in the 3-D view, position the mouse in front of the door, press Shift, and click the mouse button. Your view should change to look like the one shown in Figure 15.5. You can make the door open as you move toward it by pressing the Space bar.

DESIGN TIP

You can also set attributes for wall bitmaps by selecting settings in the Walls menu. This menu gives you a quick way to check or change an attribute setting without using the Attributes dialog box. The attributes that are currently selected will have a check mark next to their name when the Walls menu is opened.

Working with Objects

Recall that you can add objects to your game by creating bitmaps for them and assigning the objects to different locations in your game map. Of course, objects, like walls, are represented using 64x64 pixel bitmaps. Objects are a little different, however, because multiple bitmaps can be used to define different views and animation. Additionally, you can set up an object so that it has different sequences for its stages in a game (for example, creation, walking, interacting with the player, and so on).

To support all of this flexibility, the map editor provides an interactive dialog box as shown in Figure 15.6. (This dialog box is essentially the same box that is used to define attributes for a wall bitmap. The main difference is that the Walls section is now disabled.) To use this dialog box, you first must make sure the map editor is in the Objects mode. You can do this by selecting the Objects option from the Edit menu, then choosing the Object Attributes command from the Goodies menu.

The right side of the dialog box lists the bitmaps used for an object sequence. The Supply lists presents all of the object bitmaps that have been loaded into the map editor. You can select from these bitmaps to define an object sequence. The Current list to the left of the Supply list shows the object bitmaps assigned to the sequence being defined. In this case, notice that eight bitmaps are used to define the Create sequence for the object.

To define an object sequence, you click on the radio button that corresponds with the sequence you want to set up (Create, Walk, Interact, Attack, and so on). Then, you can select any of the check boxes, such as Passable,

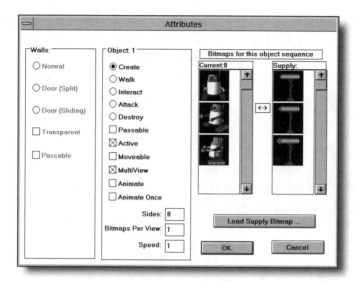

Figure 15.6   *The Attributes dialog box used to set object attributes.*

Active, Moveable, and so on to define attributes for the object sequence. The actual bitmaps for the object sequence are copied from the Supply list by double clicking on the desired bitmap to move the bitmap from the Supply list to the Current list. If you wish to remove a bitmap from the Current List, just double-click on it and it will be removed. Note that the Supply list never changes since the same bitmap can be used in multiple objects. The Current list reflects the actual bitmaps that the current object sequence uses. You also need to provide the number of Sides, Bitmaps Per View, and Speed for the object. If you need to load additional supply bitmaps, click on the Load Supply Bitmap button, and the map editor will let you select a .PCX or .BBM file to read in.

Creating a New Game Map

To start fresh with a new game map, select the Clear Map command from the Edit menu. This command clears all of the bitmaps in the map that you are currently viewing. For example, to clear out all the bitmaps for the walls, you need to be in the Edit | Map mode and the View | Map mode. To clear out all of the bitmaps used for the ceiling, you need to be in View | Ceiling mode.

If you are currently working on a game map and you want to start a new one, make sure you save the current map by choosing the Save command from the File menu before you choose the Clear Map command.

Using the 3D View Window

The 3D View window is a self-contained view that allows you to walk through your game. You can press one of the arrow keys (left, right, up, or down) to move around. You can also press and hold down the left mouse button as you slide the mouse around to move in the 3-D view. If you encounter a movable door in your path, you can make the door open by pressing the Space bar or by clicking the right mouse button. The mouse is only active for moving around the 3-D view when the 3D window is active; however, the arrow keys and Space bar work no matter which window is currently active.

One nice feature of the 3D View window is that it lets you track the position of the player in the grid map as you move around in the 3-D view. I particularly like this feature because it clarifies the relationship between the 2-D grid map and the 3-D world in which you are moving around. To use this feature, select the Track Player option from the Goodies menu. Then, as you move around, an arrow indicator is displayed in the map grid to show your location and angle of movement.

By default, the 3D View window is displayed at half its size so that you can easily view it and the Map Editor window. To increase the size of the 3D View window, select the Times Two option from the View menu. To return the window to its default size, select the Times One option.

Setting Floor, Ceiling, and Light Shading Attributes

Not only can you control how walls and objects are displayed with the map editor and view your changes with the 3D Window, you also can set different attributes to display your floor, ceiling, and light shading. But keep in mind that the attributes that you change are recorded in the game resource file created by the map editor when the resource file is saved.

To turn light shading on or off, select the Light Shading option from the Goodies menu. When this option has a checkmark next to it, you'll know that it has been selected. To choose a solid color ceiling or a solid color floor, use the Solid Ceiling or Solid Floor options from the Goodies menu. If you use a solid ceiling or floor , you can specify the color for either of these components by selecting the Global command from the Edit menu. Figure 15.7 shows the dialog box displayed when this command is selected. Use the first text box to enter a color for the solid ceiling and the second text box to enter a floor color value. The value entered (0 to 255) is used to reference the color palette table used with your game to locate an actual color. You can also click the Solid Ceiling or Solid Ceiling check box to change floor and ceiling attributes.

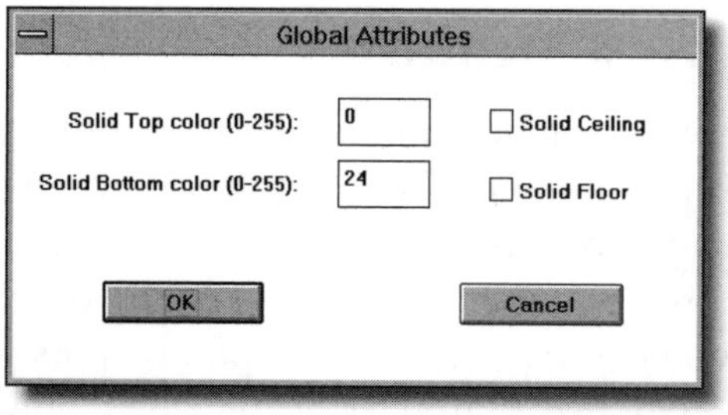

Figure 15.7 *Setting floor and ceiling colors with the Global Attributes dialog box.*

Using the Wall or Obj Window

The Wall or Obj window always displays the list of wall or object bitmaps available for use with the map editor. When the Map command is selected from the Edit menu, the Wall window is displayed. When Objects is selected from the Edit menu, the Obj window is displayed. You use the same technique for both of these windows. To select a wall or object bitmap, scroll through the list and click on the one you want. The selected bitmap is displayed with a red border.

To add a new wall or object bitmap, scroll through the Wall or Obj window to locate an empty slot and click on it. Then, choose the Load command from the Bitmap menu. The Open Bitmap File dialog box will be displayed, as shown in Figure 15.8. Enter the name of the bitmap file you want to load. Remember that this file should contain a wall or object bitmap that is 64×64 pixels.

To delete a bitmap from the Wall or Obj window, select the bitmap by clicking on it, then choose the Delete command from the Bitmap menu. You will be prompted to confirm the deletion. Choose Yes to actually remove the bitmap from the list.

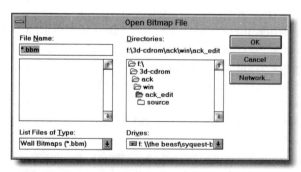

Figure 15.8 *Using the Open Bitmap File dialog box.*

Working with Game Resource Files

As I mentioned earlier, the map editor's job is to create a game resource file for you, based on the components you add to your game map. Every time you place a new wall or object bitmap in the Map Editor window, or change the ceiling or floor setting, this information is recorded internally and saved to a game resource file of your choosing. To create a resource file, select the Save As command from the File menu. The Save As dialog box is displayed so that you can enter a path and filename for the resource file. My convention is to use the extension .DTF for game resource files.

Once you've created a game resource file, you can open it at any time by selecting the Open Resource command from the File menu. After it is open, you can change it by using the Map Editor window. Save your changes by selecting the Save command from the File menu.

If you are at all curious about what the map editor does behind the scenes, you can view the script commands that the editor generates and writes to the resource file. To view the set of configuration commands being produced by the map editor as you design your game, choose the INF file command from the View menu. Figure 15.9 shows the window displayed by this command. Notice that each line of the window contains a configuration command to indicate settings, such as the player's starting position and angle, colors used for a solid floor and ceiling, light shading setting, and so on. The configuration commands also indicate which wall and object bitmaps are used to set up the game map.

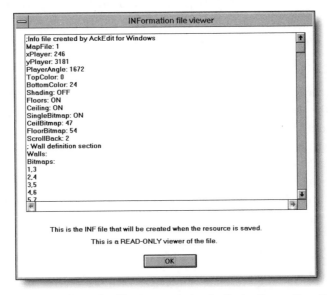

Figure 15.9 Using the INFormation file viewer window to display the configuration script.

You do not need to know the syntax of the configuration commands to use the map editor. However, you might want to write your own configuration files manually, so I've provided a detailed description of the configuration commands in Appendix A.

Mapping Your Worlds in DOS

Everything we've discussed so far in this chapter relates to the Windows version of the map editor named ACKEDIT.EXE. When I first created a map editor, I designed it for DOS. As you might guess, the original DOS-based editor was not as feature-rich as the newer Windows version. For example, it doesn't allow you to edit a map and walk around in your 3-D scene at the same time. It also doesn't automatically generate game resource files.

I've included the latest DOS version of the map editor on the companion CD-ROM in case you want to create and edit your game maps from DOS. This version of the map editor is stored in the directory \ACK\DOS\MAP_EDIT. The CD-ROM also contains some sample DOS-based games that use map files created by the DOS-based map editor. Thus, you'll need to use this editor if you wish to make changes to the game maps provided. (The complete set of demonstration games and applications provided on the companion CD-ROM is presented in Appendix C.)

When using the DOS-based map editor, keep in mind that it does not read game resource files like the Windows-based editor does. Instead, the DOS-based editor reads in an ASCII map configuration file. This configuration file tells the map editor which bitmap files you plan to use for a particular map so that you can place walls, floors, ceilings, and stationary objects in your map. You'll need to use a text editor to create a map configuration file for each map that you want to build with the DOS-based map editor. After you place the bitmap components in your map with the map editor, the editor will save a binary map file that can later be combined with all of the other game-related files to create a single game resource file. (The process of combining game files to create a resource file involves using the standalone utility BPIC.EXE, which is presented in Appendix A.)

When I created the later Windows version of the map editor, I did away with the ASCII map configuration file and designed the editor so that it could read actual game resource files.

Using the DOS-Based Map Editor

To run the DOS-based map editor, type in this command at the DOS prompt:

```
MAPEDIT filename.ext
```

where *filename.ext* is the name of an ASCII map configuration file. You must specify a file for the editor to load, otherwise you'll receive an error message. (I'll explain how map configuration files are created in the next section.) You'll also need to have a mouse installed on your computer.

A sample screen for the DOS-based map editor is shown in Figure 15.10. In this example, the MALL map configuration file (MALL.L01) has been loaded. This is the file used to build the map for the MALL demo included on the companion CD-ROM. The editor provides a 2-D view of the map, a list of the bitmaps loaded, and buttons you can click on with the mouse to edit your map. If you click on the 3D button, the editor will display an isometric view. This 3-D representation, however, can only be used to view scenes and move around in the map; you can't edit in this mode.

To edit a map, move the mouse pointer to any of the grid squares and click. The bitmap shown in the top-right edge of the screen will be placed. To place walls, click on the WALLS button—or the FLOOR or CEILING button to edit your floor or ceiling. If you want to view all of the bitmaps that are available, click the SELECT button. You can also use the following keys to perform editing operations:

Alt+B	This fills the border of the map with the currently selected bitmap. It does *not* clear the interior of the map.
Alt+C	Selects ceiling mode, just like the ceiling button.
Alt+F	Selects floor mode, just like the floor button.
Alt+M	Selects map mode, just like the map button.

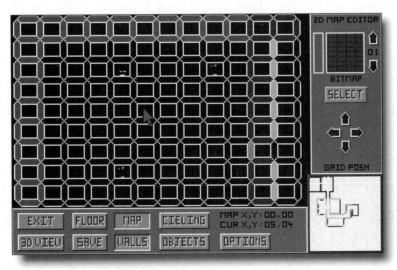

Figure 15.10 *Using the DOS-based map editor.*

After you are done editing your map, make sure you click on the SAVE button. This causes the map editor to save a binary map file so that you can later build a resource file for your game. (You can also load the binary map file in your game code by calling the **AckLoadMap()** function.)

Creating a Map Configuration File

As I mentioned, the DOS-based map editor requires a map configuration file to determine which wall and object bitmaps will be used to build a map. The file specifies the names of the bitmap files used for walls and objects, and assigns numbers to each bitmap. The syntax for creating a map configuration file is:

;	Comment line
Walls:	Identifies the start of the WALLS section
Files:	Bitmap files sub-section, these bitmaps apply to walls
1, filename.ext	Individual bitmap files associated with each wall number Up to 255 bitmaps can be loaded for the walls; each wall is assigned a unique number
n, filename.ext	More bitmaps for the walls, n can be 1 to 255
EndWalls:	Signifies the end of the WALLS section
Objects:	Identifies this as the start of the OBJECTS section
Files:	Bitmap files sub-section, these bitmaps apply to objects
1, filename.ext	Individual bitmap files associated with an object index Up to 255 bitmaps can be loaded for use by objects
n, filename.ext	More bitmaps for the objects, n can be 1 to 255
EndFiles:	Signifies the end of the OBJECTS FILES sub-section
Number: 1	Object number being identified, these numbers do NOT correspond to the bitmap numbers above
Bitmaps: 1	Bitmap number for this object
Number: 2	Another object being identified
Bitmaps: 7	Bitmap associated with object number 2
EndObjects:	Signifies the end of the OBJECTS section
MapFile: filename.map	Identifies which map file to load

Note: Comments can be included on separate lines as long as the first character of the line is a semi-colon. Blank lines are allowed. The sample file MALL.L01 can be used to experiment with the map editor and to see how map configuration files are created. This file is located in the directory \ACK\DOS\MAP_EDIT\MALL.

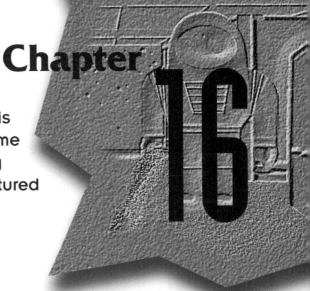

Chapter 16

Here's where we put together everything we've learned in this book and create a fun 3-D game complete with walls, stationary and movable objects, and textured floors and ceilings.

Creating a 3-D Game

Congratulations! You've made it to the last part of our journey. By now you should be armed with a lot of knowledge about the techniques of ray casting and creating the different components of a 3-D game, from a game map to textured walls to movable objects. The reward for working your way through 15 chapters is that you're now ready to create your own games. And the best part is, you have all of the tools you need—a powerful 3-D game engine, sample wall and object bitmaps you can use as is or modify to suit your needs, a visual map editor to create the layouts for your games, and even a template to build your own games. The only ingredients missing are your creative ideas, a game map, and a little C code to get your game up and running.

I'll end this book by showing you a sample game I created. *Station Escape* is a game I wrote a few years ago to demonstrate some of the features of the *ACK-3D* engine. Of course when I first wrote the game, the engine was not nearly as powerful as it is today. So, I've reworked the game a bit and even ported it to Windows to show you how to create fast 3-D Windows games. (An older version of the game that runs in DOS is also provided, if you want to compare the two.)

507

As we discuss the code for the game, we'll explore a number of useful techniques for designing 3-D games in general. Keep in mind that the game presented here does not make use of every available *ACK-3D* feature. I've purposefully designed it to be easy to follow and easily extensible. Feel free to take the game apart. Change the bitmap images. Experiment with different types of floors and ceilings. Add more movable objects. Use the visual map editor introduced in the previous chapter to change the layout for the game. If you get really ambitious, you can add another level or two to the game that can be loaded when the player successfully passes through a secret door or wipes out all of the enemies. The more you experiment with the game, the more you'll discover that the *ACK-3D* engine and visual map editor are the perfect companions to automate the process of creating and modifying your games.

I've found over and over that the best way to learn how to create games is to take a model or template of an existing game and start to change it. It's much faster and easier to create something when you don't have to start from scratch. This method also gives you a chance to see how other designers and programmers apply their craft. That's the approach we'll take in this chapter. In fact, we'll use the template developed in Chapter 14 as our starting point.

Enough said. Let's start our final adventure.

The Designer's Approach

One of the questions I am asked frequently is: How does one design a game like *Wolfenstein* or *DOOM*? If I were to sit down and sketch out all of the concepts and principles that go into designing a successful 3-D game, I'd either never get started or I'd never finish because this task is too big. I could easily fill an entire book with advice on how to create the best layouts for games, how to create impressive movable objects that really wow the player, or how to add special effects like light shading or rotating backgrounds to a game. The best single piece of advice anyone has given me is to play every 3-D game you can get your hands on and keep a close eye out for features that really excite you.

I suggest that you keep a notepad close and jot down ideas as they come to you. Often, when I'm playing a new game, I think of an idea based on something that I see in the game. Many times my idea is quite different from what is in the game I'm playing, but the *experience* of encountering something new gets my creative juices going and leads me to an original idea. Sometimes you'll encounter features in a game that you just can't figure out how to do at the moment. As an example, I was recently playing a new game called *Descent*, which allows you to "tilt" as you travel through 3-D scenes. This one feature led me to think about all kinds of extensions that I could add to the *ACK-3D* engine, which I plan to do as soon as this book is completed.

Before you start to draw bitmaps or write any of the code for your game, you should make a list of the types of games you'd like to build. Here are some examples of possible 3-D games that I'd like to create:

- The Dungeons of Bashire (A fantasy role-playing game)
- Escape from Moon Base Gamma (A futuristic space game)
- The Multimedia Museum of the World (A walk-through with art)
- Greed and Gold (A mining game with financial strategy)

As part of your list, think about the kind of artwork your game requires and the type of settings in which you would like to put your player. You also should come up with a good story line for each game. Even though the goal is to build an action-packed 3-D adventure, the better your story line is, the more interesting your game will probably be. A good story line will also help you create the visual components for your game (wall and object bitmaps, startup screen, rotating background, and so on). If you are using outside designers and artists, a good story line will also help inspire your creative help.

After you've decided on the type of game, you'll need to create bitmaps and lay out the map (or maps) for the game. The map editor comes in handy for doing this interactively, although you still may want to sketch out your game map on graph paper before you start to use the map editor. However you design it, keep in mind that the hallways and rooms, door placement, wall textures, and so on should all be believable for the setting you choose. Put some suspense into the environment, but don't frustrate the player with endless hallways that lead to tiny rooms or require super dexterity to move around. The 3-D environment is perfect for giving the impression of large areas and non-claustrophobic settings, if used in a reasonable manner.

Introducing *Station Escape*

A few scenes from the *Station Escape* game that we'll build in this chapter are shown in Figure 16.1. This game runs in a window that you can resize while you play the game. When the game starts, the default window size is 320×200. The other window sizes you can select include 480×300 and 640×400.

To start the game, run the program ACKSE.EXE, which is in the directory ACK\WIN\STATION on the companion CD-ROM. If you copy the program to your hard drive, make sure that you copy all of the files in this directory. The file KIT.OVL contains the *ACK-3D* specific resources (math tables). The file

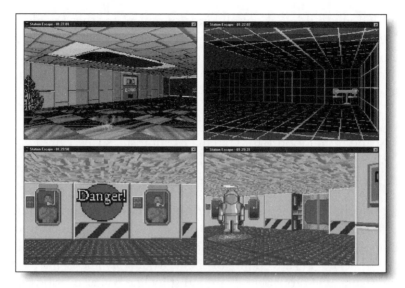

Figure 16.1   *A view of* Station Escape *running in Windows.*

PICS.DTF is the game resource created by the Windows-based map editor. You can view or edit the PICS.DTF file with the editor. Finally, the *.TXT files contain the story and help information for the game.

The object of the game is to move around in a space station and find all the parts required to repair a shuttle craft, then leave the station before the orbit decays. You only have a certain amount of time before the station falls back into the atmosphere and disintegrates. You *must* take all the repair parts to the shuttle bay and into the shuttle craft so repairs can be completed!

To move around and fight off the enemy space creatures, you use these keys:

- Up, down, left, and right arrow keys move the player
- Ctrl key with an arrow key makes the player run
- Tab fires a plasma bolt
- Space bar opens a door
- F1 displays a help screen
- F2 Toggles solid floor on or off
- F3 Toggles solid ceiling on or off

You can also navigate by using the mouse. To move, press down the left mouse button and slide the mouse in the direction you want to go. If you encounter a door, you can open it by clicking the right mouse button.

Figure 16.2 *The main menu for* Station Escape.

The game also provides a menu with options, as shown in Figure 16.2. You can open this menu by clicking the mouse at the top-left location of the menu bar. Here you'll find the commands for resizing the game window, displaying help text, viewing the story for the game, or quitting the game (closing the window).

Creating the Game

Our main theme for *Station Escape* is simple: Survival! As we've seen, the setting for the game is in a space station. By using a little imagination and the *ACK 3-D* engine, we can put the player into the role of a lone survivor aboard a space station gone berserk.

Before I created any of the artwork or wrote any of the code for the game, I came up with a good story line. I introduced part of the story in Chapter 1; you can read the whole story by selecting the Background story option in the game's main menu. You can also read the story by viewing the text file SEBACK.TXT. The last part of the story, really sums up what the game is all about:

> *"Station Escape pits you against the clock in a race to try and repair the one remaining shuttle before it's too late. Parts for the shuttle are available if you can find them and get them to the shuttle bay to make repairs. You later find that general mayhem occurred during the evacuation and certain systems are not functioning quite like they should. In fact they seem to be trying to keep you from your goal of escaping. Is there more going on than meets the eye?"*

Because our game takes place in a space station, we want to make sure the art has a space-related, "high-tech" look. If we were feeling really ambitious, we could get pretty elaborate with our station design and create one that would make NASA sit up and take notice. But for purposes of our discussion, we'll tone things down a bit and thoroughly explain what we're doing. With the map editor and some artwork, this sample game can be enhanced, much in the same way new modules would be lifted into orbit to add to a real space station that began with only a room or two and a docking bay.

The art for the game is fairly straightforward. We'll use different types of wall bitmaps, of which some are animated. The floor and ceiling are textured, and we'll use a neat lighting effect to make it look like there are skylights in the ceiling. At the object level, three types are used. The first type is the set of enemy space creatures (bad guys) that move around and come after the player. The second type of objects consists of the set of plasma bolts (bombs) that the enemies can fire at the player or the player can fire at the enemies. Finally, the last type is stationary objects, such as trees, desks, and so on, that the player can walk around. I like to use as many stationary objects as I can without making the game map too cluttered. These objects give the game a more realistic look. After all, walls can get pretty boring no matter how interesting you make them.

From Player to Engine

How the player actually plays the game is an important consideration when designing the interface. A good means of allowing movement in the 3-D environment, and one that I choose for *Station Escape*, is to use the mouse. Another possibility would be to add joystick control, but I didn't in this example. The mouse seems to give more fluid control and can also be used to select menu items. The keyboard is used as an auxiliary input device for moving around, but the mouse is recommended.

How Smart Are Those Objects?

Artificial Intelligence (AI) has been around for quite some time now and is becoming more and more apparent in computer games. The degree of AI varies depending on the application and how well it is implemented in the overall program. For the purposes of *Station Escape*, I decided to use a very simple approach to object AI mainly because this game is meant to be a demonstration of the *ACK 3-D* engine and not an exercise in the latest AI concepts. There are many ways to enhance the intelligence of the objects in the game; some we'll discuss later on. For now however, let's go through the way objects are handled within the existing game.

As the player moves around, he or she will encounter the enemy space creatures. If one of these creatures gets too close to the player, the creature will fire a plasma bolt (bomb) at the player. The bomb is essentially a set of animated objects all designed to look like a fire ball in motion. To move an enemy object in the game map, we only need to check for a few conditions and perform a few actions based on these conditions:

1. Before moving the enemy, check to see if the enemy is near a door; if so, open the door so the enemy can pass through it.
2. Move the object and check to see if the object has "hit" something. The enemy object can hit a wall, the player, or nothing.
3. If the object hits a wall, the object is turned so that it can continue to move. (You don't want an object to be stuck against a wall for the entire game!)
4. If the object encounters the player, we check to see if the object needs to fire a bomb at the player.
5. If the player fires a bomb, we check to see if the bomb hits the enemy. If it hits the enemy, the enemy is made inactive. (This is how we wipe out the bad guys.)

Step 1: Create the Bitmaps for the Game

Let's step through the process of creating the game. Our *Station Escape* world begins to come together when we create the art for the wall, object, floor, and ceiling bitmaps. Many of the bitmaps used in the game are shown in Figure 16.3. Notice that most of the bitmaps are needed to create the walls. The floor and ceiling, on the other hand, only require a few bitmaps. But if you look closely at the floor and ceiling bitmaps, you'll see that some of the bitmaps are drawn with a lighting effect, as if a light is shining on them. I made these bitmaps so that I could put skylights in the ceiling and have the light display on the floor directly below. When you place these bitmaps in the map, you must make sure that a floor and ceiling bitmap with the lighting effect are in the same grid square.

The Windows-based map editor provides a feature to show you actual map coordinates as you are placing bitmaps in the map. To use this feature, select the Show coordinates command from the Goodies menu.

DESIGN TIP

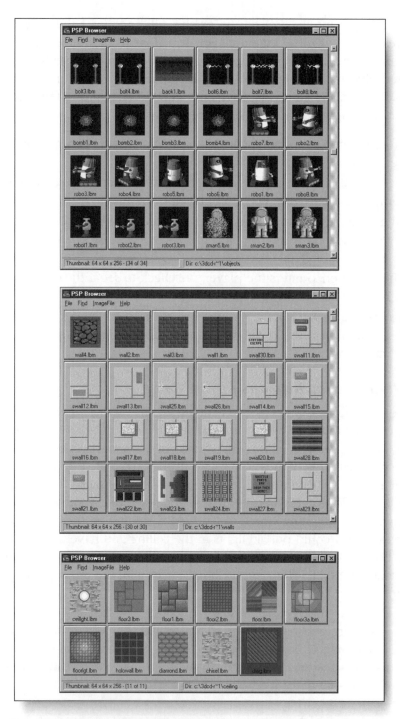

Figure 16.3   *The bitmap art used in* Station Escape.

The objects are arranged into two categories: stationary and movable. Movable objects, such as the enemy space creature and plasma bolt, are processed within the code of the game application. The stationary objects are static and are left unchanged once they are placed in the map grid. Both stationary and movable objects can be animated by assigning more than one bitmap to the object and turning on the **OF_ANIMATE** flag for that object sequence. Likewise, movable objects are really no different than stationary ones except they have the **OF_MOVABLE** flag on, which allows further processing of the object within the *ACK-3D* engine.

Step 2: Create the Game Map

Next, we need to create a map of the overall station. This step is accomplished by using the Windows-based map editor (ACKEDIT.EXE) as shown in Figure 16.4. When the editor starts, it loads the resource file PICS.DTF, which I have already created for the game. (If you were creating a new map, you would clear the map editor, load in the bitmap files you want to use, and begin laying out your map.) You can see only part of the map in the editor window at one time, but you can use the scroll buttons to check out the entire map. We have a good selection of artwork that can be used for the walls so we have many options from which to choose. I suggest you walk through the map and look at each of the walls. If you want to change a wall, select a new bitmap from the list

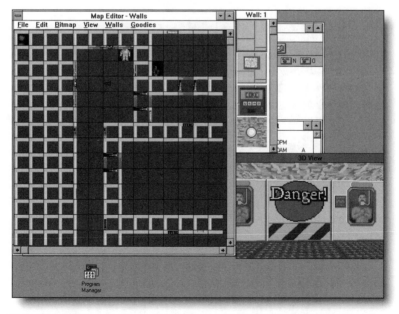

Figure 16.4 *Viewing the map for* Station Escape *with the Windows-based map editor.*

provided. But if you make changes, don't forget to save them and copy the file PICS.DTF to the directory where the *Station Escape* program is located.

We've seen the wall map for the game but what about the ceiling, floor, and objects? To view or edit the floor or ceiling, select the Floor or Ceiling option from the View menu. Figure 16.5 shows how the editor looks when it is in the floor editing mode. Each grid square contains a bitmap. These are the bitmaps that will be displayed overhead as the player moves around in the map. To change one of the bitmaps, select a new bitmap form the list and click the left mouse button on one of the grid squares. The ceiling bitmaps in *Station Escape* are essentially the same for each grid square; however, if you look closely, you'll see that some of the bitmaps are drawn with the skylight in them. If you were to switch to the floor editing mode, you'd see that each corresponding floor grid square is assigned a floor bitmap that has a light shadow in it.

The last component we need are our objects. To view them, select the Objects command from the Edit menu and the bitmap window will change to show the first bitmap assigned to each object. Also, if you were in floor or ceiling view mode, the map grid will change back to displaying walls and objects. Figure 16.6 shows an example of one section that contains objects. The stationary objects are easy to place. You just select an object from the list provided and click on the desired grid square. Movable objects are placed in the map grid the same way, except they must have the Moveable checkbox checked in the Objects Attributes dialog box under the Goodies menu. To

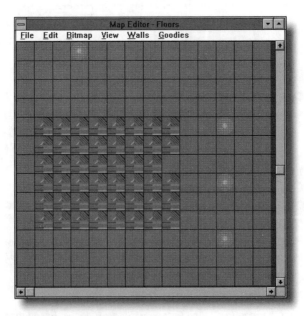

Figure 16.5 *Editing the floor with the map editor.*

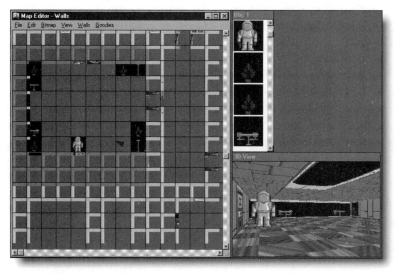

Figure 16.6   *Adding objects to the* Station Escape *map.*

animate an object, you can assign several bitmaps to a single sequence and check the Animate checkbox in the Attributes dialog box. This technique is discussed in more detail in Chapter 15.

As you view the objects in the editor, you can see them displayed as stationary objects. To bring them to life and animate them, you need to write your own code.

Step 3: Just Add Code

We now have a great story, a collection of bitmaps, and a game map with wall, floor, ceiling, and object bitmaps placed. Now comes the fun part, or the hard work, depending on your outlook. Essentially, we need to write a program to display our map and control how the player interacts with the objects in the game. Fortunately, a lot of this work is already done because we can use the Windows template program that we developed in Chapter 14. If you recall, this source file (ACKEXAM.CPP) contains all of the essential code to display views using WinG. All we need to do is change a few of the functions in ACKEXAM.CPP, such as **CreateAll()**, **AckPaint()**, and **AckWndproc()**, and add a few simple functions to control object movement.

The Complete Game Program

The source file we'll create to implement the *Station Escape* game is ACKSE.CPP. This source file also requires the header file ACKSE.H. The only new functions required are listed in Table 16.1.

Table 16.1 *Action-Related Functions in Station Escape*

Function	Description
CheckBadGuys()	Checks to see if a bomb has hit an enemy (bad guy). If it has, the bad guy is made inactive.
CheckFiring()	Checks to see if a bomb should be fired by a bad guy and sets up the bomb.
CheckStatus()	Checks the status of the game play and determines if the game has timed out or the player has won.
FindBombObject()	Locates the first inactive bomb bitmap in the object sequence.
LightOnOff()	Toggles the light shading on or off.
MoveBombs()	Moves the active bombs in the game.
MoveObjects()	Moves the enemies and the bomb objects. This is the main function that is called to control object movement. This function calls other functions such as CheckFiring() and MoveBombs().
ShootBomb()	Sets up a bomb for shooting.
SetNewWindowSize()	Changes the size of the game window and adjusts the window to account for borders and a caption bar.

Let's look at the complete program and then we'll discuss how some of the unique features, such as movable objects and light shading effects, are coded.

```
// Header file for Station Escape Demo Program
// (c) 1995 Ack Software (Lary Myers)
BOOL Register(HINSTANCE hInst);
BOOL CreateAll(HINSTANCE hInst);
int MessageLoop(void);
LRESULT  CALLBACK _export AckWndProc( HWND hWnd, UINT iMessage, WPARAM wParam,
                               LPARAM lParam );
int LoadBackDrop(void);
int AckProcessInfoFile(void);
int DoInfoDlg(HINSTANCE hInst, HWND hWnd);
#define IM_HELP       1     // Display help dialog box
#define IM_BACK       2     // Display background story
#define IM_TIMEOUT    3     // Ran out of time
#define IM_WON        4     // Won the game!
#define REPAIR_OBJECTS_NEEDED 3     // Number of parts needed to win
#define REPAIR_POSITION       3769  // Location on map to win
#define BOMB_START_INDEX      32    // Starting object number
#define BOMB_END_INDEX        40    // Ending object number

// Example source for using ACK-3D in Windows
// (c) 1995 ACK Software (Lary Myers)
#define  STRICT
```

```cpp
#include <windows.h>
#pragma hdrstop
#include <stdlib.h>
#include <string.h>
#include <wing.h>
#include "wingdll.h"
#include "ackwin.h"
#include "ackse.h"
#define IDM_RES1    1100
#define IDM_RES2    1101
#define IDM_RES3    1102
#define IDM_HELP    1103
#define IDM_BACK    1104

extern "C" {
#include "keys.h"
#include "ack3d.h"
void AckDoubleBuffer(UCHAR *Src,UCHAR *Dest);
extern  UCHAR    colordat[];
};

// Some globals to use
ACKENG  *ae = 0;          // Interface structure
HWND   hwndApp;
UCHAR kbPressed[128];
WinGdll WinG;
header  BufferHeader;
void  *pAckBuffer = 0;
HDC AckBuffer = 0;
HPALETTE   hpalApp;
RGBQUAD ColorTable[256];
pal LogicalPalette = {0x300,256};
HBITMAP gbmOldMonoBitmap = 0;
int StretchFactor = 1;
int nBitmapW;
int nBitmapH;              // WinG bitmap dimensions.
int nWindowW;
int nWindowH;
short nMoveSpeed;
short nTurnSpeed;
short nIntroCount;
short nInfoMode;
HINSTANCE hInstGlobal;
BOOL   bNoShow;           // Do not display if TRUE
BOOL   bInStatus;         // Recursive flag for status checks
UCHAR *pIntroBuf;
short nSecondsLeft;
BOOL   bUpdateTime;
UINT   nTimerID;
WORD   nTimerCount;
short nRepairObjectCount;
UCHAR SavePal[768];
```

```
ColorRange   ranges[64] = {
  {16,15},
  {32,16},
  {48,16},
  {64,16},
  {80,16},
  {96,8},
  {104,8},
  {112,8},
  {120,8},
  {128,8},
  {136,8},
  {144,8},
  {152,8},
  {160,8},
  {168,8},
  {176,8},
  {184,16},
  {200,16},
  {216,16},
  {232,16},
  {248,16},
  {0,0}
  };

// Keeps the list of movable objects
short   nMoveObjectList[] = {
  6,7,8,9,10,11,12,
  18,19,
  0}; // Denotes end of table


//****************************************************************************
// The main program window
//****************************************************************************
#pragma argsused
int PASCAL WinMain( HINSTANCE hInstance, HINSTANCE hPrevInstance,
                    LPSTR lpszCmdLine, int nCmdShow )
{
  int     result;
  long    now;
  HBITMAP hbm;
  char    szBuf[40];

pIntroBuf = NULL;
// Register our Window class if this is the first time in
if (!hPrevInstance)
  if (!Register(hInstance))
    return(-1);

// Prime the ACK-3D engine with our startup parameters
if (InitACKEngine())
  return(-1);
```

```
hInstGlobal = hInstance;
// Open our default resource file and load bitmaps, etc.
AckOpenResource("pics.dtf");
result = AckProcessInfoFile();
if (result)
  {
  wsprintf(szBuf,"Error %d in resource",result);
  MessageBox(NULL,szBuf,"Error",MB_OK);
  AckCloseResource();
  return(-1);
  }

srand(time(&now) % 37);
memcpy(SavePal,colordat,768);
pIntroBuf = AckReadiff((char *)2);
AckCloseResource();
bUpdateTime = FALSE;
nTimerCount = 0;
nRepairObjectCount = 0;
nSecondsLeft = (60 * 60) + (60 * 30);
AckSetupPalRanges(ae,ranges);

// Create the actual window to display the rendered view
if (!CreateAll(hInstance))
  return(-1);

nIntroCount = 0;
if (pIntroBuf != NULL)
  {
  nIntroCount = 500;
  }
// Here we loop until the application closes
result = MessageLoop();

// Free up our buffers we used from WinG
if (AckBuffer)
  {
  hbm = (HBITMAP)SelectObject(AckBuffer, gbmOldMonoBitmap);
  DeleteObject(hbm);
  DeleteDC(AckBuffer);
  }

if(hpalApp)
  DeleteObject(hpalApp);

// Shutdown WinG DLL
WinG.Free();
return(result);
}

//***************************************************************************
// Registers the window class.
//***************************************************************************
```

```
BOOL Register(HINSTANCE hInst)
{
  WNDCLASS wndclass;

wndclass.style          = CS_HREDRAW | CS_VREDRAW | CS_OWNDC;
wndclass.lpfnWndProc    = AckWndProc;
wndclass.cbClsExtra     = 0;
wndclass.cbWndExtra     = 0;
wndclass.hInstance      = hInst;
wndclass.hIcon          = LoadIcon(hInst,"ackicon");
wndclass.hCursor        = LoadCursor( NULL, IDC_ARROW );
wndclass.hbrBackground  = (HBRUSH)GetStockObject( WHITE_BRUSH );
wndclass.lpszMenuName   = NULL;
wndclass.lpszClassName  = "ACK3DVIEW";

if (!RegisterClass(&wndclass))
  return(FALSE);
return(TRUE);
}

//***************************************************************************
// Loads the WinG DLL and creates the display window for the application.
//***************************************************************************
BOOL CreateAll(HINSTANCE hInst)
{
  int     windx, windy;
  HMENU   hMenu;

if (!WinG.Load())
  {
  MessageBox(0,"Can't find WING32.DLL","Error!",MB_OK);
  return(FALSE);
  }

nBitmapW = 319;           // Default size (window client size to use)
nBitmapH = 199;

windx = windy = GetSystemMetrics(SM_CXBORDER)*2;
windx += nBitmapW;
windy += nBitmapH + GetSystemMetrics(SM_CYCAPTION) - 1;
nWindowW = windx;
nWindowH = windy;

// Note that in this example we're not allowing any resizing borders
// This helps to keep things alittle more constrained with the current
// ACK-3D engine.
hwndApp = CreateWindow ("ACK3DVIEW", // Class name
        "ACK-3D Station Escape",     // Caption
        WS_POPUP|WS_BORDER|WS_CAPTION|WS_VISIBLE|WS_SYSMENU,
        0,                           // Position
        0,
        windx,windy,                 // Size
        (HWND)NULL,                  // Parent window
        (HMENU)NULL,                 // use class menu
```

```
            hInst,                        // handle to window instance
            (LPSTR)NULL );                // no params to pass on

    if (!hwndApp)
      {
      MessageBox(NULL,"Unable to create 3D window","ERROR",MB_OK);
      return(FALSE);
      }

    // Now we'll display the window and setup the WinG buffer when we
    // receive the WM_SIZE message.
    ShowWindow(hwndApp,SW_NORMAL);
    hMenu = GetSystemMenu(hwndApp,FALSE);
    // Add in the menu items for the game window
    AppendMenu(hMenu,MF_SEPARATOR,0,NULL);
    AppendMenu(hMenu,MF_STRING,IDM_RES1,"320 x 200");
    AppendMenu(hMenu,MF_STRING,IDM_RES2,"480 x 300");
    AppendMenu(hMenu,MF_STRING,IDM_RES3,"640 x 400");
    AppendMenu(hMenu,MF_SEPARATOR,0,NULL);
    AppendMenu(hMenu,MF_STRING,IDM_HELP,"&Help");
    AppendMenu(hMenu,MF_STRING,IDM_BACK,"&Background story");
    return(TRUE);
    }

//****************************************************************************
// Here is where we loop until the application terminates.
//****************************************************************************
int MessageLoop(void)
{
  MSG msg;

  for (;;)
    {
    if (PeekMessage(&msg, NULL, 0, 0,PM_REMOVE))
      {
      if (msg.message == WM_QUIT)
        break;
      TranslateMessage(&msg);
      DispatchMessage(&msg);
      }
    else
      {
      DoCycle();  // Display the 3D window
      }
    }
  return msg.wParam;
}

//****************************************************************************
// Turns light shading on and off.
//****************************************************************************
void LightOnOff(short nMode)
{
  BOOL    bSet = FALSE;
```

```
if (!nMode && ae->LightFlag == SHADING_OFF)
  {
  ae->LightFlag = SHADING_ON;
  bSet = TRUE;
  }

if (nMode && ae->LightFlag == SHADING_ON)
  {
  ae->LightFlag = SHADING_OFF;
  bSet = TRUE;
  }

if (bSet)
  {
  AckSetupPalRanges(ae,ranges);
  AckRegisterStructure(ae);
  }
}

//***************************************************************************
// Checks to see if the bomb thrown by the player hits one of the bad guys.
//***************************************************************************
void CheckBadGuys(UCHAR nIndex)
{
  short    i;
  UCHAR    ObjIndex;
  NEWOBJECT    *pObj;
i = 0;
while (nMoveObjectList[i])  // Check the list of movable objects
  {
  ObjIndex = nMoveObjectList[i++];
  if (ObjIndex == nIndex)
    {
    pObj = ae->ObjList[ObjIndex];
    if (pObj != NULL)
      {
      pObj->Active = 0;  // Bad guy has been hit—make inactive
      }
    break;
    }
  }
}

//***************************************************************************
// Locates the first inactive bomb.
//***************************************************************************
UCHAR FindBombObject(void)
{
  UCHAR        index;
  NEWOBJECT    *pObj;

for (index = BOMB_START_INDEX; index < BOMB_END_INDEX; index++)
  {
```

```
    pObj = ae->ObjList[index];
    if (pObj != NULL && pObj->Active == 0)
      return(index);
    }
return(0);
}

//***************************************************************************
// Moves the active bombs.
//***************************************************************************
void MoveBombs(void)
{
  UCHAR     Index;
  UCHAR     nHitIndex;
  short     nResult;
  NEWOBJECT *pBomb,*pSman;

for (Index = BOMB_START_INDEX; Index <= BOMB_END_INDEX; Index++)
  {
  pBomb = ae->ObjList[Index];
  if (pBomb != NULL)
    {
    if (pBomb->Active)
      {
      nHitIndex = 0;
      // See if bomb will hit something
      nResult = AckMoveObjectPOV(Index,pBomb->Dir,pBomb->Speed);
      if (nResult != POV_NOTHING)
        {
        if (Index == BOMB_END_INDEX && nResult != POV_PLAYER)
          {
          pBomb->Active = 0;
          if (nResult == POV_OBJECT)
            CheckBadGuys(AckGetObjectHit());
          }
        else
          {
          if (nResult == POV_OBJECT)
            nHitIndex = AckGetObjectHit();
          if (nHitIndex != pBomb->id)
            {
            pBomb->Active = 0;
            pSman = ae->ObjList[pBomb->id];
            if (pSman != NULL)
              pSman->id = 0;
            pBomb->id = 0;
            }
          }
        }
      }
    }
  }
}
```

```c
//***************************************************************************
// See if a bad guy is not currently firing a bomb. If so, set up the bomb
// for firing.
//***************************************************************************
void CheckFiring(short nObjIndex,NEWOBJECT *pObj)
{
  UCHAR       Index;
  NEWOBJECT   *pBomb;
  long        dx,dy;

if (pObj->id)    // Bad guy is currently firing
  return;

Index = FindBombObject();  // Get the first inactive bomb

if (Index)
{  // Set all of the attributes for firing the bomb
  pObj->id = Index;
  dx = ae->xPlayer - pObj->x;
  dy = ae->yPlayer - pObj->y;
  pBomb = ae->ObjList[Index];
  pBomb->Dir = AckGetObjectAngle(dx,dy);
  pBomb->x = pObj->x;
  pBomb->y = pObj->y;
  pBomb->id = nObjIndex;
  pBomb->Speed = 32;
  pBomb->Active = 1;
  pBomb->mPos = (short)((pBomb->y & 0xFFC0) + (pBomb->x >> (short)6));
  }
}


//***************************************************************************
// Move the objects in the game.
//***************************************************************************
void MoveObjects(void)
{
  short       i,nIndex,nResult;
  short       nRow,nCol;
  NEWOBJECT   *pObj;

i = 0;
while (nMoveObjectList[i])
  {
  nIndex = nMoveObjectList[i];
  i++;
  pObj = ae->ObjList[nIndex];
  if (pObj != NULL && pObj->Active && (pObj->Flags & OF_MOVEABLE))
    {
    AckCheckDoorOpen(pObj->x,pObj->y,pObj->Dir);
    nResult = AckMoveObjectPOV(nIndex,pObj->Dir,pObj->Speed);
    if (nResult != POV_NOTHING)
      {
      if (nResult == POV_XWALL || nResult == POV_YWALL)
        {
```

```
        nResult = AckGetWallHit();
        if (nResult & DOOR_TYPE_SPLIT)
          {
          continue;
          }
        }
        // Turn object to get away from the wall
        pObj->Dir += (short)((rand() % INT_ANGLE_180));
        if (pObj->Dir >= INT_ANGLE_360)
          pObj->Dir -= (short)INT_ANGLE_360;
        }
    else
      CheckFiring(nIndex,pObj);
    }
  }

MoveBombs();  // Move the active bombs
// This code determines if the player is in a special location
// of the game map and toggles the light shadding if the player
// reaches this region. This is used to create a unique
// dynamic light shading effect
nRow = (short)(ae->yPlayer >> 6);
nCol = (short)(ae->xPlayer >> 6);
if (nRow == 33)
  {
  if (nCol == 8)
    LightOnOff(0);
  else
  if (nCol == 10)
    LightOnOff(1);
  }
if (nCol == 24)
  {
  if (nRow == 5)
    LightOnOff(0);
  else
  if (nRow == 7)
    LightOnOff(1);
  }
}

//***************************************************************************
// Fires off a bomb from the player.
//***************************************************************************
void ShootBomb(void)
{
  NEWOBJECT    *pBomb;

// Get the bomb to fire
pBomb = ae->ObjList[BOMB_END_INDEX];
if (pBomb == NULL)
  return;
if (pBomb->Active)
  return;
```

```
// Set the bomb up so that it will come from the player
pBomb->Dir = ae->PlayerAngle;
pBomb->x = ae->xPlayer;
pBomb->y = ae->yPlayer;
pBomb->Speed = 32;
pBomb->Active = 1;
pBomb->mPos = (short)((pBomb->y & 0xFFC0) + (pBomb->x >> (short)6));
}


//***************************************************************************
// Checks the status of the game and determines if the game should be
// timed out or if the player has won.
//***************************************************************************
void CheckStatus(HWND hWnd)
{
  BOOL    bResult = FALSE;
  short   nPos;

if (bInStatus)
  return;
bInStatus = TRUE;

if (!nSecondsLeft)
  {
  nInfoMode = IM_TIMEOUT;
  DoInfoDlg(hInstGlobal,hWnd);
  bResult = TRUE;
  }

if (nRepairObjectCount == REPAIR_OBJECTS_NEEDED)
  {
  nPos = (short)((ae->yPlayer & 0xFFC0) + (ae->xPlayer >> 6));
  if (nPos == REPAIR_POSITION)
    {
    nInfoMode = IM_WON;
    DoInfoDlg(hInstGlobal,hWnd);
    bResult = TRUE;
    }
  }

if (bResult)
  {
  PostQuitMessage(0);
  }
bInStatus = FALSE;
}


//***************************************************************************
// Displays the current scene in the opened window.
//***************************************************************************
#pragma argsused
void AckPaint(HWND hWnd,HDC hdc)
{
```

```
  short    nHours,nMin,nSec,t;
  char     szBuf[40];

if (ae != NULL && nIntroCount == 0)
  {
  AckCheckObjectMovement();    // Check object animation
  MoveObjects();               // Application object movement
  AckBuildView();              // Render the 3D view
  }

// Check for any introduction graphics to display
if (nIntroCount)
  {
  if (pIntroBuf != NULL && AckBuffer != NULL)
    {
    memcpy(pAckBuffer,&pIntroBuf[4],64000);
    AckFree(pIntroBuf);
    pIntroBuf = NULL;
    }
  nIntroCount—;
  }
// Let WinG display the buffer into our window. We can use a StretchFactor
// to display larger windows if so desired, at the cost of speed. The
// fastest way is to simply BitBlt the buffer into our window.
if (StretchFactor != 1)
  {
  WinG.pStretchBlt(hdc,0,0,nWindowW,nWindowH, // Use current window size
              AckBuffer,0,0,nBitmapW,nBitmapH);
  }
else
  WinG.pBitBlt(hdc,0,0,nBitmapW,nBitmapH,AckBuffer,0,0);

if (bUpdateTime)
  {
  bUpdateTime = FALSE;
  nHours = (short)(nSecondsLeft / 3600);
  t = (short)(nHours * 3600);
  nMin = (short)((nSecondsLeft - t) / 60);
  nSec = (short)(nSecondsLeft - t - (nMin * 60));
  wsprintf(szBuf,"Station Escape - %02d:%02d:%02d",nHours,nMin,nSec);
  SetWindowText(hWnd,szBuf);
  }
}


//*************************************************************************
// Adjust the actual window size to account for borders and a caption bar
//*************************************************************************
void SetNewWindowSize(HWND hWnd)
{
  int      windx,windy;

windx = windy = GetSystemMetrics(SM_CXBORDER)*2;
nWindowW += windx;
nWindowH += windy + GetSystemMetrics(SM_CYCAPTION) - 1;
```

```
SetWindowPos(hWnd,NULL,0,0,nWindowW,nWindowH,
SWP_NOMOVE|SWP_NOZORDER|SWP_NOCOPYBITS);
}

//***************************************************************************
// Message handler for the 3D window
//***************************************************************************
LRESULT CALLBACK _export AckWndProc(HWND hWnd,UINT iMessage,
                                    WPARAM wParam,LPARAM lParam)
{
  HDC         hDC;
  PAINTSTRUCT ps;

switch (iMessage)
  {
  case WM_CREATE:
    nTimerID = SetTimer(hWnd,1,1000,NULL);
    break;

  case WM_DESTROY:
    if (nTimerID)
      KillTimer(hWnd,nTimerID);
    nTimerID = 0;
    PostQuitMessage(0);
    break;

  case WM_TIMER:
    nTimerCount++;
    bUpdateTime = TRUE;
    if (nSecondsLeft)
      nSecondsLeft—;
    CheckStatus(hWnd);
    break;

  case WM_SIZE:
    AckDoSize(hWnd,lParam);
    break;

  case WM_PAINT:
    BeginPaint(hWnd,&ps);
    AckPaint(hWnd,ps.hdc);
    EndPaint(hWnd,&ps);
    break;

  case WM_KEYDOWN:
    if (wParam == VK_F1)
      {
      nInfoMode = IM_HELP;
      DoInfoDlg(hInstGlobal,hWnd);
      break;
      }

    if (wParam == VK_F2)
      {
      ae->SysFlags ^= SYS_SOLID_FLOOR;
```

```
        AckRegisterStructure(ae);
        break;
        }

    if (wParam == VK_F3)
        {
        ae->SysFlags ^= SYS_SOLID_CEIL;
        AckRegisterStructure(ae);
        break;
        }

    if (wParam == VK_TAB)
        {
        ShootBomb();
        break;
        }
// Fall through here
  case WM_KEYUP:
    nIntroCount = 0;
    ProcessKeys(iMessage,wParam);
    break;

case WM_RBUTTONDOWN:
    AckCheckDoorOpen(ae->xPlayer,ae->yPlayer,ae->PlayerAngle);
    break;

case WM_LBUTTONDOWN:
    nIntroCount = 0;
    ProcessMouse(hWnd,1,LOWORD(lParam),HIWORD(lParam));
    SetCapture(hWnd);
    break;

case WM_MOUSEMOVE:
    if (wParam & MK_LBUTTON)
        ProcessMouse(hWnd,1,LOWORD(lParam),HIWORD(lParam));
    break;

case WM_LBUTTONUP:
    ProcessMouse(hWnd,0,LOWORD(lParam),HIWORD(lParam));
    ReleaseCapture();
    break;

case WM_PALETTECHANGED:
    if (hWnd == (HWND)wParam)
        break;
    // Fall through here
case WM_QUERYNEWPALETTE:
    hDC = GetDC(hWnd);
    if (hpalApp)
        SelectPalette(hDC,hpalApp,FALSE);

    RealizePalette(hDC);
    ReleaseDC(hWnd,hDC);
    return FALSE;
```

```
case WM_SYSCOMMAND:
  switch (wParam)
    {
    case IDM_RES1:
      if (StretchFactor != 1)
        {
        StretchFactor = 1;
        nWindowW = 320;
        nWindowH = 200;
        SetNewWindowSize(hWnd);
        }
      break;

    case IDM_RES2:
      if (StretchFactor != 2)
        {
        StretchFactor = 2;
        nWindowW = 480;
        nWindowH = 300;
        SetNewWindowSize(hWnd);
        }
      break;

    case IDM_RES3:
      if (StretchFactor != 3)
        {
        StretchFactor = 3;
        nWindowW = 640;
        nWindowH = 400; SetNewWindowSize(hWnd);
        }
      break;

    case IDM_HELP:
      nInfoMode = IM_HELP;
      DoInfoDlg(hInstGlobal,hWnd);
      break;

    case IDM_BACK:
      nInfoMode = IM_BACK;
      DoInfoDlg(hInstGlobal,hWnd);
      break;

    default:
      break;
    }
  return DefWindowProc( hWnd, iMessage, wParam, lParam );

  default:
    return DefWindowProc( hWnd, iMessage, wParam, lParam );
  }
return 0;
}
//**** End of Source ****
```

A Closer Look at the Game

The start up function in ACKSE.CPP is **WinMain()**. This function is essentially the same as **WinMain()** in the ACKEXAM program presented in Chapter 14 except that it initializes a few extra variables:

```
bUpdateTime = FALSE;
nTimerCount = 0;
nRepairObjectCount = 0;
nSecondsLeft = (60 * 60) + (60 * 30);
```

These variables are used to set up a counter to determine when the game should end. The goal is to let the player move around in the game to collect three objects that are needed to repair the shuttle craft. If the player can't locate the objects in time, the game times out. The variable **nRepairObjectCount** keeps track of the number of objects found. I'll show you how this variable is used when we explore the code for checking the game status.

Once **WinMain()** performs all of the necessary initialization work—registering the window class, calling **InitACKEngine()** to set up the engine, opening the game resource file, initializing the counter variables, and creating a window to display the view, it starts the message loop which takes over the game control:

```
// Here we loop until the application closes
result = MessageLoop();
```

We've seen how **MessageLoop()** operates in Chapter 14. It looks for a message and processes the message when the message comes in. If a message is not received, **MesssageLoop()** calls the **DoCycle()** function which processes a drawing cycle.

Processing Game-Related Messages

The function that has changes quite a bit from it's counterpart in the WINEXAM program is **AckWndProc()**. The version for the *Station Escape* game is essentially one big case statement with new message processing code added to handle game control (**WM_TIMER**), new keyboard inputs (**WM_KEYDOWN**), and menu selections (**WM_SYSCOMMAND**). As an example, notice the code that has been added for processing the keys that the player can press (F1, F2, F3, and tab):

```
case WM_KEYDOWN:
  if (wParam == VK_F1)
    {
    nInfoMode = IM_HELP;
```

```
   DoInfoDlg(hInstGlobal,hWnd);
   break;
   }

if (wParam == VK_F2)
   {
   ae->SysFlags ^= SYS_SOLID_FLOOR;
   AckRegisterStructure(ae);
   break;
   }

if (wParam == VK_F3)
   {
   ae->SysFlags ^= SYS_SOLID_CEIL;
   AckRegisterStructure(ae);
   break;
   }

if (wParam == VK_TAB)
   {
   ShootBomb();
   break;
   }
```

If the player presses F1, the game help text is displayed by calling **DoInfoDlg()**. This function, which is defined in ACKSUP.CPP, displays a text file in a simple window. In this case, the text file displayed is the help notes for the game which is stored in the file SEHELP.TXT. If the player presses F2 or F3, the floor or ceiling is tuned on or off, respectively. Notice that whenever we make a direct change to one of the engine variables such as **SysFlags**, **AckRegisterStructure()** must be called.

The last input processed by this code is the tab key. When the player presses this key, the function **ShootBomb()** is called to set up a bomb so that it can be shot from the player.

If you want to add other features to the game that are triggered by keyboard input, you need to add the processing code to **WM_KEYDOWN**. As an example, assume you want to add a feature so that if you press the Shift key the player will fire off a different type of object. You would need to add an **if** statement to check for **wParam==VK_SHIFT** and then call a new function to move the object.

Checking the Game Status

The function that determines the status of the game is **CheckStatus()**. This function is called by the main message handler function **AckWndProc()** whenever a **WM_TIMER** event occurs:

```
case WM_TIMER:
  nTimerCount++;
  bUpdateTime = TRUE;
  if (nSecondsLeft)
    nSecondsLeft--;
  CheckStatus(hWnd);
  break;
```

Before the function is called, the timer counter is incremented to later display the actual time in the window's title bar and the game counter is decremented. One of the first operations **CheckStatus()** performs is to check the **nSecondsLeft** variable to see if the game should be terminated:

```
if (!nSecondsLeft)    // See if the game has timed out
  {
  nInfoMode = IM_TIMEOUT;
  DoInfoDlg(hInstGlobal,hWnd);
  bResult = TRUE;
  }
```

If **nSecondsLeft** is equal to 0, a flag is set and **DoInfoDlg()** is called to display this message:

> Tick...Tick...Tick....
>
> Oh No! You've run out of time! You feel the heat begin to rise as the station begins to enter the upper atmosphere. If only you had found those parts and made it to the shuttle in time.
>
> Tick...Tick...Tick....
>
> Thank you for playing Station Escape!
> An *ACK-3D* Windows Demonstration

The other condition that **CheckStatus()** tests for is to see if the player has gathered all of the parts to repair the shuttle craft:

```
// See if the player has won
if (nRepairObjectCount == REPAIR_OBJECTS_NEEDED)
  {
  nPos = (short)((ae->yPlayer & 0xFFC0) + (ae->xPlayer >> 6));
  if (nPos == REPAIR_POSITION)
    {
    nInfoMode = IM_WON;
    DoInfoDlg(hInstGlobal,hWnd);
```

```
    bResult = TRUE;
    }
 }
```

In order to win, the player must collect all of the missing parts *and* he or she must be in the correct location of the game map. If these conditions are met, **DoInfoDlg()** is called to display the winning message. This code illustrates how you can test the position of the player in the game map at any time and perform an appropriate action.

Controlling Objects

We've already seen how the player can fire a bomb by pressing the tab key. This action causes **ShootBomb()** to be called which in turn determines the position and angle of the player to set up a bomb object so that it can be fired. The bomb object is taken from the object list that the game maintains:

```
pBomb = ae->ObjList[BOMB_END_INDEX];
```

The game uses a list of bomb objects and dynamically assigns a bomb to one of the bad guy objects. When **FindBombObject()** is called, it returns an index to an available bomb object which is then linked to a bad guy object using the **id** field of each object. If no bombs are available, the bad guy doesn't shoot! The constants **BOMB_START_INDEX** and **BOMB_END_INDEX** are used to define the range of bomb object numbers that were created in the map editor. The last bomb object (**BOMB_END_INDEX**) is reserved for use by the player when the tab key is pressed. Each of the bomb objects has a series of bitmaps assigned to it in order to produce animation.

So what about the bad guys? How do we move them around and have them fire at the player? To control the bad guys, we'll need to add a function call to the version of **AckPaint()** we developed in Chapter 14:

```
if (ae != NULL && nIntroCount == 0)
  {
  AckCheckObjectMovement();    // Check object animation
  MoveObjects();               // Application object movement
  AckBuildView();              // Render the 3D view
  }
```

Recall that **AckPaint()** is called by the main message handler to display the current view. In previous applications, we simply called **AckCheckObjectMovement()** to update any objects in the view and then we called **AckBuildView()** to update the 3-D scene. But now we've added a function—**MoveObjects()**—between the two calls.

MoveObjects() is responsible for moving all of the bad guys and making sure that the bad guys fire at the player whenever a bomb object is available. One enhancement to this routine would be for the bad guys to fire only if the player was within a certain distance. For this demo, they will fire a bomb no matter how far away they are from the player, even if they are on the other end of the map! Not very efficient, but simple. Within the **MoveObjects()** function a **while** loop is used to step through the list of movable objects to determine which objects need to be moved:

```
while (nMoveObjectList[i])
  {
  nIndex = nMoveObjectList[i];
  i++;
  pObj = ae->ObjList[nIndex];
  ...
```

The variable **pObj** references the current object in the list and this variable is tested to see if the object (bad guy) is near a door or getting too close to a wall. If the object gets too close to a wall, we need to turn it some so that it can continue to move about and come after the player:

```
pObj->Dir += (short)((rand() % INT_ANGLE_180));
  if (pObj->Dir >= INT_ANGLE_360)
    Obj->Dir -= (short)INT_ANGLE_360;
```

We also need to check if the bad guy we are processing in the loop needs to be set up to fire at the player. This is done by calling **CheckFiring()**. This function tests to see if the bad guy is currently firing a bomb. If it isn't, the first inactive bomb object is located in the list of objects, and the bomb is set up so that it can be fired from the bad guy toward the player.

Once all of this set up work has been completed, the function **MoveBombs()** is called to move all of the active bombs. We can easily tell if a bomb is active by checking the **Active** flag stored in the object structure:

```
if (pBomb->Active)
  {
  nHitIndex = 0;
  nResult = AckMoveObjectPOV(Index,pBomb->Dir,pBomb->Speed);
  ...
```

Just Add Light Shading

The last operation performed by **MoveObjects()** involves setting up a neat light shading trick. The game map is designed so that there are two unique areas—one is a lounge and the other is a holodeck. If the player moves into one of these areas, light shading is turned on to change the mood of the game. This task is performed by checking the position of the player in **MoveObjects()** and calling the function **LightOnOff()** whenever the player moves into or out of one of these areas. This light shading effect is kind of subtle, so when you play the game and move into the light shading areas, keep your eyes peeled.

We're Done!

Wow! We've made it to the end. You now have at your disposal a generic 3-D engine that you can expand upon and build all those exciting games you've been thinking about. There are still many that could be explored further—from the way ray casting is used in general, to the final applications and uses, such as the map editor. My plans are to continue improving on the map editor and engine, with the overall goal being to develop a complete gaming toolkit that anyone can use to create 3-D applications. But don't wait for me! Jump in there and start experimenting, improving, and enhancing the *ACK-3D* engine. That's why I've provided all the code, so you have a starting point to work from. Good luck with your adventures, and I hope you keep the project growing. I look forward to seeing your achievements out there on the store shelves!

Everything You Need to Know about Resource Files

In Chapter 11 I showed you a number of different techniques to initialize the game engine and load in game components such as the map file, object bitmaps, wall bitmaps, and so on. For example, to load in a map file from your application, you call the function:

```
result = AckReadMapFile(&ae, "DEMOMAP.MAP");
```

To read in a bitmap and assign it to an object number, you call

```
result = AckLoadObject(&ae,1,"OBJECT1.PCX");
```

and then you can call this function to create the object:

```
result = AckCreateObject(&ae,1);
```

There are two problems with this system. If you use a number of wall and object bitmaps in your game, your application will require numerous .BBM or

.PCX bitmap files. When you distribute your game, you'll need to make sure that all of these files are included. If one file gets lost or corrupted, you're out of luck. This method is not the best way to develop or distribute software!

The other problem is that your actual application will need to make all of the initialization calls to set up each wall and object bitmap and create the objects used in your game. This approach could make your source files rather large! So, wouldn't it be nice if you could set up a configuration file to specify which components you want to include in a game and then have the engine do the mechanical work of setting up everything for you? You want it, you got it!

There are actually two ways to combine the resources needed to create a game. The easy way is to use the Windows version of the *ACK-3D* map editor and save the output from the editor to a resource file. (This is the method that I recommend you use.) You can also use the DOS version of the *ACK-3D* map editor that creates a game map file that you can in turn manually combine with other game-related files such as wall bitmaps, object bitmaps, and so on. The DOS version of the *ACK-3D* map editor is stored in the directory \ACK\DOS\MAP_EDIT on the companion CD-ROM.

A game resource file created by the Windows map editor actually consists of two parts:

- **Resource data** The resource data is a combination of all of the different files used in a game, such as the map data, wall bitmaps, object bitmaps, and so on.
- **Configuration script** The configuration script serves as the set of instructions that tells the engine which components to use in a game and how the components should be set up. This is the list of commands created by the Windows version of the map editor when you select the INF file command from the View menu.

Usually, game resource files are given the extension .DTF. Once a .DTF file has been created it can be read in by the Windows version of the map editor.

Creating and Using a Resource File

You've already seen how you can create resource files using the interactive Windows map editor. But you might not realize that you can also put a game resource file together manually. The *ACK-3D* engine provides a stand-alone tool called BPIC.EXE for creating resource files in this manner. This program is located in the \TOOLS\BPIC directory on the companion CD-ROM. Essentially, this program is a *resource compiler* that consolidates all of the map, bitmap, and screen files into a single binary resource file. Once the resource file has been created, your application can load it by calling **AckOpenResource()**. After the resource file has been opened, functions that need to read in data from files can get the data directly from the master resource file.

Any of the *ACK-3D* library routines that accepts a filename as a parameter can also accept a resource index number if a resource file is currently opened.

DESIGN TIP

Let's look at an example. Assume that you've combined all of your files into a resource file named PICS.DTF. In your program, you first initialize the *ACK-3D* engine by calling **AckInitialize()** and then you call **AckOpenResource()** to open the set of game resources combined in the binary resource file. Next, functions that set up game components, such as **AckLoadWall()**, can be called, which in turn use the opened resource. When you are finished with the resource file, you close it by calling **AckCloseResource()**. Here's an example of how a program performs these steps:

```
result = AckInitialize()
...
result = AckOpenResource("PICS.DTF"); // Open the resource file
...
// Include code here to process the resource file

AckCloseResource();
```

The resource compiler, BPIC.EXE, uses an ASCII file for input and generates the binary resource file as output. The input file tells the resource compiler which files should be combined. To create the ASCII file used by the resource compiler, you need to gather all of the your game files together in one directory. This list should include:

- The game configuration file that provides the script commands (we'll discuss this file later in the appendix)
- The map file created by the game editor
- Bitmap files to be used for a screen background and scrolling background

- Bitmap files for walls
- Bitmap files for objects

Next, you need to determine the order in which you plan to load these files. Finally, you can use a text editor and create a list of filenames you wish to include in the final resource file. Here's an example list of some of the files I used to create a demo 3-D program called MALL:

```
MALL.INF
MALL.MAP
MALL.LBM
MNTBACK2.LBM
WALL1.BBM
WALL.BBM
WALL2.BBM
WALL3.BBM
STONES.BBM
STONE.BBM
STONE1.BBM
```

The filename listed first is the configuration file that provides the script commands for setting up a game. I've made it sort of a standard to always place this file first in the list so it can be called upon by any application and is always in the same place in the resource file. (I'll show you how these configuration files are created in the next section.) The second file is the game map file, also something of a standard, which is created by the DOS-based visual map program. It contains all of the information about where objects and walls are placed in the map. The other files are the bitmap files used to display background screens, wall sections, and object sections.

The order of the filenames tells the resource compiler the order in which to place the files into the final resource file. By convention, all of the resource files begin with the configuration file, which we'll discuss in the next section. The information file must include the index numbers for the other files in the resource (such as the map file). This way your application can be a little more generic in how it retrieves the individual files that make up the *ACK-3D* environment.

The resource compiler is very easy to use. You call it by going to the DOS prompt and running a command in this format:

```
BPIC infile.ext outfile.ext
```

where *infile.ext* is the name of the ASCII file that contains the list of filenames to be placed in the resource and *outfile.ext* is the actual name of the resource file that is created. The resource file will contain the data for all of the individual files listed in the *infile.ext*. The file *outfile.ext* is overwritten each time you run BPIC. Thus, make sure you specify a new filename if you do not want to overwrite the existing file.

Using the Resource File

To use a resource file in your applications, you'll need to include code to process the configuration script stored in the resource file. I've included a function named **ProcessInfoFile()** to automate the process of using a resource file with an application. If you recall from Chapter 14, we called this function from the WINEXAM program. This function is also used in the Windows version of the *Station Escape* game presented in Chapter 16. The Windows version of this function is defined in the source file ACKINFO.CPP. You can also use this function with your DOS applications. If you need more information on how to use this function, review the Windows example presented in Chapter 14.

Creating a Game Configuration File

The game configuration (or information) file is a text file that provides special commands that *ACK-3D* uses to determine how to set up the **ACKENG** data structure and which initialization functions to call, such as **AckCreateObject()** and **AckReadMapFile()**. These are the instructions that are automatically generated by the Windows map editor. Creating a game configuration (.INF) file manually is a three step process. The first two steps are the same as the ones used to create a resource file:

1. Gather all of the user-specific input files that are needed.
2. Decide the order that these files will be placed in the resource file.

It's important that you determine the order of the game files before you create your configuration file, because some of the configuration commands require parameters that specify where a particular resource, such as a wall or object bitmap, will be located in the main resource file. Once you have all of this worked out, you can create the configuration file using the commands listed in Table A.1. These commands come in three flavors:

- Value specifiers
- Section labels
- Resource indexes

Table A.1   *Commands Supported in the Configuration File*

Label	Description
;	Specifies a comment line. Must be the first character on the line.
MAPFILE:	Specifies the index into the resource file where the map data is located.
PALFILE:	Specifies the index into the resource file where the color palette data is located, if one is used.
XPLAYER:	Specifies the player's starting x coordinate.
YPLAYER:	Specifies the player's starting y coordinate.
PLAYERANGLE:	Specifies the player's starting angle.
SCREENBACK:	Specifies the index into the resource file where the image is stored for the screen background picture.
SCROLLBACK:	Specifies the index into the resource file where the image is stored for the scrolling background.
TOPCOLOR:	Specifies the color used for the top part of the display.
BOTTOMCOLOR:	Specifies the color used for the bottom part of the display.
SHADING:	Specifies if light shading is turned on or off. The settings supported are "ON" or "OFF".
FLOORS:	Specifies how floors are drawn. A setting of "OFF" indicates a floor should be drawn as a solid. A setting of "ON" indicates the floor should be drawn as a textured bitmap.
CEILING:	Specifies how ceilings are drawn. A setting of "OFF" indicates a ceiling should be drawn as a solid. A setting of "ON" indicates the ceiling should be drawn as a textured bitmap.
RESOLUTION:	Specifies the resolution used to display walls, floors, and ceilings. A setting of 1 indicates that a lower resolution mode is used to display walls, floors, and ceilings. A setting of 2 indicates that the resolution is low only for floors and ceilings.
LOADTYPE:	Specifies the type of bitmap files that are to be loaded for wall and object bitmaps: 0=BBM files (default), 1=GIF files, and 2=PCX files. Note: The GIF file processing routines are currently stubbed out.
WALLS:	Specifies the start of a wall bitmap specification section.
ENDWALLS:	Specifies the end of a wall bitmap section.
OBJECTS:	Specifies the start of an object bitmap specification section.
ENDOBJECTS:	Specifies the end of an object bitmap section.
OBJDESC:	Specifies the start of an object description section. This section must be included within an OBJECTS: section.
ENDDESC:	Specifies the end of an object description section.

(continued)

Table A.1 *Commands Supported in the Configuration File (continued)*

Label	Description
BITMAPS:	Specifies the start of a bitmap section. Bitmap sections are included within wall and object sections. Each bitmap within this section is defined by using two parameters: The wall or object number and the resource index that references where the bitmap data is stored in the resource file.
ENDBITMAPS:	Specifies the end of a bitmap section. This command must be included after all of the bitmap definitions have been listed within a WALLS: or OBJECTS: section.
END:	Specifies the end of the configuration file. This label *must* be placed at the end of the file. The entire process won't know when to stop unless this label is used!

DESIGN TIP

Notice that you can use a semicolon to create a comment line in the configuration file. Here's an example:

```
; Set the initial angle of the POV to 0
PLAYERANGLE: 0
```

Comment lines must be placed on a line by themselves. Also keep in mind that the commands and labels are not case sensitive. That is, **XPLAYER:**, **xPlayer:**, and **xplayer:** can all be used to specify the same command.

The first type of command listed in Table A.1 includes commands like **XPLAYER:**, **YPLAYER:**, and **TOPCOLOR:**. They are called *value specifier* commands because they are used to provide initialization values for the engine. When the engine is initialized, these commands are read in and the values provided are assigned to the interface structure. As an example, to specify a starting position for your player at 100,200, you would include the statements:

```
XPLAYER: 100
YPLAYER: 200
```

The second type of command is called *section labels* because they are used to set up a definition section within the configuration file. These commands always come in pairs and include **WALLS:** ... **ENDWALLS:**, **OBJECTS:** ... **ENDOBJECTS:**, **BITMAPS:** ... **ENDBITMAPS:**, and **OBJDESC:** ... **ENDDESC:**.

The third type of command listed in Table A.1 serves as a *resource index*. Essentially, these commands are used to specify a resource that needs to be loaded. Because the resource itself is stored in the main user-definable resource file (along with the configuration commands), the resource index command must specify the offset into the resource file where the resource is located. This may sound confusing so let's look at an example.

Assume that you've set up your resource file using the following set of files:

```
MALL.INF
MALL.MAP
MALL.LBM
MNTBACK2.LBM
.
.
.
```

Recall that the first file is the configuration file—the place where you put the configuration commands we are now discussing. The second file is the game map output file created by the visual map editor. The configuration command to link to this file is **MAPFILE:**. Because this file is the first one in the list (listed after the configuration file MALL.INF), the actual command to link to it would be

```
MAPFILE: 1
```

where the parameter 1 specifies the index into the resource file where the map data is stored. This is why you need to know the order of the files to be combined in your resource file before you write the commands for your configuration script.

Defining Walls

All of the wall sections used in a game are defined using the **WALLS:** ... **ENDWALLS:** pair. Within this section, you include the list of wall numbers and the resource index that references where the wall bitmap data is located in the resource file. Here's an example:

```
; Define the walls used in a game
WALLS:
; Specify the wall numbers and bitmap resources
BITMAPS:
1,5
2,6
3,7
...
ENDBITMAPS:
ENDWALLS:
```

The **BITMAPS:** command is required to set up the bitmaps section. Here, each wall component is specified by providing the wall number and the number of the bitmap resource. For example, the first bitmap defined (1,5) indicates that wall number 1 uses the bitmap data located at the fifth index position in the resource file. When the *ACK-3D* engine processes a command like this in the configuration file, it essentially executes the following function:

```
AckLoadWall(ae,1,5);
```

As you can see, this method is an easy way to load all of the different wall bitmaps that you use in your game without having to include a bunch of function calls in your code.

Defining Objects

Defining objects is similar to defining walls in the sense that they are defined in their own section: **OBJECTS:** ... **ENDOBJECTS:**. However, because objects require more attributes, additional configuration commands are needed to define them. These commands are listed in Table A.2. Note that this table includes both object definition commands and labels to specify flag settings when objects are created.

Let's look at a sample script that creates an object using some of these commands and labels. The start of the objects section is indicated using the **OBJECTS:** command. This step is mandatory. Next, bitmaps are assigned to object numbers using the **BITMAPS:** ... **ENDBITMAPS:** section. For each bitmap definition, the object number must be provided along with the resource index

Table A.2   *Commands and Flag Settings Supported in the Configuration File*

Label	Description
NUMBER:	Specifies the object number of the object being defined and its speed.
CREATE:	Specifies that a "create" object sequence should be defined.
DESTROY:	Specifies that a "destroy" object sequence should be defined.
WALK:	Specifies that a "walk" object sequence should be defined.
ATTACK:	Specifies that an "attack" object sequence should be defined.
INTERACT:	Specifies that an "interact" object sequence should be defined.
ANIMATE	Indicates object bitmaps will be animated.
MOVEABLE	Indicates object can be moved.
PASSABLE	Indicates object can be walked through.
MULTIVIEW	Indicates object has multiple sides.
SHOWONCE	Indicates object will be animated once and then it will stop.

number that specifies where the bitmap data is stored in the master resource file. Inside the bitmaps definition section, I've placed a couple of object definitions that specify which bitmap data sections in the resource file are assigned to specific objects:

```
; This is the start of the objects section
OBJECTS:
; This indicates object bitmaps will follow
BITMAPS:

; The format for object bitmaps are Bitmap number, Resource Number
1,36
2,37
ENDBITMAPS:

; This indicates an object description section will follow
OBJDESC:

; The format for an object description is Object Number,Speed
; Here we are setting up object # 1
NUMBER: 1,1

; Specifies that the object should be created
; The parameters for this command are Flags, Number of Views,
; Bitmaps per view, and Bitmaps
CREATE: 0,1,1,1

; End object description section
ENDDESC:
; End object section
ENDOBJECTS:
```

After the **BITMAPS:** section (notice **ENDBITMAPS:** is used to end the section), the object description section is defined. The command pair **OBJDESC:** ... **ENDDESC:** is needed to define this section, which sets up the object that is used to specify attributes for a single object. The **NUMBER:** command defines the object number and speed for the object. After this command come the commands to define the sequences for the object, which include create, destroy, walk, attack, and interact. Each of these sequences is defined by including the appropriate command along with the parameters that specify the flag settings, number of views (or sides), number of bitmaps per view, and the bitmap numbers of the bitmaps used. Our example defines a "create" sequence using the **CREATE:** command. With this command, we are defining a sequence that has only one side and one bitmap per side. If we were creating a sequence that had more sides or more bitmaps per side, we'd need to specify additional bitmap numbers. For example, the following command defines a "create" sequence for the object where two sides are used, each having two bitmaps:

```
CREATE: ANIMATE,2,2,1,4,3,7
```

The bitmap numbers used are 1, 4, 3, and 7. Notice also that the label **ANIMATE** is used to define the flag setting. You can use any of the five labels listed in Table A.2 for this parameter; just combine them by using an "or" symbol (I) as in the case **ANIMATE I SHOWONCE**.

The other object sequences supported, destroy, walk, attack, and interact, are set up in the same manner that the create sequence is defined. That is, you must provide the flag settings, number of sides, and number of bitmaps per side, and list the bitmap resource numbers. When the *ACK-3D* engine processes one of these configuration commands (**CREATE:**, **DESTROY:**, and so on), it allocates memory for an **OBJSEQ** structure and links in the structure with the main **NEWOBJECT** structure.

A Sample ACK-3D *Configuration File*

Here is a sample configuration file that shows how commands are used to specify the key components for a game. You can use this template to help you set up your own games. If you'd like to see other examples, check out the .INF configuration files that are provided on the companion CD-ROM with some of the sample games.

```
; Comments can be placed in the file if the line starts with a semi-colon.
; Filename: MALL.INF
; Configuration file for Mall Demo
; This is the index into the resource file to indicate where the map file
; is located
MapFile: 1

; Initial coordinates of POV when first starting the engine
xPlayer: 192
yPlayer: 640

; Initial angle of POV; if omitted, a random angle will be used
PlayerAngle: 0

; Colors for solid top and bottom
TopColor: 0
BottomColor: 24

Floors: ON
Resolution: 2
```

```
; Full screen picture index into the resource file
ScreenBack: 2

; Scrolling mountains in the background
ScrollBack: 3

; This is the start of the wall bitmap section
Walls:
; This indicates wall bitmaps will follow
Bitmaps:

; The format for wall bitmaps are Wall Number, Resource Number
1 ,4
2 ,5
EndBitmaps:
; End the wall section
EndWalls:

; This is the start of the objects section
Objects:
; This indicates object bitmaps will follow
Bitmaps:

; The format for object bitmaps are Bitmap number, Resource Number
1,36
2,37
EndBitmaps:

; This indicates an object description section will follow
ObjDesc:

; The format for an object description is Object Number,Speed
Number: 1,1

; Specifies that the object should be created
Create: 0,1,1,1
; The parameters for this command are Flags, Number of Views,
; Bitmaps per view, and Bitmaps
; These other flag settings can be used to specify attributes for
; objects. You can use one of these labels for the first parameter.
; ANIMATE
; MOVEABLE
; PASSABLE
; MULTIVIEW
; SHOWONCE

; End object description section
EndDesc:
; End object section
EndObjects:
; This is a MANDATORY end statement
End:
```

Appendix B

ACK-3D Function Reference Guide

This appendix provides a description for all of the main *ACK-3D* functions that you can call from your applications. The functions are listed by their usage category to make this reference guide easy to use. Each function description provides the name of the function, its calling syntax, and a discussion of the required parameters and the return value.

Engine Initialization Functions

You must initialize the *ACK-3D* engine before it can be used. This section describes the functions that perform all of the major initialization operations, including opening and closing resource files, reading the math data and loading the required look-up tables, and reading and loading game-specific resource data such as the user-defined game map.

```
short AckInitialize(ACKENG *ae);
```

Initializes the various look-up tables (arrays) used by the *ACK-3D* engine. It reads and processes the file TRIG.DAT. It also allocates memory for an off-screen buffer, calculates internal viewport variables based on the initial dimensions provided by your application, sets up the color palette table for performing light shading, and creates the data structures and tables to display floors and a background screen. *This is the first* ACK-3D *function that should be called from your application.*

Defined in: ACKINIT.C

Parameter:

*ae   Pointer to the interface structure. This structure must be allocated by your application program before calling **AckInitialize()**.

Return Values:

0 if successful; otherwise one of the initialization error codes defined in ACK3D.H is returned.

```
short AckReadMapFile(ACKENG *ae, char *MapFileName);
```

Reads and processes an *ACK-3D* game map file created with the DOS-based editor. The game map file is a binary file created by the DOS-based visual map editor. This function can be called directly from your application to load a game map file, or you can combine the game map file into a resource file and call the **ProcessInfoFile()** function to perform this task.

Defined in: ACKINIT.C

Parameters:

*ae   Pointer to the interface structure.
*MapFileName   Name of the binary game map file to read.

Return Values:

0 if successful; otherwise the error code **ERR_BADMAPFILE** is returned if the map file cannot be opened; **ERR_READINGMAP** is returned if the game map data is not in the correct format; or **ERR_NOMEMORY** is returned if memory cannot be allocated for multi-height wall data.

Notes: This function sets up the **xGrid[ ]** and **yGrid[ ]** arrays with the wall bitmap numbers stored in the map file. Once these arrays are loaded, your application can alter them directly if you need to change any of the walls stored in the map. If you use the Windows-based map editor, which generates an actual resource file, you won't use this fiunction.

```
short AckOpenResource(char *fName);
```

Opens a resource file for reading by the *ACK-3D* functions. Only one resource file can be open at a time.

Defined in: ACKINIT.C

Parameter:

*fName   The name of the resource file to be opened.

Return Values:

0 if successful; otherwise the error code **ERR_BADFILE** is returned if the file cannot be opened or **ERR_NOMEMORY** is returned if memory cannot be allocated to store the data read in from the resource file.

```
void AckCloseResource(void);
```

Closes a resource file if one is open.

Defined in: ACKINIT.C

Return Value: None

```
void AckSetupPalRanges(ACKENG *ae, ColorRange *ranges);
```

Fills in the light shading color palette table. The incoming ranges are in a 16 by 256 array where there are 16 different distance levels. Each level provides a full set of colors for light shading.

Defined in: ACKUTIL.C

Parameters:

*ae   Pointer to the interface structure.

*ranges   Provides the set of color ranges.

Return Value: None

```
short AckWrapUp(ACKENG *ae);
```

Frees up memory buffers used by the *ACK-3D* engine. This is the final *ACK-3D* function that your application should call.

Defined in: ACKWRAP.C

Parameter:

*ae   Pointer to the interface structure.

Return Value: 0 (always)

```
int ProcessInfoFile(void);
```

Reads the commands from a configuration file and makes calls to appropriate *ACK-3D* functions and assigns values to the **ACKENG** interface structure. This version is used with DOS applications.

Defined in: ACKINFO.CPP

Return Values:

0 if successful; otherwise an error code is returned to indicate that an error has occurred while calling one of the *ACK-3D* functions.

Bitmap Processing Functions

ACK-3D provides several functions to load bitmaps for walls and objects. These functions can be called directly by your application, or they can be called indirectly by setting up a configuration file as discussed in Appendix A. Two functions are also provided for reading bitmap data directly from .PCX and .BBM (or .LBM) files.

```
short AckLoadWall(ACKENG *ae, int WallNumber, char *bmFileName);
```

Reads in wall bitmap data from a specified bitmap file or resource file and assigns the data to a wall number ID. This function loads the bitmap data by calling **AckLoadBitmap()** and supplying the **TYPE_WALL** flag as the **BitmapType** parameter.

Defined in: ACKLDBMP.C

Parameters:

*ae	Pointer to the interface structure.
WallNumber	Specifies the wall number ID to which the bitmap data will be assigned. This value serves as an index into the wall bitmap array.
*bmFileName	Name of the bitmap file to read or an index into the opened resource file.

Return Values: See **AckLoadBitmap()**.

```
short AckLoadObject(ACKENG *ae, int BmpNumber, char *bmFileName);
```

Reads in object bitmap data from a specified bitmap file or resource file and assigns the data to a bitmap number ID. This function loads the bitmap data by calling **AckLoadBitmap()** and supplying the **TYPE_OBJECT** flag as the **BitmapType** parameter.

Defined in: ACKLDBMP.C

Parameters:

*ae	Pointer to the interface structure.
BmpNumber	Specifies the bitmap number ID to which the bitmap data will be assigned. This value serves as an index into the object bitmap array.

*bmFileName   Name of bitmap file to read or an index into the opened
                     resource file.

Return Values: See **AckLoadBitmap()**.

`short AckLoadBitmap (ACKENG *ae, int BitmapNumber, int BitmapType, char *bmFileName);`

This is the general purpose bitmap function to read in data for a wall or object
bitmap. The bitmap data read can be in either a .PCX or .BBM format (Deluxe Paint
II file). This function allocates memory for the bitmap, reads it in, and rotates the
bitmap 90 degrees. A pointer to the bitmap is assigned to either the **bMaps[ ]** (for
walls) or **oMaps[ ]** array (for objects), based on the value in **BitmapType**.

Defined in: ACKLDBMP.C
Parameters:
*ae   Pointer to the interface structure.
BitmapNumber   The bitmap ID that will be assigned to the bitmap data read.
BitmapType   Specifies the type of bitmap being assigned, either
                     TYPE_WALL or **TYPE_OBJECT.**
*bmFileName   Name of the bitmap file to read or an index into the opened
                     resource file.

Return Values:
0 if successful; otherwise the error code **ERR_LOADINGBITMAP** is returned
if an error occurs while reading in the bitmap data; **ERR_INVALIDFORM** is
returned if the bitmap data is not the correct size; or **ERR_NOMEMORY** is
returned if memory cannot be allocated to store the bitmap data read.

`short AckSetNewBitmap(short index, unsigned char **Maps, unsigned char *NewBitmap);`

Assigns a new wall or object bitmap ID to one of the map arrays.

Defined in: ACKUTIL.C
Parameters:
index   Index into the map array to assign the new bitmap ID.
**Maps   The pointer reference to the map array to assign the new
                     bitmap.
*NewBitmap   A pointer to the bitmap to assign to the map array.

Return Value: 0 (always)

`unsigned char *AckReadiff(char *filename);`

Reads in a Deluxe Paint picture (.LBM) or brush (.BBM) file, allocates a buffer
for the image, and returns the buffer pointer to the calling function. The

image in the buffer will contain four bytes at the beginning to store the width and height of the image in integer format. This function is provided so that your applications can read in their own images.

Defined in: ACKIFF.C
Parameter:
*filename   Name of .LBM or .BBM file to read.
Return Values:
Pointer to buffer if successful; otherwise a NULL value is returned to indicate that an error occurred while reading the bitmap data.

```
unsigned char *AckReadPCX(char *filename);
```

Reads in a 256 color .PCX image, allocates a buffer for the image, and returns the buffer pointer to the calling function. The image in the buffer will contain four bytes at the beginning to store the width and height of the image in integer format. This function is provided so that your applications can read in their own .PCX files.

Defined in: ACKPCX.C
Parameter:
*filename   Name of .PCX file to read.
Return Values:
Pointer to buffer if successful; otherwise a NULL value is returned to indicate that an error occurred while reading the bitmap data.

Object Support Functions

ACK-3D provides a set of functions to create and set up objects, as well as functions to handle object animation and movement. Animation is performed by switching the displayed bitmap for an object. Your application is responsible for setting up an object structure to provide the engine with the necessary information to animate or move the object once the object has been created.

```
short AckCreateObject(ACKENG *ae, short ObjNumber);
```

Creates a new object and adds the object to the list kept by the interface structure. Once an object has been created, it can be moved, animated, or assigned attributes.

Defined in: ACKLDBMP.C
Parameters:
*ae   Pointer to the interface structure.

ObjNumber   Object ID for the object being created. This value serves as an index into the object list array (**ObjList[ ]**) kept by the interface structure.

Return Values:

0 if successful; otherwise the error code **ERR_NOMEMORY** is returned to indicate that memory cannot be allocated for a new object structure.

```
short AckSetupObject(ACKENG *ae, short oNum, short oType, OBJSEQ *os);
```

Places the object sequence data provided in the specified parameter (***os**) into the object structure. If the object currently does not have any bitmaps, the object sequence is selected as the active sequence by calling **AckSetObjectType()**.

Defined in: ACKLDBMP.C

Parameters:

*ae	Pointer to the interface structure.
oNum	Object ID for the object being set up.
oType	Specifies the object sequence type being set up (**NO_CREATE**, **NO_DESTROY**, **NO_WALK**, **NO_ATTACK**, or **NO_INTERACT**).
*os	Pointer to the object sequence.

Return Values:

0 if successful; otherwise the error code **ERR_BADOBJECTTYPE** is returned to indicate that an invalid object sequence is specified.

```
short AckSetObjectType(ACKENG *ae, short oNum, short oType);
```

Selects an object sequence for a specified object. Each object can be assigned five different object sequences: create, destroy, walk, attack, and interact.

Defined in: ACKLDBMP.C

Parameters:

*ae	Pointer to the interface structure.
oNum	Object ID for the object being set up.
oType	Specifies the object sequence type being set up (**NO_CREATE**, **NO_DESTROY**, **NO_WALK**, **NO_ATTACK**, or **NO_INTERACT**).

Return Values:

0 if successful; otherwise the error code **ERR_BADOBJECTTYPE** is returned to indicate that an invalid object sequence is specified.

Note: This function is called by **AckSetupObject()**; however, you can call it directly to select an object sequence for an object.

```
short AckDeleteObject(ACKENG *ae, int ObjectIndex);
```

Sets an object's **Active** flag to 0 so the object will no longer be processed by the engine. This function does not deallocate memory for the object.

Defined in: ACKUTIL.C

Parameters:

*ae	Pointer to the interface structure.
ObjectIndex	Index number (object ID) of the object to "delete."

Return Values:

0 if successful; otherwise -1 is returned if the object is already deleted (inactive).

```
short AckMoveObjectPOV(short ObjIndex, short Angle, short Amount);
```

Moves a specified object a given angle and distance.

Defined in: ACKPOV.C

Parameters:

ObjIndex	The object number of the object to move.
Angle	The angle to move the object—must be in the range 0 to 1800.
Amount	The distance to move the object—must be in the range 1 to 4095.

Return Values:

POV_OBJECT	Indicates the object encounters another object while being moved.
POV_NOTHING	Indicates the object doesn't encounter anything while being moved.
POV_SLIDEX	Indicates the object is sliding along an x wall.
POV_SLIDEY	Indicates the object is sliding along a y wall.
POV_PLAYER	Indicates the object encounters the player while being moved.

```
void AckCheckObjectMovement(void);
```

Checks the list of objects used in an application and sets up the current bitmap for each object that can be animated. This function should be called before calling the **AckBuildView()** function.

Defined in: ACKPOV.C

Return Value: None

Note: This routine is used mainly to animate objects that have multiple bitmaps. Your application should devise its own movement algorithms and call **AckMoveObjectPOV()** to carry them out.

```
short AckGetObjectHit(void);
```
Returns the object ID of the last object hit by the player.

Defined in: ACKUTIL.C
Return Value: The object ID (index) of the last object hit.

```
short AckGetObjectAngle(long DeltaX, long DeltaY);
```
Returns the angle between two objects.

Defined in: ACKVIEW.C
Parameters:
DeltaX   The distance between the x coordinates of the two objects.
DeltaY   The distance between the y coordinates of the two objects.
Return Value:
The angle between the objects. This value can range from 0 to 1800.

View Processing Functions

Displaying views in *ACK-3D* is simply a matter of moving the player around and calling the **AckBuildView()** function to create a new view based on the player's new position. To add other features to your games, such as secret doors or background screen overlays, you'll need to call other *ACK-3D* functions. This section includes all of the functions that can help you build dynamic scenes for your application.

```
void AckRegisterStructure(ACKENG *ae);
```
Sets up the process of displaying a new view by tranferring some of the data in the **ACKENG** structure to global variables. Each time a new view needs to be processed, this function *must* be called by your application program.

Defined in: ACKVIEW.C
Parameter: *ae   Pointer to the interface structure.
Return Value: None.

```
void AckBuildView(void);
```
Constructs the current POV and places the new view into an off-screen buffer. The view is not displayed on the screen at this time. To display the view in a DOS application, the off-screen buffer must be written to video memory by calling **AckDisplayScreen()**. To display the view in a Windows application, the WinG bitmap display function must be called.

Defined in: ACKVIEW.C
Return Value: None

Note: The best place to put this function is in your application's main loop so that it is repeatedly called whenever the player's POV is moved or your objects are moved or animated.

```
short AckMovePOV(short Angle, short Amount);
```

Attempts to move the player by a specified angle and amount. If the player is successfully moved, the player's coordinates are updated in the interface structure.

Defined in: ACKPOV.C

Parameters:

Angle   Angle to move player's POV.
Amount   Amount to move player's POV.

Return Values:

POV_NOTHING   Indicates player was moved and nothing was hit.
POV_XWALL   Indicates player has hit an x wall.
POV_YWALL   Indicates player has hit a y wall.
POV_OBJECT   Indicates player has hit an object.
POV_SLIDEX   Indicates player is sliding along an x wall.
POV_SLIDEY   Indicates player is sliding along a y wall.

```
short AckCheckHit(short xPlayer, short yPlayer, short ViewAngle);
```

Allows the application to determine if an obstacle is close to the player's POV. This function checks for collisions with walls (not objects).

Defined in: ACKVIEW.C

Parameters:

xPlayer   Current x coordinate of the player's POV.
yPlayer   Current y coordinate of the player's POV.
ViewAngle   Current angle the player's POV is facing.

Return Values:

POV_NOTHING   Indicates nothing nearby.
POV_XWALL   Indicates an x wall is close.
POV_YWALL   Indicates a y wall is close.

```
short AckCheckDoorOpen(short xPlayer, short yPlayer, short PlayerAngle);
```

Determines if the player's POV is close enough to trigger the process of opening a door. If so, the door is placed in the Doors sub-structure of the interface structure and the door opening process begins. Subsequent calls to **AckBuildView()** will automatically continue to open or close the door, depending on the door's state.

Defined in: DOOR.C

Parameters:

xPlayer   Current x coordinate of the player's POV.

yPlayer   Current y coordinate of the player's POV.

PlayerAngle   Current angle the player is facing.

Return Values:

POV_NODOOR   Indicates no door was opened.

POV_XDOOR   Indicates door along an x wall was opened.

POV_YDOOR   Indicates door along a y wall was opened.

POV_XSECRETDOOR Indicates a secret door along an x wall was opened.

POV_YSECRETDOOR Indicates a secret door along a y wall was opened.

```
short AckGetWallHit(void);
```

Returns the map location of the last wall hit.

Defined in: ACKUTIL.C

Return Value: The map index of the last wall hit.

```
short AckCreateOverlay(ACKENG *ae, unsigned char *OverlayScreen);
```

Reads an overlay file and compiles it into the overlay buffer. This function also determines which part of the screen is within the viewport and sets up the overlay buffer so that it can later be combined with the off-screen buffer that stores the current view.

Defined in: ACKOVER.C

Parameters:

*ae   Pointer to the interface structure.

*OverlayScreen   Pointer to 64K overlay buffer that is assigned to the interface structure.

Return Values:

0 if successful; otherwise the error code **ERR_NOMEMORY** is returned if memory cannot be allocated for the overlay buffer.

```
short AckBuildBackground(ACKENG *ae);
```

Builds a background buffer using a solid ceiling and floor.

Defined in: ACKBKGD.C

Parameters:

*ae   Pointer to the interface structure.

Return Value: 0 (always)

DOS Screen Support Functions

To use the *ACK-3D* engine with DOS, you'll need to use the functions presented in this section to put the screen in VGA Mode 13h and send the off-screen view buffers to display memory.

```
short AckDisplayScreen(void);
```
Displays the current view stored in the off-screen buffer. The view is displayed using VGA Mode 13h.

Defined in: ACKRTN.ASM
Return Value: 0 (always)

Notes: If your application uses an overlay, it must call the function **AckDrawOverlay()** before calling **AckDisplayScreen()**.

```
void AckSetTextMode(void);
```
Places the screen into standard 80x25 text color mode 3.

Defined in: ACKRTN.ASM
Return Value: None

```
void AckSetVGAmode(void);
```
Places the screen into standard 320x200 VGA Mode 13h.

Defined in: ACKRTN.ASM
Return Value: None

Note: Your DOS application can set the screen to graphics using its own routines if desired. The *ACK-3D* engine does not depend on mode 13h unless the **AckDisplayScreen()** function is called to display scenes.

```
short AckLoadAndSetPalette(char *PalName);
```
Reads the specified palette file and sets the palette of the VGA.

Defined in: ACKUTIL.C
Parameter:
*PalName   Name of the palette file to load.
Return Values:
0 if successful; otherwise the error code ERR_NOMEMORY is returned to indicate that memory has not been allocated.

Note: This is a utility function to read a palette file (768 bytes) and set the VGA video palette for Mode 13h using the values read. Your application can use its own function if desired, or it can use **AckSetPalette()** to provide its own values to set the VGA video palette.

`void AckSetPalette(unsigned char *PalBuffer);`

Sets the VGA Mode 13h color palette using a specified buffer that contains the color palette settings.

Defined in: ACKRTN.ASM
Parameter:
*PalBuffer   The 768 byte buffer containing the palette data.
Return Value: None

Note: Use this function to set a palette that has already been read into a buffer. Use **AckLoadAndSetPalette()** to read *and* set a palette by reading the palette data from a file.

Windows Support Functions

To use the *ACK-3D* engine with Windows, you need to create your own Windows-specific functions to initialize the engine and display WinG bitmaps. The source file ACKWIN.CPP provides sample Windows-specific functions that you can use as is or modify to suit the needs of your own applications.

`short InitACKEngine(void);`

Initializes the *ACK-3D* engine by calling the main **AckInitialize()** function, opening required resource files, and displaying any error messages in Windows.

Defined in: ACKWIN.CPP
Return Values:
0 if successful; otherwise -1 is returned to indicate an error has occurred. When an error occurs, a Windows message box displays the error.

Note: This function is essentially a wrapper function to call the required functions to set up the *ACK-3D* engine in Windows. It does not allocate any WinG specific bitmaps.

`int ProcessInfoFile(void);`

Reads the commands from a configuration file and makes calls to appropriate *ACK-3D* functions and assigns values to the **ACKENG** interface structure.

Defined in: ACKINFO.CPP

Return Values:
0 if successful; otherwise an error code is returned to indicate that an error has occurred while calling one of the *ACK-3D* functions.

Note: This function must be used in combination with **AckOpenResource()** and **AckCloseResource()**.

```
void CreateAckPalette(void);
```
Creates a screen palette to be used for a Windows application.

Defined in: ACKWIN.CPP
Return Value: None

```
void AckDoSize(HWND hWnd, LPARAM lParam);
```
Processes a Windows **WM_SIZE** message. When this message is generated, **AckDoSize()** uses WinG function calls to display the current view in the window that has been resized.

Defined in: ACKWIN.CPP
Parameters:
hWnd   Handle to the current view window.
lParam   Specifies the size of the new Window.

Return Value: None

```
void DoCycle(void);
```
Processes a Windows drawing cycle of the engine. This function checks the current state of user input (mouse and keyboard) and moves the player's POV accordingly.

Defined In: ACKWIN.CPP
Return Value: None

Resources for Developing 3-D Games

When I first started to develop the *ACK-3D* engine, resources such as magazine articles, books, utilities, sample artwork, demo engines, and so on were scarce. Fortunately, this situation has changed and now there are numerous resources available to help you create your 3-D games.

This guide is provided to help you locate some of the better resources for developing 3-D games. It features the software provided on the companion CD-ROM for this book, and it also presents additional resources, such as books and magazines. In putting together the companion CD-ROM, I tried to gather some of the better tools, samples, source code, artwork, and demonstration programs that will help you design and create your own games. I included many of the sample programs to show you what you can accomplish with the *ACK-3D* engine. My goal with the companion CD-ROM is to provide a complete construction kit; all you need to add is your creative ideas (and a little code, of course).

Using the Companion CD-ROM

On the companion CD-ROM you'll find all the source code presented in this book, but that's only a small part of what's included. In addition you'll find:

- Source code for the complete *ACK-3D* engines for DOS and Windows. (I've even provided an earlier 32-bit version of the engine that can be compiled with Watcom.)
- Source code for the Windows and DOS versions of the interactive map editor.
- Sample game maps that you can use with the game editor.
- Source code for the resource compiler and other standalone game development tools.
- A Windows game template to help you easily create your own 3-D Windows games with the engine.
- A complete set of object and wall bitmap art for creating 3-D games. All of the artwork for the sample games provided on the companion CD-ROM, except the art for the commercial *Slob Zone* game, is included.
- Artwork for title screens and background images.
- DOS and Windows demonstration games created with the *ACK-3D* engine, with complete source code.
- WinG DLLs and a custom WinG class interface.
- Win32s DLLs.
- Demos created by other developers who have made modifications to the *ACK-3D* engine.
- Programs for creating game bitmaps (walls and objects) and converting bitmap images from one format to another.

How the CD-ROM Is Organized

You'll find the main directories that are on the companion CD-ROM listed in Table C.1. Each of these directories contains subdirectories to keep all of the files organized. For example, the ACK directory contains WIN and DOS subdirectories to store the Windows and DOS versions of the *ACK-3D* software, respectively.

Notes About the Source Code

The source code provided on the companion CD-ROM for the *ACK-3D* engine comes in three flavors: a Watcom version for DOS, a Borland version for

---

Table C.1   *Main Directories on the Companion CD-ROM*

ACK   This directory is the home for all of the subdirectories that contain the source code for the DOS and Windows versions of the *ACK-3D* engine and source code and executables for both versions of the interactive map editor. The sample programs created with *ACK-3D* and featured in this book are also included under this directory.

BORLAND   This directory contains DLLs that you'll need to copy to your WINDOWS\SYSTEM directory to run the Windows versions of the sample games and map editor. Runtime DLLs are provided for both Borland 4.0 and 4.5.

CHAP_13   This directory contains the sample WinG game developed in Chapter 13, as well as class support libraries for WinG. The source code in this directory is designed to be compiled with Borland 4.5.

DEMOS   This directory contains an assortment of demonstration programs that have been created by other developers by using the *ACK-3D* engine presented in this book or a modified version. Here you'll also find source code for a version of the engine ported to Visual C++ which uses WinG and supports sound under Windows.

TOOLS   This directory provides tools and utility programs to help you create games with the *ACK-3D* engine. Here you'll find the *ACK-3D* resource compiler, a viewer for displaying .BBM bitmaps, and programs for drawing bitmaps and converting bitmap files. The WinG and Win32s DLLs are also provided under this directory.

IMAGES   This directory provides an assortment of artwork to help you create your own 3-D games. Artwork for both startup screens and wall and object bitmaps are included. Bitmap files are provided in both a .PCX and .BBM format.

Note: *Remember that if you copy files from the companion CD-ROM to your hard disk, you'll need to change the attributes of the files so that they are no longer set to "read only." Because of the read-only nature of CD-ROMs, all files are stored as read-only.*

DOS, and a Borland version for Windows. The main ACK directory contains a DOS and WIN directory to help organize the source code. You'll also find example programs that have been created with each version of the engine.

The very latest version of the source code and the compiled *ACK-3D* library is in the directory \ACK\WIN\ACK_LIB. This code is set up to be compiled with Borland 4.0 or Borland 4.5. This is the library and source code I use to create Windows applications with the engine. A version of the engine source code is provided in the \ACK\DOS\WATCOM directory that can be compiled and used with Watcom. If you wish to create DOS applications with the engine and you are using Borland C++, use the library and source code in the directory \ACK\DOS\BORLAND.

Playing Games

The first thing you probably want to do is play with the sample games included on the CD-ROM, right? That's what I'd be doing.

I've provided a number of different games to show you the types of worlds that can be created with the *ACK-3D* technology. Some of the games and demos provided have been created using the *ACK-3D* engine right out of the box. I've also included other games and demos that have been developed using modified versions of the engine. After I developed the original version of the engine, I made it available to game developers on on-line services such as CompuServe. Some of the more enterprising programmers have added new features and made some significant changes to the engine. By playing with some of their creations, you'll get an idea of the kinds of games that can be developed and the extensions that can be added.

Slob Zone

One of my favorite games developed with *ACK-3D* is *Slob Zone*, which I've presented throughout the book. *Slob Zone* is a commercial game published by Deep River. The main developer for the game was Ken Lemiux, and Andrew Hunter created the art. Figure C.1 shows one of the views from this game, the goal of which is to grab all the trash you can to accumulate points (cash). You can then use the cash to buy "safe" weapons at a vending machine. These weapons include water balloons, soap, and deodorant. You use these weapons to throw at your enemies.

Figure C.1 *A scene from* Slob Zone.

Directory: DEMOS\SLOBZONE
Program: SLOB.EXE
Platform: DOS

The basic instructions and hints for playing this game are as follows:

1. To pick up trash, just run over the item. This action gives you money that you can trade for weapons at any vending machine. Here's the "pecking order" of the weapons:
    - Water balloons are good and cheap.
    - Soap is better.
    - Deodorant is powerful but expensive.
2. Watch out for those crazy animals; they just hate seeing you so nice and clean. They will start throwing disgusting stuff at you unless you clean them up first.
3. Pick up the colored keys; you'll need them to open locked doors.
4. When your dirt meter rises, it's time to think about cleaning yourself. You can use a pay shower or look around for raincoats, umbrellas, and moist towelettes. If you don't, you'll get "slobbed" and have to start the level over again.
5. Save your game often; that way you can always come back.

This section explains how to control the game with the mouse and keyboard.

Mouse Support:
- The right mouse button fires your currently selected weapon.
- Moving the mouse forward, back, left, or right causes you to move in the game.

Keyboard Support:
- The arrow keys cause you to move in the game.
- The *Ctrl* key slides you left or right (press this key while holding down the left or right arrow key).
- The *Alt* key throws your currently selected weapon.
- The *1, 2,* or *3* key selects one of the weapons: water balloon, soap, or deodorant.
- *Enter* causes you to spin 180 degrees—a good technique for running away.
- *Space bar* operates doors, showers, vending machines, and so on.

- *Tab* turns the game map on and off.
- *Esc* displays the menu.
- The *P* key pauses the game.
- The *D* key turns off floor and ceiling (increases speed on slow PCs).
- The *Q* key quits the game.
- The +/- key increases or decreases the sound volume. (This comes in handy when your boss is hanging around outside your office.)

Slob Zone requires an IBM PC or compatible system, 33 MHz 80386 SX minimum. Deep River recommends a 25 MHz 80486 or better with the following hardware and software:

- CD-ROM drive
- VGA Graphics
- 4 MB RAM minimum with 4MB free
- 500K of free base memory
- Sound Card (optional)
- 100% Microsoft-compatible mouse (optional)

More detailed instructions for installing *Slob Zone* and troubleshooting tips are provided on the companion CD-ROM in the directory DEMOS\SLOBZONE.

The version of *Slob Zone* provided on the CD-ROM contains the first level of the game. You can purchase the complete game by contacting Deep River at 207-871-1684 (Monday through Friday, between 9 a.m. and 5 p.m. Eastern time); FAX: 207-871-1683; or CompuServe: 71055,3436.

FDEMO—A Fun Demonstration Game

I created this demonstration game with a 32-bit version of the *ACK-3D* engine. The game was compiled with Watcom originally and features multi-height walls, movable objects, stationary objects, a number of different wall styles, and other goodies. I also use a rotating background to show you how backdrops can be used with your games.I have also provided a version of the source code that works with Borland.

Figure C.2 shows a scene from this demonstration game. Notice the large green monster. He was created by Andrew Hunter using the clay model technique discussed in Chapter 12.

Directory: ACK\DOS\FDEMO
Program: FDEMO.EXE
Platform: DOS

Figure C.2   *A scene from* FDEMO.

- You'll need a mouse to run this game.
- You can move around by using the arrow keys or sliding the mouse.
- Click the left mouse button to throw a fireball.
- Press the *Esc* key at any time to quit.
- Press the *C* key to turn the ceiling on or off.
- Press the *F* key to turn the floor on or off.
- Press the *I* key to turn on an information display that shows current coordinates.

The game does not provide much "shoot-em-up" action, but it does show you how many of the features provided in the *ACK-3D* engine can be used.

I've included the complete source code for this game so you can experiment with it. I've also included a DOS version of the map editor and all of the bitmap files and map files that you need to make changes to the game map. The source code is in the directory ACK\DOS\FDEMO\SOURCE. The map editor and map files are in the directory ACK\DOS\MAP_EDIT\FDEMO. If you make changes to the game map, you'll need to use the BPIC utility, which is described in Appendix A, to rebuild the resource file for the game.

Mall Demo

This useful demonstration program shows how you can create 3-D applications that are not just games. This program simulates a shopping mall, as

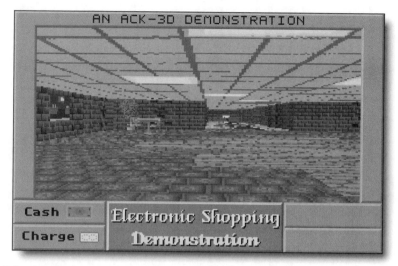

Figure C.3 *A scene from the Mall demo.*

shown in Figure C.3, in which you can walk around. You start outside and then you walk into the mall. Inside, you'll encounter stationary objects— desks, tables, and trees, transparent walls you can look through, and door- ways through which you can walk. You could use this type of 3-D navigation system to create an electronic shopping environment.

Directory: ACK\DOS\MALL
Program: MALL.EXE
Platform: DOS

You can exit at any time by pressing *Esc.* Source code and the map files are provided on the companion CD-ROM. (See directory \ACK\DOS\MAPEDIT\ MALL for more information.)

Explore a Library

If you're like me, you probably have a passion for books. And what could be better than having your own virtual library? This next demo, created by some developers in Germany, features a unique 3-D library setting, as shown in Figure C.4. Here you'll find walls represented as bookcases, unique stationary objects, transparent walls, sliding doors, and a few surprises. After you walk around for a while, you'll even encounter a floating green ball that really caught me offguard. See if you can find it.

Figure C.4 *A scene from the VR demo.*

Directory: DEMOS\LIBRARY
Program: VR.EXE
Platform: DOS

You can navigate in this 3-D world using the mouse and keyboard. No source code is provided.

ACK—The Next Generation

This demonstration game really surprised me. I encountered the developers (JC/oP Group of Germany) on CompuServe. They mentioned that they had created a new generation of the *ACK-3D* engine. And did they ever! The sample 3-D adventure included on the CD-ROM as shown in Figure C.5 runs in a 320×480 screen resolution! You can climb stairs, jump into water, swim, or dive, and don't forget to listen to the sound—very cool!

Directory: DEMOS\ACKNEX
Program: WRUN.EXE
Platform: DOS

To navigate you can use the arrow keys. To go up or down, use PgUp/PgDn or try Home/End. There are three secret rooms to discover, one of which can only be entered underwater.

This is an excellent demonstration because it will stir your imagination and give you an idea of the types of extensions that can be added to the *ACK-3D*

Figure C.5   *A scene from the ACKNEX demo.*

engine technology. I especially like the added feature that allows the player to physically go up or down levels.

Something Cool for Visual C++ Developers

John Lundy, who is active in the GAMDEVS forum on CompuServe, decided that the world needed a Windows/Visual C++ version of the original *ACK-3D* engine I created a few years back. He ported the code to Visual C++ and incorporated WinG. I just found out about it a week before we went to press, and he allowed us to include his creative work on the companion CD-ROM. Figure C.6 shows a sample game running in a window.

Directory: DEMOS\WIN_DEMO
Program: FD.EXE
Platform: Windows

As John states, "This is an MFC Windows based adaptation of the *ACK 3-D* engine, highly modified, updated and optimized, using WinG to achieve up to 18 frames per second." This version includes the complete source code to play .MID or .RMI music, sound effects using .WAV files, support for low resolution (160 by 100) and high resolution (320 by 200) modes, and support

Figure C.6 *A sample game created with the Visual C++ version of ACK-3D.*

for screen sizes from 320×200 up to 640×400. His demonstration game provides weapons (fists, pistol, rifle, machine gun, and rocket launcher), doors, keys, and ammo. You can also save your game.

All source code is provided for you. But keep in mind that John's Windows version is different from the one presented in the book. John has added some key features such as support for .BMP bitmaps.

DOS MAP Editor

In Chapter 15 I presented the Windows version of the *ACK-3D* map editor. This editor is the latest and greatest, and I'm especially proud of it because it allows you to walk through 3-D scenes as you build them. This feature was much easier to code in Windows because of WinG and Windows' multiple windows feature.

I have also provided the DOS version of the *ACK-3D* map editor on the companion CD-ROM. You'll need to use this editor if you plan to modify any of the game maps for the DOS demonstration games included on the companion CD-ROM such as FDEMO or MALL.

The DOS version of the map editor is in the directory ACK\DOS\MAP_EDIT. To run the editor, you must include the name of an ASCII map configuration file. For example, to run the editor and view the map for the MALL demo, enter this command at the DOS prompt:

```
MAPEDIT MALL.L01
```

I have also included a batch file in the ACK\DOS\MAP_EDIT\MALL directory called MALLEDIT.BAT. This program will start the editor and load the correct map configuration file.

The map configuration file essentially tells the map editor which bitmaps are used to create a map. It also provides a filename for the actual map created by the editor. More detailed instructions for using the DOS-based map editor are presented at the end of Chapter 15.

Other Utility Programs

The companion CD-ROM also contains some standalone utility programs to help you create your game resource files and view bitmap files. I've provided the source code for these programs in case you need to modify them to incorporate additional features.

Program: BPIC.EXE
Directory: \TOOLS\BPIC

This is the program used to create the .DTF resource file for a game. The syntax for using this program is:

```
BPIC filename.dat filename.dtf
```

where *filename.dat* is an ASCII file containing a list of files to put into the .DTF file and *filename.dtf* is the actual resource file created.

Program: VBBM.EXE
Directory: \TOOLS\VBBM

This is a useful program for viewing Deluxe Paint II brush (.BBM) files.

Other Resources

Many magazines now publish articles on game development, and there are a number of books in publication that cover graphics and game programming. I've included this list to recommend the books, magazines, and online services that I think you'll find to be of most use.

Books

Advanced Graphics Programming Using C/C++ by Loren Heiny (John Wiley & Sons, New York, NY, 1993, ISBN 0-471-57159-8). This is a great book produced by the Coriolis Group on ray tracing, light modeling, animation, morphing, image processing, and so on. Complete source code is provided for doing extensive work with .PCX and .TIF files.

Animation Techniques in Win32 by Nigel Thompson (Microsoft Press, Redmond, WA, 1995, ISBN 1-55615-669-3). Very little has been published on animation programming under Windows—especially for the 32-bit platform. This recently published book has some solid background material on WinG, DIBs, sprite animation, the palette manager, and Windows sound. It's not a very extensive book, but it is a great start.

The Art of Computer Game Design by Chris Crawford. This classic book is out of print now but you can order unbound copies from the author. If you weren't one of the lucky ones to get a copy of this book when it was first published by McGraw-Hill, I suggest that you write to Chris and get a copy. The book features practical game design techniques from an experienced designer. To order, send $30 plus $5 for shipping and handling to: Chris Crawford, 5251 Sierra Rd., San Jose, CA 95132.

Bitmapped Graphics by Steve Rimmer (Windcrest, 1993, ISBN 0-8306-3558-0). Many game developers refer to this book while working with bitmap images.

Encyclopedia of Graphics File Formats by James Murray and William VanRyper (O'Reily and Associates, Sebastopol, CA, 1994, ISBN 1-56592-058-9). This book is *the* bible on graphics file formats. It covers everything you'll need to know and then some about graphics files. This book is especially useful for creating game development tools to work with different file formats and platforms.

Gardens of Imagination by Chris Lampton (Waite Group Press, Corte Madera, 1994, ISBN 1-878739-59-X). This is the first book published (and the only other book I know of) devoted to the art of ray casting. Many topics are covered well, including texture mapping, lightsourcing, height mapping, and even some basic optimization techniques. The code examples are educational, but you'll need to change the code quite a bit if you plan to use it to develop any real applications.

PC Game Programming Explorer by Dave Roberts (Coriolis Group Books, Scottsdale, AZ, 1994, ISBN 1-883577-07-1). This book takes a powerful tool-oriented approach to the art of game programming. If you are interested in adding additional mouse, keyboard, joystick, or basic sound support to your game applications, I recommend you get a copy of Dave's book.

PC Video Systems (second edition) by Richard Wilton (Microsoft Press, Redmond, WA, 1994, ISBN 1-55615-641-3). This is a classic PC video programming book recently updated to cover VESA-compliant VGA modes. If you need to know what's going on under the hood at the video level, this is the book to read.

Visual C++ Multimedia Adventure Set by Peter Aitken and Scott Jarol (Coriolis Group Books, Scottsdale, AZ, 1995, ISBN 1-883577-19-5). If you plan to do any game or multimedia development with Visual C++, this forthcoming book will be a good asset. It covers WinG, animation, sound, video, hypertext, and all kinds of other goodies you might be able to use to develop your games.

Windows Graphics Programming with Borland C++ (second edition) by Loren Heiny (John Wiley & Sons, New York, NY, 1994, ISBN 0-471-30930-3). This book created by the Coriolis Group doesn't cover WinG, but it is still one of the best books out on graphics programming for Windows. The code in the book is amazing—thousands of lines of application code for texture mapping, 3-D rendering, shear transforms, and lots of other Windows graphics programming examples you won't find anywhere else.

Zen of Code Optimization by Michael Abrash (Coriolis Group Books, Scottsdale, AZ, 1994, ISBN 1-883577-03-9). One of the strengths of the *ACK-3D* engine and any powerful 3-D engine is the level of optimization found in the code. I've learned a lot about optimizing code by reading Michael Abrash's articles over the years. Now he's published a complete book on the subject that you can't afford to be without if you plan to develop your own engines.

Zen of Graphics Programming by Michael Abrash (Coriolis Group Books, Scottsdale, AZ, 1995, ISBN 1-883577-08-X). This book is the bible on *fast* VGA graphics programming. It covers everything from texture mapping, 3-D animation, hidden surface removal, anti-aliasing, and fast polygon drawing. This is also the place to go for detailed explanations of VGA memory mapping, color DACs, color palettes, 256-color, Mode X, and so on.

Magazines, Newsletters, and Articles

PC TECHNIQUES publishes a number of articles on game programming throughout the year. Noted game developer Diana Gruber writes regular articles, and Michael Abrash writes a monthly column on optimization techniques. The April/May 1995 issue is devoted to game programming with articles on WinG programming and other topics. Also check out the Dec/Jan 1995 issue, which featured a great article on BSP trees by Michael Abrash.

PC TECHNIQUES
7339 E. Acoma, Suite 7
Scottsdale, AZ 85260-6912
(602) 483-0192

Game Developer is a relatively new magazine that covers both technical and game industry-related information. I haven't seen a lot of code or 3-D technical discussions yet but the articles seem to be getting better.

Game Developer Magazine
600 Harrison Street
San Francisco, CA 94107-9602
(415) 905-2308

Microsoft Systems Journal doesn't have a reputation for publishing articles on game development or entertainment programming; however, they have published some recent articles on WinG and WinToon that you'll find to be very valuable. Try to pick up a copy of the January 1995 issue, which features a great WinG article with lots of source code.

Microsoft Systems Journal
600 Harrison St.
San Francisco, CA 94107
415-905-2200

The *Journal of Interactive Entertainment Design,* a bimonthly newsletter published by Chris Crawford, features articles on design issues for entertainment software.

Journal of Interactive Entertainment Design
5251 Sierra Rd.
San Jose, Ca 95132

For more information on 32-bit codes segments, refer to the following articles:

Finnegan, James. "Implementing Games for Windows Using the WinG API and the WaveMIX DLL." *Microsoft Systems Journal*, January 1995, p. 61.

Pietrek, Matt. "Windows Q&A." *Microsoft Systems Journal*, February 1995, p. 83.

"QA32: Demonstrates 32-Bit Assembly-Language Code." Microsoft Developer Network Developer Library, October 1994.

Getting Online

By far the best source of leading-edge information can be found on services like CompuServe or the Internet. If you know where to go, you can download game engines with source code and sample art, and you can discuss 3-D techniques with other master game developers.

The best place to hang out is in the GAMDEVS forum on CompuServe (GO GAMDEVS). This is the forum I hang out in the most, and you can find other noted game developers there also including Diana Gruber and Chris Crawford.

Here are Internet sites from which you can download (using FTP) various development oriented software and documents:

USENET NewsGroups
rec.games.programmer
rec.games.announce
rec.games.design
rec.games.video.programmer
rec.games.frp.misc
comp.sys.ibm.pc.games.misc

Anonymouse FTP Sites for Game Developers
x2ftp.oulu.fi
ftp.uml.edu
ftp.microsoft.com

Web Sites for Game Developers
http://www.coriolis.com/coriolis

The Coriolis Group is developing this Web site to provide resources for game developers as well as information on their books. Check it out and stay tuned.

Index

READ THE MAGAZINE OF TECHNICAL EXPERTISE!

Published by The Coriolis Group

For years, Jeff Duntemann has been known for his crystal-clear, slightly bemused explanations of programming technology. He's one of the few in computer publishing who have never forgotten that English is the one language we all have in common. Now he's teamed up with author Keith Weiskamp and created a magazine that brings you a selection of readable, practical technical articles six times a year, written by himself and a crew of the very best technical writers working today. Michael Abrash, Tom Swan, Jim Mischel, Keith Weiskamp, David Gerrold, Brett Glass, Michael Covington, Peter Aitken, Marty Franz, Jim Kyle, and many others will perform their magic before your eyes, and then explain how *you* can do it too, in language that you can understand.

If you program under DOS or Windows in C, C++, Pascal, Visual Basic, or assembly language, you'll find code you can use in every issue. You'll also find essential debugging and optimization techniques, programming tricks and tips, detailed product reviews, and practical advice on how to get your programming product finished, polished, and ready to roll.

Don't miss another issue—subscribe today!

CORIOLIS GROUP BOOKS
Order Form

Name _____

Company _____

Address _____

City/State/Zip _____

Phone _____

VISA/MC # _____   Expires: _____

Signature for charge orders: _____

Quantity	Description	Unit price	Extension
	PC Games Explorer	$19.95 U.S.	
	Action Arcade Adventure Set	$39.95 U.S.	
	Free Stuff From the Internet	$19.99 U.S.	
	Mosaic Explorer	$34.99 U.S.	
		TOTAL	

**FAX, Phone, or
send this order form to:**

The Coriolis Group
7339 E. Acoma Drive, Suite 7
Scottsdale, AZ 85260

**FAX us your order at (602) 483-0193
Phone us your order at (800) 410-0192**

Adventure Set License Agreement

Please read this Coriolis Adventure Set software license agreement carefully before you buy this product and use the software contained on the enclosed disk.

1. By opening the accompanying software package, you agree that you have read and agree with the terms of this licensing agreement. If you disagree and do not want to be bound by the terms of this licensing agreement, return this product in whole for refund to the source from which you purchased it.

2. The entire contents of the disk and the compilation of the software contained therein are copyrighted and protected by both U.S. copyright law and international copyright treaty provisions. Each of the programs, including the copyrights in each program, is owned by the respective author, and the copyright in the entire work is owned by The Coriolis Group, Inc. You may copy any or all of this software to your computer system.

3. The disk contains source code presented in the book, utilities, tools, and pictures. You may use the source code, utilities, tools, and pictures presented in the book and included on the disk to develop your own applications for both private and commercial use unless other restrictions are noted in the book or on the disk by the author of the file.

4. You may not decompile, reverse engineer, disassemble, create a derivative work, or otherwise use the programs except as stated in this agreement.

5. The Coriolis Group, Inc., and the author specifically disclaim all other warranties, express or implied, including but not limited to warranties of merchantability and fitness for a particular purpose with respect to defects in the disk, the program, source code, and sample files contained therein, and/or the techniques described in the book, and in no event shall The Coriolis Group and/or the author be liable for any loss of profit or any other commercial damage, including but not limited to special, incidental, consequential, or other damages.

6. The Coriolis Group, Inc. will replace any defective disk without charge if the defective disk is returned to The Coriolis Group, Inc. within 90 days from the date of purchase.

What's on this CD-ROM

The bound-in CD-ROM contains everything you will need to design and create your own 3-D games with the *ACK-3D* engine. You'll find all of the source code presented in the pages of this book, but that's only a small part of what's included. In addition you'll find:

- Source code for the complete *ACK-3D* engines for DOS and Windows. (I've even provided an earlier 32-bit version of the engine that can be compiled with Watcom.)
- Source code for the Windows and DOS versions of the interactive map editor.
- Sample game maps that you can use with the game editor.
- Source code for the resource compiler and other standalone game development tools.
- A Windows game template to help you easily create your own 3-D Windows games with the engine.
- A complete set of object and wall bitmap art for creating 3-D games. All of the artwork for the sample games provided on the companion CD-ROM, except the art for the commercial *Slob Zone* game, is included.
- Artwork for title screens and background images.
- DOS and Windows demonstration games created with the *ACK-3D* engine, with complete source code.
- WinG DLLs and a custom WinG class interface.
- Win32s DLLs.
- Demos created by other developers who have made modifications to the *ACK-3D* engine.
- Programs for creating game bitmaps (walls and objects) and converting bitmap images from one format to another.

Some of the sample programs require that you install WinG and Win32s on your system. The complete instructions for using the CD-ROM are provided in Appendix C.